NEAL-SCHUMAN
COMPLETE INTERNET
COMPANION
FOR LIBRARIANS

SECOND EDITION

ALLEN C. BENSON

NEAL-SCHUMAN NETGUIDE SERIES

Neal-Schuman Publishers, Inc.
New York   London

Published by Neal-Schuman Publishers, Inc.
100 Varick Street
New York, NY 10013

Printed and bound in the United States of America

Library of Congress Cataloging-in-Publication Data

Benson, Allen C.
    Neal–Schuman complete Internet companion for librarians / by Allen C. Benson.— 2nd ed.
        p. cm.
    ISBN 1–55570–414–X
    1. Internet —Handbooks, manuals, etc. I. Title.

TK5105.875.I57B46   2001
004.67'8'024092—dc21   2001030033

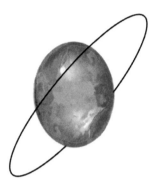

Contents

18: Integrating Tools into Traditional Reference Practice 289

19: Integrating Internet Tools into Other Library Services 315

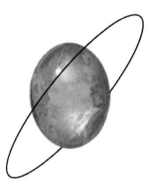

List of Tables and Figures

TABLES

FIGURES

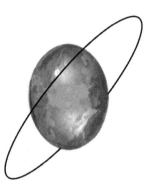

Acknowledgments

There are a number of people whose assistance I wish to acknowledge. My thanks to Greg Watson who has been so supportive offering sound advice and expert hardware and software support, especially in the areas of Linux and search and indexing systems.

I would like to thank my staff at the Norma Wood Library, Arkansas State University Mountain Home, for their commitment to excellence in helping the individuals and communities they serve. I appreciate their dedication and enthusiasm in implementing many of the ideas presented in this book. I wish to give special recognition to Laurie Ditzfeld, Candy Barnes, Deborah Benson, and Robin Harris.

I continue to be grateful to the faculty at the University of Alabama's School of Library and Information Studies, especially Dr. Marion Paris for all of her efforts on my behalf. I'm especially grateful to Professor S. Michael Malinconico, who has been so supportive in all my writing endeavors.

The development of this book resulted from the combined efforts of many talented professionals in the publishing industry. I would like to thank Charles Harmon, Neal-Schuman's director of publishing, and Gary J. Albert, editor, for their tremendous dedication and hard work.

Allen C. Benson

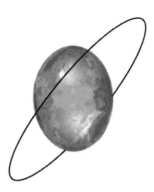

Introduction

More than seven years have elapsed since I submitted the manuscript for the original edition of *The Complete Internet Companion for Librarians*. At that time, "complete" meant describing the Internet tools and resources of the day and explaining how they could be effectively integrated into traditional library practices. The world's first graphical Web browser was just coming into its own—a program named Mosaic developed by the National Center for Supercomputing Applications (NCSA). Gopher, invented at the University of Minnesota Microcomputer and Workstation Networks Center, was at that time the primary tool for organizing and disseminating files on the Internet. Its search mechanisms were named Veronica and Jughead.

Now librarians face greater challenges as they cope with new information technologies, evolving copyright laws, access rights, Internet security, and social and cultural change. The purpose of this new edition of the *Neal-Schuman Complete Internet Companion for Librarians* is to provide librarians with the cutting-edge information they need to meet these challenges. This edition includes new sections devoted to topics such as multimedia and introduces a CD-ROM that makes the companion itself a multimedia tool.

AUDIENCE

Although invaluable to any reader interested in telecommunications and Web technologies, the *Companion* is targeted to librarians. The meaning of the word *librarian* has changed since the original edition, so naturally the scope of the *Companion* has changed. Today, librarians are involved with digital library design and implementation, Web design, metadata, online privacy, computer security, digital video production, streaming audio, information architecture, and more. The *Companion* exists to inform librarians about these new areas of interest.

Librarians can mean school media specialists in charge of computer labs and local area networks, instructional librarians teaching patrons how to use productivity tools and Internet applications, reference librarians accessing the Net several times a day to answer reference questions, special librarians who design and build searchable databases, and administrators who do strategic planning and budgeting for Internet services. Librarians can mean students aspiring to become librarians, enrolled in graduate schools all around the world preparing for their professions. The *Companion* was also written for library support staff, individuals involved with every aspect of library operations from serials to circulation, from cataloging to Website development.

ORGANIZATION

The *Companion* is arranged in seven parts. The basic building blocks are presented in Part I, "Essential Background." This section explains the librarian's role in technology and lays down the framework necessary to get libraries ready to operate in a global network environment.

Part II, "What You Need to Get Ready," covers technical information relating to hardware, software, and connecting methods—the information needed to provide your users and staff with appropriate levels of Internet services.

Part III, "Tools and Resources," remains the heart of the book. The Gopher chapter has been dropped, but the other tools are still explained in detail including telnet, FTP, Archie, online libraries, Free-Nets, Lynx, search engines, and directories.

Part IV is new to this edition. "The Multimedia Experience" covers all aspects of the multimedia marvel, from capturing images with scanners and digital cameras, to building Web-based databases containing video and sound clips.

Part V, entitled "Communication Systems," is dedicated solely to popular communication services—namely e-mail, mailing lists, and Usenet news.

The Internet continues to have a significant impact on the librarian's role as an electronic publisher. Thus, Part VI, "Your Library as an Electronic Publisher," contains three chapters covering Web publishing, Web-based search engines and databases, and digital publishers and digital libraries.

Appendixes, Part VII, include "A Glossary of Terms," "Library Discussion Lists," "Online Access to Schools of Library and Information Science," "Job Hunting Online for Librarians," "File Types and the Software That Creates Them," "Organizations Involved in Network Activity," and "Keeping Up with What's New."

NEW AND EXPANDED CONTENT

The knowledge base on which librarians make decisions and implement new Internet resources and services has changed dramatically. To accommodate these changes, the second edition of the *Neal-Schuman Complete Internet Companion for Librarians* offers expanded content in all areas related to Web technology. New chapters have been added and other chapters have been reorganized and brought up-to-date.

- Linking to library-related Web resources through subject directories is made easy with the new addition of a CD-ROM. Traditional topics are included along with new topics like Website development, information architecture, and knowledge management.

- Completely revised chapters on History, the Librarian's Role, Connection Methods, Hardware and Software, Resource Discovery, Reference Practices, and Digital Libraries reflect current Internet technologies.

- New sections in the Copyright chapter help you understand the impact of computer and communications technology on the creation, reproduction, and distribution of copyrighted works on the Internet.

- Domain name registration, purchasing domain names, and finding out which domain names are in current use are new elements of the librarian's responsibilities in today's libraries.

- New e-mail security coverage is presented in the e-mail chapter.

- New chapters on Creating and Editing Multimedia, Multimedia on the Web, and Implementing Web-Based Search Engines and Databases address new challenges in Web technology for librarians.

- There are numerous online resources that complement the print material in the *Companion*. New Online Resource boxes alert readers on where they can find special online resources and services.

- A thorough discussion on Internet security addresses firewalls, hostile scripts, ActiveX and Java, cookies, e-mail bombs, ping flooding, and cryptography.

- The invisible Web is all of the information that is invisible to basic search engines. A thorough description of the invisible Web has been added to the Resource Discovery chapter.

- The Linux operating system is gaining considerable popularity worldwide. The UNIX chapter has been expanded to include an explanation of what Linux is all about, whether your library should use it, as well as installation and security tips.

- Staying current on new hardware and software is a unique challenge. New links to hardware and software reviews on the CD-ROM alert librarians to the latest innovations in these areas.

- New e-book and online out-of-print book dealers are added to the chapter on Integrating Tools into Other Library Services.

- A new chapter, Virtually Yours for Free, shows you where to find FREE search and indexing systems, Webspace, metatag generators, statistical services, and much more.

CONVENTIONS USED IN THE *COMPANION*

This book applies the following conventions relating to typography, special word meanings, and formats for displaying certain types of data:

- Characters that you type—commands or statements—are shown in **boldface** type and the computer response is in sans serif font to set it apart from regular text. The following example shows that when you type the phrase **type recent-files.txt** at a system prompt ($), the computer responds with "This is a list of all the files . . . ."

```
$ type recent-files.txt
;This is a list of all the files which have been created or modified in the
;past three weeks. It is created every night at 2AM Pacific time.
;
;Flags Size        Modified              File Name
;
-r    187          May 12 02:00         ./help/recent-files.txt
-r    154          May 12 02:00         ./help/all-files.txt
-r 559872          May 11 20:59         ./util/DW_w.1.sea.bin
-r 116447          May 11 20:07         ./help/popular-files.txt
```

- Unless stated otherwise, pay careful attention to upper- and lowercase letters when entering data. Special keys such as SHIFT, CTRL, ENTER, and ESC are shown in uppercase letters.
- When you read the phrase "enter the command . . . ", you should type whatever expression follows and then press the ENTER or RETURN key.
- In specifying the form of a command, words enclosed in angle brackets (< >) indicate variables. In other words, you are to insert your own input in place of the bracketed information. For example, if you are asked to enter the command **get <filename>**, you supply the name of the file. If the file name were *net.bib.txt*, you would enter **get net.bib.txt**. If you are asked to type **subscribe <your_name>**, you would type **subscribe John Doe** (assuming that your name is John Doe).
- For ease of reading, computer addresses and user IDs are printed in lowercase *italic* type. For example, *abenson3@ua1vm.ua.edu* and *cse.ogc.edu/*. When an Internet address comes at the end of a sentence, please note that the last dot is a period, not part of the address.
- File names and directory pathnames are printed in *italic* type. For example, you may be told to go to the */pub/history/doc* directory and retrieve a file called *constitution.txt*.
- New terms also are presented in *italic* type. These are terms being introduced and defined for the first time.
- By convention, the computer system you connect to is referred to as the *host* system. If it is your dial-up host—the computer you dial up to as your link to the Internet—it is referred to as a *local host*. If it is a host you springboard to from the local host (that is, reach by means of the local host), it is referred to as a *remote host*.

  The terms *local* and *remote* have no significant meaning in geographic terms. The local host may be in the same room as you and the remote host may be on the other side of the globe, or your local host may be in another city and the remote host you use may be in the building adjoining your library.
- Depending on which host shell account users connect with, prompts will vary. A *prompt* is a symbol, word, or phrase that appears on the screen to inform the user that the computer is ready to accept input. Common prompts are $ and %, but they may also consist of names or parts of Internet addresses. The terms *system prompt* or *host prompt* refer to the prompt used on a local or remote computer, a computer other than your own personal computer.
- *Command prompts* are prompts that appear when you run a particular program on a host computer. Examples of typical command prompts that you'll see include

FTP>, *MAIL>*, *TELNET>*, *archie>*, etc. When these and other prompts, such as *help>* prompts are included in the text, they are printed in *italic* type. For example, you will see the phrase, "enter the command **help** at the *archie>* prompt."

- Four address formats are used in this book and each will be explained in more detail as they are introduced in the text. Briefly, they are

  1. Electronic mail (e-mail) addresses, whether they are e-mail addresses for individuals or pieces of software running on a computer. E-mail addresses consist of two parts separated by an "at" sign (@). Here are a few examples:

     username@domain.com

     listserv@domain.edu

     info-server@domain.gov

  2. Domain name addresses, which are computer addresses:

     dra.com

     sklib.usask.ca

  3. Internet Protocol addresses, which are also computer addresses, consist of four numbers separated by dots, such as

     128.174.252

     135.108.42.125

  4. Web addresses start with a reference to a protocol, for example, *http://*, *gopher://*, *ftp://*, and *telnet://*, etc. A domain name or IP address such as *www.yahoo.com* follows the protocol. This may in turn be followed by a pathname and file name such as */business/magazines/time.html*. To save time and space, the third edition of the *Companion* drops the "http://" on Web addresses. For example, the address *http://www.barnesandnoble.com/* becomes simply *www.barnesandnoble.com/*.

- Many terms used in this book are synonymous with the word *computer*. These include *remote host*, *local host*, *machine*, *personal computer*, *server*, and *system*. The term *server* can also refer to software.

- The word *site* refers to a computer's location or address on the Internet. For example, to say that a file is available at site *netcom.com* means that the file resides on a computer whose address is *netcom.com*.

- When the term *argument* is used, it refers to the word(s) or number(s) that are entered on the same line as the command and modify or expand the command. For example, in the Archie expression "**find mpeg**," *find* is the command and *mpeg* is the argument. When running another special Internet application called FTP, you might type the phrase "**get *echo.zip*.**" The word *get* is the command and the file name "*echo.zip*" is the argument.

- When the term *string* is used, it refers to any series of alphanumeric characters (any character you can type—for example, A to Z, a to z, 0 to 9, and punctuation marks). The term *substring* refers to a series of alphanumeric characters that occur anywhere within the file name or directory name. For example, the substring *to* matches any of the following: *to*, *stop*, *toe*, *stove*.

Part I

ESSENTIAL BACKGROUND

The Internet is changing our lives in remarkable ways, becoming more central to libraries and librarians with each passing year. The Internet experience is widening its hold on librarians' everyday routines—everything from delivering documents and purchasing books to searching databases and delivering distance education. In this first part of the book, I explain what this interactive experience is all about. I provide you with a brief outline of its evolution, explain the different addressing systems used on the Internet, discuss copyright in a digital environment, and present a variety of roles librarians play in a networked environment.

In Chapter 1, I start by discussing how the Internet began and provide a brief outline of its history leading up to the development of the Web, intranets, and Internet 2. I provide a brief overview of how librarians are using the Web to make their resources and services available to the public. I also introduce the concept of network etiquette and explain how organizations communicate what they consider acceptable and unacceptable use of their services.

In Chapter 2, I describe the global addressing system that enables Internet users to connect with other objects (text files, images, sound files, etc.) and people on the Internet.

In Chapter 3, I focus on copyright issues and address concerns relating to intellectual property rights in a digital environment.

In Chapter 4, I discuss in detail the librarian's role as a navigator, educator, publisher, intermediary, information evaluator, information organizer, planner, and policymaker in a global network environment. Examples are given of librarians who are demonstrating their skills in all of these areas.

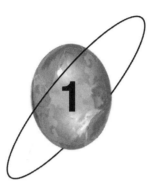

What Is the Internet?

The Internet is a worldwide network of computers and people. Built upon state-of-the-art technology, the Internet makes it possible for thousands of dissimilar physical networks that are not connected to one another and that use diverse hardware technologies to connect and operate as a single communication system.

HISTORY OF THE INTERNET

The Internet began as an effort by the Advanced Research Projects Agency (ARPA) to create a large-scale network so the computer systems of government agencies and universities could be interconnected. In 1969, the first four connection points were linked together with 56Kbps (56,000 bits per second) lines forming what was called the Advanced Research Projects Agency Network (ARPANET). The four sites that were selected included the University of Utah, the University of California at Los Angeles, the University of California at Santa Barbara, and Stanford Research Institute (now SRI International).

The Department of Defense (DoD) was interested in the early development of the Internet as a framework for building an indestructible command and control network. ARPA was to invent a system for transferring data across its network in such a way that if parts of the network were destroyed as the result of a nuclear attack, alternate paths would be available.

Online Resource
Leonard Kleinrock oversaw the installation of the first ARPANET node. The event is described in Kleinrock's personal history/biography at *millennium.cs.ucla.edu/LK/Inet/birth.html*.

This goal led to the development of a technology called *packet switching*. In packet switching, one large piece of data, such as a book, is divided into smaller chunks before being routed to its destination. Each one of these chunks, called *datagrams*, "knows" its final destination, but in getting there the datagrams take different paths and go in different directions at different times. Eventually they all end up at the same place and are put back together in the correct order to form the original book.

Another development that came out of the ARPANET project was called *dynamic rerouting*. In the preceding example, if this book were being transmitted during an enemy attack and one of the network links was destroyed, the datagram traveling on that particular link could be recovered and automatically rerouted to other links.

During its early years, ARPANET experienced continued growth as it recognized the need to communicate with other developing networks. In 1983, it became known as the ARPA Internet, and the DoD divided it into two connected networks: MILNET, a network of military computers, and ARPANET, the network of research computers.

In the mid-1980s, the National Science Foundation (NSF) created a network of supercomputers called NSFnet and in 1986 connected to ARPANET. NSFnet's sophisticated communications technology surpassed ARPANET's and, as a result, ARPANET was phased out in 1990. Those computer systems that had been a part of ARPANET joined NSFnet.

In 1987, the first commercial access company, UUNET Technologies, was founded. Uunet, along with PSINet and General Atomics, created the Commercial Internet eXchange (CIX). These were the first companies to provide commercial access to NSFnet, which made it possible for individuals not connected with research or education and commercial enterprises to access the Internet's resources.

In 1989, the number of hosts connected to the Internet exceeded 100,000 and NSFnet was upgraded to a 1.544Mbps (1.544 million bits per second) T1 backbone. During 1991 alone, the host count jumped from 376,000 in January to 617,000 in October, the National Research and Education Network (NREN) was established, the University of Minnesota developed Gopher, Thinking Machines released WAIS (Wide Area Information Service), and the High Performance Computing Act was passed.

In 1990, scientists at CERN began developing the World Wide Web and in 1991 CERN began distributing its Web software over the Internet. The Web is a collection of cross-linked documents, or "pages," stored on computers all around the world. The spider web analogy comes from the imaginary web created by the links in one document on one computer connecting to other documents on other computers all around the world.

It is remarkable to think that in the first months of 1993, Internet users could access only 50 or so registered Web servers worldwide and the Web accounted for only 0.1 percent of NSF backbone traffic. The explosive growth of the Web began later in the fall of 1993 when the National Center for Supercomputing Applications (NCSA) released Mosaic, the first graphical Web browser for Windows and Macintosh computers. By mid-1994, registered Web servers had jumped to 1,500.

In 1995, the year the first edition of this book was published, the Internet was starting to receive broad coverage in national, state, and local news media. In April 1995, the government-sponsored NSFnet backbone was shut down and replaced by a new Internet architecture called the very high speed Backbone Network Service, or vBNS *www.vbns.net/*. It originally consisted of four official network access points or NAPs. These were located in San Francisco; Chicago; Pennsauken, New Jersey; and Wash-

---

> **Online Resources**
>
> The Telecommunications Act can be viewed in plain text format at the Library of Congress *ftp://ftp.loc.gov/pub/thomas/c104/s652.enr.txt*. The Benton Foundation Telecommunications Act home page *www.benton.org/Policy/96act/* provides information and analysis on all aspects of the Act.

ington, D.C. In that same year, Netscape Communications Corp., the Web browser company founded by entrepreneur James H. Clark and software developer Marc Andreessen, debuted on Wall Street.

In 1996, the United States Congress passed the Telecommunications Act of 1996. Major provisions of the act included the controversial Communications Decency Act that was later declared unconstitutional; the embedding of V-chips into new televisions; and deregulation of the telecommunications industry. Early in 1996, Network Wizards *www.nz.com/* counted about 9.5 million hosts on the Internet. (The Internet Software Consortium *www.isc.org/ds/* now attempts to find every host on the Internet by searching the Domain Name System.) In April of 1996, Yahoo! Inc., held its public stock offering. Its stock rose from the initial offering price of $13 a share to $33 a share at the close of the next day's trading.

Push was one of the hottest buzzwords in 1997. PointCast Network, the pioneer in push technology, became famous for delivering news and information directly to your desktop through their own specialized software. (In 1999, PointCast was acquired by Launchpad Technologies and is now called EntryPoint *www.entrypoint.com/*.) In an effort to protect children from indecent materials on the Internet, President Clinton signed the sharply criticized "Child Online Protection Act" into law. In 1999, U.S. District Judge Lowell Reed declared the law unconstitutional.

> **Online Resources**
>
> "A Brief History of the Internet" is written by those who made the history, including Barry M. Leiner, Vinton G. Cerf, David D. Clark, Robert E. Kahn, Leonard Kleinrock, Daniel C. Lynch, Jon Postel, Lawrence G. Roberts, and Stephen Wolff. You can find it at *www.isoc.org/internet-history/*. Other histories include:
>
> - BBN Timeline *www.bbn.com/roles/researcher/timeline/*
> - Global Networking: A Timeline by Dr. T. Matthew Ciolek *www.ciolek.com/PAPERS/milestones.html*
> - Hobbes' Internet Timeline v4.2 *info.isoc.org/guest/zakon/Internet/History/HIT.html*
> - Netizens: On the History and Impact of Usenet and the Internet by Michael and Ronda Hauben *www.columbia.edu/~hauben/netbook/*
> - Janet Abbate's *Inventing the Internet* (The MIT Press, 1999; ISBN 0–262–01172–7) traces the history of the Internet from its early development in the 1960s to the introduction of the World Wide Web in the 1990s.

Online Resource

Visit the Nielsen//NetRatings service *www.nielsen-netratings.com/* to find out how many members of U.S. households have access to the Internet. Nielsen//NetRatings's statistics also track how many sites are visited each week and how much time is spent viewing each site.

THE INTERNET TODAY

In the early days of the Internet, ARPANET was the only backbone network available. *Backbone networks* are designated as such because of their ability to transfer data at very high speeds and with great reliability. Today, the Internet is a collection of high-speed networks composed of major backbones with the capacity to transfer data at rates over 600Mbps (600 million bits per second).

National backbones interconnect at the NAPs, Federal Internet Exchange points (FIX-EAST and FIX-WEST), and Metropolitan Area Ethernet systems known as MAEs. Some of the serious players on the national backbone level are InternetMCI, UUNET, PSINet, IBM Global Network, and Sprint IP Services. The vBNS connects 101 sites including supercomputing centers and universities and it continues to grow. In Europe, there are international backbone services provided by networks such as EuropaNET, TEN-34, and Ebone. Various smaller networks have formed alliances with each other and support the Internet on a regional level. CERFnet in San Diego and Colorado Supernet are examples of regional networks.

The Web has permeated our lives, even those of us who are non-technical. It is the most important service on the Internet. The Web includes standard formats for text, graphics, sound, and video. Web documents are indexed by Web robots and are searchable by all computers on the Internet. The Web has left the confines of the scholastic world and become a colorful, user-friendly information and entertainment resource found in offices, homes, school media centers, and libraries all around the globe.

OVERVIEW OF THE WEB

In 1990, Tim Berners-Lee and Robert Cailliau submitted a proposal to their management at CERN (European Laboratory for Particle Physics *www.cern.ch*) to develop a hypertext system called the World Wide Web. In the following year, the first U.S. Web server was launched at the Stanford Linear Accelerator Center *www.slac.stanford.edu*.

The Web is a hypertext system made up of millions of documents, each of which is called a *Web page*. *Hypertext*, first envisioned by Theodore Holm Nelson in 1965, is a system of managing textual information by creating associations between different docu-

---

Online Resource

"The World Wide Web FAQ" is an introduction to the Web in which author Thomas Boutell answers many common questions about browsers, Web page design, and HTML authoring. For more information, connect to site *www.boutell.com/openfaq/browsers/*.

Online Resources

"The Electronic Labyrinth" home page at *jefferson.village.virginia.edu/elab/ elab.html* is a study of hypertext and its use by literary artists. For other links to hypertext-related resources, see Eastgate Systems' home page "Selected Hypertext Resources on the Web" at *www.eastgate.com/ Hypertext.html.*

---

ments. In hypertext systems, one or more words in a document or the entire document itself are *linked* to other words or groups of words in the same document or other documents. This linking enables you to move easily back and forth from the original document to the linked document.

WEB CLIENTS AND SERVERS

The Web is based on a client/server architecture. The end user runs a program called a *client*. You can formulate a request for information using a client program and send it over the Internet to a server program running on an information provider's computer. The server program delivers the requested data back to your client program that in turn displays it on your monitor. Client programs on the Web—the programs you use to view Web pages—are called *browsers*. Two well-known browsers are Internet Explorer and Netscape Navigator.

The client/server communications operate by following a set of rules, or *protocols*, thus enabling clients like Web browsers to communicate with many and varied servers. Some of the more popular protocols supported by Web browsers are HTTP (HyperText Transfer Protocol), Gopher, telnet, FTP (File Transfer Protocol), and News.

HTTP was designed specifically for the Web and it enables clients and servers to communicate by transmitting hypertext over networks. Gopher is a protocol that uses a hierarchical menu structure to share information. Gopher has slowly been replaced by the more popular HTTP. Telnet is used to login to remote computers. FTP enables clients and servers to transfer text and binary files over the Internet. News, which follows a set of rules called NNTP (Network News Transfer Protocol), governs the distributions of Usenet Newsgroups over the Internet.

LIBRARIES AND THE WEB

In Chapter 4, I explore the roles of librarians in a global information network. With the advent of the Web, the librarian's role as information organizer has extended beyond the confines of his or her own library's collection. Librarians now are indexing resources owned by libraries other than their own. As publishers, librarians are designing and writing home pages, mounting them on Web servers, and making them freely available to

---

Online Resource

"The World Wide Web: Origins and Beyond" is a paper written in 1995 by Lenny Zeltser that discusses the historical aspects of the Web. See *www.seas.upenn.edu/~lzeltser/WWW/.*

---

anyone with access to the Internet. One particularly well-known library site is named the Internet Public Library.

The Internet Public Library

The Internet Public Library, or IPL for short, exists only on the Web. Built around a public library metaphor, the IPL began as a class project at the School of Information and Library Studies (now the School of Information) at the University of Michigan in 1995. Currently under the direction of David S. Carter, the IPL has a full-time staff and works in partnership with Bell & Howell Information and Learning (formerly UMI).

When you link to the IPL's homepage at *www.ipl.org/*, click on the link labeled "About the Library" to learn more about the library's mission, Statement of Principles, e-mail discussion list, and FAQ. The IPL organizes a wide variety of information including reference resources, exhibits, magazines, newspapers, online texts, and resources and services for librarians, teens, and youths.

Thomas Dowling's Libweb

One of the best sites for accessing hundreds of other library home pages is Libweb. Thomas Dowling maintains Libweb at *sunsite.berkeley.edu/Libweb/* where he lists over 3,000 library home pages in over 90 countries. Dowling's directory can be browsed starting with any one of the following subject headings:

United States
Europe
Africa and the Middle East
Asia
Australia, New Zealand, and the Pacific
Canada
Mexico, the Caribbean, Central America, and South America
Library-Related Companies

The heading "United States" is further subdivided into "Academic Libraries," "Public Libraries," "National Libraries and Library Organizations," "State Libraries," "Regional Consortia," and "Special and School Libraries." Libweb is indexed and supports keyword searching. To conduct a search, click on the link labeled "Keyword Search" found on the home page.

Reference Libraries on the Web

The phrase *reference library*, when used on the Web, has come to mean a collection of electronic resources or links to electronic resources gathered in one place. A wide variety of electronic resources are available at reference sites, including dictionaries, maps, phone books, currency exchange tables, and even search engines for tracking UPS and FedEx packages. The IPL offers original reference materials, including a Web searching guide, facts about the American states, and a guide to researching and writing a paper.

To see firsthand what online reference libraries are like, point your browser to any of the following samples:

Accurate Eye — *www.accurate-eye.com.au/*

AOL Reference Desk — *http://www.aol.com/webcenters/research/ reference.adp*

Research-It! — *www.iTools.com/research-it/research-it.html*

The Virtual Reference Desk at Purdue University — *thorplus.lib.purdue.edu/ reference/index.html*

Xplore Reference — *http://www.xplore.com/xplore500/medium/reference.html*

Yahoo! Reference — *dir.yahoo.com/Reference/*

The Australian Libraries Gateway

The Australian Libraries Gateway (ALG) *www.nla.gov.au/libraries/* attempts to list every library in Australia by providing this directory of more than 5,200 Australian libraries. In an effort to keep resources and services as current as possible, the ALG gives each library listed in the directory their own password. When libraries want to change or amend information, they login and make the changes themselves. The directory can be searched by subject, keyword, and phrase. Two special services offered by ALG include a browsable collection of links to online Australian library exhibits, and a collection of links to specialized directories and databases. An advanced search option lets you search for exhibits as well as online image collections. The specialized directories and databases are all Australian-based and include information on publishers, booksellers, online journals, books and writers, and more.

The Canadian Library Index

The Canadian Library Index is a service maintained by Peter Scott at *www.lights.com/ canlib/*. This directory of libraries is organized by geographic location and then alphabetically within each of these categories. Scott includes libraries of all types, from public and governmental, to university and medical. A link called "Other Library Web Resources" takes you to other top-level sites, such as Yahoo!'s index of libraries and Michael Sauers World Wide Web Library Directory *www.webpan.com/msauers/libdir/* that indexes over 6,000 library-related Websites in 102 countries. Sauers' site can be either browsed by geographic location, or searched by keyword.

School Libraries on the Web: A Directory

Linda Bertland's School Libraries on the Web *www.voicenet.com/~bertland/libs.html* lists Web pages maintained by K–12 libraries in the United States and around the world. The directory can be browsed by country. Special collections at this site include Websites maintained by School District Departments of Library/Media Services, State Department of Education Pages Relating to Library/Media Center Services, and Internet-Related Resources for Librarians. Bertland's resources page covers these main topics:

- Current awareness sites
- Writing your own library Web page
- Web page policies K–12
- Intellectual freedom, acceptable use policies, and filters
- Evaluating the Web
- Copyright Issues
- Learning and teaching the Web
- Other directories of library and education related Websites

Public Libraries of Europe

Sheila and Robert Harden maintain the Public Libraries of Europe Website at *dspace.dial.pipex.com/town/square/ac940/eurolib.html*. The Hardens are working on a complete, country-by-country listing of European public libraries. Their directory also includes general library links for many of the countries. These links focus on library associations and national libraries.

Yahoo!'s Library Sites by Subject

Yahoo! has assembled links to thousands of libraries organized under topics such as academic libraries, digital libraries, libraries for the blind, military libraries, presidential libraries, religious libraries, sports libraries, U.S. state libraries, and more. To access these sites and Anthony Wilson's *Libraries FAQ*, point your browser to *dir.yahoo.com/Reference/Libraries/*.

THE ARRIVAL OF INTRANETS AND EXTRANETS

An *intranet* is a Web-based architecture used for managing internal information. It is an organization-wide information system that usually resides behind a firewall and uses Internet tools, protocols, and technology to gather, store, and disseminate information. An intranet could be something as simple as a single HTML document made accessible on a Local Area Network, or it could be as complex as one or more dedicated Web servers with thousands of HTML documents linking together a worldwide network of corporate offices.

Intranets take the same features that make a World Wide Web useful—absence of geographic and time barriers, integrating multiple information services into a single interface, interactive multimedia applications, etc.—and bring them into the office. *Intranet Design Magazine* is an excellent online resource covering intranet and extranet development, tools, and tutorials. To learn more, visit their site at *idm.internet.com/index.html*.

As intranets become ubiquitous in the corporate world, there is no reason that these same concepts can't be applied to libraries' internal information systems. Nonprofit library systems that are "single" library systems or multiple library systems confined to relatively small geographic areas—a city, county, or college campus—may not realize

---

> **Online Resource**
>
> "Intranets: Readings and Resources," a resource guide compiled by Carolyn Kotlas of the Institute for Academic Technology, will steer you to dozens of intranet-related resources accessible both on and off the Web. To learn more about this resource guide, go to *www.unc.edu/cit/guides/irg-34.html.*

the same benefits national and international corporations realize, but there are still benefits to be gained.

Intranets in libraries can be used to link staff to copies of departmental handbooks, personnel manuals, copies of the library's mission statement, goals and objectives, annual reports, and staff white pages, etc. The intranet also can serve as a bulletin board where the library staff posts interesting news stories, job announcements, monthly reports, and training schedules. With applications like RealAudio, messages can be heard, not just read. Corporate library intranets can be used to manage proprietary information resources for their company's employees or other authorized individuals.

An *extranet* is like an intranet in that it uses Internet protocols to share information. It's different in that it also uses the public telecommunications system to allow various levels of access to outsiders. Outsiders, such as business partners, can only access an extranet if they are given a valid username and password. Corporate librarians might use an extranet to exchange data with librarians in partner companies. Extranets are extensions of private intranets with many security features added, such as the use of digital certificates, e-mail encryption, and VPNs. VPNs, or Virtual Private Networks, are networks that *tunnel* through public networks.

E-COMMERCE ON THE NET

E-commerce, now a billion dollar business, stands for electronic commerce—the buying and selling of products and services over the Internet. Corporations have discovered the value of Internet connectivity in their day-to-day operations. For many, the Internet offers better convenience and lower overhead. Companies like Bank One are launching their virtual counterparts, in this case WingspanBank *www.wingspanbank.com/.* At WingspanBank, customers can invest online, pay bills online, and even *chat* with financial advisors.

> **Online Resources**
>
> Intranets.com *intranets.com/* offers free intranet hosting. You are assigned your own URL in the format http://<your name>.intranets.com/. Features include the ability to build your own group members and group contacts databases, maintain a calendar, post announcements, and store, search, and retrieve documents. The intranet you create can only be accessed by individuals who know the proper username and password. IntraGenics *www.intragenics.com/* also offers free intranet hosting that supports employee directories, discussion boards, news, suggestion boxes, and more.

Online Resource

Nielsen/NetRatings is an Internet measurement service of Nielsen Media Research and NetRatings, Inc. Go to their site *www.nielsen-netratings.com/* to find out what the hottest ten Web properties, banner adds, and advertisers are each week.

Online Resources

Banner exchanges are programs where Web page owners make a banner and trade it with other Website owners. One person promises to show another person's banner on his/her site as long as that other person shows his/her banner on their site. There are a lot of different banner exchange programs from which to choose.

When choosing a site, consider what the *ratio of impressions* is. For example, for every two banners you show on your site, if one of your banners gets shown on someone else's site, the ratio of impressions is 2:1. With BannerExchange *www.bannerexchange.com/*, the ratio is 2:1.

Business managers use the Internet's global communications capabilities for maintaining contact with customers and employees, for staying on top of international developments that relate to their business, and for collaborative projects in the areas of research and development. Businesses large and small are setting up shop in cybermalls and virtual storefronts. Hundreds of Internet services like Yahoo! *www.yahoo.com* and AltaVista *www.altavista.com/* are able to provide their services free of charge by selling advertising space to companies with Web pages.

Individuals can now set up their own e-stores on the Web without any technical training. Two of the best sites for establishing a virtual storefront offer basic services for free. These sites, *www.bigstep.com* and *www.freemerchant.com*, walk you through the steps of building your own storefront. They offer free auction tools, shopping cart services, package tracking, and more.

WHAT IS SSL?

A major concern for customers using credit cards online is security. SSL is a protocol developed by Netscape Communications Corporation that uses encryption for securely delivering data over the Internet. SSL, which stands for Secure Sockets Layer, creates a secure connection between the Web browser and server. Once the connection is made, any amount of data can be transmitted in a secure setting. Web pages that require an SSL connection begin with https://. For a thorough introduction to SSL, see *developer.netscape.com/docs/manuals/security/sslin/contents.htm.*

Online Resource

The Hermes Project *www-personal.umich.edu/~sgupta/hermes/* is a research project that analyzes the commercial uses of the World Wide Web.

> **Online Resource**
>
> Brint.com *www.brint.com/ISJournal.htm* is a directory listing dozens of business and technology magazines and journals that link to thousands of articles. Topics center around technology industry news and research.

INTERNET-STYLE BROADCASTING

As the volume of information on the Internet continues to grow at a staggering pace, business executives believe that searching for information will become less and less effective. Websites are having a hard time selling banner ads because advertisers know they must wait for surfers to stumble onto a site before their banner ads will be visited.

Webcasting addresses these issues by creating customized content and delivering it directly to viewers. The process typically works like this:

1. You download Webcasting software
2. You choose which channels you're interested in (information is organized into *channels*)
3. You decide how often you would like updates
4. The Webcasting service stores your profile and searches the Web for relevant information and sends it out

This kind of information delivery is called *push delivery*. Webcasting is a service that appeals to the masses and it enables marketers to send animated ads to targeted customers. Webcasting technology has also found its way into corporate settings. Information is downloaded to corporate servers and then relayed to employees. Companies can set up their own channels for broadcasting company news.

EntryPoint Incorporated recently acquired the pioneer of Webcasting, PointCast, Inc. It offers a free *Internet toolbar* that can be downloaded at *www.entrypoint.com/*. Toolbar buttons link you to shopping, news, sports, and more. BackWeb *www.backweb.com* is a push technology company that offers software for e-commerce. For example, Charles Schwab & Co. uses BackWeb to deliver information to its retail branch offices and customer service centers.

HOW MANY PEOPLE USE THE INTERNET?

ISC (Internet Software Consortium) *www.isc.org/* administers grants of money and equipment to software developers who maintain software used on the Internet. The ISC sponsors the Domain Survey that is subcontracted to Network Wizards. Network Wizards *www.nw.com/*, a computer and communication products company in Menlo Park, California, keeps track of the number of hosts on the Internet by counting the number of IP (Internet Protocol) addresses that have been assigned a name. A thorough explanation of their survey techniques, which are somewhat complicated, can be found at *www.isc.org/ds/new-survey.html*.

As of this writing, the most recent Internet Domain Survey was completed in July 1999 and can be accessed through ISC's home page. The survey is taken twice a year.

The current survey shows the host count on the Internet to be at 56,218,000. Network Wizards defines *host* as any domain name with an IP address associated with it.

MIDS (Matrix Information and Directory Services), a corporation founded by John S. Quarterman et al., offers various services including a monthly newsletter called *Matrix News*, quarterly statistical maps, and animated maps called The Internet Weather Report. To create this report, which looks something like a weather map, Quarterman pings thousands of Internet sites six times a day, seven days a week, and creates a database showing the location of each site and the time in milliseconds the ping took. *Ping*, short for *Packet Internet Groper*, is a program used to determine whether specific Internet addresses are accessible. Each day, the results are compiled into geographic maps that show time lag. Maps can be viewed at */www.mids.org*.

NUA Internet Consultancy and Developer is an Irish firm that offers many interesting surveys, graphs, and charts relating to Internet growth. You can access this information free of charge at their Website *www.nua.net/surveys/*.

In addition to the statistics stored on MIDS and the Domain Name Survey home pages mentioned earlier, other interesting facts can be found on GVU's home page. The Graphics, Visualization, & Usability (GVU) Center is a research lab affiliated with Georgia Tech's College of Computing. GVU runs Web surveys and publishes the results on their home page at *www.gvu.gatech.edu/user_surveys/*. Their surveys give interesting insight into Web users, such as the age of the average Web user, marital status, political profile, and more. To stay abreast of matters relating to Internet growth, continue to check in with MIDS, Network Wizards, NUA, and the GVU survey team.

INTERNET 2 PROJECT

The transition from government supported backbones to a totally privatized system in the U.S. has led to the development of a new system of backbones called *Internet 2*, or I2 for short. Proponents of Internet 2, sometimes referred to as the *Next Generation Internet (NGI)*, believe that privatization of the Internet has detracted from the Internet's development, putting the focus more on business profits and less on researchers' needs. Internet 2 addresses this problem by focusing its attention on the next generation of university networks—a system that promises to be one hundred times faster than today's system.

The current Internet provides a *best-effort* level of service for technologies we are generally familiar with today. Emerging technologies and anticipated future applications are driving the requirements of the next-generation Internet. And who is building the next-generation Internet? In the early 1990s, Web servers were designed at the CERN particle physics lab. Mosaic, the first graphical-interface Web browser, was invented at the National Center for Supercomputing. Today, scientific research centers are building the next-generation Internet. The National Computational Science Alliance (NCSA), centered at the University of Illinois at Urbana-Champaign, is a partnership of researchers developing a high-speed national network (the National Technology Grid). The *Grid* brings together massive databases and high-performance computers. The National Partnership for Advanced Computing Infrastructure (NPACI) at the University of California–San Diego is also working on advanced networking.

The goals of Internet 2 are to create a world-class network that will support the national research community; develop a new generation of applications that push the en-

---

Online Resources

Learn more about the high-performance research and education networks connecting institutions all around the world at *www.ucaid.edu/abilene/html/peernetworks.html.*

There are over 170 Internet 2 universities. You can link to all of them at *www.internet2.edu/html/members.html.*

---

velope of this new leading edge network; and make the new services resulting from Internet 2 available to every level of education and to the Internet community at large.

At the heart of this collaborative effort between universities, private industry, and federal agencies is a new technology called a gigaPoP. *GigaPoPs* are the connection points that link one or more institutional members of the Internet 2 project with one or more service providers. The highly advanced equipment located at these sites will enable data transfer rates of at least 622 megabits/second. What will the next generation of I2 applications be? What will the next high-performance *killer app* be? Hard to say, but it may be something in the teleimmersion field. *Teleimmersion* is a combination of teleconferencing, virtual reality, and telepresence. *Telepresence* is a term used to describe the sense of being present in a mediated virtual environment. By combining teleconferencing, telepresence, and virtual reality, teleimmersion enables teachers and students to interact with three-dimensional models, point, gesture, converse, and see each other.

To stay abreast of the latest developments relating to Internet 2, set a bookmark on the Internet2 news site at *www.internet2.edu/.* This site, maintained by Greg Wood, offers access to Internet2 technical reports, news items, and FAQs. A government accounting of the Next Generation Internet initiative can be found at */www.ngi.gov/.* Highlights of this site include presentations, publications, workshops, and more. Many participating universities have set up their own I2 Websites; for example, The University of Alabama at *bama.ua.edu/~i2/.* The University Corporation for Advanced Internet Development (UCAID) *www.internet2.edu/ucaid/* is guiding many universities' networking efforts. The UCAID site has the latest information on advanced research networking.

NETWORK ETIQUETTE

The rules of the Internet are referred to as network etiquette, or *netiquette*. These rules relate to courtesy, politeness, and consideration for others when using Internet services, especially e-mail and newsgroups. If you're new to the Internet, take a few minutes to learn about netiquette before you become actively involved.

Much has been published online about Internet etiquette and customs. Using a Web search engine and searching on the terms *etiquette* or *netiquette* will lead you to many of these resources. The Centre for Policy Research on Science and Technology at Simon Fraser University maintains a Web server *edie.cprost.sfu.ca/* that describes their research and programs. Included on this site is an online tutorial called "A Roadmap to the Internet" which has a chapter on netiquette. Arlene Rinaldi of Florida Atlantic University maintains an award-winning Internet netiquette home page at *www.fau.edu/netiquette/netiquette.html.*

With the recent growth of commercial enterprises on the Internet, *business netiquette* has become a specialized subcategory of Internet netiquette. WestHost, a well-known virtual Web server site *www.westhost.com*, publishes an Internet marketing manual at *se.westhost.com/mmanual.html*. This manual describes what is considered acceptable behavior for commercial development and use of the Internet.

Networks and Internet hosts have developed what are called *Acceptable Use Policies* and *Terms of Service*. These are policy statements that outline an organization's core principles and explain what they consider acceptable and unacceptable use of their services. When you obtain your Internet account, you will be asked to sign and/or read an Acceptable Use Policy or some form of membership agreement whereby you agree to adhere to the service provider's rules.

When using another system besides your own, either through FTP or telnet, remember that you are a guest on that system and you should conduct yourself appropriately, complying with any stated restrictions.

When you login to a remote computer and establish a continuous connection (as occurs when using telnet), do your work and then logoff when you're finished. Don't leave the connection open unnecessarily.

When logging in to a public FTP site, login as "anonymous" and enter your e-mail address when prompted for a password. (Some FTP sites can be accessed only if you have proper authorization.) To copy files to or from these sites, you will need a user ID and password. Good examples are FTP sites that allow you to upload files to their free Web hosting services, such as Geocities *geocities.yahoo.com/home/*. To successfully upload files, you must enter the user ID and password you registered with Geocities. FTP sites that require no special registration are referred to as *anonymous FTP sites*. These are sites where the system administrator has set the FTP server up with a special user ID named "anonymous" that anyone is permitted to use.

When possible, avoid logging in to remote machines during periods of heavy usage such as peak business hours. The best time to login without running into a lot of traffic (which results in slow response times) is on weekends or very early in the morning and late at night on weekdays.

Online Resources

Netiquette Home Page *www.albion.com/netiquette/* presents "The Core Rules of Netiquette," "The Netiquette Quiz," a netiquette mailing list, and links to excerpts from the book *Netiquette* by Virginia Shea.

Newsgroup Netiquette *www.vonl.com/vtab24/news102.htm* offers tips on how to avoid network news flames and mail bombs.

Many universities offer netiquette guides. For example, the University of New Mexico posts one of the earlier explanations of what netiquette is all about at *redtail.unm.edu/cp/netiquette.html*. If you are looking for a netiquette guide that you can post on your library site, consider RFC 1855 published on Delaware Technical and Community College's Website at *www.dtcc.edu/cs/rfc1855.html*. This document offers unlimited distribution.

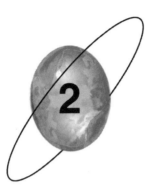

Internet Addressing Systems

Every computer on the Internet, referred to as a *host*, has its own unique address. Every person who uses the Internet e-mail system is given a user ID, which is used in combination with a host address. Every home page on the Web has its own unique address, too. In identifying where all of these entities are located on the Internet, three addressing systems have evolved: A hierarchical naming system called the *Domain Name System*; a numerical system called *IP addressing*; and an addressing system called *URLs*, which are used for identifying sites on the Web.

In this chapter, I explain how each of these addressing systems work and tell you how to find out more about the individual or organization behind the address.

THE DOMAIN NAME SYSTEM

Domain names have taken on new meaning since the first edition of this book. They provide a unique identity for individuals and businesses. Individuals use domain names like customized license plates. Domain names have become critical to successful Internet marketing. A company's domain name, corporate identity, brand, and product are often one and the same thing.

Domain names have an intrinsic value. In November 1999, the Industrial Bank of Korea *www.ibk.co.kr/*, in partnership with a domain name registration service, began offering mortgages on domain names. The bank treats domain names as if they were real estate, or *virtual* real estate in this instance. In that same year, Congress began tackling a new phenomenon called cybersquatting. *Cybersquatters* are individuals or organizations that register several domain names, including popular trademark names, in hopes of selling them off at a later date to the highest bidder.

A domain name looks like this: *opac.sfsu.edu*. As you can see, domain names consist of a series of subnames separated by periods or *dots*. When you read the address

---

Online Resource
RFCs (Request for Comments) that relate to the Domain Name System include these: RFC 1034, Domain Names–Concepts and Facilities; RFC 974, Mail Routing and the Domain System. An easy way to access these RFCs and others is by going to the Internet RFC/STD/FYI/BCP Archives at *www.faqs.org/rfcs/*.

from left to right, the subnames go from most specific to most general. Subnames refer to values such as country, type of organization, organization name, and computer name. The above address tells you that there is a computer named "opac" located at San Francisco State University (*sfsu*), which is an educational institution (*edu*).

TOP-LEVEL DOMAIN

The *top-level* domain is the name located furthest to the right in the domain name. In the domain name *uafsysb.uark.edu*, the top-level domain is *edu*, which refers to an educational institution. Other top-level domain names look like these:

com:	commercial businesses and for-profit organizations
gov:	U.S. government organizations
int:	international organizations
mil:	U.S. military organizations
net:	networking organizations
org:	nonprofit organizations

You can view an up-to-date breakdown of domain names managed by InterNIC at */www.domainstats.com/internic.cfm*.

FIRST-LEVEL DOMAIN

Just to the left of the *edu* is the first-level domain. In the example *uafsysb.uark.edu*, the first-level domain is *uark*, which stands for the University of Arkansas.

HOST NAME

The lowest level in the domain name system is the *host name*. The host name is to the left of the first dot of the host's first-level domain name. Host names identify a computer on the Internet. In our example, the host's name is *uafsysb*, which is short for the University of Arkansas at Fayetteville, System B computer. Network Wizards *www.nw.com/zone/WWW/firstnames.html* lists the top one hundred host names. Their survey shows that the top five host names in order of popularity are *www*, *host*, *mail*, *dummy*, and *router*.

In some instances, there are second-level domains delegated to organizations such as K–12 schools, community colleges, private schools, libraries, museums, as well as city and county governments. Examples of second-level domains are shown here:

     CC: Community colleges
    TEC: Technical colleges
    LIB: Libraries
    K12:   Kindergarten through 12th grade schools and districts
STATE: State government
    MUS: Museums

GEOGRAPHIC TOP-LEVEL DOMAINS

Some top-level domains describe countries. They are referred to as *geographical top-level domains* and are based on a country's two-letter international standard abbreviation. Thus, the domain name *hydra.uwo.ca* has as its top-level domain *ca*, which stands for Canada, and *saline.lib.ar.us* has as its top-level domain *us*, which stands for United States. Examples of other geographical top-level domains include these:

    Ar: Argentina (Argentine Republic)
    aq: Antarctica
    au: Australia
    be: Belgium
    cl: Chile (Republic of)
    fi: Finland (Republic of)
    de: Germany (Federal Republic of)

The name space under *us* is the state name space that is based on the two-letter state codes assigned by the U.S. Postal Service. For example, *Microsoft.Redmond.WA.US* denotes the state of Washington. For more information on the U.S. Domain Registration Services, including how to get a U.S. domain name, consult the Official Registry United States Top-Level Domain Website at *www.nic.us*.

One of the newer top-level domain names, *.tv*, has been assigned to Tuvalu, a small island nation located in the southwest Pacific Ocean. Because "tv" is an international abbreviation that stands for television, anyone using the ".*tv*" top-level domain tends to attract a lot of consumers. This is why the .TV Corporation, the exclusive registrar for the *.tv* domain, is able to charge $1,000 or more for the first year registration fee.

Larry Landweber at the Computer Sciences Department of the University of Wisconsin—Madison maintains a complete list of country codes and levels of connectivity. You can find the latest version of this list in the *connectivity_table* directory at FTP site *ftp.cs.wisc.edu*. The phrase *FTP site* refers to both a protocol and a computer. *FTP* stands for *File Transfer Protocol*, which is a method used for transferring files from one computer to another. A computer that makes files available on the Internet via FTP is referred to as an FTP site. FTP sites have Internet addresses—in this case, *ftp.cs.wisc.edu*.

As you can see by this reference to Landweber's list, understanding how to use an Internet address is essential if you want to retrieve any information from the Internet. The procedures for using FTP and connecting with FTP sites will become clearer when you read Chapter 13, "Transferring Files on the Internet."

Online Resource

DomainGames *www.domaingames.com/* supports a name search engine that enables you to search for specific or partial names using wild cards. This site also provides daily reports on dropped domain names and new domain names.

WHAT DOMAIN NAMES ARE IN CURRENT USE?

Several sites on the Internet enable you to search domain name databases to determine whether a particular domain name has been reserved. For example, NetNames.com *www.netnames.com/*, an international domain name registration company, provides a free search engine for searching domain names. On NetNames.com's home page (they also maintain a U.S. site at *www.netnameusa.com/*), there is a text box labeled "domain search." Enter a domain name, for example, *librarybook.com*, and press ENTER. The search results screen lists two top-level domains that use the name *librarybook*. You can jump to "whois" information on each name to find out who registered the domain name, contact information, when the name was registered, and when it was last updated. When you search on a more obscure name, such as *tambour-militaire.com* (French for "military drum"), the system informs you that *tambour-militaire.com* is available, as is *tambour-militaire.net* and *tambour-militaire.org*.

HOW CAN I PURCHASE A DOMAIN NAME?

Purchasing domain names is quite simple. First you must establish that the domain name you wish to register is not already in use. Once you establish that, you can go ahead and register your name. As a result of free market competition, there are numerous sites that offer .com, .net, and .org domain name registration services, online name availability checking, whois services, and more.

The Internet Corporation for Assigned Names and Numbers (ICANN) lists accredited domain name registrars currently taking domain name registrations at *www.icann.org/registrars/accredited-list.html*. Network Solutions *www.networksolutions.com/* is one of the better known Internet domain name registration service providers. It acts as the exclusive registrar for and maintainer of second-level domain names within the .com, .org, and .net top-level domains. Network Solutions provides an e-mail based registration template application process for the registration of domain names. The basic charge is $70 per address for the first two years.

WHOSE DOMAIN ADDRESS IS IT?

A service called *whois* provides you with information about who administers a particular domain name. You can access the whois service various ways. If you have a Web

---

Online Resource

DotStreet.com offers free posting services for domain names that are for sale or lease. If you have a domain name you would like to trade, visit their site at *www.dotstreet.com*.

---

browser, the simplest method is to point your browser to *www.networksolutions.com/ cgi-bin/whois/whois*. This registry database contains only .com, .net, and .org domains. Enter the domain name in question, press a search button, and moments later the results are returned. If this site is busy, try namedroppers.com at *www.namedroppers.com/*.

For a more comprehensive search, use Allwhois.Com. This service lists all currently accepted domain name extensions (top-level domains) and also lets you search them. You can reach Allwhois.Com at *www.allwhois.com/*.

An example of the kind of information provided by the whois service is shown below. When you search on the name *applepie.com*, this is what you get:

Registrant:

Fisher Zvieli (APPLEPIE5–DOM)
18034 Ventura Blvd No 225
Encino, CA 91316
US

Domain Name: APPLEPIE.COM
Administrative Contact, Technical Contact, Zone Contact:
     Fisher, O (OF176) america@INSTANET.COM
     818–8816058
Billing Contact:
     Fisher, O (OF176) america@INSTANET.COM
     818–8816058

Record last updated on 20–Mar-1998.
Record created on 20–Mar-1998.
Database last updated on 22–Jan-2000 13:59:13 EST.

Domain servers in listed order:
NS.ZF.NET 205.216.134.37
DNS.ZF.NET 216.102.246.43

E-MAIL ADDRESSES

E-mail addresses incorporate domain names and they include a user ID and an @ ("at" sign). If you wanted to send e-mail to an individual with an account on a computer host named *uafsysb.uark.edu*, you would insert his or her user ID in front of the domain name and it would appear like this: *jgitshaw@uafsysb.uark.edu*. This can be translated as meaning, "There is a person named *jgitshaw* at a computer named *uafsysb.uark.edu*." User IDs usually are assigned to you and they may include all or part of your first name, last name, or anything else for that matter.

Some computer names have an extra subdomain, showing even more specificity. For example, in the e-mail address *acbenson@engrserver.engr.uark.edu*, the *engr* stands for the College of Engineering. Mail addressed to this address goes to user id *acbenson* at a computer named *engrserver* housed in the College of Engineering at the University of Arkansas. Other examples of domain names are shown in Table 2–1.

Table 2–1: Examples of Internet addresses and their meanings	
brain.biblio.brocku.ca	*brain* is the name of a computer hosting the library catalog at Brock University in Canada.
Fire-Dept.CO.Ventura.CA.US	*Fire-Dept* is the host name of a computer located in Ventura County, California.
innopac.liswa.wa.gov.au	*innopac* is the host name of a computer (running Innovative Interfaces, Inc. automation software) located at The Library and Information Service of Western Australia.
prs.k12.nj.us	*prs* (Princeton Regional School District) is the host name of a computer located somewhere on a K–12 network in New Jersey.
online.chemek.cc.or.us	*online* is the host name of a computer that supports an online BBS at Chemeketa Community College located in Oregon.
ind.doe.state.in.us	*ind* is the host name of a computer located somewhere on the Indiana State Department of Education (DOE) network.

IP ADDRESSES

Every host on the Internet is also assigned a unique identifier called an *IP address* or *Internet Protocol address*. The IP address is a numerical address consisting of four numbers separated by periods. An IP address looks like this: *128.86.8.7* and is read as, "128 dot 86 dot 8 dot 7."

In actuality, your computer system uses only numbers, turning all domain name addresses into numbers. This translation process is taken care of behind the scenes by software, so it isn't necessary to discuss the details of how it's done. The reason domain names exist in the first place is because names are more convenient for people to use and easier to remember than numbers. For this reason, you are more apt to use domain names for addressing hosts than IP addresses.

Each domain name address has a corresponding IP address and you can use either one when contacting other hosts. For example, the Carl System can be reached with either the domain name *pac.carl.org* or with its IP address *192.54.81.128*. The details of how you can contact another person or computer on the Internet by using domain name addresses and IP addresses will become clearer when the various Internet services are discussed in subsequent chapters.

THE WORLD WIDE WEB ADDRESSING SYSTEM

Objects on the Web, including textual documents, graphics, and sound files, are assigned addresses called *Uniform Resource Locators*, or URLs for short. A *URL* is a string of text that includes information on the type of resource that's being described (Gopher,

---

FTP Addresses on the Web

When writers refer to files on the Internet, FTP Uniform Resource Locators (URLs) may be presented as a directory path only or as a full path right to a specific file name. For example, suppose a writer is giving you instructions on downloading a copy of a telnet program called *trumptel.exe*, which is stored at FTP site *ftp.asu.edu* in the directory */pub/windows/apps/*. The writer might say, "You can download a copy of *trumptel.exe* by connecting to site *ftp://ftp.asu.edu/pub/windows/apps/*." Here he or she gives you the directory path only. When you connect, you can view all of the files stored in the *apps* subdirectory. You would have to click on the *trumptel.exe* file name before your browser would start the download process.

If you had been given the full path to the file *trumptel.exe*, it would have been written as *ftp://ftp.asu.edu/pub/windows/apps/trumptel.exe*. In this instance, immediately upon connecting, your browser would ask you where you would like to save *trumptel.exe* and then the download process would begin.

HTTP, FTP, or telnet, etc.), the computer's Internet address, and where the item is located on that computer. In other words, a URL is a pathname.

Here are four examples that illustrate this addressing format:

1. *http://www.nwu.edu/research/policies.html*
   This URL refers to a Web server named *www.nwu.edu* (*nwu* stands for Northwestern University and *edu* tells you the computer is located at an educational institution). The *http* at the beginning of the URL indicates that the client and server will be communicating using HyperText Transfer Protocol (HTTP). On this Web server there is a directory called *research* and within that directory a document called *policies.html*.

2. *ftp://ftp.eff.org/pub/CAF/library*
   This URL refers to a computer host named *ftp.eff.org* (*eff* stands for Electronic Frontier Foundation and *org* tells you that the organization is nonprofit) that can be accessed using File Transfer Protocol (FTP). The URL points to the */pub/CAF/library* directory on that host. This happens to be a directory filled with documents—library policy statements including the American Library Association's Freedom to Read Statement. When your browser connects to an FTP site, it automatically logs in using the login ID of *anonymous* and a password that is your e-mail address.

3. *gopher://gopher.std.com*
   This URL refers to a host named *gopher.std.com* (*std* stands for Software Tool & Die) that can be accessed using the Gopher protocol. Visitors arrive at the *root*, or main menu, when accessing this Gopher site.

4. *telnet://library.wustl.edu*
   This URL refers to a telnet server named *library.wustl.edu* (*wustl* stands for Washington University Libraries, St. Louis, MO). This server can be accessed using a telnet client.

The part of the URL that comes before the colon identifies the protocol being used by the server providing the information. For example, when the URL begins with *http://*, the resource being described is a hypertext document. The second part of the URL (the part after the two forward slashes) gives the Internet address of the host computer where the information is located. The third and fourth parts provide the directory paths and file names.

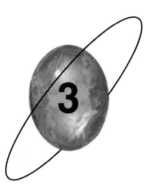

Copyright and Digital Information

The potential for copying digital works on the Internet appears to be unlimited. New Internet users soon recognize the ease and speed with which data can be transferred all around the world. They quickly see how a file can be easily downloaded from one computer and redistributed to another or many hundreds of other computers with no degradation in the quality of successive generations of copies. New users also discover how easy it is to manipulate a digital work by deleting or modifying copyright notices or other portions of text.

Copyright issues are important for librarians for several reasons. Librarians should be aware of and help safeguard intellectual property rights on the Internet. They must also be familiar with the exclusive rights held by copyright owners and know what constitutes "fair use" when reproducing digital works. These key issues are dealt with in this chapter. These issues should be given careful consideration when librarians add value to Internet services by repackaging existing information, creating Community Wide Information Systems, or establishing online local history archives.

Online Resources
For an overview of copyright law, consult the U.S. Copyright Office home page at *www.loc.gov/*. The U.S. Copyright Law is available at this site in PDF format. (To view this document, you need Acrobat Reader loaded on your PC. You can download a free copy from *www.adobe.com/*.) Another excellent resource is the Copyright Management Center of the University of Texas System Administration. The University's Office of General Counsel offers several learning aids including "The Crash Course Tutorial" on copyright law.

THE IMPORTANCE OF INTELLECTUAL PROPERTY RIGHTS

The United States copyright law tries to balance the intellectual property interests of authors, publishers, and copyright owners with society's need for the free exchange of ideas. Although most Internet users believe in the free flow of information, questions have been raised about the importance of copyright protection and how it applies in a network environment. In a free-market economy such as ours, it is clear that the elements of compensation and/or permission stimulate the creation and organization of information. For some people, producing information is a livelihood and they take risks and invest time and money to produce their information. If their intellectual property rights go unprotected on the Internet, they may be less likely to contribute. They believe that it is just as important in a network environment to preserve the protections that copyright affords as it is in a traditional print environment.

There are others, especially in the field of education, who make their information freely available and grant unlimited redistribution of their works over the Internet. Their primary interests are the widespread distribution of their work and the personal recognition that results. Due to an increasing amount of unauthorized modifications and reproductions without proper credit, some of these authors are now attaching a notice to their digital works with the proviso that they be redistributed in full, without modification, and with proper credit given to the author.

Under current copyright law, the moment a work is created it is copyrighted, even if it is distributed without a copyright notice. (Exceptions are works created by the federal government or when the owner of a work expressly states that it is dedicated to the public domain.) To prevent people from making a false assumption that a work is public domain, it makes sense for anyone claiming copyright protection to include the copyright notice. Librarians should not assume a work is in the public domain simply because there is no copyright notice attached to the work. Older works published without a notice may be in the public domain, but works created after March 1, 1989, without a notice means virtually nothing.

EXCLUSIVE RIGHTS OF COPYRIGHT OWNERS

In 1993, the Information Infrastructure Task Force (IITF) was formed to articulate the purpose of President Clinton's National Information Infrastructure (NII). The IITF is organized into various committees and working groups, and one of these working groups deals with key issues relating to intellectual property rights.

When considering what impact the latest innovations in digital technology have had on copyright protection, the Working Group on Intellectual Property Rights concluded that, " . . . with no more than minor clarification and amendment, the Copyright Act, like the Patent Act, will provide the necessary protection of rights—and limitations on those rights—to promote the progress of science and the useful arts." In July 1994, this Working Group issued a preliminary draft, popularly known as the "Green Paper" (*ftp:// ftp.aimnet.com/pub/users/carroll/law/ipnii/ipwggp.txt*). This preliminary draft was widely debated during the public comment period following its release.

The "Green Paper" was the first draft of the Working Group's "White Paper," which became the final report. The "White Paper," released in September 1995 (*www.uspto.gov/ web/offices/com/doc/ipnii/*), recommended substantial changes to U.S. copyright law.

It contained recommendations to amend the Copyright Act of 1976 (*www.arl.org/info/ frn/copy/summary.html*) and presented a lengthy legal analysis of current copyright law. The *Green Paper*'s recommendations for changes included adding "transmission" to the means by which a copyright owner may distribute his or her work.

To better understand the impact of computer and communications technology on the creation, reproduction, and distribution of copyrighted works in a network environment, it is important to review the list of exclusive rights currently granted to copyright holders in Section 106 of the copyright law. These exclusive rights exist in both the online world and the analog world. No one else may exercise these rights unless permission to do so is obtained from the copyright holder. These rights are:

- To reproduce the copyrighted work in copies or phonorecords;
- to prepare derivative works based upon the copyrighted work;
- to distribute copies or phonorecords of the copyrighted work to the public by sale or other transfer of ownership, or by rental, lease, or lending;
- in the case of literary, musical, dramatic, and choreographic works, pantomimes, and motion pictures and other audiovisual works, to perform the copyrighted work publicly; and
- in the case of literary, musical, dramatic, and choreographic works, pantomimes, and pictorial, graphic, or sculptural works, including the individual images of a motion picture or other audiovisual work, to display the copyrighted work publicly.

EXCLUSIVE ELECTRONIC RIGHTS

Electronic publishing occurs when you take print material, such as books and magazines, and make it available for use on computers. Other materials are created exclusively for electronic publication, especially multimedia works that incorporate sound, image, and motion. Making copies of a digital work violates the exclusive right of the copyright holder, unless permission is obtained or copying is considered fair use (discussed below). Digital audio, graphics, and images are considered no different than text for copyright purposes. Reproducing a work in the digital world can occur in any one of the following circumstances:

- Converting a work to digital format and saving it to a permanent storage medium, such as a floppy disk, CD-ROM, hard drive, or other computer disk.
- Converting a work to digital format and reproducing it in an electronic database.
- Downloading a copy of a digital work to a permanent storage medium.
- Transferring a copy of a digital work to another location over the Internet; for example, as an attachment to an e-mail message and sending it to one or many individuals.

E-mail and Web pages are also protected by copyright. A Web page that meets the requirement of containing a minimal amount of creativity may be protected by copyright and can contain a copyright notice. This requirement may also apply to compilations of links if the selection and arrangement of the links satisfy the creativity requirement. Telephone directory white pages, for example, do not qualify for copyright pro-

---

Online Resource

"A Guide to Copyright for Music Librarians" *www.musiclibraryassoc.org/ Copyright/copyhome.htm* helps keep interested parties up-to-date on the latest issues surrounding intellectual property rights and its relevance to music librarians. From here you can link to a statement by the Music Library Association, "Music Library Association's Statements on the Copyright Law and Fair Use in Music."

---

tection because they lack creativity. Every person with a phone number in a given geographic area is included in the phone book, so no selectivity is being exercised. In addition, the data is listed in alphabetical order, a purely mechanical process. To increase your chances of protecting a compilation of Website links, employ selectivity and exercise judgment when deciding which links to include and how to present them on your site.

Most e-mail is inconsequential and frivolous. The person who writes about a funny incident on the way to work probably isn't concerned about copyright protection. Scholars may, however, be concerned about the information they exchange pertaining to their research. An e-mail message that is original (not a copy of one created by someone else) is protected by copyright law the moment it is created and stored in a physical medium, such as a hard disk drive. If the e-mail message is created by someone within the scope of his or her employment, the employer is considered the copyright owner. It is less clear how the copyright law treats e-mail messages that are posted to systems such as Usenet newsgroups or mailing lists. One function of these services is to widely distribute the messages they receive. Once posted, many readers can copy, modify, and forward the contents of the message. To be on the safe side, obtain permission from the author of an e-mail message before copying or distributing that message.

RAM COPIES

It isn't clear whether works stored in computer RAM (Random Access Memory) are copies. RAM can be considered temporary storage because a digital document in RAM ceases to exist once the computer is shut down. In this instance, viewing a document online would not constitute copyright infringement. The other side of the argument is that computers can be left running for very long periods of time—months, even years. In these instances it is questionable whether RAM is a temporary or permanent storage device. There is no question, however, that when you make a hard copy printout, or you save a copy to disk, you are infringing on the copyright holder's reproduction rights unless you do it with the copyright owner's permission or it qualifies as fair use.

When working with computers, digital information, and online services, unless authorized or specifically exempt, infringement of the reproduction right can occur, for example, when

- a printed work is scanned into a digital file;
- a digital file is uploaded to a server or downloaded from a server;
- a digital file is transferred from one computer to another; or
- an e-mail message posted to a discussion list is captured to a disk.

If your use of information is clearly not fair use, or you are uncertain, get permission to use it. If you know who the author and the publisher are, you can contact them directly. If you are not certain who the copyright holder or publisher is, follow the suggestions put forth by Elizabeth Gadd and Adrienne Muir in Project ACORN's *Manual of Procedures on Gaining Electronic Copyright Clearance for Journal Articles* (*acorn. lboro.ac.uk/acorn/access.htm*). The Office of General Council at the University of Texas System presents a sample letter for requesting permission at *www.utsystem.edu/OGC/ IntellectualProperty/permmm.htm*.

THE FAIR USE DOCTRINE

Just as there are exclusive rights granted to copyright owners, there is also a "fair use" provision in the 1976 law (17 U.S.C., Section 107) that places certain limitations on the rights of copyright owners. The following excerpt from Section 107 presents some of the guidelines for determining whether a copyrighted work may be used without gaining permission from the copyright holder:

"Notwithstanding the provisions of sections 106 and 106A, the fair use of a copyrighted work, including such use by reproduction in copies or phonorecords or by any other means specified by that section, for purposes such as criticism, comment, news reporting, teaching (including multiple copies for classroom use), scholarship, or research, is not an infringement of copyright."

In addition to these guidelines, courts evaluate the following four factors in detail when determining whether the use made of a copyrighted work in any particular case is a fair use:

1. The purpose and character of the use;
2. the nature of the copyrighted work;
3. the amount and substantiality of the portion used in relation to the copyrighted work as a whole; and
4. the effect of the use upon the potential market for or value of the copyrighted work.

If you are not sure whether your intended use of a copyrighted work is fair use, get permission from the copyright holder or seek legal advice.

A group known as CETUS (Consortium for Educational Technology in University Systems) makes their pamphlet *Fair Use of Copyrighted Works* available online at

---

Online Resources

Stanford University Libraries maintains a Copyright and Fair Use site at *fairuse.stanford.edu/*. Here you can find links to primary materials, legislation, Internet resources, and copyright law. This site is an excellent resource for keeping up-to-date on current copyright legislation, as is the U.S. Copyright Office home page at *lcweb.loc.gov/copyright/*. Stanford's links to primary materials include U.S. Code and Regulations, International Treaties and Conventions, Case Law and Judicial Opinions, and U.S. Supreme Court Opinions.

Website *www.cetus.org/fairindex.html*. This site also has links to the U.S. Copyright Act, the Copyright Clearance Center, and other sources of copyright information.

RECENT REVISIONS TO THE COPYRIGHT LAW

In 1998, three major revisions took place in the copyright law: The Digital Millennium Copyright Act, The Sonny Bono Copyright Term Extension Act, and the Fairness in Music Licensing Act. The Digital Millennium Copyright Act (DMCA), signed into law by President Clinton on October 28, 1998, updates the copyright law to include issues of concern in the digital environment. Section 404 amends Section 108 of the copyright law to permit libraries to digitize analog materials without permission for archival purposes.

There are many provisions in the DMCA that are not discussed in this book; for example, Title II, Section 512, which establishes limitations on liability for online service providers, and the rights of copyright owners for distance education through digital networks, covered in Title IV, Section 403. For details relating specifically to distance education, see Georgia Harper's *Copyright Law for Distance Learning* at *www.utsystem.edu/ OGC/IntellectualProperty/distance.htm*. For an introductory article on the DMCA and how it defines "service providers," see *The New Digital Millennium Copyright Act Provides Safe Harbors for Service Providers* by Mark F. Radcliffe *www.legalseminars.com/ programs/members/business/library/03.htm*.

The Sonny Bono Copyright Term Extension Act (SBCTEA), Public Law 105–298, 112 Stat. 2827 (1998), amended the copyright law to extend the term of copyright protection in the United States for an additional 20 years. Signed into law by President Clinton on October 27, 1998, the SBCTEA lengthens the term of life of a copyright from "life of the author plus 50" years to "life of the author plus 70" years. In the case of works for hire created by employees or certain contracted workers, copyright lasts 95 years from the date of first publication or 120 years from date of creation, whichever ends first. Based on these new rules, it should be comparatively easy to determine how long new works are protected by copyright: Just assume everything is protected for the rest of your life and the life of your children!

Online Resource

The Coalition for Networked Information (CNI) supports a discussion list dedicated to copyright issues. To subscribe, send the following e-mail message to *listproc@cni.org*: **subscribe cni-copyright <your name>.** You can search their message archive interactively by telneting to *d5000.cni.org*. (If you don't have a particular telnet client you want to use, simply enter **telnet://d5000.cni.org** in the URL address box of your Web browser and press ENTER. This automatically starts the Windows telnet client.) Once you connect to *d5000.cni.org*, follow these steps:

1. Login with brsuser
2. Select your terminal type (vt100)
3. Enter number 1 to choose *1. Search/select a database*
4. Enter COPY to select the Copyright and Intellectual Property Forum database

It's a little more complicated figuring out the extended life of older works. Works that were created before January 1, 1978, and protected on that date now have a life extending 95 years from the date of original copyright. Old works that were not published or registered before 1978 are protected until at least the end of 2002.

SBCTEA also added a limited new exemption for certain libraries and archives in section 108 of the copyright law. (See references to Section 108(h) below.) You can view a copy of this Act in PDF format at *lcweb.loc.gov/copyright/legislation/s505.pdf*. (To view this document, you need Acrobat Reader loaded on your PC. You can download a free copy from *www.adobe.com/*.)

Do you want to play a radio or television in your store or workplace? If so, you may benefit from the Fairness in Music Licensing Act of 1998. This Act states that, as of January 25, 1999, it is not a copyright infringement to let customers hear the radio or television music in certain stores. For businesses that don't meet certain criteria, licensing may still be required.

THE RIGHTS OF LIBRARIES AND ARCHIVES

Additional exemptions of the Copyright Act are provided specifically for libraries and archives under Section 108. Under this section, libraries are given the right to reproduce or distribute three copies of a copyrighted work. Before libraries can exercise this right, however, the following conditions must be met:

1. The reproduction or distribution is made without any purpose of direct or indirect commercial advantage;
2. the collections of the library are open to the public or available not only to researchers affiliated with the library, but also to other persons doing research in a specialized field; and
3. the reproduction or distribution of the work includes a notice of copyright.

To avoid infringing on the rights of the copyright owner, certain circumstances are in place under which some libraries may reproduce or distribute copyrighted works. These circumstances are explained under Sections 108(b) through 108(i). As stated in subsection (a)(1), these rights only apply if the library doing the copying or distribution is doing so "without any purpose of direct or indirect commercial advantage." Also note the importance of including with each copy made a notice of copyright as required under subsection (a)(2).

In the previous edition of this book, it was not yet clear whether the exceptions listed in Section 108 applied to copies made in digital formats. The Digital Millennium Copyright Act has since made allowances for limited fair use for digital preservation, electronic loan, and distance-education purposes. For complete details on each of the subsections outlined below, consult the law itself. You can conveniently keyword search Title 17 of the United States Code at the Legal Information Institute, Cornell Law School *www4.law.cornell.edu/cgi-bin/fx*. To pull up an entire section, for example Section 108, simply enter **Sec.108** as your search term.

The circumstances under which copies may be made or works distributed include:

- Section 108(b) states that a facsimile copy of an unpublished work can be made if the sole purpose is preservation or security and if the reproduced copy is housed

---

Online Resource

The Copyright Clearance Center (CCC) is a nonprofit organization that helps organizations comply with U.S. copyright law by providing a wide range of services. For example, the CCC's Transactional Reporting Service (TRS) provides customers with the immediate authorization to make photocopies from over 1.75 million publications from more than 9,200 copyright holders worldwide. Their home page can be accessed at *www.copyright.com/*.

---

in the library's collection. This exemption includes the right to reproduce works in digital format as long as "any such copy or phonorecord that is reproduced in digital format is not otherwise distributed in that format and is not made available to the public in that format outside the premises of the library or archives." (See Subsection (b)(2))

- Section 108(c) states that three copies of a published work may be made if the original copy is damaged, deemed lost or stolen, "or if the existing format in which the work is stored has become obsolete," and it can be shown that an unused replacement copy priced fairly cannot be found. The provisions of the Digital Millennium Copyright Act further added, if "any such copy or phonorecord that is reproduced in digital format is not made available to the public in that format outside the premises of the library or archives in lawful possession of such copy." (See Subsection (c)(2))

- Section 108(d) states that a copy can be made if a user requests a copy of an article from a periodical issue or a small part from any other copyrighted work.

- Section 108(e) states that a copy can be made and distributed of an out-of-print work if the library can show that the copyrighted work cannot be obtained elsewhere at a fair price. (Note: The preceding two exemptions require that three conditions must be met: (1) The copy must become the property of the user; (2) The library must not receive any notice that its intended use will be for anything other than private study, research, or scholarship; and (3) A warning of copyright must be displayed where the library takes orders and on any order forms that are used.)

- Section 108(g) states that single copies of copyrighted works may be made for interlibrary loan purposes.

- Section 108(h) states that "during the last 20 years of any term of copyright of a published work, a library or archives, including a nonprofit educational institution that functions as such, may reproduce, distribute, display, or perform in facsimile or digital form a copy or phonorecord of such work, or portions thereof, for purposes of preservation, scholarship, or research, if such library or archives has first determined, on the basis of a reasonable investigation, that none of the conditions set forth in subparagraphs (A), (B), and (C) of paragraph (2) apply." The conditions referred to here are:
  (A) The work is subject to normal commercial exploitation;
  (B) a copy or phonorecord of the work can be obtained at a reasonable price; or
  (C) the copyright owner or its agent provides notice pursuant to regulations promulgated by the Register of Copyrights that either of the conditions set forth in subparagraphs (A) and (B) applies. (See Subsection (h)(2))

WHAT WORKS CAN BE COPIED FREELY?

Under certain circumstances, works can be copied freely without regard for the fair use provisions of the law. These include:

- Government publications—Title 17, Chapter 1 of the U.S. Code covers the subject matter and scope of copyright. In Section 105, it states, "Copyright protection under this title is not available for any work of the United States Government, but the United States Government is not precluded from receiving and holding copyrights transferred to it by assignment, bequest, or otherwise."
- Ideas, processes, and methods—In Section 102b, it states, "In no case does copyright protection for an original work of authorship extend to any idea, procedure, process, system, method of operation, concept, principle, or discovery, regardless of the form in which it is described, explained, illustrated, or embodied in such work.
- Works in the public domain—For a clear outline of what constitutes public domain, consult Lolly Gasaway's Web page "When Works Pass into the Public Domain" located at *www.unc.edu/~unclng/public-d.htm*. The duration of copyright has changed over the years, but most recently (before January 1978) copyright could be renewed for 28 years. For works created in 1949 or earlier, the normal copyright term would have expired before 1978. But copyright could have been renewed, thus keeping the protection alive. To be sure copyright has expired, publication of the work would have to go back to 1921. Project Gutenberg *www.promo.net/pg/* publishes public domain literary works on the Internet. These are perfectly legal and can be downloaded free of charge.
- Freeware—Freely distributed software, such as the software distributed by *www.free-programs.com*. This does not include shareware.
- Facts—Lists of facts and comprehensive compilations like phone books.

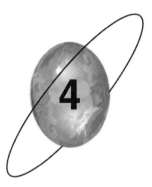

Librarians' Roles in a Global Network Environment

As every librarian utilizing the Internet knows, the Internet by itself does not create change in libraries. Librarians do. Libraries need more than a simple Internet connection to utilize the power of the Internet. It takes creative librarians to remove technological barriers and design innovative systems that make it easier for patrons to find and retrieve the information they need. Librarians have made remarkable progress in integrating the Internet into their core operations. They are beginning to understand the applications that enhance productivity and the tools that effectively distribute information across interconnected networks.

This chapter explores the role librarians play in this global network environment. As you read through this chapter, you can see links between certain roles and certain departments within the library. For example, the role of information organizer links to the cataloging department; the role of navigator and intermediary links to the reference staff; and the role of planner and policymaker has its connection with the library administration. These links are further expanded upon in Chapters 18 and 19, which examine implementing Internet services in-house.

Chapter 4 closes with an examination of the potential benefits an Internet connection can bring to library patrons and staff. Several questions are raised that can be addressed as part of the planning process when setting up an Internet connection.

LIBRARIANS' INTERNET-RELATED ACTIVITIES

In exploring what roles librarians play in relation to the Internet, I categorize all of the Internet-related activities with which libraries and librarians are involved in eight headings:

1. Role as Internet access providers
2. Role as navigators
3. Role as educators
4. Role as publishers
5. Role as intermediaries
6. Role as information evaluators
7. Role as information organizers
8. Role as planners and policymakers

Whether your library has just installed its first Internet-capable computer or you are a seasoned Internet service provider, it can be a worthwhile endeavor reviewing and discussing what these various roles mean to you and your organization. Each section helps to answer the question, "Why are we here?"

GUIDELINE FOR PLANNING SERVICES

Library planners can use this section as a guide for making decisions about which Internet resources and services their library offers. Clearly, some roles are very basic, such as serving as a community access point to the Internet. Without access, there is little reason to discuss most of the other roles librarians play. Once access is provided, however, a larger set of issues must be addressed. For example, are you going to offer training for staff and tutoring for the public in how to use Internet applications? If so, are resources available to support this endeavor?

Another question that you might address after reading about the librarian's role as publisher is this: Is your library going to create and maintain its own home page? If so, who is going to create it and keep it up-to-date? What level of training does this individual receive? Does he or she get handed an HTML manual for self-teaching or is formal training offered in planning and designing a Website?

In each of the eight sections that follow, I give examples of what librarians are doing today as educators, navigators, and publishers, etc. Resources are listed at the end of each section that enable you to explore a particular topic in greater detail.

THE ROLES OF LIBRARIANS

This section gives you a closer look at the many roles librarians have in providing Internet access and services for library patrons.

AS INTERNET ACCESS PROVIDERS

By offering access to the Internet, librarians help to remove the barriers of cost and complexity that impede many people from accessing the Internet at home. Some libraries support dial-up services enabling patrons to dial-in and access the Internet. Other libraries make available one or more public access PCs connected to the Internet. The library can serve another purpose to those who already have systems connected to the

Internet at home. By providing access to the newest information technology, these patrons can test software and hardware before investing in it for their own systems.

There is a responsibility that goes along with supporting this technology. Librarians are expected to have a certain basic understanding of how hardware and software works and in some cases, how to repair it when things quit working. Many of us have been approached by patrons asking questions about what to buy, how to get connected to the Internet, or what is a good Web authoring tool. Working in an environment where the Internet is accessible and PCs are a visible part of the landscape invites these kinds of questions.

Technical information found in the following resources are basic tools for assisting patrons with their hardware and software related questions. If patrons ask you for advice on other Internet-related questions, consult the index found in the back of this book for possible answers.

- "The Internet Technology Channel" on *www.internet.com* links you to a variety of sites specializing in hardware and software technology. To stay abreast of all that is happening in the Internet world, point your patrons and yourself to BrowserWatch, ServerWatch, SharkyExtreme.com, Hardware Central, Internet ProductWatch, Internet World, and Internet Discussion Forums.
- Forrest Stroud has been writing for *Boardwatch Magazine* (*www.boardwatch.com*) since 1994, reviewing Internet software each month in his column titled, "Consummate Winsock Apps." The applications he reviews can be found on the Web at Stroud's CWSApps(TM) *cws.internet.com/*. Go here to stay up-to-date on the latest and most popular Internet applications.
- At About.com *www.about.com* see what expert guides have to say about operating systems, hardware, and software. While you're there, save some time and subscribe to one of their Computing/Technology newsletters. Experts send news and information right to your e-mail box.
- Check out Ziff-Davis's home page at *www.zdnet.com* for reviews of the latest software and hardware. Keyword search ZDNet's entire site, or browse "Reviews," "Tech News," "Downloads," "Tech Life," "Shopping," "Help & How-To," and "Developer." Link to any one of their ten computer publications: *PC Magazine, PC Computing, PC Week, FamilyPC, Computer Gaming World, Inter@ctive Week, Sm@rt Reseller, Yahoo! Internet Life, Macworld,* and *Computer Shopper. Computer Shopper* reviews most hardware components and most brand names.

AS NAVIGATORS

Navigating information is one of the traditional roles librarians are already familiar with and it is one that can be carried forward and applied in a world of interconnected networks. Most of the information on the Internet is unstructured; that is, it isn't part of a database, spreadsheet, or other system that organizes information. All of the various indexes, catalogs, bibliographies, and databases that do exist on the Internet are fragmented and detached from each other. Many databases are invisible, a topic that is addressed in Chapter 12. It is impossible for library patrons to know about all of these resources Approaches used for searching these tools differ and the languages used to conduct the searches also differ.

With the aid of a librarian, a patron can start with any tool and be led to other tools as needed without needing to know ahead of time which is the appropriate path to follow. Librarians can help patrons find the best and fastest route to reports, software applications, news items, letters, and other files. As the Internet evolves, it will be important for librarians to become experts at finding archived copies of original sources and certifiably authentic copies of files.

The following resources offer search strategies and discuss the different tools used for indexing and accessing information on the Web.

- Kathleen Webster and Kathryn Paul's *Beyond Surfing: Tools and Techniques for Searching the Web* available at *magi.com/~mmelick/it96jan.htm.*
- Martijn Koster's *The Web Robots Pages* is available at *info.webcrawler.com/mak/ projects/robots/robots.html.*
- *How to Search the Web—A Guide to Search Tools* by Terry A. Gray is available at *daphne.palomar.edu/TGSEARCH/.*
- Read reviews comparing popular search engines, see which search engines are the most popular, and check out various tests and statistics at *searchenginewatch.com/.*
- Jian Liu, reference librarian at Indiana University Libraries, has written the *Guide to Meta-Search Engines* at *www.indiana.edu/~librcsd/search/meta.html.* This guide briefly introduces 13 different search engines.

AS EDUCATORS

Librarians should be well equipped to explain services such as the Web and telnet and serve as netiquette advisors. Assistance can be offered in the form of Internet classes, tutoring, and online manuals.

Patrons who use the Internet as an information resource or as a conduit for accessing commercial online services may need instructions in how to use browsers and other applications; do such things as cut and paste from an Internet application to a word processor; save files to floppy disks; join e-mail discussion groups; find access points to local Internet service providers; properly cite electronic documents, and more.

Librarians all around the world are currently offering their services as Internet educators. Here are a few examples of how some librarians are teaching others about the Internet:

The Library, University of California at Berkeley, provides patrons with Internet guidance through online tutors and guides at a site maintained by Patricia Davitt Maughan called "Starting your research with Library Research Guides" *www.lib.berkeley.edu/ TeachingLib/Guides/.* One guide in particular, *Finding Information on the Internet: A TUTORIAL*, thoroughly introduces newcomers to the Internet, the Web, and Netscape. The site explains strategies for searching the Web, introduces search tools, offers pointers on where to begin searching, and where to access high-quality subject guides and databases. In addition, this site serves as a central access point for dozens of subject guides and information on how to use the Library catalogs and California Digital Library-hosted databases.

All of these resources are part of a well-organized, collaborative project called The Teaching Library. The Teaching Library, based at the University of California at Berkeley, has as their mission, " . . . to ensure that every graduate of the University of California at Berkeley is thoroughly familiar with the information resources and tools in their major field of study, is trained to use them effectively, and is prepared to conduct a search strategy in any field." In addition to the online resources mentioned earlier, workshops are provided on a variety of topics, including finding online journals, online news sources, and power Web searching. To learn more about The Teaching Library's mission, goals, and services, explore their site at *www.lib.berkeley.edu/TeachingLib/*.

The Concordia University Libraries *juno.concordia.ca/concordia.html* provide online "Help and Instruction" by offering links to other online tools including search engines, Canadian search tools, image search tools, subject directories, meta-search tools, software search tools, academic subject guides, discussion groups, and new Web sites. In addition, their "Virtual Reference" site offers links to almanacs, citation guides, grammar guides, and more.

The Reference Department of Davis Library, University of North Carolina at Chapel Hill, offers links to a variety of resources including subject indexes, Website reviews, and information on how to cite electronic documents, all of which are included in their "Virtual Reference Desk" home page at *metlab.unc.edu/reference/quickref.html*.

Some librarians are offering more formal instruction on the Internet in the form of online tutorials. Academic librarians are covering subject-specific and even course-specific Internet resources in their Bibliographic Instruction sessions for faculty and students. Sessions being offered online are listed in Table 4–1.

Public libraries are offering online tutorials filled with all sorts of tips on using the Internet and computers. The Chicago Public Library *www.chipublib.org/007internet/ 007internet.html* has created "About the Internet," which links its patrons to Internet news, copyright information, Internet organizations in Chicago, and a variety of Internet tools and resources. It offers a special feature covering details on how to use the text-based Web browser Lynx. The library at Nueva School, a PreK–8 school in the San Francisco Bay Area, supports an online tutorial *nuevaschool.org/~debbie/library/ research/research.html* that offers search strategies and an interactive citation builder. Students enter author's name, title of resource, place of publication, etc., click on a button, and an MLA style format is automatically produced. Students can then cut and paste the citation into their word-processing document. Several different formats are covered, including books, e-mail messages, CD-ROMs, interviews, mailing lists, magazines, newspapers, and Websites.

For a larger sampling of sites offering library instruction online, visit the Website maintained by the Library Instruction Round Table (LIRT), a roundtable of the American Library Association *diogenes.baylor.edu/Library/LIRT/lirtporj.html*. Resources are categorized under seven headings:

1. Website Evaluation Criteria for Libraries
2. General Guides to Research
3. Subject-Specific Guides
4. Interactive Tutorials
5. Guides to the Internet & Evaluation of Resources
6. Designing Tutorials
7. Bibliography

As electronic resources become more integral to library instruction programs, the demand for instructional computer classrooms increases. Librarians involved with design-

Table 4–1: Sampling of university libraries offering Web-based tutorials		
Library	**Service**	**Address**
Cornell University	*Library Research at Cornell: A Hypertext Guide* Presents students with seven steps for conducting library research. Other tutorials and skill guides include "Distinguishing Scholarly from Non-Scholarly Periodicals," "How to Critically Analyze Information Sources," and "How to Prepare an Annotated Bibliography."	*www.library.cornell.edu/ okuref/tutorialsguides. html*
New Mexico State University	*NMSU Library Shortcuts* Interactive tutorial offer guidance in how to use the library and develop basic research skills.	*lib.nmsu.edu/projects/ tutorial/*
Rutgers University	*Library Research* Online tutorial addresses issues such as Picking a Topic, Locating Quick or Background Information, Locating Books, Understanding Call Numbers, and more.	*www.libraries.rutgers.edu/ rulib/abtlib/camlib/ libres.html*
University of Delaware	*The Virtual Library Tutor* Teaches students how to find periodical articles, newspaper articles, how to evaluate sources, and how to find subject resources on the Internet.	*www.lib.udel.edu/tutor*
University of Iowa	*Library Explorer* Computer-assisted instruction based on a book metaphor. The book is presented in a hypertext format and includes a table of contents, glossary, index, and help button. Subjects include library research and exploring the Internet.	*Explorer.lib.uiowa.edu/*

ing instructional classrooms can find a bibliography compiled by Lisa Janicke Hinchliffe on this subject in *The Journal of Academic Media Librarianship*, Volume 6 Number 1, Spring 1998 *wings.buffalo.edu/publications/mcjrnl/v6n1/index.html.*

Librarians in charge of training might consider joining NETTRAIN, a mailing list for individuals involved in teaching others how to use the Internet. The list is geared toward experienced users, not beginners looking for help with basic questions. Topics covered include teaching methods and resources and access policies. NETTRAIN also serves as a clearinghouse for Internet training materials. To subscribe, send an e-mail message containing the following line in the body of the message:

SUBSCRIBE NETTRAIN <Firstname Lastname>

to *listserv@listserv.acsu.buffalo.edu*. Leave the subject line empty. To unsubscribe, send the command **UNSUB NETRAIN**. Other useful LISTSERV commands are introduced in Chapter 24.

AS PUBLISHERS

Librarians can add content and editorial value to the Web by designing and writing home pages that help patrons access information of local interest. For instance, Don Napoli, the Director of the St. Joseph County Public Library (SJCPL) located in South Bend, Indiana, established a home page for his library back in March 1994. The SJCPL offers library patrons a searchable database of over 1,200 local community organizations and services; a searchable index of articles that are of local interest appearing in the *South Bend Tribune* newspaper; a monthly events calendar; and more. SJCPL's home page is still going strong and can be accessed at *sjcpl.lib.in.us/.*

You can explore other libraries' home pages worldwide on the Web by linking to a page maintained by Thomas Dowling called LIBWEB at *sunsite.berkeley.edu/Libweb/*. When the previous edition of this book was published, Dowling had organized links to about 1,000 libraries in 45 countries. Today, LIBWEB lists over 3,000 pages in more than 90 countries! Thomas J. Hennen's index that rates American public libraries can be accessed online at *www.haplr-index.com/main.html*. Libraries supporting Websites are hyperlinked to their respective home pages. Linda Bertland, a librarian at Stetson Middle School, Philadelphia, Pennsylvania, maintains a list of K–12 school libraries with Web pages situated all around the world. Check out *School Libraries on the Web: A Directory* at *www.voicenet.com/~bertland/libs.html*. Peter Milbury maintains a large directory of K–12 school library-related sites at *wombat.cusd.chico.k12.ca.us/~pmilbury/lib.html*.

In addition, librarians can publish papers describing Internet resources and services or professional papers describing projects with which they are involved. Examples include the following:

Roderick A. MacLeod of Edinburgh, Scotland, edits a free monthly electronic newsletter called *Internet Resources. Internet Resources* is published by the Heriot-Watt University Library Internet Resource Centre *www.hw.ac.uk/libWWW/libinfo/irchtml*. The newsletter can be viewed at *www.hw.ac.uk/libWWW/irn/irn.html*. The purpose of the *Internet Resources Newsletter* is to keep university faculty and students up-to-date on Internet resources and services, especially those that are relevant to research taking place at the university.

The library's Internet Resource Centre offers links to standard Internet resources, University member's-only resources, and specialized subject trees maintained by the Heriot-Watt University Library Staff. MacLeod's writings, for example "Running on Empty, Looking for the Virtual Service Station" (*Information World Review*, 153, December 1999, p. 62), *How to Find Out in Chemical and Process Engineering*, and *How to Find Out in Mechanical Engineering*, are cited, and when possible, hyperlinked on his home page at *www.hw.ac.uk/libWWW/libram/roddy.html*.

Wilfred Drew, Systems and Reference Librarian at State University of New York, College of Agriculture and Technology, offers links to his Internet projects and publications, including *Not Just Cows: A Guide to Internet Resources in Agriculture and Related Sciences* and *Reaching the OPAC —Java Telnet,* published in the Web version of *Ariadne* (Issue 8, March 1997). Drew also has links to his online training manuals *Internet: Learn to Surf the Net* and *Internet for Non-Beginners*.

On a lighter note, there are sites like librarian.net *www.librarian.net/* and LISNews.com *www.lisnews.com/*. LISNews.com publishes news and information stories of interest to library and information specialists. Blake Carver, site creator and maintainer, serves up articles on topics ranging from e-books and filtering, to conference information and book industry news. Librarian.net, which follows the format of a *weblog*, is the creation of librarian Jessamyn West. When West finds interesting library-related news and information on the Net, she pops it into her weblog for the day, adding her own touch of humor along the way.

Associations like the Association of College and Research Libraries (ACRL) publish portions of their newsletters online, in this case *C&RL NewsNet*, which can be accessed from the ACRL's home page at *www.ala.org/acrl/*. Other ideas for librarians serving as publishers include holding writing contests where they publish the winner's story or poem on the Internet. During National Library Week, librarians can celebrate by inviting children to paint pictures that follow a particular theme. The winner's artwork can then be published on the Internet.

And finally, there are the librarians like the team at Berkeley (*sunsite.berkeley.edu/CurrentCites/team.html*) that contribute to *Current Cites* each month. *Current Cites*, edited by Teri Andrews Rinne, is a free, annotated bibliography containing selected literature about information technology. Each month, a team of librarians pulls together ten to twenty annotated citations of current literature and distributes it to subscribers via e-mail. You also have the option of viewing current issue and all back issues at *sunsite.berkeley.edu/CurrentCites/*. A second service, *Bibliography on Demand,* indexes the contents of *Current Cites* and allows you to search all of the citations and create your own "bibliography on demand." A third feature is called *Article Search*. Powered by an indexing and search service called Swish-E, *Article Search* allows you to search the full text of over 200 Web-based documents that are cited in *Current Cites*.

AS INTERMEDIARIES

In certain situations, some activities are too complicated or too time-consuming to teach to patrons. In these instances it is far better for the librarian to step in as an intermediary with experience to do searching or other operations. Examples of when this might be appropriate or necessary include:

- Scanning photographs and attaching images to e-mail messages
- Searching online for patrons who have never learned to use a computer and are not interested in learning
- Uncompressing files using PKUNZIP for DOS or STUFFIT for Macs
- Downloading software applications and saving them to floppy disks
- Connecting to remote libraries via telnet and doing author, title, keyword, or subject searches on a variety of automation systems

No matter how accurate an Internet search engine claims to be, there's no guarantee that the documents it finds are actually relevant to the user's information needs. Problems may result from poorly defined queries or the patrons' unfamiliarity with the subject they're searching. Librarians can help make sense of the individual pages of text by examining their content and, in the case of hypertext documents on the Web, by examining the context of interlinked pages.

AS INFORMATION EVALUATORS

Most people think of traditional "ink and paper" publishing as an enormous commercial industry consisting of millions of journals, textbooks, newsletters, books, brochures, reports, magazines, and newspapers. Traditionally, the role of the publisher has been to acquire what they believe to be the best, most relevant, and most entertaining material and then improve, promote, and finally distribute it. The people that read this information pay for all of this value-added service because it saves them a lot of time not having to read humdrum research and uninteresting articles and books.

When people publish information on the Internet, they aren't always publishing with the same level of integrity, accuracy, and artistic intent that reputable commercial publishers use. Instead, many people simply post their family photos, recipes, home remedies, stories, and opinions as if they were sticking notes up on a large, global bulletin board.

Where most of the information distributed by commercial publishers goes through a filtering process, the vast majority of information published on the Internet is unfiltered. It is also difficult to tell at times what something is, where it came from, and who the author is.

Librarians can help evaluate information by questioning the authenticity of what they're reading. Here are standard guidelines for librarians to follow when appraising information they find on the Net:

- Who is the author and is he or she qualified to be writing about the subject?
- Is the information issued by a reliable organization?
- Compare what you are reading to other information in the field. Does it appear to be credible?
- Has the information been evaluated by experts, or reviewed by peers or an authority?
- Is the information original, or is it altered or quoted out of context?
- Look at the context in which the information is being presented. Does it appear biased or directed toward a particular audience?
- Look at the document itself to see whether any of these five elements are present:

1) Author's name
2) Author's affiliation
3) Date the document was created
4) Date the document was last updated
5) The name of an institution or commercial organization

Several librarians have begun publishing online guides to assist library patrons with evaluating Websites. Hope N. Tillman, Director of Libraries, Babson College, presents a thorough treatment of the subject in her article, "Evaluating Quality on the Net." You can find the full text of this article online at *www.tiac.net/users/hope/findqual.html*. The reference department at McIntyre Library, University of Wisconsin—Eau Claire, offers a concise guide, "Ten C's for Evaluating Internet Sources." You can find the Ten C's at *www.uwec.edu/Admin/Library/Guides/tencs.html*. Esther Grassian, UCLA College Library, publishes an excellent outline for reviewing Web resources at *www.library.ucla. edu/libraries/college/instruct/web/discp.htm*. Grassian considers four major criteria when evaluating Web resources:

1. Content and evaluation (What claims does the site make in terms of the quality of its content? Is it based on research? Is it commercial or non-commercial?)
2. Source and date (Who created the site and is it up-to-date?)
3. Structure (Considers reporting style and whether references are included)
4. Other (Is the source fee-based? Does it offer an alternative text-only view?)

Other resources provide evaluations aimed at librarians and other information professionals. For example, *Ariadne*, an online magazine published quarterly by the U.K. Office for Library and Information Networking, evaluates Internet resources and services that are of potential use to librarians. In the December 1999 issue, Philip Hunter writes an editorial that takes a look at the access statistics for *Ariadne*. In October 1999, the number of user sessions totaled 34,119 for the whole month. (They define a *user session* as hits from the same IP address within a single thirty-minute window.) Articles in this issue discuss distributed approaches to cataloging, streaming video on the Web, public libraries and community networks, metadata for digital preservation, and more. You can access the most recent issue and browse through back issues at *www.ariadne. ac.uk/*.

AS INFORMATION ORGANIZERS

Prior to the existence of the Internet, librarians indexed only items that were owned and housed within the four walls of their library. With the advent of the World Wide Web, librarians began indexing items owned and not owned by their library. Where traditional library catalogs contain only surrogate records describing books and serials, the Web enables librarians to provide deeper access—access to chapters in electronic texts or paragraphs within hypertext documents. In the news division of the Special Libraries Association *metalab.unc.edu/slanews/surveys/profit.html*, survey results showed newspaper librarians generating revenue from data mining their archives and creating commercial image and text databases.

There are a number of bibliographic databases and indexes accessible on the Internet. Most of the bibliographic databases are library catalogs. These catalogs can be accessed either through telnet or the World Wide Web. Depending on the brand of automation software a particular library uses, library patrons are faced with varying types of interfaces when linking to catalogs via the Net. Thanks to systems librarians, Z39.50 gateways offer patrons a consistent, user-friendly interface to catalogs for libraries, archives, and museums worldwide regardless of what the underlying automation software is.

The following projects are examples of how librarians have put their talents to work as information organizers making Internet resources easier to locate and access:

InterCAT: A Catalog of Internet Resources is an Internet cataloging project headed-up by OCLC (Online Computer Library Center, Inc.). InterCAT is a searchable index of Internet-accessible resources selected and cataloged by volunteer librarians nationwide. InterCAT utilizes USMARC-formatted bibliographic records with Field 856 being used to describe how the electronic resource can be accessed. (Guidelines for using Field 856 can be found at site */www.loc.gov/marc/856guide.html.*)

What follows is a description of Deaf World Web, a Web-based resource at *dww.deafworldweb.org/*, as it appears in USMARC format. This example was taken from InterCAT, which presently contains over 92,000 bibliographic records for Internet resources. You can search or browse InterCAT at *orc.rsch.oclc.org:6990.*

000		cmm la
001		39802778
003		OCoLC
005		19990108211328.0
008		980904m19959999xx u eng d
040		$a TNT $c TNT $d OCL $d TNT
090		$a HV2502.D434 $b (INTERNET)
049		$a llll
245	0	$a Deaf world web $h [computer file] .
256		$a Computer data.
260		$a [S.l.] : $b Jolanta Lapiak, Deaf World Web, $c [1995—
500		$a Description based on content as of September 1998.
500		$a Title from opening screen.
505	2	$a Deaf world news — ASL dictionary online – Encyclopedic resources — Deaf cy berkids — Discussions & chats — Deaf email directory — Nations — Products & services.
516		$a Text (HTML), graphics
538		$a Mode of access: World Wide Web.
650	0	$a Deaf $x Computer network resources
650	0	$a Hearing impaired $x Computer network resources.
700	1	$a Lapiak, Jolanta.
710	2	$a Deaf World Web.
856	7	$2 http $u http://purl.oclc.org/OCLC/OLUC/39802778/2 $z http://dww.deafworldweb.org/
994		$a 00 $b (UNKN)

If you have questions about InterCAT, read their FAQ at *www.oclc.org/oclc/man/catproj/catcall.htm*, or contact Erik Jul, *jul@oclc.org*.

The Berkeley Public Library (BPL) has created an "Index to the Internet" which you can reach by clicking on the link labeled "Librarians' Index to the Internet" found on their home page at *www.infopeople.org/bpl/*. BPL's well-known index demonstrates how librarians can offer value-added services by carefully selecting a handful of resources they think are relevant to their community from the millions of resources that are available; arranging them under subject headings listed alphabetically; providing descriptions; developing a search and indexing system; and publishing the information in HTML format so it can be easily accessed on the Web.

"Best Information on the Net" is an important link cited on the O'Keefe Library Website, St. Ambrose University *www.sau.edu/bestinfo/*. Originally maintained by librarian Marylaine Block and affectionately called "WHERE THE WILD THINGS ARE: Librarian's Guide to the Best Information on the Net," this resource continues to evolve and is now maintained by the reference staff of O'Keefe Library.

On the main page, librarians offers links to various indexes including one that lists Internet resources organized by major field of study. A link is offered for faculty and students called "Hot Paper Topics," which is a collection of links to article files and indexes relating to the hot topics of the day. Each topic heading is accompanied by a short description of what it is you'll find once you connect. The "Faculty and Administration Resources" link includes a pointer to sites that demonstrate how individuals can incorporate the World Wide Web into their traditional teaching practices. "Resources for Librarians" links to dozens of indexes organized under the headings: Book Reviews and Reading Lists, Children's Literature, Cataloging and Technical Services, and more.

Eric Lease Morgan, Network Technologies Development Librarian at North Carolina State University Libraries, offers a model home page where he demonstrates his talents not only as a systems librarian, but also as an educator, navigator, publisher, and information organizer. When you link to Morgan's home page at *www.lib.ncsu.edu/staff/morgan/*, you are greeted with a short introduction followed by contact information and bio. He organizes information on his site under these five headings (beginning with zero!):

1) Presentations—Professional talks
2) Publications—Formal and informal articles
3) Software—Applications and scripts
4) Services—Collections and search engines
5) Travel Logs—Notes from conferences

Clicking on "Presentations" takes you to full-text versions of Morgan's professional talks, including *DBMs and Web Delivery*, *I Like FileMaker Pro*, *Cataloging Internet Resources: A Beginning*, *On Being a Systems Librarian*, and *Introduction to the WWW* to name a few.

Clicking on "Publications" links you to Morgan's professional writings. Here you'll find, for example, full-text versions of *Marketing Through Usability*, *Catalogs of the Future*, *Adaptive Technologies*, *Possible Solutions for Incorporating Digital Information Mediums into Traditional Library Cataloging Services*, and *Adding Internet Resources to our OPACs*.

Under the heading "Software," Morgan describes his experiments with information systems software, for example, Mr. Serials Harvests—an experiment in indexing and organizing electronic serials.

The "Services" category lists the collections and search engines Morgan supports, for example, *Alex Catalogue of Electronic Texts*, *Index Morganagus*, and *ListWebber Lists*.

Morgan's "Travel Logs" is a collection of notes describing the conferences and meetings he attends listed in reverse chronological order.

To top it all off, Morgan offers you the opportunity to run keyword searches on his Web pages or to browse his Web pages by clicking on the link labeled "Subject Index."

Many of you may be familiar with a service offered by Yahoo! called My Yahoo! It lets you create your own customized front door to the Web. A *front door* is a personalized start page that allows you to pick your own weather cities, track the stocks you invest in, read the news, find local movie show times, and follow your favorite sports teams and place them all on a Web page. Now libraries are offering similar services. For example, North Carolina State University *www.lib.ncsu.edu/* hosts a service called MyLibrary@NCState. Faculty and students can create their own custom information service by creating a Web page with resources they choose. You can login as a guest and create a MyLibrary@NCState page for yourself, but you cannot save your settings.

AS PLANNERS AND POLICYMAKERS

Library administrators are responsible for advising local boards and administrative bodies on several issues relating to planning and policies:

- Will access to the Internet be free or should libraries charge a fee for this service?
- Will you offer unlimited access, or will there be time restrictions placed on patrons and/or staff? How will time limits be enforced?
- On which computers will Internet access be made available?
- Which Internet services will be made available to the public and to the staff?
- Will public and school libraries limit children's access to the Internet by running filtering software?
- Will all staff members or only some staff members be given personal e-mail accounts?
- Will the library maintain its own Web server(s)?
- What issues surrounding hardware and software security need addressing?
- Will training be offered to patrons and staff?
- Where will hardware be located?
- Will funds be budgeted for future growth and planning in the area of telecommunications? This would include funding for
  1. continuing education for keeping staff trained and up-to-date on latest technologies;
  2. purchasing software updates as new versions are released;
  3. replacing old hardware when it becomes functionally obsolete;
  4. expanding services to keep up with demand by adding more computers, computer furniture, phone lines, and greater bandwidth; and
  5. new staff members to handle the increase in demand for more assistance with computers and peripherals.

WHY SHOULD YOUR LIBRARY CONNECT TO THE INTERNET? AND OTHER GOOD QUESTIONS

Maybe you haven't decided yet whether an Internet connection is feasible. To help you with your analysis, consider these questions:

1) Why should your library connect to the Internet?
2) How can the library staff benefit from a connection?
3) How does the community you serve benefit from Internet access?
4) What is the cost of connecting?

The rest of this chapter addresses each of these questions individually. Considering your answers now will help you focus your Internet efforts in a way that will bring the biggest benefit to your library, its patrons, and the staff.

WHY SHOULD YOUR LIBRARY CONNECT TO THE INTERNET?

In the final analysis, you may decide that the overriding factor that compels you to connect is not a tangible benefit such as cost savings, but rather a simple need to remain competitive.

Today, many people set as their benchmark basic CD-ROM and communications technologies. Parents and their children are already accessing these services at work, in their schools, and at home. They expect the same and more from their library. If the challenge is there—if your library can offer them an extension of their home information systems—then your library will be a viable resource for them.

HOW CAN AN INTERNET CONNECTION BENEFIT THE STAFF?

To begin with, it helps to understand what your role as a librarian is in an inter-networking environment. For further insight into this, refer to the earlier sections in this chapter. When answering the question, "How will the Internet benefit staff?" it may be helpful to look at each department separately. Chapters 18 and 19 describe a variety of ways Internet services can be used by staff.

WHAT BENEFITS DOES AN INTERNET CONNECTION BRING TO THE COMMUNITY?

In the beginning, the Internet was mostly populated by computer scientists, academics, graduate students, and engineers. As the Internet grew, access became easier and a more diverse group of people got involved. Now, with the advent of the World Wide Web, millions of people from all walks of life, young and old, access the Internet daily.

The following discussion details six of the most important benefits offered by the Internet:

- Communicating with Others. The Internet impacts individuals, communities, and whole regions by changing the way people communicate with one another. E-mail, Free-nets, mailing lists, Usenet news, and IRC are examples of communication systems on the Internet that make it possible for individuals to share information anytime, anywhere.

- Entertainment. Surfing the Internet can be like browsing through a used-book store filled with hidden treasures. Discoveries can be unpredictable and surprising. You can surf alone browsing through subject trees and cybermalls or take on a computerized persona and join in role-playing adventure games called MUDs.
- Education. The Internet is a place where you can find educational resources, information on educational institutions, home-school discussions, curriculum materials and ideas, adult literacy, and more. The Net is something like a large, global library that provides learning opportunities for everyone who visits. Students living in large metropolitan areas work hand-in-hand with students in isolated rural areas. Schools, large and small, share the same opportunities for learning.
- Publishing. The Internet brings freedom of the press right into your home. The Internet offers citizens from all walks of life the opportunity to publish. Kids are publishing their local histories, poetry, stories, and artwork. Professors are publishing papers on genetic algorithms in computing. Businesses are publishing electronic brochures and classified advertisements introducing their businesses to prospects worldwide.
- Doing Business. The Internet started out as a research tool used mainly by academic and government institutions. Today it has evolved into a tool for doing business. For many businesses, the Internet has made it possible to provide more and better information to customers and vice versa. In industries such as stock photography, where the product can be digitized, every aspect of the transaction from purchase to delivery can take place online.
- Benefits to Kids. The Internet removes some basic barriers for kids and makes resources available to them that would otherwise be unavailable. For example, the Internet provides kids with the following benefits:

  A Storehouse of Information. Kids can find information about their community or special interests and hobbies through local or distant information systems. They can keep up-to-date on festivals and events pertaining to a particular family interest.

  A Source of Freeware and Shareware. Kids can get copies of software applications including games for entertainment purposes as well as math and science programs for help with their class assignments and research papers.

  Research. The Internet makes it possible for kids to login to their local public and university libraries to check whether an item is available and to do research for homework assignments. Through e-mail, newsgroups, and mailing lists, kids can ask experts questions and work with people of all ages all around the world. Kids can ask adults to tutor or participate in a research project.

  Visit with Other Kids. Kids can talk in real-time as fast as they can type with kids on different continents simultaneously, or they can join mailing lists dedicated just to children. On the Internet, kids discover that they are valued by what they say and how well they say it rather than by their age, appearance, dialect, ethnic background, race, or gender.

HOW MUCH WILL IT COST TO CONNECT?

Internet service providers have different charges for their services. This is addressed in the next chapter. You should also figure into your operating expenses the cost of initial training and continuing education; books and journals for keeping up-to-date on the latest technologies; and purchasing software updates. Capital expenses include furniture, the hardware devices required for establishing the connection, and the cost of replacing old hardware when it becomes functionally obsolete. Operating costs include connection fees, service contracts (if needed), and software updates.

What Are the Cost Savings?

E-mail is one of the most common uses of the Internet in libraries. When you establish an Internet connection, e-mail won't replace all written and verbal communications, nor should it; but it will replace many.

Measuring the potential cost savings resulting from e-mail is difficult. One approach might be to ask your library's department heads to estimate what percentage of their long distance phone calls and next day deliveries could be made via e-mail. Keep in mind that not everyone you communicate with will be equipped to receive e-mail. For example, patrons receiving overdue notices—a source of one of the largest postage expenses in libraries—may not have e-mail capability. Distributing overdue notices via e-mail is a more likely prospect in systems where all participants are assigned e-mail accounts by a centralized authority, such as students attending colleges and universities.

Determining the cost savings resulting from other Internet services is fairly straightforward. If you currently have a phone line dedicated to a modem for dialing into an online database such as FirstSearch, you can determine the ongoing expense associated with this dial-up connection by reviewing your monthly phone bill. An Internet connection would provide you with alternative means of accessing FirstSearch. One of these services is telnet and the other is the Web. Not all, but most, online databases provide interfaces through the Web these days. A limited number of library catalogs are still only accessible via telnet. Once your basic Internet connection is established, there are no additional charges for using the Web or telnet, unless, of course, your service provider charges you a usage fee for time online.

What Are the Intangible Benefits?

Often times the benefits gained by having an Internet connection cannot be directly measured. There are the intangible benefits of using Internet services. The speed at which e-mail is delivered and files are transferred may be an advantage especially when you compare it to the regular postal service. Will a patron who is limited by time or physical barriers benefit by receiving a document the same day he or she requests it instead of days later through the U.S. Postal Service? Will a youngster benefit by receiving a shareware program called *Treasure Hunt Math* while he or she waits at the reference desk—a resource that would otherwise be unavailable if it weren't for the Internet? With Internet access, it only takes a few minutes to download software applications from sites that are hundreds or thousands of miles away.

Once you decide to move forward with your plans to connect, the next step is to take a look at what your hardware and software needs will be. In Part II, I explore these issues and the options available for linking up with Internet service providers.

Part II

WHAT YOU NEED TO GET READY

In Part II, I define basic computer concepts and terms, explain what hardware and software are required for connecting to the Internet, and discuss issues surrounding PC security.

In Chapter 5, I explore methods of connecting to the Internet. Special attention is given to do-it-yourselfers who are installing dial-up connections using modems. I discuss the pros and cons of using commercial online services versus ISPs (Internet Service Providers). I also introduce emerging technologies and alternative methods of connecting to the Internet including the high-speed broadband services DSL, ISDN, and cable.

In Chapters 6 and 7, I address issues relating to hardware and software. I define basic computer concepts and terms, describe what hardware is needed for connecting to the Internet, and introduce general-purpose communications software.

In Chapter 8, I describe dozens of programs that help you find and retrieve information on the Internet. I introduce you to tools that make a variety of tasks easier including editors and file conversion programs.

Finally, in Chapter 9, I offer practical information on system security covering several areas of concern, including password protection, computer viruses, and Internet-related concerns. This is followed by an introduction to menuing systems and a discussion on controlling outgoing access to the Internet by using filtering software.

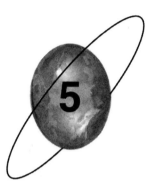

Connecting to the Internet

Connecting computers in libraries and around the world extends the power of the computer as a tool for sharing information. Libraries that are not yet connected to the Internet are feeling more and more pressure to become a part of the Internet community. For some libraries, this means getting a domain name, connecting their Local Area Network (LAN) with a T1 circuit, and setting up a Web server. For others, especially small, rural libraries, linking to the Internet means establishing a single dial-up connection with one modem and one computer. In Chapter 4, I explored the potential benefits an Internet connection brings to library patrons and staff. In this chapter, I explain the various methods of establishing an Internet connection and introduce you to commercial online services and Internet service providers that offer links to the Internet.

METHODS OF CONNECTING

Connections to the Internet fall under two basic categories: dial-up and dedicated. Of the dial-up variety, there are two that I discuss in this section: analog and digital. *Analog* refers to data transmissions that use a continuous wave form (or *sound*) to transmit data. *Digital* transmissions pass data along using discrete, on/off pulses. Unlike analog connections, digital connections do not require a modem at each end of the connection. (Analog connections use modems to convert digital, the language of computers, to analog and then analog back to digital.) For an overview of the various dial-up and dedicated connection methods, see Table 5–1.

Table 5–1. Common carrier technologies and their corresponding speeds	
Modem on regular telephone system	**Up to 56 thousand bits per second (56Kbps)**
ISDN	BRI is 64 thousand bits per second (64Kbps) to 128 thousand bits per second (128Kbps)
	PRI delivers speeds up to 1.544 million bits per second (1.544Mbps) for a T1 line and 2.048 million bits per second (2.048Mbps) for an E1 line. (E1 is the European equivalent of North America's T1 line.)
DSL (Digital Subscriber Line)	512 thousand bits per second (512Kbps) to 8 million bits per second (8Mbps)
Cable Modem	512 thousand bits per second (512 Kbps) to 52 million bits per second (52Mbps)
Frame Relay	56 thousand bits per second (56Kbps) to 1.544 million bits per second (1.544Mbps)
T1 or DS-1	Equivalent to 24 phone lines. It can handle 1.544 million bits per second (1.544Mbps)
T2 or DS-2	Equivalent to four T1s. The capacity is 6.312 million bits per second (6.312Mbps)
T3 or DS-3	Equivalent to 28 T1s. The capacity is 44.736 million bits per second (44.736Mbps)
T4 or DS-4	Equivalent to six T3s. The capacity is 274 million bits per second (274Mbps). Sprint currently uses DS-4 for the backbone
OC-1	51.84 million bits per second (51.84 Mbps)
OC-3	Equivalent to 155 million bits per second (155Mbps). MCI currently runs a few of these on their backbone
OC-12	622.08 million bits per second (622.08 Mbps)
OC-24	1.244 gigabits per second (1.244Gbps)
OC-48	2.488 gigabits per second (2.488 Gbps)
OC-192	10 gigabits per second (10 Gbps)
OC-256	13.271 gigabits per second (13.271Gbps)

> **Online Resources**
>
> Are you one of the lucky libraries located at an Internet 2 site? You can find out which schools are linked to the Abilene network at *www.ucaid.edu/ abilene/html/participating_institutions.html* and the vBNS network at *www.vbns.net/nodecount.htm*.

DIAL-UP SERVICES

Dial-up connections to the Internet use switched circuits. A *switched circuit* sets up a dedicated communication channel between two end systems. Voice calls and dial-up connections using modems are examples. For a home or library connection, the circuit starts out on a pair of twisted wires from the caller's location to a local telephone-switching center. You *switch* the service on by dialing a number that opens a number for your transmission. When you want Internet service, you dial up to your service provider, switching the service on. You have access to that switch for the duration of your call. When you are finished, you hangup and your connection is broken. The difference between dedicated and switched circuits is that a dedicated circuit is always connected and a switched circuit can be set up and disconnected at any time, reducing connect charges.

Analog Dial-Up Connections

Analog dial-up connections are the simplest and least expensive connections to make. They use the Plain Old Telephone System, or POTS for short. Today, almost all of the circuit switching systems are digital except for the *last mile* connecting to the subscriber. The signal coming out of your telephone or modem is analog (sound) and travels along a *twisted pair cable* as an analog signal. Once it arrives at your telephone company's office, the signal is usually digitized. When the signal arrives at the receiving end, it is converted back into analog and delivered to the telephone or modem.

The only hardware that's required besides your computer is a modem. The speed of an analog dial-up connection is determined by several factors including the speed of your modem. Other factors affecting speed can include line noise or compatibility with other modems to which you are trying to connect. Modems are discussed in detail in Chapter 6, "Tips on Choosing Hardware." The software used for establishing an analog dial-up connection is described in Chapter 7, "Software for Establishing a Basic Connection."

There are two types of accounts that you can establish with an analog dial-up connection: SLIP/PPP and shell accounts.

SLIP/PPP CONNECTIONS

SLIP/PPP connections are dedicated dial-up connections made with high-speed modems using software called SLIP (Serial Line Internet Protocol) or PPP (Point to Point Protocol). With SLIP and PPP connections, a minimum 28.8Kbps modem is highly recommended.

With this type of connection, you have a full Internet connection with the capability of sending and receiving data directly with any other machine on the Internet. Unlike a dedicated connection, which remains up and running at all times, SLIP and PPP connections are up and running only when you call in and make a connection, and then they are down and non-operational when you disconnect.

With a SLIP/PPP connection, your own personal computer has a full Internet connection and you work directly with other hosts on the Internet, sending and receiving data straight from your personal computer. There are differences between SLIP and PPP connections. SLIP isn't capable of detecting and fixing errors in data transmissions. If you have a connection that's prone to errors, SLIP may not be a good choice. PPP has advantages over SLIP, including the ability to set up a link to a remote network and test whether the link works.

If you are part of a university system, you may discover that it not only offers direct, dedicated access to students and faculty through an Ethernet connection on campus, but also through a SLIP/PPP connection to users with modems located on or off campus.

SLIP/PPP dial-up connections are within financial reach of most libraries, but they can be difficult to set up and run properly. If you have minimal computer skills, you might consider enlisting the services of a computer hobbyist or professional to configure this kind of system. For more details on configuring software, see Chapter 7.

SHELL ACCOUNTS

Connecting to the Internet via a shell account means you are going through an intermediary computer to access the Internet. The primary disadvantage of a shell account is that it limits you to the Internet applications running on the service provider's computer to which you connect. These applications are not as friendly as the Windows clients designed to run on your personal computers. In addition, you have to learn to use the operating commands on the host computer, which are quite different from those on your personal computer.

When you transfer information to or from the Internet using a shell account, you have to go through a two-step process. When you transfer a file from a remote machine on the Internet to your own personal computer, you first have to download the file to your service provider's machine and then download it one more time from there to your own personal computer.

In some situations, this two-step process can be advantageous. If you download a large text file to your local host and are not sure whether it is relevant to your needs, you can first view it on the local host, and then decide whether you want to download it to your personal computer. Viewing the file on your local host first gives you the option of editing the file before downloading, downloading the file as-is, or discarding it.

Transferring files from your local host to your personal computer takes much longer than transferring files from the remote host to your local host. This is because you are linked to your local host with a standard telephone wire and, at tops, a 56Kbps modem. Your local host, however, is linked to the Internet via high speed dedicated lines transferring data at rates of 1.544Mbps, or faster. For more information on shell accounts, refer to Chapter 10, where I present UNIX tips for librarians.

What are shell accounts good for? Many times librarians use a shell account in combination with standard dial-up or dedicated-access accounts. The librarian uses his or her Windows-based dedicated-access account for e-mail, transferring files, and accessing Web-based commercial databases, such as OCLC, etc. The shell account might be the only link to a UNIX computer on which the library runs a Web server. The librarian connects to the shell account on the UNIX server to manage HTML documents, bulletin boards, and other services associated with their Website. Remote access via telnet is more common than having direct access to the hardware itself.

Digital Dial-Up Connections: ISDN

ISDN, which stands for *Integrated Services Digital Network*, is an example of digital dial-up service. ISDN service is delivered to you over the same two copper wires that provide telephone service to your library. Therefore, no additional wiring will be needed in most cases. The major difference between modem dial-up connections and ISDN connections is that the ISDN connection is an all-digital connection from your end to the receiving end.

Unlike dial-up analog service, ISDN offers a higher bandwidth and is capable of transmitting voice and data simultaneously on the same connection. This means you could be surfing the Net while you are talking on the phone or sending a fax. Other typical uses of ISDN include instant image delivery, digital audio, and desktop video conferencing.

TYPES OF ISDN SERVICE

The *Basic Rate Interface* (BRI) supports a total bandwidth of 144Kbps. This channel is divided into two 64Kbps Bearer(B)Channels that can handle either data and/or voice transmissions. To attain higher throughput, the two B Channels can be combined together and used in one call to support applications such as video conferencing.

Another channel, called a "signaling" or D Channel, uses the remaining 16Kbps to control the transmissions and enables features such as conference calls, call waiting, and call forwarding. The D Channel also supports credit card authorizations and automatic teller machine transactions.

There are other kinds of ISDN connections with varying bandwidths. *Primary Rate Service* (PRI), also known as 23 B+D (23 B Channels and one D channel), is equivalent to a 1.544Mbps (Megabit per second) T1 circuit.

ALWAYS ON/DYNAMIC ISDN

As it turns out, not all of the 16Kbps D channel is used for passing signaling information. There is enough spare bandwidth left over to create a full-time 9.6Kbps connec-

Online Resource
Microsoft offers a service at site *www.microsoft.com/windows/geoids* where you can link to Pacific Bell or Southwestern Bell to learn more about their ISDN services. Go here to download ISDN software for Windows and find out if ISDN service is offered in your area.

tion between your computer and your Internet service provider. For a few extra dollars, you can maintain a continuous connection to the Internet. You can perform some of your tasks at the slower speed, such as downloading and sending e-mail. When your traffic exceeds the capabilities of the D Channel, it automatically bumps up to the faster B Channel. This new concept is called *Always On/Dynamic ISDN*, or AO/DI for short. The major phone companies, including Southwestern Bell, Pacific Bell, and BellSouth, currently support AO/DI. For additional information on how AO/DI works including a white paper, visit Access Technologies Forum (ACTEF) at *www.via-isdn.org/aodi/index.htm*.

ISDN Pricing

ISDN Basic Rate Interface (BRI) services vary in cost depending on your location and who your telephone service provider is. Monthly charges can range from $25 or $30 per month up into several hundred dollars per month. Some companies charge a flat rate for unlimited usage and others charge a usage fee. Usage fees can vary depending on time of day and whether voice or data is being transmitted.

STEPS TO CONNECTING

Usually there are four different parties involved when setting up ISDN service: your local phone company, an Internet service provider, and sources for your hardware and software requirements.

Before you begin, decide how you intend to use an ISDN connection. ISDN is digital, so analog equipment, such as your telephone, fax, and modem, won't work directly on an ISDN line. Deciding up front how many of these devices you want to operate on an ISDN helps determine hardware requirements. ISDN isn't powered like your analog telephone connection, so power outages can render your ISDN phone service unusable. For this reason, it might prove beneficial to maintain an analog phone line along with an ISDN connection. When you take all of these factors into consideration, you may want to consider adding ISDN as a second line. Use the ISDN line for high-speed digital data, and use the other line for analog voice, fax, and modem.

Contact your local phone company to see if ISDN service is available in your area. Check out their options and pricing. National carriers, such as Bell Atlantic *www.bell-atl.ocm/* and Southwestern Bell *www.swbell.com*, include ISDN information on their Websites. If you plan to use an ISDN line for long distance, you need to determine who your long distance carrier will be.

Once you decide how you are going to use an ISDN line, and you know that ISDN service is available in your area, locate an Internet service provider in your area to find out if they offer ISDN access. Ask them if they maintain an ISDN gateway with synchronous PPP on their routers.

Lastly, pick an installer for the ISDN service. One option is to do it yourself. Further details on hardware requirements are presented in the next chapter. Another option is to hire a consultant or have the local phone company install your ISDN equipment and configure any software required on your system. Software requirements include TCP/IP that supports the WinISDN standard for ISDN access. If you are running Windows98 or later, you can use an ISDN Configuration Wizard to set up ISDN support. You must

---

Online Resource

Microsoft maintains a support site for ISDN services on Windows-based PCs at *www.microsoft.com/windows/getisdn/*.

---

first have the ISDN hardware installed before running the wizard. To locate the wizard, click on "Start|Help" and browse the help index for "wizards, ISDN Configuration."

When you request ISDN services from your phone company, find out what SPID numbers are assigned to your line. SPIDs (*Service Profile Identifiers*) are sometimes needed for setting up your hardware. Other times, the hardware is capable of automatically determining the type of switch in use and configures the service provider's identification to match. For example, the 3Com U.S. Robotics ISDN terminal adapter, through a feature called *AutoSPID*, makes ISDN setup easy by automatically downloading SPIDs from switches that support it.

DEDICATED CONNECTIONS

Dedicated connections differ from dial-up connections in that they are up and running 24 hours a day. Whether anyone is using them or not, the connection remains open as long as your computer is on. Dedicated connections are sometimes called *leased lines* because you have exclusive use of the connection for a set fee independent of how much you use it. In this section, I discuss points to consider when connecting to an existing dedicated line and briefly describe two types of dedicated connections: xDSL, High-Speed Cable Access, Frame Relay, and T1 lines.

Connecting to an Existing Dedicated Line

Most universities already are connected to the Internet, as are many large government agencies and corporations. In these organizations, computing resources are often a department in themselves. Larger institutions may have multiple LANs, each with its own network administrator. Typically, these organizations use expensive, high-speed, dedicated, leased lines for connecting to the Internet.

This type of connection is appropriate for organizations that transfer large amounts of data and have many users and workstations that must be connected to the Internet. This option requires that dedicated lines be leased through a network provider and special network hardware be installed on site, making this a complicated operation.

If you are part of an organization that has a dedicated Internet connection, but for security or other reasons your library hasn't been allowed access, your best option for gaining access to the Internet is to first try linking to the existing system. You probably will need to present your proposal to a network administrator or someone in computing services.

Before approaching them, however, read through the rest of this manual and develop a clear understanding of the advantages of connecting to the Internet. When you present your request, be ready with the answers to the following questions:

1. Who will be using the Internet? Do you plan to allow access only to professional staff in the reference department or do you want to provide public access, too?

2. What services do you want to make accessible? Cover all of the available services including e-mail, FTP, telnet, the Web, and so on.

3. How will these services benefit you and your patrons? You may see e-mail as a valuable tool for keeping abreast of the most current developments in the library profession, communicating with staff and colleagues all around the world, or as a convenient method of communicating with vendors. You may determine that telnet or the Web is a more cost-effective service for connecting to commercial online databases such as Dialog or FirstSearch than is TYMNET or SPRINTNET. Or, you might see the value in allowing patrons direct, unmediated access to other libraries' online catalogs anywhere in the world.

xDSL

xDSL collectively represents all of the various types of *digital subscriber lines*, including the two main types ADSL and SDSL. xDSL technology is sometimes called the *last mile technology* because it is applied to the connection existing between your library and the telephone switching station. xDSL is like ISDN in that it runs on the copper wires you have in place for you telephone system.

ADSL stands for *Asymmetric Digital Subscriber Line* and is the most popular form of xDSL technology. ADSL differs from ISDN in its inability to transfer data at even speeds upstream and downstream. Also, ADSL transfer speeds are affected by how far you are from the telephone company's central office. Speeds can vary greatly from one service provider to the next, but you can typically expect speeds in the 400Kbps to 600Kbps range and higher.

SDSL, or *Symmetric Digital Subscriber Line*, offers the same speed in both directions. The download speed may not be as fast as ASDL, but the upload speed can be much faster. SDSL is more suitable for connections where you are running your own Web server or network.

VDSL, or *very high-speed DSL*, is on the horizon and promises to carry several services on a single twisted pair line, including multiple dial tones, data, and digital television.

Before subscribing to DSL service, make sure you find an Internet service provider that can support it. When you set up service, be sure to ask the DSL provider if your line will be capable of supporting a dial tone and data, or only data.

HOW MUCH DOES DSL SERVICE COST?

Concentric Network Corporation, a national Internet service provider, offers *ConcentricDSL* service starting at $69/month for connection speeds comparable to ISDN. Costs increase to around $500/month for high-speed connections at T1 speeds. Your

Online Resource
Visit Everything DSL *www.everythingdsl.com/* for free access to FAQs, news, tips on hardware, a glossary, message board, and links to other DSL-related Websites.

> **Online Resource**
>
> Visit the DSL Center *www.dslcenter.com/index.html* for news, glossary, and FAQ relating to DSL technology.

local phone company charges connection fees for installing a circuit. Fees range from $225 to $325 to install the circuit. The cost of hardware, like the DSL modem and network interface card, adds an additional $450 to $500. Lastly, expect the Internet service provider to charge an activation fee in the range of $200.

High-Speed Cable Internet Access

Cable technology shares the same coaxial cable and fiber optic lines that bring cable television into your home. The data transfer rate of a cable modem is phenomenal compared to an analog modem. Depending on equipment and where you live, you could expect an upload speed of 256Kbps and download speed twice that fast at 512Kbps. That makes it a better choice than ISDN if you live in an area where both are available.

WHAT TYPES OF CABLE SERVICE ARE AVAILABLE?

Depending on how cable lines were installed in your area, you can choose between One Way and Two Way cable service. With *One Way* service you use an analog modem to upload information to the Internet, while information is downloaded over the cable. *Two Way* service provides for uploading and downloading over the cable. If you currently use an analog modem, don't get rid of it just yet. You may live in an area where you must continue dialing up to your service provider in order to upload information to the Internet. Call your cable service to find out what services are available to you.

Frame Relay

When you subscribe to frame relay services, you specify what line speed you want, for example 56Kbps or 1.544Mbps (T1). One advantage of frame relay is that the distance of the call does not affect cost. Not being "distance sensitive" means a main library can use frame relay to connect to a branch library that is far away for the same price as a nearby branch.

> **Online Resources**
>
> To learn more about cable modem basics, explore Cable Modem Information at *www.cablemodeminfo.com.* Here you find links to sites describing how cable modems work and links to resources for software and tools.
>
> CNET's "Burn the Wires" is an easy-to-understand tutorial for newbies on how cable modems work, where you can get them, and how much they cost. Read more about it at *coverage.cnet.com/Content/Features/ Techno/Cablemodems/index.html.*

Online Resources

The Frame Relay FAQ, maintained by Dennis Baasch of Emerging Technologies, Inc. *www.etinc.com/frfaq.htm*, offers a detailed description of frame relay.

The Frame Relay Resource Center at Alliance Datacom *www.alliance datacom.com/frame-relay-tutorials.htm* offers an excellent collection of tutorials on frame relay.

Frame relay sources are listed on the Web at *www.mot.com/ networking/frame-relay/resources.html*. Topics include frame relay products, frame relay network providers, white papers, and articles.

Frame relay uses circuits called *virtual circuits*. In most frame relay equipment, the circuits are *permanent virtual circuits* or PVCs. PVCs are similar to private phone lines. Each one is dedicated to a single user. Unlike dedicated connections with real wires connecting your library to the Internet, "virtual" connections are maintained in a frame relay computer's memory. Frame relay is a permanent connection because a PVC is able to send data all the time. As long as the computer is running, the connection is in place.

Another type of virtual circuit is the *"switched" virtual circuit*, or SVC. These circuits exist only as long as there is data flowing on the line. Carriers that offer SVCs will likely set their pricing based on usage. Frame relay PVCs would benefit libraries that maintain fairly steady traffic and SVCs would be a benefit to libraries that have changing connection requirements.

Frame relay has the advantage over T1 lines in that they can offer networks to multiple PVCs. For example, your library's LAN could have one PVC for inbound traffic and another for outbound traffic. This could guarantee in-house library users a certain bandwidth irrespective of how many outside users were logging in to use resources. You could also designate certain PVCs for certain Internet applications.

A service available with frame relay is called *Committed Information Rate*, or CIR. PVCs are assigned a CIR measured in bits per second. They represent the average throughput a PVC should maintain. If you want some guarantees that transmission speeds will not fall below a specified level, you should specify a certain CIR. If, for example, you set up a 56Kbps frame relay connection with a 28Kbps CIR, the telephone company will guarantee transmission rates of 28Kbps at all times and allow you to burst up to 56Kbps if demand is low and traffic is light.

If you send data faster than the CIR, the data gets flagged with a special bit that signals the network to discard any of those packets if there is congestion on the network. There is a built-in protection mechanism that attempts to prevent the discarding of packets before it takes place. When the network is becoming congested, frame relay notifies the application transmitting the data to slow down.

You arrange for frame relay service through your Internet service provider. They also assist with setting up service with your local access provider. Charges for using a 56Kbps frame relay circuit run between $200 and $300 per month. Setup costs can be as high as $1,000.

Online Resource

If you want to learn more about T1 lines, go to Bob Wachtel's Website "All You Wanted to Know About T1 But Were Afraid to Ask." You can find it at Data Comm for Business, Inc. *www.dcbnet.com/notes/9611t1.html.*

T1 Lines

T1, or T-1, service is a point-to-point, dedicated service in the U.S., Canada, and Japan T-carrier system. It is appropriate for libraries that need a high-speed, permanent connection that supports outbound and inbound Internet connections.

Also referred to as a *digital signal level 1*, or DS-1 for short, T1 lines carry a 1.544Mbps digital signal. This consists of 24 64Kbps channels. For libraries that don't have a need for this much throughput, telephone companies offer *Fractional T1* (FT1) services. Fractional T1 services are usually offered in multiples of 64Kbps.

To arrange for T1 service, contact your telephone company or Internet service provider. T1 line prices are determined by the distance between your LAN and your Internet service provider or their nearest POP. A POP or *Point of Presence* is a point where a person can attach to a service provider locally. Companies charge fixed rates for T1 and FT1 service. Like other services, prices on T1 lines vary greatly depending on your location. Pricing may be as low as $600 to $1,000 per month or as high as $10,000 to $15,000 per month.

CHOOSING A CONNECTION METHOD

Determining your needs is the first step in deciding which type of connection method to use. Here are some basic questions to consider:

- Are you going to be providing service only to one person at a time on the staff or to one publicly accessible workstation? Many smaller libraries choose analog dial-up service when their goal is to link a single computer to the Internet. This is an easy platform to set up and inexpensive to run and maintain. Your basic requirements are a computer and modem and Internet access can usually be established for around $20/month.

- Do you have a Local Area Network (LAN) you want to connect or just individual machines? If you want to connect a network, an analog dial-up connection would be inefficient unless you limited users to e-mail services only. In this scenario, you would also need to restrict users from attaching large files to their e-mail messages. All of this, in addition to the fact that many people are now expecting multimedia access to the Web, makes dial-up access for networks a bad idea. The best options for linking a network to the Internet are one of the dedicated connection methods discussed earlier.

    You could link any number of individual computers on a LAN to the Internet using analog dial-up connections, each PC with its own individual modem. There is a point, however, where this system is no longer cost effective. Determine the total cost of all the modems, private phone lines, and individual dial-up accounts you need and compare that to the cost of setting up a LAN (if one is not already in place) and connecting it to the Internet.

- Do you want to provide both inbound and outbound access? Maybe your goal is to not only let your patrons and staff access the Internet, but also allow outside users access to your information services. If you want to establish inbound services, an analog dial-up connection will not be sufficient. Instead, you need to consider a dedicated connection. This makes it possible for library users to access your catalog or Web server via the Internet.
- How often do you plan to use the Internet? Only once in a while or continuously? If you plan to make your Internet-capable computers available to the public, they will certainly get a lot of use. If you want to have machines available to the reference staff at all times, they too will get used often, especially during the local information rush hours. If the public and reference staff are downloading large files and linking to graphic-rich Web pages, modem connections are going to cause a lot of frustrating bottlenecks. This can be especially true in the afternoons when Internet traffic is beginning to gridlock.
- How much throughput do you need? In other words, how fast does your connection need to be? Depending on various factors, 56Kbps V.90 modems can provide throughput reaching 56,000bps. ISDN service can transmit data at speeds ranging from 64Kbps to 128Kbps. Dedicated access offers even greater bandwidth, up to 1.544Mbps and beyond. You have to compare the costs of these services to the benefits they provide the user. If, for example, you want to offer your patrons the ability to sit down at a machine any time of the day and access real-time video, data transfer rates at 56Kbps are going to be inefficient. You need to begin your pricing with fractional T1 services. These usually begin at 64Kbps and move by increments of 64Kbps all the way up to 1.544Mbps.

MAKING THE CONNECTION

In the section that follows, I introduce various ways of connecting to the Internet. The two most popular methods are by going through a commercial online service such as America Online, CompuServe, or Microsoft Network, or by going through a local or national Internet service provider, also known as an ISP. I describe the pros and cons of each of these options and provide you with contact information for connecting with the major commercial online services and ISPs.

The decision you make about ISPs and commercial online services doesn't necessarily have to be an either/or decision. You may decide to use both. For example, you might connect your LAN to the Internet using a national ISP or statewide education/ research network and run Internet Explorer or Netscape Navigator as your public access interface to the Internet. Your youth services department may also decide that for just $9.95 per month it's worthwhile having access to Homework Help on AOL or Prodigy's Homework Helper.

COMMERCIAL ONLINE SERVICES

If your library is still looking for a way to establish its first link to the Internet, commercial online services might be the answer. America Online (AOL), CompuServe, Prodigy, and Microsoft Network (MSN) offer commercial online services with a full

Table 5–2:	Commercial online services		
Name	**Unlimited Monthly Access Fee**	**Searching for Access Numbers in Your Area**	**Contact Information**
AOL	$21.95	*access.web.aol.com/index.html*	*www.aol.com/*
Compuserve	$19.95	*www.compuserve.com/content/ phone/phone.asp*	*www.compuserve.com/*
EarthLink	$19.95 (Only $17.95/ month if you also choose Sprint long distance)	*www.earthlink.com/* (Local dial-up numbers are determined as part of the registration process.)	*www.earthlink.com/*
MSN	$21.95	*memberservices.msn.com/ supportandhelp/accessnumbers/ accessnum.htm*	*www.msn.com/*
Prodigy Internet	$19.95	*www.prodigy.com/pcom/ prodigy_internet/pi_index.html*	*www.prodigy.com/*

line of their own information products including national news services, full-text magazines and newspapers, and special entertainment and educational forums. It is these "members only" and "pay as you go" services plus a feeling of community that make commercial online services uniquely different from ISPs. In addition to their proprietary information services, commercial online services provide portals on the Web with the usual array of free services, and dial-up access to the Internet. If you already have access to the Web and you'd like to establish an account with a commercial online service, you can download their proprietary software from the Web addresses listed in Table 5–2.

EarthLink started in 1994 and is one of the newer contenders in the commercial online service market. The value-added services they offer include toll-free phone support (guaranteeing a wait time of five minutes or less), and a CD each quarter that is filled with full-version software, such as Adobe PageMill, Eudora Pro e-mail, and Norton AntiVirus. In September 1999, MindSpring, another national Internet service provider, and EarthLink announced their agreement to merge.

COMPARING COSTS

Each commercial online service offers a slightly different pricing plan. As you can see in Table 5–2, the basic unlimited access account doesn't vary much, staying between $19.95 and $21.95/month. AOL and Prodigy give special discounts when paying for one year in advance.

AOL offers five pricing options:

- $21.95 per month—Standard plan provides access to AOL and the Internet.
- $19.95 per month—For subscribers who pay one year in advance ($239.40 one-year prepaid subscription). Provides access to AOL and the Internet.
- $9.95 per month—AOL calls this service the "bring-your-own-access" plan. You provide your own connection to the Internet, but have access to all of AOL's special services.
- $4.95 per month—A light usage plan that provides only three hours/month of AOL and dial-up access to the Internet. Additional time costs $2.95 per hour.
- $9.95 per month—Another limited usage plan. This one provides you with five hours of AOL and dial-up access to the Internet. Additional time costs $2.95 per hour.

In February 1998, CompuServe became a wholly owned subsidiary of America Online, Inc. CompuServe offers services that target an audience of adults with advanced education, high incomes, and professional careers. CompuServe offers services to match this clientele that includes a mix of research and communication tools, news and information, and business and personal forums. Both AOL and CompuServe offer U.S. nationwide 800 access numbers. AOL and CompuServe members pay a surcharge of $.10/minute, or $6.00/hour when they connect using 800 numbers.

CompuServe's pricing for five hours per month is $9.95. For each additional hour, add $2.95. Unlimited monthly access is $19.95.

MSN offers one rate, $21.95/month unlimited access, as does EarthLink at $19.95/month.

Prodigy Internet charges $19.95/month for unlimited Internet service. If you pre-pay for one year of unlimited access in advance, you pay the equivalent of just $16.50/month, or $198.00 total.

Other major national service providers in this category are listed in Table 5–3. These companies don't include any significant value-added services beyond their freely accessible Websites. AT&T's site offers a subject directory, news, and information sources.

THE WELL

Compared to the Big Four commercial online services just discussed (AOL, CompuServe, MSN, and Prodigy), The WELL is refreshingly simple and straightforward in what it has to offer. In a class all its own, The WELL (Whole Earth 'Lectronic Link) is a cozy little virtual community where folks from all walks of life come to carry

Table 5–3:	Major national Internet service providers	
Name	**Address**	**Access Rates**
AT&T WorldNet	*www.att.net/*	$9.95/month for ten hours; $19.95/month for 150 hours; Unlimited access is $21.95/month.
Concentric	*www.concentric.com*	Concentric offers dial-up and dedicated access. Their DSL service costs are listed above in the section on xDSL. Unlimited dial-up access is $19.95/month; $7.95/month for five hours; $170.70/6 months paid in advance.

on public conversations and exchange private e-mail. Since the last edition of this book was published, The WELL discontinued selling dial-up Internet access as part of its service plan. If you want to join The WELL today, you first have to establish your own connection to the Internet along with an e-mail account through a school, business, or Internet service provider. Once that's done, you can participate in The WELL's conferences via the Web for $10.00/month.

For $15.00 a month you can purchase membership in a Complete WELL.com account. This carries with it a *well.com* e-mail address, a place to park your personal Web pages on *www.well.com*, which includes 10MB of storage space, and the right to create one private or personal WELL Conference.

PROS AND CONS OF COMMERCIAL ONLINE SERVICES

Before the Internet began busting its britches with one-stop sites offering weather, horoscopes, sports, classifieds, stock quotes, chat, e-mail, auctions, free reference resources, and more, commercial online services were providing a distinctly unique service. You went to AOL and CompuServe because you could find most of what you needed all in one central location. Full-text reference libraries could be easily searched with one interface. Commercial online services offered access to up-to-date encyclopedias and almanacs. You could rely on these services to help you get your e-mail account up and running.

Now, many of these same services are available at little or no cost elsewhere. Today, you can access Britannica Online *www.britannica.com/* free of charge. You can search almanacs at *www.infoplease.com* free of charge. You can read highlights and selected articles from most major newspapers and magazines free of charge. If you are a member of one of the online investment services, like TD Waterhouse, for no additional charge you are given unlimited access to *Standard & Poors Stock Reports* and *Zacks Investment Research*.

So what is it that still makes the commercial online services a choice worth considering? Aside from being another service choice for dial-up users, they still do a good job of bringing many resources together into an integrated package. Where the global matrix called *the Internet* is a collection of loosely interconnected computer networks, AOL, Prodigy, CompuServe, and MSN form something more akin to a virtual community. Their proprietary services are up-to-date and selected for *their* audience. Commercial online services continue to offer their members specialized services, such as the ability to conduct banking and stock purchases online.

If you choose to use the proprietary Web browsers these services offer, setting up your first dial-up account can be a breeze. Most of the software you need comes on a free CD-ROM. These browsers keep improving with time, but their mail programs and other features are not always as robust as commercially available applications.

INTERNET SERVICE PROVIDERS OR ISPs

As the popularity of the Internet has grown, so has the number of companies offering access to the Internet. *Internet service providers*, or ISPs, are companies that specialize in offering Internet access.

Unlike the commercial online services discussed earlier, ISPs don't necessarily offer proprietary software for accessing their services and they don't maintain fee-based services such as full-text newspaper and magazine databases. Some ISPs only offer a connection point to the Internet, either a shell account, a SLIP/PPP account, or both. Services are minimal and prices are low. Others offer value-added services that enable them to compete somewhat with the commercial online services and other ISPs. Table 5–4 lists directories that track ISPs worldwide.

REGISTRATION

You can subscribe to an ISP service two different ways: online using a modem, or by calling them in person. If you already have communications software and a modem, you can usually dial-in to an ISP and register online. If you already have an Internet connection and access to the Web, you can usually subscribe through the ISP's home page. If an ISP has their own proprietary software, they usually give you the option of downloading it from their Website or ordering a disk by mail (specify Mac or Windows).

If you are calling them in person, start with the ISP's customer service number and tell them you'd like to set up a new account. Because helping new members subscribe to their service is their bread and butter, they will be most happy to help. The service provider will be able to tell you what your connection options are, local call versus 800–number access, ISDN support, etc.

Payments to online services are generally made with Visa, MasterCard, or American Express, so have your credit card number ready.

Some service providers make special arrangements with libraries, billing them for services at the end of the month instead of requiring payment by credit card.

LOCAL VS. NATIONAL ISPs

Local ISPs are "local" in the sense that they have headquarters in the town you're living in, or a town that's a local phone call away. They aren't promoting their services nationally or even regionally, and they're not busy setting up POPs (Points of Presence) in all the major cities around the U.S.

Local service providers generally don't provide you with their own proprietary software packages. Instead, they ask you to use your own commercial or shareware Internet applications or they may mail shareware that's pre-configured with the proper information for connecting to their service. Still other local ISPs ask you to download the necessary software from their online file library.

If you live in a rural community, a local ISP may be your only choice for connecting to the Internet. National ISPs might have POPs in a major city nearby, but the call may

---

Online Resource
Another valuable source of information on ISPs in the U.S. and Canada is maintained by *Boardwatch Magazine*. Their *Directory of Internet Service Providers*, now in its 11th edition, can be viewed online at *www.boardwatch.com/isp/index.htm* or you can order a print copy. Up-to-date ordering information is available at the address listed above.

Table 5–4. Directories for locating Internet service providers		
Name	**Address**	**Services Offered**
The List	*thelist.internet.com/*	Search for ISPs by area code or country code; browse ISPs offering services in the United States or Canada.
Online Connection	*www.barkers.org/online/ index.html*	Lists national ISPs; includes links to major magazines discussing ISPs.

not be within your local calling area. Newspapers, yellow pages, and local computer stores are the best sources for finding out if there are any ISPs operating in your area.

ISP PRICING

ISPs offer four basic pricing plans:

- Flat-rate
- Hourly
- Surcharge
- Combination

In addition to these ongoing costs, there may also be a one-time set-up fee ranging from $25 to $50.

Flat-Rate

The simplest payment plan is a flat-rate plan that allows unlimited usage. With this type of plan, you can surf the Net for as many hours as you wish and the cost remains the same. The nice thing about this is that you know in advance what your monthly online charges are going to be. If you are going to be online a lot, a flat-rate plan is best. Most Internet providers offer flat-rate plans around $20 per month for unlimited usage.

By the Hour

Another payment option ISPs offer is charging by the hour. If you aren't going to be accessing the Net more than 25 to 30 hours per month, you might be better off sub- scribing to a payment plan that charges by the hour. Typically, ISPs that offer hourly rates charge around 50 cents per hour.

Surcharge

In addition to the payment plan charged by the online service, there may also be a con- nection charge for connecting to the online service you choose. This charge may be for 800–number access or for connections via public data networks like SprintNet or Tymnet.

The added cost of a connection charge won't be an issue for you if you're within local calling distance of your service provider or one of their POPs. If you live in a rural area that's not within local calling distance of a POP or a public data network, 800–number access will be your best option.

Combination

Some service providers combine charging methods. For example, they may charge a flat rate of $15 for anything up to 30 hours and then switch to a per hour charge for time spent beyond the 30 hours.

FREE INTERNET SERVICE

There are a handful of new service providers that now offer free access to the Net. For example, with 1stUp.com *www.1stup.com*, you can access the Web for free. How, you may ask, can a company offer free dial-up service when everyone else is charging about $20.00/month? In the case of 1stUp.com, they ask you to install a program on your computer that displays a navigation bar as part of your Web browser interface. The bar, which can be moved around to different locations on the screen, displays small advertisements and buttons that hyperlink you to Web services and information sites. It's these sponsors that pay for your free Internet access, not 1stUp.com.

Be aware that free services like 1stUp.com typically provide customers with personalized advertisements. They do this by monitoring the subscriber's Web surfing habits. If you are concerned about privacy issues, be sure to read each service provider's privacy statement. 1stUp.com partners with two other services that provide the actual dial-up connection: FreeWorld, powered by Excite *freeworld.excite.com/freeworld/help/ contact.dcg*, and AltaVista FreeAccess *doc.altavista.com/help/free_access/ download.shtml*. Other examples of companies offering free dial-up access are listed in Table 5–5.

UUCP CONNECTION

UUCP is an acronym for *Unix to Unix CoPy*, a protocol that started on UNIX but is now implemented on other platforms including MS-DOS and Macintosh OS. UUCP is a program that enables the transfer of files between remote dial-up sites. If there is a

Table 5–5: Companies offering free dial-up access	
Name	**Address**
address.com	*www.address.com/*
AltaVista FreeAccess	*microav.com/*
Free ISP	*www.isps-free.com/*
FreeWWWeb	*www.freewwweb.com/*
Juno	*www.juno.com/index.html*

Online Resources

UUCP Internals FAQ answers questions about how the various UUCP protocols work. You can find a copy at *www.cs.uu.nl/wais/html/na-dir/ uucp-internatls.html.*

A copy of the UUCP Manual Page can be found at *hoth.stsci.edu/man/ man1C/uucp.html.* (UNIX Manual Pages are online help files that explain commands.)

---

college or university computer within local calling distance of your library, and it supports UUCP, there is a possibility that you could establish a low cost e-mail link with the Internet through that host. Although UUCP limits you primarily to a mail-only connection with the Internet, it will become evident in subsequent chapters that a lot of resource discovery and file transfer operations can be executed with e-mail service only. Other services that involve interactive communication like telnet and the Web are not available via a UUCP connection.

To connect to a UUCP mail network, you need to have UUCP software installed on your own personal computer. Although a UUCP connection is fairly inexpensive and easy to set up, it doesn't provide the range of services a full Internet connection provides. An excellent book for MS-DOS users that includes UUCP software is *A DOS User's Guide to the Internet: E-mail, Netnews, and File Transfer with UUCP*, by James Gardner (Prentice Hall, ISBN 0–13106–873–3).

An example of a service offering UUCP e-mail is Cyber Eye, located in the city of Philadelphia. You can access them online at *www.webhosting-sitehosting.com/email.html.* This company offers a toll-free, 800–number UUCP e-mail service. A fee of $49/month buys 50MB of e-mail traffic. Cyber Eye's UUCP e-mail service allows you to access high-capacity Internet e-mail servers via dial-up modem connections. Once connected, you can pick up or "transfer" up to 50MB of e-mail.

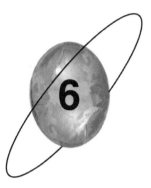

Tips on Choosing Hardware

The hardware requirements for connecting to the Internet will vary from library to library depending on the method of connection. This chapter discusses what devices are needed for the different services. I present guidelines for the do-it-yourself librarian setting up a simple, analog dial-up connection using a modem connected to a standard telephone line. In addition, I explain the hardware requirements for establishing xDSL, cable, ISDN, frame relay, and T1 connections.

Along with discussing the basic hardware components involved with setting up an Internet connection, I also explain how computers communicate, offer tips on buying personal computers and modems, and explain terminals and multiterminal systems. Software needed for connecting to the Internet is discussed in the next chapter.

If you're working in a library where Internet access is already provided through a networked PC or terminal, your link with the Internet has already been established for you. If you would also like to access the Internet's services from your home or assist a library patron with this procedure, the information in this chapter on analog dial-up services should prove helpful.

HOW COMPUTERS COMMUNICATE

The symbols you and I use to communicate, such as the 26 characters of the English alphabet, have to be translated into a form that computers can understand. Computers understand only two electrical states: on and off—a pulse of electricity or no pulse. This on/off system based on 0s (zeros) and 1s (ones) is called the *binary number system*. A single 0 or 1 is called a *bit* (short for *binary digit*), the smallest unit of information that can be represented in binary notation.

Each one of the characters you and I use are represented by a decimal number and these in turn are given a binary equivalent. For example, the character B is represented in the decimal number system by 66. The number 66 is represented in binary code by a set of on/off switches, 01000010, which are the binary equivalent of 66. These eight bits (01000010) are considered a basic unit of measurement called a *byte* (pronounced "bite"). A byte is the equivalent of one character.

A *kilobyte* is another basic unit of measurement, equal to about 1,000 bytes (1,024 bytes). The abbreviation 16KB is read as 16 kilobytes, which is roughly equivalent to about 16,000 bytes.

A *megabyte*, abbreviated as MB, is equivalent to about 1,000,000 bytes (1,048,576 bytes). This is the common unit of measurement for personal computer memory. For example, you might own a personal computer with 128MB (128 million bytes) of RAM expandable to 256MB (256 million bytes).

With the large amount of information being transferred on the Internet, it isn't uncommon to see larger measuring units, such as *gigabytes* (about 1 billion bytes) and *terabytes* (units equaling about 1 trillion bytes). These are abbreviated GB and TB, respectively.

STANDARD CODES FOR REPRESENTING CHARACTERS

ASCII (pronounced "ass-kee") stands for *American Standard Code for Information Interchange*. The ASCII character set consists of 128 seven-bit codes (the binary equivalents of the numbers 0 or "null" through 127) that represent the upper- and lowercase alphabet, numbers, standard keyboard characters, such as ?, ;, !, $, etc., and certain control characters like the carriage return and line feed.

In theory, any system that supports the ASCII standard can communicate with any other ASCII system, and it is a standard that has been accepted widely in the computer industry with the notable exception of IBM. In its tradition of doing things differently, IBM developed its own code called EBCDIC, which stands for *Extended Binary-Coded Decimal Interchange Code*.

EBCDIC is widely used in IBM mainframes, but it isn't used in non-IBM machines nor is it used in the IBM PC and PS/2 computers. The IBM PC uses what IBM calls Extended ASCII. Extended ASCII uses an 8–bit code allowing for a total of 256 characters. The standard ASCII characters are represented by values 0 through 127. Then there are 128 higher characters that define such things as diacritical marks and international punctuation.

When your PC, which supports the ASCII standard, connects through a modem to an IBM mainframe, which supports EBCDIC, there's usually a converter on the mainframe that automatically changes EBCDIC to ASCII. This is a process that takes place behind the scenes and one that you don't have to be concerned with.

PREPARING FOR MULTIMEDIA ON THE INTERNET

If you want to take full advantage of the Internet in all its multimedia splendor, you must consider certain hardware issues relating to multimedia. Tapping into the multimedia aspects of the Internet means setting up your PC for text, graphics, pictures, sound, and video. This has become somewhat easier since the introduction of Microsoft Windows Media Player. Media Player is native to Microsoft Windows and it allows you to

---

Online Resources

For online support of Microsoft Media Player, search the Microsoft Knowledge Base at *search.support.microsoft.com/kb/c.asp.*

---

play a variety of multimedia file types. These include Microsoft Windows Media formats; RealNetworks, RealAudio, and RealVideo; Moving Pictures Experts Group (MPEG); Musical Instrument Digital Interface (MIDI); Apple QuickTime; Macintosh AIFF; and UNIX .au and .snd files. To hear sound when you use Media Player, you must have a sound card.

GENERAL HARDWARE REQUIREMENTS

The challenge in discussing hardware specifications for multimedia Internet access is that there isn't a clear delineation between what works and what doesn't. Many times you get assurances from hardware and software manufacturers that anything above an Intel 486 processor with 8MB of RAM and a 14.4Kbps modem works for their software. This may be true for one application, but you might be utilizing several different applications, some simultaneously. Rather than cut corners, follow the guidelines presented in this section and invest in a fast machine with lots of hard disk drive storage and RAM (*Random-Access Memory*). If you intend to download audio and video files along with installing programs such as Windows 2000 and image-editing applications like Adobe Photoshop, RAM and hard drive space become even more important. With these considerations in mind, here are some basic guidelines to follow when buying new computers.

THE PROCESSOR

The processor, or CPU (*Central Processing Unit*) is the brains of the computer. CPUs come in a variety of speeds. Lower-end computers have slower processors. This changes about every six months, but at present, computers below $1,000 in cost use the AMD (Advanced Micro Devices, Inc.) K6–2 and Intel Celeron processors. At around $1,200 and up you begin to see Intel Pentium III and AMD Athlon processors. Top-end PCs are selling in the $2,500 price range and up and include Intel Pentium IIIs, Pentium III Xeons, and AMD Athlons. There are many variables that affect these prices, but as a general rule, the best buys are in the mid-range. For example, at this point in time the Intel Pentium III 500MHz PCs are good buys. Vendors are currently using the AMD and Cyrix CPUs in low-end model PCs to keep down prices. For general-use workstations in the library, don't be overly concerned about all the hype surrounding megahertz (MHz) and gigahertz (GHz). These are the measurements used to gauge the speed of the CPU. One megahertz equals one million cycles per second. One gigahertz equals one billion cycles per second. You and your patrons probably won't notice the increase in speed between an 850MHz and a 1GHz computer, but the cost difference may be significant. When it comes time to buy, bring yourself up-to-date by reading current issues of *PC Computing*, which can be accessed online at *www.zdnet.com/pcmag/*. In addition, go online and read reviews at Clnet *www.cnet.com/*. Follow the link to hardware, and then look for processors.

Online Resource
Consult with the CPU Info Center *bwrc.eecs.berkeley.edu/CIC/* for the latest information on CPUs. This site offers links to print resources and online technical documentation as well as historical archives.

CACHE MEMORY

Without *cache memory*, your computer won't run as quickly. When you read reviews and benchmarks evaluating PCs, you see references made to 128KB, 256KB, and 512KB of L2 cache, for example. This type of memory, while small when compared to RAM, does enhance your computer's performance. *L2 cache* provides a kind of shortcut to the information you frequently access. Sometimes it's located on the motherboard and other times it's on the same chip as the microprocessor, which offers even higher performance. When it's part of the processor, it's sometimes referred to as *on-die*, or *integrated* L2 cache. The *motherboard* is the circuit board inside your computer that holds all of the internal circuitry for the system, including memory slots, expansion slots, and so on. *Level 1 cache* is another type of "fast" memory that is built into the CPU. L1 memory also stores information that is accessed frequently. Generally speaking, the more cache memory you have, the better your computer's performance and the *integrated* cache is better than cache that is physically separate from the CPU.

RAM MEMORY

PCs use RAM (Random-Access Memory) to run programs. Ask for at least 128MB of RAM, or a minimum of 256MB of RAM if you intend to do some serious Web page graphics development using scanners, imaging editors, and illustration tools. Make sure there is room available for future expansion. Most PCs today use SDRAM, or *Synchronous Dynamic Random-Access Memory*. SDRAM is faster than DRAM (*Dynamic Random-Access Memory*), which is another type of RAM.

PCs also use video memory. Two-dimensional and three-dimensional images need sufficient video memory to produce clear, crisp images. Today's systems average 8MB to 16MB of video memory.

CD-ROM AND DVD DRIVES

CD-ROM drives (*Compact Disc Read-Only Memory*) are a necessity these days. CD-ROM drives are available in various speeds represented as multiples of ×. At present, most systems offer drives averaging 32× to 40×.

Online Resource
To stay up-to-date on Mac computers, consult Apple's home page at *www.apple.com/*. Presently, the 500MHz Power Mac G4 processor with Velocity Engine is their top performer.   The iMac and iMac DV are using 350MHz or 400MHz G3 processors.

Online Resources

You can find out more about DVD at Tristan Savatier's DVD resource page *www.mpeg.org/MPEG/dvd.html*. Jim Taylor, author of *DVD Demystified* (ISBN:0–07064–841–7), has written a DVD FAQ that can be found at *www.videodiscovery.com/vdyweb/dvd/dvdfaq.html*. In addition, DVD drive manufacturers like Sony *www.sel.sony.com/SEL/consumer/dvd/index.html* and Toshiba *www.toshiba.com/tacp/dvd_main.html* offer FAQs, glossaries, and product reviews. A meta source for DVD information is maintained by Robert Lundemo Aas at *www.unik.no/~robert/hifi/dvd/*.

Digital Versatile Discs, or DVDs, are the future of CD-ROMs. DVDs are like CD-ROMs, but hold a lot more data. CD technology allows for storing 650MB of data on a single disc while DVD holds about 4.7GB per single-layered disc. This is enough storage space to hold an entire movie including three channels of CD-quality audio and four channels of subtitles. Double-layered DVDs can store 9.4GB of data. Double-sided DVDs that are double layered on both sides can hold 18.8GB of data. DVD-RAM drives can read various CD and DVD formats including DVD-ROM, CD audio discs, CD-ROM, CD-R, and CD-RW (see below for an explanation of CD-R and CD-RW). DVD-RAM drives come in internal and external varieties, the internal being less expensive. The storage capacities of these disks will undoubtedly increase in the future.

STORAGE

Floppy disk drives still serve a useful purpose. When ordering new PCs, include a 1.44MB $3^1/_2$-inch HD (*High Density*) floppy drive.

The hard drive is where you store information "permanently." Just as you can never have too much RAM, you can never have too much hard drive real estate. Public access workstations in the library may not require as much hard drive space as a PC used in your office, or one that's used as a Web server. Presently, the low-end systems come with 8GB (gigabyte) hard drives and the higher-end systems have 20GB.

Other common storage options for supplementing your hard drive include DVD, CD-R, CD-RW, and Zip, Jaz, and Super Disks. Super Disks hold 120MB of data on a floppy disk. Zip disks come in the 100MB to 250MB range. Jaz cartridges come in 1GB and 2GB varieties and cost about $100 and $125 respectively. CD-Rs, which sell for about $1.00 each, and CD-RWs, which sell for about $3.00 each, are both capable of storing 650MB of data.

If you plan on working a lot with graphics and sound, make sure your disks can store at least 100MB. If you are working with digital video, 2GB Jaz drives are useful as are DVD, CD-Rs, and CD-RWs. The latter storage media are convenient for backing up Websites and digital library archives, especially if you want to carry projects between home and office. The single-sided DVD-R disk comes in two formats. One can store

---

Online Resource

Learn more about CD-R and CD-RW by reading Andy McFadden's CD-Recordable FAQ at *www.fadden.com/cdrfaq/*.

up to 3.95GB of data and the other can store up to 4.75GB of high-density data. The data on the DVD-R (and CD-R) is permanently recorded (write-once) and cannot be erased or altered. CD-RW discs can be rewritten, meaning you can erase and record over data already on the disc. While DVD, CD-R, and CD-RW work well for file storage, the Jaz drive reads data much faster and can be used to store and run applications.

MONITORS

Order at least a Super VGA (SVGA) 17–inch monitor. A 19–inch monitor is preferable if you can afford it. Most standard monitors provide a dot pitch of 25mm to 28mm. (*Dot pitch* is the distance between two dots of the same color. The closer the dots are to each other, the higher the resolution. More expensive monitors have dots as close as .24mm and cheaper models as far away as .52mm.) The Video Electronics Standards Association (VESA) specifies a minimum refresh rate of 70Hz for SVGA. The refresh rate determines the speed that the display uses to paint the dots on the screen.

Usually you select how much memory you want on your video card. For example, 8MB, 16MB, and 32MB of video RAM are common choices today. Choosing a greater amount of memory doesn't speed up how the video card operates. Instead, it enables your monitor to display more colors and/or higher resolutions. You need to specify the card interface type when ordering separately. There are three choices: AGP, ISA, and PCI. AGP, or *Accelerated Graphics Port*, is a high-speed standard that enables the controller card to access the computer's main memory. It is designed to handle 3–D technology. ISA, or *Industry Standard Architecture*, is a standard that handles 16–bit expansion cards. ISA cards are not as popular as the cards supporting the newer PCI standards. There are only a few peripherals that still connect through ISA ports, for example, sound cards and modems. PCI, or *Peripheral Component Interconnect*, is known for its plug-and-play capability and fast communications between the peripheral and the CPU.

SOUND CARD

Sound cards give you the ability to hear sounds with your PC. Most sound cards are designed to fit into a PCI slot (see above for details on PCI standards). Creative Labs sells one of the better-known consumer sound cards. Their high-end SoundBlaster Live! supports two to eight speaker outputs, 512–voice synthesizers, and analog and digital inputs. If you intend to support a full-featured digital audio workstation, this card would be an excellent choice. Other PCI sound cards you might consider include Turtle Beach Montego A3DXstream and Diamond Monster Sound MX200.

INPUT DEVICES

Input devices are hardware components used for entering data. The two most important input devices to consider are keyboards and mice. At a minimum, you need a 101–key keyboard. Designs range from classic to ergonomic. The Microsoft Natural Keyboard *www.microsoft.com/* is an example of a popular ergonomic keyboard. Kinesis Classic Keyboard *www.kinesis-ergo.com/* is a more radical, expensive design.

There are various types of connectors for keyboards, the preferred type being PS/2. PS/2 ports and connectors are small and round utilizing six pins. Older PCs use the larger five-pin PC/AT socket. If you want to connect a PS/2 keyboard to a five-pin socket, use a PS/2–to-DIN-5 keyboard adapter. USB keyboards are also available. USB (*Universal Serial Bus*) is the newest PC connection standard. USB uses a small, rectangular, four-pin plug. When using USB keyboards, keep in mind that when you go into Safe Mode, Windows will not recognize a USB keyboard.

You can buy inexpensive mice in the $10 range, or more expensive, innovative designs like Logitech's cordless MouseMan Wheel or Microsoft IntelliMouse Explorer. Scrolling mice, like the one Logitech makes *www.logitech.com/*, make life a little easier for Web surfers. The IntelliMouse also uses a scrolling wheel, but does not have a mouse ball. The ball has been replaced with an IntelliEye digital sensor that measures how far and how fast the pointer should move.

Mice connect to computers in a couple of different ways. They use either a PS/2 connector or serial connector. Check your computer's motherboard to see which type of connector it uses. In case your mouse doesn't match, you can use a converter connector. USB mice are also available, but they have the same problems as USB keyboards when switching to Safe Mode. If you want the convenience of a cordless mouse, these are also available.

In addition to the hardware discussed thus far, other hardware is needed for connecting your computer to the Internet. Analog dial-up services use POTS (Plain Old Telephone Service), and for this type of connection you need a high-speed modem.

INTRODUCTION TO MODEMS

The telephone system was designed to transmit audio tones like those generated in human conversations, not digital computer data. The on/off pulses of digital data must be converted into audio signals before a telephone line can carry them. Converting digital 1s ("on" switches) and 0s ("off" switches) into audio tones is called *modulation*. Converting audio tones back into digital on/off pulses that a computer can understand is called *demodulation*.

A modem (*MOdulator/DEModulator*) is a hardware device that enables one computer to communicate with another computer via telephone lines. Modems convert computer data, which consists of on/off digital pulses, into audio signals. These audio signals travel along telephone lines until they reach a receiving modem on a remote computer. The modem on the remote computer converts the audio tones it receives back into on/off pulses and sends them on to the host computer with which you are connecting.

Modems are connected to telephone lines by way of an RJ-ll plug. That's the little clear plastic telephone plug with which you are probably already familiar. Modems have two phone jacks. One phone cable runs from a modular phone jack in the wall to the modem jack labeled "line" or "telco." The second jack on the modem is reserved for your telephone's phone line connection. This allows the phone to be used, but only when the modem is not in use.

Be aware that when your computer is using the modem, it ties up your phone line. If you work in a library with only one phone line, patrons will hear a busy signal when they call in while your modem is connected. If anyone working with you picks up an extension phone while the modem is connected, it will ruin your online connection. Call waiting is another service that can't be used if a computer is sharing the line. You should consider installing a dedicated line for your computer because tying up the line will most definitely cause problems, at least during open hours.

EXTERNAL AND INTERNAL MODEMS

You can use either an external modem or an internal modem to communicate with the Internet. An external modem is a separate device that sits on your desktop next to your computer. A power adapter cord provides the external modem with electricity.

An internal modem is a circuit board (also called an *expansion card*) that fits into an expansion slot inside your computer. Internal modems connect to telephone lines in the same manner that exterior modems do, but in the case of internal modems, the two telephone jacks are part of the circuit board and are accessed from the back of your computer.

When choosing between an internal or external modem, consider the following seven points:

1. If you compare an internal modem to an external modem with the same features, you will find that the internal modem is always less expensive.
2. An internal modem will occupy one of the expansion slots inside your computer. Check to see whether you have an extra expansion slot available.
3. External modems need to plug into a serial port. A *port* is a communication channel where data flows into and out of the computer. A *serial port*, as one of its functions, transmits and receives *asynchronous data,* which is data that flows in a stream one bit after another. If you don't have a spare port, you'll need to install an expansion card with a serial port for the external modem. Then again, if you have an extra expansion slot, why not use it to install an internal modem and save on desk space?
4. Having an external modem allows you the freedom to move it from one computer to another by simply unplugging it. As long as you have the correct connecting cable, you can plug it into any other personal computer, including a Mac. (Modem cables for Macs have a round cable connector on the Mac end.)
5. Getting an internal modem for portable computers like laptops and notebooks could present special problems. They may not have expansion slots, or if they do, they may not be standard ISA (*Industry Standard Architecture*) expansion slots. You might have to get a proprietary internal modem (a modem developed by a company to be used only in the machine they create) to fit the brand of portable computer you have, or, if your portable computer supports the PCMCIA standards, you can use a PCMCIA-compatible modem. A PCMCIA (*Personal Computer Memory Card International Association*) modem is the size of a credit card and slides into a small slot on PCMCIA-compatible portable computers. Because of their unique design, PCMCIA modems tend to be more expensive than external or internal modems.
6. There are external modems for portable computers called *pocket modems,* which are ideal for portable communications. Some plug directly into the serial port. Others are packaged with acoustic couplers, allowing users to link from pay phones, hotels, and other phones where jacks aren't removable.

7. Although internal modems don't usually include a diagnostic display, external modems do. These displays, called LEDs, are located on external modem front panels. There may be an LED that lights indicating that the power is on and this is all you will ever need to check, but LEDs can also be helpful when troubleshooting. For example, you can look at the LED labeled DC (*Data Compression*) to see whether the modem is able to compress data or look at the LED labeled EC (*Error Correction*) to see if the modem is able to detect errors. Windows 95 users are given an image of an external modem in the lower-right-corner of their screen. When data is being sent or received, lights go from red to green.

If you're using an internal modem, you can run a TSR program (*terminate-and-stay-resident program*) on your computer that creates the equivalent of modem LEDs on your screen. *TSR programs* are programs that are designed to stay in the computer's RAM at all times and can be activated by the user with a keystroke. Once you have your modem and communications software running, you may want to explore local Bulletin Board Systems for this kind of program, or it may be included with the modem you purchase. Be aware, however, that TSR programs may interfere with the successful running of other applications. Unless you're experiencing modem problems, there shouldn't be any real need to run a program like this at all times.

When you add a new device to your computer it could conflict with another device for the computer's attention. If you have problems installing your modem, either have a knowledgeable friend help you or pay a little extra to have your dealer install and configure your modem so that it works properly with your software.

MODEM STANDARDS

Modems share certain things in common. Most are compatible with a standard set of commands called the *Hayes Standard AT Command Set* for controlling modem features. Modems offer different options that affect their ability to detect data errors and compress and uncompress data. Modems also transfer data at a variety of speeds. These details are all dictated by modem communication standards, and the modem you use will have to conform to these standards.

The Hayes AT Command Set

Hayes Microcomputer Products developed a set of commands called the *Hayes Standard AT Command Set*. Most modems sold today are compatible with this standardized set of commands that enable you to talk to a modem through the computer keyboard and thus control the modem's operations. The letters AT tell the modem that you are going to send it a command. For example, if you want to dial a modem, you type **ATDT** followed by the phone number you are calling. (Enter no space between the command and the numbers that you are dialing.) The D tells the modem to dial the numbers, and the T is a subcommand that tells the modem to dial in touch-tone mode. With newer versions of communications programs, you don't have to know this command to dial your modem because your program does it for you.

Speed Standards

Another detail that is governed by standards is the speed at which your modem transfers data. CCITT (Consultative Committee on International Telephony and Telegraphy), a European-based, standards-setting organization, set the technical standards for the 2400bps modem in 1985 and designated them V.22bis. In subsequent years, standards were developed for the 9600bps modems, which were designated V.32, and the 14,400bps modems that were designated V.32bis.

The ITU (International Telecommunications Union) is the successor to the CCITT standards committee. The most recent standard developed by the ITU is for the 28,800bps modem that is designated V.34. Prior to the ratification of the V.34 standard, certain companies speculated on what the final ITU standard would be and manufactured the v.Fast Class, or v.FC 28,800bps modems. These are not the same as 28.8Kbps V.34 modems. High-speed modems that meet the enhanced V.34 standard make data transfer rates up to 33.6Kbps possible.

56K Modems

In 1997, before the ITU had approved a 56K technology, various manufacturers brought 56K modems to market. Rockwell International and Lucent Technologies began production of a high-speed 56K modem chipset. Rockwell's technology was called K56Plus and Lucent's was called K56Flex. U.S. Robotics developed a competing technology called X2 that was also capable of 56K downloads. On February 6, 1998, the ITU approved a standard for 56K technology called V.90. Most modem manufacturers offer free upgrades to the V.90 standard for those owning an X2 or K56 modem. If you are a modem user, keep in mind that you can only achieve 56Kbps transmission rates if your ISP supports it.

The transfer rate of 56K is possible, but not necessarily achievable by everyone with a 56K modem. Much depends on the condition of local phone lines. 56K modems can download data at speeds up to 56Kbps, but upload speeds top out at 33.6Kbps.

Bits Per Second

The abbreviation bps stands for *bits per second*. In the telecommunications business, the speed at which modems can transfer information is measured in bits per second. A 2400bps modem can transfer information at a rate of 2,400 bits per second. The faster the transfer rate, the more quickly you can send and receive information. The phrase 28,800bps can also be stated 28.8Kbps (28.8 kilobits per second).Table 6–1 outlines the bps for different types of modems and connections.

Compression Standards

When a modem uses a compression standard, it compresses data that the computer sends to it and then transmits it in that compressed state to another modem. *Data compression* is a process that reduces the size of a file by minimizing the amount of space it requires. The data compression standard V.42bis, which is standard with 14,400bps and

Table 6–1: Data throughput speed chart			
Type of connection	**Transfer speed in bits/second**	**Transfer speed in bytes/second**	**Download time Minutes/Megabyte**
14.4 Modem	14,400	1,800	9.71 minutes
28.8 Modem	28,800	3,600	4.85 minutes
33.6 Modem	33,600	4,200	4.16 minutes
56K Modem	50,000	6,250	2.8 minutes
64k 1 ISDN B Channel	64,000	8,000	2.18 minutes
128k 2 ISDN B Channel	128,000	16,000	1.09 minutes
DSL 256K	256,000	32,000	.35 seconds
T4/DS4	276,480,000	34,560,000	0.2 seconds

28,800bps modems, compresses up to four characters into one character before sending it over the telephone lines. When the compressed character is received, it is decompressed back into its original four-character state. Theoretically, a 14,400bps modem could transmit $4 \times 14,400$bps, or 57,600 bits of data, in one second.

In reality, the potential benefits of data compression are not always fully realized. The transfer speed of textual data increases greatly after compression because all of the blank spaces it contains in its uncompressed form are removed. Executable files are packed tightly to begin with so these files can't be compressed as much as text files. Files that are already stored in a compressed state, such as ZIP files, aren't going to transfer noticeably faster than the normal connect speed of your modem.

Error Correction Standards

Another standard that is important to the operation of your modem is the *error correction protocol V.42*. Telephone lines are prone to distortion and noise, and this can garble the data being transmitted between two modems. When you're downloading information from an online database that charges for its services, it would be beneficial to have a high-speed modem that removes garbage characters resulting from line noise. To make sure your communications with a remote modem remain error free, your modem should support the V.42 error correction protocol.

Another protocol you come across is called the *MNP Protocol*, or Microcom Networking Protocol. MNP is a protocol developed by Microcom, Inc., that has the capability of performing error correction and data compression when your modem is communicating with another modem that supports MNP.

Your modem doesn't operate at a speed any faster than the top speed of the modem to which you connect. In order for these various standards to work, the modems at both ends of the telephone link have to have the same standards. If your modem is 33,600bps with error correction and data compression, but the modem that your dial-up host uses is 28,800bps without data compression, then 28,800bps will be the top speed at which you can transfer data.

Serial Cables and Plugs

The communication process between you and the Internet begins when the computer sends data (binary code) through a cable that runs from the computer's serial port to a modem. The *serial port* is a connection point, a place where data enters and leaves the computer, one bit after the other in a single file, by way of a cable leading to the modem. This cable, called an *RS-232C cable*, usually doesn't come with the modem and must be purchased separately. Make sure that your PC has a high-speed serial card to take advantage of your modem's speed.

The RS-232C cable is named after an electronic communications standard developed by the Electronic Industries Association. The RS-232C standard defines the serial port connections for terminals and communications hardware and also how data is transported over communications links. For example, an RS-232C cable connection specifies a 25–pin D-Shell connector (the pins form the shape of an elongated D) with a male plug at the terminal end and a female plug at the modem end. A few years later, IBM broke the 25–pin rule and created a 9–pin connector, and these are also commonly seen today.

The RS-232C standard also specifies that pin two sends data from the terminal to the modem and pin three receives data from the modem, while pin seven serves as the ground for both circuits. (In 1987, the official name for the RS-232C standard was changed to EIA-232D, but it is still commonly referred to as RS-232C.)

Serial Port Settings: Talking the Talk

Each byte of information, such as the character A, is sent along the phone lines as a separate data item. In order for one byte to be discernible from the next, the data is packaged with a start bit in front and a stop bit in back. The *start bit* is just an extra bit that lets the system know that what follows is a byte of information—a set of data bits. If the data you're sending is ASCII characters, seven bits is all that is needed. In this instance, you would say that your modem is "set to seven data bits." If you were sending a file that contained something other than text, you would use a setting of eight data bits. The last bit in the line is the *stop bit*, which tells the computer receiving the information that the transmission of a byte of data is complete. In communicating this idea you would say you have "a setting of one stop bit."

A special bit that comes right after the data bit and just before the stop bit is called a *parity bit*. The purpose of this bit is to make sure that all of the data bits are correct— that no garbage was inadvertently added during transmission. If *even parity* is used, the sum of all the 1s between the start bit and stop bit must be even. For example, if there were four 1s in the data bits, the parity bit would be set to 0 to keep the total number of 1s even. If you were using even parity and a byte of information arrived with an odd number of 1s between the start bit and stop bit, this would be a signal that the byte contained an error.

The above principle can be applied in reverse by using *odd parity*. The sum of all the 1s must be an odd number and so the parity bit is adjusted accordingly. *No parity* means that a parity bit isn't used to check the accuracy of the data bits. This is the most common setting for communication systems using personal computers.

Most hosts that you dial up to will use a setting of 8–N-1, which means you will have to use those same settings before your computer will communicate properly with theirs. The 8 stands for eight data bits, the N means no parity bit, and the 1 refers to one stop bit.

Because each byte of information ends up being ten bits long (eight data bits plus one start bit and one stop bit), and a byte of information equals one character, a transfer rate of 9600 bits per second equals a transfer rate of about 960 characters per second. Another common setting is 7–E-1, which means that you use 7 data bits, even parity, and 1 stop bit. A byte of information at the setting 7–E-1 also contains ten bits: one start bit, seven data bits, a parity bit, and a stop bit.

Full and Half Duplex Connections

When data is moving in both directions at the same time you have a *full duplex* connection. When you press a key on your keyboard in a full duplex connection, your computer sends the character to the remote computer, which then sends—or "echoes"—it back to your computer, where it is displayed on your screen.

When data is moving in only one direction, you have a *half duplex* connection. When you press a key on your keyboard in a half duplex connection, it is displayed on your screen and sent to the remote computer at the same time.

It is important that you use the same communications connections that the remote host is using. If you communicate in full duplex with a remote computer that's using half duplex, you won't see any characters appearing on your screen as you type. If this happens, change your settings to half duplex. If you see double letters (lliikkee tthhiiss) on your screen, change your setting to full duplex. If you're not sure how to do this, refer to your communications software user's manual or online help menus.

Flow Control and XON/XOFF Handshaking

Flow control keeps the various components of a telecommunications system from delivering more data than the receiving end can handle. The flow control takes place between your computer and the modem, your modem and the other modem, and between the other modem and the remote host to which it is connected. One modem, for example, asks the other modem how fast it can exchange information. The highest transfer rate that is common to both of them is the transfer rate upon which they agree.

Communications software enables you to set the flow control between your computer and your modem. The software usually arrives with certain default (preset) settings, but you may have to change these for your particular applications. The most common techniques used are hardware flow control and software flow control. *XON/XOFF data flow control* (sometimes called *XON/XOFF handshaking*) refers to a type of software-based method of adjusting the flow of information between a computer and modem. Your communications software and your modem need to use the same method of flow control as your modem.

Buying a Modem

The chart presented in Table 6–1 shows that the time it takes to download a file varies depending on the speed at which the data is transferred. This graph illustrates a wide spectrum of performance. On the low end, the graph shows that it takes a 14,400bps

Table 6–2: Modem manufacturers	
Name	**URL**
Hayes	*www.hayesmicro.com/*
Boca	*www.bocaresearch.com/*
Modemstore.com	*www.modemstore.com/*
Supra (now Diamond)	*www.supra.com/*
U.S. Robotics (now 3Com)	*www.3com.com/client/pcd/products/prod-modem.html*

modem operating on a standard telephone line almost 10 minutes to download one megabyte of data. On the high end, the download time is less than a second on a high-speed dedicated line.

Simple math illustrates the financial advantages of owning a modem that's capable of high connect speeds. A 56K modem transfers data about two times as fast as a 28,800bps modem and four times as fast as a 14,400bps modem. This means that a file that might take an hour to transfer at 14,400bps would only take 15 minutes at 14,400bps. If you're paying for an online connect charge, you can reduce your costs by roughly 75 percent.

When you query online databases, write e-mail, browse through menus, and so on, you use about the same amount of connect time no matter how fast your modem is. During these operations, the biggest factor that affects the amount of time you spend online is not how fast your modem runs, but rather how fast you type and read. When you're transferring files across telephone lines, you should definitely have a high-speed modem because the transfer speed effectively reduces your online time and in turn your connection costs. A 56K V.90 modem is highly recommended. Some of the better-known modem manufacturers and online modem stores are listed in Table 6–2.

In some instances, you must be able to give your modem instructions by issuing commands, telling it what to do. A good standard to follow for issuing these commands is the Hayes Command Set (also called the AT Command Set). Hayes and Hayes-compatible modems respond to these commands and are therefore the recommended models to buy.

Most modems today include fax (*document facsimile*) communication features that allow you to send and receive fax messages from your word processor or other Windows applications. This is a feature you may be interested in exploring. For more information on modems, consult the following print and online resources.

- MODEM CENTRAL *www.56k.com* is frequently updated and dedicated to 56K modem technology. Subjects include modem makers, manuals, and newsgroups. Covers other topics including ISDN, wireless modems, satellite dishes, and ADSL/xDSLs.
- *The Ultimate Modem Handbook: Your Guide to Selection, Installation, Troubleshooting, and Optimization* by Cass Lewart (ISBN 0-13849-415-0). An electrical engineer's introduction to the theory and practice of modems and data communications. Addresses 56K modems, ISDN, ADSL, and cable modems.
- *The Complete Modem Reference: The Technicians Guide to Installation, Testing,*

Online Resource

Todd Owens has compiled an extensive listing of ISDN vendors on the Internet at *www.primenet.com/~towens/ISDN/isdn.htm.*

---

and Trouble-Free Communications by Gilbert Held (ISBN 0–47115–457–1). For technicians who buy and install modems.

- *The Modem Technical Guide (Micro House Technical Series)* by Douglas Anderson, ed. (ISBN 1–88025–229–5. Information on how modems work. Includes technical details for hardware technicians.

HARDWARE FOR ISDN CONNECTIONS

When you connect to the Internet using ISDN, you use a TA or *Terminal Adapter* (sometimes referred to as ISDN modems). This is a device that attaches to your computer and provides you with a link to an ISDN-capable Internet service provider. The TA transmits computer data as digital information across an ISDN line. Just as with modems, there are internal and external ISDN terminal adapters.

The terminal adapter doesn't connect directly into your telephone jack. In the U.S. it connects to a special device called a *network termination unit*, or NT1. The NT1 can be a separate, external device or you can purchase one piece of hardware that integrates the NT1 into the terminal adapter. Today, many devices have the NT1 built right into their design. For example, the CyberSpace Internet+Plus card, marketed by ISDN*tek *www.isdntek.com/int.htm*, is a PC (ISA-bus) card with an onboard NT1.

When you purchase a terminal adapter for Internet use, make sure that it supports two data channels and that it has the ability to inverse multiplex the two channels. *Inverse multiplex* means the TA combines the two channels for higher throughput. A standard exists for inverse multiplexing called *Multilink PPP (point-to-point)*, but not all manufacturers conform to this standard. Some apply their own proprietary standard.

Online Resources

The Institute of Global Communications (IGC) *www.igc.org/igc/help/modems.htm#ISDN_Top* links you to ISDN primers and technical references. (While this site is not kept up-to-date, it still offers good background information.)

The ISDN NewsGroup FAQ can be found at *www.ocn.com/ocn/isdn/faq1/faq_toc.html.*

Intel offers ISDN tips and tricks on their support site at *support.intel.com/support/isdn/index.htm.*

Ralph Becker's ISDN Tutorial can be accessed at *www.ralphb.net/ISDN/.* Becker covers history, benefits, and links to related references and resources on the Web.

The ISDN Zone at *www.isdnzone.com/* presents a good starting point for both the beginner wishing to learn background information and the techie wanting an in-depth look at ISDN.

Table 6–3: ISDN modem manufacturers.	
Name	URL
3Com	www.3com.com/products/isdn.html
Arca Technologies	www.arcatech.com/
IDS Technologies	www.idstech.com/
ISDN*tek	www.isdntek.com/
NT1 Solutions	www.nt1solutions.com/
Sagem	www.idn
WaveRunner	www.isdnwave.com/

Because various standards do exist, it is important to match your terminal adapter to your Internet service provider's hardware. Before you make a purchase, contact your Internet service provider and ask them whether they have a specific brand of terminal adapter they want you to use.

Terminal adapters are expensive compared to modems and, depending on features, ranging in price from $300 to over $800. The more expensive models come with analog fax/modem capabilities. This allows you to transmit computer data on one channel while using the phone, fax, answering machine, or any other telephony device you want on the other channel. The less expensive terminal adapters are digital-only models.

Some of the well-known combination analog-ISDN modems include Courier I-Modem from U.S. Robotics, Modem TA 200 from Motorola Hybrid, and Impact from 3Comm. Go to *eu.microsoft.com/hcl/default.asp* to review the Microsoft Windows hardware compatibility list. Look under "Modem/ISDN" for single user modems and "Network/ISDN" for ISDN network devices. Table 6–3 lists ISDN modem manufacturers. In addition, consult Todd Owens' "ISDN Vendors on the Net" at *www.primenet.com/ ~towens/ISDN/*.

ADSL HARDWARE

The hardware requirements for establishing an ADSL connection are fairly simple. (See Chapter 5 for an explanation of the ADSL technology.) It can all operate on a single, unconditioned, twisted pair of copper wires—the same wires you use for your phone system. You need an external ADSL modem and a 10BASE-T Ethernet network card or NIC (*Network Interface Card*). The ADSL device connects to your standard RJ-11 telephone jack and to your PC's Ethernet card via the RJ-45 jack. Even if you can install all of the hardware yourself, the phone company may need to come to your site and make a small modification to your telephone line.

To determine whether you are located in a DSL service area, consult the DSL Lookup Service at the DSL Resource Center *www.2wire.com/dsllookup/finddsl.asp?id=102*. For help in configuring your Windows 95/98/NT, Mac, and Linux computers for DSL, see Carnegie Mellon's DSL site at *www.cmu.edu/computing/documentation/mac/ getstartadsl.html*.

To learn more about DSL hardware options, visit Everything DSL at *www. everythingdsl.com/*.

CABLE MODEMS

A *cable modem* is a device that delivers high-speed data transmissions via the cable TV network. Cable connections to the Internet are direct connections. When you turn on your computer, you are on the Net. Cable modems are external boxes that connect to a NIC (Network Interface Card) in your computer. There really is no choice when purchasing a cable modem. Your cable company determines the modem you need to use because your modem has to match your company's server. For example, if @Home is your service provider, your modem is going to be either a Motorola or Bay Networks modem.

Cable networks are designed to support the highest speeds in the downstream direction. Cable modem companies are promising their devices can deliver downstream speeds at rates as high as 35Mbps (35 million bits per second). This is only theoretical, however. Although your cable modem may be able to go that fast, there are some other factors present that will slow your cable modem's effective speed to 10Mbps or less, depending on the cable provider. Compared to 56Kbps modems and ISDN, this is still remarkably fast.

The upstream data transfer rate—the speed at which you can send data from your PC to another—is usually slower than the downstream rate. At present this rate is about 200Kbps to 2Mbps.

The reason it is hard to obtain transfer speeds of 35Mbps is because the data you are transferring travels across some fairly narrow roads between your home or library service provider and the host you are linking to thousand of miles away. Furthermore, there are others traveling that same road the same time you are. Cable networks are shared, which means cable providers can put hundreds of homes on a single node. This shared network architecture can also create security problems with cable modems.

Cable modems work by plugging the incoming coaxial cable into the cable wire port on the modem. The cable modem sends packets of information to the computer through an Ethernet connection. Cable modems cost anywhere from $300 to $600. Ethernet cards like the 3Com 10BASE-T can usually be purchased for less than $100. The Ethernet cable from your computer is attached to the cable modem with an RJ45 built-in plug. The cable company installs a *splitter* so you can run both your computer and TV off the single cable that enters your building.

Certain service providers, for example EarthLink, have some of their customers use

Table 6–4: Cable modem service providers and information resources	
Name	URL
@Home Network	*www.home.com/*
Road Runner Service	*www.rr.com/*
TCI Online	*www.tci.com/*
Motorola CableComm Products	*www.mot.com/MIMS/Multimedia/*
Cable Modem Info Center	*cabledatacomnews.com/cmic.htm*
David Gingold's Cable Modem Resources on the Web	*rpcp.mit.edu/~gingold/cable/*

Online Resources
Digital Nation's *cablemodems.com/* provides links to articles, vendors, and organizations associated with cable modems.   Cable Modem University *www.catv.org/modem/* covers cable modem basics, technical issues, standards, glossary of terms, vendors, and service providers.

standard analog modems or ISDN for their uplink and downloading is done through a cable line.

Cable modem service isn't offered everywhere. In fact, at the time of this writing, only about 20 percent of U.S. households with cable TV have the option of cable modem Internet access. The *Cable Datacom News* maintains an updated list of commercial cable modem launches in North America at *www.cabledatacomnews.com/cmic/cmic7.html*. Major service providers are listed in Table 6–4.

HARDWARE FOR DEDICATED SERVICES

Three pieces of hardware are needed for frame relay and T1 connections: routers, transceivers, and DSU/CSUs. You also should protect your hardware with a surge suppressor and locate it near the telephone jack.

ROUTERS

A *router* is a specialized computer that routes network traffic. Along with the router, you also need a terminal to use as a console for the router. Routers cost between $1,500 and $3,000, depending on features.

A terminal with color display monitor and standard keyboard will cost another $200 to $300. An RS-232C cable connects the terminal to the router. These run around $40. Check with your Internet service provider to see whether they require that you use a specific brand of router.

TRANSCEIVERS

A *transceiver* is a small device that supports the router's connection to your LAN. The transceiver is connected to the AUI port on the back of the router. Transceivers for 10–base-2 (Thinnet Ethernet) cost around $100–$150.

DSU/CSUs

Frame relay and T1 connections require a DSU/CSU (*Data Service/Channel Service Unit*) on the Internet side of the router in place of a terminal adapter. The DSU/CSU connects to the serial port on the router and to the telephone network (typically by means of an RJ-48S modular jack). Make sure that the DSU/CSU you purchase is capable of handling the required data transfer speed (56Kbps, T1, or FT1, etc.).

SURGE SUPPRESSORS

Two other details that apply to all the hardware devices needed for connecting your LAN to the Internet are the power strip and equipment location. You might consider getting a Tripplite line conditioner. This is a heavy-duty surge suppression and power conditioning unit that offers better protection than is typically offered by power strips sold at discount stores. The cost of a Tripplite 600W line conditioner with four outlets is about $100.

Locate the router, terminal, and terminal adapter or DSU/CSU in the same general location, which should be close to the location where the telephone company installs the jack. Keep in mind, too, that the LAN needs to extend to the router, which connects to the LAN through the transceiver.

UNDERSTANDING TERMINALS AND MULTITERMINAL SYSTEMS

Mainframe computers are very large-scale, expensive computers that require full-time staffs to keep them running. Thousands of these systems have been installed at universities and businesses worldwide. Being connected to the Internet will at some point bring you face-to-face (not literally) with one of these machines.

You may, for example, discover that a particular document you want resides on a mainframe located at the University of Alabama. The only way you can get a copy of this document is by connecting to their IBM 3090 mainframe via the Internet, sending the remote computer commands through your keyboard to locate the file you want, and then bringing a copy of the file back to your local machine.

While you are doing this, there will be several others using the same mainframe system. This illustrates a technology called *time sharing*—a system where many people, sometimes several hundred, share the same computer simultaneously. Typically, if you are a university or corporate librarian, your Internet access will be through a multiterminal system like a mainframe or minicomputer. You either will be using a terminal or a personal computer that is connected to your local host via a cable, *hardwired*, as it is often called, or you will have a personal computer that is equipped with a modem and this is how you'll access the local host. *Minicomputers* are multi-user computers that are typically more powerful than a personal computer but not as powerful as a mainframe.

TERMINALS VS. PERSONAL COMPUTERS

Exactly what is the difference between a terminal and a personal computer? Terminals, which look something like personal computers, consist of the following three basic elements:

- The monitor, also called a video display unit (VDU) or cathode-ray tube (CRT), is the screen that displays everything you see
- The keyboard is the device on which you input data
- The serial interface, consisting of the cables and plugs that connect the terminal to the host (Terminals can't do much unless they are connected to a host computer.)

Table 6–5: Thin-client resources	
Name	**URL**
History of the Network Computer by Toby Buckalew (in three parts)	*www.about.com/industry/computers/ library/weekly/aa102999.htm*
NeoStation	*www.neoware.com/*
ThinPlanet	*www.thinplanet.com/*
Understanding Thin-Client/Server Computing by Joel Kanter (ISBN 1–57231–744–2)	The first chapter of this book is pub lished online in hypertext format at *mspress.microsoft.com/prod/books/ sampchap/1518.htm*

The major element that terminals don't have, the one thing that makes them quite different from a personal computer, is the box that holds the central processing unit (CPU) and the disk drives. Because a terminal does not have a CPU—which is often referred to as the "brain" of the computer—terminals are sometimes called "dumb" terminals. In actuality, not all terminals are dumb because some do contain limited processing circuitry.

NCs VS. PCs

NCs—also known as network computers, Internet surfboxes, browser boxes, and thin-clients—are stripped-down versions of conventional PCs. They use fast, inexpensive microprocessors, run streamlined operating systems, and platform-independent applications written in languages like Java.

NCs, or thin-clients, are not replacements for PCs. NCs wouldn't work well for individuals who are installing lots of programs, who need lots of local processing power, or who operate a variety of peripherals; but they do offer an attractive option: NCs can make Internet access more affordable for networked libraries because of the reduced hardware and administration costs associated with NCs. NC prices begin somewhere in the $500 range and go up from there depending on features. In the future, instead of investing in and running monolithic applications like MS Office, libraries could be able to download only the part of the program they need in the form of small applications, called *applets*.

An efficient use of thin-clients is in local area networks (LANs) where the NCs run their applications off a server (in this case, a *fat* server). The network uses multi-user operating systems and protocols such as Citrix's ICA (Intelligent Console Architecture) to help manage all of the network traffic resulting from multiple thin-clients running applications from the server. The client hardware in a thin-client/server architecture doesn't necessarily have to be a *thin-client* per se. It also can be a PC, Mac, Windows-based terminal, or UNIX machine.

NCs could get by with dial-up Internet access using 28.8 Kbps modems or ISDN connections of 64 to 128 Kbps, but broader band-access technologies such as cable modems and ADSL may be the better choice as they become more widely available. This would enable faster downloading of applets that reside on remote network computers.

When the previous edition of this book came out in 1997, there was a prevailing attitude that Java-based networking and thin-clients would become quite popular in multi-user settings like libraries. As it has turned out, the thin-client architecture has received only moderate support. It succeeds in certain applications and in certain organizations. Thin-clients offer a consistent, single architecture that's centrally managed. This helps control the cost of service and support for distributed desktop software. Others are finding that by better managing their PC network they can still control costs while providing support for more multi-purpose, collaborative computing environments; for example, a setting where some PCs are used as image-editing workstations with attached scanners and CD-R drives. Other PCs function as video production workstations supporting firewire technology (the ability to plug-in a digital camera and capture digital video clips), and still others might be used for projects where users store information on removable disks and input sound from cassette tapes to digitize and edit for Web publishing. See Table 6–5 for additional resource information on thin-clients.

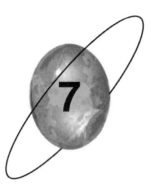

Software for Establishing a Basic Connection

Systems librarians generally are not found on the staffs of smaller libraries. For this reason, Chapter 7 concentrates on software issues that are helpful to smaller libraries or any organization where non-computer specialists are responsible for installing and maintaining analog dial-up systems.

I also introduce Internet protocols in this chapter. *Protocols* are rules computers follow for communicating with each other on the Internet, the most important of which is TCP/IP. I explain how to set up a SLIP/PPP dial-up connection for Macs and PCs and explain where to find the software you need and how to configure it. The technical details of incorporating TCP/IP into LAN environments—a job normally handled by network administrators—are beyond the scope of this chapter.

SOFTWARE AND PROTOCOLS

Software is an essential part of computers. Operating system software like Macintosh OS 9, MS-DOS 6.22, and Windows 2000 enable computers and other hardware accessories and applications to all work together. Software applications like word processors and spreadsheets enable you to write letters and create graphs. General-purpose communications programs like Procomm Plus for Windows *www.symantec.com/procomm/ index.html* enable you to connect to a variety of online services.

Software is also the key ingredient that links libraries to the Internet. There are proprietary programs you can use to access commercial online services such as CompuServe and America Online. In Chapter 8, "Developing Your Software Toolbox," you will read about many special-purpose Internet applications designed for such things as telneting, transferring files, and browsing the World Wide Web.

In addition to applications, several protocols determine how the data you process gets from your computer to another computer on the Internet.

HOW THE INTERNET IS STRUCTURED

The structure of the Internet can be thought of as a stack of flapjacks. Each flapjack in the stack performs a certain function and is governed by a different set of rules. Internet applications such as Gopher and FTP are on top of the stack, in what we'll call the *application layer*. This is where you run your Web searches, browse through Gopher menus, write e-mail, and telnet to distant libraries using popular programs like Eudora, Mosaic, and TurboGopher. The next flapjack down in the stack is the *transport layer* where rules define how your data is divided into packets. The third flapjack down in the stack is the *network layer*. This is the layer where the packets are addressed and made ready for shipment out onto the Internet. The flapjack on the bottom of the stack, the *physical layer*, is responsible for sending these packets out onto the Internet.

One of the most important sets of rules in this stack is called TCP/IP. It is the glue that binds the whole Internet together.

TCP/IP

Whether you are connecting individual computers or LAN workstations or servers to the Internet, they must all be able to communicate using TCP/IP. TCP/IP stands for *Transmission Control Protocol/Internet Protocol*, and it is the underlying principle or common language that ties together all of the thousands of networks forming the Internet.

TCP and IP are the key protocols in a whole family of protocols, thus the entire suite is named after them. The TCP/IP suite of more than one hundred communication protocols specifies the details of how computers communicate with one another, how networks interconnect, and how information is routed from one machine to another. Together they define the operations that take place within the Internet.

IP is the set of rules and regulations that determine how packets of information make their way from a source host to a destination host. TCP allows an application on one computer to connect to an application on another computer, and then to transmit data across this connection as though there were a direct hardwired link. When you transfer a file from a remote machine to your local machine, TCP ensures that pieces of the file won't be duplicated or misplaced. When you send an e-mail message, TCP keeps track of what is sent and retransmits anything that doesn't make it through. If a message is too large, TCP will divide it into smaller pieces and make sure they all arrive correctly. When computer applications need to communicate with other computer applications on the Internet, they use TCP.

CONNECTING YOUR MAC TO THE INTERNET

In order for you to connect your Mac to the Internet, you need two pieces of software: a TCP/IP stack and SLIP or PPP software.

THE TCP/IP STACK

The TCP/IP stack enables the various Internet applications you run on your Mac to communicate with other computers on the Internet. *MacTCP 2.0.x* is built into System 7.5 and the System 7.5 Upgrade. If you have an earlier system, you can get a copy of *MacTCP* by obtaining a copy of Adam Engst's *Internet Starter Kit for Macintosh*, Fourth Edition (Hayden Books, ISBN 1–56830–294–0) that sells for around $40 on *www.amazon.com*.

Open Transport is the newest addition to the Mac library of TCP/IP software. The Apple Talk and TCP/IP control panels replace the Network and MacTCP control panels used in previous versions of the Mac operating system.

SLIP OR PPP SOFTWARE

SLIP and its more advanced counterpart PPP are programs that allow your computer to connect to the Internet over a telephone line. *SLIP* or *PPP* software provides the lowest layer of communication—the flapjack on the bottom of the stack—between your Mac and other computers on the Internet. If you have a choice and your Internet service provider supports it, use PPP. It has fewer limitations than SLIP. MacSLIP, an application discussed in the previous edition of this book, is no longer being developed and is no longer available for purchase from Hyde Park Software. A MacSLIP installation FAQ can still be viewed at *www.zilker.net/~hydepark/faq.html*.

SOFTWARE DOWNLOADS

Software for the Mac can be downloaded from *asu.info.apple.com/*. Click on the "Browse" button and browse the letter M. Scroll down until you find "MacPPP." Version 2.5 was released April 10, 1996. Version 2.5.3 was released on April 24, 1997 and requires Mac OS 7.5.1 or higher. Click on the desired version to download the software. *Open Transport PPP* is compatible with Open Transport and can be downloaded at *asu.info.apple.com/*. Browse under the letter O. Version 1.0 was released on November 11, 1996.

INSTALLING AND CONFIGURING MacTCP

Once MacTCP is installed properly, you can find its icon in the Control Panel folder. Double-clicking on the icon will bring up the initial MacTCP screen.

Because some virus protection programs might think that the new files that MacTCP installs in the System folder are viruses, it may be a good idea to turn off any anti-virus software before you start.

Each box in MacTCP's setup screen requires specific information. Your Internet service provider should provide this information to you. If you don't have this information, give your provider a call, or, as another option, fax a copy of this screen to them and ask them to fill in the numbers. You must fill in the information MacTCP needs before you can make a connection to the Internet.

What follows is an explanation of the four main parts of the MacTCP Dialog Box. Again, verify this information with your Internet service provider:

- Obtain Address. Click on "Server" so MacTCP can get your IP address from the server.
- Routing Address. This field can't be edited if you have set the "Obtain Address" field to "Server."
- IP Address. Your ISP will tell you what "class" network you are. For your own information, if your IP address begins with 1 to 127, it would be Class A; IP addresses beginning with 128–191 are Class B; IP addresses beginning with 192 to 254 are Class C.
- Domain Name Server Information. Domain name servers are computers that convert a domain name into its corresponding IP address. Your ISP will tell what to enter in these fields for domain names and IP addresses for your primary and backup name servers.

MAC OS 8.5 SETUP

Mac OS 8.5 comes installed with all the software you need to connect to the Internet. When setting up a dial-up connection, the first step is to choose the type of modem you have installed.

1. From the Apple menu, choose "Control Panels," and "Modem."
2. At the Modem control panel, click on the pull-down menu next to "Connect via:" and choose "Modem Port." For "Modem:" choose the type of modem you have from the pull-down menu. Close the Modem control panel by clicking on the square in the upper left-hand corner of the window. When asked whether you want to save current configuration, click "Save."
3. Next, configure the Remote Access control panel. Beginning with the Apple menu, choose "Control Panels|Remote Access." In the Remote Access control panel, select "Guest." Enter the phone number you need to dial to connect to your Internet service provider.
4. Click once on the "Options" button. In the "Options" window, click on the "Redialing" tab. For "Redial:" select "Redial main number only" from the pull down menu. Enter **10** for Redial times and **5** seconds for time between redials.
5. Click on the "Connection" tab. In the Connection window you can check "Flash icon in menu bar while connected" if you wish. You can also check "Disconnect if idle for 10 minutes."
6. Click on the "Protocol" tab. Consult with your service provider to determine which of these options you should check. Typically, you would check "Connect automatically when starting TCP/IP applications." Check "Allow error correction and compression in modem." Check "Use TCP header compression." If you check "Connect to command-line host" and "Use terminal window," you must then login by entering a user ID and password at the system prompt.
7. When your configurations are complete, click once on "OK." At the main menu, click on the small square in the upper left-hand corner of the window to exit and save.

8. In the "Save changes to the current configuration?" dialog box, click on "Save."
9. Next, configure the TCP/IP control panel. The information you need for completing this process is obtained from your Internet service provider if you are using a dial-up connection. If you are on a LAN, this information is available from your system administrator.
10. From the Apple menu, select "Control Panels|TCP/IP."
11. From the "Edit" menu, select "User Mode."
12. Select "Advanced" and click "OK."
13. In the "TCP/IP" window, enter these settings:
    - For "Connect via:" choose "PPP" if you are using a dial-up connection.
    - For "Configure:", choose "Using PPP Server."
    - For "Starting domain name:", enter the domain name provided to you by your dial-up service provider or system administrator, for example, ***brook.asumh. edu***.
    - For "Ending domain name:", enter what your provider or system administrator tells you to enter, for example ***asumh.edu***.
    - For "Name server addr:", enter the IP numbers you are given for Name Server addresses.
14. Click on the "Options . . . " button. In the "TCP/IP Options Menu," select "Active" and "Load only when needed." Click once on "OK."
15. Click on the square in the upper left-hand corner of the TCP/IP control panel. Click on "Save."

TESTING YOUR CONNECTION AND TROUBLESHOOTING

When you run an Internet program, such as Internet Explorer or Netscape Navigator, Remote Access automatically dials. You should hear your modem dial to establish a connection. If you hear a busy tone, your software is configured to redial up to ten times. If all goes well, you can see and hear when the connection is made.

When you see the blank terminal screen come up, hit the return key until you see the Username prompt. Enter your username, press ENTER, and then enter your password and press ENTER. At the system prompt, type **CONNECT PPP** and press ENTER. This should initialize your connection. Your service provider may have more complete or slightly different instructions for you to follow.

SETUP FOR OPEN TRANSPORT

These instructions are for Open Transport users, a program that is provided with System 7.5.2 and above.

1. Close all communications programs.
2. Open TCP/IP in the Control Panel folder.
3. In the "Connect Via" pull-down menu, choose "MacPPP or Free PPP."
4. In the "Configure" pull-down menu, choose "Using PPP server."
5. In the "Name server addr" window, enter the IP addresses for your service provider's domain name servers. Your Internet service provider provides these addresses to you.

6. In the "Search domains" window, enter the domain name of your Internet service provider.
7. Leave all other boxes empty.
8. Close the TCP/IP window.
9. At the prompt, click "Save."

GETTING INTERNET PROGRAMS FOR MACS

Once you have MacTCP and InterSLIP running, you need only the applications that enable you to navigate the Internet. A good freeware and shareware archive to explore is the Umich Mac Archive. This site can be accessed via the Web at *www.ummich.edu/ ~archive/mac/* or via FTP at *ftp://mac.archive.umich.edu/.* In addition, TUCOWS *www.tucows.com/* maintains an archive of Macintosh software. MIT provides a Web interface to the Info-Mac HyperArchive at *hyperarchive.lcs.mit.edu/HyperArchive.html.*

To search a broad base of FTP servers for a particular Mac program, try using TILE.NET/FTP at *tile.net/ftp/.* Here is a sampling of new and old Internet applications for Macs.

- Internet Explorer can be downloaded from *download.cnet.com/downloads/0– 10201–108–19184.html.*
- Netscape Navigator can be downloaded from *download.cnet.com/downloads/0– 10201–108–23818.html.*
- Eudora Light 1.5.5 is an e-mail program. You can download this version of Eudora Light and find instructions for setting up this program at Doug's World of Macintosh *web2.airmail.net/cdtech/pages/Mail.html.* To get the latest version of Eudora, go to Cnet Download.com at *download.cnet.com/downloads/* and click on "Downloads for Mac."
- News Watcher 2.1.3 is for USENET News readers. You can download News Watcher and find setup instructions at Doug's World of Macintosh *web2.airmail.net/cdtech/ pages/News.html.*
- Fetch is an FTP client. You can use programs like this to explore FTP servers, or you can use your Web browser. To download Fetch 3.0.1 and find instructions for setting up and using Fetch, go to Doug's World of Macintosh *web2.airmail.net/cdtech/pages/ fetch.html.* For the latest version of Fetch (3.0.3), go to CNET DOWNLOAD.COM *download.cnet.com/downloads/.* Follow the path *"Mac\Internet\FTP."* Anarchie is another FTP client. If you're running an older Mac, you can download an early version of Anarchie and find instructions for setting up and using Anarchie at Doug's World of Macintosh *web2.airmail.net/cdtech/pages/anarchie.html.* The latest version (3.7) can also be found at CNET DOWNLOAD.COM.
- TurboGopher 2.0.3, developed by the University of Minnesota, was one of the best Gopher clients for the Mac. Gopher is all but dead, but in case you want to try it out, you can find a copy at Info-Mac HyperArchive, mentioned above.
- Apple iTools is one of the newer Internet applications to come out for Macs. Apple iTools enables you to send e-mail, create Websites, and more. It's free for Mac OS 9 users. Check it out at CNET's site *download.cnet.com/downloads/.* Look for the link to "Mac" software and then "Internet."

CONNECTING YOUR PC TO THE INTERNET

The information presented in this section is meant for Windows 3.1 users. Yes, there are still a few of you around. Microsoft's Windows 95/98 and 2000 contain everything you need to connect to the Internet including a built-in TCP/IP stack, e-mail program, dialer program, telnet program, and Web browser.

To connect your PC to the Internet using Windows 3.1, you need a program called Winsock. *Winsock* is short for Windows Sockets. This software enables your Windows PC programs to work with the SLIP software. A well-known Winsock program that is widely available on the Net is Peter R. Tattam's Trumpet Winsock.

INSTALLING AND CONFIGURING TRUMPET WINSOCK

Trumpet Winsock is shareware. When you download the program, you'll find a registration form to register your copy and pay the appropriate fee. For a single user, the program costs around $25.

If you already have access to an Internet connection, you can go to an FTP site to download a copy of Trumpet Winsock, for example *ftp.trumpet.com.au* in the *Winsock/* directory. If you are using a Web browser, enter *ftp://ftp.trumpet.com.au/Winsock/* in the location box. If you have access to one of the commercial online service providers like America Online or CompuServe, you may find Trumpet Winsock in their file library.

Trumpet Winsock is compressed using PKware's PKZIP. To uncompress the program, you need a copy of PKUNZIP. See Chapter 13 for details. Once you have the program uncompressed and in its own directory, you can then create a Trumpet Winsock Program Group.

When you first double-click on the Trumpet Winsock icon, a setup screen will appear. (If you need to get back to this screen at a later time using the Trumpet menu, select "File, Setup.") Begin the setup process by clicking on either "Internal SLIP" or "Internal PPP," depending on which protocol you will be using.

Your service provider tells you which protocol to choose and helps you with the other information you need in order to complete the set up. Most likely, the provider offers you this information without your asking, but in case you don't have it, here's what you need to ask for:

- Your Internet *IP address*, which is four numbers separated by dots. For example, 123.45.6.78.
- You probably won't have to worry about the *Netmask*, so leave it set at 0.0.0.0.
- The *Name server* address follows the same format as your Internet IP address. There may be more than one—a primary and backup.
- Your service provider's *Domain suffix* (also called a *domain name*) which looks something like this: *service.com*.
- Leave the *Default gateway* set at 0.0.0.0 or whatever your service provider requires.
- Leave the *Time server* field blank.
- Leave the *Packet vector* set at 00.
- Your service provider may give you numbers for MTU (*Maximum Transfer Unit*,

measured in bytes), TCP MSS (*Maximum Segment Size*), and *TCP RWIN* (Receive WINdow). The documentation that comes with the software suggests setting these at *MTU*=576, *MSS*=512, and *TCP RWIN*=2048.
- Leave the *Demand load timeout* and the *TCP RTO MAX* at their default settings.
- Your service provider's phone number is what you dial to make your connection.
- Your *userID* is just a string of characters that you use to login to your account.

INFORMATION YOU NEED TO KNOW

Before you connect your PC to the Internet, you need to find out several things:

- Where your modem is connected. You need to set the SLIP or PPP port to the number of the communication port where your modem is attached (COM1, COM2, etc.).
- The make, model, and speed of your modem. During setup, you will have to set the baud rate at which you would like your modem to run. If you have a 9600bps V.32 modem, set it at 38400. If you have a 14.4Kbps modem or faster, set it at 57600, and so on.
- The password for your account.

When you are done filling in the boxes, click "OK" and setup is done. You will notice that some of the fields can't be accessed. Depending on which version of Trumpet Winsock you have, checking the Internal SLIP box or the Internal PPP box may alter which fields are accessible.

If you connect using SLIP, your service provider may give you a *SLIP command*. This is a command you enter after you connect to your host machine to get your SLIP connection started. For example, you may be required to enter your user ID followed by an @ sign and then the word **slip**.

TEST RUN

Restart Trumpet. Pull down the "Dialler" menu and select "Manual login." Test your modem connection by typing **atz** and pressing ENTER. This should give you an OK reply if your modem connection is working.

Next, dial your service provider's number. Type **atdt** followed by their number. For example, if you want to dial the number 555–5555, type **atdt555–5555** and then press ENTER. If you are using a rotary/pulse phone, replace **atdt** with **atdp**.

If you get a CONNECT message, congratulations. You succeeded. If you get a busy signal, wait a minute and try again. When you connect, enter your user ID (you may have to press the ENTER key once or twice to get the *login:* prompt) and any SLIP command your service provider requires. Type your password and press ENTER. Trumpet responds with the message, "Ready to start your SLIP software." Press the ESC key and Trumpet responds with "SLIP ENABLED."

GETTING INTERNET SOFTWARE FOR PCs

At this point, you minimize the Trumpet window and start your Internet software. If you don't already have Internet applications installed on your PC, one strategy for getting started is to connect to the Internet and download a single application—a Web browser such as Netscape—and use it as your launching pad for going out and getting other Internet applications. If you are using an older PC without much RAM, for example, a 486 with only 4MB of RAM, you may have to opt for using an earlier version of a browser.

Two big sites to go to for all of your software needs are Jumbo!, once hailed as the "biggest, most mind-boggling, most eye-popping, most death-defying conglomeration of freeware and shareware programs on the Web!" at *www.jumbo.com/* and TUCOWS at *www.tucows.com/*. For links to other software archives, check the CD-ROM accompanying this book, which includes links to freeware and shareware sites. You can still find Windows 3.1 software at both of these sites.

CLOSING DOWN YOUR CONNECTION

To close down your connection, first close down any Internet applications you have running and then go to Trumpet Winsock and break your phone connection by selecting first "Dialler" and then "Bye" from the pull-down menu.

ARE THERE EASIER WAYS TO ACCESS THE INTERNET?

Yes, there are easier ways to get started with your first analog dial-up connection. The easiest is to purchase a new computer that is pre-configured to dial up a specific Internet service provider. Dell, for example, sells PCs that are pre-configured like this. The dialer program and TCP/IP settings are all ready to go when it arrives on your doorstep. Don't worry if you live in the boondocks. Dell supports a toll-free 800 number for anyone living outside the large metropolitan areas. The commercial online services, such as AOL, present you with CD-ROMs that walk you through the steps making connecting to the Internet an easy process.

INTERNET SUITES

Internet suites are bundles of Internet software that help you manage your Internet connection. Some take an integrated approach where most of the applications share a common interface. Others consist of separate modules, each with its own interface. Internet suites were popular in the mid to late 1990s. You may still come across some running on older PCs, for example, Cyberjack from Delrina, Internet Anywhere from Open Text, or NetShark from InterCon. But most, if not all, are no longer being developed. Web browsers, combined with the latest operating systems, have replaced the need for Internet suites. Web browsers now support FTP (File Transfer Protocol), Gopher (if you can even find a Gopher server still running anywhere), network news, e-mail, Java-based telnet, and, of course, the Web.

CONNECTING WITH WEBTV

When you connect to the Internet using WebTV, you can use a TV set to browse the Web and watch television. A special device called a set-top box connects to your TV and/or cable service and also to a modem and phone line.

The job of the set-top box is to convert the color technology used by computer monitors (RGB, or *red-green-blue* technology) to the NTSC technology used by televisions (National Television Standards Committee). When you want to access the Web, the set-top box connects to the *WebTV network*, for example, Microsoft WebTV Network *www.webtv.net/*. WebTV uses its own browser designed for displaying on a television set. Remote control units, including keyboards, are used to click on objects and scroll through screens.

HOME NETWORKING

The latest craze is *home networking*, a kind of do-it-yourself system of connecting two or more computers together so they can communicate with each other, share peripherals such as printers, and share a single connection to the Internet. While it may be called "home" networking, the same principles can be applied to small libraries.

WHAT YOU NEED FOR HOME NETWORKING

The basic ingredients found in a home network include:

- Cables (wires) that connect the devices together
- Network interface cards (NICs) that are inserted into the computer, sending and receiving signals that travel along the cables
- Hubs that connect cables between devices and control how they communicate
- Routers that direct traffic between your home PC and the Internet
- Computers, printers, fax machines, and other devices you connect to the network

The Cables

The cables run from the network interface cards to the hub. If your network is connected to the Internet, a cable runs from the hub to a router or modem (for dial-up connections). The cables are arranged in a *star* configuration. This means cables run from each device to a central location, such as a hub. Cable networks support a standard called *Ethernet*, which defines how the network communicates. The type of cable used in creating home networks is called *unshielded twisted pair* (UTP) and you typically use either 10BaseT or 10/100BaseT. The cables connect to the hub and NIC using *RJ45* jacks. RJ45 jacks look something like standard telephone jacks, only a little wider. Various types of UTP cable are available, but the most common and inexpensive for home networks is called *Category 5*, or *Cat 5* for short. When setting up your network, keep in mind that you can't run a single line of UTP cable longer than one hundred meters.

The Cards

Network Interface Cards, or NICs, come in a variety of models. Try to use the same card in every computer. That way you learn one card's method of installation. In addition, don't mix 10BaseT NICs with 100BaseT NICs. As was discussed earlier in Chapter 6, there are different types of slots or *buses* in which you insert cards. NICs are designed to fit in either an ISA or a PCI slot, the latter being the newer of the two.

The Hub

Cables run from your network devices, such as PCs, to the hub. Hubs come in different sizes and bandwidths. An example of a small, inexpensive hub is the Ethernet 5–port "HUBBY" made by D-Link, a pocket-sized 10BaseT hub. You can learn more about this easy-to-install hub on D-Link's Website at *www.dlink.com*. This hub's model number is DE-805TP/C. Larger, more expensive, hubs support 24 ports and are stackable.

Software for Home Networks

The last ingredient that's necessary for setting up a home network is the network operating system software. One type of software requires one computer to be designated as a *server* and it controls the network operations. This type of operating system is based on a *client/server* architecture. The workstations, or *clients*, connect to the server to share files, printers, and other services. Options in this type of operating system include Windows NT Server, Windows 2000 Server, Linux, and Novel NetWare.

The other operating system is built on a *peer-to-peer* network. Each PC in this type of system can share its hard drive, CD-ROM drive, and printer, etc. There isn't a single computer that controls the network. Peer-to-peer operating systems are generally less powerful, but easier to set up. Windows 95/98/2000 have peer-to-peer networking built right into them.

If you want to share a modem on your network, you have to install additional software. One option is *SpartaCom Internet Sharing* available for download from *www.spartacom.com/*. You load the Internet gateway software on the PC that's connected to the Internet. This PC becomes the *gateway* computer. Then you configure the other PCs to access the Internet using the gateway.

If you have one PC connected to the Internet through a high-speed ISDN, ADSL, or cable modem, etc., and you want to share that connection among other PCs on your home network, try using *Webetc* developed by Lovdahl Consulting *www.lovdahl.com/*. Webetc comes in a standard version, available for $205, that includes a firewall to protect your network and is licensed for an unlimited number of client computers. They also offer a Small Office edition licensed for eight clients, and a HOME version licensed for three clients.

Starter Kits

Starter kits are a box filled with everything you need to set up a basic home network. They usually include only the bare necessities, such as two NICs along with cables for connecting two PCs to a small hub. If that's all you want to do and your PCs are in close proximity to each other, a starter kit may be all you need. If you need to run cables through walls, you may be better off by purchasing all your basic ingredients separately. That way you can order your Cat 5 in whatever lengths you need.

D-Link *www.dlink.com/* makes a starter kit called *Home Network In a Box* that sells for around $120. Intel sells *AnyPoint* system for just under $200. *AnyPoint www.intel.com/anypoint/* uses the existing telephone system in your house for sending signals. *Aviator* by WebGear *www.webgear.com/* is capable of using radio waves to communicate and sells for about $200.

WHAT IS HomePNA?

HomePNA, short for *Home Phone line Networking Alliance*, is a set of standards developed for home networking products. The key difference between this standard and the systems described earlier is that HomePNA products use existing phone wiring instead of Ethernet cables. Instead of PCI and ISA cards, the newest generation of HomePNA kits connect to your PC via USB cables. HomePNA 1.0 operated at only 1 Mbps. The latest version 2.0 operates at 10 Mbps and competes with the 10base-T Ethernet. One drawback of HomePNA is that you must have a phone jack in every room where you want to network a PC. Other than that, the HomePNA products offer a good alternative to systems that require NICs and Ethernet cable. A typical kit includes an adapter, USB cable, and phone cable. The adapter, which is a small box, connects to a power outlet and a phone jack. The PCs connect to the adapter via a USB cable.

Some companies to explore that are currently building kits that support this standard include D-Link *www.dlink*.com, Intel *www.intel.com/anypoint*, and eCom *www.3com. com/homeconnect*.

SUMMARY OF SOFTWARE REQUIREMENTS FOR ESTABLISHING A CONNECTION

The following list summarizes the essential pieces of software you need for establishing a connection to the Internet:

- If you connect to the Internet using a dumb terminal, all the software you need is running on the mainframe, minicomputer, or other kind of large system.
- If you connect your PC to a large system via modem, you can use a terminal emulation program to simulate a dumb terminal. The most common terminal emulation is the VT-100.
- If your LAN is directly connected to the Internet, you can have full access to the Internet and run Internet applications on your personal computer. This type of access is common in libraries.
- The software needed for establishing a SLIP/PPP connection using a modem is built right into your Windows 95/98/2000 software.
- Windows 3.1x requires a Winsock TCP/IP stack such as Trumpet Winsock. Mac OS requires a TCP/IP stack such as MacTCP. (Windows 95/98/2000 and Mac OS 9 contain everything you need to establish a dial-up connection to the Internet.)

- When using commercial online services such as AOL, the company providing the service gives you the option of using their proprietary software for interfacing with the Internet. Most companies also let you use your own Internet applications.
- When you use WebTV to connect to the Internet, you need a set-top box that dials into the Internet and then displays Web pages on your TV screen. WebTV uses its own browser designed for displaying on a television set.
- Network Computers, or thin clients, access the Internet applications they need on local or remote servers.
- Helper applications are necessary additions to your Web browser for listening to certain types of audio files, viewing videos, and portable documents, etc. Specific applications are listed in Chapter 8.
- Depending on your service provider and your method of connection to the Internet, there may be other requirements.

Developing Your Software Toolbox

In this chapter, I describe applications that assist you in accessing the myriad Internet resources and services that are available. These applications, called *clients*, make it possible for you to perform special operations, such as transferring files from one computer to another or logging into remote libraries and searching their catalogs.

Keep in mind that if any of the shareware or freeware applications listed in this chapter are no longer available at the download sites I suggest, use Archie or one of the other software search engines on the Web to locate an alternate source for the software. The software search engines available on the All-In-One Search Page are a good place to start. That address is *www.allonesearch.com/*. Other software archives are described in the CD-ROM accompanying this book. Table 8–1, at the end of this chapter, provides a convenient list of all the various Internet applications discussed in this chapter.

INTERNET APPLICATIONS AND THE CLIENT/SERVER MODEL

Most of the services that are used for seeking out information on the Internet are based on the client-server model. The terms *client* and *server* refer both to the computers that function as clients and servers and to the programs that run on these computers. Client/server programs have a special relationship with one another. Client programs send requests to server programs and server programs respond. This is the reason why clients are sometimes referred to as *masters* and server programs as *slaves*. When you are learning how to use the Internet, you are actually learning how to use various client programs.

If you have a direct connection to the Internet, or ISDN or PPP dial-up, you can choose your own client programs that are designed to run on a variety of platforms ranging from Macs and PCs to Sun workstations. There are many client programs to choose from with names like HyperWAIS, WAIStation, XMosaic, Winchat, TurboGopher, Netscape Navigator, Trumptel, and others. When you have the opportunity to run your own client program, you can choose one that provides a friendly, more intuitive interface that prompts you for what information it needs.

NETWORK CLIENTS

As an Internet librarian, you are sometimes given two choices when it comes to performing certain operations: You can either perform them using a Web browser or you can run a separate, stand-alone, client program dedicated to a single function. In this section, I explain which operations offer you this choice and I show you where to find the software. The stand-alone programs that fall into this category include those that help you transfer files (FTP), find files (Archie), view files stored on Gopher servers, login to remote systems (telnet), and send e-mail.

Since the introduction of the World Wide Web, these individual, single-purpose programs are quickly being replaced by Web browsers which are a single, universal window to the Internet. In spite of this, it is still useful at times to think in terms of server-types when seeking out information on the Internet, although this paradigm is quickly becoming less relevant.

For example, it is rare that I use a separate, specialized program to download a file. Most of the time I am relying on my Web browser for this function, but there are times when a Web browser doesn't work and a simple FTP program does. There are times when I don't even have a Web browser on the computer I'm using and I have to use an FTP program to go out and *get* a browser.

Still, the day is coming when the older information looker-uppers that began with UNIX shell accounts (discussed in Chapter 10), or terminals hard-wired to IBM mainframes, will quit thinking "FTP" when they want to download a file; "Archie" when they want to find a file; and "Pine" when they want to send a message. These folks—who we might fondly refer to as "shell fossils"—will eventually be thinking "Web browser" for most everything. Only those librarians who are more technically inclined will find enjoyment and challenge in running the stand-alone applications described in this section. Only the hard-core information searchers who like the speed and complexity of text-only searching will keep their UNIX shell accounts alive.

Because there are many librarians going through the transition, I think it is worthwhile presenting tips and pointers on which stand-alone programs to try and where to find them. Equally, because many librarians at universities around the world still have access to UNIX shell accounts running FTP, Archie, telnet, and e-mail clients, it's still worthwhile explaining these programs in later chapters right along with their Web counterparts.

FTP PROGRAMS

You learn in Chapter 13 that files on the Internet can be transferred from remote computers to your own using a Web browser such as Netscape Navigator or Microsoft's Internet Explorer. You might then ask, "Why do I need a separate application for transferring files?" Specialized FTP programs offer features not found in Web browsers. You may or may not need these features to conduct your daily business. It all depends on the level to which you want to become involved with computers, software, and the Internet.

One feature that FTP programs offer is the ability to store profiles about remote hosts. You can set up a file that stores the host's name, address, login password if needed, and any other comments you think are relevant about a host's features or services. Once a profile is entered, you can simply choose a name from your custom lists of hosts and then click on a button to connect to that host.

Another feature offered by FTP programs is the ability to transfer files from a remote computer's directory to your own computer's hard drive by a process of simply clicking and dragging the file's name. The reverse is also possible. You can upload a file from your computer to a remote site by using the same process. This comes in handy when you add to or revise your home page and need to upload the new changes to your Web server via FTP.

One of the most popular FTP applications for Windows is WS_FTP. You can download a copy from CNET Shareware.com at *www.shareware.com/*, or go directly to the developer's site, Ipswitch at *www.ipswitch.com/*. Look for the link to download evaluations and then look for the latest version of WS_FTP LE. To find the most recent version, search on the keyword **ws_ftp**. The most popular WS_FTP version for Windows is WS_FTP LE, a *light* version that is free to users associated with educational institutions.

When you visit Ipswitch's Website, you find other Internet-related tools. IMail Server is an e-mail server designed to run under Windows NT, WS_PING ProPack contains a host of Internet tools including Ping, Traceroute, Lookup, Finger, Whois, and more. They also offer various terminal emulators including TNExplorer/TN2000 and VT320.

A popular FTP client written for Macs is called FETCH, by Jim Matthews. You can download a copy of Fetch from Dartmouth College at *www.dartmouth.edu/pages/softdev/fetch.html*. Dartmouth College has created other freeware and shareware products for Macs. For example, BlitzMail is a freeware e-mail system that comes with Mac and Windows clients. InterMapper is an AppleTalk and IP network mapping and management tool. MacPing is a network test tool for Macintosh AppleTalk and IP networks.

Search the InfoMac Archive at MIT for other Macintosh FTP clients. InfoMac claims to be the largest Macintosh software archive in the world. You can access this site at *hyperarchive.lcs.mit.edu/HyperArchive.html*.

WAR FTP Daemon is a freeware FTP server application. It enables you to run your own FTP server from any Windows 95/98 PC with a direct connection to the Internet. It's powerful with many security and configuration options. Versions are also available for Windows NT and Windows 2000. You can download the latest version at *home.sol.no/~jarlaase/tftpd.htm*. Find other shareware and freeware FTP servers at Tucows.Com *www.tucows.com*. Search on the keywords **ftp server**. WinFiles.Com at *winfiles.cnet.com/apps/98/servers-ftp.html* is another great source for freeware and shareware FTP server and client programs.

ARCHIE PROGRAMS

Whether you have a dial-up PPP connection, a leased line, or a shell account, the Archie implementations that are available on the Web (introduced in Chapter 15) should serve most of your needs. If you prefer running your own graphical interface, two options are David Woakes' WSArchie for Windows and Stairways Software's Anarchie for Macs. You can download a copy of WSArchie at FTP site *ftp://ftp.demon.co.uk/pub/ibmpc/ win95/wsarchie/wsarch32.zip*. To find other sites archiving WSArchie, use FAST FTP Search v4.0 at *ftpsearch.lycos.com/?form=medium*, or you can try one of the sites listed here:

> *ftp://ftp.demon.net/pub/ibmpc/win3/winsock/apps/wsarchie*
> *ftp://ftp.demon.net/pub/ibmpc/win95/winsock/apps/wsarchie*
> *ftp://ftp.yorku.ca/pub/pc/YSoft/pc/wsarchie.exe*

The most current version of Anarchie is 3.7. You can download a copy of this shareware program from the developer's Website at *www.stairways.com/*. Anarchie requires Macintosh Plus and Mac OS 7 or later. Mac OS 7.5 is recommended.

GOPHER PROGRAMS

As with the other programs described in this section, if you have a direct connection to the Internet that enables you to run your own client software, you can access Gopher sites with either your Web browser or with specialized Gopher clients, such as TurboGopher for Macs or WSGopher for Windows. Gopher services are all but gone on the Internet. If for some reason you want to implement Gopher in your library, for example, on a Windows NT server, Gopher clients may still be of some use.

WSGopher is a freeware Gopher client for Windows written by Dave Brooks, Idaho National Engineering Laboratory. As freeware, WSGopher can be used and distributed freely. The program is copyrighted, however, so it cannot be distributed for profit without permission from Lockheed Idaho Technologies. To run WSGopher, your computer must be directly connected to the Internet through a PPP or similar account, or it must be part of a LAN that has a dedicated Internet connection.

WSGopher offers a lot of features that are unavailable with the UNIX character-based clients. For example, WSGopher offers preconfigured Gopher bookmark menus organized by subject and accessible with the click of a button. (Because Gopher has been becoming less popular over the last four years or so, most of the preconfigured bookmarks no longer work.) The menu choices enable you to print files or save files to disk. They give you the ability to view the start of text files immediately when the download is in progress.

To download a copy, go to ZDNET Downloads at *www.zdnet.com/downloads/*. This is one of the few software sites where you can still get search results on the keyword **gopher**. Here you can find several Gopher clients that were popular in 1996–97, including WSGopher.

The University of Minnesota's TurboGopher 2.0 *TurboGopher* is a Mac application that works well for retrieving files from Gopher and FTP servers. You can still find a copy of this application at The Mac Orchard *www.macorchard.com/*. Two other Gopher clients you find here are MacGopher version 0.5b14 and the novel TruboGopher VR in version 2.1 alpha 4.

TELNET PROGRAMS

Telneting—connecting to a remote computer and running applications on that remote computer—usually requires that you run a separate client program. If you are running your Web browser and happen to click on a site that is accessed via telnet, your Web browser won't seamlessly connect to that site as it does to HTTP (Web) and FTP servers. Instead, your browser steps aside for a moment and lets an entirely separate program start up and take care of the telnet session. By default, this is the telnet program native to your Windows 95/98/2000 PC—a program that lacks many of the features stand-alone programs support. An exception to this is Java Telnet, a Java-based applet that runs within a Web browser. I describe Java Telnet later in this chapter.

A number of telnet programs exist for Windows and Macintosh. One difference between running telnet on a shell account and running it on your own PC is that you don't have to memorize commands. The programmers have built these functions right into their programs using menus and buttons that you can click on with your mouse. Windows telnet programs also let you store profiles on sites you visit regularly and support editing functions such as cutting and pasting.

Ewan for Windows

One of the more popular telnet applications for Windows is called Ewan. Ewan is freeware developed by Peter Zander and it can be downloaded from a number of different FTP sites. For more information on Ewan, visit their Website at *www.lysator.liu.se/ ~zander/ewan.html*. To find out which FTP sites store Ewan, use an Archie server such as *FAST FTP Search v4.0* at Website *ftpsearch.lycos.com/?form=medium*. Enter the keyword **ewan** and click on the "Search" button. Look for the latest version, which is currently 1.052.

There is no Win95 or Win32 version of Ewan per se, but in a FAQ written by Peter Zander, he stated that version 1.052 of Ewan should work in Windows 95 because he used Windows 95 while coding it. This FAQ can be found by clicking on the link labeled "Q&A/FAQ" on the Ewan home page. My own personal experience with running Ewan under Windows 95 has been good.

After downloading a copy of Ewan, UNZIP it, and then run the *Install.exe* file. After installation is complete, double-click on *Ewan.exe* to run the program.

When you first start up Ewan, you are presented with a "Connect to site" window. This window is empty because you are running Ewan for the first time. To enter a new site, click on the "New" button and an "Address" window pops up. Enter the name and Internet address of a telnet site and then click on "OK." Next, try connecting to the telnet site you specified by double-clicking on the name or by highlighting it and then clicking on the "OK" button.

Telnet for Macintosh

The National Center for Supercomputing Applications (NCSA) offers a freeware program for running telnet sessions on Mac computers. You can download a copy of NCSA telnet from *ftp://pc.usl.edu/pub/mac/telnet/*. More sites can be found by using *FAST FTP Search v4.0* at Website *ftpsearch.lycos.com/?form=medium*. Enter the keyword **telnet2.6**.

Version 2.7 might be available by the time you read this, so you might also try keyword searching on **telnet2.7**.

To connect to a site using NSCA telnet, pull down the "File" menu and click on "Open Connection." The Open Connection dialog box appears. Enter the Internet address of the site you'd like to connect to in the "Session Name" box. You can leave the "Window Name" box empty. Next, click on "OK" and NSCA telnet connects to the site you specified.

Telneting to IBM Mainframes

When telneting to IBM mainframes, you need a special telnet application that allows you to connect in 3270 mode (TN3270). Jim Rymerson designed a program called QWS3270 EXTRA that supports these connections. If you install QWS3270 EXTRA on your hard drive and then set a preference in the TN3270 Applications text box in Netscape Navigator, you find it much easier telneting to IBM mainframes.

You can download a copy of QWS3270 EXTRA from any of the following FTP sites:

> *ftp://ftp.ucsc.edu/PC/qws3270/*
> *ftp://ftp.ucsc.edu/PC/.cap/qws3270/*
> *ftp://ftp.cni.org/pub/software/terminal/windows/qws3270/*

Java Telnet

Java Telnet is a freeware program that runs within your browser. This program, developed by Matthias L. Jugel and Marcus Meißner, can be downloaded from Java Telnet's home page at *www.first.gmd.de/persons/leo/java/Telnet/*. Java Telnet offers several advantages. If your library's online catalog is accessed by remote users using telnet, this program offers a more intuitive method of connecting to the catalog. Users don't need a separate telnet program to log into your host computer. All they need is a Web browser. Java Telnet runs with different brands of browsers as long as they are *Java capable*.

You can run a test from Java Telnet's home page to see how it works before downloading. You can't log into the remote host, but you can view the telnet interface and see prompt for login and password. Versions are available for UNIX, Windows NT/95 and MAC.

SETTING UP JAVA TELNET

After you successfully unzip the program, a new folder named "Telnet" should be created. The files use long file naming conventions. If your system doesn't support this, you have to rename files. On the Java Telnet's home page there is a "help" link. Click on this for up-to-date documentation on how to set up the telnet applet.

E-MAIL PROGRAMS

In most situations, the e-mail programs that are packaged with Internet Explorer and Netscape Navigator will serve your needs just fine. If you're looking for something more specialized, you might want to explore Eudora. Eudora by Qualcomm is a graphical e-mail program that works with shell accounts as well as direct and PPP connections. There is a Windows and Mac version available for about $65. A freeware version of Eudora can be downloaded from their Website *www.eudora.com/*. Once there, check out their online tutorials for Windows and Macintosh.

Several sites on the Web provide valuable information relating to Eudora. If you would like to explore Eudora further, check out these sites:

- Eudora's home page at *www.eudora.com*
- Andrew Starr's Unofficial Eudora Site at *www.emailman.com/eudora/*
- Guide to the Eudora Mail Package at NetSpot Communications *www.netspot.unisa. edu.au/eudora/contents.html*
- Adam Engst's *Eudora for Windows and Macintosh: Visual QuickStart Guide* has a companion Website at *www.tidbits.com/eudora/*.
- Support is also offered by two newsgroups: *comp.mail.eudora.mac* and *comp.mail.eudora.ms-windows*.

Pegasus Mail is another good freeware e-mail program. Pegasus Mail is available for both Windows and Macs and can be downloaded for free from *www.pegasus.usa.com/*.

SEARCH AND RETRIEVAL VIA E-MAIL

Running search and retrieval operations via e-mail using FTP and Archie is accomplished by connecting your computer to computers that function as mail servers—machines that respond to requests they receive via e-mail. Some of the methods used in performing these searches may seem cumbersome when compared to telnet, Web, and FTP processes, but the system works acceptably well if you don't need your answers in a hurry. It can take a few minutes for the server to respond.

One convenience electronic mail offers is that you can send multiple searches in the same e-mail message and then continue with other work while you wait for the results to be sent to your mailbox. Also, those organizations with limited budgets may find that service providers offering e-mail-only connections provide a unique opportunity to connect to the Internet at a very minimal cost.

Even with mail-only access to the Internet, libraries can expand their information resources considerably. CancerNet, a database containing up-to-date information on cancer, is a very valuable resource and its file contents can be searched and downloaded via electronic mail. If you're interested in this service, FTP to one of the following sites and download the text file that explains how to obtain cancer information from the National Cancer Institute through e-mail:

- FTP to site *ftp.sdsmt.edu* and download the file called *CancerNet* in the */pub/resources/MEDICINE/* directory.

If you use a Web browser,
- FTP to site *ftp.oit.unc.edu* and download the file called *cancernet* in the */pub/academic/medicine/alternative-healthcare/general/* directory.

WEB BROWSERS

Browsers are Internet applications that enable you to search documents that are all linked together on the World Wide Web. Browsers like NCSA Mosaic, Netscape Navigator, and Microsoft's Internet Explorer are capable of presenting a variety of formats on one screen or "page" of information including sound, video, and interactive graphics.

CHOOSING A BROWSER

The two hottest graphical browsers battling for the top spot are Microsoft Internet Explorer and Netscape Navigator. Both are fast, have integrated audio and video, and can be downloaded free of charge.

WHERE TO DOWNLOAD NAVIGATOR

Currently, Communicator 4.7 is the latest release of the Internet suite from Netscape. It is available for download from Netscape Communications Corp. at *home.netscape.com/*. Navigator 4.7 is distributed for Windows 95/98/NT and Mac PowerPC (OS 7.6.1 or later). Newer versions continue to be developed.

Version 4.72 offers 128–bit strong encryption and is now available worldwide. This latest version includes Navigator (the Web browser), Messenger, Composer, AOL Instant Messenger 3.0, Netscape Radio, RealPlayer G2, Winamp, PalmPilot Synch tools, and multimedia plugins. Winamp and PalmPilot Synch tools are available with Windows versions only. You can download Netscape Navigator 4.08 if all you want is the stand-alone browser.

As new releases become available, you can find them on Netscape's home page. If you want to track down an earlier version, use Archie (see Chapter 15). Several FTP sites archive versions of Netscape Navigator, going back to version 1.0. CNET Download.Com *download.cnet.com/downloads/* offers versions of Netscape going back to version 3.01 for Windows 3.x. Once you arrive at the download site, follow this path: *PC\Internet\Browsers*.

WHERE TO DOWNLOAD INTERNET EXPLORER

The latest version of Internet Explorer (now in version 5.01) can be downloaded free of charge from Microsoft's home page at *www.microsoft.com*. Look for the "Downloads" link on their main page. The last time I visited this site, in early 2000, I also saw these products available for download:

Internet Explorer 2.0 for Windows
Internet Explorer 3.0
Internet Explorer 4.0 for UNIX
Internet Explorer 4.0 for Win 3.1, NT 3.51 and WFW
Internet Explorer 4.0 for Windows 95 & NT 4.0
Internet Explorer 4.5 for the Macintosh
Internet Explorer 5
Internet Explorer 5.01

> **Online Resource**
>
> For a list of answers to questions that have been posted in Netscape discussion groups, see The Netscape Unofficial FAQ page at *ww.ufaq.org/*. FAQs are organized under these headings:
> FAQs for all versions
> FAQs for Navigator 3.0x and below ONLY
> FAQs for Communicator 4.x and Navigator 4.0x ONLY
> FAQs for Macintosh 68K and PPC
> FAQs for UNIX — All Platforms
>
> Fixes, Patches, New and Old DLLs, etc.

OPERA

There are other browsers on the market besides these two top contenders. Opera is an excellent alternative for libraries that don't have the latest hardware to effectively run Netscape Navigator or Internet Explorer. Opera is small in size and quick to install. Without installing the Java options, it only uses up about 2MB of hard drive space. It can run on older 486 PCs with only 8MB of RAM. Opera sells for around $35 a copy with volume discounts. You can download a free trial version at *www.opera.com*.

WHERE TO DOWNLOAD OTHER BROWSERS

Most librarians are happy with the features offered by Microsoft Internet Explorer and Netscape Communicator. If you want to explore what else is available in the browser market, visit CNET Download.Com at *download.cnet.com/downloads/*. Look for a link to "browsers." Besides being a good source for alternative browsers such as Opera, NetCaptor, NeoPlanet, and NetPositive, CNET offers links to the latest versions of Netscape Communicator and Microsoft Internet Explorer.

NCSA Mosaic is also available free of charge for non-commercial use at *www.ncsa.uiuc.edu/SDG/Software/Mosaic*. Mosaic is a World Wide Web client that was developed at the National Center for Supercomputing Applications (NCSA) on the campus of the University of Illinois in Urbana-Champaign. In 1997, after almost four years of development, the Software Development Group at NCSA announced it had completed its work on Mosaic and would not be developing it any further.

> **Online Resource**
>
> Here is a fast, easy way to conduct a search when you are using Microsoft Internet Explorer version 4.0 or later. Go to the "Address" field at the top of the browser window and type in the word **find** followed by a space and the keywords for which you want to search. When you press ENTER, Internet Explorer performs the search and presents you with a condensed list of hits.

For links to other Web-related software, visit one of the software supersites, such as Jumbo! at *www.jumbo.com* or TuCows at *www.tucows.com*. At Jumbo!, begin your browsing by clicking on the link labeled "Internet." This leads you to browser plugins, e-mail clients, FTP applications, Newsreaders, telnet applications, and more. At TuCows, begin by choosing your platform, for example, Windows 95/98, Windows NT, Windows 3.x, or Macintosh, etc. Next, choose the server site closest to you. This brings you to broad Internet-related categories including "Audio," "Browsers and Accessories," "Communications," "Connectivity," "E-mail Tools," "Internet Tools," and more.

WEB SERVERS

Internet servers can run on server-class machines, or personal PCs, such as a Windows 95 PC. There are security risks and performance factors to consider when running personal Web servers connected to the Internet, but sometimes the advantages outweigh the risks. I have had good luck using OmniHTTPd for Windows 95 as a Web server for the last four years. It has proven to be an expedient method of publishing Websites on a temporary basis when I didn't have access to a UNIX or Windows NT server. The same could be said for using free Web hosting services, but the latter doesn't provide the same level of flexibility and control as building a site on your own PC.

Omnicron Technologies Corporation also makes a professional version of OmniHTTPd available. The last freeware version of OmniHTTPd was OmniHTTPd for Windows 95 and you can download a copy from *www.omnicron.ab.ca/httpd/download.html*. There are many other freeware/shareware personal Web servers to choose from, including Microsoft Corporation's Personal Web Server. You can read about this server and various others at ServerWatch *serverwatch.internet.com/*. Look for the link labeled "Web Servers or Personal Web Servers."

BASICS OF MOVING BETWEEN WEB PAGES

Netscape Communicator operates like most Web browsers. When you begin running the program, the current, or *default*, home page appears. To bring up a different Web page, you can type a new address in the bar at the top of the screen. Click on the bar to highlight the current URL. Then type in the new URL you wish to access and press the ENTER key. Clicking on the "Open" button in the toolbar also brings up a text box in which you can enter URLs. By clicking on the word "Go" in the menu, you can view a list of pages you've visited so far. The "Bookmarks" menu item displays pages you've added to your bookmark list.

If you are on a Web page, you can access other resources by simply clicking on a hyperlinked word or image. The shape of the mouse pointer changes from an arrow to a hand when you drag it over a hyperlink. Generally, blue words on the screen are hyperlinked and purple words indicate that the link has recently been accessed on your computer. These are the default colors.

While information is transferring between your browser and the Web server with which you are communicating, comets and stars are flying past the big white "N" in the upper-right corner of your screen. When the data transmissions stop, the flying comets disappear. You can stop a transfer in progress by clicking on the "Stop" button.

To go back to a site you visited previously, click on the "Back" left arrow in the navigation bar near the upper left-hand corner of the screen. To move forward, click the "Forward" right arrow button just to the right of the left arrow button.

The "Reload" button *reloads* the page you are currently viewing. Hit "Reload" when the current page only partially loads. "Home" takes you back to the page you have set as your default home page.

To learn more about the Netscape Navigator interface, consult their extensive online help system. You can access this information by clicking on the "Help|Help Contents" menu. The contents include using e-mail, creating Web pages, newsgroups, security, and more. The "Help|Reference Library" menu offers documentation on how to use most of the features offered by Netscape Communicator.

NAVIGATOR'S SETUP

For the most part, Netscape Navigator works right out of the box, provided you have your network or PPP dial-up connection working properly. There are a few extra things you have to do, however, to get the mail and news to work for you. In addition, if you want to connect to a telnet site while running Netscape, you need to install and configure a telnet application or rely on the default telnet application that comes with Windows 95/98/NT. In this section, I explain how to configure Netscape Navigator for mail, news, and telnet. If you decide to download and use Internet Explorer, you'll find that these setup operations are handled by *wizards*—friendly applications that explain everything you need to know, helping you with each step along the way.

SENDING E-MAIL

Netscape offers an easy-to-use interface to send and receive e-mail, including the ability to attach HTML documents, and more, to your messages. The application is called Netscape Messenger. Before you can use Netscape Messenger, you must designate the address of your mail servers. This is done differently depending on which version of Communicator you are running. In version 4.5, it's done in the "Edit|Preferences|Mail & Newsgroups" menu item. Open the "Mail Servers" panel. Contact your service provider to find out what your SMTP (*Simple Mail Transfer Protocol*) and POP3 mail server addresses are. You enter this information in the "Outgoing Mail (SMTP) Server" and "Incoming Mail (POP) Servers" text boxes.

Lastly, click on the "Identity" panel to enter the information that is used to identify you in your e-mail messages and news postings. Enter your name, e-mail address, reply-to address, and organization name.

NAVIGATOR'S NEWSREADER

Before you can access Usenet news with Netscape, you have to designate the name of your news (NNTP) server in the "Edit|Preferences|Mail & Newsgroups" menu item. Open the "Newsgroup Servers" panel. Contact your Internet service provider to find out what your NNTP (Network News Transfer Protocol) server address is and "Add" it in the "Newsgroup Servers" text box. Once this is done, you should be able to access Usenet news with Netscape, provided your service provider makes this service available.

Table 8–1: Internet applications to include in your toolbox

Process	Application Name	Where to Get It
Archie	WSArchie (Windows)	*ftp://ftp.demon.co.uk/pub/ibmpc/win95/wsarchie/wsarch32.zip*
Archie	Anarchie (Mac)	*www.stairways.com/*
Archiver	StuffIt Lite (Mac)	*www.aladdinsys.com/*
Archiver	StuffIt Deluxe (Mac)	*www.aladdinsys.com/*
Archiver	WinZip (Windows)	*www.winzip.com/*
Archiver	PKZIP (Windows)	*www.pkware.com*
Connection Software	Open Transport (Mac)	*devworld.apple.com/dev/opentransport/*
Connection Software	MacTCP (Mac)	*www.apple.com*
Connection Software	FreePPP (Mac)	*www.rockstar.com*
E-mail	Eudora (Mac and Windows)	*www.eudora.com/*
E-mail	Pegasus Mail (Mac and Windows)	*www.pegasus.usa.com/*
FTP	WS_FTP (Windows)	*www.ipswitch.com/*
FTP Server	WAR FTP Daemon (Windows)	*home.sol.no/~jarlaase/tftpd.htm*
FTP	Fetch (Mac)	*www.dartmouth.edu/pages/softdev/fetch.html*
Gopher	WS_Gopher (Windows)	*www.zdnet.com/downloads/*
Gopher	TurboGopher (Mac)	*www.macorchard.com/*
Telnet	Ewan for Windows (Windows)	*www.lysator.liu.se/~zander/ewan.html*
Telnet	Java Telnet (Mac and Windows)	*www.first.gmd.de/persons/leo/java/Telnet/*
Telnet	TN3270 (Windows)	*ftp://ftp.ucsc.edu/PC/qws3270/*
Telnet	NCSA telnet (Mac)	*ftp://ftp.ncsa.uiuc.edu/Telnet/Mac/*
Terminal	ProTERM (Mac)	*www.intrec.com/*
Terminal	Zterm	Shareware available from many sites including *shareware.cnet.com*
Terminal	Windows 3.1 Terminal	Native to Windows 3.1
Terminal	Windows 95/98 HyperTerminal	Native to Windows 95/98
Web Browser	Internet Explorer (Mac and Windows)	*www.microsoft.com*
Web Browser	Netscape Communicator (Mac and Windows)	*home.netscape.com/*
Web Server	OmniHTTPd (Windows)	*www.omnicron.ab.ca/httpd/download.html*

General Security and Virus Protection

Why should any of us be concerned about computer security in libraries? We're already faced with so many other pressing issues. As I think about the answer to this question, I am reminded of a book I read a few of years ago called the *Cuckoo's Egg* by Clifford Stoll. In this book, an unauthorized user gains access to one of the computers at Lawrence Berkeley Laboratory. Stoll is alerted to this when he stumbles across a 75–cent accounting error that leads him on an international chase. The FBI, CIA, and German Bundepost eventually join him in tracking down a hacker/spy named Markus Hess.

It's not likely that you are going to experience this kind of intrigue—an international spy breaking into your card catalog to see whether a Zane Grey novel is checked out or available. But there are other security issues you are going to be faced with—sometimes daily—such as

1. Virus attacks
2. Individuals guessing passwords
3. Individuals deleting files and corrupting records, either accidentally or on purpose
4. Individuals accessing programs they shouldn't
5. Stealing equipment
6. Generally messing around with program settings and desktops

Networks, and network operating systems such as Novel Netware and Windows NT, have built-in security features and, if they are properly configured, they make it pretty tough to break in. If a PC is left unprotected, however, there isn't one thing the network can to do to protect that PC. PCs that are left wide open to attack can be used as platforms to launch attacks on the network, not to mention the files and data stored on the PC itself. This chapter focuses on PC security—building strong networks from the PC up.

There are seven key concepts I address in this chapter. The first three are administrative issues and are fundamental to building a secure system:

1. Risk analysis,
2. disaster recovery, and
3. writing security policies.

Then I move on to the nuts and bolts of securing your libraries and introduce you to these concepts:

1. Front-end security
2. Back-end security
3. Protecting your library from virus attacks

I finish up with Internet-related security issues. Several security links are included on the CD-ROM accompanying this book.

RISK ANALYSIS

It is widely known that the proper level of security is determined by what it is you want to protect. For example, the server that stores your bibliographic records for your library automation system deserves your highest level of security, but an inexpensive PC that only supports word processing deserves little or no security. Risk analysis is the process of looking at every component in your system and determining whether there is anything worthwhile protecting, and, if so, determining whether it is exposed to any security threats.

I like keeping things simple if possible, and I think you can perform good risk analysis in three simple steps:

1. Take a look at your system and determine which components are at risk. Consider not only your hardware components, but also consider which applications and data would need to be replaced if disaster struck. To assist you in this step, you should begin by taking an inventory of your system. You can make a schematic drawing of your system by hand, or, if your system is large, you may want to consider using an inventory management system such as McAfee's Zero Administration Client Suite.
2. Examine how threats might manifest themselves. In other words, think about what could go wrong; for example, what would you do if the hard drive on your file server crashed this afternoon? Besides hard drive failure, threats come from a number of other sources including:
   i. Blackouts
   ii. Natural disasters
   iii. Software failures
   iv. Hackers
   v. Viruses
   vi. Human errors that result in lost or corrupted data

3. Assign cost-effective safeguards. Include safeguards that
    i.   Protect—such as protect hardware and software
    ii. Detect—such as detect viruses and attempted break-ins
    iii. Prevent—such as prevent virus attacks and attacks from hackers
    iv. Deter—such as deterring hardware theft
    v.   Recover—such as recover from virus attacks or lost data

DISASTER RECOVERY

Assigning safeguards ties in closely with the next subject: disaster recovery. It's your responsibility as librarians to maintain the accuracy and integrity of the information you provide. It's also important that you provide a safe and secure environment in which to work. If something goes wrong that jeopardizes either of these responsibilities, you need a contingency plan to fall back on. Your back-up plan should 1) help you respond to the crisis and 2) help you recover from the disaster. This whole process is called disaster recovery.

The three most important safeguards you can institute that help you recover from the majority of disasters are:

1. backing up data,
2. installing backup power supplies and surge suppressors, and
3. making emergency startup disks.

Let's briefly look at each one of these safeguards.

1. Back up data. It's important to back up critical data in case your hard drive crashes, or a tape fails, or you lose data because of a virus attack. Backing up may be as simple as taking important text files you're working on and copying them to a floppy disk and carrying the disk home with you at night, or it may be as involved as running automated tape backups of your circulation records and bib records and storing the tapes offsite.
2. Install emergency power supply systems and surge suppressors. There are some operations that don't like to be interrupted because of a blackout. For example, when you're re-indexing your library automation system, you could seriously corrupt data or lose data if your system were to crash because of a blackout. A backup battery called an *Uninterruptible Power Supply*, or UPS for short, is designed to help insure against this kind of loss.

    The most important point to consider when purchasing a UPS is something called the VA rating. The more components you want to connect to a power backup, the greater the VA rating will be and the more expensive the UPS will be. You determine the VA rating by multiplying the component's volts times its amps. For example, if you have a PC you want to back up and its plate on the back of the case says that it's rated as 115 volts and 3 amps, you multiply 115×3 and come up with a rating of 345 VA. If your hardware is measured in watts, multiply the watts $\times 1.4$ to arrive at the VA rating.

    Surge suppressors look something like power strips, but they do much more, such as condition the lines and protect against surges in electricity. When you purchase a surge suppressor, there are two important points to consider: 1) volt let-through and 2) joules rating. Underwriters Laboratory (UL) rates surge suppressors according to how much voltage they let through. UL has established 330–volt let-through as their benchmark. Joule ratings measure how well a surge suppressor absorbs surges. A joule rating of 200–600 is considered acceptable. Ratings over 500 are considered exceptional.

3. Making emergency startup disks. An emergency startup disk is a floppy disk that contains important system files that enable you to boot up your system and bypass booting up from your hard drive. Startup disks are necessary if you have to boot up your system from a clean system disk because your hard drive is infected with a virus.

Making an emergency startup disk for Windows 3.1/DOS systems is easy. Simply insert a disk into your floppy disk drive and type the command **format a:/s** at the DOS prompt. This is assuming your floppy disk drive is designated the "a:\" drive. Creating an emergency startup disk in Windows 95/98/2000 is quite simple, too. Simply click on the "Start" button and choose "Help." Then search on the keyword **startup**.

WRITING SECURITY POLICIES

After you have reduced your risks to an acceptable level, you adapt security policies to help maintain security but at the same time put your PCs to good use. Security policies define those aspects of your system that you want to protect and outlines a general approach for dealing with security problems. A basic policy might include these four sections:

1. Purpose, which is a brief statement explaining the purpose of the document
2. Scope, which explains who and what are covered by the policy
3. General policy statements, which state the rules
4. Standards, which are specific activities that support your general policy statements

Let's look for a moment at the heart of the policy—the general policy statements. Your general policy statements should be practical in nature and address questions like these:

1. Who is in charge of security?
2. Who is permitted to use the facilities?
3. What can computers be used for? For example, instructional and research purposes only and no personal use?
4. What do you want to protect?
5. What are the consequences of misusing the system?

Security polices should not detail how to protect your system. That's the job of procedures. For example, your policy may state that personnel records are confidential. Standards, which are "shall" and "will" statements, might state, "When saving personnel records to disk, they shall be encrypted." The procedures would then explain step-by-step how to encrypt text files. Procedures are generally not part of the policy.

If you have a systems librarian, you can place that person in charge of implementing your policy. If you don't have a systems librarian, break down the standards in your policy into smaller parts and assign tasks in job descriptions. For example, in a reference librarian's job description you might state that she or he is responsible for installing the antivirus software and keeping it up-to-date. The circulation clerk's job description may state that she or he is responsible for setting up new hardware and software hanging files when the need arises, and the cataloger may be made responsible for system backup, etc.

PASSWORD PROTECTION

In certain instances, you should use storage space on a host computer as a temporary holding place for files before downloading them to your personal computer. You may decide that protecting these files isn't that important, and it is not likely that you will be sending sensitive information that requires encryption through e-mail. What remains an issue, however, is your responsibility to help protect the system as a whole.

In this respect, there is a security mechanism that is of concern to you and that is your password. Passwords are an important first line of defense against intruders and it is in everyone's best interest to give this principal mode of protection some serious thought. You don't want to be the weak link in a chain because of a poorly chosen password. If an intruder can break into your host's system using your password, he or she may then be able to find other security holes in that system or use it as a means of entry into other systems on the Internet.

RULES FOR CHOOSING PASSWORDS

When you establish an Internet account, or a user account on any network, you should follow some basic rules when choosing a password. You make it easy for a cracker to decipher your password if you choose one that is easy to remember, such as your first name, your spouse's first name, or a pet's name. To help make your account more secure, consider the following principles when creating and using your password:

1. Don't use your name or a modification of your name for your password.
2. Don't use a word or modification of a word that occurs in any dictionary.
3. Don't use an acronym.
4. Once you've created an account password, don't share it with anyone.
5. Change your password often, at least every six months.
6. Don't leave your terminal unattended when you're logged in.
7. Don't write your user ID and password on a piece of paper or send it to friends via e-mail.

PASSWORD MANAGEMENT UTILITIES

IOPUS Software at *www.iopus.com/* offers some interesting freeware for managing passwords. A program called 007 WASP (Write All Stored Passwords) displays all of the passwords *(*.pwl* files) for the user currently logged in. A freeware program called 007 Password Recovery helps you manage your passwords on Windows 95/98/NT computers. If you forget a password, you can click and drag your mouse cursor over the row of asterisks (******) located in the password field in the program to reveal what the password is. Another freeware program that performs this same feat is called BeehindTheAsterisks. You can download it at *www.direct.spb.ru/bta/html.*

Password generators are programs that automatically generate alphanumeric user IDs and passwords. Segobit publishes a program called Passwords by Mask that creates random or specified alphabetic, random or specified numeric, and random or specified alphanumeric passwords. It runs on Windows 95/98/NT and can be downloaded from *segobit.virtualave.net/pbm.htm.* Segobit offers a more advanced password generator that can mix lower- and upper-case. This shareware program can be downloaded from *segobit.virtualave.net/apg.htm.*

INSTALLING FRONT-END SECURITY

Front-end security systems are right out there where everyone can see them. They are your first line of defense. Why do we need front-end security? Microsoft has made its operating systems so user-friendly, it's a challenge to maintain security. It's even difficult to keep desktop settings looking the same day-to-day, sometimes hour-to-hour.

The best front-end security for libraries is secure menu systems for a couple of reasons: They offer a basic level of security and they present a friendly interface for patrons, explaining what resources and services are available on a given PC.

Two of the better-known menu systems are CARL Corporation's Everybody's Menu and Bardon Data System's WinU.

Both offer basic security features, including disabling the CTRL+ALT+DEL key in Windows 95 and the breakout keys F8 and F5 at bootup. In addition, both offer data logging so you know which programs are being used and for how long.

Everybody's menu has a more polished interface and it allows you to create custom menu bars and icons. It's also a great program if you're running both Windows/DOS computers and Windows 95/98/2000 computers.

WinU is another top-rated menu program that runs on Windows 95 systems only. It's not quite as professional looking, but it does allow you to insert your own bitmap image in the top half of the screen for customization, or you can fill the whole screen with an image, say of your library, and then lay the buttons on top of the image. Another feature: CRTL+ALT+DEL can be password-protected, which is nice if you want to use it from time-to-time to close a program that hangs on you. Also, you can disable the right-click context menus and WinU offers a feature called "window control" that enables you to close any window when it appears, such as the Save/Open dialogs.

Learn more about Carl's Everybody's Menu Builder at *www.carl.org/pubaccess/ mb1.html.* WinU is a product of Bardon Data Systems and can be downloaded from *www.bardon.com/.*

BACK-END SECURITY

Back-end security refers to programs that run behind the scenes providing a second line of defense. PC Security, developed by Tropical Software *www.tropsoft.com/main.htm*, is a popular shareware file locking application that offers five different modes of security. One mode enables you to lock access to particular files, such as text files. Another mode enables you to lock access to programs, such as sysedit.exe and notepad.exe.

A mode called Explorer Control offers several levels of protection ranging from locking files and restricting access to control panels, to removing the "Run" command from the Windows 95 Start menu and disabling the DOS prompt.

I typically use a program like this to protect PCs from crackers that break through secure menu systems—a trick that isn't too hard to perform. Among the many features that are available, I usually use only these: disable access to DOS; disable access to the Registry; and disable the F5 and F8 breakout keys.

Menu systems usually offer the opportunity to disable the breakout keys, but it is difficult to simply toggle this feature on and off. It might be more practical to leave this feature enabled when installing secure menu systems and instead use access control software to disable the breakout keys. Then, if you want to break into the bootup sequence, it's an easy process to enable the breakout keys.

I also use back-end software to lock files hackers tend to use or alter. Some of the first files hackers go after are command.com in the Windows directory and sysedit.exe in the system subdirectory. Other files hackers go after, if you are running Netscape Communicator, include netscape.ini, located in the Windows directory, and bookmark.htm, which contains all of your Netscape program settings, such as your default homepage and bookmarks.

To illustrate how easy it is to break out of a secure menu system, and why it's important to restrict access to DOS, allow me to show you a typical security hole in Windows 95. If you have Microsoft Word available on your menu system, for example, a hacker can probably get around your menu system and access DOS a couple of different ways. The easiest way is to click on "Help" and then choose "About . . . " Next, click on the button "System Info." When the next window opens, click on "FILE|RUN." Now you can access DOS by typing **c:\command.com** in the text box that comes up. A back-end security product can protect you from this.

Besides PC Security, here are other well-known access control systems:

1. Centurion Guard from Centurion Technologies—*www.centuriontech.com/*
2. CyberSoft—*www.cyber.com/*
3. FoolProof from SmartStuff Software—*www.smartstuff.com/*
4. Fortres 101 from Fortres Grand Corporation—*www.fortres.com/*
5. Full Armor products from Micah Development Corporation—*www.fullarmor.com/*
6. Full Control from Bardon Data Systems—*www.bardon.com/*
7. GateWAY from Adafinn Software, Inc.—*www.acay.com.au/~nickw/*
8. Norman Access Control from Norman Data Defense Systems, Inc.—*www.Norman.com/*
9. Safetynet's StopLight PC—*www.safe.net*
10. PC Security from Tropical Software—*www.tropsoft.com*
11. WinLock from Boxware Inc.—*www.boxwareinc.com*

12. WINSelect KIOSK from Hyper Technologies, Inc.—*www.hypertec.com/*
13. Winshield from Citadel Technology—*www.citadel.com/default.asp*

Centurion Technologies offers a unique hardware solution called Centurion Guard. Centurion Guard works like this: You set up your PC just the way you want it with the icons in place and which programs you want available. Define a default home page in Netscape, set up bookmarks, etc., and then lock Centurion Guard. This electronically write-protects the hard drive. Now someone cannot come along and make changes to the system, including:

1. Download a virus to the hard drive
2. Delete icons on desktop
3. Delete files
4. Add screen savers and change the default home page in your browser
5. Reformat the hard drive

To restore the PC back to its original state, simply reboot and the PC restores its original settings. Keep in mind that Centurion Guard is a back-end security tool. If you want to provide patrons with a user-friendly interface that doesn't change hour-to-hour as it does when patrons move and delete icons in Program Manager or the Windows 95 desktop, you will still need to run a menu system. Centurion Guard doesn't lock these things in place. It merely makes it possible to put things back in their original state by rebooting the computer.

PROTECTING AGAINST VIRUSES

Viruses are small computer programs that attach themselves to applications and system files and can reside in your computer's memory or on its hard drive. In the case of macro viruses, data files can also be infected, most notably Microsoft Word documents. Some viruses remain dormant for an undisclosed period of time while others become immediately active. Some deliver destructive payloads, while others are fairly harmless— just placing an aggravating message on your screen or making an annoying ticking sound. In all cases, viruses have one thing in common: they replicate themselves. Their main purpose in life—their main means of survival—is copying themselves from one disk to another, one machine to another.

There are several things you can do to help avoid getting a virus, but the best single thing you can do is install antivirus software. Look for products that offer these features:

1. Periodic updates
2. Signature-based scanning (detects most known viruses before they activate)
3. Heuristics-based scanning (checks for virus-like code)
4. Memory-resident monitoring (detects viruses residing in memory)
5. Integrity checking (periodically checks the status of files to see if changes have taken place)
6. Scanning for hostile Java applets and ActiveX controls

Online Resource

Viruses *in the wild* are viruses that are out spreading in the real world and not just in a researcher's lab. While there are thousands of known viruses, only a few hundred are considered to be in the wild. The Wildlist Organization *www.wildlist.org*, headed up by Joe Wells, updates the official Wildlist *www.wildlist.org/WildList/* about every month. To get on the Wildlist, a virus has to be verified in the wild by at least two of 46 virus information experts from around the world. In February 2000, there were 182 virii listed on the main list. Another 292 virii were included on a supplemental list, which included virii reported by only one of the 46 virus specialists.

---

7. NCSA (National Computer Security Association) certification
8. West Coast Labs checkmark

WHAT IS A TROJAN HORSE?

Trojan horses are programs that have a dual purpose. They provide some useful function—for example, they may be an update to an existing program that you are running—but they also have the capability of damaging files or transferring a virus to your computer.

WHAT IS ANTIVIRUS SOFTWARE?

Antivirus software greatly reduces your chances of experiencing a viral infection in your computer. MSAV (Microsoft Anti-Virus) comes with DOS 6.22 and there are stand-alone products available like the Norton AntiVirus program. Both of these programs scan all of the files currently on your hard disk to see whether they contain any viruses. They also install memory-resident programs that keep a continuous lookout for any suspicious activity that would indicate a virus. Some of the better-known antivirus programs include these:

1. CyberMedia's Guard Dog Deluxe *www.cybermedia.com/*
2. CyberSoft antivirus software for UNIX and Windows *www.cyber.com/*
3. Dr Solomon's Anti-Virus *www.drsolomon.com*
4. EliaShim *www.eliashim.com*
5. F-Secure *www.Europe.datafellows.com/*
6. IBM AntiVirus *www.av.ibm.com/current/FrontPage/*
7. McAfee VirusScan (McAfee, Network General, PGP, and Helix have joined to form a new company named Network Associates) *www.nai.com/*
8. Norton AntiVirus *www.symantec.com/*
9. Quarterdeck's ViruSweep *www.quarterdeck.com/*
10. TouchStone PC-cillin *www.checkit.com/*

Online Resource

If you want to keep up-to-date on issues relating to computer viruses, consider joining VIRUS-L. To subscribe, send an e-mail message to *listserv@lehigh.edu*. In the body of the message, type **sub VIRUS-L <your_name>**.

KEEPING UP-TO-DATE

Today, there are thousands of known viruses and new viruses are being developed daily. To provide yourself with the best protection possible, you should update your virus protection software periodically. MSAV can't be upgraded, but other products can, like Norton AntiVirus and McAfee's VirusScan. To update, point your Web browser to the appropriate site and grab the latest release. The newest versions of antivirus software enable you to run updates automatically.

HOW TO AVOID VIRUSES

If you share floppies with others or download files from online services, there's no 100 percent guarantee that you'll always be protected against viruses. To help reduce the risk of your computer being infected, follow these tips:

1. Run an antivirus program and keep it updated often.
2. Scan floppies that you suspect might be infected.
3. Don't copy programs from one computer to another. Use the original distribution diskettes to install programs.
4. Scan your system regularly with the full scanning engine.
5. Avoid using floppies from unknown sources.
6. Write-protect your floppies by covering the notch on 5.25–inch disks or by sliding the little tab to expose the hole on 3.5–inch disks.
7. Never boot your computers from unknown diskettes. If you do and you suspect there may be a virus on the diskette, shut the computer down. Boot up from a clean system diskette and check the system with an antivirus program.
8. Utilize your antivirus program's memory resident scanners to check all files as they are accessed, even from the Internet.
9. You can warn patrons about viruses when checking out books accompanied by floppy disks by placing a warning notice near the pocket holding the disk.

Online Resource

If your Internet service provider offers access to Usenet newsgroups, check out *comp.virus* for current information on virus related issues. The VIRUS-L discussion group and the *comp.virus* newsgroup maintain a FAQ on viruses that can be downloaded from site *ftp://rtfm.mit.edu//pub/usenet-by-hierarchy/comp/virus/* or *ftp://ftp.cert.org//pub/virus-l/virus-l.README*.

INTERNET SECURITY

You build network security from the PC up by applying all of the various devices I've discussed so far, including secure menus, access control systems, backup power supplies, and antivirus software. Once your PCs are safe, then you begin implementing security controls on the information accessed across networks.

The Internet presents some unique security problems for libraries. The issues I cover in this section include:

1. Firewalls
2. Hostile Scripts
3. ActiveX and Java
4. Cookies
5. E-mail Bombing
6. List Linking
7. Ping Flooding
8. Cryptography
9. Famous Internet Hoaxes
10. Filtering

FIREWALLS

When you connect your library's network to the Internet and begin running Web servers, FTP servers, and Telnet servers, etc., crackers begin probing your site looking for weaknesses. When they find a way in, they tell all of their buddies all around the world about the security hole.

The best way to protect your network against security breaches like this is with a device called a firewall. *Firewalls* protect your network from outsiders. They can be hardware or software firewalls, but usually they consist of both. The most important aspect of a firewall, however, isn't its hardware or software; it's the architect that configures the firewall—the individual that decides who and what can access your network.

There are various types of firewalls. One type denies access based on a source's Internet address. These are called *packet filters*. You can run packet filters on a hardware device you already have in the library if you're connected to the Internet—a device called a *router*. A firewall such as this is called a router-based packet filter. These filters are fast and efficient at what they do. You can also run an auditing program in conjunction with this to track who is logging in and when.

You can find some inexpensive packet filter tools at Texas A&M University *fpt:// net.tamu.edu/pub/security/TAMU*. A PC-based screening router, Karlbridge, is available at *ftp://ftp.net.ohio-state.edu/pub/kbridge*.

Another type of firewall is called a proxy gateway. *Proxy gateways* act as agents between your network and outside networks. When a remote host sends information to your library, the proxy gateway blocks it, looks it over, and decides whether it's safe to let it through based on a set of prescribed rules. If the proxy gateway decides it is safe, it creates a bridge between the remote host and an internal host on your network.

Proxy gateways can slow processing time down and you will need a proxy server for every Internet service you offer. There are some experts in the field that argue that solid system administration practices will offer the same protection as proxy gateways without the slowdown in performance.

Another firewall, called a *callback program*, protects your network from dial-in lines. When an individual calls into your system, she enters her ID and password and then the firewall breaks the connection. The firewall then calls her back at her registered phone number. This prevents crackers from breaking in via phone lines with stolen IDs and passwords.

PERSONAL INTERNET FIREWALLS

Personal Internet firewalls are important to consider if you allow files on your PC to be accessed remotely across the Internet; for example, if you are running Microsoft's Personal Web Server or OmniHTTPd. Personal Internet firewalls are also essential if you support a direct connection to the Internet, as with cable modem and DSL connections. A personal firewall helps protect you against intruders and helps you monitor any attempts to break into your system via the Internet. ZoneAlarm 2.0 is free for individual users and can be downloaded from Zone Labs' Website at *www.zonelabs.com/*. ConSeal PC Firewall, a more advanced personal firewall, is available from Signal 9 Solutions. You can learn more about their product at *www.signal9.com/products/index.html*. If this site no longer exists when you read this chapter, try looking for ConSeal PC Firewall on McAfee's site *www.mcafee.com/*. Signal 9 Solutions was recently acquired by McAfee.

HOSTILE SCRIPTS

Website developers create interactive Websites using CGI scripts. *CGI* stands for Common Gateway Interface, which is a set of rules. These rules govern how a client passes data to and receives data from a Web server. CGI scripts are programming languages such as C++ and the language of choice—Perl. CGI scripts are used to collect and process information. For example, when you send a virtual postcard, or sign a guest book, a CGI program running on the server system receives your information and processes it. CGI scripts, such as Perl, are classified as server-side languages because they execute on the server computer, not on your personal computer. Scripting languages, such as JavaScript, run within your browser on your own computer and are considered client-side languages.

Both Webmasters and users are exposed to security risks using language technologies. Security holes can exist in CGI scripts and threaten the security of servers. In this instance, it's the job of an experienced programmer to determine whether a Website is opening itself to attack. Programmers can include "escape codes" that provide backdoors for hackers trying to break in.

JavaScript is used to deliver information to your browser and poses a threat to you when you are running your browser. If you run Netscape Navigator you are at risk if JavaScript is turned on. One security hole, for example, enables remote users to monitor your Web activities. You can disable supporting JavaScript, as well as Java and cookies, in the "Advance" preferences panel.

ACTIVEX AND JAVA

ActiveX controls are programs that your browser downloads and saves to your computer's hard drive. Java applets are small programs that run inside your Web browser.

Netscape Navigator has built-in security features that can protect you against hostile applets, but it is an all-or-nothing proposition. You are given only two choices: Java applets are either allowed in or they are kept out. This is how Internet Explorer handles Java, too. Java programs are considered secure because they run in a safe zone called a *sandbox* where they supposedly cannot cause any harm to your system. But there is nothing to prevent a programmer from writing some malicious code that freezes your browser, compromises the privacy of data stored on your hard drive, pops up outrageous windows, or freezes your computer by consuming most of its resources.

Since your only concern is to keep *hostile* applets out, you might think that enabling this security feature is too restrictive. An alternative is to run filtering devices that look for suspicious behavior. This type of filter is now being offered in some antivirus software suites. The best antivirus suites not only identify hostile Java applets and ActiveX controls, they also help you stop them from downloading. One of the better-known scanners of this type is WebScanX, which is part of McAfee VirusScan Security Suite. WebScanX is not only known for successfully recognizing hostile Java applets and ActiveX controls, but it also maintains a library of hostile Internet addresses.

Another product, called The Java Filter, also protects you against unsafe applets without having to shut off your browser's Java feature. The Java Filter, developed by the Department of Computer Science at Princeton University, offers advanced controls that enable you to specify which applets you allow into your system and which applets you block. To learn more about The Java Filter, go to Princeton University's Secure Internet Programming site located at *www.cs.princeton.edu/sip/JavaFilter/index.html*.

Internet Explorer offers a security feature called *signing* that removes some of the risk associated with ActiveX controls. The developer that creates an ActiveX control digitally signs it. Before you install and run the control, you are shown a *certificate* that tells you where the control came from and you can choose to except it or reject it. The problem with this method is knowing who to trust. How can you tell by looking at a certificate whether it is worthy of your trust?

To help address this issue, Version 4.0 of IE has built its browser security around four security zones:

> Internet
> Local Intranet
> Trusted Sites
> Restricted Sites

Online Resource

The ICSA (International Computer Security Association) *www.icsa.net* Web Certification Program requires that any programs that can be downloaded and run on the user's computer, such as Java, and ActiveX, etc., must be harmless. They also verify that any use of cookies is harmless and that data they collect and store is secure.

For each of these zones you can assign different security settings. These include "High," which is most secure; "Medium," which warns you before running potentially damaging programs; "Low," which gives no warnings; and "Custom," which allows you to define your own level of security by controlling such things as access to files, ActiveX controls, scripts, and Java applets. For example, you could configure IE so that it restricts certain sites from sending your library any ActiveX controls, and then require IE to prompt you before installing and running all other controls.

A final tip on making Web browsers more secure is to run the latest version of software available. When a new and improved version of browser software is released, it usually solves security issues that were discovered in earlier versions. Use only fully released versions, not beta versions. Beta versions don't include technical support and are likely to have more problems. Visit your Web browser's home page from time to time to download the latest patches for security holes that are discovered. For Netscape go to *www.netscape.com/download/index.html* and for Internet Explorer go to *www.microsoft.com/ie/*. To stay up-to-date on Java security, check out *java.sun.com/security*.

COOKIES

Cookies are text files that reside on your computer and are maintained by your Web browser. Web servers store information about you in the cookies.txt file—usually demographic and advertising information, but it can also be information about your surfing habits and experiences. One server might store information about you that you consider private, such as user IDs and passwords, and another invasive server may come along and steal that information. Storing login information may also be a service to you. It enables you to visit a site without entering the same login information each time you visit.

You can't avoid every problem you encounter by deleting the cookies.txt file or individual cookies files. Navigator and IE create a new cookie file the first time a server transfers a cookie to your browser. You can set your browser so that it alerts you when a server attempts to download a cookie to your hard drive, or you can stop your browser from accepting cookies altogether. You enable cookie security in Netscape 3.0 by clicking on "Options|Network Preferences." In Navigator 4.0 and later, click on "Edit|Preferences|Advanced." This solution creates a serious problem: Because so many Websites use the cookie mechanism, each time you visit one of these sites a message would come up asking you if you want to allow it. So, if you set your browser to alert you each time a cookie is to be downloaded, you would be continuously asked whether you want to accept a cookie.

You can use a utility program specifically designed to control cookies. Cookie Pal is a shareware cookie management system for Windows 95 and Windows NT 4.0. You can use it to automatically accept and reject cookies from anywhere, or user-specified Websites. This avoids the annoying Cookie Alert message that continually comes up if you disable cookies in your browser. You can download Cookie Pal from Kookaburra Software at *www.kburra.com/cpal.html*.

Where are Cookies Located on Your PC?

Cookies are stored in various places on your hard drive. The exact location depends on which Web browser you use. Here are the locations you can find cookies stored based on common combinations of browsers and platforms.

1. If you are running Internet Explorer 3.x on a Windows PC, cookies are stored in the folder *C:\WINDOWS\COOKIES.*
2. If you are running Internet Explorer 4.x, or 5.x, Windows and cookies are stored in file *C:\WINDOWS\TEMPORARY INTERNET FILES.*
3. If you are running Navigator 4.x on a Windows PC, cookies are stored as a single file named COOKIES.TXT located in the directory where Navigator is installed. (Typically this is *C:\PROGRAM FILES\NETSCAPE\USERS\DEFAULT.*)
4. If you are running Internet Explorer 2.x on a Macintosh, cookies are stored all together in one file called COOKIES.TXT in the *SYSTEM FOLDER| PREFERENCES|EXPLORER* folder.
5. If you are running Internet Explorer 3.x on a Macintosh, you find cookies stored in *SYSTEM FOLDER|PREFERENCES|INTERNET PREFERENCES.*
6. If you are running Internet Explorer 4.x on a Macintosh, then the cookies are stored in *SYSTEM FOLDER|MS|PREFERENCES PANEL|COOKIES FILE.*

DENIAL OF SERVICE ATTACKS

Denial of Service Attacks, or DoS for short, is a type of attack that brings network services down to its knees by flooding the network with excessive traffic. DoS attacks are so incredibly simple, crackers scorn their comrades who launch these attacks. There are software fixes for known DoS attacks that can be installed by your system administrator. These fixes, however, do not protect you from new DoS attack scenarios that are yet to be invented. In this section I examine three types of DoS attacks: E-mail Bombing, List Linking, and Ping Flooding. The tools for launching these DoS attacks are free and easy to obtain.

E-mail Bombing

One of these attacks, called an *e-mail bombing*, consists of sending the same e-mail message to a recipient over and over again. The messages can flood the recipient's mailbox until it is so full nothing more can fit. E-mail bomb attacks can be launched from most platforms including Microsoft Windows. PC crackers have several e-mail bombers to pick from. A program called *QuickFyre* makes e-mail bombing a simple process. The perpetrator begins by filling in the target's e-mail address, the sender's address (which can be their own or someone else's), the subject field, and the mail server's SMTP address. He or she finishes by writing their message and specifying how many copies to send (up to 32,767).

Online Resource

Surveillance tools are specialized programs that enable you to log a user's keystrokes, access times, and URLs that are visited on the Web. They run invisibly in the background. Some of these surveillance tools are capable of sending the log file to you via e-mail. One such example is 007 STARR (Stealth Activity Recorder & Reporter) from IOPUS Software. IOPUS Software makes a fully functional evaluation version available on their Website at *www.iopus.com/download.htm*. Libraries find these tools valuable if they need to track unauthorized use of PCs or printers, or record what users are doing wrong to help troubleshoot problems.

List Linking

List linking is a variant of the e-mail bomb. A cracker subscribes their victim to dozens, sometimes hundreds of discussion lists. Because lists generate a lot of mail, the cumulative effect of multiple subscriptions can be similar to an e-mail bomb. Crackers create multiple subscriptions either manually or by creating a list of discussion list addresses and subscribing the target to all of them at once using forged e-mail.

Ping Flooding

The *Ping command* sends a packet of information from your computer to a remote system. If you successfully connect, the remote system responds. Ping is normally used to determine whether a remote server is down or up and running. Ping can also be used destructively to take down a server. For this reason, many system administrators hide or remove the Ping program on their servers.

   Ping flooding floods an IP (Internet Protocol) address with repetitive Ping requests. You can flood a server or even a PC with a dial-up connection if you know its IP address. Since IP addresses for dial-up accounts are usually assigned dynamically, it would be a challenge for a cracker to know just what IP address you are using. If you are running an IRC (Internet Relay Chat) client, a cracker could find out what your IP address is by entering **/dns <theirnickname>**. If you are on a LAN (Local Area Network), a cracker could send a 'killer ping' to any number of IP addresses within a range of numbers and at least hit someone on the network.

CRYPTOGRAPHY

Another security hazard on networks is the threat of data being intercepted as it travels from one computer to another before reaching its destination. An effective method of protecting the privacy of your e-mail as it is transmitted across the Internet is encryption. Encryption is a process that takes *plaintext*, data you can read, and scrambles it up so it becomes unreadable, at which point it is called *cyphertext*.

   You encrypt and decrypt data with something called a key. Keys are secret values—typically a random string of numbers. Theoretically, you can crack any key as long as you have enough computing power and time. The greater the key's length, the more difficult it is to crack.

For example, a 32–bit key can be cracked by an amateur hacker on a home PC. A 40–bit key would require the resources of a university to crack. A 56–bit key, which is considered "strong encryption," would take the resources of a government or large corporation to crack, or maybe a grad student at Berkeley with access to some parallel mainframes!

Encryption systems come in two flavors: single-key systems and double-key systems. Double-key systems use two keys—one is private and only you know it, the other is public and it's known by everyone. PGP or *Pretty Good Privacy* is an example of a double-key system. They are very secure, but somewhat hard to learn, in my opinion.

Single-key systems are the easiest to use. Cycode shareware uses the same key whether you are encrypting or deciphering data. A drawback with single-key encryption systems is that you have to communicate the decryption key to the person receiving your message. If you do this via e-mail, there is a chance that the key could be intercepted by a third party. You can avoid this risk by conveying the information in person.

To use Cycode, simply cut and paste your text into the window on the right; click on the button labeled "encrypt"; and then it appears as cyphertext in the left-hand window. From here you can mail it off or save it to your hard drive and password protect it. Cycode can be downloaded from Cycosoft at *cycosoft.blandford.cc/programs/cycode/*.

FAMOUS INTERNET HOAXES

Statements flashing across the Net such as, "The FCC is banning all religious broadcasting," and "Some pyramid schemes are legal under the postal lottery laws" should serve as warnings that not everything you hear on the Net is true. Statements like these are Internet hoaxes designed to exploit new, unsuspecting Internet users. They are not viruses in a literal sense, but they are a kind of "social" virus. Sometimes they are referred to as junk-mail viruses because they are myths spread around the Net via e-mail.

These are some of the more famous hoaxes that have fooled new, unsuspecting Internet users:

1. The "Good Times Hoax" goes something like this: "Don't open any e-mail with 'GOODTIMES' in the subject field. It will release a computer virus that can destroy your hard drive and place your computer's processor in an nth-complexity infinite binary loop." For more details on this one, check out Good Times Virus Hoax FAQ at *www.hr.doe.gov/goodtime.html*.
2. The "Deeyenda Virus" is another hoax that carries warnings similar to the "Good Times Hoax."
3. There's a story circulating about a boy in Great Britain named Craig Shergold. He's seven years old and has a brain tumor. He has a short time to live, but he has one wish: To break the Guinness Book of World Records for receiving post cards.
4. There's a woman who was shocked to get a $250 bill for this famous chocolate chip and oatmeal cookie recipe from Neiman Marcus. She was so irate about being charged this exorbitant amount that she published the recipe on the Internet for free.
5. Ghost.exe was originally distributed as a free screen saver that advertises a com-

> **Online Resource**
>
> *A Practical Guide to Internet Filters* by Karen Schneider is available from Neal-Schuman Publishers *www.neal-schuman.com*. In her book, Schneider explains how filters work and offers case studies to guide you in making your decisions about filtering software. One chapter is devoted to information on The Internet Filter Assessment Project. You can learn more about this book and other filtering issues on Schneider's Website *www.bluehighways.com/filters/*.

pany named Access Softek. The program opens a window showing ghosts flying around the screen. Whenever Friday the 13th rolls around, the program window title changes and the ghosts fly off the window and around the screen. Someone thought that this indicated it might be a Trojan horse that could ruin the hard drive, got worried, and sent out a Ghost.exe Warning.

CONTROLLING OUTGOING INTERNET ACCESS

Restricting access to Internet content is not the role of a librarian per se, but it is a policy issue confronting librarians in school and public libraries, so I will address it here.

You have two alternatives available for controlling or restricting access to the Internet:

1. Allow individuals the right to exercise freedom of choice, to determine for themselves what they see, read, and hear on the Internet. When children are involved, their parents may get involved offering guidance and supervision as they see fit.
2. Allow one individual or group of individuals to control content or levels of access.

In the first option, librarians get involved only to the extent that they make Internet users aware of the nature of the Internet and the library's position on unrestricted access. Publishing disclaimers on home pages, offering Internet advisories, and posting notices on computer monitors help accomplish this. Librarians also need to be concerned about the physical placement of computers in their library. Patrons inadvertently may be exposed to images they find objectionable.

To aid parents in the implementation of the second option, and as an alternative to governmental regulations, software companies offer filtering software, or "control ware," and commercial online services offer kids-only services. Parental guidance and supervision is still important, even when running filtering software. Some librarians offer both options in their library: PCs with filtering software and PCs that are unfiltered. Patrons are given a choice of which to use.

> **Online Resource**
>
> Be aware that there are sites on the Net, Nurse Your Net Nanny *www.glr.com/nurse.html*, for example, that offer instructions for turning off Net censorship programs like Net Nanny and CYBERsitter. When you understand how kids disable filtering software, you have a better chance of beating them at their own game.

> **Online Resource**
>
> Stay up-to-date with the latest innovations in blocking and filtering software by linking to Yahoo! at *www.yahoo.com/Business_and_Economy/ Companies/Computers/Software/Internet/Blocking_and_Filtering/*.

The American Library Association Intellectual Freedom Committee addresses filtering issues in their online document titled "Frequently Asked Internet Questions" available at *www.ala.org/alaorg/oif/interfaq.html*. The ALA is opposed to filtering and supports Internet-use policies, parent involvement, and educating the public in policy matters and in how to use the Internet to access information. ALA's page "Filters and Filtering" provides links to First Amendment, filtering, and intellectual freedom information. Use this page to access ALA policies and statements on filtering, including *Resolution on the Use of Internet Filters* and *Statement on Internet Filtering*.

How Filtering Software Works

Filtering software restricts individuals from accessing particular sites and materials. When an individual tries to access a blocked site, a message appears on the screen stating that it is blocked. Some software is preset. The sites that the software blocks have been predetermined based on subjective evaluations by the software producer. Some programs allow users to select "stop words" from a dictionary to filter sites. Other programs use subject categories to determine if a site is accessible.

Filtering Software Choices

Filtering software isn't perfect. Some sites are banned because of a few objectionable words and other sites that are questionable get through. Part of the problem is staying up-to-date. Hundreds of new Websites are created daily and changes to existing Websites are being made around the clock. Software companies that offer monthly and even weekly updates can't keep up with the changes.

Nothing prevents a teenager from logging in and accessing a new address for pornography or white supremacy that was just handed to him or her by a friend. Nor will it prevent the teen from sending or receiving pornographic images via e-mail.

In this section I provide brief overviews of the most popular filtering programs used in libraries. These include:

1. CYBERsitter
2. SurfWatch
3. Net Nanny
4. Cyber Patrol
5. Bess
6. I-Gear
7. X-Stop

CYBERSITTER

CYBERsitter offers "intelligent phrase filtering." This means a site isn't necessarily blocked because of a single word. CYBERsitter takes into consideration the context in which the word is written. For example, if the program is working properly (nothing is perfect), "Flowerheads of plants may have both female and male organs (bisexual)," would not be blocked, but a lurid statement about human sexual organs or human bisexuality would be.

In a test I ran during the previous edition of this book, CYBERsitter did not allow access to my own home page, which contained only library-related resources. When questioned why not, CYBERsitter user support explained that my Internet service provider had over 150 adult, white supremacist, or other objectionable Web pages posted by subscribers. They went on to explain that generally, when a particular domain allows such material and the individual pages get to be over 50, they block the entire domain.

CYBERsitter keeps a log of restricted areas that your child has tried to access. CYBERsitter can also be programmed to monitor information your child sends out such as your home address and phone number. You can download a free test version from the site *www.cybersitter.com/.* Solid Oak Software sells CYBERsitter for about $40 for a single computer.

SURFWATCH

SurfWatch offers filtering in five categories:

1. Drugs/Alcohol/Tobacco
2. Gambling
3. Hate Speech
4. Sexually Explicit
5. Violence

They offer additional filtering services in areas they call *Productivity Categories*. This includes subjects ranging from Astrology and Entertainment to Travel and Usenet News. SurfWatch supports a "Test a Site" program on their Website at *www1.surfwatch.com* that enables you to verify whether a site is blocked by their software. SurfWatch costs from $40 to $50 dollars, depending on your operating system. Six months of filter updates is included in the price. An additional six months of filter updates costs $29.95.

Online Resource
Librarians who work with young children can offer parents some additional guidance on "safe surfing" by directing them to a site named CyberAngels. This international organization states that their mission is to fight crime on the Internet; protect kids from online criminal abuse; offer support to online victims; promote good netiquette and freedom of speech; and teach cyberstreetsmarts™ to new users.

NET NANNY

Net Nanny can block access to chat rooms, while at the same time allowing access to the Internet, and vice versa. It also enables you to create a "can go" list. This means that users can only go to the sites on your list and are blocked from sites that are not on your list. Filter updates can be downloaded from their Website and are free of charge to their customers. You can download a single-user copy of Net Nanny for about $27 at Net Nanny Software International Inc.'s Website *www.netnanny.com/*.

CYBER PATROL

Cyber Patrol's filtering system is structured around four *Cyber LISTs*:

1. CyberNOT List
2. Kid's List
3. Productivity List
4. Internet List

A group of professional researchers compile the lists. Cyber Patrol features a service called ChatGARD that prevents kids from giving out personal information online, such as name, address, and phone number.

Cyber Patrol costs approximately $30 for a single-user license and can be downloaded from their Website at *www.cyberpatrol.com/*. Included with this price is three months subscription to the filtering lists.

BESS

Bess, named after a dog known by the same name, offers two services that are of particular interest to librarians: an educational portal named Searchopolis and a content filtering service. Searchopolis is a free, filtered search service that weeds out "harmful or distracting" sites. You can access it at *www.bess.net/*. The level of filtering varies depending on the grade level you choose prior to running your search.

The content filtering service provides users with more than 40 filtering categories from which to choose. Both humans and computers flag inappropriate sites. The human element helps rectify unnecessary keyword blocks on words such as *breast cancer* and *sex education*. N2H2 provides the filtering services for Bess. You can learn more by exploring their site at *www.n2h2.com/solutions/filtering.html*.

I-GEAR

Unified Research Laboratories has developed a filtering solution called I-Gear that runs on a proxy server. You configure the software by telling it what users and computers can access the system. In addition, you define what should be blocked; for example, foul language and racial slurs. I-Gear comes out of the box with a database already programmed to prevent accessing over 300,000 objectionable sites.

I-Gear's proxy server basically works like this: A user requests a Web page. The Web server retrieves the page and searches its content for objectionable words and phrases. Based on this review process and the individual user's permissions, all or parts of a document may be blocked from viewing. The review process can be fine-tuned by defining words you want blocked when the word is found in a document and replacing the objectionable word with a series of dashes. When you attempt to reach a blocked site, an error message informs you the site is unauthorized. To learn more about I-Gear, visit their site at *www.symantec.com/urlabs/public/index.htm/*.

X-STOP

X-Stop filtering service can be loaded as a client on an individual PC, applied as a proxy-based filter, Microsoft Proxy Server on Windows NT, as a filter on your Ethernet, or as a filtering tool built on top of Novell's Internet Caching System.

The Client version, designed for the home or small office, gives you the ability to block access to hundreds of thousands of pornographic Websites, FTP sites, and newsgroups. A search-engine monitor prevents users from searching on objectionable words. It doesn't block access to the search engine itself. A typing filter blocks the typing of certain objectionable words that are contained in the X-Stop library. It doesn't matter whether the user types these words in a word processor, a browser, or e-mail message, X-Stop can block them. A modem filter allows access to only approved numbers. If a 900 number isn't on the approved list, dial-up access is blocked.

A blacklist of blocked sites is maintained on X-Stop's Website. Subscribers can download it manually or automatically. To learn more, visit X-Stop's Website at *www.xstop. com/products/index.html*.

CONCLUSION: SETTING YOUR SECURITY GOALS

The goal to strive for when applying all of the various security measures discussed in this chapter is *balance*—balance between your need for safety and security and the patron's need for functionality. When you offer lots of flexibility, easy access to programs and files, and offer lots of user-friendly services, you increase your library's risks because it opens security holes. Shackling your system unnecessarily with lots of restrictions and passwords makes it hard for everyone to be productive and work effectively, including your own staff.

Strive towards a point midway between these two extremes. Perform risk analysis, discussed earlier in this chapter, and consider the needs of your staff computers separately from those of your public access PCs.

Part III

TOOLS AND RESOURCES

In Part III, I cover Internet tools and resources. This part doesn't deal with the technical concepts behind the tools, but rather with the services they provide to those who use them. From this vantage point, you can view the Internet and its underlying technology as a set of application programs that are made available to you as an Internet user.

I open Part III with an introduction to UNIX shell accounts and what is fast becoming the world's hottest operating system, Linux. Chapter 10 begins with an introduction to communications software and explains what is meant by terminal emulation. I then go into basic UNIX commands followed by an introduction to Linux. Chapter 11 is for hard-core information seekers that are interested in learning Lynx—a text-based Web browser that runs on UNIX systems. Chapter 12, "Resource Discovery on the Web," introduces the tools used for finding information on the World Wide Web.

Next, in Chapters 13 through 15, I introduce three of the most time-honored tools on the Internet: FTP, telnet, and Archie. These are the basic services that enable you to login to other Internet computers and search for, access, and retrieve information stored on those computers. These tools are presented in three different environments or interfaces: UNIX shell accounts, the Web, and, in some cases, the Internet e-mail system. Each of these chapters begins with a description of the service as it is used in a UNIX shell account. This "stick-shift" approach illustrates the basics of each protocol.

The method of choice for most will ultimately be the Web and this approach is introduced second. Keep in mind, however, that using a Web browser interface to interact with these services isn't always the best choice if you're interested in speed and pictures aren't important. In other cases, such as telneting, there isn't any choice but to work in a text-based environment.

Chapters 16 and 17 cover online libraries and community information networks. The transformation from print to online is bringing reference librarians a growing number of online resources. These are discussed in detail in Chapter 18, "Integrating Tools into Traditional Reference Practice." Chapter 19 continues with a discussion of how the Internet can serve as a strategic resource for your other departments, including Acquisitions/Collection Development, Cataloging, Serials, Children's Services, and Special Collections and Archives. Part III concludes with Chapter 20, "Virtually Yours for Free," which explains how to utilize a broad range of free services ranging from conferencing systems and Web-based databases to mailing lists and fax services.

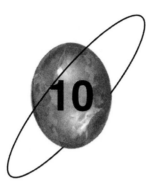

Happy Hacking in UNIX

UNIX is a multi-user, multi-tasking operating system for workstations. It is the most widely used operating system on the Internet. Its popularity is partly due to the fact that several people can use a UNIX computer at the same time and each person can run several programs simultaneously. These are important attributes in an environment like the Internet where many people are doing many things all at once.

UNIX began its development back in 1969 at Bell Labs. Since that time, many people have developed various versions of UNIX, but they all are based on either Berkeley UNIX, known as BSD (Berkeley Standard Distribution), System V, or both.

Most of these versions are commercial and include IBM's AIX, Sun Microsystems' Solaris and SunOS, and Digital Equipment Corporation's Ultrix, just to name a few. There are non-commercial versions of UNIX including one called Linux.

Because BSD UNIX is the most common version of UNIX used on commercial Internet sites, and C shell is the most commonly used shell program on BSD UNIX systems, this chapter will focus on C shell commands.

This chapter was written for librarians who access the Internet through a UNIX shell account and who like tinkering with new ideas while exploring the Net. It will appeal more broadly to anyone involved in the exchange of information on the Internet—for example, teachers. To this end, I offer suggestions to teachers on how they might share some of the ideas presented in this chapter with their students.

The chapter starts with an introduction to communications software—the software that's used to connect to shell accounts and other online services such as bulletin boards. This is followed by an explanation of what UNIX shells are and how to create files and take care of other housekeeping tasks in a shell environment. Finally, I present some of the lesser-known UNIX commands and explain how librarians and other Internet users can use these commands to expand their understanding of the Internet. The chapter closes with a special section on Linux, explaining why libraries might use Linux, its installation, and where to find it.

INTRODUCTION TO COMMUNICATIONS SOFTWARE

Communications software (sometimes referred to as terminal emulation software, or comm software for short) enables your computer to communicate with modems, phone lines, and remote computers.

Different comm applications offer varying features and although some are DOS based, others are designed for Windows and Mac environments. One feature that every comm program should offer is the capability of emulating different terminals. *Terminal emulation* is the feature that enables your personal computer to link with other types of computers that are online, including university mainframes.

Another common feature is called *file transfers*. This service involves sending and receiving data between your personal computer and a host computer. More sophisticated programs may offer other features like automatic dialing, cut-and-paste editing, scripting, and bulletin board functions.

TERMINAL EMULATION

When personal computers first came on the market in the late 1970s, they were used as stand-alone systems. Terminals were used to communicate with mainframes or mini-computers, and personal computers were used to run one or more specialized applications like word processors and spreadsheet programs.

In many libraries today, personal computers are used for more than word processing, spreadsheets, and database management. They also perform as terminals in online communications. With the aid of comm software, a personal computer can now be used as a terminal in addition to all of the other functions it serves. In fact, with the new comm programs available today, personal computers are able to offer users much more than the terminals they replace.

"Why would anyone want to make a powerful microcomputer act as though it were just a terminal?" you may wonder. The answer is simple. When you dial-in to a host computer, the host is expecting to communicate with a terminal, not a full-fledged computer like your PC or Mac. The only way your personal computer can interact with a host is if you make the host believe your computer really is a terminal.

TERMINAL TYPES

All the various hosts you'll be connecting to with your shell account on the Internet recognize a limited set of terminal types. The most common one is VT100, which stands for VAX Terminal, Model 100. When you purchase your communications software, make sure that VT100 is included among the list of terminals it emulates. You should also be able to emulate an ANSI terminal, which will aid you in communicating with bulletin board systems.

The basic goal is to make sure that your terminal emulation is set to the same terminal type as the host's. VT100 is the default setting on most hosts and it is a good one to choose if you are in doubt.

FILE TRANSFER PROTOCOLS

File transfer protocols are sets of rules that regulate how your personal computer communicates with a remote host when sending or receiving data. The comm program you choose should support the most common file transfer protocols including Kermit, ZModem, YModem, and XModem.

OTHER COMMUNICATIONS SOFTWARE FEATURES

Some communications programs offer ways to store one or more telephone numbers in a dialing directory. When you want to contact a particular host, the program retrieves the desired number and dials it automatically, making the connection for you.

Most communication programs allow you to capture information so that you can save it to a disk or send it to the printer. When the capture feature is turned on, the characters you type and receive during a session are saved to a disk. When you're being charged by the minute for online time, this is an economical way to retrieve data quickly and then disconnect. Once you're offline, you can pull your file into a word processor for reading, editing, and printing at your convenience.

Some communications programs support scripting. A *script* is a list of instructions that are written in such a way that a program can understand them. Scripting is typically used to write programs that automate routine tasks. For example, if you login to FirstSearch or CompuServe on a regular basis, a login script could be written to take care of the connecting and logging in process automatically. Instructions for writing and compiling scripts usually are explained in the user manual that accompanies your communications software.

Lastly, your communications program may have a review feature, sometimes called *scroll back* or *replay*, that enables you to go back and view data that has already scrolled off the screen. This feature is very convenient when part of a directory has scrolled off your screen and you'd like to go back and confirm a file name.

CHOICES OF COMMUNICATIONS SOFTWARE

As was pointed out in Chapter 5, the software you need depends on the kind of connection you make to the Internet. For a shell account, all you need is comm software on your end of the connection. The rest of the connection, which involves a multitude of applications, communication links, and host computers, is all outside your realm of responsibility. Other individuals put these items into place.

A few of the more popular commercial comm applications include Crosstalk, Crosstalk for Windows, Procomm Plus, Procomm Plus for Windows, and Smartcom for Macs. If you're using Microsoft Windows and looking for a recommendation, I would suggest trying Procomm Plus for Windows. Produced by Datastorm Technologies, it provides an excellent Windows interface with several useful features. Another comm application that offers all of the basic features you'll need is Hilgraeve's HyperTerminal that comes bundled with Windows 95. You can find it by clicking on "Start" and then selecting "Programs|Accessories." Next, highlight and click on the "HyperTerminal" folder.

Telneting to Your Shell Account

Even if you have a SLIP/PPP account running on your computer, you still can access your shell account without closing down your SLIP/PPP connection. You accomplish this by plugging your ISP's Internet address into a telnet application. When you connect, the screen will look just as though you were connecting via your comm software. You can maintain this telnet connection to your shell account at the same time you have a SLIP/PPP connection.

One instance where this operation comes in handy is when you are building Web pages. With your SLIP/PPP connection up and running, you can work with your HTML editor and run Netscape to view changes as you make them. If you have a need to alter files that are already loaded on your service provider's UNIX box, you can telnet into your shell account, make the changes, and then switch back to your browser and reload your home page to see the changes immediately.

There are shareware and freeware packages that can provide you with the basic requirements necessary for connecting to both the Internet and bulletin boards systems. Some names to look for are Procomm (shareware version for DOS), Qmodem, MicroLink (a simple Microsoft Windows shareware program), and White Knight and ZTerm for Macs.

WHAT IS A SHELL ACCOUNT?

When you login to a UNIX system, you are generally placed in a program called the shell. A *shell* is a program that expects you to type commands at a prompt in order to interact with the computer's operating system. More advanced operators type commands in script files, also called shell scripts. *Script files* are a lot like batch files. A list of UNIX commands is saved to a file and then the file is executed. Writing script files requires programming knowledge and a good understanding of the UNIX operating system.

This chapter only addresses entering commands at the command line prompt. This prompt, found at the bottom left of your screen, is usually a dollar sign ($) or percent sign (%). The prompt can also include other information, such as the name of your service provider (for example, CRCINET>), or the name of the Internet application you're running, such as FTP> or archie>.

The most popular shell programs are the classic Bourne Shell and Korn Shell, both of which prompt you with a dollar sign ($), and the C Shell, which prompts you with a percent sign (%). The most important difference between shells is the command language. C Shell (csh) uses a command language something like the C programming language. The Bourne Shell uses a different command language. Versions of most shells have been ported to Linux.

WHY USE A SHELL ACCOUNT?

Shell interfaces are text-based as opposed to GUI (Graphical User Interface). Working in a text-only environment has its advantages. On modem connections, librarians and other information specialists can run text-based Internet applications that execute search and retrieval operations faster than their GUI counterparts. For example, if all you are looking for is hard-core textual data and you are given an option of choosing a GUI Web browser like Netscape or a text-based browser like Lynx, depending on your connection speed, your search may go quicker running Lynx in a shell environment.

A common practice of many Web developers is to perform simple editing tasks by telneting to a UNIX shell account. While sitting at a PC, the developer logs into the computer that hosts the Website. Using a UNIX text editor, such as Vi Editor or Pico, the developer opens the HTML document for editing, makes changes, and then saves the file. By loading a Web browser and pulling up the newly edited page, the developer immediately sees the end results.

An alternative practice is to use an FTP client to download the HTML document for editing. After making changes to the file locally, the file is saved and then uploaded back to the server. Using shell accounts and UNIX text editors saves time and allows Web developers to see the results of editorial changes quickly.

Many of the companies offering virtual Web server accounts give you the option of logging into UNIX shells to maintain files. It would be valuable to have a basic understanding of how to login, view directories, change directories, and delete files. More advanced operators can explore editing CGI scripts. These are text files that enable Web developers to perform tasks such as collecting data that visitors enter into online forms, for example, interlibrary loan request forms.

WHAT DO SHELL ACCOUNTS LOOK LIKE?

Some Internet service providers present their subscribers with a custom-designed menuing system to make life a little easier when they first log into a UNIX host. A "user friendly" menu appears immediately after logging in and may look something like this:

```
Menu:
1 Readme First
2 BBS Direct
3 Internet
4 Multiplayer Games
5 Net Highlights
6 Library
7 Logoff Net
8 Feedback
Enter a command or "?" for help:
```

You arrive at the shell prompt only after choosing menu item number "3 Internet." Other service providers offer nothing more than a Welcome screen listing a phone number to call for help.

CAN YOU DIAL UP TO A SHELL ACCOUNT?

You can access shell accounts on the Internet by either dialing in with a modem, or by telneting from a computer already connected to the Internet. A distinguishing feature of a dial-up is that you're not connecting your personal computer directly to the Internet. Instead, you're dialing into a host computer that *is* connected to the Internet. All of the Internet services you access, you will access through this host. When you compose e-mail messages, you use a mail program running on the host—probably Pine or Elm. Internet applications like telnet and FTP also run on the host computer, which is a mixed blessing. It means you don't have to concern yourself with installing and configuring client software, but then you're limited to using whatever program your service provider happens to have available, which are text-based UNIX applications.

There are times when it is advantageous to run UNIX clients from a shell account. If you are logged into your UNIX host doing maintenance on your account, it's easy to jump to another remote system by simply telneting from the shell. At least some would find it easier to maneuver in this manner rather than starting up a Windows-based telnet client and making the connection.

BASIC UNIX COMMANDS

Table 10–1 describes some of the basic UNIX commands that help you manage your working environment. Virtually every utility found on standard implementations of UNIX has been ported to Linux—the UNIX clone introduced later in this chapter. This includes basic commands such as **ls**, **more**, **passwd**, **cd,** and so on.

There are times when you may want to stop a program temporarily, start another program, kill it, and then go back and resume the original program. The first four commands listed in Table 10–1 enable you to exercise this kind of job control. *Job control* is a UNIX facility that allows you to start a program running and then suspends, views, resumes, or kills the process.

The following session illustrates the basic commands associated with job control. In this example, I start the Pine mail program, suspend it, then start an FTP session, suspend it, then view what jobs are running, kill the FTP session, and then go back to Pine mail. Commands are presented in boldface type and the computer response is in plain text. Each command is numbered (1., 2., 3., etc.) and explained later.

```
1.  % pine
    PINE 3.90 MAIN MENU  Folder: INBOX 1 Message
    ?   HELP                        -Get help using Pine
    C   COMPOSE MESSAGE             -Compose and send/post a message
    I   FOLDER INDEX                -View messages in current folder
    L   FOLDER LIST                 -Select a folder OR news group to
                                     view
    A   ADDRESS BOOK                -Update address book
    S   SETUP                       -Configure or update Pine
    Q   QUIT                        -Exit the Pine program
    Copyright 1989–1994. PINE is a trademark of the University of Washington.
       [Folder "INBOX" opened with 1 message]
```

Table 10–1: Basic UNIX commands for shell account users		
Command	**Purpose**	**Example**
jobs	Tells you what jobs are running	jobs
kill %n	Kills job *n*, where *n* is the number of the job	kill %1
%n	Resumes job *n*, where *n* is the number of the job	%1
^Z (ctrl-Z)	Suspends the current process	^Z
sz	Sends text file via ZMODEM	sz readme.txt
sz-b	Sends binary file via ZMODEM winpkt.com	sz-b
rz	Receives text file via ZMODEM	rz word.doc
rz-b	Receives binary file via ZMODEM	rz-b photo.gif
cd	Changes directories	cd /pub
cp	Copies files	cp .plan plan.copy (The .plan file remains and a new copy name plan.copy is created.)
date	Displays date and time of day	date
ls	Lists files in a directory	ls
ls-l	Lists files along with their size, dates, and other information	ls-l
man	Displays online help information	man pico
more	Displays data one screen at a time	ls-l I more
mv	Moves files and renames files (To move a file named logo.gif to a directory named public_html)	mv logo.gif public_html
pico	Starts Pico, a simple text editor	pico
pine	Starts Pine mail program	pine
pwd	Tells you what directory you're currently in	pwd
passwd	Changes password	passwd
rm	Deletes a file	rm .signature
rmdir	Removes a directory (directory must be empty)	rmdir Mail/
rmdir-r	Removes a directory and all files and News/ subdirectories it contains	rmdir-r
touch	Creates new file (contains 0 bytes) resume.htm	touch

```
? Help       P PrevCmd     R
RelNotes
[KO OTHERCMDS L [ListFldrs]        N NextCmd      K
KBLock
```

2. **^Z**

   Pine suspended. Give the "fg" command to come back.
   Stopped (signal)

3. % **ftp ftp.unt.edu**

   Connected to mercury.acs.unt.edu.
   220 mercury FTP server (Version wu-2.4(1) Tue Oct 10 00:19:29 CDT 1995) ready.
   Name (ftp.unt.edu:anonymous): anonymous
   331 Guest login ok, send your complete e-mail address as password.
   Password:
   230–Please read the file README
   230– it was last modified on Wed Jul 6 11:59:09 1994 —576 days ago
   230 Guest login ok, access restrictions apply.

4. ftp> **^Z**

   Stopped

5. % **jobs**

   [1] —Stopped (signal) pine
   [2] + Stopped   ftp ftp.unt.edu

6. % **kill %2**

   [2] Terminated   ftp ftp.unt.edu

7. % **%1**

   pine
      PINE 3.90 MAIN MENU Folder:
   INBOX 1 Message

?HELP	-		Get help using Pine
C	COMPOSE MESSAGE	-	Compose and send/post a message
I	FOLDER INDEX	-	View messages in current folder
LFOLDER LIST		-	Select a folder OR news group to view
A	ADDRESS BOOK	-	Update address book
S	SETUP	-	Configure or update Pine
Q	QUIT	-	Exit the Pine program

   Copyright 1989–1994. PINE is a trademark of the University of Washington.
   ? Help   P PrevCmd   R
   RelNotes
   O OTHER CMDS L [ListFldrs] N NextCmdK
   KBLock

The following commands were used in the session illustrated above.

1.	pine	starts Pine mail
2.	^Z	suspends Pine mail
3.	ftp	starts FTP program
4.	^Z	suspends FTP program
5.	jobs	lists what jobs are running

6. kill %2   kills job 2, the FTP program
7. %1   resumes job 1, Pine mail

The next set of commands listed in Table 10–1 (sz, sz-b, rz, and rz-b) are used for transferring files between the host and your personal computer using a program called ZMODEM. The point to remember here is that the command sz, which stands for send zmodem, moves files from the host computer to your personal computer. Another name for this is *downloading*. The rz command, which stands for receive zmodem, is used when you want to move files from your personal computer to the host. Another name for this process is *uploading*.

For more detailed explanations of these and other UNIX commands refer to Christopher C. Taylor's *Unix is a Four Letter Word*, which can be accessed at *www.msoe.edu/taylor/4ltrword/*. Details for accessing this manual online are given at the end of this chapter.

UNIX COMMANDS FOR INTERNAUTS

Teachers and librarians can do only so much with basic UNIX commands on the Internet. For instance, the commands used when running FTP only allow you to login to another system, view that system's directories, and transfer files. In the following section, you'll be given new ideas to try out and an opportunity to explore UNIX a little further.

THE TRACEROUTE COMMAND

Librarians may find it interesting to look at the route their computer takes on the Internet to get to another computer with the traceroute command. The command is easy to use. Just enter the command **traceroute** followed by the address of another computer. For example, to see what route your computer follows when it connects to *ecn.purdue.edu*, enter **traceroute ecn.purdue.edu** at the system prompt.

Your computer traces all the steps it takes to get to the remote site and prints it to your screen. Note how fast connections are made and how indirect the route can be. Routes will vary depending on the time of day and other circumstances. If you start in California, it may look something like the output shown in Figure 10–1.

As you trace the path shown in the example, it's interesting to see all of the places one computer visits before it finally reaches its destination—Washington, New York, Hartford, Cleveland, Chicago, and so on.

If you're a teacher or youth services librarian, you can use the traceroute command to demonstrate to students the speed at which information travels on the Internet. You can make it more challenging by asking students to translate the domain names and IP numbers into geographic locations and then plot them on a map. The whois command, described next, can be used to help students pinpoint the city and state in which a particular computer is located.

Figure 10–1: The traceroute command lets you see the route your computer takes when linking to another computer on the Internet

% **traceroute ecn.purdue.edu**

traceroute to ecn.purdue.edu (128.46.128.76), 30 hops max, 40 byte packets

  1   wfbcn1–fddi.cris.com (199.3.12.188) 2 ms 1 ms 2 ms

  2   199.3.98.22 (199.3.98.22) 30 ms 44 ms 43 ms

  3   aads.agis.net (198.32.130.19) 27 ms 48 ms 103 ms

  4   washington.agis.net (204.130.243.36) 66 ms 57 ms 52 ms

  5   mae-east.ans.net (192.41.177.140) 86 ms 108 ms 101 ms

  6   t3–3.cnss56.Washington-DC.t3.ans.net (140.222.56.4) 106 ms 70 ms 91 ms

  7   t3–0.cnss32.New-York.t3.ans.net (140.222.32.1) 78 ms 92 ms 115 ms

  8   t3–0.cnss48.Hartford.t3.ans.net (140.222.48.1) 74 ms 96 ms 86 ms

  9   t3–2.cnss43.Cleveland.t3.ans.net (140.222.43.3) 90 ms 113 ms 118 ms

 10   t3–1.cnss27.Chicago.t3.ans.net (140.222.27.3) 119 ms 107 ms 96 ms

 11   cnss29.Chicago.t3.ans.net (140.222.27.194) 116 ms 238 ms 203 ms

 12   enss152–2.t3.ans.net (199.221.97.70) 250 ms 193 ms 289 ms

 13   cisco1–oc.gw.purdue.edu (192.5.102.3) 275 ms 280 ms 201 ms

 14   nscmsee.ecn.purdue.edu (128.46.201.99) 208 ms 178 ms 218 ms

 15   harbor.ecn.purdue.edu (128.46.129.76) 229 ms * 177 ms

THE WHOIS COMMAND

The whois command runs a program called whois that in turn runs on whois servers located all around the world. For now, we will use the server at InterNIC (*rs.internic.net*).

The following syntax would be used to query the server at InterNIC: **whois-h rs.internic.net <search string>**, where *<search string>* is the domain name, IP number, or user name for which you are searching. The session illustrated in Figure 10–2 searches for the domain name *cris.com*—the first domain name listed above in the output resulting from the traceroute command.

THE WHO COMMAND

The who command enables you to find out who else is on the computer you're using. Type **who** at the system prompt and press ENTER. The response will look something like that shown in Figure 10–3.

Output from the who command shows userIDs, terminal names, and login times. From the output shown in Figure 10–3, you can see that userID *Rx7guy* has been logged into terminal *ttyp6* for a long time. The output from the who command will vary depending on which version of UNIX is running.

Figure 10–2: Output from the whois command includes mailing addresses and administrative and technical contacts

% **whois -h rs.internic.net cris.com**
Concentric Network Corporation (CRIS-DOM)
    105900 N. Tantau Avenue
    Cupertino, CA 95014
    USA

Domain Name: CRIS.COM

Administrative Contact:
    Kotacka, Chris (CK24) arch@CONCENTRIC.NET
    (408) 342–2836
Technical Contact, Zone Contact:
    Schairer, David R. (DRS9) njal@CONCENTRIC.NET
    (408) 342–2817

Record last updated on 27–Dec-95.
Record created on 21–Oct-92.

Domain servers in listed order:

NAMESERVER.CONCENTRIC.NET 199.3.12.2
NAMESERVER1.CONCENTRIC.NET 199.3.12.3

The InterNIC Registration Services Host contains ONLY Internet Information
(Networks, ASN's, Domains, and POC's).
Please use the whois server at nic.ddn.mil for MILNET Information.

THE FINGER COMMAND

You use the finger command to find information about users on your system and remote systems. When you *finger* a system, the command produces output similar to the who command—user IDs, how long each user has been idle (how long it has been since they last touched their keyboard), and the current process they are running. Entering **finger** at your system prompt produces results similar to those shown in Figure 10–4.

Figure 10–3: Output from the who command

% **who**

Shelbyh	ttyp1	Dec 14 08:28	(SHELBYH)
Spanners	ttyp3	Dec 14 08:17	(SPANNERS)
Cbodmer	ttyp4	Dec 14 08:49	(CBODMER)
Tbeymer	ttyp5	Dec 14 06:27	(TBEYMER)
Rx7guy	ttyp6	Dec 13 10:38	(MICHAELAHARMON)
Forever	ttyp7	Dec 14 08:35	(FOREVER)
Kahuna	ttyp9	Dec 14 08:46	(KAHUNA)
Belmont	ttypa	Dec 14 08:49	(BELMONT)

Figure 10–4: The finger command entered by itself provides information on users logged into your system

---

%**finger**

Ait	ttypD	8:37am		file transfer
Alwright	ttysD	9:05pm	1:29	SLIP
Bangor	ttyqP	9:04am		file transfer
Beagle	ttysC	9:01am		
Beavis	ttyqN	Sat 1pm	5days	pine
Bellevue	ttysP	9:00am		file transfer
Belmont	ttypA	8:49am	1	telnet
Bertec	ttyqJ	9:03am		pine
Bill2nd	ttyqM	7:06am		trn

Today, you can finger someone from the Web using a Web-Finger gateway. HyperFinger can be accessed at POPULUS *www.POPULUS.net/cgi-bin/HyperFinger*. Enter the name e-mail address of the individual you are searching and click "Search."

Fingering Individuals

You can finger a specific user by entering **finger <userID>**. For example, if you were to finger Bertec's user ID listed above, you'd be presented with the output shown in Figure 10–5.

The last line of output, reading "No plan.", makes note of the absence of a file called *.plan*. This file and one called *.project* are explained further in the sidebar. Although many individuals have no *.plan* file, others have created elaborate "plans." Figure 10–6 illustrates what I found when I fingered author Dave Taylor's e-mail address.
% finger taylor@netcom.com

As a project idea, media specialists might have students collect e-mail addresses for interesting and informative "plans" and assemble them in a notebook that other students can access. Teachers might consider placing students in charge of drafting the text for a *.plan* file. It could describe an annual festival unique to their community. Ad-

---

Figure 10–5: Details are provided on individuals when fingering a user ID.

% **finger Bertec**
Connected…
Login: Bertec   Name: Barnes
Directory: /U/B/Bertec   Shell: /bin/csh
CRCNet User-ID: SBARNES
Email address: Bertec@cris.com
Logged in on machine: viking
New mail since Thu Dec 14 20:16:56 1995
Mail last read Thu Dec 14 12:37:54 1995
No plan.

The .*plan* and .*project* Files

UNIX was designed in an academic environment where most folks were involved in research projects. Students and faculty would write about their current and future plans in a file called .*plan* and they'd describe their projects in a file called .*project*.

When someone would finger them, the contents of their .*plan* would be displayed and a portion of their .*project* file would also be displayed. This way, everyone on campus could keep up with what others were doing. When you finger yourself, you'll most likely see the comment "No Plan" displayed and no mention of a .*project* file, as you saw in Bertec's printout in Figure 10–5.

You can create these files with a text editor (vi, pico, emac, etc.) and give them the proper permissions so they can be read. File permissions are changed with the chmod (change mode) command. If you want to let anyone read, but not modify, your .*plan* files, enter the command **chmod 644 .plan**. If you have both a .*plan* and .*project* file, enter the command **chmod 644 .plan .project**.

If you don't want to be fingered, create a file .*nofinger* in your home directory. Once this file is created, the following message will be generated when you're fingered: "User <user ID> does not exist or does not wish to be fingered." The easiest way to create this file is to type this command at your system prompt: **touch ~/.nofinger**.

If you create a file named *FingerLog* in your home directory (with the command **touch ~/FingerLog**), every time a user fingers you, it will be recorded in this file. The user's name won't show up but his or her site address will. If you've included some important information in your .*plan* file, this is a good method of keeping track of how many times it gets accessed.

---

vertising the event could be as simple as sending out a notice to finger their e-mail address. Librarians might consider creating a .*plan* file describing a unique service offered by their library that appeals to a broad audience.

Fingering Remote Computers

You can sometimes find out who's on other computers on the Internet by entering the command finger followed by a space, an "@" sign, and then the domain address of the computer you're targeting. (If the computer doesn't want to be fingered, it will tell you so with a response: "User does not exist or does not wish to be fingered," or it might say "connection refused.") Suppose that you'd like to see who's logged into the computer called *ecn.purdue.edu* at Purdue University. You'd enter the command **finger @ecn.purdue.edu**. The output would look something like that shown in Figure 10–7.

You could then finger one of the user IDs—for example, *lejohn*—with the command **finger lejohn@ecn.purdue.edu**. The results would be similar to those shown in Figure 10–8.

Figure 10–6: A .plan file can be simple, or more elaborate like this one belonging to Dave Taylor (used with permission)

% **finger taylor@netcom.com**

[netcom.com]
Dave Taylor (taylor)
Home: /u1/taylor
Shell: /bin/csh
Mail forwarded to "l/usr/local/bin/filter".
Dave Taylor (taylor) is not presently logged in.
Last seen at netcom7 on Thu Feb 8 06:57:43 1996

Plan:
Hello! If you're looking for a copy of The Internet Mall(tm) list of commercial Internet shops and services, then you're at the right place!

There are a variety of ways to visit the Mall:

   FTP ftp.netcom.com look in */pub/Gu/Guides*
   EMAIL taylor@netcom.com use subject *send mall*
   USENET news.answers   posted twice monthly
   GOPHER peg.cwis.uci.edu look in peg/internet assistance
   WWW   http://www.internet-mall.com/

Finally, there are a couple of mailing lists that you'll want to know about too: join IMALL-L and you'll get the Mall every two weeks automatically delivered to your mailbox (it's big, so make sure you can accept 300,000+ byte messages first), and join IALL-CHAT and you can discuss commerce on the Internet, and specific vendors, with others. To join either, please send email to listserv@netcom.com with the message containing *subscribe <list>*

If you're wondering whether I'm the same Dave Taylor who wrote The Elm Mail System, Embot, the books "Global Software", "Teach Yourself UNIX In A Week", "Creating Cool Web Pages with HTML", co-authored "The Internet Business Guide" and writes for Marketing Computers and more, well, I am. :-)

If you'd like to receive free information on my books, I invite you to send me an email message with **send coolweb send TYU send GS** or **send intbiz** for helpful informative blurbs on the books. Or, even better, pop over to my home page, where you can also see a picture of me and even some photos of my girlfriend, parents and dogs! All this, and more, on the Web at http://www.intuitive.com/taylor

Also, feel free to drop me an email message if you have any questions, thoughts, ideas or just want to say Hi. Thanks!

Figure 10–7: The finger command can be used to finger an entire site

finger @ecn.purdue.edu

Login	Name	TTY	Idle	When	Office	
lejohn	John A. Le	pts/10		5:26 Thu 08:29	f lejohn	49–44326
moyman	James M Moya	pts/1		3:10 Thu 10:50	MSEE 104J	49–42349
ralph	Ralph L McCallister	pts/2		12: Mon 14:42	POTR 304C	49–48742
jmoore	James D Moore	pts/0	1d	Tue 08:11	CIVL 3158	49–62496
mjs	Maryjane Scharenberg	pts/3		Thu 21:22	MSEE 104E	49–43648
dsm	Digital Services Mai	pts/9	7d	Thu 10:31	MSEE 130	49–43376
ghg	George Goble	pts/19	2d	Thu 08:05	MSEE 104C	49–43545
trs	Thomas R Statnick	*pts/8	4:16	Thu 09:01	MSEE 104G	49–43546
wb9omc	Duane P Mantick	pts/7	3:38	Mon 09:10	MSEE 130A	49–49942
moyman	James M Moya	pts/13	10:	Thu 10:47	MSEE 104J	49–42349
dsm	Digital Services Mai	pts/6	1d	Tue 10:33	MSEE 130	49–43376
rice	Ken Rice	pts/11	1d	Tue 10:33	MSEE 130B	49–46678
dsm	Digital Services Mai	pts/14	1d	Mon 09:15	MSEE 130	49–43376

Figure 10–8: Results from the finger command when applied to an individual's e-mail address

% **finger lejohn@ecn.purdue.edu**
[ecn.purdue.edu]
Login name: lejohn   In real life: John A. Le
Office: f lejohn, 49–44326   Home phone: 555–5555
Directory: /home/harbor/a/lejohn   Shell: /bin/csh
Affiliations: ecn   Uid: 4264
Expires: December 1999   Login group: other (1)
Department: Engineering Computer Network Classification: Staff
Authorized by: Moya
Member of groups: root, ecnstaff, moymac, pcnfs
On since Dec 7 08:29:18 on pts/10 from liberty.ecn.purdue.edu
                                        5 hours 31 minutes Idle Time
Unread mail since Thu Dec 14 21:46:53 1995
No plan.

Table 10–2: Finger servers and descriptions	
When you enter this:	The server returns this:
finger copi@oddjob.uchicago.edu	Daily list of events and birthdays in history, and sports schedules
finger help@dir.su.oz.au	Access to databases, find newsgroups, access Archie, etc.
finger spyder@dmc.iris.washington.edu	Earthquake information from around the world
finger nasanews@space.mit.edu	Recent press releases from NASA
finger robc@xmission.com	Scores and standings for baseball and football
finger aurora@solar.uleth.ca	Auroral activity warnings/watches/sightings
finger solar@solar.uleth.ca	Solar and geophysical report
finger info@cdrom.com	Annotated list of Walnut Creek CD-ROM products
finger magliaco@pilot.njin.net	Weekly publication of space news

Finger Servers

Table 10–2 lists some interesting finger servers on the Net that provide more than just user information. Finger servers are computers that are set up to provide specific information when you contact them with the finger command.

THE PING COMMAND

Things go wrong at times and the trouble isn't always on your dial-up host computer. It's possible for a remote system to have things go wrong. The ping command sends a request to a remote system. If the system responds, the link from your computer to the other computer is good. If there's something wrong with the remote system, ping will fail to respond, or it will return an error message.

To use the ping command, type the word **ping** followed by a host name. For example, if you type **ping mercury.acs.unt.edu** at your system prompt, and the computer named *"mercury"* is alive, *mercury* will return with the message "mercury.acs.unt.edu is alive." In other words, mercury is up and running and you can communicate with it.

A slightly different variation on this command enables you to see the time in milliseconds that it takes a packet of information to make a round trip. Figure 10–9 illustrates how to run this test by sending three packets of 100 bytes each to *ualr.edu*.

Figure 10–9: Ping statistics include the host's IP address and round-trip times

% **ping -s ualr.edu 100 3**
PING ualr.edu: 100 data bytes
108 bytes from mbox.ualr.edu (144.167.10.38): icmp_seq=0. time=151. ms
108 bytes from mbox.ualr.edu (144.167.10.38): icmp_seq=1. time=146. ms
108 bytes from mbox.ualr.edu (144.167.10.38): icmp_seq=2. time=146. ms

——mbox.ualr.edu PING Statistics——
3 packets transmitted, 3 packets received, 0% packet loss
round-trip (ms) min/avg/max = 146/147/151

> **Online Resource**
>
> The UNIX command called man (short for manual) is used to view online manual pages explaining UNIX commands. To view a manual page, type the command **man** followed by the name of the UNIX command you're interested in learning more about. If your system scrolls through the manual page too fast to read, use the more command to display one screen at a time. For example: **man finger Imore**

Certain forms of the ping command can take down a server. Because of its potential destructiveness, Internet service providers sometimes hide the ping program so you can't easily find it. If you enter the ping command followed by a host name and your shell account responds with "command not found," **try /usr/etc/ping <hostname>**

THE NSLOOKUP COMMAND

Every host on the Internet is assigned a unique IP (Internet Protocol) address in addition to its domain name address. The *IP address* is a numerical address consisting of four numbers separated by periods (also referred to as *dotted decimal representation*). An IP address looks like *130.184.8.7* and is read as "130 dot 184 dot 8 dot 7." Domain Name Servers (DNS) are computers that have the job of taking a domain name (the address we humans can remember and prefer using) and resolving it to an IP address (the address computers understand and use).

When the DNS is working, you can contact other hosts on the Internet by using domain names like *ualvm.ua.edu*. If you can't connect to a host using its domain name, either you haven't designated the correct DNS in your software setup, or possibly the DNS isn't working. If the DNS isn't working, you might try using the host's IP address instead.

To determine which IP address a given host resolves to, use the nslookup command. For example, to find out what IP address *ualr.edu* resolves to, type **nslookup** at your system prompt, followed by the host's domain address, as shown in Figure 10–10.

If this service isn't available on your system, use the *SWITCH Internet Domain Name Service* by telneting to *nic.switch.cu*. At the *Login:* prompt enter **lookup**. Type a domain name, press ENTER, and SWITCH will return either the corresponding IP address or an error message if no information is available.

Figure 10–10: The nslookup command tells you which domain name server the local host uses

CRCINET 20> **nslookup ualr.edu**
Server: ptolemy-fddi1.concentric.net
Address: 199.3.12.175

Name: ualr.edu
Address: 144.167.10.38

THE ALIAS COMMAND

The alias command lets you make up nicknames for commands you frequently execute. For example, if you often finger the Earthquake Bulletin provided by the National Earthquake Information Service (NEIS) of the U.S. Geological Survey, you could set up a short nickname like "quake" to take the place of **finger quake@gldfs.cr.usgs.gov**.

Creating an Alias

At the shell prompt, type **alias [name [command]]**, where *name* is the nickname you want to give to the command, in this case "quake," and the command itself is **finger quake@gldfs.cr.usgs.gov**. The command is placed within single quotation marks, which tells the shell to treat the characters like the "@" sign literally. This is a good practice when creating aliases because certain punctuation characters have special meanings to the shell and you don't want the command misinterpreted. Now when you type the nickname **quake** at your system prompt, **finger quake@gldfs.cr.usgs.gov** will be executed.

Removing an Alias

If you want to remove an alias, use the unalias command. For example, to remove the "quake" alias, type **unalias quake** at the shell prompt.

Table 10–3: Useful aliases that make working in a shell easy	
Command	**Result**
alias whois 'whois -h rs.internic.net'	Enables you to type **whois <search string>** at the shell prompt, where **<search string>** is the domain name, IP number, or user name. This particular alias is set up to search the Internet Registry at InterNIC.
alias weather 'telnet 141.213.23.10 3000'	Connects you to the University of Michigan Weather Underground when you type **weather** and press ENTER.
alias dir 'ls -l'	Enables you to use the DOS dir command in place of the UNIX ls -l command to display a "long" listing of files.
alias del 'rm -i'	Enables you to use the DOS del command in place of the UNIX rm -i command, which asks your permission before removing a file.
alias type 'more'	Enables you to use the DOS type command in place of the UNIX more command, which displays data one screen full at a time. (Press the spacebar to page down.)

> **Online Resources**
>
> *What Is . . . Linux (a definition)* from whatis.com, one of the largest
> techno-speak encyclopedias on the Internet (or anywhere) *www.whatis.com*.
> You can listen to the author of Linux, Linus Torvalds, give his definitive
> pronunciation for Linux at *metalab.unc.edu/mdw/links/mm.html#sounds*.

Displaying Aliases

If you want to display all of the aliases on your system, type **alias** and press ENTER. Additional aliases that you might like to create are shown in Table 10–3.

Running Aliases Automatically

When you type any of the above aliases directly to the shell, they will last only as long as you are logged in. If you want the shell to remember your nicknames, you need to edit your shell's initialization file and create a file called *.aliases*. An *initialization file* is a file in which you store commands that you want to have run automatically each time you log into your shell account. The C shell initialization file we're concerned with here is called *.cshrc*.

First of all, if you don't already have a file called *.aliases*, create one that contains the following text:

    #finger NEIS earthquake bulletin
    alias quakes **finger quake@gldfs.cr.usgs.gov**

Note that in shell scripts, lines that begin with "#" are comments that are ignored by the shell. Next, add the following statement to the end of your *.cshrc* file if it isn't already part of that file:

    #Invoke aliases file
    Source $HOME≠ .aliases

> **Creating and Editing Text Files**
>
> You can use a simple UNIX text editor like Pico to create your *.aliases*
> file. At your system prompt, type **pico .aliases** and press ENTER. Now
> type the text just as it is presented above using the Pico text editor. When
> finished, press CTRL+X. When the system asks you whether you want
> to save, press **y** for Yes. The system will then ask you to confirm the file
> name is *.aliases*. Press ENTER to confirm.
>
> To edit your *.cshrc* (C-shell run Commands) file, type **pico .cshrc** at
> your system prompt and press ENTER. Now scroll down to the bottom
> of the file and add the following text:
>
> **#Invoke aliases file**
> **Source $HOME≠ .aliases**
>
> When finished, press CTRL+X. When the system asks you whether you
> want to save, press **y** for Yes. The system will then ask you to confirm
> the file name is *.cshrc*. Press ENTER to confirm.

INTRODUCTION TO LINUX

Linux (pronounced lin-nucks) is a UNIX-like operating system that is gaining considerable popularity worldwide. Originally developed by Linus Torvalds at the University of Helsinki in 1991, Linux is multi-user, multi-tasking, Internet ready, and free for everyone to use. Linux is an operating system much like Microsoft Windows and Macintosh are operating systems. Linux, however, behaves quite differently with its own set of tools, games, rules for saving files to your hard drive, and displaying pictures on your screen.

WHY SHOULD MY LIBRARY USE LINUX?

Libraries are in the business of managing information, and if your library manages lots of information, Linux offers powerful tools for helping you store, retrieve, manipulate, and share it across networks. All of the applications are free, including Apache, the most widely used Web server on the Net. There are other information organizing applications, such as the Swish-e search engine *sunsite.berkeley.edu/SWISH-E/* and ROADS Web-based database software *www.ilrt.bris.ac.uk/roads/*, that are free and run under Linux.

If stability is a high priority, Linux comes out way ahead of Windows. You won't see the familiar "blue screen of death" or experience the usual lockups common with Windows. Uptimes last longer and can be measured in months, not days or hours as with Windows PCs. This is not to say that you can expect Linux, or any other implementation of UNIX for that matter, to run trouble-and maintenance-free.

Linux does many things equal to or better than other operating systems, and some things not as well. Depending on your computing needs, it may or may not be a good replacement for your current operating system. At present, your favorite Windows programs, such as Office 2000, will not easily work in Linux. Corel WordPerfect 8 will, however. Kids won't have any reliable way of viewing their favorite Windows multimedia encyclopedia using Linux. Medium- to small-sized libraries may find the high-performance, multi-user nature of Linux overkill for their operations. While Linux has it's own word processing, spreadsheet, image editing, and database applications, it also requires that you understand and apply a certain amount of UNIX-style system administration. For many librarians, it would be a formidable challenge to even install and configure Linux.

Online Resources

What is...Linux (a definition) from whatis.com, one of the largest techno-speak encyclopedias on the Internet (or anywhere).

    You can listen to the author of Linux, Linus Torvalds, give his definitive pronounciation for Linux at *metalab.unc.edu/mdw/links/mm.html#sounds.*

The term *Linux* refers to the core or kernel of the operating system and also to the operating system itself. A *kernel* only handles basic tasks such as memory allocation, user access, security, file management, and so forth. If you are new to Linux, it's not likely that the kernel itself will be of much use to you. Instead, get the entire Linux system, called a distribution.

A *Linux distribution* combines the Linux kernel with thousands of programs and software support packages. There are a variety of Linux distributions from which to choose. Each distribution offers its own special features including desktop interfaces, word processors, spreadsheets, image editors, browsers, and more.

WHERE TO GET LINUX

There are many distributions of the Linux software available free via anonymous FTPs. You can find various distributions in UNC's MetaLab FTP archives *ftp://metalab.unc. edu/pub/Linux/distributions/*.

While the core, the basic utilities, and much of the Linux software is free, extra, value-added features do have costs. Added features that come with commercial distributions include product support, CD-ROMs, and books. Nowadays, it's possible to walk into a bookstore and find a Linux book that includes a CD-ROM for under $30. Some of the mainstream distributions of Linux include:

- Red Hat *www.redhat.com/* (the most popular Linux distribution)
- Slackware *www.slackware.com/* (free and a favorite of hackers)
- Debian GNU/Linux *www.debian.org/* (you can either buy a cheap CD-ROM set, or download it for free)
- SuSE *www.suse.com/* (originating from Germany and popular in Europe)
- TurboLinux *www.turbolinux.com/* (popular in Asia because it makes it possible to run Linux in Japanese and Chinese)
- Caldera OpenLinux *www.tcu-inc.com/* (aimed towards businesses with an easy installation feature)

You can download these distributions from each company's Website. Go to the home page listed above and look for the appropriate download link. Many of the Websites list CD-ROMs and books that are available. Distributors like Linux Systems Labs *www.lsl.com/* in Chesterfield, Michigan, are a central clearing houses for RedHat, Mandrake, Debian, Slackware, Caldera and SuSE distributions of Linux.

There are various other Linux distributions. DragonLinux *www.dragonlinux.nu/* is based on a file system called UMSDOS. The UMSDOS File system enables DragonLinux to reside on your DOS partition, which means you don't have to re-partition your hard drive to install Linux. DragonLinux is a small distribution of Linux, only 150MB installed. Armed Linux *www.armed.net/* and WinLinux 2000 *www.winlinux.net/* also install directly to your Windows PC without the need to re-partition your hard drive. For a list of well-known and not-so-well-known distributions of Linux, go to *kernelnotes.org/dist-index.html*.

Online Resources

ASL Workstations, Inc. *www.aslab.com/* sells pre-installed Linux workstations and servers. AmNet Computers LLC *amnet-comp.com/* builds Red Hat systems utilizing Intel Pentium and AMD Athlon processors. Both companies offer systems starting in the $1,500 range. The Computer Underground, Inc. *www.tcu-inc.com/* sells pre-installed Linux computers for under $1,000. For a complete list of companies selling Linux computers, see *www.linuxhq.com/vendors/systems.html.* Companies are organized geographically.

Use GLUE (Groups of Linux Users Everywhere) *www.ssc.com/glue/groups/* to find a Linux-savvy friend to help you with installing and running Linux. If there's no one in our area, try starting your own Linux User Group (LUG) *www.ntlug.org/archive/lug-howto/lug.html* with advice from Kendall Grant Clark.

CAN LINUX RUN ON MY SYSTEM?

Linux has been ported to a variety of platforms, including Intel and compatibles, Alphas, Sun Sparcs, DEC, PowerPC chips, and others. It can run on a desktop or a laptop. For Intel-based PCs, the basic requirements are a 386 processor with 200MB of hard disk space and 4MB of RAM. If you are going to use Linux on a server, you should have at least 32MB of RAM, a 486 processor, and as much hard drive real estate as you can afford.

It is possible to run Linux and Windows on the same computer by partitioning the hard drive. Partitioning is a destructive process, so proceed with caution. It's risky re-partitioning an existing hard drive while hoping to preserve the information that is already stored on it.

Plan on re-installing Windows after you install Linux and back up all of your important data before you start. Another solution is to install a second hard drive in your computer to run Linux alongside Windows or Mac OS. If you plan to replace your current operating system with Linux (as opposed to running it alongside Linux), then you need not consider re-partitioning or adding a second hard drive.

Chances are, Linux can run on your motherboard/CPU, but there may be problems getting it to run with your peripherals (printers, modems, network adapter cards, scanners, Jaz drives, etc.). To research hardware compatibility before you get started, go to Linux Online at *www.linux.org/* and click on the button labeled "Hardware." This link connects you to details about systems with Linux pre-installed, companies offering Linux drivers for their products, and tips for installing Linux on laptop computers.

INSTALLING LINUX

Installing Linux can be frustrating if you are a novice. If you fall into this category, consider enlisting the help of someone with a background in UNIX. If you take on the task yourself, you can go online for support. The Linux Documentation Project at *www.linuxdoc.org/* presents a generic set of instructions for installing Linux. If you succeed in getting your system running, your journey has just begun. When you delve into

---

Online Resources

When you need help, try *Linux Frequently Asked Questions with Answers* maintained by Robert Kiesling at *www.linuxdoc.org/FAQ/Linux-FAQ.html*. Another good source is the Linux Documentation Project (LDP) *www.linuxdoc.org/*. LDP is filled with reliable documentation for the Linux operating system. Go there to find HOWTOs, FAQs, and current and back issues of the *Linux Gazette*, which are filled with tips and tricks.

---

the more complex tasks of running Linux—installing new software, recompiling the kernel, and so forth—having background knowledge in UNIX is going to be a necessity.

DOES LINUX HAVE A GRAPHIC MODE?

Linux has a character-based mode that looks a lot like MS-DOS, and a graphical mode called the X Window System (also called X11, or simply X). Most distributions of Linux automatically install the X Window System along with drivers that support your video card. Once you correctly install Linux, you begin an X session by using the startx command at the shell or command prompt.

READY TO GET STARTED?

If you want to try your hand at installing and running Linux, and you are a first-timer, here are some closing thoughts to help you get started.

The first time I installed Linux was back in 1992. I downloaded a free copy and I had a software engineer, hardware specialist, and UNIX guru all huddle around my PC for a couple of hours to help with the installation. Eight years later I tried it again. This time I used a commercial distribution of Linux that consisted of a CD-ROM and "how-to" book (*How to Use Linux* by Bill Ball ISBN 0–672–31545–9). This particular distribution was Caldera OpenLinux Version 1.3. The CD and book cost only $24.99. I didn't have anyone with me this time, but someone who had gone through many installations of Linux was just a phone call away. In addition, I bought a new computer, the sole purpose of which was to run Linux. I made sure all of its hardware was compatible with Linux because I wanted everything going in my favor!

My choice of distributions came down to Red Hat and Caldera. I decided either one would work fine or be a total disaster, depending on the hardware in my computer and what settings I chose. Both offered their own advantages and supported a certain amount of hardware detection during installation. Automatic hardware detection is advantageous because defining the hardware components in your PC—a necessary step during installation—can be very challenging. When possible, use the autoprobe feature. If you need to configure a component manually, look in the manuals for the information you need. Configuring your video card and monitor correctly are very important. It's not too difficult to recover from an incorrect configuration on other hardware, but you might have serious problems trying to recover from bad settings on your video display devices.

I hoped to avoid unnecessary installation problems by purchasing a new machine. When I wrote the specification for the new computer, I consulted with the vendor telling them up front that all components had to be compatible with Linux. Linux supports

System Administration

Installing and configuring Linux is only part of the equation. After you set up your service, you have to keep it running. Invest in a Linux system administration manual and read about what is involved. As a bare minimum, you should check log files for errors and unusual events. Depending on what services you run, system administration can become a full-time job.

If you open up your server to network access, you open yourself up to security risks. It is essential that you guard yourself against various types of attacks. A useful Linux tool for helping in this matter is called tcpd. It works like this. When a host requests to use one of your Internet services, for example, FTP, tcpd logs the request and checks to see if the requesting host has permission to use that service. If the host does have permission, it executes the server program.

There are two files, *hosts.allow* and *hosts.deny*, that help you implement access control. Both of these text files are located in the */etc* directory and you use an editor, such as Pico, to change their contents. In the example that follows, I explain how to deny access to everyone by default and allow only those hosts with authorization to access your system. The *hosts.deny* file describes the names of the hosts that are not allowed to use the local INET services. In the *hosts.deny* file, add the line **ALL:ALL**. "ALL" is a universal wildcard. It denies all services to all hosts, unless they are permitted access in the *hosts.allow* file.

The *hosts.allow* file describes the names of the hosts that are allowed to use the local INET services. Each entry lists three items:

1. The process name, for example, *in.telnetd* for telnet services and *in.ftpd* for FTP services
2. The host's address, for example *145.209.125.5*
3. A comment that helps the system administrator remember the meaning of the file

If you have a PC in your library with the IP address *145.209.125.5* assigned to it and you want to be able to telnet from this PC to your Linux box and transfer files using FTP, here are the entries that should be inserted in the *hosts.allow* file:

```
in.telnetd :145.209.125.5      #computer in the media lab
in.ftpd : 145.209.125.5        #computer in the media lab
```

When you want to give another computer on the network permission to access the Linux box, you add another line with that PC's IP address.

most hardware, but not all. The hardware components that have been around for a while have a better chance of being supported. Brand new, cutting edge components, especially sound cards and video cards, tend to create problems. To find out whether a certain device is compatible with Caldera, go to *www.caldera.com.* Even though I gave the vendor a specific list of hardware components, Linux did not support the video card that came with the computer. The card I requested was too old and no longer available. Instead of asking me for another option, the vendor chose one and didn't inform me of the change. The one they chose wasn't on the compatibility list, so my first attempt at installing Linux came to a halt when I tried to install the video card.

LINUX IN SUMMARY

The reasons for and against using Linux in your library are many. On the one hand, Linux is inexpensive to install and can run on numerous platforms, from Apple Macintoshes to Intel-based PCs and high-end Sun servers. For some purposes, it runs more efficiently than other operating systems, which can translate into using less-expensive hardware. In addition, Linux is based on open standards and so it is vendor-neutral. On the other hand, Linux's ongoing administrative costs are going to be pretty much the same as those of any other UNIX operating systems. If you introduce Linux into your library, you have to provide some additional training to anyone who is going to use it, including those who are already well versed in UNIX or Windows NT. Hardware compatibility, especially for printers, has posed serious problems for those running Linux on their PCs. Except for WordPerfect Office, it's difficult to find popular business and personal applications that run on Linux.

If your PC does everything you need it to, then switching to Linux makes little sense. If you want to use Linux to run a Web server because you are tired of rebooting and reinstalling drivers and applications on your Windows system, then perhaps it is worth a try. Remember that getting it to work properly takes some work and may even require that you replace hardware. You can't install Linux on just any PC and expect it to work without a glitch. To be on the safe side, back up all of your important data on removable media before beginning the Linux installation.

Lynx for Hard-Core Searching

Many Internet users still access the Web using a dial-up connection to a UNIX or VAX/ VMS shell account. Accessing the Web in this manner requires that you use a Web browser running on your service provider's computer or that you telnet to a remote computer and use a public site. The easiest way to determine whether your Internet service provider is running a Web client is to call them up and ask. You might also want to try entering the command **Lynx** at your service provider's system prompt and see whether that runs a program called Lynx.

TELNETING TO A PUBLIC SITE

If your service provider doesn't offer a Web browser, try telneting to the University of Kansas by typing **telnet lynx.cc.ukans.edu** at your system prompt and then pressing ENTER. Login with the word **lynx.** When prompted for a password, press the ENTER key. Next, enter the terminal type, press ENTER (vt100 is the default terminal type). This site uses a text-based browser called Lynx as shown in Figure 11–1. Note that using the Go command (by pressing the **G** key) to go to a random URL is disallowed at this site.

Online Resource
Help for beginning Lynx users can be found in a document maintained by Philip Webb at *www.chass.utoronto.ca/~purslow/lhfb.html.* This site also features links to information on Lynx for the blind and visually impaired.

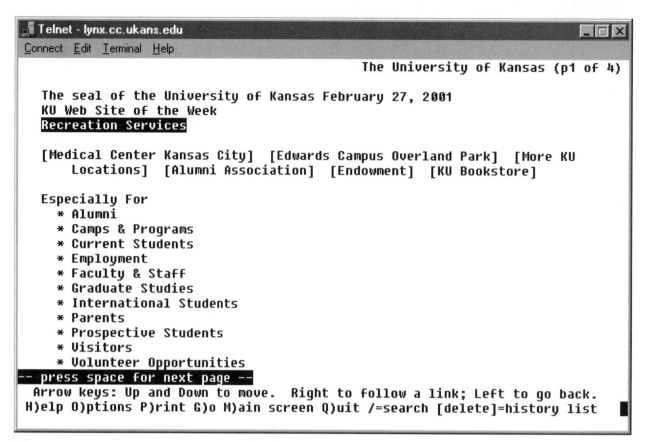

Figure 11–1: A view of Lynx at the University of Kansas

Online Resource

The Lynx Users Guide Versions 2.3 is made available online by Academic Computing Services at the University of Kansas. You can find it at *www.cc.ukans.edu/lynx_hlep/Lynx_users_guide.html*.

LEARNING ALL ABOUT LYNX

Lynx uses boldfaced text to show you which words and phrases link to other documents on the Web. The single word or phrase that is shown in reverse highlighting or normal text (depending on the foreground and background colors of your terminal) is the link that is currently selected and, when you press ENTER, that link is activated. Use the procedures described in this section when working with Lynx.

- Press the down arrow to move to the next link.
- Press the up arrow to move to the previous link.
- Press the right arrow or ENTER key to jump to the highlighted topic.
- Press the left arrow to return to the previous link.
- Press the "+" key to scroll down and the "-" key to scroll up.
- To page down, press the spacebar.

Online Resource

The Lynx FAQ at *www.savyon.com/ellen/lynx.htm* offers basic information on how to get started using Lynx.

- Press the "=" key to display information on the current document and the current link, if you've selected one.
- For complete information on keystrokes, press **H** for Help.
- To exit Lynx, type **q** and press ENTER. When asked whether you want to quit, enter **y** for yes or **n** for no. To quit without verification, enter an uppercase **Q.**

SEARCHING THE WEB USING LYNX

The following search is based on a true situation and demonstrates the basic skills involved in utilizing a text-based browser. To begin with, I already had set up one important bookmark establishing a quick link to the Lycos search engine. Using the bookmark feature is an essential part of effectively searching the Web. Bookmarks help you quickly zero in on resources that you know handle specific tasks well, such as searching the Web for information. I'll go through the procedure for setting up bookmarks before proceeding on to the search itself.

SETTING UP BOOKMARKS IN LYNX

Bookmarks are a feature of Web browsers that enable you to "flag" interesting sites and then add their addresses to your own customized bookmark list. To connect to one of your bookmarked sites, simply select the bookmark you're interested in and press ENTER.

To use the bookmark feature, begin by setting up a bookmark file on your local host. To do this, connect with a Lynx client and press **o**. This enables you to set the options where you tell Lynx the name of the file in which you want to store your bookmarks. The default bookmark file name is usually something like *lynx_bookmarks.html*. If you want to change the default, press **b** and enter the file name of your choice. Press **>** to save. To leave the Options menu, press the left-arrow key or **r** for return.

BOOKMARKING THE LYCOS SEARCH ENGINE

Next, set up a bookmark for the Lycos home page or any other search engine of your choice. The site address for Lycos is *http://www.lycos.com/*. To get to Lycos from your current Web page, press **g** to bring up the *URL to open:* prompt, which appears in the lower left portion of the screen as shown in Figure 11–2. At the blinking cursor, type in the URL and press ENTER. If your browser isn't running, you can get to the Lycos site by entering **lynx http://www.lycos.com/** at the system prompt.

Once you connect to Lycos, add it to your bookmark list by pressing **a.** Depending on which version of Lynx you are running, you may get a message something like this: "Do you wish to save this document in your current bookmark file? (y/n)." Alternatively, you may see a list of options, one of which will be "Save D)ocument to book-

```
                                                    Online Documentation

   Caldera Systems, Inc. [Website Resources] Go!
   ───────────────────────────────────────────────────────────

Online Documentation

     * Looking Glass Desktop Interface User's Guide
     * Linux Installation and Getting Started Guide
     * The Linux Kernel
     * Network Administrators Guide
     * Programmer's Guide
     * System Administrator's Guide
     * CRiSPLiTE Editor User's Guide
     * Linux HOW-TO documents
     * What's installed on this computer?
       A web server must be running on this computer for this link to
       work.




URL to open: http://www.lycos.com
  Arrow keys: Up and Down to move. Right to follow a link; Left to go back.
 H)elp O)ptions P)rint G)o M)ain screen Q)uit /=search [delete]=history list
```

Figure 11–2: After pressing g **for** go, **Lynx users can type in the URL they want to visit**

mark file," in which case you'd enter **d.** You then press **v** to view the bookmark list as shown in Figure 11–3.

CONDUCTING A SIMPLE SEARCH IN EIGHT STEPS

This is the scenario for search using Lynx: A student requests information on the Ebola virus. You use Lynx because images aren't critical in this search and text-only browsers are faster than browsers that are also trying to download graphics.

Follow these eight steps to find resources about the Ebola virus using Lynx:

1. Start Lynx and then press **v** to view the bookmarks file.
2. Highlight the Lycos search engine link and press ENTER. This brings you to the Lycos search screen illustrated in Figure 11–4.

Online Resources
Programmers who develop Lynx maintain a Website at *lynx.browser.org/*. You can communicate with the developers via the lynx-dev listserv at *lynx-dev@sig.net*. To access the message archive for lynx-dev, point your browser to *www.flora.org/lynx-dev/*. Documents date back to 1994.

```
                                                             Bookmark file

You can delete links using the remove bookmark command. It is usually
the 'R' key but may have been remapped by you or your system
administrator.
This file may also be edited with a standard text editor. Outdated or
invalid links may be removed by simply deleting the line the link
appears on in this file. Please refer to the Lynx documentation or
help files for the HTML link syntax.

   1. http://www.lycos.com/
```

```
Commands: Use arrow keys to move, '?' for help, 'q' to quit, '<-' to go back.
  Arrow keys: Up and Down to move. Right to follow a link; Left to go back.
 H)elp O)ptions P)rint G)o M)ain screen Q)uit /=search [delete]=history list
```

Figure 11–3: Here there is a single entry for the Lycos search form displayed while viewing a bookmark file in Lynx

3. Press the down-arrow key until the "Query:" line is highlighted. Enter the search term **ebola**. Press the down-arrow key one more time to highlight the word "Search." Press ENTER to start the search. The resulting list of hits included titles including "Occurrences of Ebola," and "Ebola Outbreaks." Each entry includes an abstract.

4. Move down through the list using the down-arrow key. When you came to an abstract that looks interesting, press ENTER and go to that link. If, upon further investigation, it isn't relevant, press the left-arrow key to bring you right back to the original list of hits.

5. When you choose a document and after the page loads, press the forward slash (/). This brings up a prompt for entering a search string in the lower left corner of the screen as illustrated in Figure 11–5.

6. Type the word **ebola** and press ENTER. This takes you to a spot in the Web page where links to the ebola virus are located.

7. Select the link you are interested in, link to it, and when you connect, press **p.** This gives you three options for saving the document:
   i.   Save to local file
   ii. Mail the file
   iii. Print to the screen
   If you print the document to the screen, turn on the screen capture feature that comes with your communications program (Procomm Plus, for example). Lynx asks you to confirm that you want to print. Press **y** for yes and then press

```
                                                            Lycos (p1 of 6)

REFRESH(300 sec): http://www.lycos.com/

                            Lycos My Lycos | Site Map
         Meet and Flirt With Fun People [LINK] Free Dido Download and Videos

                                Search for:
              ebola█_____    Search    Advanced Search
                            Parental Controls

                                Feb. 27, 2001

                                Free Cell Phone
                                Free Cell Phone
           CONNECT:    Browser  Calendar  Chat  Clubs  Dating  Email
       Instant Messaging  Message Boards  Photos  Videos  WAP/SMS  MORE »
       FIND:    Downloads  FTP  Jobs  LycosTV  Maps  MP3  Multimedia  News
         People  Stocks  Top 50  Translate  Weather  Websites  Yellow Pages
                                MORE »
           SHOP:    Auctions  Books  Cell Phones  Classifieds  Services
      (Text entry field) Enter text.  Use UP or DOWN arrows or tab to move off.
              Enter text into the field by typing on the keyboard
        Ctrl-U to delete all text in field, [Backspace] to delete a character
```

Figure 11–4: The Lycos home page

ENTER. The document's pages scroll by, all of which are captured in a file on your hard drive.

Many patrons now have their own e-mail addresses, so this may also be an effective means of delivering the file. When you choose "Mail the file," you are prompted to enter a valid e-mail address. Enter the address and then press ENTER.

8. The last step is viewing the captured file in a word processor and printing it out for the patron. You also have the option of saving the file to a floppy disk and giving it to the patron to take home in digital format.

AN ALTERNATIVE TO LYNX CALLED CERN'S WWW

If the Web server at *lynx.cc.ukans.edu* is busy, try telneting to *telnet.w3.org*. This connects you to a public Website at CERN. CERN runs a slightly different text-based browser called www. (Note that the "www" refers to a piece of software, not the World Wide Web itself.)

Unlike Lynx, where you move a cursor to the desired link, you find information on a www browser by following references. *References* are numbers enclosed in brackets next to words or phrases. Numbers are placed in square brackets next to a word or group of words signifying that a link exists between that word or group of words and another document. To follow the link, you type the appropriate number and then press ENTER.

```
                                               Outbreak: Ebola Update (p1 of 4)

Medical Sciences Bulletin

█Medical Sciences Bulletin Contents█
   ─────────────────────────────────────────────────────────────────────

                          Outbreak: Ebola Update

   Reprinted from the August 1995 issue of Medical Sciences Bulletin ,
   published by Pharmaceutical Information Associates, Ltd.
   ─────────────────────────────────────────────────────────────────────


   In April and May of this year, a large outbreak of Ebola viral
   hemorrhagic fever occurred in Kikwit, Zaire, a city located 240 miles
   east of Kinshasa. The outbreak came to the attention of authorities
   when a laboratory technician in Kikwit was hospitalized with fever and
   bloody diarrhea, and 10 days later medical personnel at the hospital
   where he was treated also showed similar symptoms. One of these
   patients was transferred to a hospital in another city, and a similar
   outbreak occurred there among caregivers. Blood samples from 14
█Enter a whereis query:█ebola█
 Arrow keys: Up and Down to move. Right to follow a link; Left to go back.
 H)elp O)ptions P)rint G)o M)ain screen Q)uit /=search [delete]=history list
```

Figure 11–5: When you press the "/" key in Lynx, you are given a prompt for entering a search string

You can display the list of available www commands by entering the **help** command. The following list shows you the most common commands used with the www browser program.

> ENTER key moves down one page within the document.
> Typing **bottom** and pressing ENTER takes you to the last page of the document.
> Typing **top** and pressing ENTER takes you to the first page of the document.
> Typing **up** moves up one page within the document.
> Typing **list** lists the references (hyperlinks) found in the document.
> Typing **z** and pressing ENTER interrupts a request.
> **Go <address>** takes you to another Web page where "<address>" is the URL, for example: **go http://www.lycos.com/**
> Typing **quit** closes the www program.

Online Resource
Lynx Links Digest reviews Internet resources and services that are Lynx friendly. You can read back issues and subscribe at *Lynx Links Digest members.tripod.com/~lynxlinks/.*

Resource Discovery on the Web

There are basically two ways to find information on the Web: searching and browsing. When you *search*, you use the brute force of computers to dig up information. Computer applications designed to do this sort of work on the Web are called *search engines*.

Browsing requires that you do a lot of the work yourself. You can find answers to specific questions by browsing, but many times it's more accidental than planned. The best places to go for this kind of information hunting are subject trees or directories. A *subject tree* is a list of subject terms arranged hierarchically or alphabetically. In a hierarchical listing, subjects start out very broad in scope (at the root of the tree) and as you branch out the terms become narrower.

It used to be enough to know which search engines were best at indexing the Web and to know how to express what it is you wanted to find in a language the search engines could understand. Today you must also know how to tap into the invisible Web. The *invisible Web* is all of the information that is invisible to basic search engines.

In this chapter, I introduce the invisible Web and explain how to find resources that are invisible. In addition, I discuss using directories and search engines to find information on the Web. In Chapter 20, I describe search and indexing systems that are free of charge and that you can run from your own PC or server.

SEARCH STRATEGIES

It is important to understand at the outset that information accessible on the Internet is chaotic. Conduct a search on the phrase "herbal medicine" in *britannica.com*. Do the same search in the archives at *www.newsweek.com*. Compare these searches to a search for books on the subject of herbal medicine at *www.amazon.com*. Repeat your search

---

Online Resource

Econtent www.ecmag.net/ (formerly *DATABASE*) and *online www.online inc.com/onlinemag/* magazines are written for serious searchers and other information technology professionals. They provide how-to information on using database systems, reviews, and product comparisons. Their coverage includes online databases, CD-ROMs, and Internet resources. When you visit their Websites, you find selected full-text articles and news from each issue of the magazine.

---

on CARL's document delivery database *UnCover* at *uncweb.carl.org* or a specialized search engine like EBSCOhost Health Source Plus. Lastly, run this search on a popular Internet search engine, such as Lycos or AltaVista. What becomes apparent is that there is not one universe of information, but rather several unrelated universes of information existing online. Each service is designed to reach a different audience and contains a different set of resources relating to herbal medicine.

No single resource is 100 percent complete, so it is essential to include several resources in your search strategy. When you conduct a search on the Web, utilize two or more search engines and subject directories. Understand what the invisible Web has to offer. The invisible Web is discussed in greater detail later in this chapter. Avoid using meta search engines that search several databases simultaneously because you lose the ability to use the powerful search features individual search engines offer.

To learn more about search engines and strategies for searching on the Internet, refer to Greg R. Notess's home page Search Engine Showdown: The User's Guide to Web Searching at *www.notess.com/search/*. Notess, a reference librarian at Montana State University, provides Internet access to excellent training materials free of charge. Explore his site to learn more about search engine features and capabilities. I strongly encourage you to read his two articles from *Online*: "Internet Search Techniques and Strategies" and "More Internet Search Strategies." Both are available online on his Website under the heading "Learning|Strategies."

IS IT A SEARCH ENGINE OR A DIRECTORY?

The distinction between search engines and directories has blurred since the last edition of this book. In the early days of the Web, directories were collections of links organized alphabetically or by subject. As these sites grew, they added search engines. For example, Yahoo! offered searching, but it was limited to the contents of Yahoo!'s own database. Yahoo!'s database was created by humans who gathered entries and cataloged them. Adding a search engine made it a searchable directory.

Today, Yahoo! incorporates the AltaVista search engine and database into its site. Now when you run a keyword search on Yahoo!, you search Yahoo!'s database and then Yahoo! forwards your query to AltaVista. AltaVista searches its database and sends the search results back to Yahoo!. You are then presented with AltaVista's search results along with Yahoo!'s advertisements at the top of the page.

Many systems, such as ERIC *ericir.syrr.edu/Eric/*, only index their own site and provide a search engine that searches their own materials. Some sites, such as The Argus

Clearinghouse *www.clearinghouse.net/*, not only give you the option of searching their own materials, but also the rest of the Web using a major Web-based search engine.

The WWW Virtual Library *www.vlib.org/*, discussed later in this chapter, allows you to search a system of distributed directories. The WWW Virtual Library uses a search engine called ht://Dig, which isn't as powerful as Internet-wide systems like AltaVista; instead, ht://Dig indexes information on intranets and company-and campus-wide systems.

THE INVISIBLE WEB

The part of the Web that is invisible to the major Web-based search engines has been nicknamed the invisible Web. The invisible Web consists of information stored in databases. Spiders, robots that search the Internet for Web pages, generally can't access database information. For example, when a spider comes across The Library of Congress, it indexes the home page *lcweb.loc.gov/index.html*, but it doesn't index the approximately 12 million database records found in the Library of Congress Online Catalog. When you want to learn about a company's products or services, you find the *Thomas Register of American Manufacturers'* online by searching with AltaVista, but you can't access the 156,914 companies found in the Thomas Register database unless you go to the site itself and register to use their search system. Other information found in the invisible Web includes discussion list message archives, product reviews, auction databases like eBay, medical databases like Cancernet, and much more.

HOW DO YOU FIND RESOURCES THAT ARE INVISIBLE?

You find resources on the invisible Web by browsing directories that list invisible resources. Some of these *invisible resource* directories have search engines, but they search only their own materials. On the CD-ROM accompanying this book, I offer descriptions with links to some popular databases under the headings "Databases" and "Reference." Recommended tools for finding other invisible Web resources are listed in Table 12–1. In addition, be sure to check out Gary Price's "Direct Search" site at *gwis2.circ.gwu.edu/~gprice/direct.htm*. Price, a librarian at George Washington University, has put together this up-to-date list of hundreds of specialized databases.

Online Resources

Chris Sherman, an About.com guide specializing in Web searching, hosts a forum that focuses on search engines. To learn more about The Web Search Forum, read their FAQ at *websearch.about.com/internet/websearch/mbbfaq.htm*. Participation requires that you register and become a member of About.com. Membership gives you access to other tools and services including free e-mail and personal Web page.

The I-Search Digest is a discussion list moderated by Marshall D. Simmonds that focuses on Internet directories and searching. To browse their archives, go to *www.audettemedia.com/i-search/archives/*.

Table 12–1: Invisible Web resources	
Name	Address
AlphaSearch	*www.calvin.edu/library/searreso/internet/as/*
Beaucoup	*www.beaucoup.com*
The BigHub.com	*www.thebighub.com/*
Direct Search	*gwis.circ.gwu.edu/gprice/direct.htm*
Finder Seeker	*www.finderseeker.com*
Infomine's Multiple Database Search	*infomine.ucr.edu/search.phtml*
InvisibleWeb.com	*www.invisibleweb.com*
The Invisible Web Catalog	*dir.lycos.com/Reference/Searchable_Databases/*
InvisibleWeb.com	*www.invisibleweb.com/*
Little-Red-Schoolhouse Library	*www.westmark.pvt.k12.ca.us/LRCweb/specialtysearch.html*
Search.com	*Search.cnet.com/*
SearchPower.com	*www.searchpower.com*
Virtual Search Engines	*www.virtualfreesites.com/*
WebData.com	*www.webdata.com/webdata.htm*

LINK ROT AND DEAD LINKS

Before I explain the details of browsing and searching, consider these helpful pointers on solving a problem known as dead links and link rot. *Dead links* are addresses for resources that are out of date and no longer valid. This happens when a Web page gets deleted or moves to a new address. In the case of Planet Earth Home Pages—a reference link introduced in the previous edition of this book—the site was terminated by the Defense Department because it was "no longer in compliance." *Link rot* is another name for links that die or move to a new address.

In Chapter 18, for example, I point you to an Internet-Draft called *Specification of Uniform Resource Characteristics* written by Michael Mealling and tell you that it is located on the Web at *www.acl.lanl.gov/URI/urc_draft.txt*. If the document is no longer at that address when you go to look for it, the address has become a dead link.

Although the *Neal-Schuman Complete Internet Companion for Librarians* is primarily a book of concepts and techniques, there are numerous instances where I provide lists of resource addresses or tell you to go to a specific site to download a file. Until URLs (Uniform Resource Locators—the addressing system used on the Web) are replaced by something more effective, it is important to separate in your mind the *names* of these resources and files from their *locations*. This may help you get around the problem of dead links being dead ends.

For example, the Internet-Draft introduced earlier has as its URL *www.acl.lanl.gov/ URI/urc_draft.txt*. If this ends up being a dead link when you go to look for it, take the file name *urc_draft.txt*, which is the last string of text in the pathname, and search for that file name using one of the following search tools:

- Use Archie for files stored on FTP servers. Archie is explained in detail in Chapter 15. If you have access to the Web, use Fast FTP Search v4.0 at *ftpsearch.lycos.com/?form=medium* or search with Nexor's ArchiePlex at *archie.emnet.co.uk/*.

Online Resource

Online tutorials can help you sharpen your information hunting skills. *Finding Information on the Internet: A Tutorial* from the Teaching Library at University of California, Berkeley *www.lib.berkeley.edu/TeachingLib/ Guides/Internet/FindInfo.html*, offers beginning, intermediate, and advanced lessons in finding Internet resources.

- Use a Web search engine for files stored on Web servers. Lycos at *lycospro.lycos .com/* and AltaVista *www.altavista.com/* are good choices.

A second technique that may help you resolve dead links is shortening the pathname. Begin at the end of the URL and delete the characters going to the left until you arrive at the first slash. Now enter this address and see whether it connects you to a source. In the preceding example, you would remove *urc_draft.txt* and end up with *www.acl.lanl.gov/URI/*. If the shortened URL connects you to a page, look for a link that may lead you down a new path to the *urc_draft.txt* file.

BROWSING SUBJECT TREES

In this section, I introduce two of the more comprehensive subject trees on the Net: Yahoo! and The WWW Virtual Library. Both of these services can be accessed with either text-based browsers like Lynx or graphical browsers such as Netscape Navigator or Microsoft Internet Explorer.

YAHOO!

To connect to Yahoo!, point your Web browser to *www.yahoo.com*. The opening screen shown in Figure 12–1 is the "root" of the subject tree. Here you find 14 broad subject headings listed in alphabetical order ranging from Arts and Business to Social Science and Society. Find a topic that interests you, point-and-click (or, if you're using Lynx, use the up- and down-arrow keys and then press ENTER) and you link to another Web page with several subject headings, much narrower in scope. Select one of these and continue pointing-and-clicking (or pushing arrow keys—whichever the case may be), working your way down through the categories until you come to a document. Presently, Yahoo!'s directory links to more than half a million sites divided into more than 25,000 subject categories.

When to Use Yahoo!

If you are offering Web access in your library and are limited in how much support you can offer, Yahoo! is a great place to start novice Web users. (Computers dedicated to children can have their home page set to Yahooligans!—a version of Yahoo! designed just for kids—at site *www.yahooligans.com/*.) A short, personal introduction to browsing the Web can include:
- Introducing Yahoo! by saying, "If you don't have any particular place you want to go on the Internet, Yahoo! is a great place to browse just to see what's out there."

Auctions

Messenger

Check Email

What's New

Personalize

Help

My Yahoo!
create your own

Get the Y! Stock Market Toolbar!
••• click here

Yahoo! Mail
free email for life

[Search] advanced search

Y! Auctions - millions of items - unwanted gifts, autos, PlayStation 2, PDAs, digital cameras, coins, stamps

Shop Auctions · Classifieds · PayDirect · Shopping · **Travel** · Yellow Pgs · Maps **Media** **Finance/Quotes** · News · Sports · Weather
Connect Chat · Clubs · Experts · GeoCities · Greetings · Invites · **Mail** · Members · Messenger · Mobile · Personals · People Search
Personal Addr Book · Briefcase · Calendar · **My Yahoo!** · Photos **Fun** Games · Kids · **Movies** · Music · Radio · **TV** **more...**

Yahoo! Shopping   Thousands of stores. Millions of products.

Departments	Stores	Features
· Apparel	· Electronics	· Kodak	· Post Holiday Sale
· Beauty	· Music	· eToys	· ShoppingVision
· Books	· Sports	· RitzCamera	· Yahoo! Gift Card
· Computers	· Super Value	· Costco	· Shop Assistant
· DVD/Video	· Toys	· More Stores...	· More Features

ValueVisionTV - Watch & Buy on Yahoo! ShoppingVision

Arts & Humanities
Literature, Photography...

News & Media
Full Coverage, Newspapers, TV...

Business & Economy
B2B, Finance, Shopping, Jobs...

Recreation & Sports
Sports, Travel, Autos, Outdoors...

Computers & Internet
Internet, WWW, Software, Games...

Reference
Libraries, Dictionaries, Quotations...

Education
College and University, K-12...

Regional
Countries, Regions, US States...

Entertainment
Cool Links, Movies, Humor, Music...

Science
Animals, Astronomy, Engineering...

Government
Elections, Military, Law, Taxes...

Social Science
Archaeology, Economics, Languages...

Health
Medicine, Diseases, Drugs, Fitness...

Society & Culture
People, Environment, Religion...

In the News
· Bush names campaign aides to senior White House posts
· Arab ministers back right to return
· Calif. utilities to raise rates
· Report: Children's mental health 'crisis' in U.S.
more...

Marketplace
· Bid on 'Cast Away' memorabilia
· Yahoo! PayDirect - send and receive money online
· Looking for a car? job? house?
· Y! Travel - buy tickets, check arrival times

Broadcast Events
· 7pm ET : Duke vs. Florida St.
· 8pm : Magic vs. Knicks
· 8:30pm : Stanford vs. Arizona St.
· 9pm : Sharks vs. Avalanche
more...

Inside Yahoo!
· Yahoo! Radio - tune in to your favorite station
· Y! Photos - post your holiday pics online
· TV Listings - what's on tonight

Local Yahoo!s
Europe : Denmark - France - Germany - Italy - Norway - Spain - Sweden - UK & Ireland
Asia Pacific : Asia - Australia & NZ - China - HK - India - Japan - Korea - Singapore - Taiwan
Americas : Argentina - Brazil - Canada - Chinese - Mexico - Spanish
U.S. Cities : Atlanta - Boston - Chicago - Dallas/FW - LA - NYC - SF Bay - Wash. DC - **more...**

More Yahoo!s
Guides : Autos - Careers - Health - Living - Outdoors - Pets - Real Estate - Yahooligans!
Entertainment : Astrology - Events - Games - Movies - Music - Radio - TV - more
Finance : Banking - Bill Pay - Insurance - Loans - Taxes - Live market coverage - more
Local : Classifieds - Events - Lodging - Maps - Restaurants - Yellow Pages - more
News : Top Stories - Business - Entertainment - Lottery - Politics - Sports - Technology - Weather
Publishing : Briefcase - Clubs - Experts - Invites - Photos - Home Pages - Message Boards
Small Business : Business Marketplace - Small Business Center - Store Building - Website Hosting
Access Yahoo! via : Pagers, PDAs, Web-enabled Phones and Voice (1-800-My-Yahoo)

Make Yahoo! your home page

How to Suggest a Site - Company Info - Copyright Policy - Terms of Service - Contributors - Jobs - Advertising

Copyright © 2001 Yahoo! Inc. All rights reserved.
Privacy Policy

Figure 12–1: The Yahoo! home page
Text and artwork copyright (c) 2001 by YAHOO!, Inc. All rights reserved. YAHOO! and the YAHOO! logo are trademarks of YAHOO!, Inc.

- Tips on using the mouse
- Basics on using toolbar buttons to move "Back" and "Forward," "Print" the current page, "Reload" the current page, and "Stop"
- How clicking on highlighted words takes you to other documents
- Instructions on how to enter keywords in the Yahoo! search forms located at the top of each page.

Using Yahoo!'s Search Engine

Yahoo! gives you the option of switching to a keyword search at any time. At the top of the screen, you see a place to enter your keywords for searching either the subject you're currently in or all of Yahoo!'s subjects categories.

If you don't need to run a very refined search, simply enter your keywords in the text entry box that's located on the home page or on any one of the results pages. By default, Yahoo! matches all words in your search statement. Keywords are treated as substrings instead of entire words (*cat* will match *cat*s and *cat*amaran) and matches are case-insensitive (*Cat* will match *cat*). Only the first one hundred matches are returned. These options may be changed and other parameters set by using Yahoo!'s search forms.

Using Yahoo!'s Advanced Search Forms

If you'd like to fine-tune your search, click on the link called "Advanced Search" located just to the right of the text entry box. When you click on the words "Advanced Search," you link to a search form that offers more in-depth searching. Search syntax options include the following:

"+" requires that word be included in all search results, for example, "farming +diary"

"-" requires that word not be found in any of the search results, for example, "hiking –hitch"

"t:" restricts your search to document titles only, for example, "whale watching" vs. "t:whale watching." Use this syntax when you know the title of the site you are trying to find.

"u:" restricts your search to document URLs, for example, "herbs" vs. "u:herbs" (The latter finds sites with domain names such as *natures-herbs.com*, *all-about-herbs.com*, and *herbs-spices-flowers.com*.

Use (" ") quotes for an exact phrase search. Use phrase searches when you are looking for a specific topic.

The (*) asterisk is a wildcard symbol. When added to the right-hand side of "lib*," for example, the search engine finds "library," "librarian," and "libraries," etc.

Other features include the ability to limit your search by the age of the listing (one day, three days, one week, one month, three months, six months, three years) and the ability to expand your search to newsgroups. In addition, you can change the number of search results displayed on the results page.

The WWW Virtual Library

- **Agriculture**
  Agriculture, Gardening, Forestry, Irrigation...

- **Business and Economics**
  Economics, Finance, Marketing, Transportation...

- **Computing**
  Computing, E-Commerce, Languages, Web...

- **Communications and Media**
  Communications, Telecommunications, Journalism...

- **Education**
  Education, Applied Linguistics, Linguistics...

- **Engineering**
  Civil, Chemical, Electrical, Mechanical, Software...

- **Humanities**
  Anthropology, History, Museums, Philosophy...

- **Information & Libraries**
  General Reference, Information Quality, Libraries...

- **International Affairs**
  International Security, Sustainable Development, UN...

- **Law**
  Arbitration, Law, Legal History...

- **Recreation**
  Recreation and Games, Gardening, Sport...

- **Regional Studies**
  African, Asian, Latin American, West European...

- **Science**
  Biosciences, Health, Earth Science, Physics, Chemistry...

- **Society**
  Political Science, Religion, Social Sciences...

Search the WWW VL: [   ] [Search]

Match: [All ▼]   Format: [Long ▼]   (help)

Mirrors: vlib.org (USA), East Anglia (UK) Geneva (CH), Geneva-2 (CH), Argentina

About | Alphabetical Listing | Keyword Search | News

Copyright © WWW Virtual Library, 1994-2000. Last update Dec 12, 2000

Figure 12–2: The WWW Virtual Library at *vlib.org/*

How Yahoo!'s Search Machine Works

When you run a search using Yahoo!, it presents results in three different ways. It looks in its own database for matches in categories, matches in Websites, and it utilizes an outside (external) search engine for Web-wide searching. Yahoo!'s own database consists of Yahoo! categories containing Yahoo! sites. Depending on your search term(s), the search results may include categories to click on, or take you directly to a list of Yahoo! sites. The results are ranked in order of relevancy with the most relevant hits listed first.

Online Resource

ht://Dig Search Engine software can be downloaded from *www.htdig.org*.
The ht://Dig system is a UNIX-based Web indexing and searching system
designed for intranets. Developed at San Diego State University, ht://Dig
was released under the GNU General Public License, which means it's
licensed free of charge.

The external search engine results are provided by Inktomi, a search engine that indexes the full text of every page it can find on the Web. To see what the results are of
an Inktomi search, click on the text link "Web Pages" listed on the top of the search
results page. You can move between Yahoo! Categories, Yahoo! Websites, and Inktomi
Web Pages.

THE WWW VIRTUAL LIBRARY

Another important subject tree on the Net is the WWW Virtual Library, or WWW VL
for short. It can be reached by pointing your Web browser to *vlib.org/*. The WWW VL
is one of the oldest directories on the web, originally started by Tim Berners-Lee (the
Web's founder) in 1991. Subject indexes are compiled by specialists in their respective
fields and stored individually on servers all around the world. They are linked together
by a directory maintained by Gerard Manning at *vlib.org/* with mirror sites at these locations:

* Penn State University—*www.meteo.psu.edu/~owens/VL/*
* East Anglia—*www.mth.uea.ac.uk/VL/Overview.html*
* Geneva—*cuisung.unige.ch/vl/Home.html* and *cuiwww.unige.ch/vl/Home.html*
* Argentina—*www.vlib.org.ar/*

If you're viewing the WWW VL through a graphical browser like Netscape Navigator, the opening screen appears as illustrated in Figure 12–2.

Services Offered by the WWW VL

The WWW VL offers browsing through subject indexes and searching. You can browse
the holdings of the WWW VL starting at the top of a concise, hierarchical index located on the main page, or you can link to a list of some 300 subject headings arranged
alphabetically beginning with Aboriginal Studies and ending with Zoo.

You can search the WWW VL using the text box and search button located at the
bottom of the main page. The WWW VL uses the ht://Dig indexing and search system
to create a searchable database of their holdings. The ht://Dig system supports matching all of your search terms, any of your search terms, and Boolean operators. The search
engine is configured to search for any terms with the same root as the terms you enter,
but with different endings.

Library Resources by Libraries and Librarians

The Library subject index, named "Library Resources by Libraries and Librarians," contains over 350 links, all accompanied by brief annotations. Maintained by Anne Graham and Celestina Wroth of Indiana University Bloomington Libraries *www.indiana.edu/~libweb/*, the directory is broken down into four subject categories:

- Directories
- Bibliographies
- Digital Libraries
- User Guides

In addition to these services, visitors can search the libraries database using keywords, phrases, and Boolean operators. Search results provide site title and descriptions with keywords and phrases bolded for easy recognition. Another link lets you submit suggestions for adding new links to the site.

Information Management

Interestingly, Information Management is listed on the front page as a major subject heading. This term links to narrow subjects including Information Quality, Electronic References and Scholarly Citations of Internet Sources, Evaluation of Information Resources, and Knowledge Management.

Dr. T. Matthew Ciolek from the Research School of Asian and Pacific Studies, maintains the Information Quality site at *www.ciolek.com/WWWVL-InfoQuality.html*. Dr. Ciolek focuses on collecting links to resources that are relevant to networking scholarly information. Many of his links should be of interest to information professionals, including these:

- Alastair Smith's site *Evaluation of Information Resources*
- Greenhill's *Electronic References & Scholarly Citations of Internet Sources*
- Dr. T. Matthew Ciolek's *Electronic Publishing and Information Quality*

Knowledge Management

The Knowledge Management site, maintained by Dr. Yogesh Malhotra, includes links to "Information Policy," "Intellectual Property," and white papers defining knowledge management.

Computing: World Wide Web Development

The Virtual Library's WWW Development page links to several carefully selected resources. The main page is divided into six broad categories: 1)Authoring, 2)Internet, 3)Location, 4)Multimedia, 5)Software, and 6)Web References. Within each of these categories you can explore many sub-topics, each with its own description. For example, the "Authoring" category covers CGI, forms, graphics, HTML, Java, tutorials, XML, design, and so forth. If you are looking for Internet-related magazines or statistics, explore the "Internet" link.

Table 12–2: General interest subject trees	
About.com	*home.about.com/*
The Argus Clearinghouse	*www.clearinghouse.net/*
Britannica Online	*www.britannica.com/*
The BUBL Subject Tree Project	*bubl.ac.uk/link/*
The BUBL Subject Tree — Arranged by Universal Decimal Classification	*bubl.ac.uk/link/ddc.html*
Chicago Public Library: selected subject information resources	*cpl.lib.uic.edu/008subject/008subject.html*
The Free Internet Encyclopedia — Macro Reference Index (comprehensive treatment of subjects)	*www.clever.net/cam/enc/macro.a.html*
The Free Internet Encyclopedia —Micro Reference Index (brief explanations of topics)	*www.clever.net/cam/enc/micro.a.html*
Galaxy	*galaxy.einet.net/galaxy/index.html*
HOT SHEET Web Quick Reference	*www.hotsheet.com/*
Infomine	*infomine.ucr.edu/*
Librarian's Index to the Internet	*www.lii.org/*
LookSmart	*www.looksmart.com/*
MyStartingPoint	*www.stpt.com/*
Paginas Amarillas	*www3.satnet.net/amarillas/Contents.htm#abc*
Virtual Information Center (UC Berkeley Internet resources by subject)	*www.lib.berkeley.edu/Collections/acadtarg.thml*
WWW Virtual Library	*vlib.org/*
Yahoo!	*www.yahoo.com/*
Yelloweb: The European World Wide Web Source	*www.yweb.com/index2.html*

Table 12–3: Library-related subject trees	
The Best Information on the Net	*vweb.sau.edu/bestinfo/Library/libindex.htm*
LIBCAT:A Guide to Library Resources on the Internet	*208.249.120.62/lc/lc1.cfm*
Librarian's Index to the Internet	*lii.org/*
Northwestern University Library: Resources on the Internet	*www.library.nwu.edu/resources/library/*
Online Resources for the Solo Librarian	*www.unc.edu/cit/guides/irg-44.html*

The Magazine of Digital Library Research

By following the path *Libraries/D-Lib Magazine*, you can explore the latest issues of an electronic magazine called *D-Lib*. *D-Lib* offers a forum for researchers and developers of digital libraries. There is no subscription fee and CNRI (Corporation for National Research Initiatives) grants users permission to copy the materials contained in *D-Lib* for research or non-commercial purposes. They only ask that you cite the individual authors or *D-Lib Magazine* and that you do not alter or abridge the materials in any way.

The Category Subtree

If you go back to the Virtual Library's home page, you see a link at the bottom of the page called "Alphabetical Listing." This is an interesting place to start, too. It gives you a little different view of the "root" because it includes narrower terms right at the outset.

Links to Other Subject Catalogues

In addition to Yahoo! and the Virtual Library, there are other subject trees of general interest. These are shown in Table 12–2. Table 12–3 lists library-related subject trees.

The BUBL Subject Tree Project listed in Table 12–1 offers an interesting approach to subject tree design. BUBL, which stands for the Bulletin Board for Libraries, has organized Internet resources according to Universal Decimal Classification.

WEB SEARCH ENGINES

As I mentioned earlier, when you search the Internet for information—as opposed to browsing—you use search engines that do most of the work for you. Web search en-

Online Resource
The Glossary of Search Engine Terms *www.cadenza.org/search_ engine_terms/* covers specialized language used by search engines.

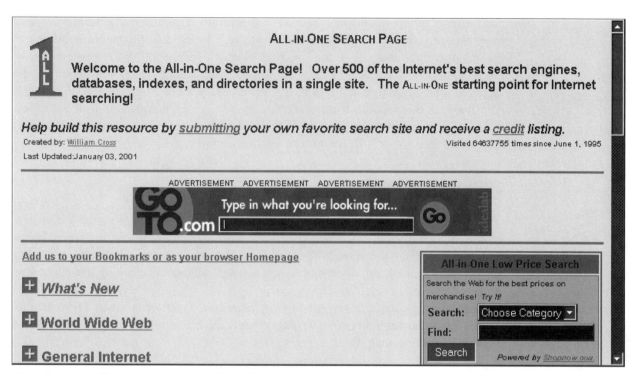

Figure 12–3: William Cross's All-In-One home page

FEATURED SEARCH
Goto.com No hierarchies or complex search expressions, just type what you want and goto it.

Search [   ]

FEATURED SEARCH
Ask Jeeves Ask your question in plain English...

Search [   ]

100hot.com Search for the top web sites on the Internet (Enter keywords)

Search [   ]

1Blink.com Metasearch of 11 popular search engines

Search [   ]

411 Locate Locate a Web site or e-mail address by a phone number, name, company name, or keywords lookup.

Figure 12–4: All-In-One forms-based search tools

gines offer a variety of services. Some are general in scope and index millions of Web pages on every subject imaginable. Others are very focused. For example, some search engines only hunt down the e-mail address of employees working for a single organization. Others only search FTP sites for software applications. And still others are designed to search message archives or the text of a single book like the *1995 CIA World Fact Book*. In this section, I introduce you to the Grand Central Station of search engines—William Cross's All-In-One Website. Another site listing many search engines and subject directories is Beaucoup! at *www.beaucoup.com/*.

CROSS'S ALL-IN-ONE

William D. Cross has created a popular All-In-One searching center on the Web where you can search a variety of resources online from one common starting place. When you connect to the All-In-One Website at *www.allonesearch.com* (shown in Figure 12–3), you are presented with dozens of search engines capable of searching just about anything on the Internet.

When you first arrive at the All-In-One home page, you see a list of 11 broad subject headings that are linked to other pages where the actual search engines exist. These 11 subject headings include:

* *What's New*—-Listing of new and updated search engines organized by month.
* *World Wide Web*—About 200 Web search engines ranging from About.com to Zeeks.
* *General Internet*—-A broad spectrum of search engines including those for searching newsgroups, Net classifieds, Internet service providers, business yellow pages, and more.
* *Specialized Interest*—-Information relating to astronomy, games, Discovery Channel, Compaq, and IBM.
* *Software and Images*—-Links to various Archie servers, commercial and free software, image, and sound files.
* *People*—-Services for finding people including Finger gateways and e-mail address search programs.
* *News/Weather*—-Information on current weather conditions, weather forecasts, and skiing conditions.
* *Publications/Literature*—-A rich collection of full-text documentation, including WAIS searching, current U.S. legislation, White House publications, Senate documents, Shakespeare's works, various online newspapers, magazines and catalogues, and more.
* *Technical Reports*—-Includes such things as computer science technical reports and the Alex catalog of electronic texts.
* *Documentation*—-Search resources such as FAQs, Man pages, RFCs, computer support-related information, and various Web documents.
* *Desk Reference*—-A rich collection of online ready reference books (see below for more details).
* *Other Interesting Searches/Services*—-Everything else including airline flight information, anagram generator, map server, CD music titles, FAA aircraft registration, radio station database, Federal Express, and more.

When you click on one of these headings, you link to a Web page listing several forms-based search tools. *Forms-based* means that you need to fill out a form to run a search. These forms, pictured in Figure 12–4, look the same on all Web browsers that support forms. Web browsers that don't support forms, like Lynx, will instead present you with text and a single line upon which you enter your search terms.

In the opening list of subjects shown on the All-In-One home page, there is one heading called "Desk Reference." When you click on "Desk Reference," you discover several interesting ready reference tools with links to specialized databases. These include the following:

- 555–1212.COM Area Code Directory
- Acronyms and Abbreviations
- Acronym Finder
- Area Code Search
- At Hand Yellow Pages
- AT&T Tollfree 800 Directory
- Bartlett's Quotations
- BigBook Directory (millions of U.S. businesses listed w/maps)
- BigBook Map Server (displays a map when given U.S. address)
- BigYellow Yellow pages
- Biographical Dictionary
- Biography.com
- Britannica.com
- Calculators Online
- Calendar Server (displays a full-year calendar)
- Canadian Address Lookup—-by Postal Code
- Canadian Postal Code Lookup—-by Street Address
- CEDAR National Address Server
- CNET Help.com
- Computing Dictionary
- DICT Online Dictionary
- Encyclopedia.com
- Encyclopedia of the Orient
- Funk and Wagnalls
- Geographic Name Server
- Goto.com
- Hacker's Jargon
- Harvest TollFree (800) Directory
- Homework Central
- Information Please

Online Resource

Read about searching tips and techniques from the pros in *Searcher Magazine www.infotoday.com/searcher/default.htm*. Subscriptions in the U.S. are $69.95/year. You can freely access a combination of abstracts and full text when viewing their current issue online. In addition, you are given access to past issues, currently for the years 1998–99.

- Information Please Kids' Almanac
- Infospace Reverse Address Search
- Infospace Reverse Phone Searches
- Infospace Yellow Pages
- Language Identifier
- LawOffice.com
- Lives, the Biography Resource
- Logos Dictionary
- Love Quotes
- Maps On Us
- Merriam-Webster Online
- OneLook Dictionaries
- PC Webopedia
- Quotations and Sayings Database
- Quotations Page
- Rhyming Dictionary
- Roget's Thesaurus
- Switchboard: Business Nationwide (U.S.) Yellow-Page Database
- Switchboard: People Nationwide (U.S.) White-Page Database
- U.S. Gazetteer Tiger Map Server
- USPS City/State Lookup
- USPS Zip Code Lookup
- USPS Zip+4 Lookup
- WebElements Periodic Table
- Webster's Dictionary
- West's Legal Directory (search for law firms and lawyers)
- WhatIs.com
- Xerox Map Server
- Yellowpages.Net

By going back to the All-In-One home page and clicking on the words "World Wide Web," you link to about 200 search engines—each one designed just for searching resources on the Web. One of the more popular search engines found here is called Lycos.

NEW IDEAS IN SEARCHING

Some companies are developing new applications for searching the Web. For example, Infoseek offers Express Search *express.infoseek.com/*, a desktop search application you can download for free and install on your desktop. Express Search helps you organize your search results and allows you to search by category. AltaVista offers a desktop utility named Discovery *discovery.altavista.com/* that enables you to index and search the contents of your local hard drive in combination with searching the Web.

Copernic 2000 is a multi-Website search agent that is capable of retrieving information from the Web, newsgroups, and e-mail directories. The newest version, 4.1 at the time of this writing, allows you to search content in various languages including English, French, German, Italian, and Spanish. You can download a free copy from Copernic Technologies' Website at *www.copernic.com/*.

Other companies are providing access to other services, such as Open Web Directory and Direct Hit, to help augment their base of information.

OPEN DIRECTORY PROJECT

Lycos, AltaVista, HotBot, Netscape, and others, utilize the Open Directory Project for its data. The Open Directory Project, currently hosted at *www.dmoz.org*, is a directory of Web resources assembled by thousands of different volunteer editors. It's a menu consisting of 15 general topic categories. Netscape Communications Corporation owns the copyright and makes the Open Directory available to anyone free of charge under the terms of their license agreements. You can view the Open Directory License at *dmoz.org/license.html*.

DIRECT HIT

Search engines, such as Infoseek and Inktomi, are author-controlled search engines. *Author-controlled search engines* compare words entered in the search statement with words contained in all of the Web pages that are indexed. They are author-controlled in the sense that the author can include words in the Web documents that lead to more traffic and higher rankings. *Direct Hit* is a search technology that ranks Websites based on popularity. Direct Hit monitors which sites in the search results list users click on, how much time users spend visiting those sites, and several other factors. They attempt to combine the best of both worlds: the depth and breadth of a search engine, and the relevancy of an editor-controlled directory, such as about.com.

SEARCHING THE WEB USING LYCOS

Lycos is one of my favorites because it's fast, easy to use, and makes it easy to expand searches to sound files, images, and their ever-growing list of searchable databases. The technology used for the Lycos search and index system was originally developed at Carnegie Mellon University. Lycos has since moved into international markets and now uses Basis Technology *lycos.basistech.com* to search and index Asian text.

When you search Lycos, each record it returns includes a linkable title, the first few words of text from the corresponding home page, and a URL. Lycos can be accessed by connecting to *www.lycos.com/*. From this site, you can link to other versions of Lycos in languages from Europe, Asia-Pacific, and the Americas.

Lycos Basics

Lycos offers three places from which to launch a search:

1. The text entry box on the home page (the box at the top of the screen)
2. A more advanced search form that you can access by clicking on the link labeled "Advanced Search"
3. Multimedia searching for pictures, sounds, movies and streaming multimedia

Simple searches that you run from the text entry box match any of the words in your query. In other words, the default for Lycos is to search using the OR operator. A search using the keywords **white water rafting Colorado** will retrieve documents containing either "white" OR "water" OR "rafting" OR "colorado" or any combination of those words. Lycos assigns a score to each document it returns; the higher the score, the more relevant the document. A perfect score of 100 percent would contain all or a significant number of the keywords you specified.

Simple searches also support + sign for requiring certain terms and – sign for excluding certain terms. You can match your word pattern exactly by using quotes ("").

Using the Lycos Search Form

The search form that appears on the All-In-One home page and Lycos home page is fairly straightforward. You use a single text entry box to enter your search terms. If you search from the Lycos home page, you can access more options that help fine-tune your search. SearchGuard is a service available to anyone who wishes to attempt filtering adult, violent, hate, and weapons-related materials from search results.

The Lycos Advanced Search form offers options to use the AND and OR operators, or you can select exact phrase searching. Lycos also enables you to use a variety of languages to select specific categories in which to conduct your search, for example, FTP sites, home pages, newsgroups, and multimedia, etc.

Lycos Features

Lycos has evolved from a search-only site into a service that also offers a wide range of browsing opportunities. For example, patrons who are interested in learning more about how the stock market is performing can click on Lycos's "Stock" link located at the top of the page. The link labeled "People" demonstrates several other Lycos features: the ability to find out where someone lives; see their location on a street map; search for e-mail addresses and phone numbers; look for ancestors and people in the news; seek out government officials, and a lot more. The PeopleFind index is neither up-to-date nor comprehensive, but in some cases it has proven to be a valuable tool for locating friends from the past. In the Lycos Advanced Search screen, click on "LINK REFERRALS" to search the Web for documents that link to your Website.

SEARCHING THE WEB USING ALTAVISTA

AltaVista, developed by Digital Equipment Corporation, is one of the newer search engines and considered by many to be the largest, fastest, and most sophisticated search engine on the Web. At the time of this writing, AltaVista claims it is indexing 250 million general Web pages, up 220 million since the last edition of this book was published. Of course, these figures change daily and if Internet growth continues at its present rate, there will soon be hundreds of millions more pages being indexed by search engines like AltaVista.

BASIC SEARCHES USING SIMPLE QUERIES

To begin a search, go to site *www.altavista.com/*. AltaVista offers five query forms: Default, Advanced Search, Images, MP3/Audio, and Video. When you link to AltaVista's home page, you are accessing the default query form. To link to the advanced search form, click on the link at the top of their home page labeled "Advanced Search."

To run a simple search, enter the keywords describing the subject that interests you. AltaVista retrieves documents matching any of the keywords you enter, listing matches in order of relevancy. For example, if you enter the keywords **organic gardening**, AltaVista places those documents containing both words at the top of the results list. Documents containing only "organic" or only "gardening" would be at the end of the list.

Words presented in lowercase match words in lower- or uppercase. For example, "diet" will match "Diet," "DIET," or "diet," etc. Words presented with uppercase letters only retrieve an exact match.

You can fine-tune your simple queries by using the + and – signs. Use the + sign in front of any word that must be included in the documents AltaVista retrieves. Use the – sign as a NOT operator to exclude documents containing specific words. For example, **+water +systems –wells** retrieves documents containing the words "water" and "systems" and excludes any documents containing the word "wells." The search statement **+cats –dogs** retrieves documents that contain the word "cats" and not "dogs." Note that there is a space between each search term.

Word phrases should be enclosed in quotation marks. For example, "automatic weapons" and "4th of july" retrieve more accurate search results than *automatic weapons* and *4th of july*.

Constraining searches are searches that focus on certain parts of HTML documents. For example, if you're interested in finding documents that have the word *star* in their image tag, enter the search statement **image:star**. Running a search like this may help you zero in on a particular image. When I ran this search, the search results contained home pages that included images of stars. The file names accompanying the image tag had names such as *star.gif* and *star.jpg*. More help with simple queries can be accessed by clicking on the link labeled "Help."

TIPS ON ALTAVISTA ADVANCED QUERIES

You can connect to AltaVista's Advanced Query form by clicking on the tab labeled "Advanced Search" at the top of the home page. Once connected, clicking on the link

Table 12–4: Meta search engines	
Name	Location
AskJeeves	*www.aj.com/*
BigHub	*www.thebighub.com/*
C4	*www.c4.com/*
Dataware	*queryserver.dataware.com/general.html*
Ixquick	*www.ixquick.com/*
Metacrawler	*www.metacrawler.com/*
Redesearch	*www.redesearch.com/*

labeled "Help" connects you to help for advanced queries. Here are some basic pointers to keep in mind when submitting Advanced Queries:

- As with simple queries, it's recommended that you type words in lowercase because lowercase letters indicate a case-insensitive match.
- The operators AND, OR, NEAR, and NOT can be used to show relationships between words and phrases. NEAR is a proximity operator. In the query **public NEAR library**, AltaVista matches queries where "public" and "library" occur within ten words of each other.
- Search statements in AltaVista can become complex when you enter a statement that has both AND and OR operators. For this reason, it's a good idea to place parentheses around synonymous concepts (words joined with OR operators) so AltaVista processes them first. For example, in the search statement **sustainable and (agriculture or farming)**, AltaVista retrieves documents containing the word "sustainable," and, in the same document, either "agriculture" or "farming."

META SEARCH ENGINES

A new breed of search engines is evolving called "multi-threaded" or "meta search" engines. These search tools examine multiple databases for matches to your query. Meta search engines may or may not maintain their own internal database of indexed terms. Those that don't maintain their own database rely entirely on indexes created by other search engines. For example, MetaCrawler at *www.metacrawler.com* doesn't maintain an internal database, but relies on other Web-based search engines, including Lycos, WebCrawler, Infoseek, Excite, AltaVista, GoTo.com, LookSmart, and Thunderstone.

The advantage of using a meta search engine is that it can take your set of search terms and run them on several sites all at once. The results are organized into a uniform format, usually in order of relevancy. Furthermore, you can familiarize yourself with a single search form rather than several different search forms. Several meta search engines are listed in Table 12–4.

METACRAWLER

MetaCrawler offers a basic search option and a Power Search option. The basic search is presented on the home page. You can specify any one of the following options:

- Search for words as a phrase: This treats your search statement as a single phrase.
- Search for all words: This attempts to find each word of your search statement somewhere in the retrieved documents. It is equivalent to the AND operator.
- Search for any words: This attempts to find any word of your search statement in the retrieved documents. It is equivalent to the OR operator.

A Power Search Option allows you to specify which search engines you use. The list includes:

1. AltaVista
2. Infoseek

3. WebCrawler
4. Thunderstone
5. Excite
6. Google
7. Lycos
8. LookSmart
9. GoTo
10. About.com
11. DirectHit
12. RealNames

In addition, Metacrawler lets you direct your search to various geographical locations, or .com, .gov, or .edu sites only. The results list can be viewed in order of relevancy, by top-level domain (*.com*, *.edu*, etc.), or by source, for example, Excite, Webcrawler, Google, etc.

IXQUICK

Ixquick is one of the newest and fastest meta search engines on the Net. Ixquick searches 14 search engines simultaneously. It ranks results according to relevancy and the results list includes source information. Ixquick supports both natural language searches and advanced Boolean searches. You can direct your search towards one of four subject categories:

1. Web
2. News
3. MP3
4. Pictures

When searching for news, you can specify searching in one or more of the following sources:

a. Associated Press
b. CNN
c. *Los Angeles Times*
d. Reuters
e. *San Francisco Chronicle*
f. *Washington Post*

Online Resource

To learn more about the various search engines available on the Net, check out "How to Search the Web: A Guide To Search Tools" by Terry A. Gray at *daphne.palomar.edu/TGSEARCH/*. Gray discusses AltaVista, Excite, WebCrawler, Lycos, Opentext, Infoseek, Yahoo!, NlighteN, Internet Sleuth, and Magellan.

ASKJEEVES

AskJeeves *www.askjeeves.com* works especially well for general, natural language searching. Search results are gathered from its own database and AltaVista, WebCrawler, Excite, and About.com. I posed the following question to AskJeeves: "How can you get a grease stain out of your tie?" AskJeeves responded with four closely related questions for which it had answers. These included:

1. How can I remove grease and cooking oil stains?
2. How can I contact stain manufacturers?
3. How do I remove a stain from my clothes?
4. Where can I buy ties online?

Each question included a drop-down list of optional keywords. For example, in question number one, you could replace "grease and cooking oil" with acid, alcohol, blood, chewing gum, ice cream, or dozens of other options. The matches included from other search systems may also include drop down lists that offer optional keywords.

FINAL TIPS ON WWW SEARCHING

Here are a few more tips that help librarians search the Web more effectively:

1. Alter the keywords you use as a way of fine-tuning your search. For example, when a student asked one of our reference clerks "How does 3–D work?," the reference clerk first entered **3–D** as the search statement. AltaVista found 100,000 documents with "3" and "D" occurring in them. AltaVista, like most search engines, lists the most relevant hits first. The first two matches retrieved on this search were not relevant.
2. The reference clerk then narrowed the search by entering the phrase **"how does 3–D work"**. Enclosing the phrase in double quotation marks retrieved documents where all of the words in the phrase occurred next to each other and in the exact order they were typed. This second search resulted in two hits, the first hit's title being: "You Can — 3–D: Three D. Question How does 3–D work? Answer: You need . . . " This linked to a document that explained in simple terms how 3–D worked and it provided a real-life example.
3. Try running your search in different search engines. Entering the same search statement in different search engines yields varying results. For convenience, bookmark at least two different search engines—for example, AltaVista and Lycos. When one doesn't yield satisfactory results, try the other. You could also run your search on a meta search engine, such as Ixquick or AskJeeves (both listed in Table 12–4).
4. Some information professionals apply the 80:20 rule of thumb when searching for information. When they have a question, they go to the resource that has historically given them the best results and the highest probability of finding an answer. If they strike out, they move onto the next most effective resource. By applying this principle, they find 80 percent of their answers in 20 percent of their available resources.
5. When you connect to a link and you get an error message, go on to the next title that's listed. The reason for the error might be:

1. The page has been renamed or removed by the owner
2. Access restrictions may exist
3. The server may be so overloaded that attempts to connect to it time out
4. The server may be down at the moment
5. It's possible that the Internetworking structure isn't working; for example, your browser may not be able to connect to a domain name server that's down
6. Maybe you have put a slash at the end of a URL containing a file name. This kind of error may look like this: *www.concentric.net/~Acbenson/ etext.htm/*. The final "/" is wrong.
7. Maybe you entered an incorrect URL. For example, some addresses end with ".html" and you entered ".htm"
8. Most Web servers are UNIX-based, which means they are case-sensitive. If you use incorrect capitalization, you may run into problems.

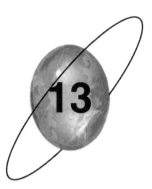

Transferring Files on the Internet

File transfer is one of the most frequently used Internet applications, enabling you to copy files from over a thousand different archives around the world. You can think of these archives as libraries—electronic libraries housing digitized information. Although information in traditional paper-based libraries is stored in books and magazines, the file is the unit of storage in electronic libraries. These files hold such things as text, images, sound, and executable programs. Tools like Archie assist you in exploring the staggering number of files that reside in these archives. (Archie is discussed in detail in Chapter 15.)

The set of conventions that govern how this file transfer process takes place on the Internet is called *File Transfer Protocol,* or FTP. The FTP protocol enables you to list directories on remote machines and to transfer files in either direction. When a file is transferred, it is not actually moved; rather, the file is copied from one machine to another. The computer from which the file is copied is sometimes referred to as the *source host* and the computer to which the file is copied is called the *destination host*.

RUNNING FTP FROM A SHELL ACCOUNT

Like most of the Internet applications discussed in this book, FTP is based on a client/server model. You run a program on your local machine called an *FTP client,* which in turn connects to another program running on a remote machine called a *server.* The client application can be either a character-based program or GUI (Graphical User Interface) program. In this section I focus on the former. You can run a simple, character-based FTP client from the DOS prompt on Windows 95/98/2000 PCs, or from the system prompt on UNIX systems. As with other Internet protocol names, FTP is sometimes used as a verb. For example, you may see a sentence like this one: "You can obtain a copy of *The Library Bill of Rights* by FTPing to the Electronic Frontier Foundation's Library Policy Archive."

ANONYMOUS FTP

Some sites enforce a strict FTP authorization that prohibits you from accessing files until you obtain a login name and password for their computer. Many other sites, the ones you will most often be connecting to, allow *anonymous FTP*, which provides unrestricted access to public files. Anonymous FTP access means that you don't have to be a registered user to connect to the remote host. You login by entering **anonymous** as your user ID and your e-mail address as your password. This process is covered in more detail later in the chapter.

MIRROR SITES

In order to provide a reasonable level of performance and to avoid overloading their system, popular FTP sites install user limits for anonymous FTP. When one site is busy, one or more archive sites around the world are usually available that can provide the same files. These archives are referred to as *mirror sites*.

FOLLOWING REFERENCES TO FTP SERVERS

Throughout this book, you find numerous references to files located on FTP servers all around the world. Directions for accessing these files always include three elements:

1. The remote computer's Internet address, either the domain name address (*archive.latrobe.edu.au*) or IP address (*131.172.2.2*);
2. the pathname that tells you the path of directories you must follow to get from the root directory to the directory where the file resides, for example, *archive.latrobe.edu.au/pub/music/;* and
3. the file name itself, for example, *README*.

The complete set of details are presented a few different ways:

1. When FTPing from a UNIX system or your DOS prompt in Windows, I usually direct you by saying, "FTP to site *ftp.eff.org* and download the file named *README* located in the */pub/academic/civics* directory." All of this information could be written simply as *archive.latrobe.edu.au/pub/music/README*
2. When FTPing on the Web, I present the information in the form of a URL—an address you enter in the location box at the top of your Web browser: *ftp:// archive.latrobe.edu.au/pub/music/README*

In Appendix E of this book, you find explanations of the various file types that you encounter on the Internet for both PCs and Macs. Appendix E can serve as a handy reference guide anytime you work on the Internet and you confront a file name extension that is foreign to you.

DOWNLOADING ASCII TEXT FILES

In this section, I present examples of anonymous FTP sessions that demonstrate how to download ASCII text files. ASCII text files contain plain text and are usually given the extension *.txt*, *.doc*, or in some cases, no extension at all. You are downloading a text file when you transfer it from a remote computer to a local computer. When you transfer a text file from your local computer to a remote computer, you are uploading the text file. The details of transferring other file types are discussed later in this chapter.

The text files you create with a text-editing program such as DOS Editor are plain text files. Usually, these files don't create any problems when being sent over a network. A file saved in word processing programs such as Microsoft Word or Corel WordPerfect usually includes ASCII text, but it also includes formatting codes for such things as bold, italic, and underlining. These formatted files are actually binary files, not ASCII text files, and cannot be easily moved from computer to computer without encountering some difficulties. If you were to view a file with formatting in another application that couldn't read and interpret these codes, you would see unrecognizable characters mixed in with the text.

Most word processors offer the option of saving text as a plain ASCII file or text only. If you plan to send your word processing files over the Internet and you want them to be universally accepted and readable, make sure that you save them using one of these options. Most word processing programs also enable you to save your file with all the formatting intact so that it can be transferred from one application to another. A process called Rich Text Formatting (RTF) is used to convert the formatting into instructions that other applications can read and interpret. This allows you to transfer formatted files between, for example, a DOS system and a Macintosh system. RTF files are generally given an *.rtf* extension.

CONNECTING TO AN FTP SITE AND DOWNLOADING A TEXT FILE

In the first exercise you FTP to an archive containing historical texts maintained by the Electronic Frontier Foundation (EFF). Once there, you download a copy of The Declaration of Independence, which is a text file named *dec_of_ind* residing in the */pub/Censorship/Academic_edu/CAF/civics* directory. The name of the computer on which all of this is found is *ftp.eff.org*. If the FTP server at EFF is down, try looking for the *dec_of_ind* file at one of the following mirror sites:

ftp.cerias.purdue.edu/mirrors/ftp.eff.org
ftp.auscert.org.au/pub/coast/mirrors/ftp.eff.org
ftp.rge.com/pub/security/coast/mirrors/ftp.eff.org

Making the Connection

To make a connection to the FTP server, begin by typing **ftp** at your system prompt and then pressing ENTER. (Remember, this section focuses on character-based FTP clients running on UNIX systems or Windows PCs.) Depending on how you connect to the Internet, there may be slight variations in how to issue the ftp command. If an *ftp>* prompt is displayed after issuing the ftp command, type the **open** command, followed by the destination host's address, for example:

ftp> **open ftp.eff.org**

Some systems allow you to type **ftp ftp.eff.org** all on one line from the system prompt. The first "ftp" is the command that runs the FTP client. The second "ftp" is part of the host address.

Once connected, you must first enter your username, which is **anonymous**. (Some systems require that you type **user anonymous**). You then are prompted to provide a password, at which point you enter your e-mail address. (Passwords are not echoed, which means that as you type characters, they don't appear on the screen.) You then see the *ftp>* prompt or some other prompt such as *FTP.EFF.ORG>,* indicating you have connected and can begin communicating commands to the server. So far, the session looks something like this:

CRCINET 3> **ftp ftp.eff.org**
Connected to ftp.eff.org.
220 kragar.eff.org FTP server (Version wu-2.4(26) Wed Dec 13 11:23:34 PST 1995) ready.
Name (ftp.eff.org:anonymous): **anonymous**
331 Guest login ok, send your complete e-mail address as password.
Password:
230–**************** Welcome to the EFF Online Library *****************
230–Electronic Frontier Foundation files & info: /pub/EFF
230–* Get README for info on this server, including auto-decompression
230–* Send questions to ftphelp@eff.org if you have any difficulties
230– This is a person, not an infobot! Please be detailed & specific.
230–* Remember: use binary mode on .tar, .z, .gz, .zip, .exe, .lha files!
230–Current local time is Tue Jul 9 11:51:50 1996.
230–***
230–WWW USERS: Try http://www.eff.org/pub/ instead! Same files, better site
230–***
230–Looking for EFF'S GUIDE TO THE INTERNET (formerly Big Dummy's Guide)?
230–Do this, EXACTLY as shown here, to get the regular text version:
230–[These instructions presume a commandline Unix-style FTP browser.]
230– cd /pub/Net_info/EFF_Net_Guide
230– ascii
230– mget netguide.*
230–Troubles? Send any message to netguide@eff.org for a copy of the Guide.
230–***
230–
230–You are connected from host mariner.cris.com.
230–You have been given group USA permissions.
230–
230–
230–Please read the file README
230– it was last modified on Mon May 6 19:16:20 1996 - 64 days ago
230–Please read the file README.incoming
230– it was last modified on Thu Dec 7 19:39:03 1995 - 215 days ago
230 Guest login ok, access restrictions apply.

Issuing the dir (Directory) Command

To better understand how directories and files are organized, type **dir** at the prompt and press ENTER. This displays the following directory, called the *root directory*:

```
ftp> dir
200 PORT command successful.
150 Opening ASCII mode data connection for /bin/ls.
total 634
-rw-r--r--      1 root       daemon      0          Oct 17 1991    .notar
-rw-r--r--      1 mech       mech        1327       Apr 26 1995    00-INDEX.ftp
lrwxrwxrwx      1 root       daemon      8          Apr 13 20:42   00-MASTER.FILELIST.
                                                                   gz -> ls-lR.gz
-rw-rw-r--      1 brown      doc         487        Jun 18 16:24   00-index.txt
lrwxrwxrwx      1 root       daemon      7          Apr 13 20:41   EFF -> pub/EFF
drwxr-xr-x      7 mech       doc         512        Jun 4 16:37    Mech
-rw-rw-r--      4 mech       doc         32393      May 7 02:16    README
-rw-rw-r--      1 mech       doc         1495       Dec 8 03:39    README.incoming
-rw-rw-r--      3 106        doc         44909      Jun 24 20:10   about.eff
drwxrwxr-x      2 root       daemon      512        May 29 1993    bin
lrwxrwxrwx      1 root       daemon      7          Apr 13 20:42   eff -> pub/EFF
drwxrwxr-x      3 root       daemon      512        Jun 7 1995     etc
drwxrwx-wx      4 mech       doc         512        Jul 9 17:34    incoming
-rw-rw-r--      1 brown      doc         2891       Jun 18 16:24   index.html
-rw-r--r--      1brown       brown       218483     Jul 9 10:26    ls-lR.gz
drwxrwxr-x     21 brown      doc         1024       Jun 18 16:24   pub
drwxrwxr-x      3 root       daemon      512        Jun 1 1995     usr
226 Transfer complete.
1126 bytes received in 3 seconds (0.36 Kbytes/s)
```

The DOS command **dir** works on a UNIX machine because the system administrator set up something called an *alias* to make life easier for everyone. When you enter the dir command, the alias points to the actual UNIX command for a long directory listing, which is "ls -l." You can use the ls -l command to display the directory instead of dir.

Working in UNIX Directories

The directory shown in our example is one displayed on a computer running the UNIX operating system, the most prevalent operating system on the Internet. UNIX organizes files into directories, which are in themselves a special kind of file. In the directory illustrated in the example, the system has stored information about other files and directories.

Each line, read left to right, displays information about a particular file or directory. The type of file is listed in the left column. A "d" in this first column indicates a directory and a "-" indicates a file of some kind. Next is information relating to access modes for different users ("-rw-rw-r—"). The letters "r," "w," and "x" stand for read, write, and execute. Depending on their position in line, they are rights given to individuals, groups, or everyone.

The next column lists the number of files or directories linked to the particular file. For example, on the 12th line of output shown above, the *README* file has four links. The column after this lists "mech" as the creator or owner of the file. The next word, "doc," refers to the group that owns the file. Next, the file's size is given in bytes ("32393"), and just past this is the date the file was created or last modified. Current year entries are expressed in month, day, and time. The file and directory names are listed in the last column.

UNIX file and directory names are case-sensitive. This means that in order to successfully change directories or transfer files, you must type the name of the directory or file just as it is shown. You cannot download a file called *INDEX.rfc* if you ask for "index.rfc," nor can you change to a directory called *XFree86* if you type "xfree86."

UNIX organizes files into a hierarchical structure. This way of organizing files has been compared to a family tree. When you first connect to an FTP server, you are in the parent directory, which is the top, or "root," of this imaginary tree. The root directory is designated with a slash (/) in path statements.

Pathnames and Subdirectories

As you can see in the root directory of *ftp.eff.org* illustrated in the example, there are directories under the root called "bin" and "pub," etc. These are called *subdirectories* of the root. Each directory, except for the root, has one parent directory and one or more subdirectories.

The file you are looking for (*dec_of_ind*) resides in the */pub/Censorship/Academic_edu/CAF/civics* directory. This series of directory names separated by slashes is called a *pathname*. Note that UNIX directory path separators are forward slashes (/), not backslashes (\) as they are in DOS. The pathname tells you the path you must follow through the hierarchical file structure to find the file you want. For example, the root directory is the first "/." The directory *pub* is a subdirectory of *root*. The directory *CAF* is a subdirectory of *pub*, and so on.

Changing to a Different Directory

You can change your working directory (the directory you are currently working in) by using the cd (change directory) command. The cd command uses the form *cd <pathname>*, where the argument "<pathname>" is the pathname for the directory to which you want to change. The command cd .., or cdup, will move you up one directory.

Moving ahead with the first exercise, type the following command and pathname, and then press ENTER:

ftp>cd /pub/Censorship/Academic_edu/CAF/civics

You can use the command cd to change only directories, not files. That is why the file name *dec_of_ind* was not included in the above pathname.

In the preceding example, you moved through all the directories at one time by issuing the cd command once, followed by a pathname that included all the necessary subdirectory names. You could have moved one directory at a time by typing **cd pub** and pressing ENTER, **cd CAF** and pressing ENTER, and **cd civics**, and so on. Either way, you arrive at the desired destination.

Now you can enter the **dir,** or **ls –l**, command to confirm that you are indeed in the directory that contains the file *dec_of_ind* along with several other interesting files.

```
ftp>dir
<Opening ASCII mode data connection for /bin/ls.
total 1064
```

lrwxrwxrwx	1 ftp	caf	6	May 28 19:32	Index -> README
-rw-r–r–	1 kadie	caf	8690	Oct 18 17:38	README
-rw-rw-r–	1 ftp	caf	1076	Sep 2 1992	administration.address
-rw-rw-r–	1 ftp	caf	16488	Jan 12 1993	affirmative-action.info
-rw-rw-r–	1 ftp	caf	9918	Aug 5 03:32	alawon-2–31
-rw-rw-r–	1 ftp	caf	192	Mar 14 19:36	bill.status.pointer
-rw-rw-r–	1 ftp	caf	2517	Mar 20 03:00	cabinet.contact-info
-rw-rw-r–	1 ftp	caf	125	Apr 4 22:16	cabinet.resumes.pointer
-rw-rw-r–	1 ftp	caf	1071	Feb 8 1993	campus-news.pointer
-rw-rw-r–	1 ftp	caf	82640	Nov 16 1992	canada.constitution
-rw-rw-r–	1 ftp	caf	20354	Nov 16 1992	canada.meech-accord
lrwxrwxrwx	1 ftp	caf	18	May 28 19:32	charter.can ->../law/charter.can
lrwxrwxrwx	1 ftp	caf	34	May 28 19:32	civil-disob -> ../../EFF/newsletters/
					effector4.04
-rw-rw-r–	1 ftp	caf	5879	Aug 5 03:32	clinton-appointees
-rw-rw-r–	1 ftp	caf	1387	Mar 14 19:37	clinton.press.pointer
-rw-rw-r–	1 ftp	caf	1304	Dec 11 1992	columnist.contact-info
-rw-rw-r–	1 ftp	caf	307	Mar 20 03:09	congress.info.pointer
-rw-rw-r–	1 ftp	caf	34709	Aug 24 14:59	congress.phones
-rw-rw-r–	1 ftp	caf	879	Aug 14 1992	constitution.az.us
-rw-rw-r–	1 ftp	caf	45483	Jun 10 1992	constitution.us
-rw-rw-r–	1 ftp	caf	8496	Oct 4 1991	dec_of_ind
-rw-rw-r–	1 ftp	caf	1428	May 24 01:52	executive.phone-numbers
-rw-rw-r–	1 ftp	caf	1653	Oct 31 1991	fcc
-rw-rw-r–	1 ftp	caf	11442	Jul 24 19:35	fed-register.internet
-rw-rw-r–	1 ftp	caf	18114	Nov 16 1992	federalist-paper-10
-rw-rw-r–	1 ftp	caf	11812	Nov 16 1992	federalist-paper-51
-rw-rw-r–	1 ftp	caf	1875	Nov 14 1992	federalist-papers.pointer
-rw-rw-r–	1 ftp	caf	8874	Dec 4 1992	foia.insight
-rw-rw-r–	1 ftp	caf	37138	Feb 27 1992	foia.nlg
-rw-rw-r–	1 ftp	caf	2830	Mar 21 1992	gov.contact
-rw-rw-r–	1 ftp	caf	866	Jan 12 1993	historical-documents.pointer
-rw-rw-r–	1 ftp	caf	3122	May 24 01:52	judiciary-comm.phone-numbers
-rw-rw-r–	1 ftp	caf	865	May 24 01:52	library-of-congress.pointer
-rw-rw-r–	1 ftp	caf	5703	Mar 1 1992	media.fax
-rw-rw-r–	1 ftp	caf	181	Aug 14 1992	umd.edu
-rw-rw-r–	1 ftp	caf	5725	Nov 16 1992	virginia.decl-of-rights
-rw-rw-r–	1 ftp	caf	1225	Feb 8 1993	white-house.email-address
-rw-rw-r–	1 ftp	caf	10785	Apr 4 22:16	white-house.pr.pointer
-rw-rw-r–	1 ftp	caf	139671	May 5 22:18	wtp.zip
drwxrwsr-x 2 ftp	caf		1536	Aug 5 03:34	zzz

```
<Transfer complete.
```

The pwd (Print Working Directory) Command

While you are in the *civics* directory, you can practice another useful FTP command. At the FTP prompt, type **pwd**. The server responds by telling you the name of the working directory.

FTP>**pwd**
"/pub/Censorship/Academic_edu/CAF/civics" is current directory.

Transferring a File Using the get Command

Now you are ready to transfer a copy of the *dec_of_ind* file from the remote computer to your local computer. You do this by issuing the command **get <file name>**. To download a copy of The Declaration of Independence, for example, you would enter the command **get dec_of_ind**. Some systems will prompt you for a "local" file name after you have entered the remote host's file name. You may need to rename the file when you transfer it in order to follow DOS conventions that limit file names to eight or fewer characters plus a three-character extension. Enter **get dec_of_ind declar.txt** (notice that there is only one space separating the original file name and the shortened file name you have assigned it). When the transfer is complete the *FTP>* prompt reappears.

You may be wondering to which computer does this file get transferred. The file is transferred to your local hard drive. If you are working on a PC in your office running UNIX, for example, the file is transferred to that computer. If you dialed-up or telneted to a remote UNIX computer, the file were transferred to that computer.

Viewing Text Files During FTP Sessions

The following UNIX command enables you to view a text file before downloading it: **get <file name> -**
To view the text file *dec_of_ind*, type the following command while you're in the *civics* directory: **get dec_of_ind -**
The hyphen at the end of the command transfers the text to your terminal instead of to the directory space on your dial-up host. To prevent long text files like this one from scrolling off your screen, you can use the command **get dec_of_ind |more**
This command enables you to transfer the file to a "pager" program. To move through the document one page (screen full) at a time, press the space bar.

Using the statistics Command

Just how long does a file transfer take? One way to find out is to use the statistics command. The statistics command turns the print timing statistics for file transfers off and on. When this feature is turned off and you use the get command to download a file, the following information is displayed on your screen:

FTP>**get dec_of_ind**
    To local file: declar.txt
Opening ASCII mode data connection for dec_of_ind (8496 bytes).

Transfer complete.
FTP>

If you type **statistics** at the *FTP>* prompt and press ENTER, you then switch the print timing statistics feature on. Now when you get a file, the screen will also display information describing the file transfer rate in bits per second (bps) and the elapsed time in milliseconds (ms).

FTP>**statistics**
[Transfer statistics printing is ON]
FTP>**get dec_of_ind**
    To local file: **declar.txt**
<Opening ASCII mode data connection for dec_of_ind (8496 bytes).
<Transfer complete.
8659 bytes transferred at 1135 bps.
Run time = 0. ms, Elapsed time = 61006. ms.

To turn this feature off, enter the statistics command once again.

Checking Your Local Directory with the ldir Command

You may be able to confirm that the file arrived on your local dial-up host without closing your FTP session by entering the **ldir** command at the *FTP>* prompt. This command displays the working directory on your local computer without breaking the FTP connection. In the following example, you can view the working directory on my local computer and see that I did indeed download The Declaration of Independence as file *DECLAR.TXT* (see line three).

FTP>**ldir**
DISK$USER:[ACBENSON]

00–ABSTRACT.TXT;1	70	5–DEC-1993	09:52	[ARKNET,ACBENSON]	(RWED,RWED,,)
00–INDEX.TXT;1	75	5–DEC-1993	09:52	[ARKNET,ACBENSON]	(RWED,RWED,,)
DECLAR.TXT;1	18	5–DEC-1993	09:59	[ARKNET,ACBENSON]	(RWED,RWED,,)
GOPHERRC.;5	4	22–JUN-1993	20:56	[ARKNET,ACBENSON]	(RWD,RWD,R,)
MAIL.MAI;1	36	3–DEC-1993	16:13	[ARKNET,ACBENSON]	(RW,RW,,)
NEWS-EXTRACTS.DIR;1	1	31–OCT-1993	09:22	[ARKNET,ACBENSON]	(RWE,RWE,,E)
PROC.;1	6	4–DEC-1993	09:25	[ARKNET,ACBENSON]	(RWED,RWED,,)
SEND.EXE;2	8	8–SEP-1993	11:31	[ARKNET,ACBENSON]	(RWED,RWED,RE,)
SEND.EXE;1	8	8–SEP-1993	11:30	[ARKNET,ACBENSON]	(RWED,RWED,RE,)

TT.;2	1	5–DEC-1993	09:56	[ARKNET,ACBENSON]
				(RWED,RWED,,)
TT.;1	8	5–DEC-1993	09:51	[ARKNET,ACBENSON]
				(RWED,RWED,,)

README Files

Before leaving the Electronic Frontier Foundation FTP server, you should go back to the root directory and download two potentially important files, which also gives you an opportunity to practice two new commands. Entering the **cd /** command will take you all the way back to the root directory. (Note that there is a space between the "cd" and the "/.") Once there, you can enter the **pwd** command just to confirm that your working directory is now the root ("/").

FTP>**cd /**
FTP>**pwd**
<"/" is current directory.

If you enter the **dir** command, you display the holdings of the root directory as illustrated earlier. Notice the files listed in the right column with "*README*" and "*index*" in their names. Some special-purpose files located in FTP archives assist you in understanding what things are stored at that particular site. *Readme* files are usually text files describing the contents of a directory, special instructions, or a brief explanation of the archive's contents and/or purpose. The files with "index" in their name usually describe the contents of various directories located on the FTP server. These explanatory files are also called *index.txt*, *abstract.txt*, *00–INDEX.TXT*, or something similar. Another file to look for at each site is the *LS-LR* file. This file contains the entire directory structure of a site.

Using the mget (Multiple Get) Command and Wildcards

To transfer all of these readme files at once, use the command mget (multiple get). Along with this command, you can use the wildcard characters "?" or "*." The question mark represents a single character and the asterisk represents one or more characters. Because there are no other file names beginning with the letter R, simply enter **mget R*** at the *FTP>* prompt and you successfully transfer both of the readme files.

Sample Session Uploading Files from an NT Server to a UNIX System Using FTP

In this exercise you have an NT server in the library with several files stored on it and you want to move these files to a UNIX system in your office. Both systems are on the Internet, but you don't have the UNIX system on your NT network. The solution is to use FTP to communicate between the two computers.

Begin by going to the system prompt on the NT server. Open the FTP session by entering the **ftp** command followed by the IP address or domain name of the UNIX system in your office. For example C:\> **ftp 150.120.45.165**

When prompted, enter the user ID and password for logging into your UNIX system. This assumes you are running the FTP service on the UNIX system and that you have an account setup for yourself. (You cannot login as *root* in this operation.)

Once you have successfully logged in, check to see what directory you are currently in on your local NT server. Enter the command **lcd**. If you are not in the directory you want to be in—the folder that contains the files you intend to transfer—then move to the desired destination. Use the **lcd** command to change directories. The system will return with something like *Local directory now C:\Windows.* If you are using file names with spaces in them on the NT computer, place your path statement within double quotes. For example, if all of the files you want to move are located in the *C:\Library Staff\Joe's Project* folder, then you would enter this command: FTP> **lcd "c:\Library Staff\Joe's Project."** After executing this command, the system returns with *Local directory now C:\Library Staff\Joe's Project.*

Next, find the destination folder on the UNIX system. If you logged into the Guest directory, for example, and you want to place the files in a subfolder called "docs," then change directories by entering **cd docs**. To make certain you are in the /Guest/docs directory, enter the **pwd** command (print working directory).

If there are binary files included in the set you wish to upload, enter the **bin** command to change the transfer mode to binary. Next, enter the **hash** command so hash marks (#) appear during longer file downloads. Enter the **prompt** command to set the interactive mode *off.* The last step is to enter the **mput** command. Since you want to upload all of the files in the folder, you can save a lot of time by using wildcards. Enter the command FTP> **mput *.***

After all of the files have transferred, you return to the FTP prompt. Enter the **quit** command to end the session. You should now find all of the files located in the destination folder on the remote computer; in this case, the UNIX system in your office.

Using the bell Command

Enter the pathname for moving back to the *civics* directory:

FTP> **cd /pub/Censorship/Academic_edu/CAF/civics**.

Next, type the command **bell** and press ENTER. This causes a tone to sound when you complete your operation—a handy device if you are transferring a large file and want to work on something else during the downloading process. The beep will let you know when the transfer is complete. To turn the bell off, simply type **bell off** at the prompt. Practice this procedure by downloading the file called README after issuing the bell command and then turn the bell off when you are finished. Type **quit** at the prompt to end your session and close the connection. Your session should look something like this:

FTP>**bell**
[Bell will now ring when operations complete]
FTP>**get README**
Opening ASCII mode data connection for README (8690 bytes).
Transfer complete.
FTP>**bell off**
[Operations will complete silently]

FTP>**quit**
Goodbye.
$

DOWNLOADING TEXT FILES AND SAVING DIRECTORY INFORMATION

In the next search exercise, you download a file called *proclamation-of-neutrality* in the subdirectory */pub/gutenberg/freenet* at FTP site *ftp.gutenberg.org*. To retrieve a copy of this file, go to your system prompt (DOS prompt if you are on a Windows PC, or log into your host computer) and then execute the following commands:

west:~$ **ftp ftp.gutenberg.org**
Connected to jib.gutenberg.org.
220 jib FTP server (Version wu-2.4.2–academ (1) Fri Apr 16 11:19:28 EDT 1999) re
ady.
Name (ftp.gutenberg.org:star-host): **anonymous**
331 Guest login ok, send your complete e-mail address as password.
Password: **guest**
230–The response 'guest' is not valid
230–Next time please use your e-mail address as your password
230– for example: joe@westhost.westhost.net
230–*** All transfers are logged with your host name and email address.
230–*** If you don't like this policy, please disconnect now.
230–_____
230–
230– Sailor's FTP Server
230–_____
230– sailor.gutenberg.org
230– ftp.sailor.lib.md.us
230–
230– This is a service of
230– Sailor, Maryland's Online Information Service
230–_____
230–
230–Our ftp server can do on-the-fly compression to convert files
230–to many different compressed file types; not all file types will
230–appear in directory listings. See the file README for more information.
230–
230–Project Gutenberg texts are found in the directory pub/gutenberg .
230–
230–We welcome your comments and suggestions. Please mail any input
230–to ftpadmin@sailor.lib.md.us
230–
230–
230–
230–Please read the file README

230– it was last modified on Thu Feb 27 15:31:06 1997 - 1136 days ago
230 Guest login ok, access restrictions apply.
Remote system type is UNIX.
Using binary mode to transfer files.
ftp> **cd /pub/gutenberg/freenet**
250 CWD command successful.
ftp> **bell**
Bell mode on.
ftp> **get proclamation-of-neutrality proc.txt**
local: proc.txt remote: proclamation-of-neutrality
200 PORT command successful.
150 Opening BINARY mode data connection for proclamation-of-neutrality (2586 bytes).
226 Transfer complete.
2586 bytes received in 0.0704 secs (36 Kbytes/sec)
ftp> **bye**
221 Goodbye.

Renaming a File While Downloading

In the preceding exercise, you first connected to an archive containing historical texts; next you moved to the *freenet* directory and issued the bell command; and you then downloaded a copy of *The Proclamation of Neutrality (1793)*. The 26–character file name was renamed *proc.txt* before transferring. If everything went as planned, you should have a file on your host computer named *proc.txt* that reads as follows:

THE PROCLAMATION OF NEUTRALITY (1793):
BY THE PRESIDENT OF THE UNITED STATES
A PROCLAMATION
Whereas it appears that a state of war exists between Austria, Prussia, Sardinia, Great Britain, and the United Netherlands, of the one part, and France on the other; and the duty and interest of the United States require, that they should with sincerity and good faith adopt and pursue a conduct friendly and impartial toward the belligerent Powers;
I have therefore thought fit by these presents to declare the disposition of the United States to observe the conduct aforesaid towards those Powers respectfully; and to exhort and warn the citizens of the United States carefully to avoid all acts and proceedings whatsoever, which may in any manner tend to contravene such disposition.
And I do hereby also make known, that whatsoever of the citizens of the United States shall render himself liable to punishment or forfeiture under the law of nations, by committing, aiding, or abetting hostilities against any of the said Powers, or by carrying to any of them those articles which are deemed contraband by the modern usage of nations, will not receive the protection of the United States, against such punishment or forfeiture; and further, that I have given instructions to those officers, to whom it belongs, to cause prosecutions to be instituted against all persons, who shall, within the cognizance of the courts of the United States, violate the law of nations, with respect to the Powers at war, or any of them.
In testimony whereof, I have caused the seal of the United States of America to be

affixed to these presents, and signed the same with my hand. Done at the city of Philadelphia, the twenty-second day of April, one thousand seven hundred and ninety-three, and of the Independence of the United States of America the seventeenth.
GEORGE WASHINGTON
April 22, 1793

France declared war against Great Britain and Holland early in April, 1793. President Washington called a special cabinet meeting, which resulted in this declaration of neutrality.

Prepared by Gerald Murphy (The Cleveland Free-Net - aa300)
Distributed by the Cybercasting Services Division of the National Public Telecomputing Network (NPTN).
Permission is hereby granted to download, reprint, and/or otherwise redistribute this file, provided appropriate point of origin credit is given to the preparer(s) and the National Public Telecomputing Network.

Saving Remote File Names to a Local Machine

Another FTP command that is quite useful enables you to take the output of the dir command and put the output in a file on your local machine. You can then read the file's contents after you break the FTP connection. This is useful when the directories are very long and you would like to review their contents offline, especially when you are paying by the minute for connect time.

The command for accomplishing this is **dir * <local file name>**, where "*" represents all the subdirectories and the files they contain in your current working directory and "<local file name>" specifies the name you would like to assign this file on your local machine. The following session demonstrates how this command works. After FTPing to site *ftp.cdrom.com*, I changed directories to */pub* and there I issued the dir command. After viewing the output from this command, I entered the command **dir * library.txt**, which took all of the directories shown below and the files contained in those directories and placed them in a local file named *library.txt*.

west:~$ **ftp ftp.cdrom.com**
Connected to wcarchive.cdrom.com.
220 wcarchive.cdrom.com FTP server (Version DG-3.1.37 Sun Jun 20 21:18:25 PDT 1999) ready.
Name (ftp.cdrom.com:star-host): **anonymous**
331 Guest login ok, send your email address as password.
Password: **guest**
230–Welcome to ftp.cdrom.com, a service of Digital River, Inc.
230–There are currently 4559 users out of 5000 possible.
230–
230–This machine is a Xeon/500 with 4GB of memory & 1/2 terabyte of RAID 5.
230–The operating system is FreeBSD. Should you wish to get your own copy of
230–FreeBSD, see the pub/FreeBSD directory or visit http://www.freebsd.org
230–for more information. FreeBSD on CDROM can be ordered using the WEB at
230–http://www.wccdrom.com/titles/freebsd/freebsd.phtml or by sending email
230–to orders@wccdrom.com.
230–

230–100Mbps colocation services provided by Applied Theory. For more information
230–please visit http://www.appliedtheory.com.
230–
230–NetFRAME 9201 server machine provided by Micron Electronics. Please visit
230–http://www.micronpc.com/web/walnutcreek.html.
230–
230–Please send mail to ftp-bugs@ftp.cdrom.com if you experience any problems.
230–Please also let us know if there is something we don't have that you think
230–we should!
230–
230 Guest login ok, access restrictions apply.
Remote system type is UNIX.
Using binary mode to transfer files.
ftp> **cd pub**
250 CWD command successful.
ftp> **dir**
200 PORT command successful.
150 Opening ASCII mode data connection for 'file list'.
total 101
lrwxr-xr-x 1 root wheel 13 Oct 3 1998 3dfiles -> ../.1/3dfiles
lrwxr-xr-x 1 root wheel 14 Sep 23 1999 3dportal -> ../.2/3dportal
lrwxr-xr-x 1 root wheel 14 Oct 3 1998 3drealms -> ../.1/3drealms
lrwxrwxrwx 1 root wheel 11 Oct 1 1998 4.4BSD-Lite -> bsd-sources
lrwxr-xr-x 1 root wheel 11 Oct 3 1998 4cust -> ../.1/4cust
lrwxr-xr-x 1 root wheel 13 Oct 3 1998 FreeBSD -> ../.2/FreeBSD
lrwxr-xr-x 1 1003 wheel 17 Nov 18 17:51 ImageMagick -> ../.2/ImageMagick
lrwxr-xr-x 1 root wheel 16 Oct 3 1998 MacSciTech -> ../.1/MacSciTech
lrwxr-xr-x 1 root wheel 12 Oct 3 1998 NetBSD -> ../.3/NetBSD
-rw-r–r– 1 root wheel 5493 Jul 1 1998 README
lrwxrwxrwx 1 root wheel 14 Oct 1 1998 UPLOADS.TXT -> ../UPLOADS.TXT
lrwxr-xr-x 1 root wheel 9 Oct 3 1998 X11 -> ../.3/X11
lrwxr-xr-x 1 root wheel 13 Oct 3 1998 XFree86 -> ../.1/XFree86
lrwxr-xr-x 1 root wheel 11 Oct 3 1998 abuse -> ../.1/abuse
lrwxr-xr-x 1 root wheel 13 Oct 3 1998 ada -> languages/ada
lrwxr-xr-x 1 root wheel 16 Oct 3 1998 algorithms -> ../.1/algorithms
lrwxr-xr-x 1 root wheel 12 Jul 27 1999 applix -> ../.2/applix
lrwxr-xr-x 1 root wheel 14 Oct 3 1998 artpacks -> ../.1/artpacks
lrwxrwxr-x 1 root wheel 9 Oct 9 1998 ase -> ../.1/ase
lrwxr-xr-x 1 root wheel 10 Oct 3 1998 asme -> ../.3/asme
lrwxr-xr-x 1 root wheel 11 Oct 3 1998 audio -> ../.3/audio
lrwxr-xr-x 1 root wheel 12 Oct 3 1998 avalon -> ../.1/avalon
lrwxr-xr-x 1 root wheel 10 Oct 3 1998 beos -> ../.1/beos
lrwxr-xr-x 1 root wheel 15 Nov 26 1998 bluesnews -> ../.3/bluesnews
lrwxr-xr-x 1 root wheel 17 Oct 3 1998 bsd-sources -> ../.3/bsd-sources
lrwxr-xr-x 1 root wheel 11 Oct 3 1998 cdrom -> ../.1/cdrom
lrwxr-xr-x 1 root wheel 12 Oct 3 1998 cheats -> ../.3/cheats
lrwxr-xr-x 1 root wheel 10 Oct 3 1998 cnet -> ../.1/cnet
lrwxrwxr-x 1 root wheel 9 Jul 12 1999 cug -> ../.1/cug

```
lrwxr-xr-x 1 root wheel 12 Oct 3 1998 delphi -> ../.1/delphi
lrwxr-xr-x 1 root wheel 6 Oct 3 1998 delphi_www -> delphi
lrwxr-xr-x 1 root wheel 16 Oct 3 1998 delphideli -> ../.1/delphideli
lrwxr-xr-x 1 root wheel 11 Oct 3 1998 demos -> ../.1/demos
lrwxrwxrwx 1 root wheel 7 Oct 1 1998 doom -> idgames
lrwxrwxrwx 1 root wheel 7 Oct 1 1998 doom2 -> idgames
lrwxr-xr-x 1 root wheel 10 Oct 3 1998 epic -> ../.1/epic
lrwxr-xr-x 1 root wheel 15 Mar 3 00:13 forth -> languages/forth
lrwxr-xr-x 1 root wheel 11 Oct 3 1998 games -> ../.1/games
lrwxr-xr-x 1 root wheel 19 Oct 3 1998 games_patches -> ../.1/games_patches
lrwxr-xr-x 1 root wheel 17 Oct 3 1998 gamesdomain -> ../.3/gamesdomain
lrwxr-xr-x 1 root wheel 11 Oct 3 1998 garbo -> ../.1/garbo
lrwxr-xr-x 1 root wheel 9 Oct 3 1998 gnu -> ../.1/gnu
lrwxr-xr-x 1 root wheel 8 Oct 3 1998 gt -> ../.1/gt
lrwxr-xr-x 1 root wheel 9 Oct 3 1998 gus -> ../.1/gus
lrwxr-xr-x 1 root wheel 15 Oct 3 1998 gutenberg -> ../.1/gutenberg
lrwxr-xr-x 1 root wheel 14 Oct 3 1998 hamradio -> ../.1/hamradio
lrwxrwxrwx 1 root wheel 15 Oct 1 1998 hexen2 -> idgames2/hexen2
lrwxr-xr-x 1 root wheel 3 Oct 3 1998 hobbes -> os2
lrwxr-xr-x 1 root wheel 13 Jul 16 1999 idgames -> ../.1/idgames
lrwxr-xr-x 1 root wheel 14 Jul 16 1999 idgames2 -> ../.1/idgames2
lrwxr-xr-x 1 root wheel 14 May 6 1999 idgames3 -> ../.3/idgames3
lrwxrwxr-x 1 root wheel 9 May 25 1999 imm -> ../.1/imm
lrwxr-xr-x 1 root wheel 13 Oct 3 1998 infozip -> ../.1/infozip
lrwxr-xr-x 1 root wheel 14 Oct 3 1998 internet -> ../.1/internet
lrwxr-xr-x 1 root wheel 9 Oct 3 1998 irc -> ../.1/irc
lrwxr-xr-x 1 root wheel 14 Oct 3 1998 japanese -> ../.1/japanese
lrwxr-xr-x 1 root wheel 10 Oct 3 1998 java -> ../.1/java
lrwxr-xr-x 1 root wheel 9 Oct 3 1998 jn4 -> ../.3/jn4
lrwxr-xr-x 1 root wheel 15 Oct 3 1998 languages -> ../.1/languages
lrwxr-xr-x 1 root wheel 11 Oct 3 1998 linux -> ../.4/linux
lrwxrwxrwx 1 root wheel 14 Oct 1 1998 lisp -> languages/lisp
lrwxr-xr-x 1 root wheel 9 Oct 3 1998 mac -> ../.3/mac
lrwxr-xr-x 1 root wheel 10 Oct 4 1998 math -> ../.1/math
lrwxr-xr-x 1 root wheel 9 Oct 4 1998 mng -> ../.1/mng
lrwxr-xr-x 1 root wheel 13 Oct 3 1998 mozilla -> ../.1/mozilla
lrwxrwxr-x 1 root wheel 10 Apr 29 1999 mutt -> ../.1/mutt
lrwxr-xr-x 1 root wheel 12 Oct 3 1998 netlib -> ../.3/netlib
lrwxr-xr-x 1 root wheel 12 Oct 3 1998 novell -> ../.1/novell
lrwxr-xr-x 1 root wheel 9 Oct 3 1998 obi -> ../.3/obi
lrwxr-xr-x 1 root wheel 9 Oct 3 1998 os2 -> ../.1/os2
lrwxr-xr-x 1 root wheel 10 Oct 3 1998 perl -> ../.1/perl
lrwxr-xr-x 1 root wheel 17 Oct 4 1998 planetquake -> ../.3/planetquake
lrwxr-xr-x 1 root wheel 9 Oct 3 1998 png -> ../.1/png
lrwxr-xr-x 1 root wheel 12 Oct 3 1998 python -> ../.1/python
lrwxr-xr-x 1 root wheel 9 Aug 6 1999 qnx -> ../.3/qnx
lrwxrwxrwx 1 root wheel 8 Oct 1 1998 quake -> idgames2
lrwxrwxrwx 1 root wheel 15 Oct 1 1998 quake2 -> idgames2/quake2
```

```
lrwxr-xr-x 1 root wheel 8 May 6 1999 quake3 -> idgames3
lrwxr-xr-x 1 root wheel 12 Dec 20 23:43 regnow -> ../.2/regnow
lrwxr-xr-x 1 root wheel 9 Oct 3 1998 sac -> ../.3/sac
lrwxr-xr-x 1 root wheel 9 Oct 3 1998 sde -> ../.1/sde
lrwxr-xr-x 1 root wheel 14 Oct 3 1998 security -> ../.3/security
lrwxr-xr-x 1 root wheel 16 May 14 1999 setiathome -> ../.2/setiathome
lrwxr-xr-x 1 root wheel 15 Oct 3 1998 simtelnet -> ../.3/simtelnet
lrwxrwxrwx 1 root wheel 24 Oct 1 1998 slow.txt -> ../archive-info/slow.txt
lrwxr-xr-x 1 root wheel 9 Oct 3 1998 tcl -> ../.1/tcl
lrwxrwxrwx 1 root wheel 9 Oct 1 1998 tex -> ../.1/tex
lrwxr-xr-x 1 root wheel 14 Oct 3 1998 tomahawk -> ../.1/tomahawk
lrwxr-xr-x 1 root wheel 12 Oct 3 1998 unix-c -> ../.1/unix-c
lrwxr-xr-x 1 root wheel 18 Oct 3 1998 unixfreeware -> ../.1/unixfreeware
lrwxr-xr-x 1 root wheel 12 Oct 3 1998 unreal -> ../.1/unreal
lrwxrwxr-x 1 root wheel 9 Apr 29 1999 vim -> ../.1/vim
lrwxr-xr-x 1 root wheel 12 Oct 3 1998 viseng -> ../.1/viseng
lrwxrwxrwx 1 root wheel 14 Oct 1 1998 win3 -> simtelnet/win3
lrwxrwxrwx 1 root wheel 16 Oct 1 1998 win95 -> simtelnet/win95/
lrwxr-xr-x 1 root wheel 11 Oct 3 1998 x2ftp -> ../.3/x2ftp
226 Transfer complete.
ftp> dir * library.txt
output to local-file: library.txt? y
200 PORT command successful.
150 Opening ASCII mode data connection for 'file list'.
226 Transfer complete.
ftp> bye
221 Goodbye!
```

Saving a List of File Names Contained in a Single Directory

FTP to site *ftp.funet.fi* and go to the directory */pub/doc/library/* and enter the dir command.

```
west:~$ ftp ftp.funet.fi
Connected to ftp.funet.fi.
220–Hello UNKNOWN at westhost.westhost.net,
220–
220–Welcome to the FUNET archive, Please login as 'anonymous' with
220–your E-mail address as the password to access the archive.
220–See the README file for more information about this archive.
220–
220– All anonymous transfers are logged with your host name and whatever you
220– entered for the password. If you don't like this policy, disconnect now!
220–
220–THIS is a new four processor SUN 450/4GB/600+GB system under installation
220–Please mail to problems@nic.funet.fi in case of problems
220–
220–
220–ftp.funet.fi FTP server (Version 4.1486 problems@ftp.funet.fi) ready.
```

220–There are 140 (max 250) archive users in your class at the moment.

220–Assuming 'login anonymous', other userids do vary.)

220–Local time is Sun Apr 9 05:33:46 2000 EET DST

220–

220 You can do "get README" even without logging in!

Name (ftp.funet.fi:star-host): **anonymous**

331 Guest login ok, give your E-mail address for password.

Password: **guest**

230–You didn't give your Internet E-mail address as the password.

230–You gave: 'guest'

-Examples:

- Firstname.Lastname@westhost.westhost.net

230–

230– Finnish University and Research network FUNET

230– Archive FTP.FUNET.FI

230–

230–Most important file name suffixes are described at /README.FILETYPES

230–

230–Welcome, you are 141th archive user in your class (max 250).

230–Your class is named: The known world outside NORDUnet region

230–There are 168 users in all classes (max 787)

230–Your data-transfer rate has no limitations.

230–

230–Local time is Sun Apr 9 05:33:50 2000 EET DST

230–

230–You entered an invalid/improbable password, and are now accessing

230–restricted subset of files. Please read README for more information.

-Err from chroot(): 2 (No such file or directory)

230–We have special access features, see file README

230– It was last updated Wed Nov 12 22:15:21 1997 - 878.3 days ago

230

Remote system type is UNIX.

Using binary mode to transfer files.

ftp> **cd pub/doc/library**

250 CWD command successful.

ftp> **dir**

200 PORT command successful.

150 Opening ASCII mode data connection for .

-rw-r–r– 1 shem ftp 6019 Feb 6 1997 00Index

-rw-r–r– 1 shem ftp 6042 Sep 14 1992 00Index~

drwxr-xr-x 2 shem ftp 8192 Aug 11 1999 EFF

-rw-r–r– 1 shem ftp 600064 Feb 21 1993 Hytelnet6.4.sea.bin

-rw-r–r– 1 shem ftp 58839 Apr 2 1992 Index.csuvax

lrwxrwxrwx 1 root csc 7 Sep 23 1999 README -> 00Index

-rw-rw-r– 1 kiravuo ftp 998 Jun 26 1991 aaareadme.txt

-rw-rw-r– 1 kiravuo ftp 101716 Jun 26 1991 aarnet.guide

-rw-r–r– 1 shem ftp 16859 Nov 19 1992 acadlist.readme.Z

-rw-r–r– 1 shem ftp 115185 Nov 19 1992 acadlist.tar.Z

-rw-r–r– 1 shem ftp 42347 Sep 14 1992 agguide.dos.Z
-rw-r–r– 1 shem ftp 39877 Jun 24 1992 agriculture-internet.txt.Z
-rw-r–r– 1 shem ftp 34952 Apr 2 1992 anzlibraries.list
-rw-r–r– 1 shem ftp 1868 Mar 30 1992 archie_guide.txt.Z
-rw-r–r– 1 shem ftp 8938 Apr 2 1992 artbase.txt.Z
-rw-r–r– 1 shem ftp 43899 Sep 14 1992 aut103–4.txt.Z
-rw-r–r– 1 shem ftp 54723 Sep 14 1992 aut1101.txt.Z
-rw-r–r– 1 shem ftp 9033 Apr 2 1992 bailey.list
-rw-r–r– 1 shem ftp 74127 Apr 24 1990 bibliography.Z
drwxr-xr-x 2 shem ftp 8192 Aug 11 1999 connections
-rw-r–r– 1 shem ftp 31825 Apr 21 1992 cwis.txt
-rw-r–r– 1 shem ftp 10114 Mar 30 1992 cwis.txt.Z
-rw-r–r– 1 shem ftp 2441 Apr 2 1992 download.txt
-rw-r–r– 1 shem ftp 82803 Apr 2 1992 e-journals.dir.Z
drwxr-xr-x 2 shem ftp 8192 Aug 11 1999 ejournal
-rw-r–r– 1 shem ftp 106887 Sep 14 1992 ejournals.txt.Z
-rw-r–r– 1 shem ftp 5486 Mar 30 1992 email_services.txt.Z
-rw-rw-rw- 1 hakala ftp 136520 Oct 12 1994 europe.rtf
-rw-rw-rw- 1 hakala ftp 181899 Oct 12 1994 europe.wp6
-rw-r–r– 1 shem ftp 4182 Sep 14 1992 explorer.doc
-rw-r–r– 1 shem ftp 249047 Sep 14 1992 explorer.zip
-rw-r–r– 1 shem ftp 4168 Mar 30 1992 ftp_guide.txt.Z
-rw-r–r– 1 shem ftp 3793 Mar 30 1992 ftp_help.txt.Z
-rw-r–r– 1 shem ftp 3718 Mar 30 1992 ftp_how_to.txt.Z
-rw-r–r– 1 shem ftp 29673 Mar 30 1992 guide1.txt.Z
-rw-r–r– 1 shem ftp 29289 Jun 2 1992 guide2.txt.Z
-rwxr-xr-x 1 shem ftp 13414 Feb 6 1997 han
drwxr-xr-x 2 mirror mirror 8192 Aug 11 1999 hp3000
drwxr-xr-x 5 shem ftp 96 Aug 11 1999 hytelnet
-rw-r–r– 1 hakala ftp 46253 Nov 20 1995 illpres.wp5
-rw-r–r– 1 hakala ftp 54273 Nov 20 1995 illpres.wp6
-rw-r–r– 1 shem ftp 2138 Jun 3 1996 index.html
-rw-r–r– 1 shem ftp 275965 Jun 2 1992 infpop20.exe
-rw-rw-r– 1 kiravuo ftp 5166 Dec 12 1991 internet.databases
lrwxrwxrwx 1 root csc 15 Sep 23 1999 internet.libraries.Z ->
libraries.txt.Z
-rw-r–r– 1 shem ftp 14608 Mar 30 1992 internet_intro.txt.Z
-rw-r–r– 1 shem ftp 7197 Apr 21 1992 internet_svcs.txt.Z
-rw-r–r– 1 shem ftp 7529 Sep 14 1992 jnl_hunter.pl
-rw-r–r– 1 shem ftp 7711 Sep 14 1992 journal_check.perl
-rw-rw-r– 1 kiravuo ftp 109226 Sep 19 1991 libcat-guide
-rw-r–r– 1 shem ftp 9318 Apr 2 1992 libconfers.txt
-rw-rw-r– 1 kiravuo ftp 2963 Dec 12 1991 libinet.doc
-rw-rw-r– 1 kiravuo ftp 248760 Dec 12 1991 libinet.exe
-rw-r–r– 1 shem ftp 15318 Oct 11 1993 liblists.txt
-rw-r–r– 1 shem ftp 71354 Apr 2 1992 libnet.exec
lrwxrwxrwx 1 root csc 13 Sep 23 1999 libraries.adr -> libraries.con
-rw-r–r– 1 shem ftp 1858 Feb 16 1994 libraries.africa

```
-rw-r–r– 1 shem ftp 183584 Feb 16 1994 libraries.americas
-rw-r–r– 1 shem ftp 20360 Feb 16 1994 libraries.asia
-rw-r–r– 1 shem ftp 795 Oct 12 1993 libraries.con
lrwxrwxrwx 1 root csc 13 Sep 23 1999 libraries.contacts -> libraries.con
-rw-r–r– 1 shem ftp 89109 Feb 16 1994 libraries.europe
-rw-r–r– 1 shem ftp 39063 Oct 12 1993 libraries.instructions
-rw-r–r– 1 shem ftp 2884 Oct 12 1993 libraries.intro
lrwxrwxrwx 1 root csc 13 Sep 23 1999 libraries.ps -> libraries.con
lrwxrwxrwx 1 root csc 13 Sep 23 1999 libraries.tx2 -> libraries.con
lrwxrwxrwx 1 root csc 13 Sep 23 1999 libraries.txt -> libraries.con
-rw-r–r– 1 shem ftp 59199 Jun 29 1992 libs.sh.Z
drwxrwxr-x 2 shem ftp 8192 Aug 11 1999 libsearch
-rw-rw-r– 1 kiravuo ftp 23765 Jun 26 1991 libtel-unix.escape
-rw-rw-r– 1 kiravuo ftp 21902 Jun 26 1991 libtel-unix.noescape
-rw-rw-r– 1 kiravuo ftp 28336 Jun 26 1991 libtel.com
-rw-r–r– 1 shem ftp 4600 Oct 11 1993 listserv_usenet.txt.Z
**drwxr-xr-x 2 shem ftp 8192 Aug 11 1999 lori**
-rw-rw-rw- 1 hakala ftp 436627 Oct 24 1994 marc007.wp5
-rw-rw-rw- 1 hakala ftp 883405 Oct 24 1994 marc008.wp5
-rw-rw-rw- 1 hakala ftp 277923 Oct 24 1994 marccon1.wp5
-rw-rw-rw- 1 hakala ftp 322222 Oct 24 1994 marccon2.wp5
-rw-rw-rw- 1 hakala ftp 249129 Oct 24 1994 marccon3.wp5
-rw-rw-rw- 1 hakala ftp 386253 Oct 24 1994 marccon4.wp5
-rw-rw-rw- 1 hakala ftp 302425 Oct 24 1994 marccon5.wp5
-rw-r–r– 1 shem ftp 18994 Sep 14 1992 medical_resources.txt.Z
-rw-r–r– 1 shem ftp 32753 Apr 2 1992 nephis.com
-rw-r–r– 1 shem ftp 12503 Mar 30 1992 networking_biblio.txt.Z
-rw-rw-r– 1 hks ftp 44040 Mar 24 1992 nonbib.txt
-rw-r–r– 1 hakala ftp 270829 Apr 7 1995 onetask.wp5
-rw-r–r– 1 shem ftp 2716 Mar 30 1992 pacsl_dbms.txt.Z
-rw-r–r– 1 shem ftp 4768 Mar 30 1992 pacsl_intro.txt.Z
-rw-r–r– 1 shem ftp 25224 Mar 30 1992 public_unix.txt.Z
-rw-r–r– 1 shem ftp 12668 Sep 14 1992 spec_libs.txt.Z
-rw-rw-rw- 1 hakala ftp 48393 Oct 12 1994 srnett.rtf
-rw-rw-rw- 1 hakala ftp 77082 Oct 12 1994 srnett.wp6
-rw-r–r– 1 shem ftp 15651 Apr 2 1992 stanton.bib.Z
-rw-r–r– 1 shem ftp 145753 Jun 26 1991 stgeorge.ps.Z
-rw-r–r– 1 shem ftp 108889 Jun 26 1991 stgeorge.txt.Z
-rw-rw-rw- 1 hakala ftp 190480 Jan 12 1995 teimarc.ps
-rw-r–r– 1 shem ftp 84480 Apr 2 1992 thesauri.exe
-rw-rw-r– 1 kiravuo ftp 53470 Jun 26 1991 uk.lib
-rw-rw-rw- 1 hakala ftp 57136 Dec 8 1992 verkot.txt
-rw-r–r– 1 shem ftp 8418 Mar 30 1992 wais.txt.Z
drwxr-xr-x 14 hakala ftp 8192 Aug 11 1999 z3950
226 Transfer complete.
ftp> **dir libsearch libsearch.txt**
output to local-file: libsearch.txt? **y**
200 PORT command successful.
```

150 Opening ASCII mode data connection for libsearch.
226 Transfer complete.
ftp> **bye**
221–Goodbye, and thank you for using the FUNET archive.
221 You transferred 8 KBytes during this session.

As you can see by the preceding printout, this site archives lots of software and documents for librarians and library users on the Internet, although most of it is somewhat dated. Notice that in the displayed directory there is a subdirectory called *libsearch* (which is bolded in the above output so it is easier to recognize). To create a file that displays the files contained in that directory, I entered the command **dir libsearch libsearch.txt**

In this exercise, you began by typing the command dir followed by the subdirectory name *libsearch*; and then follow that with the output file name *libsearch.txt*. When you view this file, which is named *libsearch.txt* on your local host, you see a listing of the contents of the directory called *libsearch*, which should resemble this:

```
total 336

-rw-rw-rw- 1 5001 ftp 4980 May 6 1992 DATA.sites
-rw-rw-rw- 1 5001 ftp 3880 Sep 2 1992 README.libsearch
-rw-rw-rw- 1 5001 ftp 208 May 6 1992 Syntax.AFIT
-rw-rw-rw- 1 5001 ftp 216 May 6 1992 Syntax.Aberdeen
-rw-rw-rw- 1 5001 ftp 221 May 6 1992 Syntax.Aberystwyth
-rw-rw-rw- 1 5001 ftp 126 May 6 1992 Syntax.Aleph
-rw-rw-rw- 1 5001 ftp 221 May 6 1992 Syntax.Arizona.State
-rw-rw-rw- 1 5001 ftp 177 May 6 1992 Syntax.BuCAT
-rw-rw-rw- 1 5001 ftp 221 May 6 1992 Syntax.Dynix
-rw-rw-rw- 1 5001 ftp 231 May 6 1992 Syntax.GEAC
-rw-rw-rw- 1 5001 ftp 126 May 6 1992 Syntax.Karolinska
-rw-rw-rw- 1 5001 ftp 221 May 6 1992 Syntax.Libertas
-rw-rw-rw- 1 5001 ftp 123 May 6 1992 Syntax.NOTIS
-rw-rw-rw- 1 5001 ftp 323 May 6 1992 Syntax.Oulu
-rw-rw-rw- 1 5001 ftp 117 May 6 1992 Syntax.VTLS
-rw-rw-rw- 1 5001 ftp 241 May 6 1992 libsearch
-rw-rw-rw- 1 5001 ftp 1020 May 6 1992 libsearch.main
-rw-rw-rw- 1 5001 ftp 366 May 6 1992 libsearch.procedures
-rw-rw-rw- 1 5001 ftp 106 May 6 1992 libsearch.settings
-rw-rw-rw- 1 5001 ftp 643 May 6 1992 misc.problem.systems
-rw-rw-rw- 1 5001 ftp 101 May 6 1992 misc.todo
```

MOVING FILES FROM YOUR DIAL-UP HOST TO YOUR PERSONAL COMPUTER

If you executed the preceding text file transfer properly, you now have a file copied to your workspace on the local host named *libsearch.txt*. If you don't have a file on your local host for this exercise, go out and get one just for practice. For example, FTP to Wiretap Online Library at site *ftp.mc.hik.se* and go to the *pub/doc/etext/wiretap-library/*

Cyber directory and download the file named *polly.txt*. This is a copy of Jean Armour Polly's "Everything I Need to Know About the Net, I Learned in the Public Library," an interesting recounting of her experience operating a library BBS and the insight she gained from it.

If your personal computer is connected directly to the Internet, as is the case with a dial-up PPP account, the files you download using FTP come right to your personal computer. If you are using a modem and telephone line to connect to the Internet through a shell account, you have to transfer the file one more time before it actually arrives on your own personal computer. That is, you grab it from the system you dial-up to and pull it over to your personal PC. You began by transferring a file from a remote computer to your workspace on your local host using FTP.

FILE TRANSFER PROTOCOLS

Now you have to transfer the file from the local host—the intermediary computer—to your own personal computer using one of a group of other standard file transfer protocols, such as Kermit, Xmodem, Ymodem, or Zmodem. When you choose a communication program, it more than likely supports one or more of these common protocols.

These protocols are simply agreed-upon standards that govern how your personal computer communicates with another computer when exchanging files. For example, if the communication software on your personal computer supports Zmodem and the local host that you dial-up to supports Zmodem, you tell the local host to *send* using Zmodem and you tell your communication software to *receive* using Zmodem. The local host's Zmodem is not your responsibility, but you do have to confirm that it is installed.

Downloading a File Using Zmodem

To demonstrate this process, let's transfer the file *polly.txt* from the local host to your personal PC. You must first determine which of the mentioned protocols is supported by both your communication software and the local host to which you are connecting. Most communication programs support Zmodem, so I use that protocol in the following demonstration.

On most systems, the Zmodem program is called sz, which stands for *send using Zmodem*. Its companion program is named rz, which stands for *receive using Zmodem*.

To download a text file from your personal workspace on the dial-up host to your personal computer, you "send" using Zmodem. Type **sz -a <file name>**, which in this case is "sz -a polly.txt." You use the "-a" parameter when downloading ASCII text files. If you are downloading a binary file, use "-b." (Because ASCII is the default, the command would also work simply as "sz polly.txt.")

Depending on the communication software you use, as soon as you enter the sz command, your communication program may detect that you have initiated a Zmodem trans-

Online Resource
Kermit is a file transfer protocol first developed at Columbia University in 1981. You can read more about Kermit at the Kermit Project, Columbia University Website *www.columbia.edu/kermit/* .

fer and automatically start transferring the file without any further action on your part.

You may have to "tell" other communication programs to start downloading using Zmodem. The exact procedure you follow will vary from program to program; so consult the documentation that came with the particular communication program you use.

Again, depending on which communication program you use, you see different things on the screen while the file is being downloaded. Procomm Plus for Windows displays a status window that tracks the downloading process, showing the number of bytes being transferred per second, the estimated time until completion, and the percentage of the total file that has transferred at any given time. When the download is complete, the program beeps three times and the window disappears.

Most communication programs allow you to switch over to a DOS prompt without quitting the communication program or breaking your connection with the dial-up host. You can use this feature to confirm that the transfer took place successfully. Once the file is successfully transferred, you can exit back to the communication program and continue your communications with the dial-up host. A good file management habit is to delete the *polly.txt* file from your personal workspace on the dial-up host while it is still clear in your mind what that file's purpose is and that you no longer need it.

Zmodem also permits downloading multiple files with one command. If you wanted to download all files with the *.txt* extension, you could enter **sz -a *.txt**.

CONNECTING TO A VAX COMPUTER

In the next FTP exercise, you connect to a VAX/VMS computer. VAX is a family of minicomputer systems produced by Digital Equipment Corporation and VMS (Virtual Memory System) is the operating system. VAX/VMS is different from UNIX in the way it displays directory information. Directory and file names are listed in uppercase in the left column and directories are designated with a *.dir* extension. In the second column, the file size is given in kilobytes. (To translate this number into bytes, simply multiply by 1,000.) To move up one directory, use the command cdup.

Making the Connection

Begin this session by entering the **ftp ftp.wku.edu** command. This connects you with the FTP archive at Western Kentucky University, which runs on a VAX/VMS system. After logging in, enter a **dir** command. Notice how file information is displayed much differently than it is on UNIX systems. The session should look something like the following:

west:~$ **ftp ftp.wku.edu**
Connected to axp1.wku.edu.
220 ftp.wku.edu MadGoat FTP server V2.6 ready.
Name (ftp.wku.edu:star-host): **anonymous**
331 Guest login Okay, send ident or e-mail address as password.
Password: **guest**
230–
230– Welcome to the FTP archives at Western Kentucky University.
230–

230– This is the official home of the WKU VMS freeware archives, the
230– MadGoat Software archives, and the WKU mailing list archives.
230–
230– If you encounter any problems, please send mail to the archive
230– maintainer, Hunter Goatley <goathunter@PROCESS.COM>.
230–
230– This site runs Process Software's TCPware. For more information
230– on TCPware and Process's MultiNet, see www.process.com.
230–
230–Guest guest login Okay, 8–APR-2000 22:08:01 -0500, access restrictions apply.
230 Connection closes if idle for 15 min.
Remote system type is VMS.
ftp> **dir**
200 Port 209,150,128,113,30,60 Okay.
150 LIST of *.*; Started; Opening data connection.

ANONYMOUS_ROOT:[000000]

.MESSAGE;1 1 13–JAN-1999 15:34 ARCHIVES (RWED,RWED,,RE)
JOURNEY.DIR;1 1 17–OCT-1995 14:45 ARCHIVES (RWE,RWE,RE,RE)
LISTS.DIR;1 3 24–JAN-1995 09:40 ARCHIVES (RWE,RWE,RE,RE)
MADGOAT.DIR;1 3 5–JAN-1995 12:11 ARCHIVES (RWE,RWE,RE,RE)
MX.DIR;1 2 5–JAN-1995 12:11 ARCHIVES (RWE,RWE,RE,RE)
SICKTHINGS.DIR;1 1 5–JAN-1995 12:13 ARCHIVES (RWE,RWE,RE,RE)
VMS.DIR;1 1 5–JAN-1995 12:13 ARCHIVES (RWE,RWE,RE,RE)

Total of 7 Files, 12 Blocks.
226 File transfer Okay.

If you FTP to an IBM mainframe, for example *ftp.temple.edu*, you shouldn't see any difference in how the directory information is displayed on your monitor.

Downloading a Text File

For additional practice in downloading text files, explore the following FTP archives:

1. UKUNET Archive *ftp.uu.net* (Look in */doc/literary/obi/Misc/Books/*)
2. Project Gutenberg Etexts–University of North Carolina (Main Project Gutenberg FTP Site) *metalab.unc.edu* (Look in */pub/docs/books/gutenberg/*)

Continue practicing the commands for connecting, moving through directories, and downloading files that were explained in earlier exercises. At most FTP sites, you find the interesting files and directories located under */pub*.

If you find a text file you'd like to refer to later, record the following information for future reference: document title, host address, path, file size, and file name. Remember, always insert the ftp command before the host's Internet address when trying to connect.

DOWNLOADING BINARY FILES

Any data that is not plain text is binary data and a file that contains binary data is referred to as a *binary file*. Some examples of binary files are sound recordings, pictures, and executable programs.

Because binary files contain binary data, they must be transferred in binary mode. ASCII text is the default mode of file transfer in FTP, so unless you tell the program something different, the FTP application will assume you are working with text files. Switching to a binary setting is a simple process. Simply enter the **binary** command before you enter the **get** or **mget** command. When you have changed the transfer mode to binary, that mode remains in effect until you quit your session or until you enter the **ascii** command again.

If you find after transferring your files that they are corrupted, you may have failed to set the transfer type to binary before you transferred the file from the remote host to your local host. If you are using a dial-up service, make sure that you also set the file transfer type to binary when you transfer the file from your service provider's computer to your own personal computer.

CLASSIFICATIONS OF SOFTWARE

Software resources on the Internet can be divided into three classifications: public domain, freeware, and shareware. *Public domain* software carries no copyright and is made available by the programmer without any restrictions. No limitations are imposed on its distribution and it can be transformed or modified by anyone without first obtaining permission from the author or paying the author a fee.

Freeware is copyrighted software made available for public use without charge. By retaining the copyright, the author can restrict the redistribution and modification of the software.

Shareware programs are also copyrighted but are made available on a trial basis. If, after you try out the software, you decide to keep it and use it, you are required to pay the author a small fee. In return, you become a registered user and receive certain benefits such as a printed manual and technical support. If you decide not to keep the program, you must destroy the copies you have in your possession.

FILE COMPRESSION

In an effort to conserve storage space and keep related files grouped together, system managers running anonymous FTP archives use two special file formats. You must become familiar with these if you want to take full advantage of the binary holdings in FTP archives.

The first of these formatting procedures takes large files and compresses them into smaller files that require less storage space and downloading time. These are called *compressed* files and they must be transformed back into their original, or *decompressed*, state before they can be used.

The second format takes a set of related files and packs them together into a single file called an *archive*. For example, the separate documentation files and programs that constitute a piece of software are usually packed together into a single archive for easier storage and downloading. After you download an archived file to your own machine, you then have to unpack it to convert it back into its original state.

Many utilities like *tar*, *StuffIt*, and *pkzip* transform files into different formats. Most of the text and data compression programs used for performing these operations use standard public domain software that can be found at one of two sights:

1. In the United States, *http://wuarchive.wustl.edu/* or *ftp://wuarchive.wustl.edu/systems/* at Washington University, St. Louis
2. In Europe, http://*garbo.uwasa.fi* or *garbo.uwasa.fi* at the University of Vaasa, Finland.

Many other sites have the same programs, in particular *http://oak.oakland.edu/*. This is the primary mirror site of SIMTEL20 (U.S. Army Information Systems Command at White Sands Missile Range in New Mexico), which closed down in September 1993. The Oak Software Repository is an FTP archive maintained by Oakland University, in Rochester, Michigan. If you are looking for Windows applications via FTP, go to *ftp://oak.oakland.edu/pub/simtelnet/*. Mac users should try looking in the Download Zone at *http://w3.trib.com/~dwood/software.html*.

DOWNLOADING A ZIP FILE

A *zip* file is a single file in which one or more compressed files are stored. In the next exercise, you download a zip file and the software needed for transforming the zip file into a normal file (called *unzipping* the file).

To retrieve a zip file, begin by FTPing to the following site to download a copy of *balloons.zip*. I chose this file because it's small (only 150K) and it might come in handy if you ever meet a young child who wants to shoot balloons with a cursor.

1. *gatekeeper.dec.com /pub/micro/pc/winsite/win95/games/balloons.zip*
    The session will look something like this:

```
west:~$ ftp gatekeeper.dec.com
Connected to gatekeeper.dec.com.
220– *** /etc/motd.ftp ***
Original by: Paul Vixie, 1992
Last Revised: Richard Schedler, April 1994

Gatekeeper.DEC.COM is an unsupported service of Digital Corporate Research.
Use entirely at your own risk - no warranty is expressed or implied.
Complaints and questions should be sent to <gw-archives@pa.dec.com>.

EXPORT CONTROL NOTE: Non-U.S. ftp users are required by law to follow U.S.
export control restrictions, which means that if you see some DES or
otherwise controlled software here, you should not grab it. Look at the
file 00README-Legal-Rules-Regs (in every directory, more or less) to learn
more. (If the treaty between your country and the United States did not
require you to respect U.S. export control restrictions, then you would
```

not have Internet connectivity to this host. Check with your U.S. embassy
if you want to verify this.)

Extended commands available via:

quote site exec COMMAND
Where COMMAND is one of:
index PATTERN - to glance through our index (uses agrep). example:
ftp> quote site exec index emacs

This FTP server is based on the 4.3BSD-Reno version. Our modified sources
are in /pub/DEC/gwtools.

If you are connecting to gatekeeper from a VMS system running a version of
UCX earlier than V2.0, a bug in UCX will prevent the automatic login from
working. To get around this, wait for the message that says:
%UCX-E-FTP_LOGREJ, Login request rejected
and then log in by hand with the "login" command at the "FTP>" prompt. You
should also consider upgrading to the latest version of UCX.

220 gatekeeper.dec.com FTP server (Version 5.182 Mon Apr 3 17:48:00 PDT 2000) ready.
Name (gatekeeper.dec.com:star-host): **anonymous**
331 Guest login ok, send ident as password.
Password: **guest**
230 Guest login ok, access restrictions apply.
Remote system type is UNIX.
Using binary mode to transfer files.
ftp> **cd /pub/micro/pc/winsite/win95/games**
250 CWD command successful.
ftp> **binary**
200 Type set to I.
ftp> **get balloons.zip**
local: balloons.zip remote: balloons.zip
200 PORT command successful.
150 Opening BINARY mode data connection for balloons.zip (153756 bytes).
226 Transfer complete.
153756 bytes received in 0.714 secs (2.1e+02 Kbytes/sec)
ftp> **quit**
221 Goodbye.

If you can't login to this site, or the file has moved to some unknown directory, try one
of the sites listed below.

   2. *ftp.sunsite.org.uk /Mirrors/ftp.winsite.com/pub/pc/windows95/games/balloons.zip*
   3. *ftp.esat.net /mirrors/ftp.winsite.com/pub/pc/win95/games/balloons.zip*

Notice that after logging in and moving to the desired directory, I entered the binary
command before entering the get command.

You may want to enter the **ldir** command to confirm that the file arrived before quitting the FTP session. If you have a dial-up connection to a local host, the next step is to download the file from your local host to your personal computer using Zmodem or one of the other file transfer protocols mentioned earlier.

When the transfer is complete, store the *balloons.zip* file in its own directory on your personal computer and proceed to the next exercise where you download software that transforms *balloons.zip* into a usable file. If you would rather use a Web browser to download this file, point your browser to: *ftp://gatekeeper.dec.com/pub/micro/pc/winsite/ win95/games/balloons.zip*

GETTING A COPY OF PKUNZIP

The most commonly used program for transforming zip files is PKZIP. This is a shareware program produced by PKWARE Inc., 9025 N. Deerwood Drive, Brown Deer, Wisconsin 53223. It comes in both DOS and Windows varieties. The latest official 32–bit Windows version is version 2.70. The latest 16–bit version for Windows 3.1 or NT 3.5 is PKZIP 2.60.03. The latest for DOS is version 2.50. PKZIP is also available for OS/2 and UNIX. You need to have the latest version of PKUNZIP. If you have an older version, such as version 1.1, you can decompress only those files made with PKZIP version 1.1 or earlier. If you have the latest version, you can decompress any zip file made with PKZIP 2.70 or earlier. PKZIP can be downloaded from PKWARE's Website *www.pkware.com/*.

Stuffit Expander is probably the single most popular decompression utility for Macs. The program also can convert MacBinary and *.hqx* files so your Mac computer can recognize them as normal Mac files. You can download this freeware from FTP site *ftp.aladdinsys.com* in the */pub/mac* directory. Stuffit Expander for Windows is a Windows version of this software and is also available as freeware.

If you choose to get PKZIP using the FTP client native to Windows or UNIX, as you have done so far in this chapter, the session should look something like the one illustrated below. In this exercise, I FTP to Internet Connect's FTP server at *ftp.inc.net* to download the latest version for PKZIP for Windows. Remember to set the transfer mode to binary before downloading the file.

west:~$ **ftp ftp.inc.net**
Connected to ftp.inc.net.
220 ProFTPD 1.2.0pre10 Server (ftp.inc.net) [ftp.inc.net]
Name (ftp.inc.net:star-host): **anonymous**
331 Anonymous login ok, send your complete e-mail address as password.
Password:**guest**
230–Welcome to the Internet Connect, Inc. FTP Server
────────────────────────────────────

You are user 9 out of 50 possible connections.

────────────────────────────────────

Subject	Path
Internet Connect	/pub/icon
AWE-32 files	/pub/awe32
Merge Technologies	/pub/merge
Appalachian Trail	/pub/at
PK-Ware	/pub/pkware
Metrix Software	/pub/metrix
Misc. Security	/pub/security
Perry Printing	/pub/perry
Repro Graphics	/pub/repro
Protel International	/pub/protel

Please email ftpadmin@twtelecom.net if you have questions regarding this server.

Enjoy your stay!

http://www.inc.net
230 Anonymous access granted, restrictions apply.
Remote system type is UNIX.
Using binary mode to transfer files.
ftp> **cd pub**
250 CWD command successful.
ftp> **cd pkware**
250 CWD command successful.
ftp> **binary**
200 Type set to I.
ftp> **get PK270WSP.EXE**
local: PK270WSP.EXE remote: PK270WSP.EXE
200 PORT command successful.
150 Opening BINARY mode data connection for PK270WSP.EXE (1067555 bytes).
226 Transfer complete.
1067555 bytes received in 1.67 secs (6.3e+02 Kbytes/sec)
ftp> **bye**
221 Goodbye.

TRANSFERRING A BINARY FILE WITH KERMIT

Now transfer the *PK270WSP.EXE* file from your dial-up host to your personal computer, using one of the standard protocols described earlier. For demonstration purposes, this exercise illustrates how the session looks if you are using Kermit. (If Kermit isn't available to you, use one of the protocols that is.)

After quitting the FTP session and retiring to your local host, type **kermit** and press ENTER. Next, type **set file type binary** and press ENTER. Now, type **send PK270WSP.EXE** and press ENTER. Using Kermit to download the file to your personal computer will look something like this:

```
$ kermit
VMS Kermit-32 version 3.3.128
Default terminal for transfers is: _LTA5756:
Kermit-32>set file type binary
Current block size for file transfer is 512
Kermit-32>send PK270WSP.EXE
```

DECOMPRESSING THE PK270WSP.EXE FILE

Once you have PK270WSP.EXE on your local PC, create a separate directory and copy it to that directory. Because the file has an *.exe* extension, it may look as though it is an executable file. Actually it is a self-extracting MS-DOS executable file. *Self-extracting* files decompress themselves on disk when you run them.

To run the program, go to the folder in which the file is stored. At the DOS prompt, type **PK270WSP** and press ENTER. If you prefer, you can locate the file using Windows Explorer and double-click on the file name to run it. After a few moments, the directory displays over a dozen normal files, one of which will be *PKUNZIP.EXE*. If you are working on an IBM-compatible computer, this is the program you use to decompress any files you download with the .zip extension. These files have been compressed and archived with PKZIP, a companion program that is also included in the PK270WSP.EXE file.

UNZIPPING AND INSTALLING *BALLOONS.ZIP*

In this exercise, you use the PKUNZIP utility to "unzip" the file you downloaded earlier called *balloons.zip*. Click on the "Start" button and choose "Programs|Pkware|PKZIP for Windows." Once PKZIP is running, click on "File|Open" and locate *balloons.zip* and open the Zip file. This presents you with a preview of what is contained in the *balloons.zip* file. Next, click on "Extract|Extract files." Choose the files you wish to extract, in this case all of them, and choose the folder in which you wish to place them. To complete the process, click on the "Extract" button.

VIEWING THE DECOMPRESSED FILES

Once *balloons.zip* is unzipped, you see five new files as well as the original file *balloons.zip*. The original zip-formatted file was not changed and can be deleted if you see that everything is in order.

ZIPPING A FILE

PKUNZIP's companion program, PKZIP, takes one or more normal files and compresses them into a single zip-formatted file. In the next exercise you learn how to "zip" a file.

Let's say you wrote an article that you'd like to upload to a remote computer's FTP archive. First you would save the document, either as a plain ASCII text file or formatted document; next, compress it using PKZIP; and then upload it to your local host computer. From there, you would upload it to a remote computer of your choosing by using the put command.

For example, if you wrote a bibliography and named the file *BKLST.TXT*, the following process turns *BKLST.TXT* into a zip-formatted file called *BKLIST.ZIP*. Begin by opening PKZIP. Select "File|Wizard." When the PKZIP for Windows Wizard opens, select "Compress files into a new .ZIP file." Follow the onscreen instructions, selecting the files you wish to compress, and then compressing them.

AN ALTERNATIVE TO PKZIP

Another popular utility for zipping and unzipping files is WinZip. You can download a copy from WinZip's Website at *www.winzip.com/*. WinZip has received several awards including Best Utility MVP Award from *PC Computing* (January 2000 issue), 1999 Editor's Choice Award from *PC Magazine*, and the 1998 "World Class" Award from *PC World*.

FTP COMMANDS REVIEWED

The following list outlines the major FTP commands that have been introduced in this chapter. For a more complete listing online, enter **help** or **?** at the *FTP>* prompt.

ascii—This command puts FTP in the mode to transfer ASCII text files. It is the default mode for FTP.

binary—This command puts FTP in the mode to transfer binary files.

cd <directory>—The cd command changes directories on the remote host, where z "<directory>" is the name of the directory to which you want to move. When you enter a path, separate directory names with the slash character. For example, cd pub/docs/history.

cd ..—This command makes the directory above the one you're working in the current directory on the remote host.

cdup—This command also changes the directory to the directory one level up on the remote host.

dir–This is the "directory" command; it lists the contents of the current directory on the remote machine.

Online Resource
For additional information on compression, check out the Compression Pointers Website at *www.internz.com/compression-pointers.html*. Their "People" section includes a directory of people working in the field of compression.

dir <remote file name or directory> <local file name>—When you use the dir command with these two arguments, the remote file name or directory that you specify is moved to your local machine with a "local" file name that you have assigned it.

get <file name>—The get command transfers or downloads the specified file from the remote host to the local host.

get <remote file name> <local file name>—Attaching these two arguments to the get command enables you to transfer the file and also rename it with a local file name.

hash—The hash command turns hash mark printing on and off (toggle printing "#"). This feature is handy on long downloads. As you watch the rows of #s print to your screen, you know the download is taking place. Without the hash marks, your screen would not show any evidence of activity and you may wonder if you lost your connection or if the system locked up.

help—The help command prints online user help.

mget <file names>—The mget command transfers multiple files from the remote host to the local host.

mput <file names>—The mput command transfers multiple files from the local host to the remote host.

prompt—This command forces interactive prompting on the multiple commands mget and mput. The first time you enter prompt, for example, it turns the interactive mode off. That means when you run mget or mput, you are not asked whether you want to proceed with the file transfer for each individual file. The next time you enter **prompt**, it turns the interactive mode back on. Now you are asked, or *prompted*, for a "yes" or "no" before each individual file transfers. Turning the interactive mode off is highly recommended when you are downloading dozens or hundreds of files.

pwd—This command displays the current directory on the remote host.

quit—This command, or the exit command, causes the FTP program to terminate.

statistics—The statistics command acts as a toggle switch, turning on or off the feature that prints file transfer timing statistics.

ACCESSING FTP SERVICES ON THE WEB

Not too long ago, the only way to transfer files on the Internet was by using a stand-alone application called an FTP client. Thus far, Chapter 13 has discussed using an FTP client running in DOS or on a dial-up UNIX host. These are character-based (no graphics) and require that you enter commands at a prompt. This is referred to as a *command-line interface*.

The same has been true for most of Gopher's existence. If you wanted to browse Gopher menus, you had to run a separate application called a Gopher client. The Gopher interface looked and worked differently from an FTP interface. WAIS and Archie clients also had their own look and feel.

The Web has changed all this. Web browsers have simplified life by providing librarians with a common window for accessing FTP sites and running Archie searches; sending and receiving e-mail; or reading newsgroups. Now, one single window to the Internet accesses all of these services and more.

To access FTP sites using a graphical Web browser, you first must establish a dial-up PPP account or connect to the Internet via a local LAN at work or school. To gain the greatest benefit from this method of connection, run Netscape Navigator 4.5 or higher, or Microsoft's Internet Explorer 5.0 or higher.

VIEWING TEXT FILES

One of the advantages of accessing FTP sites via the Web is that you can easily view text files by clicking on their file names. Browsers such as Netscape Navigator also allow you to cut and paste text from these files to other Windows applications or save a copy of the file to your hard drive.

Follow these steps to connect to an FTP site and view a text file:

1. Launch your Web browser.
2. Enter the address *ftp://arizona.edu/* in the "Location" box. This links you to the FTP archive at the University of Arizona.
3. Click on the file named *0readme*. This links you to a document that explains the contents of the site.
   i. When you finish reviewing the document, click on the "Back" button to return to the root directory.
   ii. You can also view the "University of Arizona Network Information File" by clicking on the file named *information.txt*.

To save a text file while viewing it in your browser, click on "File|Save As." Choose a location for saving the file and click "OK."

For more practice in reading text files stored on FTP servers, point your browser to Maryland's Online Information Service "Sailor" at *ftp://sailor.gutenberg.org/pub/gutenberg/*. To begin with, click on the file named *index.html* to view the contents of Sailor's Project Gutenberg Server.

VIEWING IMAGES

Most modern Web browsers are pre-configured to display GIF and JPEG images. If you want to do more than just view images—for example, resize images or change their formats—you will need a graphics editor. You can find several freeware and shareware graphics editors at *winfiles.cnet.com/apps/98/graph-view.html*. To simply *view* a JPGE or GIF image archived at an FTP site, follow these steps:

1. Launch your Web browser.
2. Enter the address *ftp://wuarchive.wustl.edu/* in the "Location" box.
3. Scroll down through the root directory of Wuarchive until you come to the "multimedia" directory. Click on "multimedia."

    i. Scroll down through the multimedia directory and click on "images."
    ii. Scroll down through the images directory and click on "gif."
    iii. Scroll through the gif directory and click on any letter of the alphabet you wish. Each of these directories holds dozens of images.
    iv. To view JPEG images, click on the "Back" button until you are once again in the images directory. Now go down the JPEG path.
    v. If you get the following message—"Could not login to FTP server"—it's a sign that too many are logged in. Simply click on the "Back" button and try again. If a mirror address is provided, you can try that site.

To save an image you view in your browser, place the mouse cursor over the image and right-click. Choose "Save Image As" and then select a location for saving the image file.

FTP Error
Could not login to FTP server
Sorry, there are too many anonymous FTP users using the system at this time. Please try again in a few minutes. There is currently a limit of 200 anonymous users. We encourage you to access wuarchive via the World Wide Web and http rather than ftp. The web address for wuarchive is:
       http://wuarchive.wustl.edu
Web users can click here.
Thank you
User anonymous access denied.

LISTENING TO AUDIO FILES

Web browsers make listening to certain audio file formats a simple process. All of the latest browsers running under Windows 95/98/2000 support MIDI and WAVE files. While you are logged into the Washington University archive, listen to some of the MIDI files stored at that site. Begin by entering the following address in your browser's location box: *ftp://wuarchive.wustl.edu/multimedia/midi/*. Once you have connected, click on one of the many sub-directories listed in the midi directory, for example, "a-ha." This takes you to the file named *take_on_me.mid*. The URL that leads you directly to this audio file is notated as *ftp://wuarchive.wustl.edu/multimedia/midi/a-ha/take_on_me.mid*.

To save this audio file, click on "File|Save As" and choose a location to save the file.

DOWNLOADING AN EXECUTABLE FILE

Downloading executable files is an easy process with a Web browser. You don't need to run a separate program or learn UNIX commands. Follow these steps to download a file:
Launch your Web browser.

1. Make sure you have a temporary directory designated for storing files.
2. Enter the following address in the "Location" box: *ftp://ftp.cdrom.com/.1/games/windows/educate/*

3. Look in the "educate" directory for the *00_index.txt* file or *index.html* (to view as a Web page) and click on it. This text file describes the software stored in the educate directory. Decide which one you'd like to download. If you are viewing the *index.html*, simply click on the file name and the download process begins. If you are viewing the *00_index.txt* file, click on the "Back" button to take you back to the educate directory and then select the desired file.

4. When you click on a file name, a "Viewing Location" window pops up and shows you the progress of the download. If your browser doesn't know how to "display" a file—for example, a file with a *.zip* extension—it returns with an "Unknown File Type" dialog box. If this happens, click on "Save to Disk." In other circumstances, if you are simply given the option of saving the file or opening it, choose save. After you click on the save option, you are asked where you want to save the file. After you designate a location on your hard drive and click "OK," your browser shows you the download progress.

FTP MAIL

This section describes how you can access FTP services using *FTP mail servers*—programs that enable you to download text files and software using the Internet mail system. By typing special commands in the body of an e-mail message and sending them to an FTP mail server, you can accomplish the same tasks you would if you had connected to a regular FTP server. Even if you have access to an FTP program, you may choose to use an FTP mail server instead. You can send an FTP transaction off in the mail and it will process on its own while you're doing other work. This is especially convenient when the other FTP server allows only ten simultaneous logins and you are caller number eleven.

One of the better-known FTP mail services is called *ftpmail*, an application written by Paul Vixie at Digital Equipment Corporation (DEC). Here are two ftpmail sites you can try:

bitftp@pucc.princeton.edu   USA
ftpmail@ccc.uba.ar   Argentina (Server speaks in Spanish!)

When sending e-mail to a mail server, leave the subject field blank. Place the information necessary for retrieving the file in the body of the message. The basic message

---

Online Resource

The University of Michigan's Macintosh Public Domain and Shareware Archive is a very popular Macintosh FTP site and one worth exploring. Here you find a wide variety of applications for listening to sound files and viewing graphics on Macs. This archive is mirrored on dozens of sites around the world. First try AOL's mirror site in Virginia at *ftp:// mirror.aol.com/pub/mac/*. Once you arrive, read the file called *00introduction* for tips on downloading files and pointers to other mirror sites.

format for retrieving text files is illustrated as follows (the message address format may look slightly different, depending on the service provider you're using):

To: **bitftp@pucc.princeton.edu**
Subj:
FTP <host>
USER anonymous guest
ascii
chdir <path>
get <file name>
quit

The first command in the body of the message is "FTP <host>," where "<host>" is the site address of the FTP server to which you want to connect. This address should not be confused with the FTP "mail server" address. The mail server address (*bitftp@pucc.princeton.edu* in the above example) is the address to which your request is sent. In the body of your message, you list the FTP host address of the archive you'd like to search. Next comes the anonymous login sequence "USER anonymous guest" where "anonymous" is the user ID and "guest" is the password. The ascii command is used for downloading text files as opposed to binary files. The command "chdir <path>" means change the directory to whatever path you designate. The get "<file name>" command serves the same function as the get command you use when connected to a regular FTP server where "<file name>" is the name of the file you want to download. The word "quit" tells the mail server that you have finished sending commands. The following example illustrates a specific request:

To: **bitftp@pucc.princeton.edu**
Subj:
FTP ftp.uark.edu
USER anonymous guest
ascii
chdir /pub/docs/internet
get ftp.help
quit

In most cases, ftpmail is not a supported service. This means that if the system goes down, the system administrators will fix it only when time allows. This could translate into time delays lasting days if things aren't working quite right. Usually, the system administrator will inform you of these conditions by posting a warning in the help file.

After sending the above message, you may get a return message from the mail server similar to the following:

We processed the following input from your mail message:

connect ftp.uark.edu
ascii
chdir /pub/docs/internet
get ftp.help
quit

We have entered the following request into our job queue
as job number 836861600.04006:

    connect ftp.uark.edu anonymous -ftpmail/acbenson@cris.com
    reply acbenson@cris.com
    chdir /pub/docs/internet
    get ftp.help ascii

There are 168 jobs ahead of this one in our queue.

You should expect the results to be mailed to you within a day or so. We try to drain the request queue every 30 minutes, but sometimes it fills up with enough junk that it takes until midnight (Pacific time) to clear. Note, however, that since ftpmail sends its files out with "Precedence: bulk", they receive low priority at mail relay nodes.

Note that the "reply" or "answer" command in your mailer will not work for this message or any other mail you receive from FTPMAIL. To send requests to FTPMAIL, send an original mail message, not a reply. As shown in the header of this message, complaints should be sent to the ftpmail-admin@ftpmail.ramona.vix.com address rather than to postmaster, since our postmaster is not responsible for fixing ftpmail problems. There is no way to delete this request, so be sure that it has failed before you resubmit it or you will receive multiple copies of anything you have requested.

If all goes as it should, the mail server should return a message similar to the one shown here:

```
> FTP ftp.uark.edu
> USER anonymous guest
>> OPEN FTP.UARK.EDU
<<< Connecting to FTP.UARK.EDU 130.184.5.11, port 21
<<< 220 cavern.uark.edu FTP server (Version wu-2.5.0(1) Wed Jun 30 17:43:51
 CDT 1999
<<< ) ready.
>> USER anonymous
>>> USER anonymous
<<< 331 Guest login ok, send your complete e-mail address as password.
<<< Password:
>> star-host%westhost.westhost.net@pucc.Princeton.EDU
>>> PASS ********
<<< 230-Welcome to the Anonymous FTP server at cavern.uark.edu.
<<< 230-We hope you find what you are looking for.
<<< 230-Questions or comments concerning this FTP service
<<< 230-should be directed to ftpadmin@cavern.uark.edu.
<<< 230————————————————————
<<< 230-Logged in as anonymous at Sun Apr 9 22:24:31 2000.
<<< 230-You are user 2 of 20.
<<< 230————————————————————
<<< 230-
<<< 230 Guest login ok, access restrictions apply.

> ascii
>> ascii
```

```
>>> TYPE a
<<< 200 Type set to A.

> chdir /pub/docs/internet
>> CD /pub/docs/internet
>>> CWD /pub/docs/internet
<<< 250 CWD command successful.

> get ftp.help
>> GET ftp.help FTP.HELP.D ( REPLACE
>>> PORT 128,112,129,99,143,203
<<< 200 PORT command successful.
>>> RETR ftp.help
<<< 150 Opening ASCII mode data connection for ftp.help (10832 bytes).
<<< 226 Transfer complete.
<<< 11128 bytes transferred in 0.320 seconds. Transfer rate 34.77 Kbytes/sec.
>>>> "ftp.help" sent as mail.
*********************************************************************************
* You will note that the rate of transfer between BITFTP and the host *
* you are FTPing from is quite low. If possible, please choose a *
* different host in the future. Note that BITFTP is located in North *
* America and thus has the best connectivity to hosts that are also in *
* North America.
*********************************************************************************
> quit
>> CLOSE
>>> QUIT
<<< 221-You have transferred 11128 bytes in 1 files.
<<< 221-Total traffic for this session was 12122 bytes in 1 transfers.
<<< 221-Thank you for using the FTP service on cavern.uark.edu.
<<< 221 Goodbye.
```

Following this message, another e-mail message arrives containing the requested text file.

You cannot ask for only certain parts of a file to be sent. If you receive output from ftpmail that seems to be missing some parts, it is likely that some mailer between here and there has dropped them. You can try your request again. You cannot specify that your request should be tried only during certain hours of the day. If you need a file from a time-restricted FTP server, you probably cannot get it via ftpmail.

The mail server sends you a file with instructions on how to use the system if you simply type **help** on the first line and **quit** on the second line, like this:

To: **ftpmail@decwrl.dec.com**
Subj:
help
quit

Table 13–1 provides a summary of the commands discussed in this help file.

Table 13–1: Commands in the FTP mail help file	
Command	**Description**
reply <e-mail address>	Use this command if you want to make sure the mail server returns the information to the correct address. FTP uses the address in the header, but if that's wrong, you won't receive anything back from the mail server.
connect <host>	Use this command to designate the host to which you'd like to connect.
ascii	Insert this command when the files you're downloading are printable ASCII files.
binary	Use this command when you're downloading compressed and/or archived files.
chdir <path>	Use this command to change to a specified directory. Use only one chdir command per ftpmail session.
compress	Use this command to compress a binary file before sending it.
uuencode	Use this command to tell ftpmail to convert a binary file into uuencode format before transferring. You must use this command when downloading binary files or they will arrive corrupted.
chunksize <bytes>	Use this command to divide the file into chunks, where "<bytes>" is the chunk size you specify. The default size is 64,000 bytes. If your dial-up host accepts only mail messages smaller than 10,000 bytes, for example, you would insert the command **chunksize 9,000** on one of the lines in the body of your message.
get <filename>	Use this command to retrieve the file you specify. You cannot use the get command more than ten times per ftpmail session.
quit	Use this command to end your ftpmail session. It should be the last command you enter.

MANAGING FTP SERVERS IN WINDOWS

While Web browsers work nicely for viewing and downloading one file at a time, they don't permit you to manage your own FTP server—uploading and downloading multiple files, renaming and deleting files, etc.—and they don't permit you to upload single or multiple files to an anonymous FTP server.

For this kind of work you need a standalone FTP client, much like the one you used in the earlier part of this chapter, only this time it needs to be a GUI (Graphical User Interface) program.

There are several Windows-based FTP clients available. Some are freeware and others are shareware. One that I have successfully used for years is called WS_FTP. If you are associated with an educational institution, the Limited Edition version of WS_FTP is free for the asking. You can download a copy of WS_FTP Limited Edition from *www.ipswitch.com*. Click on the "Download Evaluations" button to download a copy of WS_FTP LE 5.08, the current version of the program.

Cute FTP is another popular shareware application that you can download from *www.cuteftp.com/*. Other FTP clients can be found at CNET's WinFiles.com *winfiles.cnet.com/apps/98/ftp.html*.

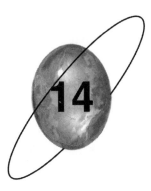

Telnet: Remote Login

Telnet is a powerful Internet application that enables librarians to access remote computer systems, including libraries' online catalogs worldwide. Accessing other libraries' catalogs can help you verify information for acquisitions, interlibrary loan, and copy cataloging. When you access systems such as CARL's UnCover (*database.carl.org*), you can search magazine article indexes online. Telnet can assist you in managing remote Web servers by allowing you to login and perform file maintenance tasks.

In this chapter, I introduce you to the basics of how to run the telnet program from a UNIX shell account and from your Web browser. I also show you how to access resources and services on the Internet that utilize telnet and where to go for telnet software.

WHAT IS TELNET?

Telnet is a powerful Internet application that is built around a client/server architecture like most of the other Internet applications introduced in this book. The client program, running on your computer, initiates the connection with a server program, running on a remote machine. Keystrokes are passed from your terminal directly to the remote computer just as though they were being typed at a terminal on the remote computer. Output from the remote computer is sent back and displayed on your terminal. Once logged into the remote server, your client program allows you to run programs on the remote computer as if your keyboard were directly connected to it.

Online Resources

Several RFC documents pertaining to telnet are available. Two that may be of particular interest are #0854 (May 1983) *Telnet Protocol Specifications* and #855 (May 1983) *Telnet Options Specifications*. To obtain copies of these documents, point your Web browser to Internet RFC/STD/FYI/BCP Archives at *www.faqs.org/rfcs/*.

WHAT IS TELNET USED FOR?

When the first edition of this book came out in 1995, telnet was the only means by which a librarian at the Denver Public Library, for example, could access the OPAC at the University of Alabama. Since then, new developments using Web-based catalogs and the Z39.50 protocol have made it possible to access library catalogs using Web browsers. The Z39.50 protocol is a set of rules that enables you to view disparate library automation systems through a common interface as long as all of the systems involved support the Z39.50 protocol. Another development that has made telneting to OPACs less relevant is Web-based automation systems, such as SIRSI Corporation's WebCat (for example, University of Minnesota, Duluth *www.d.umn.edu/lib/*) and Endeavor Information Systems' Voyager (for example, Library of Congress *catalog.loc.gov/*).

In light of all this, telnet is still a valuable and necessary tool for accessing some of the world's library catalogs, but many of the other diverse resources telnet can access are more easily accessed using a Web browser. Telnet can also be used to login remotely to UNIX systems and perform maintenance tasks. This is one of the more practical applications of telnet. For example, in your library you may use telnet to login to a UNIX system that runs your Web server. Once logged in, you can delete old files, check e-mail using a program such as Pine, or use telnet to hopscotch to yet another computer somewhere else in the world.

Many of the public telnet resources serve very specific purposes, such as the Student Computer Association BBS at the University of Iowa (ISCABBS). This forum is where the Sysops posts administrative announcements concerning ISCABBS. "Sysops" is short for *system operator*, the individual who manages a bulletin board system (BBS) or other online service. The system is a menu-driven communications tool that offers help files and it allows others to post administrative questions. The system can be reached by telneting to *bbs.isca.uiowa.edu*. You can login as "guest" just to look around, or login as "new" to set up an account. You also find systems like the Baker College of Flint Public Access Catalog that offers a full menu of services including InfoTrac, OCLC FirstSearch, Proquest Direct, Library News, and keyword searching and browsing of their bibliographic database. You can access this system by telneting to *hp.falcon.edu*.

Gateway systems, such as the CARL Corporation Network at *database.carl.org*, provide centralized access to several other systems. You are in effect telneting to reach machine A and then invoking telnet on machine A to reach machine B.

Table 14-1: Commercial databases that can be accessed using telnet		
Database Name	**Domain Name**	**IP Address**
CARL UnCover	*database.carl.org*	*[192.54.81.76]*
DIALOG	*dialog.com*	*[192.132.3.234]*
FirstSearch	*fscat.oclc.org*	*[204.151.6.106]*
Medlars	*medlars.nlm.nih.gov*	*[130.14.70.100]*
ORBIT	*orbit.com*	*[192.188.13.234]*

ACCESSING COMMERCIAL VENDORS VIA TELNET

The telnet service also enables librarians to access commercial online bibliographic utilities and services. Accessing commercial database utilities via the Internet can save the cost of local telephone service and long distance access charges from public data networks like TYMNET and SprintNet. Some examples of commercial databases and their corresponding telnet addresses are listed in Table 14–1. As noted earlier, these services have a friendlier interface when accessed via the Web.

RUNNING TELNET FROM A SHELL ACCOUNT

Telnet has a very useful and practical application when used for connecting to a UNIX shell account. This may be the only means you have for performing file maintenance tasks on remote computers. To run telnet and open the connection, you must issue the appropriate command. The command to invoke the telnet client on a UNIX computer (which you may be directly connected to, or you may be dialing into) is similar to this:

$ **telnet <domain_address>**

In this case, "telnet" is the command you enter to run the telnet software, and "<domain_address>" is the domain name or IP address of the remote machine you want to use (which may be a free service or a commercial database service like those listed in the previous section). You login to the remote host using an account number, password, or special username. For example, to connect to the telnet server at the University of Illinois Graduate School of Library and Information Science, you would enter the following:

$ **telnet carousel.lis.uiuc.edu**

A few moments later, the following text is displayed on your screen:

The Graduate School of Library and Information Science
University of Illinois at Urbana-Champaign
Welcome to carousel.lis.uiuc.edu! The following services are available:
login: Description

iris   Illinois Researcher Information Service (IRIS)
ops   Online Periodical Service (part of IRIS)
absees American Bibliography of Slavic & East European Studies
jobs   Library & Information Science Employment Opportunities
quit   log off

[Type the name of the service you want (in lowercase letters) at the login:]
[prompt below and then press <ENTER>.
login:

Next, type **jobs** in lowercase letters at the *login*: prompt and then press ENTER. This connects you to the Library and Information Science Employment Opportunities database. No password is required. The process of entering your name and password, if required, is called *logging in* or *logging on*. The next screen asks you to verify your terminal type. Enter **vt100** and press ENTER to move to the registration screen shown here.

UNIVERSITY OF ILLINOIS
GRADUATE SCHOOL OF LIBRARY AND INFORMATION SCIENCE
** PLACEMENT ONLINE SEARCH SERVICE **
The Placement Database contains professional job notices
received by GSLIS. This online service allow you to perform
searches of LIS-related jobs from our database. To post new
job announcements, please send e-mail to: lisjobs@uiuc.edu
Answer the following questions to enter the database:
Enter your last name ==> _____
Enter the last four digits of your Social Security Number ==> _____
Last updated: Unknown
- NEW - Access Jobs via the web with URL http://carousel.lis.uiuc.edu/~jobs/

Enter your last name, press ENTER, and then type last four digits of your Social Security Number and press ENTER. The next screen that appears looks like this:

M A I N M E N U
~~~~~~~~~~~~~~~~~~~~~~~~
(Enter a number or highlighted letter)
1. Introduction to the Database
2. Search Job Notices by Certain Criteria
3. Review All Job Notices in the Database
4. Review New Job Notices in the Database
5. Download New Job Notices
Q. Quit from the Database (Exit)
==>

To quit, type **q** and then press ENTER. Before logging out, you are asked if you want to leave any comments.

CONNECTING VIA YOUR WEB BROWSER OR DOS

You could connect to this same site using a basic client that comes with your Windows operating system. Enter **telnet://carousel.lis.uiuc.edu** in your Web browser's location box and press ENTER. Notice that a telnet URL begins with "telnet://" not "http://". Alternatively, you could enter the command **telnet carousel.lis.uiuc.edu** at the DOS prompt, press ENTER, and the same Windows-based client starts up and connects you to *carousel.lis.uiuc.edu*.

THE TELNET COMMAND MODE

When working in UNIX, if you enter the telnet command by itself without a target host's address, a *telnet>* client prompt appears and you are placed in what is called *telnet command mode*. You can type a question mark (?) at the *telnet>* prompt to display a list of valid telnet client commands. Among the various telnet commands that are available to you, the most common are open, quit, close, set, carriage return, and display.

The "open" command allows you to initiate a session from the *telnet>* prompt by typing "open <domain_name>." If the *telnet>* prompt is displayed on your screen, which means you are in command mode, you initiate a telnet connection by entering the command open, followed by the Internet address. For example, to connect to the San Jose State University Library and Instructional Resource Center, you would enter **open sjsulib1.sjsu.edu** at the *telnet>* prompt. If command mode is not active and the only thing displayed on your screen is the system prompt, you initiate this session by entering **telnet sjsulib1.sjsu.edu**. When you login to this site, here is the menu with which you are presented:

```
L > LIBRARY CATALOG - San Jose State University.
J > JOURNAL INDEXES & RELATED SOURCES - Uncover
O > OTHER DATABASES - Reference and Referral, Beethoven, National Gallery
of Art, Reserve Course Lists.
C > CATALOGS FROM OTHER LIBRARIES - University of California.
Hayward State University.
Q > QUIT THE SJSU ONLINE CATALOG
Choose one (L,J,O,C,Q)
```

The menu item "Other Databases" takes you to an interesting collection of books, articles, and other resources on Beethoven.

THE SET COMMAND

The set command allows you to set various operating parameters. Entering set? at the *telnet>* prompt provides you with a complete listing of these parameters. The display command displays the operating parameters in use for the current telnet session.

EXITING A TELNET SESSION

Exiting a telnet session is fairly simple. If you are provided with a menu, just choose "Quit, Exit," or whatever menu choice they offer for exiting the session. If you are in command mode, use the quit command to exit telnet. If you are currently connected to a remote machine, use the close command to disconnect from the remote machine without stopping the telnet program.

If you get stuck in a telnet session and it appears that things are locked up, try using the *telnet escape character* to quit. On UNIX systems, the telnet escape character is CTRL+]. Press the CTRL key and hold it down while pressing the right square bracket (]). This moves you into command mode. Press ENTER without entering a command to get out of command mode and get back into the telnet session with the remote computer. (Note: In some documentation, you will see the CTRL key indicated with the caret (^). For example, CTRL+Z is written as ^Z.)

Sometimes it may appear that the escape character doesn't work. This is because the remote host acts immediately on the input it receives from your keyboard, but the information it sends back to you is buffered. A little time may pass before the information appears on your screen. As a result, if you use the escape character it may seem as though it's not working because the data that has already left the remote host and found its way into the buffer will still arrive and be displayed on your screen.

PORT NUMBERS

Occasionally, you are asked to specify a port number when you make a telnet connection. *Port numbers* are positive integers that represent different destinations within a given host computer. Each destination provides a different service and these services are kept separate by giving each one a different port assignment.

Some ports are always reserved for certain standard services such as electronic mail, telnet, and FTP. Other numbers are used for special services; telnet traditionally uses port 23. If you don't designate a port in the telnet address, it connects to port 23 by default. If someone wants you to connect to a port other than 23, they must tell you.

For example, there used to be a popular host computer at the University of Michigan that provided weather reports for the United States and Canada. The system was called *Weather Underground*. In order to connect to this special service, you had to specify a port number of 3000. To specify port number 3000, type in **telnet downwind.sprl.umich.edu 3000**. If this command format for specifying the port number doesn't work at your site, check your local documentation on using telnet. On some systems, such as VAX/VMS, it's necessary to specify the port number in the following manner:

telnet downwind.sprl.umich.edu /port=3000

To see how specifying ports works, try telneting to the New Hampshire State Library using port 2000. Enter this address in your Web browser: ***telnet://199.92.250.12 2000***, or enter this command and address at your UNIX or DOS system prompt: **telnet 199.92.250.12 2000**.

Because port 23 is the default port for telnet, you can include it or leave it off. For example, both of these addresses work when you want to connect to the New York Public Library Network (login: **nypl**):

telnet nyplgate.nypl.org 23
telnet nyplgate.nypl.org

TERMINAL EMULATION

The telnet client software on your local host provides terminal emulation, and you should be aware of what type of terminal it is emulating. *Terminal emulation* means that your computer is emulating a terminal, not a full-blown computer. The PC setting on your desk is imitating a *dumb terminal*. Terminals are devices that consist of only a monitor and keyboard hardwired to a multiuser system such as a mainframe.

The remote host may ask you what type of terminal emulation you are using or give you a number of choices from which to pick. The most common type of terminal emulation is VT100 and most hosts accept VT100 emulation or something similar. Exceptions to this are IBM mainframes that neither accept nor use VT100 terminal emulation.

When you telnet into the California Digital Library at *melvyl.ucop.edu 23*, you are asked to present your terminal type. Here is the first screen with which you are presented:

```
DLA LINE 637 (TELNET) 20:06:50 04/16/00 (MELVYL.UCOP.EDU)
Please Enter Your Terminal Type Code or Type ? for a List of Codes.
TERMINAL?
```

If you are using an IBM PC or compatible and enter anything other than vt100, it may have an adverse effect on how the text is formatted on your screen.

When you are using the telnet client native to Windows, set your terminal emulation as follows: When the telnet program window opens, click on the pull-down menu named "Terminal" and choose "Preferences." Under "Emulation," choose "VT100/ANSI." This procedure varies depending on which client software you are running.

TN3270 APPLICATION FOR TELNETING TO IBM MAINFRAMES

You may need a special version of the telnet application called tn3270 on rare occasions when trying to establish a connection with an IBM mainframe. IBM mainframes are designed to interface with 3270 terminals, which work differently from others, including the vt100 terminal. For example, 3270 terminals use special *PF keys* (programmed function keys).

Sometimes, the IBM machines to which you are connecting automatically handle the appropriate terminal emulation. Other times, the system may freeze up and you must enter a telnet escape character to break the connection. In these instances, you can then try using tn3270 to reach the IBM computer.

The way the 3270 system works with input and output is different from other systems, and you may have to go through some trial and error in order to determine which keys have what functions. The 3270 runs a full-screen application, which means that you are expected to move around the screen by using the tab key and arrow keys, sometimes entering information in different fields. You will notice with 3270 systems that the screens do not scroll upward one line at a time; instead, the screen goes blank and a whole new screen appears.

Before making a connection to an IBM mainframe, you should find out which keys on your keyboard are mapped to the 3270 keys for CLEAR, ENTER, PF1, etc. With most keyboards, if you have to clear the screen, try pressing CTRL+Home or CTRL+Z.

A full list of PC key equivalents is included with a Windows application called QWS3270, described in the next paragraph. You can access the keyboard mapping chart by opening the "Help" menu and clicking on "Keyboard Mapping."

Jim Rymerson has written a telnet program called QWS3270 that supports 3270 terminal connections. If you install QWS3270 on your hard drive and then set a preference in the "TN3270 Applications" text box in Netscape, you'll find it much easier telneting to IBM mainframes. You can download a copy of *qws3270.zip* at FTP site *ftp.ucsc.edu* where it is found in the */PC/qws3270/* directory. To locate and download it using a Web browser, enter this URL: ***ftp://ftp.ucsc.edu/PC/qws3270/qws3270.zip***

Aside from the extra effort involved in telneting to an IBM mainframe in a shell account, using telnet is a rather simple operation. Once you learn the basic telnet commands and the procedure for logging on to a remote host, the only challenge you face is in making use of the resources you're accessing on the remote computer.

RECORDING INFORMATION

Telnet is not a service that makes it easy to move information from the remote computer to your own. If you want to record what occurs during a session, it's best to capture a log file of your session. Check with your computer department or the manual accompanying the communication software you use to learn just how this can be done on your system. PROCOMM PLUS for Windows, for example, gives the option of capturing to a file, Windows clipboard, or directly to the printer during a telnet session. Both methods are initiated by clicking on the appropriate pull-down menu.

The telnet client native to Windows allows you to select all and copy all under the "Edit" pull-down menu.

TROUBLESHOOTING

Sometimes, you may experience problems trying to connect to a remote host. If you fail to connect to a host using telnet, an error message appears on your screen, stating something like "?UnKnown INTERNET host." One reason this may occur is that you mistyped the domain name or IP address.

Another reason you may be unable to connect is that all the connections that the remote host supports are already in use. When this happens, you get a time-out message saying something like "Connection refused" or "There are too many interactive users at the moment."

PING COMMAND

Another cause of problems connecting to a remote host may be that the host you are trying to reach is down. Another cause is that some part of the network may be down or too congested. A command called ping can help in testing this kind of problem. You may have to find out how to do this on your particular system, but you can begin by simply typing the word **ping** at your system prompt, followed by the host address, and then press ENTER. For example, when you enter the command **ping ua1vm.ua.edu**, the host you are pinging will probably return something like "ua1vm.ua.edu is alive," or give you a continuous readout until you cancel by pressing CTRL C. You could enter a more involved command like the one shown below, which tells you how many milliseconds it takes a packet of information containing 100 bytes to make a round trip:

```
$ ping -s 100 ua1vm.ua.edu
PING ua1vm.ua.edu: 100 data bytes
108 bytes from ua1vm.ua.edu (130.160.4.100): icmp_seq=0. time=148. ms
108 bytes from ua1vm.ua.edu (130.160.4.100): icmp_seq=1. time=122. ms
108 bytes from ua1vm.ua.edu (130.160.4.100): icmp_seq=2. time=149. ms
—-ua1vm.ua.edu PING Statistics—-
3 packets transmitted, 3 packets received, 0% packet loss
round-trip (ms) min/avg/max = 122/139/149
```

The ping program sends data packets to the host, which in turn should echo them back if a connection is made. The IP address from which it is echoed back, the time it takes in milliseconds, and, sometimes, the size of the packet are given in the above report. If you receive a message that says no such host exists, there may be a problem with the domain network software and its attempt to translate the corresponding IP address. If you know the IP address, try using that to contact the host. If this works, the problem was the domain name. If neither the domain name nor IP address work, there's a good chance the server is down.

USING THE BACKSPACE KEY

One common problem occurs when the BACKSPACE key on your keyboard is not recognized by the remote system. Remember, you are emulating a terminal, so that particular key may have a new meaning. Experiment by holding down the CTRL key while you press the BACKSPACE key. You also can learn from your local telnet application how to set an erasing BACKSPACE. Type **?** or **set ?** at the *telnet>* prompt (notice that there is a space between "set" and "?") for help.

TELNET ON THE WEB

On most systems, opening a telnet URL in your Web browser launches an external telnet application. The telnet application is what connects you to the telnet site, not the Web browser. To successfully telnet using Internet Explorer or Netscape Communicator, precede the telnet address with "telnet://." In some versions of Web browsers, you can set a preference telling your browser where to find a particular telnet application on your hard drive. This is useful if you want to forgo using the telnet client that comes with Windows and replace it with another program that has more features.

TELNET RESOURCES

The following list of resources is a sampling of the kind of information that can be accessed on the Internet using telnet. Other resources are listed in Table 14–2.

1. The CARL Corporation Network and Uncover: CARL's network services offer access to UnCover, CARL System Libraries, and the following Open Access Databases. Type **telnet database.carl.org** (choose VT100 emulation):

   > OPEN ACCESS DATABASES
   >
   > 7. British Library Document Supply
   >   (Info & document delivery for 54,000 serial titles)
   > 9. Federal Domestic Assistance Catalog
   >   (List of domestic assistance grants from U.S. govt.)
   > ***NEW*** 27. Linda Hall Library (ARTICLE DELIVERY)
   > 42. U.S. Government Publications
   > 50. CONSER (serial records from the Library of Congress)
   > 58. General FirstSearch Access *Password required*

2. The FedWorld Information Network provides access to IRS tax form and information, Nuclear Regulatory Commission Online, and FedWorld. FedWorld offers a tremendous storehouse of information on subjects ranging from business and health to scientific and technical subjects. Type **telnet fedworld.gov.** Users must fill out registration form.

3. HYTELNET was a software utility created by Peter Scott that provided hypertext access to listings of Internet-accessible library catalogs, Free-Nets, CWISs (Campus Wide Information Systems), BBSs (Bulletin Board Systems), Gophers, and other telnet services.
   HYTELNET can still be accessed through the Web at *www.lights.com/hytelnet/*. The HYTELNET information page is no longer being kept up-to-date and many of the listings are dead links, but this is still a good source for accessing online library catalogs that are accessible via telnet.

4. Library of Congress Services: The Library of Congress Information System (LOCIS) offers the following services by typing **telnet locis.loc.gov** (closed during national holidays):

   > L O C I S : LIBRARY OF CONGRESS INFORMATION SYSTEM
   >   To make a choice: type a number, then press Enter
   > 1 Library of Congress Catalog   4 Braille and Audio
   > 2 Federal Legislation   5 Organizations
   > 3 Copyright Information   6 Foreign Law
   > *

Table 14–2: Sampling of telnet sites		
Name	**Address**	**Login Information**
California Digital Library	*melvyl.ucop.edu*	Enter terminal type **vt100**.
National Capital FreeNet –Canadian National Archives	*telnet.ncf.carleton.ca*	Login as **guest**.
Colorado Alliance of Research Libraries	*pac.carl.org*	Login as **PC**. Enter terminal type **5**, which represents vt100. Press ENTER to continue.
The Einstein On-Line Service—Smithsonian Astrophysical Observatory	*cfa204.harvard.edu*	Login as **einline**.
Toronto Free-Net	*torfree.net*	To register, login as **guest**.
Victoria Telecommunity Network	*freenet.victoria.bc.ca*	Login as **guest**. Enter terminal type **vt100**. Enter your name.

7 Searching Hours and Basic Search Commands
8 Documentation and Classes
9 Library of Congress General Information
10 Library of Congress Fast Facts
11 * * Announcements * *
12 Comments and Logoff
Choice:

TELNET SOFTWARE FOR WINDOWS

Throughout this chapter, references have been made to the telnet application native to Windows 95/98. This program can do the job in most situations. If you want more features, try downloading one of the applications described in Table 14–3. If you are running Windows 3.x, try using Trumptel, also listed in Table 14–3.

Table 14–3: Download sites for Windows telnet software	
Name	**Where to find**
Trumptel	*ftp://ftp.asu.edu/pub/pc/win31/utils/*
Easy Term	*www.arachnoid.com/easyterm/*
EWAN	*www.lysator.liu.se/~zander/ewan.html*
GoodTech Telnet Server for Windows NT V3.0 Beta	*www.goodtechsys.com/*
The Java Telnet Applet	*www.first.gmd.de/persons/leo/java/Telnet/*
NetTerm	*starbase.neosoft.com/~zkrr01/html/netterm.html*
Anzio Lite	*www.anzio.com/*
AnzioWin	
Anzio for DOS	
AnzioNet	

Archie

Archie is the name given to an Internet database service that consists of a collection of several computers distributed around the world called *Archie servers*. Each Archie server, independent of the others, collects data and stores it for future use. The data it collects is retrieved from anonymous FTP sites. Each Archie server stays in contact with anonymous FTP archive sites all around the world and maintains an up-to-date composite index of their holdings. Archie servers do not collect and store the actual files themselves; instead, they index only the directory names and file names.

Finding a file on the Internet by simply browsing through the directories of hundreds of FTP sites is physically impossible. Herein lies the purpose for learning how to use Archie: Archie servers provide a search mechanism for locating files. Anyone who has access to the Internet can search the indexes. Search results tell you which FTP server stores a particular file or directory and what the pathname is for locating it. Although each Archie server is a separate entity, they all perform the same service and even index close to the same FTP sites.

The following example illustrates how Archie can be an effective resource discovery tool in your library: A patron has just requested a copy of Kehoe's original *Zen and the Art of the Internet* and a copy of some software called PKUNZIP. You're confident the files are located on the Internet, but you're not sure where. Because Archie is a directory of text and software resources, Archie is one service you could consider going to for your answer.

You begin your search by connecting to an Archie server, either via a UNIX shell account or the Web. Enter the text string **zen**. You don't know what the actual file name is for this document, but maybe *Zen and the Art of the Internet* is stored in a directory named "zen." As it turns out, the document is stored in dozens of directories named "zen." The same process can be applied to the binary file PKUNZIP. You may not know the exact file name, but chances are the PKUNZIP program is stored in a directory of the same name.

After a short wait, your search results scroll across the screen, providing FTP site addresses and pathnames where copies of the files can be found.

You record the information and immediately initiate an FTP session to retrieve the desired files. You give the patron the option of downloading the files to a floppy disk, or, in the case of textual information, printing it out while he or she waits.

This illustrates how Archie can serve a practical purpose by helping patrons locate certain materials on the Internet. The search results Archie provides give you enough information that you can retrieve the necessary files at point of need.

HOW ARCHIE WORKS

Archie consists of two software tools originally developed by Alan Emtage, Bill Heelan, and Peter Deutsch at the School of Computer Science, McGill University, Montreal, Canada. One software tool keeps track of Internet FTP archive sites in a central server and is updated about once a month. Every night, the system executes an anonymous FTP connection to several of the archive sites scattered across the Internet. Archie downloads the directories at each site and then stores them in a searchable database. About one-thirtieth of the total number of sites is searched each night so the directories of each site and eventually the entire system are updated once a month.

The other tool is the Archie program itself, and this is the program you will be using. This program allows you to login to an Archie server and query two different databases. One database retrieves directory names and file names, while the other, called *whatis*, retrieves descriptions along with the file names. You can search these databases for character strings and the system searches all of its file names and directory names for entries with that string.

ACCESSING AND SEARCHING ARCHIE

You can access and search Archie four ways: On your host computer running an Archie client; interactively using telnet; through e-mail; and via the Web.

TELNET ACCESS

If the host computer you connect to supports telnet, the remote login program—or you can run your own telnet client on your personal computer—you can telnet directly to an Archie server. Before you start your session, it would be wise to open a capture file or log file (a file in which the text that's displayed on your screen is saved) because Archie's output scrolls across the screen quite fast. If your communications software has a scrollback buffer, you can use this instead to pause the display and then go back and view previously received data.

LOGIN PROCEDURE USING A UNIX SHELL ACCOUNT

Login to your local host as usual and at the system prompt, enter **telnet <server address>**, where "<server address>" is an Archie server address, such as *archie.Rutgers. edu*. The session should look something like this:

$ telnet archie.rutgers.edu
SunOS 5.6

login:

At the *login:* prompt, type **archie**, and press ENTER. The system returns with a response similar to this:

login: **archie**
Last login: Sun Apr 23 13:09:01 from ppp540.mh.centur
Sun Microsystems Inc. SunOS 5.6 Generic August 1997
———————————— Network Services ————————————
You have mail.
                  Welcome to Archie!
                  Vers 3.5
Bunyip Information Systems, Inc., 1993, 1994, 1995
Terminal type set to 'vt100 24 80'.
'erase' character is '^?'.
'search' (type string) has the value 'exact'.
archie>

When logging in to some systems, you may be asked for a password. In these situations, enter your e-mail address and that should give you access to the database. The Archie prompt generally looks like *archie>*, or it may be some variation including part of the host's domain name.

FINDING HELP

Enter the command **help** at the *archie>* prompt. To retrieve a listing of the specific help topics, enter a question mark (**?**) at the *help>* prompt. The resulting output is shown here:

archie> **help**
These are the commands you can use in help:
 . drop down one level in the hierarchy
 ? display a list of valid subtopics at the current level
 done, ^D, ^C quit from help entirely
 <string> help on a topic or subtopic
help>?
Subtopics:
about
autologout

```
# bugs
# bye
# done
# email
# exit
# find
# general
# help
# list
# mail
# motd
# nopager
# pager
# prog
# quit
# regex
# servers
# set
# show
# site
# term
# unset
# version
# whatis
# whats_new
```

The help topics listed differ somewhat from one Archie server to the next. To explore any one of the help topics online, type the topic name at the *help>* prompt and press ENTER. To return to the *archie>* prompt, press the ENTER key without entering any commands at the prompt.

LOCATING SERVERS

When you are back at the *archie>* prompt, enter the command **servers,** and the program displays a list of available servers worldwide. A sample of what this session might look like is shown here:

```
$ telnet archie.rutgers.edu
SunOS 5.6
login: archie
Last login: Sun Apr 23 13:09:01 from ppp540.mh.centur
Sun Microsystems Inc. SunOS 5.6 Generic August 1997
———————————— Network Services ————————————
You have mail.
                    Welcome to Archie!
                       Vers 3.5
# Bunyip Information Systems, Inc., 1993, 1994, 1995
```

```
# Terminal type set to 'vt100 24 80'.
# 'erase' character is '^?'.
# 'search' (type string) has the value 'exact'.
archie> servers
< List of active archie servers >>
    archie.au                 139.130.23.2        Australia
    archie.univie.ac.at       131.130.1.23        Austria
    archie.belnet.be          193.190.248.18      Belgium
    archie.bunyip.com         192.77.55.2         Canada
    archie.cs.mcgill.ca       132.206.51.250      Canada
    archie.uqam.ca            132.208.250.10      Canada
    archie.funet.fi           128.214.6.102       Finland
    archie.univ-rennes1.fr    129.20.254.2        France
    archie.th-darmstadt.de    130.83.22.1         Germany
    archie.ac.il              132.65.16.8         Israel
    archie.unipi.it           131.114.21.10       Italy
    archie.wide.ad.jp         133.4.3.6           Japan
    archie.kornet.nm.kr       168.126.63.10       Korea
    archie.sogang.ac.kr       163.239.1.11        Korea
    archie.nz                 130.217.96.24       New Zealand
    archie.uninett.no         128.39.2.20         Norway
    archie.icm.edu.pl         148.81.209.2        Poland
    archie.rediris.es         130.206.1.2         Spain
    archie.luth.se            130.240.12.23       Sweden
    archie.switch.ch          130.59.1.40         Switzerland
    archie.switch.ch          130.59.10.40        Switzerland
    archie.ncu.edu.tw         192.83.166.12       Taiwan
    archie.doc.ic.ac.uk       146.169.16.11       UK
    archie.doc.ic.ac.uk       146.169.17.5        UK
    archie.doc.ic.ac.uk       146.169.2.10        UK
    archie.doc.ic.ac.uk       146.169.32.5        UK
    archie.doc.ic.ac.uk       146.169.33.5        UK
    archie.doc.ic.ac.uk       146.169.43.1        UK
    archie.doc.ic.ac.uk       155.198.1.40        UK
    archie.doc.ic.ac.uk       155.198.191.4       UK
    archie.hensa.ac.uk        129.12.43.17        UK
    archie.sura.net           128.167.254.195     USA (MD)
    archie.unl.edu            129.93.1.14         USA (NE)
    archie.internic.net       192.20.225.200      USA (NJ)
    archie.internic.net       192.20.239.132      USA (NJ)
    archie.internic.net       198.49.45.10        USA (NJ)
    archie.rutgers.edu        128.6.18.15         USA (NJ)
    archie.ans.net            147.225.1.10        USA (NY)
```

Since the arrival of the World Wide Web, most of the above sites have become inactive. However, if you want to explore this character-based interface further, try using the archie server maintained at *archie.Rutgers.edu*.

SEARCH COMMANDS

You use the prog command to search the Archie database for a specified pattern. Prog is short for *program* and it tells Archie to run its search program. You can use the command find in place of prog. At the *archie>* prompt, enter the command **prog** or **find**, followed by a space and the character string you are searching. Capture the results of your search to a disk or make notes on paper to use later for retrieving the desired files via FTP.

Exercise Using the prog Command

To practice using the prog command, login to an Archie server and try locating a file called *archie_guide.txt*. This is a text file by Richard Hintz called "What is an Archie?" Begin by telneting to an Archie server and entering **archie** at the *login:* prompt. At the *archie>* prompt, enter the command **prog archie_guide.txt**. The database then searches all the FTP sites it tracks for any files or directories called *archie_guide.txt*. When I ran this search, Archie found one file with this exact name located at FTP site *sunsite.unc.edu*. The output is presented here:

```
SunOS 5.6
$ telnet archie.rutgers.edu
SunOS 5.6
login: archie
Last login: Sun Apr 23 13:09:01 from ppp540.mh.centur
Sun Microsystems Inc. SunOS 5.6 Generic August 1997
——————————— Network Services ———————————
You have mail.
                Welcome to Archie!
                Vers 3.5
# Bunyip Information Systems, Inc., 1993, 1994, 1995
# Terminal type set to 'vt100 24 80'.
# 'erase' character is '^?'.
# 'search' (type string) has the value 'exact'.
archie> prog archie_guide.txt
# Search type: exact.
working...
Host sunsite.unc.edu (152.2.254.81)
Last updated 14:11 30 Apr 1998
    Location: /pub/docs/about-the-net/libsoft
    FILE    -rw-r–r–    3091 20:00  7 Sep 1992 archie_guide.txt
archie>> quit
# Bye.
Connection closed
```

Setting Variables

Archie has several variables you can use to modify how searches are performed or to ensure that certain operations take place automatically. Set these variables before you conduct a search.

To control the volume of output a search produces, use the set maxhits <number> command, where "<number>" is the maximum number of hits you want Archie to return. For example, if you know you're searching for a piece of software that's probably stored at the majority of FTP sites, it would be wise to use a command something like this before conducting your search: archie> **set maxhits 10.** The results of a prog search would then stop after ten matches are found.

The set pager command causes output to be displayed one page at a time. The unset pager command allows the output to scroll across the screen.

The set mailto <email address> command is useful if you want to mail the search results to yourself or others. For example, typing **set mailto user1@ua1vm.ua.edu** sends the output to user1. Typing the command **set mailto user1@ua1vm.ua.edu, user2@foxhole.com** sends the output to both "user1" and "user2" at their specified addresses. When mailing to multiple addresses, separate the addresses with commas, but don't use spaces anywhere. After you have set the mail variable, conduct your Archie search. When you retrieve results that you'd like to send to your e-mail address, type **mail**. Archie automatically sends the output from the last command you entered. If you didn't set the mailto variable prior to your search, you can send the output to yourself by typing the command **mail** followed by your e-mail address and pressing ENTER.

The sortby variable organizes the output in various ways. For example, typing **set sortby time** displays the results of a search in order from newest to oldest; typing **set sortby filename** organizes the output alphabetically by file name.

The set search exact command determines the way Archie searches for matches in its database. For example, when you know exactly what you want, enter **set search exact** command to tell Archie to look for names that are an exact match, including upper- and lowercase. If you ask Archie to search for a file named *Ami-HyTelnet*, it would match "*Ami-HyTelnet*" but not "*ami-hytelnet*" or "*AMI-HyTelnet*." Notice that in the earlier example of using the prog command, an exact pattern search is the default setting when using TELNET to access Archie.

To search for a substring, use the set search sub command. This matches any name that contains the substring you specify, upper- or lowercase. For example, if you searched the substring *reference*, Archie matches "*REFERENCE*," "*reference.txt*," "*VMS-reference.zip*," and "*test.scr.Reference*." To make this same search case-sensitive, type the command **set search subcase**. Now the name *reference* would match "*reference.txt*," but not "*test.scr.Reference*."

Regular Expressions

The regular expression (*regex*) setting is the most complicated mode of searching. Regular expressions are used by UNIX programs to search for a sequence of characters. Regular expressions are similar in purpose to truncation, something many librarians may already be familiar with in searching commercial and other databases. *Truncation* permits variations in spelling or word length when searching for single words.

After you enter the command **set search regex** at the *archie>* prompt, you can use the following special characters to achieve specific results.

The **..** (two dots) are a regular expression that allows the character replaced by the . (dot) to vary. Typing the command **find b..p** would match "bump," "burp," and "blip"—but not "bop" or "bops."

The $ (dollar sign) is used to find a file name by matching the ending. Typing the command **find $mit** matches "kermit" and "summit," but not "*kermit311.zip.*"

The ^ (caret) is used to specify the beginning of a word. Typing the command **find ^kerm** matches anything that begins with "kerm"—for example, "*kerm311.zip*"—but it will not find "*imbkerm.zip.*"

The [ ] (square brackets) are used to find only certain single characters at a certain point in the text. Typing the command **find sl[o a i]p** matchs "slop," "slap," and "slip" but not "slep" or "slup." Typing **[a-zA-Z]**, would match any upper- or lowercase character a through z. Typing the command **find ^pkz11[0–9]** would match "*pkz110.exe*" and "*pkz112.exe.*"

Default Settings

When you first login to an Archie server, you can see what the default settings are for these and other variables by entering the command **show**. What appears will look something like this:

archie> **show**
'autologout' (type numeric) has the value '60'.
'collections' (type string) is not set.
'compress' (type string) has the value 'none'.
'encode' (type string) has the value 'none'.
'language' (type string) has the value 'english'.
'mailto' (type string) is not set.
'match_domain' (type string) is not set.
'match_path' (type string) is not set.
'max_split_size' (type numeric) has the value '51200'.
'maxhits' (type numeric) has the value '50'.
'maxhitspm' (type numeric) has the value '100'.
'maxmatch' (type numeric) has the value '100'.
'output_format' (type string) has the value 'verbose'.
'pager' (type boolean) is not set.
'search' (type string) has the value 'exact'.
'server' (type string) has the value 'localhost'.
'sortby' (type string) has the value 'none'.
'status' (type boolean) is set.
'term' (type string) has the value 'dumb 24 80'.

Consult the online help system provided by Archie for any variables that need further explaining.

USING AN ARCHIE CLIENT ON YOUR SHELL ACCOUNT

If you have your own Linux box, or you dial-up to a UNIX host that supports an Archie client, log on to your account and enter the word **archie** at the system prompt. The output from the archie command should look something like this:

$ archie
Usage: 2dia0:[sys0.syscommon.][ualr_lib]archie.exe;2 [-[cers][l][t][m#][hhost] ["L"]["N"#]] string
- -c : case sensitive substring search
- -e : exact string match (default)
- -r : regular expression search
- -s : case insensitive substring search
- -l : list one match per line
- -t : sort inverted by date
- -m# : specifies maximum number of hits to return (default 98)
- -h host : specifies server host
- -"L" : list known servers and current default
- -"N"# : specifies query niceness level (0–35765)

HOW UNIX ARCHIE CLIENTS WORK

Local client programs are the best way to access an Archie database because it takes less time away from the server than a continuous telnet session. The client links with Archie only when it has information to send or receive. Some Archie clients are menu driven, and others offer a command line interface. If you need assistance in using a particular client, try entering the word **help** at the Archie client prompt.

Searching for Files

When you use an Archie client on a UNIX system, you search the Archie database right from your system prompt. The basic format you follow is an expression beginning with the archie command, followed by the name of the file or directory for which you want to look. For example, typing the expression **archie pkzip** finds all files and directories called "*pkzip*" in Archie's database. Archie prints any matches it finds.

You can modify the archie command by using characters with special meanings called *options* or *switches*. Switches are always given after the archie command and before the search string. In the previous example (archie pkzip), Archie finds only files and directories that match that exact string. To widen the search to include files and directories that have the string "*pkzip*" anywhere in their names, follow the command name archie with the switch -s, like this: **archie -s pkzip**. The -s switch is a good tool to use if you approach Archie with a subject query rather than a specific file name.

RUNNING ARCHIE FROM THE WEB

The advantage of using a Windows-based Web browser to search FTP sites is the familiarity you have with the interface. There is no complicated search syntax to learn. You simply enter your keywords in a text box and click on the search button. Some services provide drop-down menus that enable you to refine your search. In the next section I introduce you to two resources that can help you find files archived at FTP sites.

FINDING AND DOWNLOADING FILES WITH A WEB BROWSER

Web browsers make it easy to locate and download files on the Internet. Rather than running an Archie client to first find the file, and then an FTP application to download the file, browsers provide you with a single, user-friendly interface for doing both.

ARCHIEPLEX

For a large listing of Archie servers all around the world that can be accessed via the Web, point your browser to ArchiePlex at *archie.emnet.co.uk/services.html*. ArchiePlex is a public service created by NEXOR and maintained by EMNET. At this site you find a list of Archie servers that support forms—dialog boxes in which you enter text.

FTP SEARCH 4.0

In the previous edition of this book I introduced you to a service called FTP Search, a service developed by the Norwegian University of Science and Technology. The service is still around, now at version 4.0 and part of Lycos at *www.lycos.com*. If you go to their main page you find a link to FTP near the top of the page. This takes you to a basic FTP search service at *ftpsearch.lycos.com/*. This interface offers one pull-down menu that lets you choose a class of files to search including software files that end in *.zip* or *.exe*; sound files including RealAudio, MIDI, AU, or MP3s; and image files in JPEG or GIF format.

If you want more control over your search, link to the Advanced or Normal search forms. The following exercise demonstrates how to use FTP Search 4.0 Normal Forms to find and download an education program called *Animals. Animals* is a simple numbers game for children written by Donald Pavia.

1. Once your browser is running, enter the following address in the "Location" box near the top of the screen: **http://ftpsearch.lycos.com/**. Look for the link labeled "Form: Normal" and click "Normal" to connect. This links you to a simple form-based search screen. You see several boxes in which you can enter variables. The default settings work fine for most searches.
2. Enter the file name **animals.zip** in the "Search for" box located at the top of the window.
3. Set the "Search type" at "Case insensitive multiple substrings search" for gen-

eral searching.

4. Place a checkmark in the box for "Try exact hits first."

5. Up your maximum hits to "50."

6. Use checkmarks to hide all of the files types listed; for example, Packages, Distfiles, FreeBSD, and OpenBSD, etc.

7. Click on the "Search" button.

8. In the search results screen, shown below, you notice that the file sizes vary from as low as 12.3KB to as high as 111.6KB, signifying that they may not all be the same program. It isn't uncommon to retrieve a list of hits that includes a few files other than the one you were specifically looking for. Knowing that it's an educational game for kids, look for directory names like "education," "educate," or "child" that precede the file name. As you look through the choices below, you see a few files all the same size (26KB) and in directories that appear to contain educational software.

```
1  -r--r--r--   26.0K  1993 Dec  2  ftp.cdrom.com           /.1/math/ed/animals.zip
2  -r--r--r--   26.0K  1997 Feb  8  ftp.cdrom.com           /.1/math/utk/software/msdos/k-12/animals/animals.zip
3  -r--r--r--  111.6K  1998 Sep 13  ftp.bitcon.no           /.11/pdacentral/epoc/files/series5/animals.zip
4  -r--r--r--   12.3K  1999 Mar  7  ftp.bitcon.no           /.14/themes/themeicons/zips/animals/animals.zip
5  -rw-r--r--   12.3K  1999 Mar  6  ftp.southcom.com.au     /.2/freethemes/themeicons/zips/animals/animals.zip
6  -rw-r--r--   12.3K  1999 Mar  7  ftp.labyrinth.net.au    /.3/freethemes/themeicons/zips/animals/animals.zip
7  -r--r--r--   26.0K  1999 Apr 19  ftp.cdrom.com           /.3/gamesdomain/kidstuff/pc/animals.zip
8  -r--r--r--   26.0K  1986 Jun  6  ftp.eunet.cz            /.3/msdos/educate/animals.zip
9  -r--r--r--  111.6K  1998 Sep 13  ftp.fct.unl.pt          /.3/pdacentral/epoc/files/series5/animals.zip
10 -rw-r--r--   26.0K  1986 Jun  6  ftp.cdrom.com           /.3/simtelnet/msdos/educate/animals.zip
```

9. If you click on an FTP site address in the middle of the line, such as *ftp.cdrom.com* in line one, you connect to the FTP server's root directory. Instead, scroll right until you see the full pathname and at the end of the line you see the file name *animals.zip*. When you click on the file name, you connect to the FTP server and automatically go to the directory in which *animals.zip* is stored. Click on the file name to download it.

10. At this stage, you may receive an error message something like: "FTP Error - Could not login to FTP server." If not, skip to step 11. If you do get this error message, it means that the server is either down or has reached its maximum number of allowable logins. You can try another site that's listed, or wait a few minutes and try again.

11. When you click on a file for downloading, you are asked whether you want to save the file to disk or open it. If it's a zip file or executable file, choose "Save File." If it happens to be a text file or image, you could also choose to view it if your system supports the file format.

12. After you click on the "Save File" button, your browser usually asks where you want to save the file. In the "Save as" window that appears, select your download folder, click on it to select it, and then click on "Save."

13. As soon as the download begins, your browser presents you with a saving status window. When the download is completed, the window disappears.

For additional exercises, see if you can find the following files using ArchiePlex or FTP Search 4.0.

aquiz01.zip—Quizy is a fully functional shareware program that enables you to create your own multiple-choice quizzes. Based on the machines found in arcades.

chre95.zip—Chain Reaction is an educational word game from Mace Software, Inc., based on the TV game show of the same name.

clmath.zip—Clown Math displays random math questions designed to help children and adults increase their math skills.

clspell.zip—Clown Spell is a spelling program designed to help children and adults develop their spelling skills.

dragon.zip—Create a dragon drawing program.

flshcd10.zip—Music flashcard program.

guitar3.zip—Guitar Scales is a program written by David Sampson that displays guitar notes and cords.

immouse.zip—Master your mouse technique with games and tutorials. Gives you practice clicking, double-clicking and moving the cursor.

pigs.zip—Money Pigs teaches kids how to identify coins and bills. Supports sounds and voices.

sky352.zip—Skyglobe is an astronomy program.

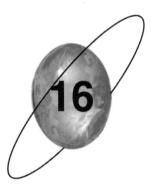

Online Library Catalogs

Libraries that can be accessed on the Internet are sometimes referred to as *virtual libraries*. The term *virtual*, as in *virtual reality*, refers to reality that's not real. By putting on some special devices, such as a head-mounted display and sensory gloves, you're able to see images and experience the sensations of sound and touch. You think you are somewhere else, not here. A true virtual library would be one where you feel you are really there. You see images of books. You can reach out and touch them. You immerse yourself totally into a synthetic world.

When someone speaks of a virtual library, typically they are talking about online databases—digital card catalogs—that can be viewed on a computer monitor. Patrons won't see any "real" books. At the most, they see text displayed on their screens or maybe graphical images of book spines.

This chapter focuses on library catalogs that are online and connected to the Internet. Although these catalogs may not be *virtual* in the truest sense of the word, they are unique in terms of accessibility. They can be accessed 24 hours a day, every day of the year; and the fact that they may be located hundreds or thousands of miles away from your computer is irrelevant.

In the sections that follow, I briefly describe three of the better-known computerized library systems on the Internet: The University of California's Melvyl Library System, the Colorado Alliance of Research Libraries (CARL), and the Library of Congress. I define the Z39.50 protocol and show you where to find directories listing hundreds of online libraries including academic, public, and K–12 libraries. At the close of this chapter, I introduce you to an innovative storage system called holographic storage.

For a comprehensive list of links to online libraries, consult the CD-ROM accompanying this book.

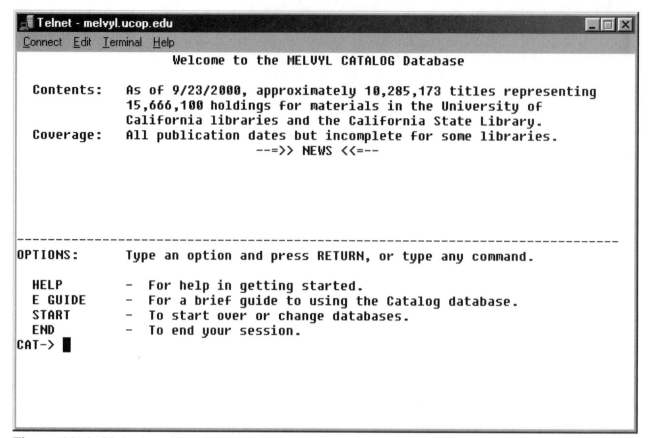

Figure 16–1: Melvyl main menu provides access to the main catalog and commercial databases

UNIVERSITY OF CALIFORNIA'S MELVYL LIBRARY SYSTEM

Melvyl, the online library of the University of California, offers access to several databases, including online catalogs, periodical databases, and other library systems. As with most campus information systems, access to fee-based databases like INSPEC and PsycINFO is generally restricted to students, faculty, and staff.

Melvyl is part of the California Digital Library (CDL), a collaborative effort of the University of California campuses.

CONNECTING TO MELVYL VIA TELNET

To connect with Melvyl, telnet to *melvyl.ucop.edu*. When asked for a terminal type, enter **VT100**. At the opening menu, you are presented with two broad classifications of

Online Resource
lib-web-cats at *staffweb.library.vanderbilt.edu/Breeding/libwebcats.html* is a searchable index of library Websites and catalogs maintained by Marshall Breeding of Vanderbilt University.

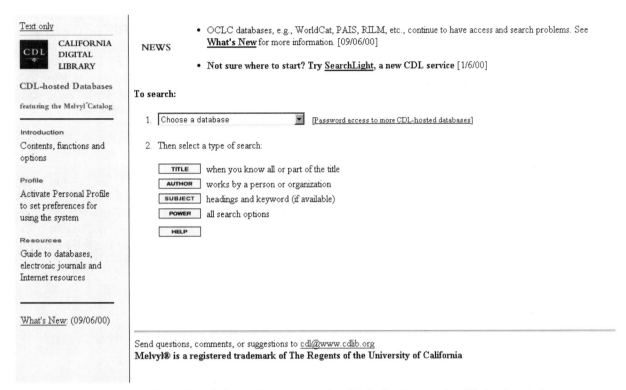

Figure 16–2: The California Digital Library on the Web features the Melvyl catalog

databases: Library databases and Indexes to recent articles. The latter is restricted to University of California users only.

You can access the Library databases by entering the commands cat or pe. Entering **cat** connects you with the full Melvyl catalog. The command **pe** connects you with the Melvyl Periodicals Database. Melvyl's opening menu is pictured in Figure 16–1.

The full Melvyl Catalog database contains, as of April 29, 2000, about 10,116,402 titles representing over 15 million holdings in the University of California libraries and the California State Library. The Periodicals Database contains 824,540 periodical titles representing 1,448,400 holdings in the Statewide Serials Database, which includes the University of California along with several other institutions. This database can be searched by title, author, subject, or keywords.

Online help is available for both databases. At the opening menu of each database, enter **HELP** for information on getting started, or **e guide** for a guide to using the database. To move back to the opening menu, type **start** and press ENTER. To end your session, type the command **quit**.

CONNECTING TO MELVYL VIA THE WEB

You can access Melvyl on the Web, shown in Figure 16–2, at *www.melvyl.ucop.edu/*. Choose either the catalog or periodicals database from the drop-down menu. Then select a method of searching by clicking on "Title," "Author," "Subject," or "Power." The Power search enables you to search specific libraries by date, language, and form. In addition, you can refine your search by combining keyword title, author, and subject terms.

THE COLORADO ALLIANCE OF RESEARCH LIBRARIES (CARL)

CARL Corporation was established in 1988 as CARL Systems for the purpose of developing and marketing the library system used by the Colorado Alliance of Research Libraries. This system offers access to several academic and public library OPACs, various indexes, and interactive word searching in various information databases.

CONNECTING TO CARL VIA TELNET

To connect with CARL, telnet to *pac.carl.org* and, at the *SELECT LINE #:* prompt, enter **5** for vt100 terminal emulation. You can also login to the CARL system at *database.carl.org*. At the *Enter Choice>* prompt, enter **PAC**. Next, you are asked to enter your terminal type—for example, VT100. Some databases are not accessible without a password or library card number. The opening menu offers you the following six choices plus a new database, Linda Hall Library (Article Delivery).

1. UnCover–Article access & document delivery–No password required
2. OPEN ACCESS Databases–No password required
3. LICENSED Databases–Restricted access
4. CARL System Library Catalogs–No password required
5. FAQ–Frequently Asked Database Questions
99. UnCover EXPRESS
27. Linda Hall Library (Article Delivery)

The first item in the main menu, "1. UnCover–Article access & document delivery," connects to a periodical index and document delivery system. You can enter the Open Access version by pressing the ENTER key several times and then following the online instructions shown in the welcome screen.

The second item in the main menu, "2. Open Access Databases," leads you to the following choices:

1. UnCover
2. Open Access Databases
3. Licensed Databases
4. CARL System Libraries
5. FAQ
7. British Library Document Supply Centre (Info & document delivery for 54,000 serial titles)
9. Federal Domestic Assistance Catalog(List of domestic assistance grants from U.S. Govt.)
27. Linda Hall Library (ARTICLE DELIVERY)
42. U.S. Government Publications
50. CONSER (serial records from the Library of Congress)
99. UnCover EXPRESS (Articles available within 1 hour)

By choosing menu item four, "CARL System Libraries," you are presented with three submenus: one leading to a list of CARL libraries in the Eastern half of the United States and two others that list CARL libraries in the Western United States. Both academic and public libraries are included in these lists.

Selecting menu item five, "FAQ—Frequently Asked Database Questions," brings you to a Frequently Asked Questions database, a file explaining how often databases are

---

> **Online Resource**
>
> Libweb at *sunsite.Berkeley.EDU/Libweb/* lists over 3,000 library Web servers worldwide. U.S. libraries are organized under the headings Academic Libraries, Public Libraries, National Libraries and Library Organizations, State Libraries, Regional Consortia, Special, and School Libraries. This site is maintained by Thomas Dowling, Berkeley Digital Library SunSITE.

updated, and a section offering new announcements regarding commercial databases. To exit the system, type **//exit** at the prompt and press ENTER.

ACCESSING CARL VIA THE WEB

To connect to CARL via the Web, point your browser to *www.carl.org*. The CARL home page provides a graphical user interface for searching CARL and UnCover.

THE LIBRARY OF CONGRESS

In the fall of 1993, the Library of Congress announced the availability of a new online system called LC MARVEL (Library of Congress Machine-Assisted Realization of the Virtual Electronic Library). LC MARVEL was like the CWIS (Campus-Wide Information System) of the Library of Congress. It offered information about the Library, its activities, and collections through a Gopher interface. LC MARVEL also provided information to the U.S. Congress and constituents throughout the world.

If you are interested, you can still connect to LC MARVEL's Gopher server. The Gopher address for LC MARVEL can be inserted in your Web browser's location box as *gopher://marvel.loc.gov*. You can access this same server using a UNIX shell account by entering *gopher marvel.loc.gov* at the system prompt. (This won't work if your system administrator on the UNIX system isn't supporting a Gopher client.)

Even though you can still access the LC MARVEL running on the Gopher server, it is no longer maintained as the CWIS for the Library of Congress. It is only used to provide access to a few documents stored in ASCII text format.

To access The Library of Congress via the Web, point your browser to *lcweb.loc.gov/*. Links to resources and services on the homepage include:

> **Online Resources**
>
> The Canadian Library Index *www.lights.com/canlib/*, maintained by Peter Scott, is a collection of Canadian libraries organized geographically and then alphabetically within each location. The index includes libraries of all types, from public and governmental, to university and medical. A link called Other Library Web Resources takes you to other top-level sites, such as Yahoo's index of libraries and Michael Sauers World Wide Web Library Directory, which indexes over 6,000 library-related Websites in 102 countries.

The LIBRARY *of* CONGRESS
Online Catalog

<u>Frequently Asked Questions</u>

*** Important Announcement ***
Due to system maintenance, regular Web and Z39.50 access to the Online Catalog will be **unavailable** on Sunday, September 24 from approximately 8:00AM-1:00PM EDT.

About This Catalog	Searching Help	Services for Researchers	Search Other Libraries' Catalogs

Select a Search Method	Description *(consult Search Examples within each search method for more information)*
Subj-Name-Title-Call#	Browse the catalog by subject, name (personal, corporate or meeting), or call number; search by title or serial title. Search limits are available only for title and serial title searches.
Guided Keyword	Use a "fill-in" form to create searches. Search words or phrases may be restricted to <u>particular indexes</u> and combined using Boolean operators. <u>Number searches</u> and search limits are available.
Command Keyword	Use Boolean operators and/or <u>index codes</u> in a command mode. <u>Number searches</u> and search limits are available.
Keyword	Search for words or exact phrases anywhere in the catalog record. Add punctuation for more precise results (see <u>search examples</u>). Results are relevance ranked. Search limits are available.
Set Search Limits	Limits restrict search results by language, date, type of material (e.g., book, music, etc.), location of material in the Library, or place of publication. Set search limits now, or prior to executing a search; they remain in effect until cleared or changed.

Information about the images: Two pendentive paintings by Edward J. Holslag are displayed from the Librarian's Room (Librarian's Ceremonial Office) located in the Thomas Jefferson Building of the Library of Congress. On the left, "Efficiunt clarum studio" (Study, the watchword of fame); on the right, "Dulce ante omnia musae" (The Muses, above all things, delightful).

<u>Library of Congress Home</u>	<u>Using the Library</u>	<u>Thomas</u>	<u>Copyright Office</u>	<u>American Memory</u>	<u>Exhibitions</u>	<u>The Library Today</u>	<u>Bicentennial</u>	<u>Help & FAQs</u>	<u>Search our Site</u>	<u>Site Map</u>

 Library of Congress
Comments: <u>lcweb@loc.gov</u> *(03/31/2000)*

Figure 16–3: Library of Congress online catalog

> **Online Resource**
>
> The Australian Libraries Gateway (ALG) at *www.nla.gov.au/libraries/* attempts to list every library in Australia. ALG provides links to more than 5,200 Australian libraries. Special services offered by ALG include a browsable collection of links to online Australian library exhibits and a collection of links to specialized directories and databases. An advanced search option lets you search for exhibits as well as online image collections. The specialized directories and databases are all Australian-based and include information on publishers, booksellers, online journals, books and writers, and more.

1. The library's catalogs and collections—The online catalog represents more than 12 million records. You can connect directly to the Library of Congress online catalog, shown in Figure 16–3, at *catalog.loc.gov/*.
2. Thomas—The Thomas database covers three major areas: Legislation, Congressional Record, and Committee Information. You can access it directly at *thomas.loc.gov/*.
3. Copyright Office—Go here to learn about the copyright law and search copyright registrations and recorded documents.
4. American Memory—Contains historical collections for the National Digital Library. Items include digital images (still and motion), sound recordings, and text.
5. Exhibitions—Online versions of current exhibits being held at the Library of Congress.
6. The Bicentennial—The Library of Congress celebrated its 200th birthday in April 2000.
7. Help & FAQs—Find general information, staff directories, services, maps, statistics, and more.
8. News and Events—Learn about international Internet projects, new books, cybercasts, and more.

FINDING OTHER ONLINE LIBRARIES

There are many other online libraries to explore besides the three mentioned here. In the following section, I introduce you to directories listing many libraries with Web-based OPACs (Online Public Access Catalogs).

WHAT IS HYTELNET?

HYTELNET was a program developed by Peter Scott of Northern Lights Internet Solutions in Saskatoon, Canada. It provided hypertext access to listings of Internet-accessible library catalogs, Free-Nets, CWISs, BBSs, Gophers, and other telnet services. HYTELNET gave you specific instructions on how to login to every system it listed. The HYTELNET program could be downloaded and run on your own PC, or you could access it on a remote host—either via telnet or the Web.

In 1997, Peter Scott announced that he would be closing down HYTELNET, but that the site would remain open for anyone that wanted to use it. Since that time, many of the resources listed in HYTELNET have discontinued their services. Many of the libraries formerly offering telnet access to their OPACs have since switched over to Web-based catalogs. However, it's still a good resource for connecting to the remaining library catalogs that are only accessible via telnet.

If you are interested, you can still download the last DOS version of HYTELNET that was produced. It's stored at *ftp://ftp.usask.ca/pub/hytelnet/pc/latest/hyteln69.zip*. You can access HYTELNET on the Web at *www.lights.com/hytelnet/*.

Z39.50 IMPLEMENTATIONS

Z39.50 is a national standard that defines a set of rules for how computers retrieve information. Z39.50 makes it possible for you to search and retrieve information on other computer systems without the need to know the search syntax that is required by those other systems.

The Library of Congress maintains a Z39.50 Gateway home page that provides access to LC's catalog and dozens of other libraries around the world, from the Anne Arundel County (Maryland) Public Library's DRA system to Western Washington University's INNOPAC system. You can reach this gateway at *lcweb.loc.gov/z3950/gateway.html*.

Harold Finkbeiner maintains an experimental Z39.50 to WWW Gateway at site *www.physics.brocku.ca/cgi-z39/dir.CGI*. Finkbeiner offers access to various online databases including ERIC's database of educational materials.

Dan Brickley of the Institute for Learning and Research Technology maintains a Website listing Z39.50 resources *www.ilrt.bris.ac.uk/discovery/Z3950/resources*. Along with general information, Brickley points you to gateways in Singapore, France, Germany, Russia, Poland, and other countries. Go here to download Z39.50 software including search modules for Web servers.

WEBCATS

WEBCATS, originally designed by Peter Scott and Doug Macdonald, is now hosted by Northern Lights Internet Solutions and maintained by Peter Scott. WEBCATS offers access to libraries with Web interfaces through a geographic index, vendor index, and library-type index. This is advantageous if you are interested, for example, in viewing only the collections of K–12 schools, public libraries, religious libraries, or governmental libraries. If you are shopping for a new automation system, WEBCATS's vendor index offers you an opportunity to view automation systems ranging from ALEPH to VTLS. You can reach WEBCATS at *www.lights.com/webcats/*.

THE LIBRARY CORPORATION'S NETPAC-Z

NetPAC-Z is a service made available by the Library Corporation—the producers of BiblioFile automation products. (You can learn more about their products and services at *www.tlcdelivers.com/tlc/.*) NetPAC places your library's Public Access Catalogs on the Web using a service called *virtual servers*. The latest version of NetPAC, named NetPAC-Z, utilizes Z39.50 server capabilities.

Information on the Internet is exchanged through a network of hundreds of thousands of computers called servers. A *server* is a high-end computer designed to communicate or "serve" out information to several users simultaneously. The library catalogs described earlier in this chapter run on their own servers.

A *virtual server* is a server that appears to be yours, but in reality is someone else's; in fact, it may not even be an individual computer, but rather a shared portion of a server that others are also using. The virtual server is run and maintained by an outside source, in this case, the Library Corporation. The Library Corporation gives your library the opportunity to have a commercial, highly sophisticated presence on the World Wide Web without having to maintain your own server or full-time connection to the Internet. By supporting Z39.50 servers, NetPAC-Z libraries can seamlessly access other online catalogs on the Internet right from their own automation system.

NetPAC libraries listed alphabetically can be viewed at *www.tlcdelivers.com/tlc/virtual/netpac.htm*. To see a sample template of a basic NetPAC interface, click on the link labeled "Basic NetPAC Template." Each library designs its own Web page that forms a framework around the basic NetPAC interface.

Around this basic interface, libraries add their logos and links to other library services, commercial full-text databases, library home pages, parent institution's home pages, and more.

NetPAC supports searching by keyword, author, title, subject, notes, or other fields specified by the individual library. NetPAC first displays findings in a compact form—single-line entries hyperlinked to bibliographic records. When you click on one of these links, you connect to a full record. This record supports hyperlinks to other works by the same author and similar materials.

HOLOGRAPHIC STORAGE

What do you think of holding an entire library's holdings in your hand? Lucent Technologies and Imation Corporation are collaborating on a new development called holographic storage. Basically it works like this: Information is stored on a 5 $\frac{1}{4}$-inch removable storage disk that holds 125GB (gigabytes) of data. This is equivalent to about twenty-seven of the current 4.7GB DVD discs. Data access speeds would increase beyond that of current hard disk drive speeds. This is partially due to the fact that data is stored and retrieved in *page format*—one million bits at a time. The holdings of a small to medium-sized library could be stored on a single holographic storage disk. Instead of data being stored only on the disk's surface, holographic storage allows recording throughout the entire thickness of the disk. As the data transfer rate increases and storage capacity reaches one terabyte (one trillion bytes), a large university library could one day be able to store its entire holdings on a single holographic storage disk.

To keep up-to-date on the latest developments in this new technology, visit Imation's home page at *www.imation.com/*.

Free-Nets

Free-Nets are computerized civic information systems. Most are linked to the Internet, and, as their name implies, there is no charge for connecting. As information, education, and communication systems, Free-Nets are set up to provide users with services such as these:

- Community bulletin boards for groups with special interests
- Access to online library services
- Connections with community profit and nonprofit organizations such as senior centers, the post office, schools, and medical centers, and businesses, etc.
- Access points to local, state, and federal government information
- Interactive access to government officials
- Educational programs
- Access to the Internet
- E-mail service
- Classified ads
- Weather and travel information
- Community calendars

Community Networks is a new term, but one that can mean the same thing as Free-Nets. These Websites provide information about a particular community, such as details about local businesses and public events. Most offer public dial-up access to the Internet. Fee-Nets are similar to Free-Nets except they charge fees for their services. Typically, connection costs are less expensive than local ISPs.

THE NATIONAL PUBLIC TELECOMMUNICATIONS NETWORK (NPTN)

The term *Free-Net* was originally a servicemark of the National Public Telecommunications Network (NPTN) based in Cleveland, Ohio. Only those civic computer information systems that followed NPTN's principles and standards were allowed to use the name *Free-Net*. NPTN offered several network services to its Free-Net affiliates, including Internet e-mail service and summaries of House and Senate Bills and U.S. Supreme Court decisions. NPTN filed for bankruptcy and began closing down its services in 1997.

In spite of NPTN's closedown, community networks are still going strong, with older systems being transformed and newer systems coming online. The original Cleveland Free-Net, for example, was sponsored by Case Western Reserve University, Community Telecomputing Laboratory. In 1999, this organization was closed down and replaced by the New Cleveland Freenet, a project of the Organization For Community Networks (OFCN). You can connect to the New Cleveland Freenet by telneting to *new.cleveland-freenet.org*.

Today, some communitywide information systems still use the name *Free-Net,* such as the Twin Cities Free-Net. Others use variations of this name including *FreeNet* and *Freenet*, or something entirely new like *CedarNet*—the communitywide information system located in Cedar Falls, Iowa.

THE ORGANIZATION FOR COMMUNITY NETWORKS (OFCN)

The Organization For Community Networks (OFCN) in some respects replaces the National Public Telecommunications Network. Based in Ohio, this nonprofit corporation serves as a central repository for information about Free-Nets and other community information systems. In addition, the OFCN houses a collection of documents that have been supplied by various community information networks. These documents are available for new and existing community networks to use for information and training purposes. The following titles are included in this library:

- Akron Regional Free-Net Articles of Incorporation
- DANEnet–Madison, Wisconsin, Articles of Incorporation
- FairNet–Fairbanks Alaska Community Network's Acceptable Use Policy
- Genesee Free-Net Acceptable Use Policy
- Akron Regional Free-Net 501(c3) Form
- Community Networking Institute (CNI) Kearney, Nebraska, 501(c3) Form
- DANEnet–Madison, Wisconsin, 501(c3) Form
- FairNet–Fairbanks Alaska Community Network's Volunteer Agreement
- FairNet–Fairbanks Alaska Community Network's Volunteers Legal Handbook
- Show-Me Net's "Guidelines for Information Providers"
- Akron Regional Free-Net Code of Regulations
- DANEnet By-Laws
- Great Lakes Free-Net By-Laws
- Greater New Orleans Free-Net By-Laws

- Lehigh Valley Free-Net By-Laws
- NPTN By-Laws
- Owensboro On-Line By-Laws
- FairNet's Parliamentary Procedures for Non-Profit Directors
- *A Critical Study of Three Free-Net Community Networks* by Ben Stallings
- 4th Community Networking

The OFCN Website at *ofcn.org/* lists community networks worldwide organized alphabetically by country and supports a legal information center that lists current legislative information relevant to community networks. Other features offered at OFCN's Website include:

- Health and Wellness Center with medical information
- Academy Center where teachers exchange lesson plans
- TeleDemocracy Program with links to The Office of Independent Counsel's Report, The White House Press Briefings, The White House Press Summaries, and State Governments
- Digital library of full-text public domain books

THE ASSOCIATION FOR COMMUNITY NETWORKING (AFCN)

The Association for Community Networking (AFCN) is another organization that supports community networking. Their mission, as stated on their Website at *www.afcn.net/ mission.html*, is to, "improve the visibility, viability and vitality of Community Networking by assisting and connecting people and organizations, building public awareness, identifying best practices, encouraging research, influencing policy, and developing products and services."

FREE-NET COVERAGE

Some Free-Nets are organized as communitywide information systems by local libraries, such as the Akron Community Online Resource Network (ACORN) *www.acorn.net*. ACORN offers free public-access and dial-up accounts to residents of Akron, Ohio, and northern Summit County. As a service of the Akron–Summit County Public Library, ACORN offers access to local information and community organizations. Others, like the Alachua Freenet *www.afn.org*, provide countywide communication, education, and information services. Alachua Freenet, headquartered in Gainesville, Florida, provides Internet access to over 10,000 people. Still other Free-Nets offer services to an entire region. For example, the Buffalo Free-Net *freenet.buffalo.edu*, which has been active since 1993, provides free Internet access to eight counties in western New York. It is funded by donations from the community and other individual and corporate sponsors.

```
                                      Twin Cities Free-Net (p1 of 3)

                       Twin Cities Free-Net (R)

        Bringing People Together through Internet Technologies

TCFN is a nonprofit organization that uses Internet technologies to
bring people together in communities of shared interest or need. We've
been linking the people of Minneapolis, St Paul and neighboring
communities since 1995. Register a custom domain name -- at a discount
-- while supporting the Free-Net, through our [1]OrgResources project.

                          Community Resources:

   [2]Neighborhoods: Read up about the cities and neighborhoods in the
   Twin Cities Metro Area and join discussions on neighborhood issues.
   [3]Organizations: More than 100 nonprofit organizations and businesses
   are members of the Free-Net. Learn more about them here.
   [4]Tools: Jump from here to the Nonprofit Management Info Library, as
   well as discussion forums on neighborhood issues and public safety.
   [5]Search: Start looking here to find anything Twin Citian or
-- press space for next page --
   Arrow keys: Up and Down to move.  Right to follow a link; Left to go back.
 H)elp O)ptions P)rint G)o M)ain screen Q)uit /=search [delete]=history list
```

Figure 17–1: The Twin Cities Free-Net telnet interface

ACCESSING FREE-NETS

Free-Net systems can be accessed via telnet, dial-up modems, or the Web. At the end of this chapter I list several examples of Free-Nets along with their Internet addresses. As with other systems, Free-Nets accessed via telnet are limited to a maximum number of simultaneous logins. When you do make a connection, you are usually given the option of browsing as a visitor or becoming a registered member.

ORGANIZATIONAL STRUCTURE

Free-Nets built around character-based interfaces (those to which you telnet) organize their information in a hierarchical fashion. You start at the top with broad topics and from there move to narrower topics through menu choices. Each Free-Net contains information relevant to its own community or region, sometimes building the main menu around a city metaphor. For example, some Free-Nets use headings in the top menu named after local buildings or streets.

Web-based Free-Nets are designed to take advantage of hyperlinks and graphics. For example, the Twin Cities Free-Net offers "clickable neighborhood maps" as a means of finding and connecting to your favorite neighborhood.

CONNECTING TO THE TWIN CITIES FREE-NET

The Twin Cities Free-Net (TCFN) has been in operation since 1995. It offers information services to folks living in Minneapolis, St. Paul, and neighboring communities. You can connect to this Minnesota-based Free-Net via telnet or the Web. To telnet, enter the following address in your Web browser's address box: *telnet://freenet.msp.mn.us*. When you connect, the system asks you to login as **guest**. After a few introductory pages, you arrive at the main menu presented in Figure 17–1.

This telnet view of the Twin Cities Free-Net is similar to the other systems offering telnet access. The interface uses a character-based Web browser known as Lynx, discussed earlier in Chapter 11. The Twin Cities Free-Net can be accessed on the Web at *freenet.msp.mn.us/*.

Every Free-Net offers its own unique set of resources and services. The Twin Cities Free-Net, unlike other Free-Nets, does not act as an Internet access provider. Instead, it focuses its attention on being an outlet for community information. When you register, you can participate in discussion forums and send and receive e-mail. The Twin Cities Free-Net Website does list public Internet access sites in Minnesota. Visitors can search Internet access sites by city, county, or zip code.

CONNECTING TO THE BUFFALO FREE-NET

The Buffalo Free-Net came into existence in October 1993. In the beginning, you could only gain access to the Buffalo Free-Net if you dialed in locally, or if you had an Internet connection you could access it via telnet. Today, the Buffalo Free-Net can be accessed through local dial-up connections, or from outside the Buffalo, New York, area via telnet and the Web. To telnet to the Buffalo Free-Net, enter the following address in your Web browser's Location box: **telnet://bfn.org**; or run your favorite telnet client application. Non-members login as **freeport**. The Welcome screen is pictured in Figure 17–2. With a non-member login you gain access to the New York State Job Service and you are given a chance to register for membership.

The Web version of Buffalo Free-Net can be found at *bfn.org/*. If you have a computer that supports graphics, this is the most effective means of connecting to the site.

CONNECTING TO BIG SKY TELEGRAPH

Big Sky Telegraph is a Free-Net that is big on lesson plans, helping rural teachers, and offering online classes. Big Sky Telegraph is useful not only to those who are part of Montana's statewide educational network, but also to anyone with a connection to the Internet.

You can connect to Big Sky Telegraph by telneting to *Telnet: 192.231.192.1*. At the *login:* prompt, enter **bbs**. After you read the opening screens and complete the login sequence for Big Sky Telegraph, you are presented with a menu of choices. By selecting menu item "(F)iles…Areas for upload and download," you are given a submenu showing all of the different topic areas that are available.

When you choose category four, "LessonPlans," as a topic to explore further, the

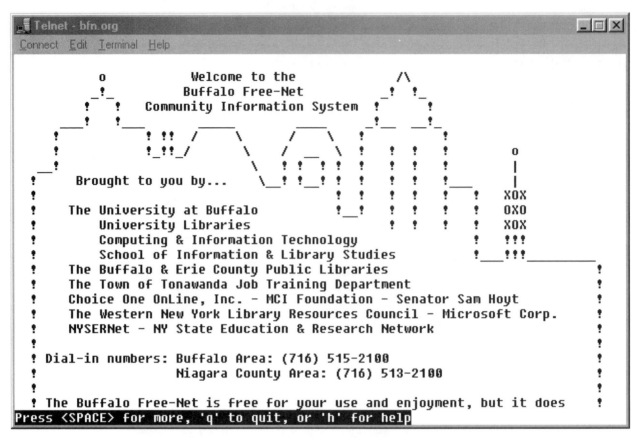

Figure 17–2: Welcome screen for telnet version of Buffalo Free-Net

system lists all of the files in that topic area. When you select "(F)iles...List of all files in THIS topic area," you are presented with a list of file names, their size, date of creation, and short description.

The list of available lesson plans is quite long. If Easter is coming up, librarians and teachers might be interested in downloading a copy of the file called *Egglessn* using Zmodem. The process of transferring a file from Big Sky Telegraph to your own computer is as simple as making a series of menu choices.

If for some reason the telnet service to Big Sky Telegraph is down or discontinued when you try to connect, go to their Website at *macsky.bigsky.dillon.mt.us/*. They offer two versions: full graphics and text only. Their front page index includes six main subject categories:

1. Self-directed learning resources
2. K–12 resources and training
3. BST Mission and Montana
4. Community networking
5. Web development
6. Family and fun learning

The K–12 resources and training is further broken down into these categories:

• School tech planning guidelines

- Censorship
- Child safety
- Privacy
- Copyrights
- Online K–12 projects registries
- Multicultural project sites
- Lesson plan archives

TELNETING TO THE HEARTLAND FREE-NET

You can connect to the Heartland Free-Net by telneting to *heartland.bradley.edu* and logging in as **bbguest**. When prompted for a password, press ENTER. Be aware that there is a 15–minute time limit on connections to this Free-Net.

To further demonstrate the depth of information available on Free-Net systems, the following list provides an index to resources found on the Heartland Free-Net System. To print this list online, type **go index** at the *Your Choice ==>* prompt.

<<< Heartland Regional Network Index >>>
-A-

Administration Building	go admin
Amateur Radio	go ham
Apple Computer Info	go apple
Audubon Society	go birds
Auto Info/Repair	go auto

-B-

Baby SIGS Incubator	go baby
Bel-Wood Nursing Home	go belwood
Better Business Bureau	go bbb
Birds	go birds
Bloomington, City of	go bloom
Bloom./Normal Calendars	go cal
Board Agendas, Peo. Cnty.	go board
Board Minutes, Peo. Cnty.	go board
Bradley University	go bradley
Bulletin Board	go public
Business	go business, go bsns
Business Statistics	go stats

-C-

Census Bureau	go census
Change Password	go passwords
Change Terminal Type	go term
Chemical Addictions	go chemical
Chemical Dependency	go chemical
Children's Events	go children
Clubs & Orgs. B/N	go bnclubs
Computer Forum	go pc, go computer

Craft Show Calendar   go craft
Cultural Events Calendar   go culture

-D-
Departments, Peo. Cnty   go pcdirectory
Disability Info   go disability
Disaster Planning   go disaster, go redcross
Drug Abuse   go drug
Drug Information   go drug

-E-
Economic Statistics   go stats
Editors   go editor
Educational Project   go projects
Elected Officials   go elected
Electronic Mail   go mail
e-mail   go mail
Environment Info   go environ
Ethics Discussion   go religion
Eureka College   go eureka

-F-
Festival Calendar   go festival
Fines, Peoria County   go peoria.county
Flight, Space & Airplane   go space
Flea Market Calendar   go flea
Forum, Personal Computer   go pc, go computer
Forum, Public   go forum
Freedom Shrine   go shrine
Fulton County   go fulton

-G-
Gambling, Compulsive   go gamble
Gardening Info   go garden
Gopher Menus   go gopher
Govt, Local   go local
Govt, Peoria County   go peoria.county
Govt, State   go state

-H-
HAM Radio   go ham
Handicap Info   go disability
Historical Documents   go shrine
History   go shrine
Home Repair   go home
Human Resources B/N   go bnss
Hytelnet Menu   go hytelnet

-I-
ICC   go icc
Illinet OnLine   go illinet

Ill. Dept. Employ. Sec	go ides
Illinois State University	go isu
IDES Jobs	go jobs
Index	go index
Internet News & Happenings	go internet
Intervention Resources	go special

-J-

Jobs (Peoria County)	go pcjobs
Jokes SIG	go jokes
Journal Star	go pjs

-K-

Knox County	go knox

-L-

Law	go law
Lawyer Help	go law
Legal Information	go law
Legal Questions	go law
Letters to Elected Off.	go elected
Library	go library
Licenses, Peoria County	go license
Lindbergh Middle School	go lind
Link to Other Systems	go mlink, go rlink, go glink
Literary Discussion	go lit
Local Govt	go local

-M-

Mail	go mail
Mailboxes	go mail
McLean County	go mclean
Media, Talk Back To	go media
Medicine	go medical
Medicine, General	go medical
Medicine, Psychology	go mental.health
Membership Info	go member
Mental Health	go mental.health
Movies Discussion	go movies
Music Discussion	go music

-N-

New SIG area	go admin
New Unread BBS	go new
Normal, Town of	go normal

-O-

Open Bulletin Board	go open
Outer Space	go space

-P-

Pager	go pager

Parameters	go parameters
Passwords	go passwords
PC Forum	go pc
Peoria Calendars	go cal
Peoria, City of	go peoria
Peoria County Depts.	go pcdirectory
Peoria County Govt.	go peoria.county
Peoria Govt Job Listing	go pcjobs
Peoria Journal Star	go pjs
Personal Computer Forum	go pc
Pest Control	go pests
Pilot, How to Become a	go pilot
Political Discussion Area	go politics
Post Office	go mail
Property Assess, Peo Cnty	go property
Psychology/Mental Health	go mental
Public Forum	go public

-Q-
(No listings under "Q" at the moment.)

-R-

Recipes	go recipe
Recreation Center	go recreation
Recycling	go recycle
Red Cross	go redcross
Registration	go registration
Religion	go religion
Resource Sharing Alliance	go rsa
Rockets	go rockets

-S-

St. Joseph Medical Center	go stjoe
Satellites	go satellite
Scouting	go scout
Science	go science
SciFi Talk	go scifi
Senior Info	go senior
Set Password	go passwords
Set System Parameters	go parameters
Sierra Club	go sierra
Social Services PIA	go ss
Space	go space
Special Needs	go special
Speeches	go shrine
Sporting Events Calendar	go sportcal
Social Security Q & A	go ssn
Star Trek	go trek
State Govt	go state

Sweeney, Father (school)	go sweeney
System Parameters	go parameters

-T-

Tax Clinic	go tax
Taxes	go tax
Teachers' Area	go teacher
Teen Center	go teen
Terminal Setup	go term
Termite Control	go termites
Theater Events Calendar	go theater
Timeline, Historical	go timeline
Travel Center	go travel
Trek, Star	go trek

-UVWXYZ-

User Services Menu	go user
Video Games	go video
Weather	go weather
WEEK TV, Channel 25	go week
WHOI TV, Channel 19	go whoi
Wildlife Prairie Park Current	go wild
Woodford County	go woodford
World Wide Web	go www
Zip Codes	go zip
Zoo, Glen Oak Park	go zoo

LIST OF FREE-NETS

The Free-Nets listed in this section can be accessed on the Internet. Each entry includes the name of the Free-Net, its Internet address, and any information you must enter at the *Logon:* prompt. Web addresses are included for those Free-Nets with sites on the Web.

Big Sky Telegraph
telnet 192.231.192.1
Login as **bbs**

Buffalo Free-Net
http://freenet.buffalo.edu
telnet Free-Net.buffalo.edu
Login as **freeport**

Calgary Free-Net
http://www.freenet.calgary.ab.ca/

Cleveland Free-Net
telnet kanga.ins.cwru.edu

Central Virginia's Free-Net (CVaNet)
http://freenet.vcu.edu/

Grand Rapids Free-Net
http://www.grfn.org/

Greater Columbus Free-Net
http://www.freenet.columbus.oh.us/

Heartland Free-Net
telnet heartland.bradley.edu
Login as **bbguest**
Press ENTER when asked for a password

London Free-Net
http://www.lfn.com/

Los Angeles Free-Net
http://lafn.org/

Mobile Alabama Free-Net (MAFN)
http://www.maf.mobile.al.us/

Omaha Free-Net
http://omahafreenet.org/

The Swedish East Coast Free-Net
http://www.lp.se/gerrie-warner/freemet.htm

Tallahassee Free-Net
http://www.freenet.tlh.fl.us/
telnet Free-Net.fsu.edu
Login as **visitor**

Three Rivers Free-Net, Pittsburgh, Pennsylvania
http://192.204.3.5/

Twin Cities Free-Net
http://freenet.msp.mn.us/

Victoria Free-Net, Victoria, British Columbia
http://freenet.victoria.bc.ca/vifa.html
telnet Free-Net.victoria.bc.ca
Login as **guest**

Integrating Tools into Traditional Reference Practice

Digital objects are slowly replacing reference books. These objects are not simply digital versions of their predecessors; they are new entities that utilize the power of the Web to deliver their contents. Reference books offered as online resources are constructed from text and image databases that support unique searching and sorting capabilities.

Companies like The Gale Group *www.galegroup.com* are combining multiple reference resources to create *mega-resources*. Their newest online resource, *Business & Company Resource Center*, brings together under one umbrella company profiles, industry rankings, investment reports, industry statistics, corporate chronologies and histories, consumer marketing data, business news and analysis, press releases, and even 20–minute delayed stock quotes. The Gale Group's *Biography Resource Center* combines 50 Gale Group biographical databases with 250 full-text periodicals. The Gale Group offers free access to specially selected resources at *www.galegroup.com/freresrc/index.htm.*

H.W.Wilson and its online *Biographies Plus* database is another example. It draws from several different resources including *Current Biography*, *World Authors: 800 b.c.– Present*, *World Artists 1980–1990*, *American Reformers*, and *Booklist/Reference Books Bulletin.*

In some instances, the contents of the reference databases are expanded through new partnerships to include resources beyond the original print version. For example, *The Grove Dictionary of Art Online www.grovereference.com/TDA/* links to more than 30,000 images from museum and other art sites.

This transformation from print to online is bringing reference librarians a growing number of resources that feature continuous updating, hyperlinking, and full-text and natural-language searching. In Chapter 18, I present ideas, resources, and tools to help librarians integrate the Internet into their reference services and to provide greater assistance to patrons in accessing Internet information resources.

I begin this chapter with a discussion about the difficulties reference librarians face when trying to locate information on the Net and then present a system for determining when and how to use the Internet in answering author/title questions, fact-finding questions, and subject questions. This chapter also spotlights full-text resources on the Internet that can be accessed free of charge and various tools that can be used for organizing information. The chapter closes with a presentation on how you can use the Internet to enhance traditional reference and instruction services.

FINDING THE RIGHT INFORMATION

Reference librarians who are responsible for locating Internet resources often view the Internet as a complex information structure, and for good reason. Finding the right information at the right time in a worldwide network like the Internet is more difficult than it is in a single online system. Most of this difficulty evolves from the fact that there isn't a centralized catalog offering controlled access to all of the Internet's resources and services.

In this section, I present the Internet in a way that, in spite of this difficulty, it becomes as practical and accessible to you as any other resource sitting on your ready reference shelf. All the various Internet resource discovery tools, services, and sources of information introduced in this book are interesting in themselves, but what do you do with it all when you're out there facing the public at the reference desk? Two closely related issues come into play here:

1. Within the context of the reference question itself, what's the best way to approach locating and accessing information on the Internet?
2. What should your role as a reference librarian be in providing these services?

PROBLEMS ASSOCIATED WITH LOCATING AND ACCESSING INFORMATION

Issues relating to locating and accessing information on the Internet were being addressed early in 1991 when OCLC (Online Computer Library Center, Inc.) initiated a project investigating the nature of electronic information stored on the Internet. OCLC's goal was to locate and identify the various types of electronic information available on the Internet, produce a descriptive taxonomy of this information, and assess the problems libraries face in handling this information. In their final research report[1], and in other leading articles on this subject, it's apparent that Internet resources are not yet an integral part of existing reference department infrastructures for two reasons:

1. Because of the difficulty in locating and accessing network information, and
2. because the reference librarian's role in a global network environment is unclear

In March 1995, OCLC and NCSA (National Center for Supercomputing Applications) sponsored a metadata workshop that focused on developing a core set of metadata elements to describe Internet resources (see *mirrored.ukoln.ac.uk/dc/workshops/dc1conference/report.htm*).

Describing Networked Resources: Questions and Answers about Metadata

1. How do search engines search?
   Search engines like AltaVista and WebCrawler use Web robots and spiders to help them find information. Robots are applications that roam the Web reading Web documents. These robots index the information they find. When you search the Web using a search engine, you are searching an index that in turn points you to a Web document.
2. What types of information do search engines gather?
   Different search engines grab different things. Lycos, for example, extracts the title, headings and subheadings, 100 most important words, and the first 20 lines.
3. What is metadata?
   Metadata is data about data, or *information about information*. For example, think of a photograph as a piece of information. The name of the person who captured the photograph, the date on which it was taken, and the subject of the photo are considered metadata—*information about information*. Full MARC records are examples of metadata—data describing the books in your library.
4. What is The Dublin Core Metadata Element Set?
   The Dublin Core is a set of 15 elements that are used to define a Web document. A lot of people all around the world got together and agreed on what these 15 elements would be. They agreed the element set should include, for example, title, author, subject and keywords, description, publisher, and date. You can find a complete description of The Dublin Core at *purl.oclc.org/dc/*.
5. After looking at the complete list of elements in The Dublin Core and the HTML code it takes to create them, is there a simpler way to get the job done?
   Yes! You can more easily create The Dublin Core Metadata Element Set using a template. A *template* simplifies the process by having you fill in data in a standard form. When you are finished, you click on a button and the template automatically converts your input into the proper HTML code.

If you are new to metadata, try this exercise:

1. Point your Web browser to this site: *purl.oclc.org/dc/*.
2. Scroll to the bottom of the page and look for the link labeled "Tools" and click on it. When the next pages loads, find the link labeled:
       "Nordic DC metadata creator (including URN generator)"
       http://www.lub.lu.se/cgi-bin/nmdc.pl
   This link takes you to a Dublin Core Metadata Template.
3. Click on the button labeled "Shore and Simple Template" and fill in these elements:

   1 Title
   2 Creator

> 3 Subject: Keywords
> 8 Type
> 10 Identifier: URL
> 10 Identifier
> 12 Language
>
> You can just make something up for this exercise if you wish. When you create The Dublin Core Metadata Element Set for your Website, fill in as many of the elements as you can.
>
> 4. When finished, click on the button labeled "Return metadata." Before doing so, be sure to select the appropriate choice from the pull-down menu: "for preview," "for inclusion in HTML-document," or "for inclusion in HTML 4–document." For this exercise, choose "for inclusion in HTML-document."
>
> 5. The data that appears on the next screen should look something like output presented in Figure 18–1.

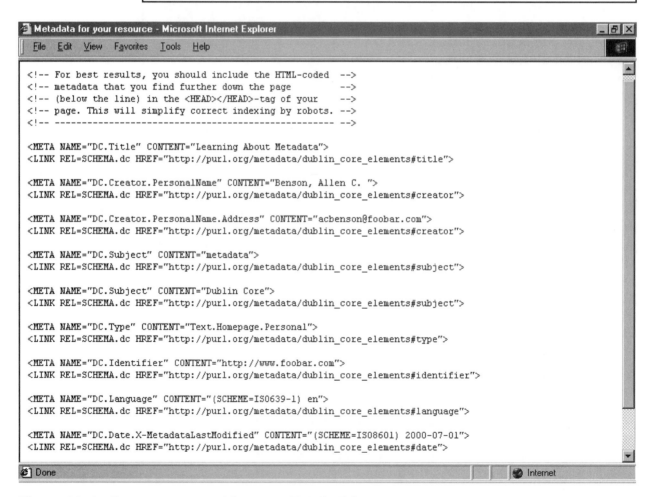

Figure 18–1: Output generated from the Nordic DC metadata creator

This set of metadata elements is known as The Dublin Core. These and other developments are helping reference librarians with more effective resource discovery on the Internet. Other developments include the Library of Congress 1994 Proceedings of the Seminar on Cataloging Digital Documents *(lcweb.loc.gov/catdir/semdigdocs/ seminar.html)*, 1994 Position Papers from IEEE Metadata Workshop (*www.llnl.gov/ liv_comp/metadata/papers/pos-papers-1994–05.html*), and The 4th Dublin Core Metadata Workshop Report (*www.dlib.org/dlib/june97/metadata/06weibel.html*). See the sidebar on pages 291-292 for additional information on metadata and The Dublin Core.

THE KNOWLEDGE APPROACH

Two fundamentally different approaches address the problem of locating and accessing information on the Internet. One approach, which is based on knowledge, seeks to improve access to files by determining the meaning and content of the files as they exist on the Internet. Once this structure is imposed on the data, access is improved. This is a familiar process to librarians, one that catalogers have been applying for years. Catalogers create bibliographic records that "fill in" for the information itself. These *surrogates*, which contain author, title, publisher, and indexing terms, etc., are joined together into a single database called a *card catalog* (unautomated) or *OPAC* (automated). An information seeker searches this database, locates what he or she wants, and then goes out and retrieves the document itself.

THE BRUTE FORCE APPROACH

The other way of providing access to information is through sheer computing power—employing powerful search engines that go right to the documents themselves, or to keyword, subject, or full-text indexes to determine relevancy. Many of the Internet resources and services are based on this model. A good example of the brute force approach is WAIS (Wide Area Information Server). Instead of searching a centralized database of bibliographic records, WAIS goes right to a full-text database that you specifically choose and conducts a keyword search on every document contained therein.

PETER DEUTSCH'S URSNs AND INFORMATION BROKERS

Peter Deutsch presented a concept that combined both methods of accessing information in a thesis that examined systems for locating and accessing distributed databases on the Internet. "Resource discovery," he explained, "is the act of discovering the existence of classes of resources in an Internet environment, locating specific instances of such resources, and accessing those resources."[2] He proposed using a method of universal encoding to identify resources on the Internet. Special resource identifiers would contain the physical information needed to actually access an item and a Unique Resource Serial Number (URSN) would be assigned identifying the item's contents. Software applications called *Information Brokers,* the mechanisms for handling this process, would manage the user's resources and control access to their information.

INTRODUCING URLs

Some of what Peter Deutsch had in mind became a reality with the creation of the Uniform Resource Locator, or URL. The *URL* is a standard for identifying any item on the Internet by means of a single expression that describes what the object is in terms of format and where it is located.

WHAT ARE UNIFORM RESOURCE IDENTIFIERS (URIs)?

URIs are schemes for naming, discovering, and retrieving resources on the Internet. URLs are one example of a type of URI. Two others are

- URNs (Uniform Resource Names) name resources and files independent of their location. (See RFC 1737 for specifications. To access a hyperlinked archive of RFCs and FAQs, go to *www.faqs.org/rfcs/.*)
- URCs (Uniform Resource Characteristics) were designed to provide meta information about resources including such things as author, title, publisher, etc. URCs could be compared to a bibliographic record. An Internet-Draft *Specification of Uniform Resource Characteristics*, written by Michael Mealling, proposed a set of requirements for URCs. This document, introduced in the last edition of this book, is now difficult to locate online. Internet-Drafts have no formal status and are only valid for a maximum of six months. They can be updated, replaced, or made obsolete by other documents at any time.

THE PROBLEM WITH URLs

In the previous edition of this book, a reference was made to the above mentioned Internet-Draft's URL as being *www.acl.lanl.gov/URI/urc_draft.txt*. This demonstrates a major weakness of URLs: They confuse the name of a resource with its location. I can give you a URL for this Internet-Draft today, but if it moves to a new location by the time you decide to look for it, the URL becomes invalid. Even though the resource may still exist on the Internet and still retains the name *urc_draft.txt*, the URL *www.acl.lanl.gov/URI/urc_draft.txt* has become what is termed a *dead link*.

A SOLUTION TO THE URL PROBLEM

The URI working group of the Internet Engineering Task Force hopes to assign names to Internet resources using URNs and to describe Internet resources using URCs. (For up-to-date information, consult *www.ietf.org/html.charters/urn-charter.html.*) Not only will the URC contain information such as author and title, but it will also contain a set of locations for the resource and they will be presented as a set of URLs. In this scenario, when your browser locks in on the URN for Mealling's Internet-Draft, it will locate the document by trying one of the URLs listed as part of that resource's meta information. If the first URL is a dead link, your browser will try another. The browser will keep trying until it locates the file or runs out of URLs.

It is not likely that there will ever be a central database containing a bibliographic record for every resource existing on the Internet. What reference librarians will have access to, in addition to their own superior abilities, are distributed database systems and numerous online resource guides such as the Argus Clearinghouse (formerly known as the Clearinghouse for Subject-Oriented Internet Resource Guides) at site *www.clearinghouse.net/*; powerful Web search engines like AltaVista; hypertext directories like The Librarian's Index to the Internet *lii.org/*; and digital libraries like American Memory *lcweb2.loc.gov/ammem/ammemhome.html*.

MOMSPIDER

MOMspider takes another approach to partially solving the problem of broken hypertext links due to documents changing location or being deleted. The Multi-Owner Maintenance spider, or MOMspider for short, was developed to address this maintenance problem. MOMspider, developed by Roy T. Fielding, is a robot that traverses the Web looking for changes. The operator tells the software which sites to visit and then MOMspider builds an index document in the form of a hypertext document. This document lists broken links, redirected links, changed link destinations, and expired documents. The program is written in Perl and should run on any UNIX-based system with Perl 4.036. To learn more, visit the MOMspider site at *www.ics.uci.edu/pub/websoft/MOMspider/*.

INTEGRATING INTERNET SERVICES

The second issue mentioned at the outset of this chapter relates to the role of reference librarians in integrating Internet services into their current reference practice. With the addition of the global Internet as yet another reference resource, librarians must make a decision at the reference question level whether or not to use it; it is at this level that they must decide whether the Internet is appropriate for a particular user or question.

THE REFERENCE QUESTION

In *Gorgan's Case Studies In Reference Work, Volume I*, Denis Gorgan describes three types of questions based on the complexity of the information required:

1. Author/title questions
2. factual or fact-finding questions, and
3. subject questions (material-finding queries)[3]

The Internet can be used to answer author/title questions by connecting to any one of several OPACs worldwide. Fact-finding questions can be answered by consulting textual documents such as *The Catalog of Federal Domestic Assistance* (*www.pr.doe.gov/gf10cat.html*) or calculators and converters, such as Oanda Corporation's currency converter at *www.oanda.com/converter/classic*. Subject requests can be handled a number of different ways: By utilizing Internet resource discovery tools such as Web search engines and subject directories, or by using word processors to conduct full-text searches on electronic books and journals.

William Katz points out in his *Introduction to Reference Work, Volume II*, that the search process for these types of questions "is more a matter of familiarity with the reference collection and the typical question than with any sophisticated process."[4] He goes on to say that when questions require more than semiautomatic reasoning coupled with memory—when they require real searching—then the structure is normally in terms of isolating the most likely sources. When information is found, it is analyzed for relevancy. If the result is satisfactory, the search is over. If the results are not satisfactory, the reference librarian begins searching again by exploring other sources.

This same process can be applied in a global network environment. At the outset, you should decide whether the patron's question can be answered by using the Internet. Your first decision is whether or not you are familiar with a specific Internet resource that is relevant to answering the question. If you are, then proceed by going online and connecting to the appropriate resource. The resource might be a text file stored at an FTP site, a database that can be searched online via telnet, or a Gopher resource that specializes in a particular subject.

The Author/Title Question

Suppose that a patron approaches you with a question that requires bibliographic verification of an author or title. Using your best judgment, you might look in one or more of the following resources held locally: *Books in Print*, *Forthcoming Books*, your card catalog or online catalog, etc. If you don't find what you need locally, the Internet provides another option. You can use telnet or the Web to connect with another library's online catalog. The type of library in which you work and the clientele you serve helps determine which remote catalogs you should become most familiar with and learn to access from memory just as you memorize where certain other resources are located in your stacks.

As an example, some librarians find CARL to be a convenient point of entry. The Internet address is easy to remember, *pac.carl.org* (for telnet access), and the login process is intuitive. CARL provides a gateway to many other library systems that are divided into two broad categories: Eastern U.S. and Western U.S.

All the libraries accessed through *pac.carl.org* use the same automated system (CARL), which means that you have to learn only one interface for searching the various library catalogs. Because it's a gateway service, you won't have to initiate a separate telnet session every time you switch to a different library; that process is done transparently for you. You could also explore Peter Scott's and Doug Macdonald's WEBCATS home page at *www.lights.com/webcats/*. This site supports three indexes: Library Type, Geographical Location, and Vendor.

Because these directories contain hundreds of OPACs from which you can choose, the issue still comes down to selecting one or two ahead of time and becoming familiar with their holdings and their automation systems before you need to use them—before a patron approaches you with an author/title question.

One last alternative is to use a *bookmark utility*, for example Internet Explorer's "Favorites" button or Netscape's "Bookmarks." You can use this feature to maintain an online record of a few select OPACs that have automation systems you are familiar with and that you find especially useful and relevant to your clientele. You can customize bookmark utilities to include special notes about library holdings and searching strategies, etc. In Netscape, click on "Bookmarks" on the "Location" tool bar. Then select "Edit Bookmarks." You can attach *metadata* to the bookmark you've chosen by selecting it and then right-click to bring up the "Bookmark Properties" window. Here you can edit the bookmark name and add a description.

The Fact-Finding Question

Several opportunities exist on the Internet for answering factual questions. Factual questions about the Internet itself are easiest to answer. Examples include "Is there a Website that specializes in law?", "Can you use the Internet to search the United States Military Academy's library at West Point?", "I'd like to join this mailing list I heard about called WOODWORK. What's their address?", and "Where can I download a copy of MacroMedia's Shockwave for Director?"

To answer these questions and other questions like them, you can either keep some basic Internet resources on your ready reference shelf in print format or bookmark online resources. In the original edition of *The Complete Internet Companion for Librarians*, I recommended downloading and printing out copies of certain resources on the Net to form the basis of an Internet-related ready reference collection. This is no longer a practical approach. A lot of the resources I mentioned at that time no longer exist in plain ASCII text, or if they do, they haven't been updated for a very long time. Today the best way to approach fact-finding questions relating to Internet topics is to use online resource discovery tools such as those described in Part III of this book.

Factual questions that pertain to issues other than the Internet itself are more difficult to answer. Resources may be available, but they are scattered all around on thousands of different information servers. Depending on the subject matter, there may be an overabundance of resources, very few, or none at all.

In the mid 1990s, your choice of tools to conduct searches on the Internet was critical. You could choose between Veronica (for Gopher servers), WAIS, Archie, or one of many Web search engines. Your choice depended upon the nature of the question. If you weren't sure where to begin, you started with a Web search engine such as Lycos. Otherwise, if you knew the resource you were looking for would be residing on an FTP server and not a Web server, for example, you went directly to Archie and ran your search.

Today, you have fewer search and retrieval tools to choose from because the Web is becoming the single, universal window for accessing everything. Still, some questions can be answered with more than one tool and, in the example that follows, you can arrive at different results depending on which search tool you use. Notice that in the author/title question example a lot of analysis was required in interpreting the search results.

In this reference question example, a teacher asks whether you know of a source on the Internet where education-related software might be found. Because the format being requested is software, it's reasonable to think that the answer can be found by searching FTP servers. You can still use Archie to run a case-insensitive substring search on the word **education** or **educational** and your search should return good results. Nowadays you can run these searches using a Web browser. You no longer have to connect to a UNIX-based Archie server and type in cryptic commands at a system prompt.

A good Web-based Archie server to try is FAST FTP Search at *ftpsearch.unit.no/ftpsearch*. A *case-insensitive substring* search retrieves records where the specified string occurs anywhere in the file name or directory name. It is the broadest search possible of the tens of thousands of FTP file names that are indexed by Archie. (You needn't be too concerned about the syntax for a case-insensitive substring search as this is usually the default setting.)

When I ran the above search using FAST FTP Search, I reset the maximum number of hits to 100 and searched on the keyword **education**. Before zeroing in on one particular FTP site, I quickly scrolled down looking through the entire list. I noticed one pattern that looked hopeful—certain sites were listed three times, one after the other, with the pathnames */dos/education*, */win3/education*, */win95/education/*, and */winnt/education*. These included *ftp.cdrom.com*, *ftp.bitcon.no*, *ftp.comp.hkbu.edu.hk*, *ftp.iif.hu*, among others. This could mean they were big sites with directories for each operating system and that the archive had been mirrored on several different servers. The sites that placed the education directories close to the root, like *ftp.cdrom.com/.1/cnet/dos/ education*, and included operating system names in the directory path, probably offered the best odds. FTP sites with path statements like *ftp.kreonet.re.kr/.7/docs/usenet-by-hierarchy/soc/culture/pakistan/education*, were probably bad bets. The word "docs" found early in the path statement implied that the contents would include education-related documents, not software.

You could approach this same question by going directly to a Web search engine. Which one might you try? The first source that came to my mind was William Cross's All-In-One Search Page because it maintains a category of search engines that specialize in software. I first chose about.com from Cross's list of search engines because about.com's information is hand-assembled by humans and could provide a better chance of producing relevant hits. I entered the phrase **educational software** and ran the search. *About.com* returned 95 hits, the first one being "Educational Software-Completely Free Educational Software (Pre-School, Jr./Sr. High-School, College and Educators)." This descriptive hit linked to *shareware.about.com* where sources of free educational software were listed by topic, including short descriptions. The whole process took less than one minute.

Another possibility for a reference question search is that you know from the start where to go to get an answer to your question. You may have to consult an online directory or print version of an Internet resource manual on your ready reference shelf to get a specific address, but essentially you know how to locate and access the resource. Over time, your knowledge of resources on the Internet that answer factual questions will grow. You can create a catalog that organizes your resources by subject using a simple HTML editor or bookmark utility.

You may want to set one of your bookmarks to a descriptive listing of ready reference resources, such as Ready Reference Resources on the Internet at *www.mcls.org/ homepages/ref/wwwref.htm*, or one of the many online ready reference collections such as the Internet Public Library Ready Reference Collection at *www.ipl.org/ref/RR/*, Refdesk.com at *www.refdesk.com/*, or Purdue University's Virtual Reference Desk (THOR) at *thorplus.lib.purdue.edu/reference/index.html*.

The Subject Question

When a patron approaches you with a subject-related question, you would again start by asking the question "Do I know of a resource on the Internet that's relevant to answering this patron's question?" I'm sure you won't be surprised when I tell you that the answer you'll come up with most often is "no" or "I'm not sure." This applies to fact-finding questions as well.

While introducing the various Internet resources and services throughout this book,

I have tried to avoid exaggerating their usefulness in answering reference questions in libraries. Certainly e-mail and FTP have proven themselves useful tools for certain types of communication and for acquiring resources that would otherwise be unavailable. Yet, the fact remains that most of the information needs expressed by library patrons cannot be met by accessing noncommercial databases on the Internet. The majority of answers will still be found in online commercial databases (though they may be reached via the Internet) and on microfilm, microfiche, CD-ROMs, and in print format materials such as books, magazines, and newspapers.

In those instances, where you do know of an appropriate Internet resource for answering a subject question, you should go to that resource and use it. If you're not aware of anything relevant existing on the Internet, you might begin by exploring your local holdings and services which offer the convenience of controlled access points such as your library catalog, CD-ROM databases, and commercial online services.

If you decide to extend your search onto the Internet, remember the frame of mind with which this has to be approached. There is no centralized database, so avoid the frustration of looking for and not finding this kind of access to Internet information. You are going to use computers running powerful search engines that are designed to go right to the heart of the data itself.

It would be nice if I could tell you that searching for information on topics relating to artificial intelligence, virtual reality, snake bites, and furniture building will get you excellent results, but searching for information on volcanoes, volleyball, and Volvos will result in zero hits. The fact is, you don't really know what you'll find until you try.

As time passes, and with continuous contact, you learn more about the strengths and weaknesses of the Internet. I have used the Internet to answer reference questions relating to all seven topics I just mentioned. With the first two—artificial intelligence and virtual reality—I was very confident from the beginning of my search that an Internet excursion would reap plentiful returns. With the other five, I was less confident; and with two of the items it was only through serendipitous discovery that I found precisely what the patron was looking for.

It helps to understand at the outset that there are certain broad subject categories that are well represented on the Internet. Knowing what these subject categories are helps guide you when you are trying to decide whether you should even approach the Internet as a resource for answering a particular reference question. Without question, the Internet remains an excellent source of freely accessible technology-related information.

Introducing Patrons to the Internet

It's not unusual to hear patrons ask "Where's your travel section?", "Where's *Value Line?*", or "Where's the *Reader's Guide?*", but it would be very unusual to hear the question "Where's the EFF Web server?" or "Where's the Labovitz e-zine list?" When you get a question that includes the word *Internet*, be sensitive to the fact that the person asking may know nothing about the Internet, but it's a way of asking for a general introduction to the global network, and what better place to come for that than the library? I'm discovering, however, that there is also a new generation of library users that are accustomed to using computers and the Internet for almost their entire resource discovery. They go to portals like Yahoo! to chat, to conduct research, to send *e-mail* to friends, to sell merchandise on auctions, to look for car parts, and more. These individuals are aggressive with their attempts at finding online information without the assistance of librarians. One day I overheard an individual who was new to the Internet yelling at his friend, "Look! Just go to *directhit.com* and punch in *tactical thigh holster* if that's what you're looking for!"

Newcomers to the Internet

The kind of service reference librarians provide for newcomers varies depending on what that person's perception is of the Internet. Some individuals see the Internet as a source of entertainment. They browse Websites just for fun; something to do to pass the time. This activity is equivalent to coming into the library and paging through *The Guinness Book of Records* or browsing the stacks—not because they have a specific question that needs answering, but because they want to be entertained. Other individuals view the Internet as a reference tool—a mechanism for document delivery or a means of communicating via e-mail. They access it only when they have a question that needs to be answered, a specific task that needs to be performed, or because they have an idea that needs to be communicated. If you offer public access to the Internet and it's your responsibility to train new users, keep these different viewpoints in perspective.

Providing Internet Reader's Advisory Service

To service patrons in the area of reader's advisory, you might try thinking in terms of formats or services. By this I mean to think of the different formats in which information on the Net is published. Information comes in the form of e-journals, e-zines, e-texts, online magazines and newspapers, messages on mailing lists, postings to newsgroups, HTML files on Web servers, and records in specialized databases. For example, if a patron expresses an interest in computers and you know they haven't explored the Internet, you might begin by offering them a list of mailing lists that discuss issues relating to computers. Prepare help sheets explaining how to subscribe and how to search message archives (see Chapter 24 for more information).

Other formats that deal with the subject of computers include e-journals such as *The Amateur Computerist* (*www.columbia.edu/~hauben/acn/index.html*). Newsgroups are a great source of news and information on dozens of different topics relating to computers (see Chapter 25). Remember, too, that search engines often have problems indexing Web pages that are delivered dynamically, such as those resulting from database programs like library catalogs and other specialized databases. This is known as the *invisible Web*—a topic covered in Chapter 12.

A useful print resource that can assist you in this area is *Harley Hahn's Internet & Web Yellow Pages,* published by Osborne McGraw-Hill (ISBN 0–072–12785–6). This book provides an index to thousands of resources including discussion lists, newsgroups, OPACs, FTP archives, electronic journals, RFCs, Web pages, and more. If you look in the index under the heading *psychology*, for example, you find references to mailing lists, Web pages, and newsgroups. This reference is by no means an exhaustive list of Internet resources, but it would serve nicely as another ready reference tool.

You could introduce fiction readers to the Internet by recommending some of the online magazines and electronic journals listed in Chapter 28. In addition, there are mailing lists and Usenet newsgroups that provide forums for discussing literature. To browse mailing lists by subject, refer patrons to TILE.NET at *www.tile.net*. Keep in mind, the Internet doesn't always yield the results you would expect. A recent search in TILE.NET on the keyword **rodeo** yielded zero hits, while a search on **bucking bronco** yielded several hits, all of which pointed to mailing lists about late model Ford Broncos. Searching newsgroup message archives by subject is easier if you use the Deja News query form at *www.deja.com/usenet*.

COMMERCIAL ONLINE SERVICES

The Internet enables you to explore online services available to libraries. By connecting to a vendor's home page, you can read a general outline of the services that are available and you can, in most cases, see a listing of titles included in a database. UMI at *www.umi.com* offers a detailed view of holdings. For example, with ProQuest databases at *www.umi.com/hp/Support/Titles/*, tables include title, ISSN, publication IDs, format availability, and first and latest dates.

Some services display these files within your Web browser window. Others require Adobe Acrobat Reader support. (Acrobat Reader is free and can be downloaded from the Net at *www.adobe.com/products/acrobat/readstep.html*.)

GRAPHIC AND TEXT-ONLY VIEWS

Many vendors offer access to their services through the Web and a text-only telnet connection. Library systems using terminals would opt for the e-text-only service, as would libraries with older PCs that don't support Web browsers. If your Internet PCs have adequate CPUs and RAM, the Web offers the friendliest interface for patrons and it supports graphics. If you need telnet software running on your PC, see the explanations in Chapter 14.

SITE LICENSES

When you set up your online services, support is usually offered for both multi-user (two or more users accessing the account simultaneously) and single-user accounts. Vendors specify in their contract the exact number of concurrent users allowed, or if it is unlimited.

PRICING

Pricing is not listed on Web pages. Vendors prefer to negotiate flexible pricing that depends on how many databases you access and the number of concurrent logins you request. Academic libraries are often billed according to their current FTE counts. Vendors such as Knight-Ridder Information, Inc., offer pay-as-you-go telnet access to a large selection of online databases through Dialog. If you access a database only occasionally, this mode of access is more economical than paying for annual subscriptions.

Table 18–1: Index, abstract, and full-text database services available on the Internet		
Name of Service	**Description**	**Web Address**
AskERIC	Internet-based education information service	*ericir.syr.edu/*
Bell & Howell Information and Learning	Features several Web-based services including ProQuest and Dissertation Services	*www.bellhowell.infolearning com/*
DIALOG@CARL	DIALOG@CARL provides end-users with an easy-to-understand interface for accessing nearly 300 DIALOG databases. Includes full-text articles from more than 3,000 journals and 100 newspapers.	*dialog.carl.org/*
EBSCOhost	Online access to a variety of general reference and subject-specific databases including 500 journals in searchable full text, over 1,000 full image journals, abstracts and indexing for nearly 3,800 journals, and current citations for over 11,000 titles. Offers access to other information providers' databases, such as Academic Abstracts FullTEXT and ERIC.	*www.epnet.com/*
ERIC Document Reproduction Service (EDRS)	The document delivery component of ERIC	*www.edrs.com/*
The Gale Group	Offers several online services including Gale's Ready Reference Shelf, LegalTrac and InfoTrac.	*www.galegroup.com/*
Lexis ®-Nexis ®	Premier information service providing legal, business, and financial information.	*www.lexis-nexis.com/*
OCLC Online Computer Library Center, Inc.	Integrated collection management, cataloging, and authorities services. OCLC's Core service is World Cat Online Union Catalog.	*www.oclc.org/*
Ovid Technologies, Inc.	Access to more than 90 scientific, medical, and technical databases including MEDLINE, Current Contents, Biosis, ABI/Inform, and PsycInfo.	*www.ovid.com/*

Table 18–1(*cont.*)		
SIRS Mandarin, Inc.	SIRS Researcher provides access to thousands of full-text articles on social, scientific, historic, economic, and political issues. Articles include text and images and are drawn from more than 1,500 newspapers, magazines, journals and government publications. Other SIRS Mandarin products include SIRS Government Reporter and SIRS Renaissance.	*www.sirs.com/*

THIRD-PARTY VENDORS

Third-party vendors, including CARL, EBSCO, and OCLC, are forming partnerships with publishers and making resources like *Books in Print* available on the Web. A sampling of these and other online databases are presented in Table 18–1.

GENERAL REFERENCE DATABASES

In this section, I introduce you to a full-text, online service called Electric Library. Electric Library is available for library- or campus-wide usage, or library patrons can subscribe to the service as individuals and access it from home.

ELECTRIC LIBRARY

Electric Library is a full-text database that contains newspapers, magazines, newswires, classic books, transcripts of television and radio shows, thousands of photos and maps, and a reference collection including a thesaurus, almanac, encyclopedia, and dictionaries.

One interesting feature of Electric Library is its association with another Infonautics Corporation resource called Researchpaper.com. Researchpaper.com offers a large collection of themes and ideas for school-related research projects. Students can browse through dozens of term paper ideas and then launch a search for pertinent articles. Searches link to holdings in Electric Library. This alone would be a valuable service if you had access to the journals and newspapers cited in your search results. Before you can link to the full-text online articles, you must become a member of Electric Library.

The subscription fee for an individual is $9.95/month or $59.95/year for unlimited access. Site licenses for libraries are also available. You can negotiate a sight license for all the PCs in you library, or all the PCs on your campus. For a free 30–day trial subscription, visit *www.elibrary.com.*

FREE FULL-TEXT DATABASES

In this section, I introduce examples of free, full-text databases available on the Internet. Included in this discussion are Index Morganagus, a searchable collection of full-text library-related e-journals; TIME.com, an example of a major news and information magazine with a full-text archive that can be searched or browsed; ZD Inc.'s ZDNet, a *portal* offering access to Ziff Davis media publications; and CRAYON, a customizable online newspaper you design.

INDEX MORGANAGUS

Index Morganagus uses FileMaker Pro (*www.filemaker.com/index.html*), a database application from FileMaker, Inc., and Harvest, an indexing and search system, to offer access to a select list of electronic serials. Eric Lease Morgan, the individual behind this project, indexes a total of 29 serials in Index Morganagus, most of which are related to the library profession. You learn more about Index Morganagus in, "Description and Evaluation of the 'Mr. Serials' Process: Automatically Collecting, Organizing, Archiving, Indexing, and Disseminating Electronic Serials", *Serials Review* 21, no. 4 (Winter 1995): 1–12. This article can be accessed on the Web at *www.lib.ncsu.edu/staff/ morgan/report-on-mr-serials.html*. You can see a title list of the serials being indexed at *www.lib.ncsu.edu/staff/morgan/serials-of-mr-serials/index.html*.

TIME DIGITAL

Time Digital is the online counterpart to *Time* magazine in print format. When you go to TIME.com at *www.time.com/time/index.html*, you can view select articles from the print version of the current issue, and full content of the print versions in the archives approximately one week after their publication date. From the home page, you can also access Time Asia, Time Europe, and Time Canada.

TIME.com's archive can be browsed or searched. You can browse by date or by viewing covers of the print version going back to 1994. You can use the simple search box located on the home page, or go to the advanced search service where you have access to the following features:

- Boolean operators AND, OR, and NOT
- Directing your search to all of TIME.com, Time Daily, Time Magazine, Time Digital, or Time Europe
- Limit results to last week, last month, last year, or don't limit results
- Display or do not display summaries
- Sort by date or relevance

Accessing a major news magazine online for free is a valuable service. Maybe your library already has access to a commercial, online, full-text journal article service. If this is the case, pointing your patrons to a single-title database like the TIME.com archive for a subject search doesn't make much sense. A more comprehensive search can be accomplished in one of your other services. However, if your patrons are young students doing research from home, you might suggest this resource as a good choice for news articles.

ZIFF-DAVIS PUBLISHING COMPANY ON THE WEB

ZDNet, a trademark of the Ziff-Davis Publishing Company, offers you an opportunity to run full-text searches on material collected from hundreds of different computer magazines. ZDNet also collaborates with Yahoo!, making *Yahoo! Internet Life* available for searching. In addition to searching full-text magazine articles, ZDNet maintains an extensive software library including games, Internet applications, and software for home and education.

All of this material can be accessed from ZDNet's Website located at *www.zdnet.com/*.

Initiating a Search

There is a search box near the top of the ZDNet home page where you can initiate a simple search covering the entire site, or the Web. Just to the right of that box is a hyperlink to "Power Search." The Power Search page lets you focus your search on specific e-magazines by using a pull-down menu. Beyond this, there are still other sections of ZDNet that have their own search engines.

On the Power Search page, look for a link called "Magazine Archive." This links you to ZDNet's Tech InfoBase—currently a collection of over 300,000 articles and abstracts taken from 293 computer-related magazines, journals, newsletters, and newspapers. Full access to this service is *not* free. You must register and pay $7.95/month to access the entire archive's holdings. What you can access for free is the current content of their e-magazine holdings. Considering the size of the database, this in itself is a valuable free service, especially for library patrons who have no other access to technical information at home. At present, you can view a complete list of available tiles at *cma.zdnet.com/texis/techinfobase/techinfobase/allmags.html*.

Clicking on "PC Magazine," or any of the other titles listed on the home page, takes you directly to that e-magazine's page on ZDNet. Along with searching and browsing capabilities of back issues, you can click on the image of the current issue's cover and browse through most of the current issue online including the cover story and feature articles.

NEWS AND INFORMATION SERVICES

News and information services are services on the Internet that enable you to create your own electronic newsstand or newspaper. With news and information services like MyZDNet, you select which resources you want to access—only the news that's important to you—and list it on a Web page you design. Your custom page is stored on the news and information service provider's computer, not on your personal computer. Other services, like EntryPoint, offer a sophisticated blend of technology and publishing. EntryPoint feeds daily news right to your home or library computers through their custom-designed software.

CRAYON

CRAYON news allows you to create your own online newspaper two different ways: in sections or as one big page all at once. Creating your newspaper in sections takes a little longer than viewing it all at once. To begin creating your newspaper, connect to *crayon.net/*, click on the "CReAte Your Free Newspaper" link, enter your e-mail address as your login ID and a password, and you are ready to begin.

The next screen that comes up asks you to name your newspaper, give it a motto, choose a page layout, decide whether you want inline images or links to images, and which operations will require input of your password. After this you begin adding news to your online newspaper.

The first section of CRAYON News contains U.S.-related news and you are given 18 newspapers from which to choose. You can customize your news section by inserting the names and URLs for any other newspapers you'd like included. When you finish a section, click on the "Next" button to continue, or you can stop at any point and create your newspaper by clicking on the "Create My Newspaper Now" button.

The headings for the various sections include:

- U.S. News
- Canada
- Local News
- World News
- Politics as Usual
- Editorial and Opinions
- Weather Conditions and Forecasts
- Business Report
- Information and Technology Report
- Science
- Religion
- Health
- Lifestyles
- Sports Day
- Snippets Corner
- Funny Pages
- Tabloid Page
- Web Spotlight

You access your CRAYON newspaper by connecting to site *crayon.net/* and entering your e-mail address and password, or you can bookmark your newspaper and access it quicker. You can go back and modify your newspaper anytime you wish by clicking on the appropriate link in the left column.

MANAGING INFORMATION ON THE NET

In the traditional search process, if sources don't come readily to mind, you consult various access points to information like bibliographies, indexes, and catalogs, or subject sources such as vertical files. In an Internet environment, these choices don't yet exist. To some degree, you can circumvent this lack of having controlled access points by creating your own index or catalog of resources.

The purpose of introducing these applications is not to imply that you should use them to create a comprehensive catalog of every resource on the Internet; instead, you should use them to create a personalized system built over time, one that meets your own needs and interests and one that focuses on local needs, preferences, and clientele.

CREATING CATALOGS WITH BOOKMARK UTILITIES

A *bookmark* is a marker you place on a remote document on the Internet so you can easily find it at some later date. A *bookmark utility* is a specialized application that's designed just for managing bookmarks. In order to operate one of these programs, you need to be connected to the Internet. In the previous edition of this book, I introduced an application called FirstFloor Smart Bookmarks. This product has since been discontinued. If you installed Smart Bookmarks and need technical support, consult their FAQ at *www.firstfloor.com/sbfaq.html*. At that time there were only a couple of bookmark utilities to choose from. Now there are dozens. The main features these programs offer include:

- Add bookmarks—Create folders and add sites to your folders for future reference.
- Save copies of Web pages—Store local copies of Web pages on your hard drive for offline viewing and updating.
- Monitor Web pages for changes—Monitor Web pages manually or automatically for changes in content or for new links.
- Run Web searches and then save the search as a bookmark. Rerun it automatically to get updated results.

As you might expect, companies are now offering Web-based bookmark services. These services allow you to store your bookmarks on a remote server so you can access them anytime from any computer connected to the Internet. They support editing, deletion, sorting, searching, and organizing your bookmarks into folders. Like most Web-based services that replace locally run applications (free Web-based e-mail is a good example), you can enjoy easy access without being tied down to one PC, but response times can be slow on dial-up connections. For example, when you click on a folder, seconds may pass before it opens.

Some bookmark managers you might like to explore are BestBookmarks at *www.bestbookmarks.com/* and Blink at *blink.com/*. Blink allows you to sort your bookmarks alphabetically, by category, by rating, or by the date you entered them or last used them. Both BestBookmarks and Blink are free.

MySpider.com at *www.myspider.com/* creates a slightly different variation on this theme by bringing in the element of *community*. With MySpider you get in touch with people who are digging for the same information you are. It enables you to access sites that have been prescreened by humans. When you search a subject, you may have the opportunity to interact with someone who has already "been there, done that."

Still another twist on the bookmark theme is offered by Jumplist at *www.jumplist.com/*. Jumplist helps you custom create a system for listing links on your Website. You have access to tools that allow you to add new icons, manage links submitted by visitors to your site, and support reciprocal linking. One of the most valuable services Jumplist offers is link validation. This service helps you keep your links up-to-date automatically.

If you are looking for a quick and easy bookmark manager that you can use without registering and one that is simple to operate, consider using URLpad at *members.tripod. com/~rtiess/urlpad*.htm. This system uses cookies to retain URLs, so it isn't portable in the sense you can walk up to any computer in the world and access your list of URLs. You could use it in a library setting, however. Cookies must be enabled on the PCs you are using in order for URLpad to work.

To learn about other bookmark managers, go to *www.webwizards.net/useful/wbbm.htm*

REFERENCE AND INSTRUCTION SERVICES

The Internet removes some limitations associated with traditional reference and instruction services. Reference personnel work the reference desk 64 hours a week, more or less. They offer reference assistance over the phone during those same hours. During the course of the year, library staff provide library tours and classes on topics such as Internet searching, finding books online, finding articles, and so on.

When students can't make it to regularly scheduled classes, the Internet makes it possible for those students to view teaching materials online for the classes they missed. Reference librarians use the Internet to give library patrons 24 hour per day access to textual information that not only covers instruction, but also describes library resources and services. Making HTML documents available on the Internet to home users or students on public access PCs any time of the day can be superior to live instruction where there is no opportunity to sit at a computer and gain hands-on experience. In addition, students are given the opportunity to learn at their own pace and hyperlink to resources that are available online.

Documents like Esther Grassian's "Thinking Critically about World Wide Web Resources" *www.library.ucla.edu/libraries/college/instruct/web/critical.htm*, are shared through hyperlinking by many libraries that utilize online instruction. The Internet and its participants have this unique ability to share and not reinvent the wheel every time a library creates its own reference resources and instruction pages. While many proprietary services are unique to single libraries, there are many general principles of research and online bibliographies that can be created by one and shared by many.

The Occidental College Library offers access to current library class Web pages and to their archives holding older class materials. This service is part of their library Web page at *www.oxy.edu/departments/library/instruction.html*. Their link labeled "Research Help" offers assistance in developing library research methods along with guides to their electronic resources. While their collection of online documents is small, they provide a valuable service to library patrons and their archives is growing with time. Larger institutions like UCLA Libraries *www.library.ucla.edu/instruc/index.htm* offer more extensive collections of online guides and tutorials. Upon closer review, you may discover that someone else's documentation can be of practical use to your own clientele. If your resources are limited, explore the possibility of linking to someone else's. For example, UCLA Libraries has excellent tutorials on such basics as "How to Use Netscape," "Web Search Tools," and "Search Strategy Tips."

The Longwood College Library at *web.lwc.edu/administrative/library/librefrm.htm* presents their students with a Virtual Reference Shelf of both free resources and commercial services that are available through the Virtual Library of Virginia (VIVA).

Like the Occidental College Library, Longwood College Library also offers in-person instruction and consultation along with online services. Their Virtual Tour lets visitors tour the library from any computer connected to the Internet, any time of the day. As part of the tour, you can click on an image map of the library's floor plan to explore any area in the library on any floor.

The Missouri State Library uses the Internet and portable documents to distribute evaluation forms from their Website at *mosl.sos.state.mo.us/lib-ser/libser.html*. They also use their Web pages to announce new additions to the State Library's book collection.

One of their feature services, called *Info-to-Go*, presents online visitors with a hyperlinked bibliography of magazine and journal articles. If the users of this service have access to EBSCOhost, they are given access to the full text of the articles.

MIT Libraries *libraries.mit.edu/* offers in-house instruction to both individuals and groups. They offer samples of instruction programs online designed to help students with their research. Their online documentation is designed to complement the human resources, not replace them. You can see samples of their HTML documents at *web.mit.edu/infolit/www/Faculty/NewInstdesc.html*.

DEVELOPING YOUR OWN ONLINE RESEARCH TUTORIAL

The following is a sample printout of an online tutor I developed at Arkansas State University Mountain Home. You can use it as a guide in developing your own library research tutorial. Hyperlinks are represented with bolded and underlined text.

Library Research at
Arkansas State University Mountain Home:
An Online Tutor
(Unless otherwise stated, hyperlinked resources are available
anywhere there is a computer connected to the Internet.)

STEP 1: CHOOSE A TOPIC.

STEP 2: OBTAIN BACKGROUND INFORMATION.

STEP 3: FINDING BOOKS.

STEP 4: FINDING ARTICLES.

STEP 5: FINDING INTERNET RESOURCES.

STEP 6: CITING YOUR SOURCES.

STEP 1: CHOOSE A TOPIC.
Think about your topic and what concepts are involved. State your topic in the form of a question, for example, "How is telecommunications used in supporting rural health programs in the United States?" Start a list of possible search terms. Include keywords (single terms) and phrases (two or more terms that belong together, as in health care). For synonyms, consult a print thesaurus and/or subject index such as Reader's Guide. Subject indexes can also be found online with products like **FirstSearch** (Authoriza-

tion: ***-***-*** Password: ******). There you can access subject and keyword indexes to multiple databases. (**FirstSearch** is only available in the library.)

Where Can I Get Ideas for a Topic? Discuss your ideas with the reference staff. Set up a research consultation meeting if your topic is lengthy. Browse the *CQ Researcher* for ideas. (CQ Researcher is shelved on the index table.) Explore the research topics that have been developed at **Researchpaper.com**. Consult a specialized encyclopedia that covers your particular subject. For example, "folk music" in *The New Grove Dictionary of Music and Musicians* and in *Folklore: An Encyclopedia of Beliefs, Customs, Tales, Music, and Art*; "nursing homes" in the *Encyclopedia of Sociology*. (A subject guide to the reference collection is available at the reference desk.) Search the tables of contents, plus abstracts and full-text articles from thousands of journals and newsletters in a variety of fields at **BUBL Journals** and **UnCover**.

STEP 2: OBTAIN BACKGROUND INFORMATION.

Once you have keywords and phrases that describe your topic, consult additional resources for background information. Common resources for this process are traditional print versions of encyclopedias and dictionaries. You can locate these in our reference collection by consulting the library's online catalog. **Britannica Online** is available in the Library and at home. For facts and figures, consult World Almanac, Information Please (in print in the library, or **online**), and collections of statistical data. (See the subject guide to our reference collection at the reference desk.)

STEP 3: FINDING BOOKS.

Access books by searching the library's **online catalog**. The library's online catalog points you to circulating books and reference books. If you don't have a particular author or title in mind, search by keyword in the title and subject field. If you don't find what you need in our collection, search OCLC's **WorldCat** through **FirstSearch**. This catalog links you to millions of titles worldwide. When you find a title you are interested in, fill out an **Interlibrary Loan (ILL) request form** and submit it to our ILL department. For help in understanding the Library of Congress classification system, check out the help guide at **about.com**. For help with subject headings, consult the **Library of Congress Subject Headings** in the big red books at the reference desk).

STEP 4: FINDING ARTICLES.

Check our **online catalog** to see what the library's periodical holdings are. A paper catalog in the periodical section of the library lists all of the holdings in the library's online full-text journal databases. The public access PCs in the library link you to CD-ROMs and online services that provide abstracts and full text articles.

How do I find articles on my topic? You find relevant articles by searching in indexes. The *Reader's Guide to Periodical Literature* and *CINAHL* (Nursing and allied health literature) are located on the index table. These are print indexes. The indexes for online services are accessed via computers.

Commercial Online Services
(Use a Web browser to access these resources):

Electric Library www.elibrary.com/s/edumark (AVAILABLE CAMPUS-WIDE)
EBSCOhost http://search.global.epnet.com/ (AVAILABLE WORLDWIDE)

Four Databases are Available:

1. Academic Abstracts FullTEXT Ultra
2. Clinical Reference Systems
3. Health Source Plus
4. USP DI Volume II, Advice for the Patient

UserID: *****
Password: *****

FirstSearch http://newfirstsearch.oclc.org (AVAILABLE WORLDWIDE)
Authorization: *****
Password: *****
Lexis-Nexis http://web.lexis-nexis.com/universe (AVAILABLE CAMPUS WIDE)
Proquest http://proquest.umi.com/pqdweb (AVAILABLE WORLDWIDE)
Account Name: *****
Password: *****
Infotrac web2.infotrac.galegroup.com/itweb/akstateu3 (LIBRARY USE ONLY)
(No login necessary)
ERIC (Education-related) www.edrs.com/default.cfm (LIBRARY USE ONLY)
(No login necessary)
JAMA: the Journal of the American Medical Association http://pubs.ama-assn.org/
(AVAILABLE CAMPUS WIDE)

CD-ROMs (Look for the icon on the PC's desktop)

SIRS Government Reporter (Government Documents)
SIRS Researcher

STEP 5: FINDING INTERNET RESOURCES.
Here are some of the best-filtered directories on the Net. They are built by human beings and include carefully selected resources.
   Infomine http://lib-www.ucr.edu/Main.html
   The Librarian's Guide to the Internet http://sunsite.berkeley.edu/InternetIndex/
   NetFirst http://newfirstsearch.oclc.org (Login: ***** Password: *****) When you reach the home page, click on Databases and then look for NetFirst (ONLY AVAILABLE IN THE LIBRARY)
   About.com http://home.about.com/
   Researchpaper.com http://researchpaper.com/
Quick links to major search engines:
   AltaVista http://www.altavista.com/
   Lycos http://www.lycos.com/index.html
   Infoseek http://infoseek.go.com/
   Google http://www.google.com/
   NorthernLight http://www.northernlight.com/

STEP 6: CITING YOUR SOURCES.
You can find style sheets in the library or on the Internet. Consult the online catalog for Turabian, APA, MLA, and others–all located in the library. For online examples of

citations, see **Modern Language Association (MLA)** or **American Psychological Association (APA)** standards.

For help specifically with citing electronic resources, go to **Nancy Crane's site at the University of Vermont**.

ONLINE REFERENCE SERVICES

Librarians continue to set up Websites offering electronic reference forms that patrons can fill out. Many fear they will be overwhelmed with requests but often report that incoming queries are small in number. Curtin University in Western Australia has been providing e-mail reference services for years and, more recently, Web-based reference services at *andre.curtin.edu.au/eclectic/eclecticinput.asp*.

Jim Robertson, Director of the Architecture Library at the New Jersey Institute of Technology, used to maintain a Web page listing libraries that use Web forms for patron input including reference questions. You can link to Robertson's home page at *hertz.njit.edu/~robertso/prof1.html*. Look under the heading "Here are some Web publications of mine:" for the link "web forms." This link has not been updated since early 1997.

The Vancouver Public Library at *www2.vpl.vancouver.bc.ca/emailRef/eRefIntro.html* makes it clear that the scope of their online reference service is broad in subject, but limited to fact-finding questions and local information. On the bottom of their *E-Mail Reference Service* page they add the caveat:

> Reference assistance to residents outside British Columbia is limited to local information and referrals specific to the Vancouver area. Please contact your local library for assistance with all other reference inquiries.

Since the last edition of this book was published, the number of commercial sites offering what is called *expert* services has grown. These services are not connected to libraries. They are businesses that solicit for "experts" in their respective fields to answer questions, either for free or for pay. This chapter closes with a selective listing of some of the more popular expert sites currently available. As with all online information services, users should view the expert and the information they receive from such sites with a critical eye. Where reference librarians and other information professionals cite their sources, many online experts speak only from personal experience.

- exp.com *www.exp.com/*—Exp.com links you to thousands of experts by subject, or you can post a public question and let qualified experts respond. Each expert listing includes a profile, service description, customer rating, and pricing schedule.
- AllExperts *www.allexperts.com/*—At AllExperts, volunteers answer questions for free. Computer-related topics range from operating systems and networking to spreadsheets and word processing.
- ASKanything.com *www.askanything.com/*—Information seekers go to this site and post questions for free or offer payment. It is a common understanding among users of this site that money can motivate experts to answer questions more quickly and more completely. The more you offer to pay, the more prominently your question is displayed.

- Ask an Expert Page *njnie.dl.stevens-tech.edu/askanexpert.html*—Ask an Expert Page provides links to experts in ten different categories including library reference and computing and the Internet.

REFERENCES

1. Dillon, Martin, et al. 1993. *Assessing Information on the Internet: Toward Providing Library Services for Computer-Mediated Communication.* Dublin, OH: Online Computer Library Center, Inc. Downloaded from FTP site *zues.rsch.oclc.org* in directory */pub/internet_resources_ project/report* as file *report.ps.tar.Z* (312328 bytes).
2. Deutsch, Peter. 1992. *Resource Discovery in an Internet Environment.* Master's Thesis. School of Computer Science, McGill University: 1. Downloaded from FTP site *archives.cc.mcgill.ca* in directory */pub/peterd/thesis* as files *cover.june30.txt* (4858 bytes) as file *thesis.june30.txt* (113945 bytes).
3. Gorgan, Denis Joseph. 1967. *Gorgan's Case Studies in Reference Work, Volume I: Enquiries and the Reference Process.* London: Clive Bingley.
4. Katz, William A. 1974. *Introduction to Reference Work, Volume II: Reference services and reference process.* (New York: McGraw-Hill Book Company.

Integrating Internet Tools into Other Library Services

As a librarian, when you think in terms of integrating the Internet into your existing services, you should view the Internet as a strategic resource for your entire operation, not just as a single, technical resource. Although the Internet functions well as a reference tool and its primary use will be in that department, it can also serve as a consulting resource and communication tool in other departments.

IMPLEMENTING INTERNET SERVICES IN-HOUSE

Once the Internet has been introduced to library staff and they are made aware of its resources and services, it slowly becomes part of the normal flow of library operations.

E-mail is used for ordering books and other materials, requesting reference assistance from colleagues, and sending claims to subscription agents for missing journals. In addition, librarians stay in touch with other librarians via discussion lists. Topics discussed include everything from library automation systems to children's story hour. The Internet is used to verify bibliographic data and to explore publishers' catalogs and online bookstores. Catalogers access other libraries' online catalogs for copy cataloging. Others use the Internet for developing bibliographies, studying collection development practices in other libraries, and as a source of book reviews.

New ideas for Internet implementations should be continuously solicited from all employees in every department. These ideas can be evaluated not just in terms of how they will benefit the overall operations of the library, but also in terms of how they can benefit the community.

This chapter is meant to be a place of departure for librarians who are just beginning to explore the Internet. In this chapter, I present a selective list of resources and services arranged by department including Acquisitions/Collection Development, Cataloging, Serials Librarians, Children's Services, and Special Collections and Archives.

ACQUISITIONS/COLLECTION DEVELOPMENT

In this section I list various Internet resources that may be of interest to library staff involved with developing collections or purchasing materials. You can find large book wholesalers like Baker & Taylor Books online, as well as small presses like Gutter Press with their "dangerous fiction" (*www.gutterpress.com/*). Each vendor's site is worth exploring for interesting services and programs. The Librarian's Guide, a feature offered by the Ingram Book Group at *www.ingrambook.com/* (look under "Programs and Services"), offers librarians tips on such things as collection development, "Opening Day" collections, Kidlist—a source for children's books, standing orders programs, and various title selection tools. A subscription service called "i Page" allows you to make title selections, check stock, and order all on the Web. This service is located at *www.ingrambook.com/ipage.* Another service, called "Sorting It Out," offers articles and interviews with authors that are of interest to librarians. Baker & Taylor and other book vendors are listed in Table 19–1.

In June 2000, Baker & Taylor announced the creation of a new business-to-business e-commerce venture called Informata.com. Informata.com builds Internet portals that host specialized services including those directed towards librarians. Informata.com's first Internet portal, theLibraryPlace.com, offers librarians access to an electronic marketplace with a wide variety of products and services including books, music, movies, library furniture, computers, and more.

Table 19–1: Sampling of library-related book vendors on the Internet	
Name	Address
Baker & Taylor	*www.baker-taylor.com/*
Bell & Howell Information and Learning Company	*www.umi.com/*
Bernan Associates	*www.bernan.com/*
Blackwell's Book Services	*www.blackwell.com/*
Blake's Books (an online used and antiquarian bookstore)	*www.blakesbooks.com/*
Brodart Co.	*www.brodart.com/*
Duthie Books (online Canadian bookstore)	*www.duthiebooks.com/*
Ingram Book Group	*www.ingrambook.com/*
John Smith & Son Bookshops International Library Services (Scotland book retailer)	*www.johnsmith.co.uk/ils/*
Moonbeam Publications, Inc.	*www.gtii.com/mpi/moonbeam/ mnbeam.htm*
Schoenhof's Foreign Books	*www.schoenhofs.com/*
Multilingual Books	*www.esl.net/mbt/*
Nolo.com, Inc.	*www.nolo.com/*
Pepper Music Network (sheet music)	*www.jwpepper.com/*
Powells.com (new and used bookstore)	*powells.com/*
Publishers' Catalogues Home Page (over 6,000!)	*www.lights.com/publisher/*
United States Government Printing Office	*www.access.gpo.gov/*
Yankee Book Peddler, Inc.	*www.ybp.com/*

R.R. Bowker has built a useful one-stop site at *www.bowker.com/lrg/home/* that offers hundreds of links to library services and suppliers. You can access their database via full-text searching and by browsing alphabetically or by subject.

Library of Congress Acquisitions

The Library of Congress Website has a special Acquisitions page that provides access to several interesting documents at *lcweb.loc.gov/acq/acquire.html*. Here you can view their Collections Policy Statements that govern the library's acquisitions and collections development. You can link to their Gopher server (one of the few Gophers still running) and read about the library's collection overviews. You can find a description of the library's surplus book program and learn how it benefits educational institutions. And you can view the library's acquisitions FAQ which covers the following topics:

1. Does the Library of Congress sell books?
2. How can I buy a book with the following LCCN (Library of Congress Card Number)?
3. I hear the Library of Congress gives away books; is this true?
4. How much is a book worth?
5. Can I sell material to the Library of Congress?
6. I sold some books to the Library. When will the LC pay my bill?
7. How does the Library of Congress obtain its books and other materials?
8. Which vendors cover which country?
9. How are vendors selected?
10. Can I donate a book to the Library?
11. I sent my book to the Library of Congress; where is it?
12. How can my institution exchange materials with LC?
13. What is the Cooperative Acquisitions Program?
14. What happened to the Exchange and Gift Division, Order Division, and Overseas Operations Division?

While the Library of Congress does not sell books from its collection, it does sell items through its cataloging distribution service (CDS). These items pertain to MARC documentation, cataloging manuals and training tools, LC classification, and authority records. LC MARC documentation is discussed in further detail later in this chapter.

E-book Sellers

Electronic books, or e-books for short, are available for download from the Web and viewable on your PC, or they may come as special hardware devices designed specifically for displaying e-books. One of the most popular such devices is the Rocket eBook. The Rocket eBook, weighing in at 22 ounces and the size of a paperback, holds the text and images of about ten average size novels in its 4MB of flash memory. It is powered by a rechargeable nickel metal hydride battery. The black and white viewing area measures approximately $4^1/_4$" × 3".

The RocketLibrarian is an application that runs on your PC or Mac that enables you to communicate to and from the Rocket eBook. It assists you in downloading

RocketEditions you purchase from online bookstores and it helps you manage your Rocket eBook library.

Rocket eBooks cost around $200 each and can be purchased from any of the following vendors:

EBookEmpire.com *www.ebookempire.com/*
Barnes & Noble *barnesandnoble.com/*
Levenger *www.levenger.com/shop/Computing/ebook3.asp*

New titles are coming out daily and can be purchased via the Internet from any of the following vendors:

Barnes & Noble *barnesandnoble.com/*
Powell's Bookstore *powells.com/*
eCAMPUS.com *ecampus.com/*

The last time I checked with Barnes & Noble, they were offering almost 4,000 different RocketEditions. Steven King's *Riding the Bullet* was selling for $2.50, L. Ron Hubbard's *Battlefield Earth: A Saga of the Year 3000* was selling for $6.39,

Rare and Out-of-Print Books

Barnes and Noble offers a central clearing house service for rare and out-of-print books at *barnesandnoble.com*. Look for the tab labeled "Out of Print" located at the top of the page. You can browse special collections, or search by title, author, or keywords. You can narrow your search by first editions, signed copies, dust jacket, and "new this week." Barnes & Noble allows you to add titles to your shopping cart, in which case they make the purchase for you and ship it to you, or you could contact the dealer yourself. Dealer names are provided in the search results list and a dealer database can be accessed by clicking on their link "Our Dealers."

Bookstores that Ship Worldwide

Evelyn C. Leeper has compiled a selective list of bookstores that ship worldwide and organizes the list into various geographic regions as shown below. You can access a hypertext version of this list online at *www.geocities.com/evelynleeper/bookshop.htm*. The stores listed here are physical bookstores, not online bookstores.

www.geocities.com/evelynleeper/na-can-e.htm	Eastern & Central Canada
www.geocities.com/evelynleeper/na-can-w.htm	Western Canada & Alaska
www.geocities.com/evelynleeper/na-nyc-m.htm	New York City (Manhattan)
www.geocities.com/evelynleeper/na-ny.htm	New York State (other than Manhattan)
www.geocities.com/evelynleeper/na-east.htm	Eastern U.S.
www.geocities.com/evelynleeper/na-dc.htm	Washington D.C.
www.geocities.com/evelynleeper/na-south.htm	Southern U.S.
www.geocities.com/evelynleeper/na-chi.htm	Chicago
www.geocities.com/evelynleeper/na-midwe.htm	Midwestern U.S.

www.geocities.com/evelynleeper/na-cent.htm	Central U.S.
www.geocities.com/evelynleeper/na-west.htm	Western U.S.
www.geocities.com/evelynleeper/na-sw.htm	Southwestern U.S.
www.geocities.com/evelynleeper/na-socal.htm	Southern California
www.geocities.com/evelynleeper/na-bay-s.htm	San Francisco Bay Area (SF and north)
www.geocities.com/evelynleeper/na-bay-b.htm	San Francisco Bay Area (Berkeley and east)
www.geocities.com/evelynleeper/na-bay-p.htm	San Francisco Bay Area (Peninsula and south)
www.geocities.com/evelynleeper/uk-nire.htm	U.K. (Northern Ireland)
www.geocities.com/evelynleeper/uk-scot.htm	U.K. (Scotland)
www.geocities.com/evelynleeper/uk-engl.htm	U.K. (England, not London)
www.geocities.com/evelynleeper/uk-lond.htm	U.K. (London)
www.geocities.com/evelynleeper/uk-wales.htm	U.K. (Wales)
www.geocities.com/evelynleeper/eu-benl.htm	Benelux
www.geocities.com/evelynleeper/eu-fr.htm	France
www.geocities.com/evelynleeper/eu-de.htm	Germany
www.geocities.com/evelynleeper/eu-nord.htm	Nordic Countries
www.geocities.com/evelynleeper/eu-misc.htm	Europe (various)
www.geocities.com/evelynleeper/africa.htm	Africa
www.geocities.com/evelynleeper/asia.htm	Asia
www.geocities.com/evelynleeper/japan.htm	Japan

A sample listing from the "Central United States" category is presented in the following example. Notice that one of the five entries includes a Website addresses.

Cummings Books (318 14th Ave SE (University Ave SE & 14th Ave SE in Dinkytown), 55414, 612–331–1424). General used bookstore, with first floor and basement full of books. Has a cat. Open Mon-Thu 10AM-7PM, Fri-Sat 10AM-9PM, Sun 12N-5PM.

Dinkytown Antiquarian Book Store (1316 SE 4th, 612–378–1286). This store is located near the University of Minnesota. Modern first editions, Western fiction, decorated covers, somewhat disordered. There are several other used bookstores in the area. Irregular hours; call ahead.

DreamHaven Books (912 West Lake 55408, 612–379–8924; 1309 4th SE, 612–379–8924, dreamhvn@icicle.winternet.com). Truly fantastic new and used SF, fantasy, horror selection. Accepts telephone credit card orders. Will ship worldwide. Open Mon-Fri 11AM-8PM, Sat 11AM-6PM, Sun 12N-5PM.

Great Books (3919 W Broadway, Robbinsdale, 612–535–9682). Used paperbacks, large selection of SF. Open Tue-Fri 10AM-6:30PM, Sat 12N-5PM.

Half Price Books (2041 Ford Parkway, Highland Village, 612–699–1391). One of the larger and better-run stores in this chain, selling used and publisher's overstock. The selection is good, and some real bargains can be obtained. A nice complement to the new Barnes and Noble across the street. Sections include, among others, technical, mystery, SF, children's (good selection) and art (good selection). Some very good deals can be found. There are branches of this store in the suburbs of St. Louis Park and Maplewood. Open Mon-Sat, 9AM-9PM Sun 10AM-6PM.

ACQNET

ACQNET (The Acquisitions Librarians Electronic Network) is a mailing list for acquisitions librarians and others interested in acquisitions and collection development work to share information, exchange ideas, and ask questions. To subscribe, send the following command in the body of an e-mail message to *listproc@listproc.appstate.edu*: **subscribe <your name> ACQNET-L**

You can send postings to the list at *ACQNET-L@LISTPROC.APPSTATE.EDU*. To access copies of back issues, go to the ACQNET stacks maintained by the North Carolina State University libraries at Website *hegel.lib.ncsu.edu/stacks/serials/acqnet/*. You can either search the archives or browse by volume number. The archives contains messages going all the way back to 1991, Volume 1.

AcqWeb

AcqWeb, a sister site of ACQNET, offers links to some extraordinary resources for librarians with acquisitions or collection development responsibilities. The scope is international. The editor is Anna Belle Leiserson (Collection Development Librarian, Vanderbilt Law Library), and associate editors are: David Marshall (Head of Acquisitions and Serials, Georgetown University Library) and Peter Scott (Manager, Small Systems, University of Saskatchewan Libraries).

The contents of AcqWeb can be accessed at *www.library.vanderbilt.edu/law/acqs/acqs.html* and include:

Web News for Acquiring Minds—includes press releases, conference announcements, and new vendor links added to their list of publishers.

Verification Tools and Resources—this category lists bookstores with searchable in print lists of books, price comparison searching services, cross-store comparison shopping for CDs, videos, and DVDs, and links to serials resources, including Faxon Guide to Serials *www.faxon.com/guide/*, MediaFinder *www.mediafinder.com/*, and PubList.com *www.publist.com/*.

AcqWeb's Directory of Publishers and Vendors—a treasure trove of contact information. Includes links to an international directory of e-mail addresses of publishers, vendors and related professional services, publishers Websites, and new title notifications. Resources can be browsed by geographic location, alphabetically by name, or keyword searched.

Associations and Organizations—hyperlinked listing of associations for librarians interested in acquisitions and collection development.

Library and Information Science—a gold mine of resources covering schools, employment, news, acquisitions, cataloging, collection development, copyright issues, gifts and exchanges, microforms, preservation, serials, software, and statistics.

Journals, Newsletters, and Electronic Discussion Archives—links to newspapers, Web directories, Usenet newsgroups, mailing lists, and electronic journals and newsletters.

Reference Resources—a ready reference shelf of electronic resources covering awards information, bibliographic information, dictionaries, thesauri, glossaries, multilingual resources and translating services, geographic information, and much more.

Guides to Getting Started on the Web—includes a general introduction to using the Internet along with links to resources for librarians organized under several categories from art librarians and children's and young adult librarians, to East Asian librarians and music librarians.

CATALOGING

Catalogers are facing new challenges as they push to stay on the leading edge of information technology. One of the biggest challenges is migrating their library's bibliographic records into new automation systems like Endeavor's Voyager system (used by the Library of Congress). Systems like Voyager are fully integrated with the Web. Users can access electronic reserves from home, search their library's catalog on the Web, and link to multimedia objects, such as images, sound, and video clips stored in remote digital libraries.

Catalogers also face the challenge of identifying and describing digital resources found on the Web. One of the better-known projects focusing on this issue is CORC—OCLC's Cooperative Online Resource Catalog *www.oclc.org/oclc/corc/index.htm.*

In addition, catalogers are now considering alternative methods of cataloging electronic resources. While MARC has been effective in cataloging digital documents, it carries with it a high labor cost. Some catalogers now use the Dublin Core metadata framework for describing resources. You can read more about metadata in the ALA report, *Committee on Cataloging: Description and Access. Task Force on Metadata and the Cataloging Rules. Final Report (August 21, 1998)* located at *www.ala.org/alcts/organization/ccs/ccda/tf-tei9.html.*

In this section, I explain where to find newsletters and how to subscribe to mailing lists that discuss issues relating to cataloging. You can browse or search the contents of their message archives as explained in Chapter 24. I also describe resources relating to cataloging that are available on Web servers maintained by the Library of Congress and other sites. See Table 19–2 for a sampling of projects that are involved with cataloging Web-based resources.

Table 19–2: Projects involved with organizing information on the Web

Name	URL	Description
ADAM (Art, Design, Architecture & Media Information Gateway)	www.adam.ac.uk/	Catalog of Internet resources selected and cataloged for the U.K. higher education community.
Beyond Bookmarks: Schemes for Organizing the Web	www.public.iastate.edu/ ~CYBERSTACKS/CTW.htm	Links to various systems that organize Internet resources using alphabetic, numeric, alphanumeric, and controlled vocabulary.
BUBL Information Service	bubl.ac.uk/	Information service for higher education in the U.K. Uses the DDC to provide browsing access to their archive.
CliniWeb International	www.ohsu.edu/cliniweb/ browse.html	Database of clinical information for health care education and practice. Indexing terms are taken from the MeSH anatomy and disease classifications.
Cooperative Online Resource Catalog (CORC)	www.oclc.org/news/oclc/ corc/index.htm	Libraries cooperating in the creation, selection, organization, and maintenance of Web-based resources, currently numbering over 200,000. Search the catalog at corc.oclc.org/.
CyberDewey: A Catalogue for the world Wide Web	ivory.lm.com/~mundie/ CyberDewey/CyberDewey.html	Internet sites organized by Dewey Decimal Classification. Maintained by David A. Mundie.
Infomine	infomine.ucr.edu/	Virtual library containing annotated listings of thousands of university-level Web resources. Uses Library of Congress subject headings.
Librarians' Index to the Internet	lii.org/	Carefully selected and anno-tated resources to meet the needs of public library patrons.
Mathematics Index	archives.math.utk.edu/	Mathematics-related materials categorized and cross-referenced. Supports full-text searching.
Mr. Dui's Topic Finder	www.oclc.org/oclc/research/ publications/review96/duiart.htm and www.oclc.org/oclc/research/ publications/review96/dui.htm	Database built around the Dewey Decimal Classification system. The Topic Finder links you to OCLC's NetFirst data-base of Internet Resources.

Table 19–2 *(cont.)*		
OMNI (Organizing Medical Networked Information)	*omni.ac.uk/*	Includes a number of Internet-based biomedical resources. Uses the U.S. National Library of Medicine's Medical Subject Headings (MeSH).
PHOAKS	*www.phoaks.com// index.html*	Automatically reads, classifies, abstracts, and tallies opinions people post to Usenet news.
The Scorpion Project	*orc.rsch.oclc.org:6109/*	OCLC project exploring the indexing and cataloging of electronic resources.
Signpost	*www.signpost.org/signpost/*	Testbed for the Isaac Network that seeks to integrate distributed information systems through a single search interface.

The Cataloging Directorate at the Library of Congress

The Cataloging Directorate at the Library of Congress is responsible for the bibliographic control of their collections. They also develop cataloging theories and practices and share their knowledge with the national and international library community. The Web has made it possible to disseminate this information to a broad audience, some of it free of charge.

Descriptions of MARC documentation can be found at the Cataloging Distribution Service at *lcweb.loc.gov/cds/marcdoc.html*. Ordering information is also available at this site. Titles currently available include:

- Understanding MARC: Bibliographic
- USMARC Concise Formats
- MARC 21 Format for Bibliographic Data
- MARC 21 Format for Authority Data
- USMARC Format for Holdings Data
- MARC 21 Format for Classification Data
- MARC 21 Format for Community Information
- MARC 21 Code Lists: Languages, Countries, Geographic Areas, Organizations, Relators
- USMARC Specifications for Record Structure, Character Sets, and Exchange Media
- MARC Format: Proposed Changes

The Library of Congress Cataloging home page can be found at *lcweb.loc.gov/catdir/ catdir.html*. Several services are available free of charge. Like the Acquisitions site described earlier, the Cataloging page includes its own FAQ. The following topics are covered:

1. Which types of materials are cataloged at the Library of Congress (LC)?
2. Can I search the Library's catalogs over the Internet?
3. Where is the cataloging completed?
4. How may I contact the LC with cataloging questions, comments, and queries?
5. How may I direct questions to the LC about the use of the MARC formats, including which fields to use for specific types of data?
6. Who is responsible for cataloging policy at the LC?
7. What is "cooperative cataloging"?
8. How is the LC involved in cooperative cataloging programs?
9. Is the LC's cataloging used by other libraries?
10. What is the difference between monographs (e.g., books) and serials (e.g., periodicals)?
11. How many titles does the LC catalog in one year, and how much money is spent on cataloging?
12. How can I order cataloging documentation from the LC?
13. Who publishes the Library of Congress Rule Interpretations?
14. Are Library of Congress Classification (LCC) schedules available on the Internet?
15. What cataloging rules and publications do LC catalogers use?
16. What levels of cataloging are used at the LC?
17. Is Dewey Decimal Classification used at the LC?
18. What cataloging-related standards are developed and maintained at the LC?
19. Which of the MARC (machine-readable cataloging) formats are used by cataloging staff at the LC?
20. How can publishers obtain information about cataloging services such as Cataloging in Publication (CIP), International Standard Serial Number (ISSN), and other services that supply standard numbers for publications?
21. Is cataloging completed when a title is deposited for copyright registration?
22. How can I get my publication cataloged?
23. What is "initial bibliographic control" (IBC)?

Also available at this site are the Library of Congress Subject Headings Weekly Lists. These are lists of changes to existing headings, proposals that have been approved, and proposals submitted by cooperating libraries.

The Library Corporation's *Cataloger's Reference Shelf* consists of a collection of reference manuals and other works published by the Library of Congress. The resource is free and can be accessed at *www.tlcdelivers.com/tlc/crs/*.

AUTOCAT

AUTOCAT is a library cataloging and authorities discussion list. To subscribe, send the message **subscribe autocat your_name** to *LISTSERV@LISTSERV.ACSU.BUFFALO.EDU*. To retrieve a listing of the files contained in their message archive, send the command **get autocat filelist** in the body of a message to *LISTSERV@LISTSERV.ACSU. BUFFALO.EDU*. Leave the subject line blank. An excerpt from the output resulting from this command is presented in the following example. To retrieve any one of the files listed, send the command **get filename filetype** to *LISTSERV@LISTSERV.ACSU. BUFFALO.EDU*. For example, if you'd like to retrieve the first one listed, send the command **get autocat log 9101**.

```
*
* Archive files for the AUTOCAT list at LISTSERV.ACSU.BUFFALO.EDU
* (weekly logs)
*
```

* filename	filetype	GET PUT	size (bytes)	date	time
AUTOCAT	LOG9101	LOG OWN	241,170	1996–11–21	08:25:16
AUTOCAT	LOG9102	LOG OWN	387,716	1996–11–21	08:25:19
AUTOCAT	LOG9103	LOG OWN	315,454	1996–11–21	08:25:21
AUTOCAT	LOG9104	LOG OWN	318,684	1996–11–21	08:25:23
AUTOCAT	LOG9105	LOG OWN	377,086	1996–11–21	08:25:25
AUTOCAT	LOG9106	LOG OWN	228,828	1996–11–21	08:25:27
AUTOCAT	LOG9107A	LOG OWN	183,803	1996–11–21	08:25:29
AUTOCAT	LOG9107B	LOG OWN	179,526	1996–11–21	08:25:30
AUTOCAT	LOG9108	LOG OWN	285,086	1996–11–21	08:25:32
AUTOCAT	LOG9109	LOG OWN	284,279	1996–11–21	08:25:33
AUTOCAT	LOG91101	LOG OWN	208,133	1996–11–21	08:25:35
AUTOCAT	LOG91102	LOG OWN	201,073	1996–11–21	08:25:37
AUTOCAT	LOG91103	LOG OWN	255,362	1996–11–21	08:25:39
AUTOCAT	LOG9111	LOG OWN	487,260	1996–11–21	08:25:41
AUTOCAT	LOG9112	LOG OWN	239,729	1996–11–21	08:25:42
AUTOCAT	LOG9201	LOG OWN	426,879	1996–11–21	08:25:45
AUTOCAT	LOG92021	LOG OWN	149,422	1996–11–21	08:25:48

SLA-TECH

SLA-TECH is concerned with technical services in special libraries and information centers. To subscribe to SLA-TECH send the following command in the body of an e-mail message to *listserv@ukcc.uky.edu*: **subscribe sla-tech <your name>**

LC Marvel

LC Marvel is a Gopher server maintained by the Library of Congress at *gopher:// marvel.loc.gov*. This Gopher server provided access to the Library's resources and services before its sister Website at *lcweb.loc.gov/* came into existence. The Gopher site is still running and is being used to store certain ASCII text documents. The Library of Congress continues to maintain this site, although it is somewhat slow in removing out-of-date materials. Unless you have a particular need to access this text-only service, it's best to use the Web server.

If you are interested in exploring documents on the Gopher server pertaining to cataloging, at the main menu shown in Figure 19–1, follow this path: */Libraries and Publishers (Technical Services)/ Cataloging at the Library of Congress: Programs & Services /*. This brings you to a menu that links to these topics:

- Cooperative Cataloging Programs at the Library of Congress
- LC Cataloging Directorate: Reports and Papers
- Library of Congress Cataloging Policy and Practice

Gopher Menu

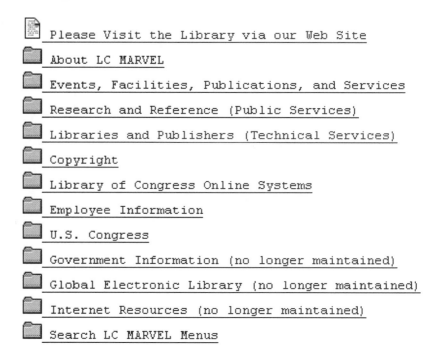

Figure 19–1: The root menu on the Library of Congress Gopher server

- LC Subject Headings Weekly Lists
- Library of Congress Cataloging Newsline (LCCN)

USMARC is a forum maintained by the Library of Congress Network Development and MARC Standards Office for discussing issues relating to USMARC formats such as maintenance and development. While you're on the MARVEL Gopher server, begin at the opening menu and follow the *path I /Libraries and Publishers (Technical Services)/ MARC 21 Standard*. This brings you to an archive of messages that can be both browsed and searched. The messages are only archived up to March 1998. A sample search on the keywords **856 guidelines** returned a long list of hits, the first few of which are shown here:

```
08/26/1997: Je Re: 856 \u Question
12/20/1997: Jo Re: Discussion Paper No. 106
01/05/1998: ac Re: Re: Proposal 98–1
02/20/1998: Su Re: MARC OFFICE SOUTH AFRICA
03/06/1996: account fo Re: Guidelines for the Use of Field 856
01/28/1998: Jo Re: RLG comments on MARBI Midwinter DPs
04/23/1998: Ra Re: Technical notice, 03–31–1998
08/26/1999: "L Re: linking records
02/23/1999: Be Re: TOP33 USMARC elements
05/28/1998: "M Re: Coding of USMARC field 853–855, subfield "y"
```

06/28/1996: "D Re: Updated list of source codes
01/28/1999: ac Re: MARBI paper available
02/29/2000: "R Re: MARC Language codes
04/12/2000: Ro Re: Re: XMLMARC Software Released
06/26/1997: "D Re: Importing MARC to MS_Access
03/30/1998: "J Re: 246/notes final period
03/29/1997: Pa Re: Reply: 052 & 043
02/12/1996: Mitch Turi Re: 95–6
10/30/1996: "M Re: Re: How to represent the delimiter in Microsoft Word

SERIALS LIBRARIANS

If you work in serials, you can utilize the Net in a number of different ways. You can access product information online, for example, EBSCO Subscription Services at *www.ebsco.com/home/*, Faxon Company at *www.faxon.com/*, and the United States Book Exchange for back issues of periodicals at *www.usbe.com/*; correspond with others in your discipline by joining relevant discussion groups, such as SERIALST at *listserv@list.uvm.edu*; or develop an electronic journal collection that can be accessed online.

SERIALST is a great way to network electronically with other like-minded professionals. You can learn about the origins of SERIALST and what goes into moderating mailings lists in an article by Birdie MacLennan called "SERIALST and the Global Serials Community: The Five Year Evolution of an Electronic Discussion Forum." Go to *www.uvm.edu/~bmaclenn/serialst5.html* for a hypertext version of this document. The SERIALST home page can be found at *www.uvm.edu/~bmaclenn/serialst.html*.

IESCA

Northwestern University Library has developed an interactive training tool to assist librarians in cataloging electronic serials on the Internet. The Interactive Electronic Serials Cataloging Aid, or IESCA for short, gives you access to cataloging rules, sample MARC records, rule interpretations, and a glossary of terms. When you visit their site at *www.library.nwu.edu/iesca/*, you can browse the following categories:

- Examples of Interactive MARC records
- Rules, Guidelines, and Local Interpretations
- Glossary of Cataloging and Internet Terminology
- Useful Sources, Acknowledgements, and Credits

In addition, IESCA provides a search engine for accessing information.

ISSN International Centre

Search or browse the ISSN (International Standard Serial Number) International Centre Website at *www.issn.org/index.html* for information on a wide variety of topics relating to ISSN. Subjects include basic explanations of what ISSN is, what serial publications are, ISSN related standards, using ISSNs, ISSN and barcoding, and more. This

---

Figure 19–2: HTML code used for presenting a journal title and annotation

```
<HTML>
<HEAD>
<TITLE>Electronic Journal Collection</TITLE>
</HEAD>
<BODY>

<DL>

<DT><A HREF=" http://arcrs4.saed.kent.edu/Architronic/homepage.html">
Architronic</A>

<DD>Architronic is a scholarly electronic journal disseminating ideas about
architecture. It is written for architects, architectural historians, educations,
and students. Articles cover subjects ranging from 3–D space to German
architectural nationalism.

</DL>
</BODY>
</HTML>
```

site supports both browsing and searching.

Electronic Magazine Racks

Depending on your clientele, you may find it a worthwhile project building a custom electronic newsstand or virtual magazine rack for your library. Web pages are the perfect platform for making this information available. The simplest form of presentation would be a list of links to electronic journals. Value can be added by annotating the listing and, if the list is long enough, organizing entries under subject headings.

One method of presenting annotated entries on a Web page uses Definition Lists. The opening and closing tags look like this: "<\DL>" and "<\/D>".

The Definition Term "<\DT>" places the journal title flush left in the display window. The journal title is linked to its home page. The Definition Data "<\DD>" creates a separate, indented paragraph for the annotation. This paragraph is placed on a new line below the Definition Term. A sample Definition List might look like the example shown Figure 19–2. This HTML code, when read by a Web browser, presents a simple example of an electronic journal collection with a single entry. When viewed in a browser

---

Figure 19–3: The Definition List presented in Figure 19–2 as it appears when viewed in a Web browser

Architronic

Architronic is a scholarly electronic journal disseminating ideas about architecture. It is written for architects, architectural historians, educations, and students. Articles cover subjects ranging from 3–D space to German architectural nationalism.

it appears as shown in Figure 19–3.

CHILDREN'S SERVICES

In this section, I point you to resources for children's literature on the Internet and introduce you to the concept of chat rooms. In Appendix B, you can find details on how to join KIDLIT-L and PUBLIB—discussion lists of interest to children's librarians.

Children's Literature

Several sources on the Web relate to children's literature. You can begin by visiting the Children's Literature Web Guide at *www.ucalgary.ca/~dkbrown/index.html*. This resource will be of interest to teachers, librarians, and parents alike. Their "What's New" feature keeps you up-to-date on conferences, children's bestsellers, and children's book awards. From this page you can link to Children's Booksellers on the Internet *www.ucalgary.ca/~dkbrown/booksell.html*, where the site's creator, David K. Brown, has put together a selective list of Internet bookshops catering to those interested in children's literature.

The Children's Literature Web Guide lists Internet resources related to books for children and young adults and provides a forum where people meet and discuss children's literature online. Brown has been able to build a feeling of community by offering the following forums where people can come and share their ideas:

- Readers Helping Readers is where people meet and talk about children's books
- Children's Book Conferences and Events posts information about upcoming children's Literature conferences, lectures, and workshops

Links to children's literature are also provided at the Association for Library Service to Children site at *www.ala.org/alsc/notable97.html*. Here you can read about Notable Children's Films and Videos, Newbery Medal Home Page, Caldecott Medal Home Page, The Laura Ingalls Wilder Medal, Notable Children's Recordings, and more.

Kids Chatting

It's hard to escape the fact that kids of all ages like chatting online. *Chatting* is real-time conversations taking place on the Internet. Kids talk to each other by typing messages at their keyboards and listen by reading what they type. Chatting is similar to talking on the phone, but much less expensive. Two individuals or many people can talk, all at the same time. If you have an Internet computer in the children's services area of your library, chat is one of the services kids ask for and one you can support. Chat is even popular with students in college and university libraries.

Chat, also called Internet Relay Chat, or IRC for short, is primarily used for entertainment and has no practical use for librarians during a normal workday. One instance where it may be useful is if you want to communicate with another individual privately, online, in real time to avoid making a long distance phone call. IRC conversations can be either free-form public conferences or private conversations between two individuals.

Chat is popular because it enables individuals from all walks of life from all around

Table 19–3: Moderated chat rooms for kids	
Name of Service	**Address**
AcmePet Community - Chat	*www.acmepet.com/chat/index.html*
FreeZone's ChatBox	*freezone.com/index.html*
Talk City Kids Chat	*www.talkcity.com/chat/kids.htmpl*
WebPilot	*worldkids.net/chat.htm*

the world to communicate with each other in real-time. Like most other Internet applications, it is built around a client/server architecture. On the server side there are several networks, or *nets*, of IRC servers. The function of these server computers is to allow users to connect to the IRC system. Some of the more popular nets are Efnet, Undernet, IRCnet, DALnet, and NewNet. The largest nets can have tens of thousands of users logged in all at the same time. Individual nets are further subdivided into channels. *Channels* group people together with similar interests. The larger nets have as many as 12,000 channels to choose from, each one devoted to a different topic.

The client side of the equation is handled by your personal computer. You use an IRC client to connect to a server on one of the IRC nets. The server communicates with your client and other servers on the same net. Two of the most popular PC clients are mIRC and PIRCH. Macintosh users prefer Ircle, and a popular UNIX shell client is ircH. You can learn more about mIRC and download a copy from the official mIRC home page at *www.mirc.co.uk/*. A more sophisticated product, called CoolTalk, supports audio, graphics, images, and text. For this application, you need a sound card. A full duplex sound card is needed if you want both users to speak and be heard simultaneously. For more information, see *home.netscape.com/navigator/v3.0/cooltalk.html*.

Chatting can also take place on the Web without running a separate chat client. All you need is a Web browser that supports Java in order to use this feature. The current versions of Netscape and Internet Explorer support Java. You can get kids started with chatting on the Web by pointing them to one of the moderated kids' sites shown in Table 19–3. Let parents know ahead of time what precautions should be taken.

Here are some simple rules for kids to follow:

Don't tell anyone in a chat room:

- Your real name
- Names of any family members or friends
- How old you are
- Where you live
- Your telephone number
- Any personal information about yourself

The most recent development in the area of IRC is a service called voice chat. *Voice chat* joins real-time, text-based conversations with voice. You can experience public and private voice chat rooms at *www.excite.com/communities/chat/voicechat*. FireTalk at *www.firetalk.com/* supports voice chat rooms and a technology that allows you to conduct voice conferences through a particular Website. PalTalk at *www.paltalk.com/* enables instant voice messaging between two people.

SPECIAL COLLECTIONS AND ARCHIVES

You can begin your online journey in this department by exploring the Rare Books and Manuscripts Section of the Association of College and Research Libraries at *www.rbms.nd.edu/* and the Society of American Archivists home page at *www.archivists. org/*. From here, you should go to the University of Houston Libraries Special Collections Web Resources page at *info.lib.uh.edu/speccoll/specres.htm*. You can explore everything from associations and book dealers to online exhibits and reference materials—all relating to special collections and archives on the Web.

Next, take a look at the Abbey Newsletter, which focuses on the preservation of library and archival materials. When you visit their site at *palimpsest.stanford.edu/byorg/ abbey/an/index.html*, you can browse or search their archives going back to 1975. Each issue contains feature articles plus news, literature reviews, and job announcements. Conservation Online, or CoOL for short, is a project of the Preservation Department of Stanford University Libraries. The site is located at *www.palimpsest.stanford.edu* and covers a wide variety of topics including those in the list that follows:

- Copyright and intellectual property
- Digital imaging
- Disaster planning and response
- Documentation
- Education and training
- Electronic media
- Electronic records
- Environment
- Ethics
- Conservation/Preservation information for the general public
- Health and safety
- Library binding
- Mass deacidification
- Mold
- Preservation-related organizations
- Pest management
- Reprographics
- Suppliers
- Survey results
- Bibliographies and resource guides
- Dictionaries, thesauri, glossaries, abbreviation lists, etc.

Other sites to explore include Berkeley Digital Library's Finding Aids for Archival Collections and Sarah Spurgin's Archives and Manuscript Collections Outside Columbia *www.cc.columbia.edu/cu/libraries/subjects/speccol.html*. At Finding Aids you can access inventories and indexes to collections held by archives and manuscript repositories, libraries, and museums. Archives and Manuscript Collections Outside Columbia provides access to information about the archives and manuscript holdings of more than

The LIBRARY *of* CONGRESS

PRESERVATION

Minerva by Herbert Adams
Vestibule of Great Hall

Caring for the Library of Congress Collections

Caring for Your Collections

Frequently Asked Questions

What's New:
Specifications for Preservation Supplies

Bach to Baseball Cards:
Preserving the Nation's Heritage
at the Library of Congress

Library of Congress Preservation Directorate
Washington, D.C. 20540-4500
Voice: 202-707-5213 | Fax: 202-707-3434 | Email: preserve@loc.gov

Using the Library: Collections and Services - Library of Congress Home Page
Search or Browse the Library of Congress Web Site

 Library of Congress
Comments: lcweb@loc.gov (07/13/2000)

Figure 19–4: Publications available online from the Library of Congress Preservation Directorate

200 repositories.

OCLC's Preservation Resources home page at *www.oclc.org/oclc/presres/preshome.htm* offers imaging samples in grayscale and color along with links to a wide variety of preservation resources, including:

- Bibliographic Control of Preservation Microfilm
- Color and Preservation Microfilm
- The New Generation of Cameras for Preservation Microfilming
- Preparation of Materials for Preservation Microfilming
- Preservation Microfilming of Non-Book Formats, Rare Materials, and Items Requiring Special Handling
- Preservation Quality Continuous Tone Microfilm

Online Resource

To learn more about book arts resources on the Internet, check out *A Guide to the Book Arts and Book History on the World Wide Web libraries.cua.edu/bookarts.html.* Andrew K. Pace of the Catholic University of America offers links to everything from book arts courses and exhibits to discussion lists and imaging projects. His list of *Finding Aids & WWW Guides* offers important links to resources for archivists and general conservation and preservation information.

- Preserving Microfilm
- Protection for Preservation Microfilm

Lastly, stop off at the Library of Congress preservation site at *www.loc.gov/preserv/* for information relating to the preservation of library materials. You can begin exploring information pamphlets and documents covering a wide range of topics under the heading *Caring for Your Collections.* The preservation menu for this page is shown in Figure 19–4.

They also offer a FAQ on preservation that covers the following topics:

1. How should I store my books?
2. How should I display documents or works of art on paper?
3. Can I save wet books? What if my books are moldy?
4. How can I get rid of the smell of mildew in my books?
5. How can I preserve my family photographs for my grandchildren?
6. I have an infestation. How can I get rid of bugs in my books?
7. How can I preserve my newspaper clippings?
8. The leather on my books is worn and scuffed. Should I oil my leather bindings?
9. Will the Library of Congress restore or appraise my books?
10. Will the Library of Congress deacidify my book collections?
11. What if I have other questions about preservation of library and archives materials?

USEFUL INTERNET SERVICES

This chapter introduced several resources and different ideas for implementing Internet services in-house. To reinforce the usefulness of maintaining an Internet connection for library operations, I offer the following list of Internet services that I have found beneficial in my own work. At one time or another, each of these services has contributed to the overall improvement of the organizations with which I have been involved. They have also directly or indirectly expanded the services made available to the communities served by these organizations.

- Using Web servers to publish online tutorials and help sheets to assist patrons with using print and electronic resources
- Publishing PowerPoint presentations on Web servers for bibliographic instruction classes

- Building searchable image, text, and sound archives on the Web
- Placing orders with vendors for software, books, and other materials
- Accessing technical support for computer software and hardware
- Researching solutions to problems in preservation
- Searching for and advertising employment opportunities
- Corresponding with other librarians via e-mail
- Accessing and searching library catalogs worldwide for author/title verification copy cataloging, and the creation of bibliographies
- Keeping abreast of current events and innovations in the library profession through e-journals and LISTSERVs
- Accessing public domain, shareware and freeware programs, text files, image files, and sound files to assist patrons with specific needs
- Interactively searching dozens of free online databases worldwide via telnet
- Connecting with government agency bulletin boards that cover topics ranging from environment and health to business and law
- Offering library patrons local and remote access to full-text commercial databases via the Web

Virtually Yours for Free

The concept of offering free services on the Internet has been around on a small scale for a long time. In certain localities, free access to the Internet has been available for years through community information networks, such as Free-Nets. Software released under the GNU General Public License (*www.fsf.org/copyleft/gpl.html*) has always been available free of charge.

Today, there are attempts to make a wide range of services available for free, or almost free. All it takes is enough customers to sell the amount of advertising needed to stay afloat. Let's face it. The end goal is for these companies to make money. For example, companies like NetZero, a national Internet service provider, offers free 56K dial-up access. They make their money by having you use their dial-up software. After you connect with NetZero's system, a dial-up program loads a floating window onto your system's desktop that displays advertising. When you click on an ad, you connect with the advertiser's site.

In Chapter 20 I introduce a broad range of free services ranging from conferencing systems and Web-based databases to mailing lists and fax services. Some of the services introduced in this chapter, such as virtual conferencing systems and mailing lists, have practical applications in libraries. They help us communicate with colleagues. In other situations, you can make recommendations to your patrons when useful applications of these services make sense. For example, in an academic library, free mailing list servers can be valuable to distance education faculty who wish to communicate with students. Public library patrons without their own home computers and Internet accounts may be excited to learn about free Webspace, Fax services, and Web storefronts.

Keep in mind that some of the companies described in this chapter may be gone by the time you go to look for them. If a company doesn't get the critical mass of customers they need to stay in business, they disappear like several before them. Because the Internet's services are ever changing, try to focus more on the tools used for finding these services than on the services themselves. The last section in this chapter provides basic tools for staying up-to-date in this ever-changing environment.

PORTALS

Web portals are the hottest thing in the Internet industry right now. Portals are sites on the Web where consumers come to read the news and find other useful information. Portals offer free e-mail services, message boards, e-commerce, and they let you personalize their Web pages to your liking. Yahoo! *www.yahoo.com* is one of the better-known portals. While you read about classic cars on Yahoo!, you can link to classified ads for Corvettes and Mustangs, visit classic car chat rooms, and ask to be alerted via e-mail when new articles matching *classic cars* are indexed by Yahoo!. Other popular portals include Excite *www.excite.com*, Snap.com *www.snap.com*, Netcenter *www.netcenter.com,* and Lycos *www.lycos.com.* One of the newest portals for librarians, developed by Baker & Taylor, is LibraryPlace.com at *www.libraryplace.com/.* An example of a university library portal is the University of Utah Spencer S. Eccles Health Sciences Library at *medlib.med.utah.edu/.*

Portals began as destinations for the general consumer. Now they are focusing on the special needs of specific groups of people. They want you to visit them first thing in the morning and last thing before calling it a day. *Vertical portals* refer to sites that provide more than just e-commerce and news. They create workspaces for professionals and provide content and services that support specific business processes.

A company named *everyone.net* offers a plug-in-portal service that helps you create your own online community. Once you have a Website set up and running, go to *www.everyone.net* to add discussion boards and chat, a search engine, plug-in e-mail, and ad space. Registration requires that you provide your name, e-mail address, zip code, the address of your Website, and a password. After registering, you arrive at everyone.net's Control Center. Here you can choose between Express Setup and Advanced Setup. The former only takes one to five minutes and you choose from 15 pre-existing themes. The latter takes 15 to 30 minutes to complete and allows you to customize your text and navigation bar colors, create text messages, customize images and backgrounds, and rotate banner ads.

FREE E-MAIL SERVICES

Free e-mail services have come a long way since the original edition of *The Companion*, both in terms of features offered and the number of companies offering free e-mail services. You now have hundreds of services to choose from with features ranging from free voicemail and faxing, to private conferencing and file storage. Full-featured e-mail services include Visto and Zkey. Zkey.com *www.zkey.com* offers 30MB of file storage space, calendar, discussion board, address book, and e-mail. Visto *www.visto.com* gives you 15MB of file storage space, address book, bookmarks, calendar, and two external POP e-mail accounts. Optional pay services include access to information via telephone, telephone conferencing, and additional file storage space.

FREE MAILING LISTS

eGroups, or *e-mail groups*, is a new word for an old concept known as mailing lists. Mailing lists enable you to correspond with other individuals who share common interests. Once your list is created, anyone who signs up can send mail to the list address. Their messages are forwarded to all other members of that list. eGroups *www.egroups.com* supports daily digests that merge all e-mails into one full-text message. Your list is given its own main page and you can customize the HTML code to change your main page's appearance. In addition, this service archives old messages and gives you 20MB of private storage space for saving and sharing files, photos, and other documents.

When you go to the eGroups Website, you can create your own mailing list and you can join any one of the thousands of other lists already formed. Search for other lists by subject or browse their subject tree, which is organized hierarchically like other directories on the Internet.

FREE TELEPHONY SERVICES

There are two pieces of hardware you may hear about in the Internet-based telephone industry: Internet PhoneJacks and Call Quality Enhancing Headsets. The *Internet PhoneJack* (IPJ) is a plug-and-play card that allows you to use your regular telephone to place PC-to-phone calls. Once installed, you plug your phone into the card to make your call. A *Call Quality Enhancing Headset* is another alternative for PC-to-phone conversations. Unlike the IPJ, the headset doesn't require any installation. Both hardware devices can help improve the quality of your call.

There are a number of companies that offer free long-distance calling from one PC to another using the Internet. One of the newest services offers PC-to-phone calling. Callrewards.com *www.callrewards.com* lets you make calls from your computer, which may be in any country in the world, to any telephone in the U.S. There are plans to expand this to any telephone in the world. Callrewards.com currently offers 20 minutes of free calling time just for joining and five minutes additional calling time for every friend you refer, up to a total of ten friends. They plan to offer additional calling time based on your interaction with advertising.

To utilize the service requires that you register online and download their software. You have the option of using the specialized hardware mentioned earlier for improving the PC-to-phone communications, or you can use a microphone and speakers. If you don't have an Internet phone jack, you can dial using a virtual telephone on your screen.

BuzMe *www.buzme.com/*, founded in May 1999, is an Internet-based call manager that provides call screening and caller ID, home answering, voicemail, and more. BuzMe's beta release was made available only in the San Francisco Bay Area. Go to BuzMe's Website to see if their service is available in your area, or pre-register to be notified if BuzMe becomes available in your area.

Internet telephony has its downside—a latency problem. The quality of the connection is not that good, primarily because of delays and inconsistencies with the hardware at each end of the connection, or with the flow of data over the network. A PC can convert analog signals to digital and vice versa quite well. The processor speed, however, may not be fast enough to avoid a delay between the time a word is spoken and when it is heard. And how often do you pick up your telephone receiver and hear a dial tone? If you are like most, this happens almost 100 percent of the time. Can you say the same thing for your data network? When data networks are under heavy use and the flow of traffic is high, slowdowns in data transmission speeds are inevitable. Internet technology improves continuously and the next generation of hardware and communication protocols may improve Internet telephony and other real-time technologies considerably.

BeeCall uses PC-to-PC telephony to let you send and receive voice messages over the Web for free. You use your PC microphone to talk and speaker system to listen. Before you can take advantage of this service you must download and install BeeCall's software. Once installed, you can add a BeeLink to your Web page and greet visitors with a spoken message and use your PC as an online intercom system. To learn more about BeeCall, check out their site at *www.beecall.com/*.

Net2phone, another PC-to-PC telephony service, offers free phone calls between computers anywhere in the United States. The last time I checked, Net2phone was offering a free headset for your PC (with an additional shipping and handling fee) if you registered to use their service. You can download the Net2phone software at *www.net2phone.com/jump/switchboard/*.

FREE WEB-BASED FAXING

Fax4Free *www.fax4free.com* provides free fax service from anywhere in the world to the U.S., Canada, and Australia. Fax4Free also gives you an address book in which you can enter up to 20 names for free. With Fax4Free you can compose faxes online, or attach Word, Excel, Works, or WordPerfect documents. For an additional fee ranging from 5 cents to 50 cents per page, depending on destination, you can fax to countries outside of the U.S.

To receive faxes on your PC without a dedicated fax line, use FaxWave *www.callwave.com*. FaxWave gives you a private fax number. Sending faxes to this number is no different than sending faxes to a standard fax machine. FaxWave routes your faxes to your e-mail inbox as an e-mail attachment.

Another fast and easy fax service is eFax.com at *www.efax.com*. You can receive and view faxes for free, but you have to hand over $2.95 per month for the eFax Plus service which lets you send, forward, and preview faxes from any PC on the net.

FREE INTERNET ACCESS

NetZero *www.netzero.net/* is a national Internet service provider offering free dial-up access in many of the major cities and their surrounding areas. This service could be a money saver for librarians on the road who normally dial long distance numbers to access their Internet service providers back home. Before traveling, check *www.netzero.net/customer/access.html* in advance to see if NetZero has a number that will be local to you. Check back often as they are always adding more numbers.

NetZero makes its money by having you use their dial-up program. After you connect to their site, NetZero uploads an ad window to your computer which remains visible on your desktop. This leads to one of the drawbacks of using NetZero. If you don't click on an ad at least once very 30 minutes, a window pops up that must be clicked to stay connected to the Internet. Screen resolution might be another problem. If you are running at 640 × 480, you need to run your computer at the highest resolution your eyes can stand, or the ad window can intrusively take up a large portion of your screen. NetZero recommends an SVGA monitor at 800 × 600 screen resolution.

If NetZero offers a local dial-up in your area, start by downloading their software at *www.netzero.net/download/index.html* or ordering it on a CD *www.netzero.net/download/ order_info.html*. The software is about a 4.8MB download and runs on Windows 95, 98, and NT. They're currently charging $6.95 shipping and handling for the free CD that takes about two weeks for delivery. NetZero's software runs best on a Pentium system with 32MB of RAM, about 12MB of free disk space, and a 56K modem.

Juno Online Services *home.juno.com/* announced 100 percent free Internet access on December 20, 1999. Juno's automated information can be contacted at 800–654–JUNO. If you're already a member of the free e-mail service then you may sign up for Juno Free Web at 888–829–5866. Significant differences between Juno's Free and Premium (paid) services include:

1. $9.95/month charge for Premium (paid) service.
2. Free service has 897 POPs available—expect busy signals. The paid service has access to an additional 1,321 POPs. The e-mail-only service has access to 1,310 POPs. Eliminating overlap, Juno has a total of about 2,300 POPs.
3. Paid service gets free 24–hour tech support. Free service pays $1.95/min at 900–370–5866
4. Constant ad displayed in a banner on your screen with free service.
5. Free service requires Juno version 4.0 and MS Internet Explorer 4.0 or better. Paid service may use earlier Juno versions and does not require Internet Explorer.

Juno is the granddaddy of free e-mail services that are still offered. Juno's unique free e-mail service does not require Internet access, only a modem. Their proprietary e-mail software is complete, but not compatible with POP3/SMTP servers. Older software version 1.49 will run with Windows 3.x, but has no Internet capability. Limitations of the free e-mail service include, but are not limited to: 64 kilobytes per message, 1MB mailbox, no attachments, no binary files, limited number of connects per day.

Juno offers a DSL service called JunoExpress in the New York City metro area for $49.95 per month. Juno is planning a nationwide rollout of DSL service. Covad supplies some of the infrastructure.

Juno Online Services (JWEB:N) is publicly traded. D.E. Shaw provided Juno's initial financing and remains the majority shareholder. Recent SEC filings can be found here. Extensive online help is available, but customer service is generally reported as poor.

FreeInternet.com *www.freeinternet.com/* (formerly FreeI.net) provides nationwide, 100 percent free Internet access. Advertiser supported, a banner is constantly displayed. They claim more then 1,500,000 accounts. They expanded from Northwest regional to nationwide coverage on October 10, 1999. FreeiClient software for Windows requires installation of Microsoft's Internet Explorer version 5, although you may use any browser after installation. Call 1–253–796–6505 to obtain a free CD-ROM.

Fanz.net *www.fanz.net/home.html* offers 100 percent free, nationwide, Internet access.

Registration uses a "fake" Visa card. Ignore any credit card messages. An "Info bar" displays cycling advertisements on your screen. Technical Support can be contacted at 206–652–9365.

Warning: The installation makes Fanz.net your default ISP and sets your home page to point to Fanz. They configure Internet Options for "dial whenever a network connection is not present." Fanz's name is inserted into the title-bar of both Outlook Express and Internet Explorer.

Fanz.net is a division of Brigadoon which bought the failed Bigger.net domain from TGGH, Inc., and transformed it into the new Fanz.net domain.

dotNow! *www.dotnow.com/* offers Internet dial-up access to customers in hundreds of U.S. cities—totally free! Their aggressive placement of access lines means that they have over 2,400 points of presence (POPs) in all 50 states, with over 98 percent penetration. dotNow! lets nearly everyone in the U.S. get what they need on the Internet without a single charge.

> Q: How can they do this?
> A: Simple. They use their patent pending methodology of providing free Internet service entirely supported by ads. The dotNow! bar™ is shown during the entire time that you're online and displays ads that refresh periodically.
> Q: Can you still use your current browser?
> A: You can still use Netscape Communicator/Navigator or Internet Explorer, or any other Web browser. The only difference is that the dotNow! banner bar is placed on your PC window when you are online.

ProNet USA *www.pro-usa.com/main.htm* offers free, nationwide, Internet access after a one-time $29.95 setup fee. There are no banner ads, no session limits, and no e-mail tag lines. ProNet's free plan, which began January 2000, is the same as the $17.95/month "Standard" service except for the monthly market survey you are required to complete. Warning: If you fail to return the monthly marketing survey for any reason you will be billed the normal monthly fee.

A full range of services is offered by ProNet USA, such as 56K or ISDN access via 1,300 POPs, including some Canadian cities. Optional setup software is available for Windows, but manual instructions are provided for other operating systems. Call toll-free 1–877–PRO-NET5 (1–877–776–6385) Monday-Friday, 8am-5pm Eastern.

ProNet USA is a subsidiary of GBM Technologies. The market surveys are done by New Millennium Concepts, which operates RhinoPoint.

SYSTEMS FOR DISTANCE EDUCATION

One of the most exciting areas of development on the Net is the area of online educational services. Librarians now have access to free tools for creating Web-based courses using virtual server software and course management tools. Some products, such as Blackboard, are capable of supporting an entire virtual campus on your own dedicated server, or a single course you design and offer by yourself for free on Blackboard's Website. You can use these free services to present bibliographic instruction, knowledge management courses, online searching techniques, or any other online course you might think of. Virtual classroom software lets you present learning materials online, communicate with students (bulletin board systems or real-time chat), give quizzes to students, and take surveys.

Blackboard, Inc. offers two products: CourseInfo, a commercial product that allows entire institutions to build virtual campuses, and Blackboard.com, the free Web-based service. You can find Blackboard.com on the Web at *www.blackboard.com*. Their site guides you step-by-step through the process of building your own virtual classroom on 5MB of disk space. Their online tutorials are excellent. You can view demo programs at *company.blackboard.com/Bb/demo.html* and get additional information from their FAQ *company.blackboard.com/Bb/faqs.html*. If you are interested in making your course available to a broader audience, a registration fee of $100 buys you e-commerce capabilities, technical support, and 10MB of disk space.

LEARN ANYWHERE, ANYTIME, FREE

Blackboard.com not only allows you to set up your own distance education course, you can go there as a student and take online courses. Free online courses are available once you register. You can study at your own pace, any time of the day, and from any location in the world where there is a computer connected to the Internet. Classes have limits on the number that can enroll. From their main home page, you can access the list of study topics that are available and how many courses are still open for enrollment.

Jobs University at *www.jobsuniversity.com/* offers free online courses that focus on topics relating to career changes, management, and job seeking. You also can find courses here that pertain to technology. For example, advanced Adobe Photoshop, introduction to C++, and how to build Web pages.

IETF/TERENA Training Materials Catalogue is a catalog of mostly free training materials for use by Internet trainers. You can add your own materials to this catalog by filling out the appropriate forms included on their site at *www.trainmat.ietf.org/*. The current list of titles includes:

1. Internet Passport: NorthWestNet's Guide to Our World Online
2. The Net: User Guidelines and Netiquette
3. Emily Postnews Answers Your Questions on Netiquette
4. Surfing the Internet
5. A Guide to Electronic Mail
6. Course Notes and Exercises: Networked Information Services 1
7. SURFnet Guide 96/97
8. A Cruise of the Internet
9. Information Sources: the Internet and Computer-Mediated Communication
10. The Whole Internet User's Guide and Catalogue (2nd ed.)
11. Network Training Pack
12. Janet Hunt
13. An Introduction to Using the Internet at St. Louis University School of Law
14. "Where to Start" for New Internet Users
15. Introduction to the Internet II
16. Internet Hunt
17. LIBCAT
18. A Guide To Internet/Bitnet v.2.0

19. Network Services on Janet and Internet: A Lunch Time Seminar for Library Staff
20. SOSIG Documentation and Training Materials
21. University of Washington Internet training
22. Global Quest Video
23. Introducing the Internet: A Trainer's Workshop
24. All About Internet FTP: Learning and Teaching to Transfer Files on the Internet
25. The Computer Chronicles
26. The Video Guide to the Internet
27. INTERNET, The Video Tape
28. Crossing the Internet Threshold, 2nd ed.
29. Charm Net's Learning Page: Books, Tutorials, Hint Sheets
30. Internet Training and Tutorials
31. Internet Resources
32. Network Training Materials Gopher (trainmat)
33. Computers: Internet: Beginner's Guides
34. Internet Web Text
35. Using KULeuvenNet and Internet
36. TONIC: The Online Netskills Interactive Tutorial

Each of these entries links you to a record with information about title, author, language, organization name, and other metadata elements. If the document is available online via the Web, a URL is included in the URL field. For example, resource number 30, titled "Internet Training and Tutorials," links you to a record containing the URL *lcweb.loc.gov/global/internet/training.html*. This links you to the Library of Congress Internet Resource Page that contains an up-to-date collection of guides, online courses, and tutorials.

Librarians who are new to the Internet may find Ellen Chamberlain's and Miriam Mitchell's *Back to School: The Electronic Library Classroom 101* helpful. This is an online classroom that can be accessed free of charge at *www.sc.edu/bck2skol/fall/fall.html*. The course consists of 30 lessons covering many aspects of Internet resources and services. Some of the topics covered are no longer relevant—for example, Jughead and Veronica—and there are several broken links. Other topics that are covered still have relevancy in today's libraries, including telnet and FTP.

FREE STATISTICAL SERVICES

RealTracker FREE at *free.realtracker.com/* is a statistical tracking service that tells you how many people visit your home page and what their point of origin is. You can even learn details about such things as the most popular browser being used by visitors to your site. There is an option that allows visitors to leave their opinions about the content of your home page. RealTracker FREE is free for non-commercial users except in Amsterdam where commercial users can use them for free. For all other commercial users, check out their proprietary business tracking service at *business.realtracker.com/*

WEB-BASED FILE STORAGE

Running out of local disk space? Do you want to share files among many individuals at different locations? Free, Web-based file storage may be a solution. Before you decide, consider the pros and cons. If you work with files that you need to access both at home and the office, storing them on the Web might be easier than transporting them by disk. In fact, you could access your files from any location that provides Internet access. Another possible use would be temporary storage of files while you are away on business. When you return home, you could login to your Web-based storage system and transfer the files back to a local hard disk or removable disk. Free Web-based file storage is not meant to be a reliable backup system. Some companies retain the right to close out inactive accounts. If your data is important, keep backups on disk space you control.

File Monkey *www.filemonkey.com* offers 10MB of disk space free to its members. Registration is a snap and transferring files is as easy as clicking on an upload or download button. Be careful how long you go before visiting your site. File Monkey states in their license agreement that any account remaining inactive for 60 days may be deleted at File Monkey's sole discretion. In their FAQ, File Monkey shortens this wait to 30 days.

Driveway *www.driveway.com*, formerly the iFileZone service, offers a lot of storage space for the money—25MB at no cost to you. Additional file space is sold in 100MB increments, or you can try to obtain additional space for free by participating in some of their promotions. With a Driveway account you can save any file type, including Web pages. If you want to collaborate with someone and share your files, Driveway lets you do it. You can set various levels of access control on your files.

NetFloppy.com gives away 3MB virtual floppy disks. Actually, the service is no different than the other online file storage services, but the metaphor is original. You *eject* rather than logout when you leave your account. Owners of iMacs have picked up on the concept of a virtual floppy disk since they don't have a floppy disk drive. Watch out for the little trashcan sitting in the lower right hand corner of the screen. When you click on it, selected files are "trashed." (The current interface will likely change by the time you read this.)

FreeDrive at *www.freedrive.com* offers a *tree structure* view of your files, making it easy to navigate and find what you are looking for. FreeDrive gives you 50MB of storage space absolutely free. They support a clever feature that allows you to save Web pages to your FreeDrive account while you surf the net.

Bitlocker at *www.bitlocker.com/* is more than just another file storage site. Bitlocker offers free access to Web-based database applications. You can gather and store almost anything, including graphics, audio files, and bibliographic records. Registering takes less than a minute and, once your account is activated, you can begin studying their online tutorial. Learn how to create a database, or *Bitlocker* as they call it, and modify, sort, and delete records. Develop custom views of your database and control who can access it.

The tab labeled "My Bitlocker" has links to blank templates you can use to create your first *Bitlockers*. Use *DatabasePlus Blank Template* to create a new database from scratch, or choose from the templates listed on the home page. You begin by naming and describing your database and determining who can access it. Then you move on to creating the various fields where you choose a name, description, and type (text, number, true/false, date, time, file, currency, etc.). To add more fields, use the menu on the left side of the screen, choosing "Author" and then "Fields." When the Fields windows opens, click on "Create."

You can use Bitlocker to build a simple digital library. Create a "container" field in which you place your *object*. Your object can be any file type supported by your Web browser; for example, JPEG images and HTML documents. Create a "Title" and "Description" field where you tell viewers something about the object. The program automatically thumbnails your image and links it to the full-sized image. Other file types are represented by a small icon that looks like a sheet of paper with its upper left corner turned down. If you store records with file types not supported by your browser, you are asked if you want to download and save the file instead of viewing it.

Records can be modified or deleted at any time. The disadvantage of building a database in this manner is the time it takes for processes to run on a wide area network. Depending on the speed of your Internet connection, and the size of the files you catalog, the system could be slow. For a more detailed look at Bitlocker, see Chapter 27.

FREE SURVEYS

What do your young adult readers *really* think about your new paperback racks? Why not ask them to use SurveyHeaven.com? Login to *www.surveyheavy.com/* and find out just how easy it is. Enter your survey question and as many as five possible answers. Provide your name or nickname and e-mail address. Choose a category for your survey and click on the "Preview" button. After previewing it, save the survey and SurveyHeaven provides you with a hyperlink that can be used in your home page. After taking the poll, visitors are given the option of sending it to a friend.

WEBSPACE FOR FREE

Librarians and library patrons alike may find that free home page providers serve a useful purpose. Depending on who controls the server at your institution, a free home page provider could be a quick, easy solution for quickly getting a page up and running. For example, you've prepared a PowerPoint presentation on imaging technology in the library for a group of students. Some students couldn't attend, but still want to view the presentation. You could quickly save the presentation in HTML format and then publish the presentation to free Webspace, making it available to anyone with an Internet connection. Your ability to publish information quickly and without going through a lot of red tape might prove advantageous at times.

Most companies offering free Webspace allow you to use their site for personal or business use. Few sites tolerate hacking, porn, or warez. Some place restrictions on whether you can run banner ads. There are four things to consider when choosing which company to go to for free Webspace:

1. Does the service put banner ads on every page?
2. How much disk space are you given for free?
3. How do you upload files? With a browser, FTP, or both?

4. What domain name is servicing the account?
5. What special features are offered?

Consider each one of these issues carefully. With few exceptions, most services place logos, banner ads, or pop-ups on your site. This is how companies make their money. Crosswinds *www.crosswinds.net* is an example of an exception to this rule. Crosswinds lets you set up your own home page free of any advertising. Crosswinds makes their money by selling advertising space on the pages of their main site.

Disk space is free and varies in size among Webspace companies, ranging from less than 3MB to over 20MB. All services offer you some means of uploading files to your Webspace. If you are not accustomed to FTP, subscribe to a service that lets you upload files using a browser interface.

Why is a service's domain name important? The BigAssWeb *www.bigassweb.com*, for example, offers 5MB of free disk space, and the ability to create and edit your pages with an online editor, or by using a wizard. Nice features, but your site has to carry banner ads and your home page URL follows the format *freepages.BigAssWeb.com/ freepages/User_Name*. The domain name *BigAssWeb.com* may not be the image you are looking for.

ProHosting *free.prohosting.com*, on the other hand, doesn't force banner ads or pop-ups, gives you 15MB of free disk space, one FTP account, and assigns you a URL that is respectable: *lightning.prohosting.com/User_Name*.

Freeservers at *www.freeservers.com/* lets you choose your own custom domain name beginning with a name or phrase you choose followed by one of several options they offer in a drop-down list. Choices include *freeservers.com*, *freehosting.net*, or less descriptive names like *8k.com* or *gq.nu*. Everyone signing up is given 20MB of disk space for free. If you already have your own registered domain name, Freeservers is offering to host it for free. Freeserver offers its services free of charge because each time you build a page, an advertising banner is added to the top margin. For $5.95/month you can have ad-free pages.

A similar service is offered by eSmartStart.com at *50m.esmartstart.com/*. You get customized domain names and free Web-based e-mail. A difference comes in the amount of disk space provided. eSmartStart starts you out with 100MB of free space on their server along with FTP access. They also offer some interesting tools and utilities, including Web-board discussion forums.

BUILDING A VIRTUAL CARD SITE

There are hundreds of sites that offer free postcard services. One of the most popular is Blue Mountain at *www.bluemountain.com*. Typically, you go to a site to build a custom

---

Online Resources

The Free Webpage Provider Review (FWPR) *fwpreview.ngworld.net/* categorizes sites by subject and by country. Visitors can post reviews of any of the sites listed.

Looking for your own source of banner ads? Try these Web advertising agencies: *www.doubleclick.com* or *www.flycast.com*.

card choosing images, words, and sometimes music. In this section I focus on a different type of postcard site. These Web services make it possible to build your own virtual postcard site. Each service has its own unique features and you can choose which one fits your style best.

To get started, you should have some background in HTML and also have images available for designing postcards. Remember that any images, sound files, multimedia animation files, Java applets, poems, or text, etc., made available on your site can only be used after obtaining permission from the owner of the copyright to those files.

123 Greetings *associates.123greetings.com/index.html* lets you build a customizable electronic greeting card site on any corporate, personal, or professional site. You are given the option of adding your own logo, background, and text color to the service. You can add further customization by including your own images, quotations, and music.

The 123 Greetings server works as the back end for your site. The interface you offer is easy to use for visitors who come to your Website to create and view their cards. To make it all work, you must insert an HTML Tag in your Website. Once you are set up, users can design their cards and schedule when cards are to be delivered.

At All Yours, you follow two easy steps and you are on your way to building a virtual card site. First you must send an e-mail message to an auto-responder at *response@all-yours.net* and then register for the services. You can leave the subject line and body of the message blank when e-mailing the auto-responder. In a few moments you receive an answer. The auto-responder sends you a URL giving instruction on how to create your card site using their interface. You can go directly to this help sheet at *www.all-yours.net/postcard/faq20.html*. All Yours' services support many languages, so your visitors have a choice of which language to use at the opening page.

My Postcards at *mypostcards.com/* is another great service designed to help you build your own postcard site. For commercial enterprises that are interested in a more full-featured postcard site, My Postcards offers My Postcards PRO service. This service allows you to expand your postcard site beyond the single page available to those using the free service. My Postcard offers full multimedia support, so bring on your JPEG and GIF images, MIDI and WAV sound files, and text! You can introduce your site on their home page for free. To see what other folks are doing with their postcard sites, visit the My Postcard home page.

After completing registration, you are sent an e-mail message notifying you that you can now set up your virtual postcard shop using an interactive program called Cardshop Creator. To begin, you must login with the user ID and password found in your e-mail message. You start by editing your profile, entering your Website's URL and the location of your picture folder and MIDI folder, if you have one. When this is completed, you generate your HTML code for your postcard page. This is done with the click of a button. Save the HTML code to a file and upload it to your Website and you are set to go.

Services like this can serve many purposes in libraries. You can create custom cards promoting your library, or you can hold a special workshop teaching others how to set up their own card site.

Online Resource

For links to free graphics and sounds, check out one of the biggest freebie sites on the Net, TheFreeSite.com at *www.thefreesite.com/*.

FREE CONFERENCING SYSTEMS

Conferencing systems, also known as forums or Bulletin Board Systems (BBSs), offer you an opportunity to set up a virtual community where any number of individuals can meet and share information online. If you are not familiar with conferencing systems and how they work, point your Web browser to Assembly Web Discussions at *assembly.nerdworld.com/* for a quick introduction. Basic services include the ability to read and post messages as well as create your own conferencing system for free. After registering, you can view and participate in other members' message boards, too.

Assembly Web Discussions organizes its members' message boards by subject. Visitors can browse or search by keyword to find a particular conferencing system. If you are teaching a class and want to create an environment online where students can post questions and answers, Assembly Web Discussions might be the answer. Assembly provides graphics that you can insert in an HTML document if you want to link to an "Assembly" from your library's home page.

Special features offered by Assembly include weekly e-mail updates that announce new services, notification of recent messages posted on your message board, and the ability to control who has access to your system.

You also have the option of installing forum software on your own server. For a comprehensive index of Web conferencing software, see Thinkofit at *thinkofit.com/webconf/*. If you have access to a UNIX system, you can install and run WWWBoard for free. This CGI script, developed by Matt Wright, can be downloaded from Matt's Script Archive at *www.worldwidemart.com/scripts/*.

If you don't want to mess around with CGI scripts locally, you can use a service like *www.hostedscripts.com*. HostedScripts.com handles all of the CGI scripts remotely. You do not need to know anything about CGI programming to use their free services, which include message boards.

Other free message board sites include:

Boardhost *www.boardhost.com/*
Delphi Forums *www.delphi.com/*
Inside the Web *www.insidetheweb.com/*
Boards2Go *www.boards2go.com/*

ONLINE DIARIES

Online, interactive diaries are another form of conferencing system. You have the ability to read someone else's writings and add your own writings if you wish. I first became acquainted with digital diaries and journal writing when I stumbled across The Open Diary at *www.opendiary.com/*. I set up an account that invited older folks in the surrounding area to share their memories and stories about the past. I was involved with a digital library project that was capturing local history and this was one tool we used to invite participation by folks living in remote locations.

Online diaries are now being used by individuals from all walks of life to post their daily ramblings—from artists and addicts to teachers and farmers. They all come to tell the world about their triumphs and defeats. You can link to several different diary sites at MetaJournals *www.metajournals.com/*.

FREE SEARCH ENGINES

Adding search capabilities to your Website is becoming quite easy with hosted-site search engines. A *hosted-site search engine* is a search engine that resides off-site. It is run by someone else other than yourself or your organization. Some are free and all are fairly easy to set up. You don't have to configure and run scripts on a Web server. All of that work is done for you. The setup you do have to perform is done through an easy-to-use Windows interface. One of the more popular search engine services, called whatUseek, is explained in detail in Chapter 27. You can access this service at *www.whatuseek .com/*.

Atomz.com at *www.atomz.com/* is a free search engine that you can add to your site if your site has less than 500 pages. Atomz doesn't place banner ads on your search results page, just a logo. Indexing can be performed weekly.

BeSeen *mysearch.looksmart.com/*, a product of LookSmart, is another basic search engine service supported by banner ads. You can modify how the search results page looks and the system will index up to 5,000 pages. LookSmart also sponsors free Webspace and a service that helps you build a free e-commerce site at *shops.looksmart.com/isroot/ orbitres/look/apps/marketing_website/center/index.html*.

As with all search engine services, remember to *re-index* your site every time you add new information. Some spiders crawl your site automatically at prescribed intervals. Others require direct interaction. After you login to BeSeen, click on the "Spidering Options" tab. Next, click on the first menu option titled "Re-Spider Your Site | Update Search Index." The member's login page is *mysearch.looksmart.com/login/*.

FreeFind *www.freefind.com/* indexes up to 32MB of data for free and offers lots of opportunities for customization using wizards. FreeFind provides you with site maps, what's new lists, and allows you to schedule indexing up to once a day. Search reports provide you with keyword counts and recently performed searches.

PicoSearch *www.picosearch.com/* indexes 1,500 pages for free. A professional plan lets you index up to 3,000 pages for $199/year. PicoSearch supports multi-site search capabilities, advanced searches (keywords, phrases, and Boolean logic), and is highly customizable. Like all of the other search engines, there is no coding required and no software. Indexing is done for you and you are given reports on visitors' keyword searches.

SearchButton *www.searchbutton.com/index1.html* indexes up to 1,000 pages for free, supports metatags, case-sensitive searching, sound-alike matching, synonym-search support, and fuzzy and wild card matching. Indexing can be performed automatically or on demand and you can exclude certain documents from being indexed.

METATAG GENERATOR

Information City provides a free metatag generator at *www.freereports.net/metatags.html*. Using metatags helps optimize your Web pages for indexing by robots. You simply enter your information for title, author, subject, description, and keywords, and then click the "Create Metatags" button. The metatag generator automatically creates the HTML code you need to copy and paste between the Head Tags at the top of your page.

It was pointed out in Chapter 18 that you also can create metadata free of charge using the Nordic DC metadata creator at *www.lub.lu.se/cgi-bin/nmdc.pl*.

E-MAIL ENCRYPTION

PGP is the de facto standard for e-mail encryption and is available in both commercial and freeware versions. The latest freeware version can be downloaded from MIT at *web.mit.edu/network/pgp.html* or from the International PGP home page at *www.pgpi.org/ download/*.

The Robots Exclusion Protocol

Some of the search and indexing systems introduced in this chapter support exclusion of certain HTML documents while their spider crawls your Website. The files that are excluded won't be indexed. If a service doesn't support exclusions, you may be indexing pages on your site that for some reason should not be visited by the spider. To address this problem there are a couple of methods you can use to limit what robots and spiders do.

1. Store a special file on your site called *robots.txt* that specifies which parts of your site should not be visited by robots.
2. Use a Robots metatag that indicates a page may not be visited and indexed by robots.

In the first method, if your WWW directory is *http://www.library.org/*, you would place the *robots.txt* file here: *http://www.library.org/robots.txt*. It must be placed here in the top level of your Webspace. Typically, on a UNIX server this is located in the */usr/local/etc/httpd/ htdocs/* directory—the same directory where your *index.html* file is located. When a robot visits your site, it examines the *robots.txt* file and analyzes its content. There can be only one *robots.txt* file on a Website. To learn more about the text you should include in the *robots.txt* file, see *info.webcrawler.com/mak/projects/robots/exclusion-admin.html*. It is fairly basic and can be demonstrated in the following example.

```
User-agent: Swish
Disallow:
User-agent: WebCrawler
Disallow: /
User-agent: *
Disallow: /forms
Disallow: /personal
```

In the first paragraph, a robot called Swish is allowed to index the entire site. In the second paragraph, a robot called WebCrawler is closed off from searching the entire site. In the third paragraph, the *robots.txt* file tells all other robots that they should not visit URLs starting with "/forms or /personal."

If you are using a service provider's Web server, there may not be an opportunity to perform this customization in the top level URL space. In this instance you can try implementing the second option and use the robots metatag. These metatags are not recognized by all robots. Any HTML document that contains the following metatag should not be searched and indexed by a robot:

```
<META NAME="ROBOTS" CONTENT="NOINDEX, NOFOLLOW">
```

For complete details on adding these metatags, see *info.webcrawler.com/mak/projects/ robots/meta-user.html*. You can access the Web Robots FAQ at *info.webcrawler.com/mak/ projects/robots/faq.html*.

Part IV

THE MULTIMEDIA EXPERIENCE

My first introduction to multimedia and its possibilities in libraries came as a result of working on the South Shore Memory Project. This project was a multimedia, digital library project built around the premise that computers are integral parts of children's lives. The primary purpose of the South Shore Memory Project was to enable kids in the public school system to document and preserve the local history and culture of their region. Their tools included computers, digital video and still cameras, scanners, sound recorders, and various applications for creating and editing sound, images, and text.

Librarians can bring their expert skills to multimedia projects like this. Librarians can help with the specifications for hardware and software, design electronic classrooms, writing help guides and offer group and individual training. They can archive and preserve the digital documents created by students. Librarians can attach metadata to the audio and video clips, to the images and text, and build search and indexing systems that provide access to these digital libraries. In addition, librarians can help students build Websites that display their multimedia exhibits online.

In Part IV, I focus on the tools and techniques for creating and viewing multimedia documents. The information presented in this section has a direct relationship to other sections in this book. If you use a digital camera and scanner to build a collection of historical images, for example, you must then consider how to make this collection available to others. In Chapter 27 "Implementing Web-Based Search Engines and Databases," you can learn how to use simple, Web-based tools to add search capabilities to your collection. Throughout this book there are references to metadata and the importance of adding meaning to the multimedia documents you publish. Refer to the index in the back of this book for pointers to these metadata entries. In addition, find the "metadata" link located on the CD-ROM accompanying this book.

Creating and Editing Multimedia

There are many ways to add multimedia to your work. You can use it to enhance an online help guide for library patrons, or to assist the local history society build a multimedia Website. You can use multimedia tools to record the life of a local historical figure, or to convert that shoebox filled with old library photographs and correspondence into a multimedia exhibit on your library's Website.

In Chapter 21, I explain what multimedia tools are available to you and how they function. In addition, I cover concepts you must understand to successfully work with imaging and audio technology; for example, resolution, which is applicable in creating both image and audio files. The chapter is roughly divided into two sections that cover these two technologies, image and sound. A detailed discussion on how to use specific pieces of hardware is outside the scope of this chapter, but I do cover general principles that apply to most hardware devices, including scanners, digital cameras, and audio recorders.

DEVELOPING GRAPHICS FOR WEB PAGES

Librarians have the option of contracting graphics jobs out to professional art studios or doing the work in-house. One side benefit of investing in the hardware and software to do the work in-house is that the equipment can also be made available to the public for their use. The downside, of course, is that you must be able to support this new software and hardware. If everyone is already stretched to their limits with understanding and applying new technology, there may not be enough resources to formally support yet another application or hardware peripheral.

In a small library where Web development is the responsibility of the director, or maybe an individual on the staff or volunteer that has the reputation of being the local "computer expert," it may be best to invest in applications that are designed for the

---

> **Online Resources**
>
> If you are one of those individuals who are addicted to Paint Shop Pro, check out some of these Paint Shop Pro users groups at *www.pspug.org/* and *www.pspiz.com/* for tutorials, online classes, contests, tips and tricks, reviews, and more.

casual user. Medium- to large-size libraries that have several professional librarians working as a team on Web page development may choose to go with applications that are designed for graphics professionals.

ILLUSTRATION SOFTWARE

If you intend to do original artwork for your home page, you should consider investing in illustration software. *Illustration software* consists of a set of programs that enable you to create images, such as flow charts, diagrams, custom maps, logos, signs, and other graphics.

Illustration software ranges in price from absolutely free to $600 and more. Macromedia FreeHand 9 *www.macromedia.com/software/*, CorelDRAW 9 Graphics Suite *www.corel.com/products/graphicsandpublishing/index.htm*, and Adobe Illustrator 9 *www.adobe.com/products/illustrator/main.html* are the three applications most often chosen by graphics professionals. For libraries on a budget, CorelXara *www.xara.com/corelxara/* offers several of the features these more expensive applications offer, but at a reduced price. You can download a free, 15–day trial version of CorelXara 2 from Xara's Website. Last time I checked, CorelXara 2 was selling for $79.95.

One of the most popular, low-end illustration programs is Paint Shop Pro from Jasc Software *www.jasc.com/*. You can download it from the Net for about $99, or buy it in a shrink-wrapped box for around $109. This program worked well in the South Shore Memory Project with which I was involved. Students quickly learned how to use this program to create icons, buttons, line drawings, and original animated GIFs.

Another tool you need for repairing, resizing, and cropping scanned photos is an image editor.

IMAGE EDITORS

Image editors are tools that allow you to edit images and line art. Programs like Adobe Photoshop 5.5 *www.adobe.com/products/main.html* make it possible to merge and edit color photographs, retouch proofs, create original works of art, optimize JPEG images for Web publishing, and more. Although Adobe Photoshop is considered "tops" by graphics experts, it is also fairly expensive, with a street price of around $600. Keep in mind that it takes a lot of time and dedication to learn how to use an advanced imaging program like Adobe Photoshop.

> **Online Resources**
>
> Photoshop tutorials are available at Deepspaceweb *www.deepspaceweb.com/* and Adobe's own Website *www.adobe.com/products/tips/photoshop.html*.

Attaching Metadata to Files

Adobe Photoshop allows you to attach meaningful data to images using a standard developed by the Newspaper Association of America (NAA) and the International Press Telecommunications Council (IPTC). This standard, known as XMLNews, supports fields describing captions, keywords, credits, categories, and origins. Some of these fields can be searched by third-party image text applications. XMLNews consists of two parts, XMLNews-Story, a format for textual news stories, and XMLNews-Meta, a format for metadata records for any kind of news objects including textual news stories, audio and video clips, photos, and virtual 3–D works.

The XMLNews standard is based on SGML (Standard Generalized Markup Language), which allows the same information to be used by different media with only minor changes in formatting. You can find more information about XMLNews at *www.xmlnews.org/*.

Other Windows applications allow you to add descriptive data (also known as *metadata)* to TIFF, JPEG, EPS, and PDF file formats. In Mac OS, you can add file information to files in any format.

Before you invest, decide what it is you want to accomplish with an image editor. If time and money are considerations, for about half the cost of Adobe Photoshop, you might consider Corel Photo-Paint 9 *www.corel.ca/paint9/index.htm.* If you are not interested in doing anything more than basic cropping and resizing of photographs, and fixing and repairing scanned photos, explore Adobe PhotoDeluxe Home Edition selling for about $49 or the Business Edition that sells for around $79. The later is designed more for business-related projects, such as printing to Avery paper for labels and cards. Another good editor to explore is Microsoft Picture It *www.microsoft.com/.*

WHAT IMAGING SOFTWARE DO YOU NEED TO GET STARTED?

As a bare minimum, you need image-editing software to prepare photos for publication on the Web or for creating a digital image archive. If you are just starting out, Adobe PhotoDeluxe Home Edition should provide you with everything you need. As your abilities increase and your projects become more advanced, you can graduate to a more sophisticated editor like Adobe Photoshop.

Some digital still cameras come with software that assists you in downloading images from your digital camera to your PC. Depending on the make of your camera, Adobe PhotoDeluxe may be capable of transferring image files from your camera to your PC. If you have a camera that captures images straight to a storage medium, for example, a floppy disk, then you simply insert the floppy disk in your PC's floppy disk drive and open the images with your editing software.

Other specialized software is needed for creating and editing digital audio clips. These applications are discussed later in the chapter.

CAPTURING IMAGES

You use digital cameras and scanners to capture images in digital format so you can get them into your computer. Once digitized, you can publish images to the Web, attach them to e-mail, or catalog them in digital libraries. If you don't have a digital camera, you can use a scanner to convert photos into a format that can be used by a computer. Scanners are also useful for optical character recognition (OCR).

There are four basic types of scanners. The *flatbed scanner* has a horizontal glass plate on which you place photographs, newsprint, and other flat documents for scanning. A scanning head moves beneath the glass plate. A *sheet-fed scanner* works something like a fax machine. The document moves over the scanning head. Some sheet-fed scanners only take one sheet at a time. Others have built-in document feeders that can scan multiple documents automatically. *Drum scanners* consist of glass cylinders on which the original document is mounted.

The next five sections present some points to consider before purchasing a scanner.

IMAGE RESOLUTION

Image resolution is the size of an image measure in pixels per inch. Today, the typical resolution of an inexpensive scanner is 600×600 for every square inch of the image. Generally speaking, scanners that offer higher resolutions cost more. If you have a printer that is capable of printing 1200 dpi (dots per inch), then it might pay to invest in a scanner that has an optical resolution of 1200×1200. If your output is going to be a printer as opposed to monitor, for example, then you can take full advantage of the printer's high resolution by matching it with a scanner that can capture high-resolution images.

Optical resolution is based on the number of pixels a scanner can actually see. *Interpolated resolution* is an artificially enhanced system of resolution. The scanner scans an image at its maximum optical resolution, say 600×600, and then adds pixels in between those pixels, guessing at what might be appropriate. This usually results in lower-quality images.

When you are deciding how much resolution you need, consider your output device. Is it going to be a printer, and if so, what is the printer's dpi (dots per inch)? Will your image be displayed on a Web page? Images that are only viewed on a computer monitors don't require high-resolution scans. Most monitors can only display 72 to 80 dpi. In most cases, a 600 or 1200 dpi scanner can take care of most of your needs.

BIT DEPTH

Another consideration is the scanner's bit depth. *Bit depth* is a measurement of how much information it takes to define a pixel. The higher the number, the better the image quality and the more colors the scanner can recognize. A scanner with 4–bit color can recognize 16 colors and a scanner with 24–bit color can recognize over 16 million different colors. A scanner that advertises having 36–bit color is theoretically capable of capturing billions of colors. However, due to certain limitations, not all systems can take advantage of the higher bit depth. For example, your monitor may only be capable of displaying 24–bit true color, or less if it is an older monitor. Currently, 24–bit to 36–bit scanners are reasonably priced and offer high-quality scanning.

SCANNING SPEED

Another consideration besides resolution and color quality is performance. Expect to pay more for scanners that scan at higher speeds. There isn't a standard unit of measurement for this, so go to review sources that provide comparisons between different models and brands of scanners. Try *www.zdnet.com*, *www.cnet.com*, and those sources mentioned in the Hardware-Product Reviews section on the CD-ROM accompanying this book. Buying a scanner that supports a Universal Serial Bus (USB) connection can significantly increase the speed at which data transfers between your scanner and computer.

DYNAMIC RANGE

The more expensive scanners specify their dynamic range. The *dynamic range* is the range of colors a scanner can record. Dynamic range is measured on a scale from 0.0, which is perfect white, to 4.0, which is perfect black. A single number is given which represents how much of this range the scanner can recognize. High-end scanners have dynamic ranges in the area of 3.3 to 3.8.

SCANNING AREA

Scanning area refers to the document size that can be scanned. This is a fairly non-technical specification and is given in inches. Most flatbed scanners for home and small offices support an 8.5" × 11.7" scanning area.

DIGITAL STILL CAMERAS

Scanners can only capture images from photos or other documents that are very flat. Digital cameras, on the other hand, can capture images of three-dimensional objects.

TERMINOLOGY

Digital cameras sometimes go by the shorter name *digicam*. When you snap the shutter, you don't take a picture. You *capture an image*. Digital cameras have other terms associated with them that are unique and may be new to you. So, before you go shopping, here are some terms with which you should become familiar:

Acquire—The process of importing an image from your digital camera into your software.

Aperture—The size of the lens opening that the light comes through. The aperture size can be either fixed or adjustable. It is calibrated in F-Stop numbers; the smaller the number, the larger the lens opening.

Auto Focus—Camera lens that focuses automatically on the subject.

CCD—Charged Coupled Device, the light sensitive chip in digital cameras

Digital Zoom— Digital zoom is not as detailed as a true optical zoom and uses electronics to take an image from the center of a frame and resize it at twice its actual size. The image is not as sharp and the digital zoom introduces noise (grain).

Exposure—Making an exposure is taking a picture. Exposure can also refer to the quantity of light that is allowed in when capturing an image. This is determined by the shutter speed and aperture.

Firmware—The operating software that processes data in your digital camera.

ISO—ISO stands for International Standards Organization and it is used as a prefix to film speeds; that is, the film's sensitivity to light. Slow films have ISO ratings of 100 or less. Fast films are 400 and higher.

LCD Panel—Liquid Crystal Display on digital cameras shows captured images along with information such as remaining exposures, and flash status.

Megapixels—High-resolution digital cameras that offer more than one million pixels are referred to as *megapixel* cameras. For example, a camera that is only capable of capturing an image at 640×480 pixels *is not* a megapixel camera. ($640 \times 480 = 307,200$ pixels). A camera with 1280×960 resolution produces an image with over one million pixels—1,228,800 to be exact. This camera is considered a megapixel camera. Cameras that capture images with a resolution of more than 3 million pixels are called 3 megapixel cameras.

Pixelization—This refers to the *stair-step* appearance of curved and angled lines in digital images. Also known as "jaggies."

Red-eye Reduction—The process of shining a light into a subject's eye before taking a flash picture. This causes the pupil to shrink and prevents the red-eye effect.

Shutter speed—The length of time your camera has to look at what you are taking a picture of.

SLR—Single-lens reflex, through-the-lens viewing. This means that when you look through the optical viewfinder, you are actually looking through the lens of the camera. You see what the sensor sees when the shot is taken.

WHAT IS A GOOD ALL-AROUND CAMERA?

Libraries can make digital cameras available for check-out and they can use them internally for various projects, such as Website development or to capture images for a digital library. Different cameras meet different objectives.

No matter what the purpose, look for a camera that offers removable memory op-

---

Online Resources

Most of us won't ever have the opportunity to borrow 20 or 30 digital cameras to try before we buy. Access to the Web makes it possible to at least compare image quality between the various brands and to read reviews. Two of the best sites for finding this kind of information are CNET and ZDNet. To link to CNET's site, point your browser to *www.cnet.com/* and find the link labeled "Hardware Reviews." The hardware page has links to various components including cameras. If you go to ZDNet's Website at *www.zdnet.com*, look for a link labeled "Reviews." When this page loads, look for a category called "Hardware" and within this, a sub-category called Digital Cameras. Here you can find several digital camera reviews and comparisons of images captured by different cameras. In addition, you can view samples of individual cameras by visiting their respective sites. For example, if you'd like to see how well the Canon PowerShot S100 captures images, check out their site at *www.powershot.com/*.

Visit Deja.com at *deja.com/usenet* and search on the phrase rec.photo.digital canon S100. This search statement enables you to focus your search on a single newsgroup named *rec.photo.digital* while at the same time searching that newsgroup's messages for the keywords *canon S100*.

---

tions because you or library patrons may be out in the field shooting for long periods. The camera needs to offer good image quality in automatic mode so users do not have to waste time adjusting settings. If software is required, look for software that is user friendly and intuitive so students can easily move images from camera to computer.

The six factors that you should consider when deciding on a digicam are:

1. Price
2. Functionality
3. Software
4. Storage
5. Image quality
6. Battery life

PRICE

Photo quality continues to climb dramatically as prices slide. If your budget requires that you stay in the $700–$1,000 price range, you are looking at business class cameras—one step above the home user/PC hobbyist category and one step below the semi-professional digital cameras. As with most products, there is a correlation between the price and quality of a digital still camera. Keep in mind that prices not only vary between brands, but the same camera may vary in price among different vendors.

FUNCTIONALITY

The functionality of a camera refers to its features. This covers a lot of territory, but the most important features include the ease with which you can capture, review, and erase images and whether it has a built-in flash with red-eye reduction, and zoom capabilities. Exposure on some cameras can be set automatically or manually. If convenience is important and you want a camera that can fit in your pocket, then size and weight features should also be considered.

Look for controls that are easy to operate and intuitive, especially those associated with the LCD monitor. Consider how much "on camera" information is available and whether it's easy to understand. For example, what is the remaining life of the battery, how many shots are remaining, different flash mode settings, image resolution, self-timing, and image resolution.

SOFTWARE

In the world of digicams, you sometimes need software to move your images from camera to computer. The minimum requirements your software should meet include selecting, saving, and printing photos. Software should also recognize your camera automatically and allow you to view thumbnail images before transferring full images to your computer. Make sure your software package includes a TWAIN driver for Windows. This enables you to pull your images into most programs. If you are interested in more options, you can go beyond what your digicam comes bundled with and invest in image-editing software.

STORAGE

When a digicam captures an image, it compresses the image and stores it in memory. Cameras store their images on different media. Find out how many shots at various resolutions can be stored before running out of space. The most common forms of memory cards are CompactFlash, SmartMedia, Memory Sticks, and floppy disks. A 4MB CompactFlash can hold approximately 40 low-resolution images and maybe only eight superfine, high-resolution images.

If your main purpose for owning a digital camera is Web publishing, you will have lower resolution requirements and you can fit more images into a smaller space. Resolution settings of 640 × 480 pixels are acceptable on cameras used for Web applications.

IMAGE QUALITY

When you consider what good image quality is, you are comparing the quality of your camera's output to a 35mm film camera or a professional-quality digital camera. While some of the factors are objective, two critical numbers play an important role in whether your camera will produce quality photos.

1. Color Depth—The picture's realism and color richness is determined by how many colors your camera can capture. The more bits per pixel your camera

records, the richer the color. It is the same principle discussed earlier with scanners. Cameras that record 24 bits of information per pixel create images in a possible combination of 16.7 million colors.

2. Resolution—Resolution is the other number to watch. Resolution determines the maximum image size you can display or print without enlarging the photo. Enlarging a photo can result in pixelated images—images that look blocky.

BATTERY LIFE

Most cameras come bundled with batteries and an AC adapter. Battery life is important when you are taking lots of snapshots. You are better off with a camera that uses easily replaceable batteries, such as AA or AAA batteries. You can save on battery power by doing your downloading to the computer under AC power.

PRINTERS

After you are done creating those snazzy graphics with your illustration software, or taking the perfect shot with your digital camera, your next step might be outputting your results to a printer. If you are on a limited budget, an ink-jet color printer is your best choice. *Ink-jet printers* use containers filled with liquid ink that is sprayed through a nozzle onto the page. It is a low-cost printing solution for low-volume printing.

Color laser printers offer higher speeds and higher qualities than ink-jet printers. They use a technology similar to that used in photocopiers. A photoelectric belt transfers the toner to a drum that in turn transfers the image to paper using heat and pressure.

If professional output is a necessity and you are willing to invest the money, investigate thermal wax and dye-sublimation printers. The *thermal-wax printer* uses a ribbon coated with wax and a thermal print head melts tiny dots of wax on coated paper. The cost is not high, but continuous tone images are not as good as those created by dye-sub printers. The *dye-sub printer* uses a transfer ribbon made of plastic film. A thermal print head transfers the dye from the ribbon to specially coated paper. Dye-sub printers produce high-quality images, but the output costs can be as high as $4 per 8.5 × 11–inch page.

DIGITAL VIDEO CAMERAS

Today you can use high-speed computers with video capture cards and powerful editing software to edit digital videos right in your library. Is there a place for PC-based video editing in libraries? In academic libraries and school libraries, students could be given an opportunity to add motion pictures to their multimedia documents. Librarians can enhance their Websites and teaching aids with video clips. Librarians can help build digital libraries that not only include still images, but also video clips.

WHAT YOU NEED

Before you can consider supporting this service, there are a few items you must make available.

1. Video Camera—You can use either an older analog camcorder or one of the newer digital video cameras. The more expensive digital video cameras, such as Sony's TRV900, have three CCDs for better color reproduction.

2. Capture Card—A capture card enables you to import video from your camcorder to your PC. With analog camcorders, the capture card converts the analog video signal into a digital format. If you use a digital video camera, you are making a digital-to-digital transfer and this is done through a capture card that supports a FireWire. A *FireWire* (IEEE 1394) is a special high-speed connection that transfers data at speeds up to 400Mbps. Sony has a proprietary name for this connection which they call *i.Link*.

3. Computer—Editing video on a PC requires enormous amounts of memory and a fast processor; a Pentium II or equivalent with at least 128MB of RAM is minimum. The hard drive should be rated 5400–rpm or faster, UDMA 33 or 66, and be as large as you can afford. With one 60–minute digital video recording, you could easily use up several gigabytes of hard drive space storing uncompressed video clips. Consider having two hard drives, one reserved exclusively for video clips and the other for applications and other files.

   Some companies offer turnkey systems that come bundled with a capture card, basic editing software, IEEE 1394 cable, and CD-RW drive. Examples are the Sony VAIO desktop and laptop PCs. Advantages of systems like these are that you know all of the components are compatible and they are easier to set up and service. When you make a call for technical support, you can get assistance from someone who knows how all of the components in your system are configured.

4. Video Editing Software—Digital non-linear editing (NLE) software is used for adding special effects, linking video clips together, adding sound tracks, and applying transitions between clips. Adobe Premiere *www.adobe.com/* costs several hundred dollars and is aimed towards video professionals. Other competing software includes EditDV *www.digitalorigin.com/*, MediaStudio Pro *www.ulead.com/*, and Vegas Video *www.sonicfoundry.com/*.

MORE ABOUT EDITING

In traditional videotape editing, you don't have the option of splicing a clip into the middle of an existing tape. To insert the clip, you have to re-edit everything that comes after it. With non-linear editing (NLE) systems, you can add a clip anywhere and the rest of your presentation automatically adjusts. NLE systems also give you the ability to create titles, make interesting transitions between clips, and add audio tracks.

Online Resources

The DV.com Forums, launched in April 2000, offers a platform for sharing digital video problems and solutions with your peers. Topics include Reader Reviews of Products, Cameras, Editors, Audio Solutions, The Craft of Lighting, Web Video, Motion Graphics/Special Effects/3D/ Animation, Production and Technology Issues, Equipping a Studio, and more. To join a discussion group, go to *www.dv.com/community*.

NON-LINEAR EDITING SYSTEMS

If you are looking for an easy solution, consider investing in a turnkey system that has the hardware and software you need to edit digital video. Entry-level systems can be purchased for around $3,000 and include everything you need except the digital video camera. An entry-level system that I've had success with in digital library projects with students is produced by Sony. The basic component is a computer called VAIO and comes in desktop and laptop configurations. The VAIO desktop comes with dual drives, DVD-ROM and CD-RW, 10/100 Base-T Ethernet Port, modem, i.Link interface (IEEE-1394), Microsoft Word 2000, and video editing software. Depending on the size of your hard drive and processor speed, these systems can run anywhere from $800 to $3,000. Monitors are sold separately. Expect to pay around $600 for a good 19" monitor. If you can afford a larger monitor, go for it. When editing video, you will appreciate the larger monitor size for viewing multiple clips. To learn more about the Sony VAIO system, go to Sony's Website at *www.sony.com/* and follow the path from "electronics" to "computing."

The software that comes bundled with Sony's VIAO workstations is called DVgate Motion. This basic digital video software, along with their i.Link (IEEE 1394) connection, allows you to stream the video directly onto your PC where you can capture clips by marking "in" and "out" points. More precise editing of the "in" and "out" points is performed with a companion program called DVgate Clip. Lastly, you use DVgate Assemble to join all of the clips together for your final cut.

Sony also makes a professional-level editing system called the ES-3 EditStation. This system is targeted towards corporate and institutional users, multimedia producers and small postproduction houses. IBM produces a comparable system called AvidXpress DV on IntelliStation. Professional non-linear editing systems like these can cost $10,000 or more depending on the exact specifications.

MORE ABOUT CAPTURING

Captured video is compressed with either hardware or software. If it's compressed with hardware, special chips on the capture card compress the video before it's stored on the hard disk. Hardware-compressed videos are only viewable by computers that use the same capture card. For example, if you use a Targa card to capture your video, the same card has to be installed on the viewing computer to watch the movie properly. The chip that is used to code and decode the compressed video is installed on the card. To avoid this situation, you can use software compression.

When you capture video using software compression, you use special capture software to save individual images or video clips to a disk. You begin by connecting the video source to your computer's capture board.

When you play the videotape on your camcorder, the footage appears in a viewing window on your computer monitor. To transfer that video to your hard drive, you click on a capture button and the video capture card and software work together to save the video to your hard drive. The sequence of events may vary depending on your software, but essentially, you click on buttons to mark the "in" and "out" points for your clip and you set up the capture files.

Once you have captured a clip, you use editing software to whittle the clip down

---

Online Resource
There are many capture cards on the market. One of the most popular capture cards is the Osprey 100 capture card. You can order these from RealNetworks at *www.realnetworks.com/developers/capture.html*. This is a low-cost, full-motion, PCI capture card for Windows 95/98/NT/2000. With this card you can capture video and encode it in Real, WindowsMedia, and Quicktime.

frame-by-frame to a more exacting size. You also use editing software to add special effects; for example, adding transitions between clips like fade-ins, slide right, and checkerboard out.

If you are connecting a digital video camera to your computer, the connection is made with a Firewire (IEEE 1394 cable). In the case of digital video cameras, data is captured as the video is being shot, it is compressed and converted to digital format in the camcorder. The data is stored on a digital videotape. This digital tape can be played on a digital tape drive, like the one in your camcorder.

When you transfer the digital video data to your PC, it is more like a file transfer, not a capture in the sense that you are converting analog to digital. When the video data is saved to the PC's hard drive, it is done so in a format that can later be processed by a video editor, such as Adobe Premier. Typically, this format is AVI for Windows or Quicktime for Macs.

VIDEO COMPRESSION

Digital video files can be quite large. Transferring these files over modem connections could take hours. The solution is to use compression to reduce the file size. When you shrink the size of your file using compression, you may alter the quality of the picture. In *lossy* compression, for example, some information is lost; hence the name "lossy". When you decompress one of these files, some of the detail is missing. Generally speaking, as you decrease the size of the file, the degradation increases. (In *lossless compression* the information content isn't changed between compression and decompression.)

A subcommittee of the ISO/IEC called the Moving Picture Expert Group developed an audio and video compression standard called MPEP. MPEG uses various compression techniques to make video and audio look and sound as good as possible, while keeping the file size as small as possible. One technique MPEG uses is called *motion compensation*, where frames are examined sequentially, looking for places where the scene has changed. Only the parts that move or change are transmitted to build each frame from previous frames. To accomplish this compression, the capture card in your PC uses a special algorithm called a *codec* (COmpression/DECompression algorithm). *Intel Indeo* compression is available on most systems that offer choices of video compression. Different versions of QuickTime use various codecs, including Cinepak and Motion JPEG. Cinepak is widely used for video stored on CD-ROMs. Cinepak doesn't work well in environments where the data transfer rate is slow, for example, modem dial-up connections. Motion JPEG can produce smaller file sizes for slower data transfer rates. This makes it a good choice for Web use.

Table 21–1: Compression formats and their uses		
Format	**Applied to**	**Details**
GIF (Graphics Interchange Format)	Still images	A lossless format owned by Compuserve. Requires a licensing fee.
JPEG (Joint Photographic Experts Group)	Still images	More lifelike colors than GIF. Uses lossy compression.
PNG (Portable Network Graphics)	Still images	Uses lossy compression. More lifelike colors than GIF.
MPEG-1	Video images	Video resolution of 320×240 at 24–30 frames per second.
MPEG-2	Video images	Video resolution of 720×480 and 1280×720 at 60 frames per second.
MPEG Layer-2 audio	Used for audio with both MPEG-1 and MPEG-2	Used for high-bandwidth MPEG audio at near-CD quality.
MPEG Layer-3 audio (MP3)	MPEG audio format popular on the Internet	Generally used in audio-only files (.mp3 files); a lower-bandwidth format than MPEG.
MPEG-4	Audiovisual media	Object-based; provides interaction and hyperlinking capabilities.

Table 21–1 further explains some of the different compression formats and how they are used.

WHAT IS A VIDEO PRODUCTION APPLIANCE?

A *video production* or *editing appliance* is a "box" that looks a lot like a PC (minus the monitor). It even has its own CPU, memory, hard disk drive, and sometimes a CD-ROM drive. Appliances are wired for a keyboard and mouse and can connect directly to a TV/Monitor. It differs from a PC in that it only does one thing—video editing. It doesn't let you do spreadsheets and word processing and you can't connect peripherals like printers and scanners.

There are a few video production appliances on the market and you can find them priced under $2,000. Explore Casablanca and Avio by Draco *www.draco.com/* and Sequel and ScreenPlay (a more expensive model) by Applied Magic *www.applied-magic.com/*. These devices provide everything you need to edit your videos.

Online Resource
You can find the Moving Picture Experts Group's home page at *www.cselt.it/mpeg/*.

ARE APPLIANCES BETTER THAN COMPUTER-BASED EDITING?

Computers and appliances each have their pros and cons. Computers are more flexible and allow you to run a variety of programs. In addition, you can use a PC to compress video into streaming formats. Appliances don't allow you to do this. Computers, on the other hand, can crash from time to time because they *are* doing so much.

Editing software is another consideration. Appliances come with only one option—the software installed by the manufacturer. You can't load other programs on an appliance, such as Adobe Premiere. Appliance software is easy to use and can render effects and transitions in real or near-real time. Computers usually have to build their transitions before they can be played back at full speed. This takes time.

PUBLISHING DIGITAL VIDEO ON THE WEB

Digital video files can be quite large. Transferring these files over modem connections could take hours. The solution to this problem is to use compression to reduce the file size. Compressed video is made up of two kinds of frames: key frames and delta frames. *Key frames* present complete images. *Delta frames* contain only visual information that is different from the frame before it. Factors such as fast cuts, handheld cameras, transitions, and busy sets all absorb bandwidth like a sponge. When filming for Web publication, the general rule is to make each frame look as much like the frame before it as possible. This helps to keep the file size down. You can accomplish this by shooting scenes similar to a news broadcast: static cameras on tripods, cuts instead of dissolving transitions, and sedate motion. Shooting video scenes like this yields smaller delta frames.

Today, if you decide to add streaming video to your Website, you can choose from a variety of proprietary formats. Each format requires the use of a different player. There is, however, a movement by Microsoft to offer a single standard and delivery platform in a product called NetShow. This is a streaming video component being developed for Internet Explorer.

The software for encoding streaming video can be a standalone program, or it may be part of your editing software. Some editing packages have encoding options built-in

Table 21–2: Turnkey systems that are full-function computers prepackaged for video editing, including FireWire support

Company	Price Range	Preloaded software
Apple Computer *www.apple.com*	$1,300–$6,000	iMovie or Apple Final Cut Pro
DVGear *www.dvgear.com*	$2,300–$6,000	Adobe Premiere LE or Adobe Premiere 5.x
Mina Systems *www.minasystems.com*	$5,000	Adobe Premiere 5.x
Sony VAIO *www.sony.com/*	$1,400–$4,000	Sony DVgate

Table 21–3: Streaming video encoders		
Company	**Name**	**Price**
Apple *www.apple.com/quicktime/*	QuickTime	$30
Microsoft Media Technologies *www.microsoft.com/windows/windowsmedia/*	Windows Media Technologies 7	Free
RealNetworks *www.realnetworks.com/products/producer*	RealProducer	Free
Xing Technologies	XingMPEG Encoder	$249

to their output options. Cleaner 5 from Terran Interactive, for example, saves to all the streaming formats: QuickTime, RealSystem, Windows Media, and MP3, as well as MPEG-1 and MPEG-2. You can learn more about their software by visiting *www.terran.com/*.

One issue that can be confusing for novice videographers is understanding the difference between codecs (discussed earlier in this chapter) and the software packages that allow you to create, store, and playback various streaming formats. In the case of QuickTime, the application has one name, "QuickTime," but the codecs it supports have different names. Depending on which version of QuickTime you are using, it may compress video using Cinepak, Sorenson, or Motion JPEG, for example. QuickTime is not in itself a codec.

Tables 21–2 through 21–4 offer pointers to digital video production workstations, encoders, and hosting services.

THE WORLD OF DIGITAL AUDIO

In this section, I explain how to convert analog recordings into digital sound files. An analog recording is a recording saved to tape. For example, a cassette recording is con-

Table 21–4: Web hosting services for streaming video		
Name	Services	Cost
Earthnoise *www.earthnoise.com*	Editing and posting videos for streaming. 50MB storage space for free.	Free or $50/year for 200MB of storage space
ClipShow *www.clipshow.com*	Translates your video into digital and streaming formats for Web viewing.	Free
Undergroundfilm *www.undergroundfilm.com*	Makes your videos available for viewing as streamed or QuickTime downloads.	Free

---

What is Sample Rate?

A sound wave has two important characteristics: amplitude and frequency. Amplitude is equivalent to volume. The greater the amplitude, the louder the sound. Frequency is the speed of the sound wave; that is, the number of waves that move past a given point in a certain amount of time. Higher frequencies (high-pitched sounds) result from faster waves and lower frequencies (low-pitched sounds) result from slower waves.

An analog sound wave is a continuous line with infinite amplitude values along its length. When your computer converts it into digital sound, it takes several measurements of the wave's amplitude at particular points in time. The measurement it takes is called a *sample*.

Because the original sound wave has an infinite number of amplitudes along its length, it's impossible to measure them all. The number of samples taken per second is called the *sample rate*. These are measured in Kilohertz (KHz). The most popular sample rates are 11KHz, 22KHz, and 44KHz (actually, they are precisely 11.025KHz, 22.050KHz, and 44.100KHz). The higher the sample rate, the closer the digital recording is to the original sound.

44.100KHz means that you are taking 44,100 samples of the sound wave every second. 22.050KHz means you are taking 22,050 samples of the sound wave every second, and so on.

---

sidered analog. I also show you in this section how to create digital sound files using microphones. I explain how to convert digital sound files into various formats for publication on the Web. In addition, I introduce you to basic digital sound editing techniques, such as fade-in, fade-out, and normalization.

CREATING DIGITAL SOUND FILES

Special collections librarians sometimes work with original recordings of interviews on cassette tapes. The first step in creating sound files for distribution in a digital environment is to convert these cassette recordings into digital WAV files. The WAV files are created at the highest possible sample rate and resolution. They are unaltered and saved on CD-RW discs or hard drive discs for archival purposes. All subsequent editing, downsampling, and file conversions are made from these high-quality, archival copies.

WAVeform-audio, or WAV for short, is an audio file format developed by Microsoft and IBM. It is the standard audio format used on PCs. One way you can create WAV

What is Sample Size or Sample Resolution?

Sample size (also called *sample resolution*) is the increments between the bottom and the top of the waveform. You can have either 8–bit or 16–bit wave sample resolutions. The 16–bit sample size offers the highest resolution, or finest details in the sound. 16–bit means you are using 2 bytes, or 16 bits of data to define a value. 8–bit sample size only uses 1 byte, or 8 bits of data to define a value.

The process of converting analog sound into digital sound is called *sampling*. A digital waveform is made up of millions of single digits that create a jagged line. When you listen to digital sound over a speaker, filters are used to smooth out the jagged edges of the digital sound wave and sending analog sound waves to your speaker.

files is by using a digital sound recorder on a PC to record the cassette recording as the tape player plays the tape back.

WHY NOT RECORD DIRECTLY INTO A PC?

Recording to a cassette and then encoding it into digital format creates a *second-generation* recording. Connecting a microphone to a PC and recording directly into the PC creates a *first-generation* digital recording. A first-generation recording is better because you have avoided the noise and distortion that invariably accompanies an analog recording. The noise and distortion on the cassette recording transfers to the digital recording. If you made copies of copies in the analog world, the noise would increase with each successive copy. In the digital world, each successive copy is exactly like the original.

With all of these good reasons for recording directly to your PC, you may still find it necessary to use a cassette recorder. Maybe you have to go to a remote site to record and you don't have access to a laptop. Another issue of concern is that digital audio files can be quite large. If a laptop were available, the length of an interview or musical performance may exceed the computer's disk storage capacity.

CHOOSING A DIGITAL EDITOR/RECORDER

There are several digital sound recorders from which to choose. The easiest and most convenient sound recorder to use is the one that comes with Windows 95/98. If you don't plan to do any sound editing—for example, cutting out silence or removing "hiss" sounds from a recording—then the basic sound recorder that comes with Windows can do the job. Most recordings, however, require some editing. At the very least, you have to "cut" short clips from long recordings—interesting, one-minute clips from taped interviews, for example. The best tool for this is a program that both records and edits.

The following instructions guide you through the process of recording and editing using a program called CoolEdit96 from Syntrillium Software Corporation *www.syntrillium.com/*. Other, more expensive, sound editors you can explore include Sound Forge *www.sonicfoundry.com/* and Steinberg's WaveLab *www.steinberg.net/*.

RECORDING WITH COOLEDIT

There are three ways you can record sound using CoolEdit: 1) using a microphone, 2) a cassette recorder, or 3) using the computer to generate the sound. Table 21–5 describes when you might use one input device over another. To use a microphone, first plug the microphone jack into the recording jack (red) located in the sound card. The sound card can be accessed from the back of the computer.

Recording with a Microphone

If the microphone has a switch, be sure it is switched "On."

1. To begin recording, click on the "Record" button located in the lower left-hand portion of the CoolEdit window. Then begin speaking into the microphone.

Table 21–5: List of input devices for recording with CoolEdit	
Input Device	Advantages
Microphone	Use a microphone when you can sit right next to the computer and record yourself speaking, singing, or playing an instrument.
Cassette recorder	Use a high-quality recorder when you record off-site and store the recording on a cassette tape. (Marantz cassette recorders are good choices.) Examples of off-site locations would be recording a concert or an interview at a remote site.
The computer itself	Sound files are stored on computers all around the world and can be accessed via the Internet. There are sound archives containing recordings of works by most well-known composers. When you play one of these files, you can record the sound while the file is playing. There are programs like NoteWorthy Composer that enable you to create music. This music can be recorded using CoolEdit96.

2. When you finish speaking (or singing, or playing an instrument), click on the "Stop" button to stop the recorder.
3. Click on the "Play" button to hear the recording you just made.

Recording with a Cassette Recorder

Before getting started, run a patch cord from the *line out* jack on the tape recorder to the *line in* jack on the computer's sound card. Next, run a line from the tape player's line in jack to the sound card's line out jack.

1. Now insert the cassette recording into the machine and cue it up; in other words, find the point on the cassette tape where you would like to begin recording with CoolEdit. Once you find it, rewind a little ways so that you give yourself some lead time.
2. When you are ready to begin recording, click on CoolEdit's record button and then press the "Play" button on the recorder.
3. To stop recording, click on CoolEdit's "Stop" button.

Recording Sound from the Computer

In this exercise you are going to find a sound file on the Internet and play the sound file while recording it with CoolEdit. First, go to the following site on the Internet using a Web browser: *http://piano-midi.de/midicoll.htm*

1. This Web page lists works by various composers. Find a musical work and double-click on its name to begin playing the music. After a few seconds, the music starts playing.

Controlling the Recording Level

You can check the recording level by looking at the VU meter located at the bottom of the CoolEdit screen. To activate the meter, click on "Options|Monitor VU Level." Red lines appear at the bottom of the screen. As you are recording, the red lines move to the right as the volume increases and to the left as the volume decreases. Try to maintain a recording level where the meter runs between –3 and 0. If it goes too far to the right, some distortion in sound will occur (called "clipping").

To control the recording level, double click on the speaker icon located in the system tray in the lower right-hand corner of the screen. Adjust the slide control under "Wave Balance." Move it up to increase the recording level and down to decrease the recording level. If you don't see the speaker icon in the system tray, you can start it through the programs menu. Click on "Start|Programs|Accessories|Entertainment|Sound Recorder."

---

2. Click on CoolEdit's "Record" button to begin recording the music as it plays.
3. Click on CoolEdit's "Stop" button to stop recording the music.
4. Click on CoolEdit's "Play" button to hear the music played back.

EDITING DIGITAL SOUND FILES WITH COOLEDIT

After you finish converting an analog recording to WAV format, the next step is to save the WAV file to a CD-R disc or hard disk drive. In the future, when you prepare files for distribution over the Net, you work from the original files stored on CD-Rs or hard disk drives. When you get ready to extract a short sound clip, entire melody, or interview from the disc, you edit the WAV file using a program called a *digital editor* like CoolEdit. CoolEdit can apply dozens of special effects to a digital recording. This section focuses on four:

1. Cropping your sample to remove parts of sentences that might occur at the beginning or end of a sound clip
2. Increasing the volume of the overall recording if the original recording level was too low
3. Removing tape "hiss" or other unwanted background noise
4. Fading in and/or fading out

To begin, start CoolEdit and open the WAV file. (If you are using an unregistered version of CoolEdit, make sure you select the "Save, External . . . " and "Amplify, Envelope . . . " functions when opening the program. These are necessary for the first three editing procedures, described next.) WARNING: If you are working with a large WAV file, say a taped interview that lasts 30 minutes, be sure you are on a PC that has enough memory to handle such a large file.

1. Crop the sample
   After opening the WAV file you wish to edit, click on the PLAY button so you can hear the recording. As it plays back, make mental notes of where you would like to precisely crop the recording so that it starts without a delay and doesn't hang on at the end. After the playback stops, click-and-drag from left to right on

the sound WAV image you wish to remove. Once selected, choose "Edit|Cut." For detailed work, click on the "ZOOM IN" button. The software zooms in closer each time you click the button. You can move left or right viewing the WAV by using the *hand* to grab the ruler below the WAV image.

When finished, replay the recording to see if you've accomplished what you set out to do; if so, save the edited file. If not, go back and do your editing again until you get it just the way you want it.

2. Increase volume

Make sure the entire recording fills the viewing window. (Click the "FULL" button.) Click-and-drag the portion of the WAV image you wish to make louder (usually the entire recording). Click on "Transform|Amplitude|Amplify." Click on the "Constant Amplification" tab. Move the slide bar to the right to a number higher than 100 percent. Click "OK" and test your volume level. When finished, save the edited file.

3. Fading in and fading out

Click-and-drag on the portion of the recording you wish to edit. Click on "Transform|Amplitude|Amplify." When the "Amplify" window opens, click on the "Fade" tab. If you are fading in, set the "Initial Amplification" to 0 percent and the "Final Amplification" to 100 percent. If you are fading out at the end, set the "Initial Amplification" to 100 percent and the "Final Amplification" to 0 percent. Click "OK."

Listen to your final result. If satisfied, save the file. If not, click on "Edit|Undo Amplify" and do over.

4. Noise Reduction (If you are using an unregistered version of CoolEdit, you must close CoolEdit and reopen it making sure you select the "Save, External . . . " and "Filter and Noise Reduction" functions for the next operation.)

When you first played back your recording, did you hear background noise, such as tape hiss? If so, determine which portion of the recording is creating the noise or "hiss" sound. Click and drag on that portion of the WAV image in CoolEdit. (Zoom-in for detail if necessary.)

Click on "Transform|Noise Reduction." When the "Noise Reduction" window opens, click on the button labeled "Get Noise Profile from Selection."

Move the "Noise Reduction Level" slide to the right. The closer you get to 100, the greater the noise reduction. Click "OK" when finished.

Play the file back and listen for the changes. If satisfied, save the file. If not, click "Edit|Undo Noise Reduction" and try again.

CREATING AUDIO CLIPS FOR PUBLICATION ON THE WEB

There are many options for distributing files over wide area networks, but the best options are those that enable quick transfers over limited bandwidths while maintaining a level of quality that is as close to the original WAV file as possible.

Table 21–6 offers a comparison of file sizes among the most popular formats used on the Web. The original recording used in this comparison study was created with a program called NoteWorthy Composer, or NWC for short. NWC enables you to place music notation on a staff and then convert that notation into a MIDI file. The tune I recorded is named "We're Coming Arkansas," taken from *Songs of the Ozark Folk* by Leo Rainey, Orilla Pinskston, and Olaf Pinkston (1987. Branson, MO: The Ozarks Mountaineer). The tune lasts approximately 50 seconds. Note how many megabytes of disc space is required to store just 50 seconds of music in WAV format as compared to MIDI format.

ADDING STREAMING AUDIO TO HTML DOCUMENTS

To publish streaming audio on the Web using RealAudio compression, two files are required: a metafile with the extension *.ram* and the audio clip itself with the extension *.ra*. To better illustrate this process, let us say that you have named your audio clip *johnston.ra*. You can create a RealAudio file using CoolEdit. When you have a WAV file open, choose "File|Save As . . . " and choose the file type "RealAudio."

The metafile is a text file you create with a simple editor like Notepad. The file name should end with *.ram*. If the audio clip is named *johnston.ra*, it makes good sense to name the metafile *johnston.ram*.

The metafile should contain this line of text: *pnm://www.foobar.com/realaudio/johnston.ra*

The first variable, "*pnm://*" is the protocol you use to stream the files. The protocol RealNetworks uses is called pnm (Progressive Networks Media). Replace "*www.foobar.com*" with your Website address. Before your visitors can hear streaming RealAudio, your ISP (Internet service provider) must install RealServer. The path statement */realaudio/Johnston.ra* is set by your system administrator. It is determined when RealServer is installed configured. Ask your system administrator or ISP where you should store your RealAudio files. Now use WS_FTP, or any other FTP client to upload the *johnston.ra* and *johnston.ram* files to a Web server. Save both of them to the /realaudio directory, or whatever directory your ISP specifies. The *.ram* file should be uploaded as an ASCII text file and the *.ra* file should be uploaded as a binary file.

When you create the hyperlink linking to this RealAudio file, point the link to *www.foobar.com/realaudio/johnston.ram* not the **.ra* file.

Other Formatting Options

Remember, the higher the fidelity, the larger the file and the longer the download time. If you choose to make WAV, AU, MP3, or AIFF files available for distribution on the Web, you should downsample and convert the original file in such a way that it can be accessed in a reasonable length of time. You can do this by creating a mono recording sampled at a rate of 11KHz or 22KHz with 8–bit resolution. The recording should last only a few seconds to keep the download time to a minimum.

In some situations, it is also beneficial to create MIDI music files and TrueSpeech files for spoken words. If you want to convert sheet music into digital audio, MIDI is a good choice. If you would like to present a longer-than-usual speech on your Web page, TrueSpeech is an excellent choice because of its high compression ratio. MIDI files and TrueSpeech files are relatively small in size and transfer well over modem connections.

Table 21–6: Comparison of file sizes for different digital audio file formats		
Format	**Program Used to Produce, Render, or Convert File**	**File Size**
MIDI (*.mid*)	NoteWorthy Composer V1.55a	3KB
TrueSpeech (.wav*)	TrueSpeech Converter, DSP Group, Inc.	51KB
RealAudio (*.ra*)	RealEncoder V3.1	95KB
RealMedia (*.rm*)	RealProducer G2 V6.0	130KB
MP3 (*.mp3*)	Blade's MP3 Encoder	753KB
Next/Sun AU (*.au*)	CoolEdit	2,073KB
WAV (*.wav*) 44,100 sample rate, 16–bit resolution	WAVmaker III	8,291KB
AIFF (*.aif*)	CoolEdit	8,291KB

* TrueSpeech is not designed for compressing music. The resulting sound quality is rather poor, but still it was included in this comparison because it shows you the resulting file size relative to the other file formats. Using it to compress speech can be quite effective.

ADDING NON-STREAMING AUDIO TO HTML DOCUMENTS

The simplest way to add non-streaming audio to an HTML document is with an anchor tag. Locate the spot in your document where you want to insert a link to the audio file. Type **<A HREF="** followed by the URL of the sound file to which you want to link, then close the tag by typing **">**. Type some descriptive text, known as *link text*, or insert an image after the anchor tag. Finish the anchor tag by typing **</A>** on the same line.

Here are two examples of how it might look:

1. This first example demonstrates linking to a MIDI sound file located on a remote server. I used MDID.COM's search engine at *www.midi.com/* to hunt down a MIDI file on the Internet. A search on the keyword **vivaldi** resulted in several hits including this one: *ftp://ftp.inria.fr/misc/music/midifiles/allegro.mid*. The HTML code for linking to this MIDI file would look like this:

<A HREF="ftp://ftp.inria.fr/misc/music/midifiles/allegro.mid">Vivaldi's Allegro</A>

2. This example demonstrates how the HTML code would look if the *allegro.mid* file was located in the same directory as the HTML document that links to it:

<A HREF="allegro.mid">Vivaldi's Allegro</A>

In both instances, when a visitor clicks on the linked text, their Web browser either opens an external program to play the audio file or a plug-in player is launched right in the browser window.

A second method for linking to audio files uses the <EMBED> tag. This tag places a control panel on the page that can provide play, stop, pause, and volume control buttons. The following example demonstrates how to create a link to the Vivaldi sound file using the <EMBED> tag. The sound file plays when the user clicks on the control panel's play button.

> <EMBED SRC="allegro.mid" CONTROLS="console" HEIGHT=60 WIDTH=145 AUTOSTART="false">Vivaldi's Allegro</EMBED>

The <EMBED> tag supports several attributes. In the preceding example, the CONTROLS attribute determines what image appears on the page. For example, "console" gives you a control panel with play, stop, pause, and volume control buttons. If you replace this with **CONTROL="smallconsole"**, a smaller version with just play, stop, and volume control appears. The HEIGHT and WIDTH attribute determines the size of the console image. The AUTOSTART attribute determines whether the audio clip starts playing automatically when the page loads (AUTOSTART="true"), or if the user must click on the play button to hear the audio clip (AUTOSTART="false").

BUILDING A DIGITAL AUDIO TOOLBOX

In this section, I offer examples of software packages that perform various specialized tasks. While editing applications can perform many different operations, there may be situations where you want a program that performs a specific task. Included in this listing are programs that play, record, edit, enhance, organize, convert, and create digital sounds in all types of formats.

Audio Players—Play CDs and all types of audio files (MP3, WAV, MIDI, etc.).

> Winamp—*www.winamp.com/*
> Winamp, freeware from Nullsoft, Inc., is a high-fidelity music player that supports MP3, MP2, CD, MOD, WAV and other audio formats. It offers custom interfaces called skins and audio visualization and audio effect plug-ins.

Audio Recorders—Record audio from your sound card's inputs.

> Total Recorder—*www.highcriteria.com/trinfo.htm*
> Total Recorder, shareware from High Criteria, Inc., records from any sound card input line. For example, you can record from CD or you can hook up a cassette player and record from it. In addition, Total Recorder converts different sound formats to WAV.
> The evaluation version is fully functional except that your recordings are limited to 40 seconds each. Unlimited recordings require a registration fee of $11.95.

Audio Editors—Play, edit, and fine-tune audio files in detail.

> CoolEdit—*www.syntrillium.com/cooledit/index.html*
> CoolEdit, shareware from Syntrillium, is a full-featured digital audio editor. It allows you to record through your sound card from a microphone, CD player, or other source. CoolEdit supports a wide variety of special effects that enable you to touch-up your sounds, for example, reverberation, noise reduction, echo and delay, flanging, filtering, and many others. The unregistered shareware version

disables save and clipboard functionality after 30 days and limits you to using only a subset of the features per session. This is nice, because you can still evaluate all the features, just in separate sessions. Full functionality requires registration fee of $69.

Audio Restoration—Clarifies, filters, and restores noisy and corrupt audio recordings.

Pristine Sounds 2000—*www.accuratesound.net/prissouncdma.html*
Pristine Sounds is a digital audio editor and restoration tool. The software comes in two versions: Lite $99 and Pro $199. Supported file formats include: AU, MPG, MP2, PCM, RAW, SND, TXT (save only), and WAV. The free demo version disables batch processing, audio-CD splitting, real-time previewing, and limits processing to a maximum of 30 seconds.

Format Converters—Convert between various audio file formats.

WIDI—*www.chat.ru/~andreenk/english/widi.htm*
WIDI is a WAV to MIDI converter. It takes a WAV recording and converts it to a MIDI score containing notes. At present, the process has not been perfected, so the results are not always accurate.
   The unregistered shareware version has no trial limitations, but as with all shareware, registration is encouraged to help fund future improvements. To register, send $22.

Digital Ear—*digitalear.iwarp.com/*
Digital Ear analyzes recorded WAV file (a singing human voice or musical instrument) and converts it to a standard MIDI file. Digital Ear can translate events such as vibrato, tremolo, pitch-bending, and portamento effects. The demonstration version limits the duration of wave file processing, disables Auto Correct, Pitch Quantize, and the In-Tune Wizard. The demo does not expire and you can save and load your work. Send $75 to register.

TiMidity—*www.goice.co.jp/member/mo/timidity/*
TiMidity converts MIDI files to WAV audio files. It is also a real-time MIDI player.

Audio Encoders—Encode audio to highly compressed files such as MP3.

BladeEnc—*bladeenc.mp3.no/*
Blade's MP3 Encoder (BladeEnc) is a freeware MP3 encoder.

CD Rippers—Copy audio CD tracks to audio files (WAV, MP3, etc.).

Cdex—*cdex.n3.net/*
Cdex is a freeware utility that can record digital audio tracks from CD into files. The recorded audio tracks can be stored as WAV or MP3 files.

Plug-ins—Process audio using add-on software effects.

Beatnik Player—*www.beatnik.com/*
Beatnik is a digital audio music and sound effects plug-in for Netscape, Internet Explorer, and AOL browser. Beatnik supports many music and audio file formats, including RMF (Rich Music Format), MIDI, MOD, AIFF, WAV, MP3, and AU files.

MIDI/Audio Sequencer—Software designed to record, play, and edit music using MIDI and/or audio.

Cakewalk Pro Audio—*www.cakewalk.com/*
Cakewalk Pro Audio is a full-featured, professional MIDI/Audio sequencing software for composing music. It enables you to compose, edit, and produce original music. You can use Cakewalk to create CDs, soundtracks for videos, music for multimedia applications, and Internet content. The demo version disables the save, print, and edit plug-in functions. Cakewalk Pro costs around $429. Cakewalk Home Studio is for non-professionals and runs $129.

Notation—Software used to read, write, and print music scores.

NoteWorthy Composer—*www.ntworthy.com/composer/*
NoteWorthy Composer is a software music composition and notation processor. It allows you to create, record, edit, print, and play back your own musical scores. The unregistered shareware version has a 30–day trial period. To register, pay $39.

Multimedia on the Web

With the proper equipment, you can experience sound, images, motion pictures, animation, and text while exploring the Web. In this chapter I introduce you to some of the basic plug-ins that can extend the capabilities of your Web browser so you can take advantage of the variety of data that exists on the Web.

The latest versions of browsers make it easy to view most images and listen to most sound files on the Web. In Internet Explorer, click on "Tools|Internet Options" and then click on the "Advanced" tab. Scroll down until you come to the multimedia area. Here you can check one or more of the "Show pictures," "Play animations," "Play videos," and "Play sounds" choices. Windows Media Player is native to Windows 98 and supports the following types of media files:

- Microsoft Windows Media formats
  File name extensions: *.avi, .asf, .asx, .rmi, .wav*
- RealNetworks' RealAudio and RealVideo (version 4.0 or lower)
  File name extensions: *.ra, .ram, .rm, .rmm*
- Moving Pictures Experts Group (MPEG)
  File name extensions: *.mpg, .mpeg, .m1v, .mp2, .mpa, .mpe*
- Musical Instrument Digital Interface (MIDI)
  File name extensions: *.mid, .rmi*
- Apple QuickTime®, Macintosh® AIFF Resource
  File name extensions: *.qt, .aif, .aifc, .aiff, .mov*
- UNIX formats
  File name extensions: *.au, .snd*

You can install additional components to support file formats that are not already supported by your browser or built-in media player. This is explained later in the chapter. At a minimum, you should configure your system to display portable documents—files with a *.pdf* extension. Today, many files come in this format, from support manuals for your automation system, to ERIC documents. Details of how to make your browser capable of reading PDF documents are also presented in this chapter.

HELPER APPLICATIONS

Helper applications are programs that run separately from your browser. These are external programs that have no connection to the Web. Your Web browser relies on helper applications for playing sound files and displaying unfamiliar image and video file formats. When your browser comes across a file whose MIME type is unknown—a RealAudio sound file, for example—the browser automatically locates the RealAudio Player you installed and loads it so you can hear the sound file played

It's up to you to find, download, and install helper applications on your computer. As part of the installation process, your browser settings are automatically reconfigured so it knows where to find the new helper application. (Settings are usually changed automatically.) Figure 22–1 presents a view of the helper applications panel in Netscape. You can find it by choosing "Preferences" in the "Edit" pull-down menu. Once the Preferences window is open, click on "Navigator|Applications."

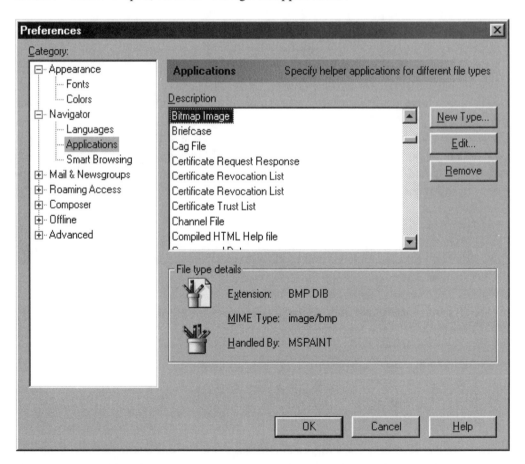

Figure 22–1: Applications Netscape uses for various file types

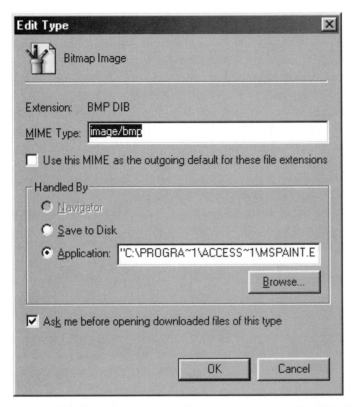

Figure 22–2: The "Edit Type" window allows you to customize helper application settings

Note the file type details shown in Figure 22–1 that read

Extension: BMP DIB
MIME Type: image/bmp
Handled By: MSPAINT

If you click the "Edit" button shown in Figure 22–1, you discover where the helper application is located. You are given a path statement that points you to the program that handles the particular MIME type. In this case, the browser is all set to match file types with the extensions *.bmp* by launching the necessary helper application. *MIME* is an Internet standard used to represent data formats. MIME designates a major type and a minor type—two words separated by a dash. In the example shown in Figure 22–1, the major type is "image" and the minor type is "bmp." Other major MIME types include video, audio, text, and application.

If you want to be asked before Navigator downloads a file of a certain type, you can specify this in the "Edit Type" window shown in Figure 22–2. Put a check mark in the box preceding the "Ask me before opening downloaded files of this type."

Browsers can tell which applications to run based on the file type extensions; that is, the three letters that come after the dot in the file name. For example, when you click on a link to a WAV-format sound file, your browser goes to a table of helper applications and determines which application should be launched to run a file with a *.wav* file name extension.

PLUG-INS

Where helper applications provide a separate window or interface for displaying multimedia, plug-ins display multimedia content in-line. This means that the application runs right in the browser window as part of the Web page. Plug-ins are designed to communicate with any browser that supports the plug-in interface. In Windows, plug-ins are DLL files that load into memory when the browser starts up.

A list of plug-ins can be found on Netscape's home page at site *home.netscape.com/ plugins/index.html*. Some of the more popular plug-ins currently listed include:

- Internet Postage by Stamps.com—gives you the ability to print postage for mail
- Macromedia Flash Player—displays vector graphics and animation
- Shockwave by Macromedia—offers interactive multimedia, streaming audio, and graphics
- RealPlayer by RealNetworks—plays real-time (streaming) audio, video, and animations.
- Net2Phone—enables you to place calls from your PC to a phone

A good way to find plug-ins on Netscape's site is to click on the "Search Plug-ins" link. The next page that comes up gives you the options of searching by type of platform (Win95, Win98, Macintosh, Linux, etc.), by file extension (*.au*, *.bmp*, *.pdf*, etc.), and by MIME type.

The Plug-in Gallery & Demo Links at *www2.gol.com/users/oyamada/* offers plug-ins organized under the following subject headings:

- Multimedia
- VRML & 3D
- Sound Player
- Video Player
- Image Viewer
- Document
- Misc.

BrowserWatch's Plug-In Plaza *browserwatch.internet.com/plug-in.html* offers a comprehensive list of plug-ins organized by category and platform. Categories include:

- The Full List
- Multimedia
- Graphics
- Sound
- Document
- Productivity
- VRML/3–D

SOURCES OF HELPER APPLICATIONS AND PLUG-INS

Helper applications are available as shareware or freeware and can be found at various software sites all around the Internet. There are a variety of helper applications available including video players, portable document viewers, sound players, and image viewers. In the lists that follow, some of the applications come in the form of plug-ins, running seamlessly within your browser window. If you are running the latest version of Netscape, the job of updating is made much easier. When you come across a file Netscape doesn't understand, it guides you in finding a helper application.

If a specific program I describe is no longer at the site I list, run a search using one of the search engines linked to the All-In-One Search Page at *www.AllOneSearch.com/*, or try going to a Web-based software archive and search on the application's name. Two good sites for this are TUCOWS at *www.tucows.com/* and CNET's shareware.com at *www.shareware.com/*.

The following are four basic helper applications/plug-ins you should consider installing if your system doesn't yet support them.

> Name: QuickTime
> Developer: Apple, Inc.
> Description: Watch movies and listen to music.
> Download site: *www.apple.com/quicktime/*
>
> Name: Acrobat Reader
> Developer: Adobe Systems, Inc.
> Description: View portable documents
> Download site: *www.adobe.com/products/acrobat/*
>
> Name: Shockwave/Freehand
> Developer: Macromedia, Inc.
> Description: Access interactive multimedia
> Download site: *www.macromedia.com/software/downloads/*
>
> Name: RealPlayer
> Developer: RealNetworks, Inc.
> Description: plays RealAudio sound files
> Download site: *www.real.com/player/index.html*

STREAMING AUDIO AND VIDEO

When you retrieve audio and video files with your Web browser, you have the option of either downloading them in their entirety and then playing them, or using a continuous delivery technology called streaming. *Streaming* is a technology that compresses audio and video files before sending them on to the user. By compressing the data streams, users can listen to audio or view video in real-time. Before you can take advantage of this technology, you must install on your PC one or more media players designed just for this purpose. RealPlayer, for example, supports both streaming audio (RealAudio) and streaming video (RealVideo). In fact, the G2 Player is capable of playing many different file formats. This enables you to access most standard sound and video files found on the Web. Below is a list of file types that the RealPlayer can handle:

AIFF	(Audio Interchange File Format)
ASF	(Advanced Streaming format, type 1 only)
AU	(Audio)
AVI	(Audio/Video Interface)
MIDI	(Musical Instrument Digital Interface)
MOV	(QuickTime 1 & 2, uncompressed files only)
MPEG-1	(Moving Pictures Experts Group)
RA	(RealAudio)
RV	(RealVideo)
RM	(RealMedia)
VIV	(Vivo)
SWF	(RealFlash)
WAV	(Waveform Audio)

REALAUDIO SITES

A good way to try out your RealAudio player is to connect to a Website that supports RealAudio. Yahoo! Broadcast at *www.audionet.com* offers a variety of RealAudio files. Music lovers can listen to the "Nashville Pickin' Party" live from the Bluebird Cafe on WRLT or jazz music on WWOZ in New Orleans. Other topics of interest include hourly updates from the NASDAQ stock market; Art Bell's "Coast to Coast" show featuring science, current events, and mysterious occurrences; and "On A Roll with Greg Smith," a talk show on disability issues that is produced entirely by people with disabilities.

The World Radio Network (WRN), formed in 1992, is a 24–hour news and information network that broadcasts segments of programming from 25 public and international broadcasters. WRN's home page can be accessed at *www.wrn.org/*.

Note that as you begin exploring streaming media, the quality of both the sound and image depend greatly on the speed and quality of your connection. Don't be surprised if sound becomes distorted or even stops occasionally. Also, if you are short on RAM, you may not be able to continue browsing the Internet while a RealAudio file is playing in the background. RealAudio isn't likely to gain widespread acceptance in libraries until the content of the available audio archives improves and broader bandwidths become more common.

STREAMING VIDEO

Companies continue to experiment with streaming video over modem connections. One of the most important factors that determine whether you can view video in real time is your connection speed. You also need a central processing unit (CPU) and graphics card capable of processing data quickly. At present, the best streaming video technology has to offer with 28.8Kbps dial-up connections is low-resolution video with some distortion playing at only one or two frames per second. This would best be described as "near" real-time video.

Xing Technologies offers a product called the XingMPEG Player that is a combination audio/video player that enables you to watch and listen to live concerts, radio broadcasts, and other events over the Internet. In August of 1999, RealNetworks, Inc., merged with Xing Technology Corporation. The XingMPEG line of software products now includes the XingMPEG Encoder for the creation of MPEG-1 video and the XingMPEG Player for viewing MPEG1 video. A 30–day trial version of the XingMPEG Player can be downloaded from Xing Technology's home page at *www.xingtech.com/video/*.

For other software choices in the field of streaming video, run a keyword search on **streaming video** at CNET's site at *www.shareware.com/*.

HOW TO CONFIGURE NETSCAPE NAVIGATOR TO WORK WITH REALPLAYER

If RealPlayer installs properly, it automatically configures Netscape Navigator to recognize RealPlayer as a helper application. If you click on a RealAudio file and Netscape prompts you to save the file, rather than starting up the player, you need to manually configure Netscape to recognize RealPlayer.

To set up RealPlayer as a viewer in Netscape 3.0x, follow these steps:

1. Start Netscape Navigator and click on the "Options" pull-down menu and select "General Preferences."
2. In the Preferences window, select the "Helpers" tab.
3. Click on the "Create New Type" button. When the dialog box appears, enter **audio** in the Mime Type field and **x-pn-realaudio** in the MIME subtype field.
4. Under "file extensions", enter **ra, rm, ram**
5. Select the "Launch Application" radio button and find the directory where RealPlayer was installed. By default, this is in the *C:\RealPlayer* folder. Select *REALPLAY.EXE* as the application to launch.

To set up RealPlayer as a viewer in Netscape Communicator 4.0x, follow these steps:

1. Click on the "Edit" menu and choose "Preferences."
2. In the Preferences window, under Navigator, click on "Applications."
3. Scroll until you find "RealPlay File". (If the "RealPlayer File" doesn't exist, see below.)
4. Click on "RealPlay File" to highlight the text.
5. Verify if the following information is correct:
   Extensions: RA, RM, RAM
   Mime-Type: audio/x-pn-realaudio
   Handled by: REALPLAY
6. Click "Ok".

If the "RealPlay File" option wasn't available, follow these steps:

1. Click on the "New Type" button.
2. Enter the following information:
   Description of type: RealPlay File
   File extension: RA, RM, RAM

> **MIME Type: audio/x-pn-realaudio**
> **Application to use: C:\Program Files\Real\RealPlayer\realplay.exe**
> If the location of *realplay.exe* is different from the description above, use the browse feature to locate the *realplay.exe* file.

3. Click "OK."
4. Click "OK."

If you followed the above procedures, RealPlayer should launch next time you click on a RealAudio file.

HOW TO CONFIGURE INTERNET EXPLORER TO WORK WITH REALPLAYER

As with Netscape Navigator, the RealPlayer installer should automatically configure Internet Explorer so that it starts RealPlayer and begins playback whenever you click on a RealMedia link. If RealPlayer does not start when you click a RealMedia link, manually configure Internet Explorer 4.x–5.0 by doing the following:

1. Click on the "Start" menu, choose "Programs," and then "Windows Explorer."
2. After Internet Explorer starts, click on the "View" pull-down menu and select "Options."
3. Click on the "File Types" tab.
4. Scroll to see if "RealMedia File" is in the list. If you find it, double-click on it to open the edit dialog box. If it is not listed, click on the "New" button.
5. In the dialog box that appears, enter the following information:
   Description of Type: RealMedia File
   Content Type (MIME): application/vnd.rn-realmedia
   Default Extension for Content Type: .rm
6. Click on the "Edit" button and enter the following information in the Action dialog box:
   Action: open
   Application used to perform action: (Browse to locate the *realplay.exe* file. The default location is *C:\Program Files\Real\Realplayer\Realplay.exe*)
7. Click "OK."

Repeat the above steps for each of the following file types:
   Description of Type: RealAudio File
   Content Type (MIME): audio/vnd.rn-realaudio
   Default extension for content type: *.ra, .ram*

   Description of Type: RealVideo File
   Content Type (MIME): video/vnd.rn-realvideo
   Default extension for content type: *.rv*

   Description of Type: RealAudio File
   Content Type (MIME): audio/x-pn-realaudio
   Default extension for content type: *.ra, .ram*

PLUG-INS THAT LISTEN AND READ

Apple Computers have been in the forefront of designing software that helps Mac users who have difficulty operating a standard mouse and keyboard. Apple's PlainTalk technology is able to interpret text and produce computer-generated speech. This is known as Speech Synthesis. Furthermore, it enables users to control Mac computers with certain spoken phrases the computer interprets as mouse clicks or keystrokes.

Netscape plug-ins that incorporate the PlainTalk extension enables Web pages to, in effect, "listen" and "read." Websites that support speech-recognition plug-ins make it possible for users to verbally command their browsers to link to another Web page. Speech-recognition plug-ins will work only if you have a microphone (which is bundled with most Macs) and you need to install the PlainTalk components. You can learn more about PlainTalk from Apple's home page at *www.apple.com*. Look for the search engine on their home page, enter the words **plain talk** in the search window, and then click on the "Search" button.

EXPERIENCE INTERACTIVE MULTIMEDIA WITH SHOCKWAVE

Shockwave plug-ins provide you with the capability of accessing movies and interactive images created with Macromedia's Macromedia Shockwave and Flash programs. You can download the latest release of Shockwave by visiting Macromedia's Download Center at *www.macromedia.com/software/downloads/* or *sdc.shockwave.com/shockwave/download/*. Macromedia Authorware Web Player is also available as a free download from this site.

One application of Shockwave that I found particularly interesting was the FrogSpeller created by Yue-Ling Wong. This Shockwave file combines the Frogger game, which requires good eye-and-hand coordination, with the Hangman spelling game. Librarians that are looking for a good Shockwave site that demonstrates interactive multimedia to both children and adults should check this one out at *www.knowledgebydesign.com/cg2/cg2.html*

VIEWING VIRTUAL REALITY

A Web publishing format called VRML (pronounced "ver-mul") has helped bring 3–D to the Internet. VRML, which stands for Virtual Reality Modeling Language, enables programmers to create virtual worlds with interactive animations. VRML has the potential to extend the Web's resource discovery tools beyond directories and search engines to an environment where you can navigate three-dimensional sites intuitively by walking through the site. A VRML world can be interactive and animated, and include hyperlinks to other Web documents.

The current revision of the VRML standard is called VRML97. The official name is "International Standard ISO/IEC 14772–1:1997". While VRML97 was a draft international standard, it was known as VRML 2.0. VRML 1.0 is an older version of the standard.

Before you can view 3–D online, you need to install a VRML plug-in or stand-alone VRML browser. In this section, I briefly describe some of the tools that are available for viewing virtual reality on the Web. For additional information, go to the VRML Repository *www.web3d.org/vrml/vrml.htm* maintained by the Web3D Consortium. Here you find VRML education, information, documentation, software development resources, authoring, and browsing tools. VRML 1.0 and VRML97 browsers or plug-ins are available for most platforms at this site.

Cosmo Player is a Netscape and Internet Explorer 4.0 compatible plug-in from Cosmo Software and can be found at the VRML Repository or *www.cai.com/cosmo/*. WorldView by Intervista Software is another free virtual reality viewer. You can find it by searching *home.netscape.com/plugins/search_pi.html*. If you have trouble finding either of these viewers at the recommended sites, use your favorite search engine to search on the phrase **vrml viewer**.

The Cosmo Player runs in your Web browser as a plug-in letting you interact with 3–D worlds and objects and is supported by both Windows and Macintosh. To run Cosmo Player properly, make sure Internet Explorer is configured to enable ActiveX controls and plug-ins. In Internet Explorer 3.0, make sure the "Enable ActiveX controls and plug-ins" item is checked on the "View|Options|Security" page. In Internet Explorer 4, if you configured your browser for a "Custom" security level, make sure the "Run ActiveX controls and plugins" item is enabled.

If you are not sure whether your browser is equipped to view VRML, go to *cic. nist.gov/vrml/vbdetect.html* and find out. This site is designed to detect VRML browsers.

One interesting application of VRML can be found at *cic.nist.gov/vrml/equip.html* where you can interact with several pieces of construction equipment including an excavator, tower crane, and dump truck. This site gives you the opportunity to see how well you can handle the equipment driving over rough terrain and moving objects.

EXPLORING JAVA SITES

Java is a programming language that is used to create small mini-programs called *applets*. Applets on the Web cannot run by themselves, they need a compatible Web browser like Netscape Navigator or Internet Explorer in order for them to run. These small, single-purpose programs can be such things as a Web page wizard where you fill out a form and click on a button which in turn translates all of your input into a custom Web page. Or it might be a loan calculator, painting program, or games like those made available at *www.funschool.com/*.

More sophisticated applets enable you try out different options on Land Rovers; changing the color, adding a roof rack, or steel running boards. The JavaMan applet, developed by the Neurovisualization Laboratory at the University of Virginia, allows you to view sequential MRI images of a 3–D brain. Cherwell Scientific has developed a tool called ChemSymphony that uses applets to assist in visualizing molecules and processing chemistry data.

Sometimes you may not know that you have encountered a Java applet. If you see something animated on the page, such as a stock tickertape scrolling across the bottom of the screen or some other blinking or scrolling text, you have probably encountered a Java applet.

To explore Java applets, you can go just about anywhere on the Web, but here are a two select sites to explore:

java.sun.com/applets/—Here you can find samples, resources, and free applets available for use on your own Website.

gamelan.earthweb.com/—This site offers discussion, free downloads, reference library, glossary, and an opportunity to "ask the experts."

A sampling of the educational Java applets that can be accessed at JavaSoft include these:

- 3–D Chemical Models
  http://java.sun.com/applets/applets/MoleculeViewer/example1.html
- Fractal Figures
  http://java.sun.com/applets/applets/Fractal/example1.html
- Animated Sorting Algorithms
  http://java.sun.com/applets/applets/SortDemo/example1.html

Part V

COMMUNICATION SYSTEMS

The Internet impacts individuals, libraries and other organizations, communities, and whole regions by changing the way people communicate with one another. E-mail, Free-Nets, mailing lists, Usenet news, and IRC are examples of communication systems on the Internet that make it possible for individuals to share information any time, anywhere. In Part V, e-mail, mailing lists, and Usenet news are introduced.

Electronic mail, or e-mail, is the Internet's most popular service. E-mail is electronic messages that are transferred automatically between computers. Transfers may take place over telephone lines using modems and/or over computer networks. E-mail gives you the means to send and receive messages to and from just about anyone with access to the Internet. Your message may consist of text only, or you can attach files to it; for example, images and audio clips. Since the last edition of this book was published, new issues have become concerns for e-mail, including unwanted spam and malicious viruses that spread via e-mail.

A mailing list is a group or "list" of people with e-mail addresses. A message from one person on the list can be sent to everyone else on the list. The person sending the message has only to send one message rather than a lot of individual messages to a whole bunch of people. It's difficult to estimate just how many mailing lists are in existence. Liszt, a popular online mailing list directory at *www.liszt.com/*, currently has in its main directory over 90,000 mailing lists discussing every imaginable topic.

Usenet newsgroups are electronic bulletin boards on which millions of people exchange ideas by leaving messages. Newsgroups are the coffee houses, meeting halls, and bulletin boards of the Internet. Some newsgroups remain active for years, while others disappear without ever getting off the ground. You may find over 10,000 newsgroups to choose from at any given point in time.

E-mail

Electronic mail, or *e-mail*, is the most widely used service on the Internet. E-mail enables people to exchange electronic messages much as they would using conventional mail, but with certain added conveniences. In Chapter 23 I cover the essentials of using the Internet mail service and explain its underlying protocols. Along with the basics, I show you how to deal with junk mail, also known as *spam*, how to protect yourself against e-mail viruses, and maintain your privacy with anonymous remailers and encryption.

THE BASICS OF HOW E-MAIL WORKS

The standardized system for delivering Internet mail is called *Simple Mail Transfer Protocol (SMTP)*. SMTP is the part of the TCP/IP protocol suite that makes it possible for an individual with one computer system to exchange e-mail with someone who has an entirely different computer system. This protocol describes how e-mail messages are to be handled during delivery and what their format should be.

E-MAIL ADVANTAGES

One of the more notable conveniences is the speed with which e-mail travels. E-mail messages travel on high-speed networks and usually arrive at their destination within minutes of being sent. As a result, Internet users have come to refer to the regular postal service as *snail mail* when comparing it to the speed at which e-mail travels.

Unlike a paper letter, e-mail can be stored in file form on a computer, which in turn enables you to pull it into a word processor for editing and printing. E-mail can be for-

---

Online Resource

Details on SMTP are explained in J. Postel's *Simple Mail Transfer Protocol, RFC 821*, USC/Information Sciences Institute, August 1982. (To access a hyperlinked archive of RFCs and FAQs, go to *www.faqs.org/rfcs/.*)

---

warded easily to another person without the inconvenience and cost of making a paper copy, stuffing it in an envelope, affixing a stamp, addressing it, and taking it to the post office. Further, one e-mail message can be directed easily to multiple recipients. No more printing out multiple paper copies and mailing each one separately.

Location and distance are irrelevant factors when you are communicating via e-mail. If you live in a remote area of the Ozark Mountains and have access to the Internet e-mail system, you find that it is just as easy to send a message to a colleague in Switzerland as it is to send one to your closest neighbor just a hollering distance away.

In addition to these conveniences, e-mail also serves as a powerful tool for discovering and transmitting various kinds of information. You can attach files to your messages including video and audio clips, still images, and word-processing documents. Because of its ability to access FTP servers, e-mail can be used to download text and binary files. E-mail can even be drafted as HTML documents and sent as Web pages over the Internet.

TRANSPORT AND USER AGENTS

Two different operations are involved when you exchange e-mail. One of these operations involves a program called a *transport agent* that runs in the background without direct contact from the user. This is the program that is actually responsible for sending and receiving e-mail via the SMTP standard. The Internet mail system works because every network that is part of the Internet has at least one computer that runs a transport agent.

The other operation involves a program called a *user agent*. This is a program that serves as your interface with the Internet e-mail system. Many different user agents are available, and each one looks and feels a little different from the next. All the various

---

Online Resources

For further reading on the subject of multimedia data such as bitmaps, voice, and graphics being transported via computer mail, see J. Postel's *A Structured Format for Transmission of Multi-Media Documents, RFC 767*, USC/Information Sciences Institute, August 1980; J. Reynolds, J. Postel, A. Katz, G. Finn and A. DeSchon, *The DARPA Experimental Multimedia Mail System*, IEEE Computer, Vol. 18, No.10, October 1985; and *MIME (Multipurpose Internet Mail Extensions) Mechanisms for Specifying and Describing the Format of Internet Message Bodies, RFC 1341*, PS, June 1992. (To access a hyperlinked archive of RFCs and FAQs, go to *www.faqs.org/rfcs/.*)

---

user agents offer mail management features for handling basic tasks such as reading messages, composing messages, sending messages, deleting messages, and so on.

SENDING AND RECEIVING MESSAGES

The process of sending and receiving e-mail is fairly simple. The operation begins when you enter a command that starts the user program (user agent). The user program provides an editor you use to compose the message you want to send. The user agent then sends the completed message to a mailer program (transfer agent). The mailer program works behind the scenes and is responsible for transmitting the message to the remote host.

The remote host's mailer program receives the message and stores it in a file system. The last step of the process comes when the person to whom the message was addressed receives it and views the message by running his or her own user program.

The file system where messages are stored is called the user's *mailbox*. If you send a message to a user who doesn't have a mailbox at the Internet address you specify, the transport agent at that address creates an error report and sends it back to you as a message. When this happens, your mail is described as having been *bounced back*.

E-mail enables you to connect not only with other Internet hosts, but also with non-Internet systems through *mail gateways*, special-purpose computers that transfer information to and from the Internet. The non-Internet systems include such networks as FidoNet, and UUCP Mail Networks. FidoNet is a worldwide network made up of hobbyists using PCs to send and receive e-mail and download files. UUCP, or UNIX-to-UNIX Copy Program (or Protocol), is a set of rules used to send e-mail and Usenet news between UNIX computers.

ANATOMY OF AN E-MAIL MESSAGE

E-mail messages contain lines of text that follow a certain format. As illustrated in the sample message below, the opening section consists of a list of field names (each of which is followed by a colon) and one or more items of information. These field names are referred to as *message headers*, or collectively as a *message header*.

The message header is followed by another section called the *body* of the message. The message body, which is separated from the header by a blank line, is where the actual text is entered by the person composing the message. You do not see the header as part of the message when you compose it. The header is attached automatically when you send your message. A sample header is shown in Figure 23–1.

You don't need to understand what every field in the header means before you can use the Internet mail system effectively. The following brief descriptions provide basic definitions of the different header fields.

- The "From" field describes the person who sent the message. Note that e-mail addresses consist of two parts separated by the at (@) sign. The part that comes before the @ is usually the username—the name that a person uses when logging on. The part after the @ is the domain name.

Figure 23–1: An example of an e-mail message's header

Received: from SpoolDir by BROOK (Mercury 1.44); 2 Jul 00 04:37:08 -600
Return-path: <4ap4MMjhD@msn.com>
Received: from imail.maxcontrols.com (209.71.90.125) by brook.asumh.edu
(Mercury 1.44) with ESMTP;
 2 Jul 00 04:37:05 -600
Received: from dOSINgdv5 [216.123.100.84] by imail.maxcontrols.com
 (SMTPD32–6.00) id AD1ECC400B6; Sun, 02 Jul 2000 05:36:30 -0400
DATE: 02 Jul 00 5:25:19 AM
FROM: 4ap4MMjhD@msn.com
Message-ID: <cAq5Hn2R16>
TO: acbenson@foobar.com
SUBJECT: Your Driving Record - Details

- The "Return-Path" field provides information about the address of the person who originated the message.
- The "Received" field tells when the message was received by a particular computer, the path that the message took, and which mail programs were being used. In Figure 23–1, Mercury Mail was being used. Depending on how many computers handled your message along the way, your message header may show one or more of these Received fields.
- The "Date" field shows the time and date the message was sent. After the Date field, there is another From field which is different from the first From field in that it gives the real name of the person who sent the message.
- The "Subject" field is specified by the sender and summarizes what the message is about.
- The "To" field gives the names of all the people who are to receive copies of the message. If the message is sent only to you, only your address appears here.
- The "Message-id" field is meaningless to us humans, but it does contain a unique identifier that computers find interesting.
- The "CC" field shows the address of anyone who has received a copy of the message.
- The "Status" field tells the status of the message. "R" means the message is being read for the first time; "N" means the message is new; "O" means the message is old; and "U" means the message is unread.

Online Resource

The format of e-mail messages is discussed in D. Cocker's *Standard for the Format of ARPA Internet Text Messages, RFC 822*, Department of Electrical Engineering, University of Delaware, August 1982. (To access a hyperlinked archive of RFCs and FAQs, go to *www.faqs.org/rfcs/*.)

TRACING JUNK MAIL

Learning to decode mail headers can help you understand the source from which your message was delivered. Programs like Sam Spade can make that job easier. Sam Spade is a freeware program that helps you track down unsolicited mail. In addition, Sam Spade is a Website that offers free services that can help you decipher mail headers by adding meaning to their content. You can download a free copy of the Sam Spade decoding utility at *www.samspade.org*. It is simple to use. Copy your header from your e-mail message and paste it into Sam Spade.

To view your e-mail header in Netscape Messenger, open a message and click on "View" and then select "Page Source."

Sam Spade offers several tools, including these:

- *Ping* enables you to test whether a host on the network is alive and how long it takes for information packets to get there and return.
- *Nslookup* gives you a computers IP address when presented with the domain name, or the domain name when presented with the IP address.
- *Whois* lists information associated with the entity that owns the domain name you are querying.
- *IP block whois* can tell you who owns a block of IP addresses.
- *Dig* requests a DNS server for all the information it has about a host.
- *Traceroute* traces the path information takes from your computer to a remote computer.
- *Finger* checks on user information stored on a Unix system. For security reasons, the *finger* service has been disabled on many Unix systems.

Figure 23–2: Sample mail header before it is analyzed by Sam Spade freeware

Received: from SpoolDir by BROOK (Mercury 1.44); 2 Jul 00 16:05:16 -600
Return-path: <acbenson@star-host.com>
Received: from westhost.westhost.net (209.150.128.113) by brook.asumh.edu
(Mercury 1.44) with ESMTP;
  2 Jul 00 16:05:09 -600
Received: from Allen.asumh.edu ([150.208.145.123])
        by westhost.westhost.net (8.8.5/8.8.5) with ESMTP id QAA06157
        for <acbenson@brook.asumh.edu>; Sun, 2 Jul 2000 16:00:53 -0500
Message-ID: <395FAC84.ECB8CF9D@star-host.com>
Date: Sun, 02 Jul 2000 15:56:36 -0500
From: "Allen C. Benson" <acbenson@star-host.com>
X-Mailer: Mozilla 4.0 [en] (Win95; U)
MIME-Version: 1.0
To: acbenson@brook.asumh.edu
Subject: Confirming Meeting Date
X-Priority: 3 (Normal)
Content-Type: text/plain; charset=us-ascii
Content-Transfer-Encoding: 7bit

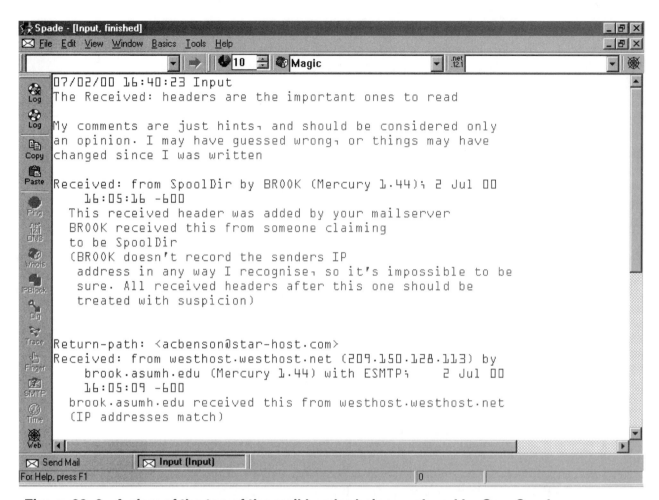

Figure 23–3: A view of the top of the mail header being analyzed by Sam Spade

Online Resources

If you are having trouble viewing your full e-mail header, try sending a message to the echo processor at Technical University Berlin, Germany *echo@tu-berlin.de*. An *echo processor* is an automatic response program that you can use to test whether your e-mail is working. You send a blank message to the address shown above and in a few minutes you receive an automated response. Another autoresponder to try is *ping@stamper. itconsult.co.uk*. In both instances, the message sent back to you contains a copy of the full message header the autoresponder stripped from your e-mail. The autoresponder at *test@alphanet.ch* also responds with a verbose header and it includes a rather humorous message.

- *SMTP VRFY* command asks mail servers whether an e-mail address is valid and whether it is being forwarded.
- *E-mail header analysis* helps you determine the source of forged e-mail.
- *Blacklist lookups* crosschecks the host addresses in your e-mail header against the Realtime Blackhole List *mail-abuse.org/rbl/*, Dialup User List *mail-abuse.org/dul/*, and Relay Spam Source List *mail-abuse.org/rss/*.

The message header displayed in Figure 23–2 was copied from an e-mail message and pasted into Sam Spade. A portion of the output from Sam Spade's interpretation is presented in Figure 23–3.

SPAM EATERS

To mass distribute an e-mail message to many different mailing lists, individuals, or newsgroups, is called *spamming*. In most instances, the people who get spammed are not interested in receiving the e-mail and it was inappropriate sending it to them in the first place.

You can address the problem of spam in a number of different ways. Some ISPs (Internet service providers) offer spam filters as part of their services. MindSpring *www.mindspring.com* is one such company. If your ISP doesn't, you can try using Brightmail, which is free, or a program like Novasoft SpamKiller, which can be purchased for $29.95.

Brightmail doesn't delete your spam, but it does move it to your Brightmail Inbox. You get a weekly report that lists the spam that has been forwarded there. You can learn more about Brightmail's services at *www.brightmail.com*. Novasoft SpamKiller is a commercial application that custom filters. Using a Filter Wizard, you can filter on any part of a message including the sender's address, the subject line, or the body of the message. SpamKiller costs $29.95, but you can download it and try it out for 30 days before you have to buy.

Microsoft Outlook has the capability of searching for commonly used phrases in junk mail and can automatically move junk mail from your Inbox to your Deleted Items folder, or any other folder you designate. The list of terms that Outlook uses to filter questionable e-mail messages can be found in a file called *Filters.txt* located in the *c:\Program Files\Microsoft Office\Office directory*. The first few lines of this file are displayed in Figure 23–4.

MICROSOFT OUTLOOK EXPRESS FILTERING

If you are running Outlook Express, you can use the built-in filtering options to stop spam, coming through either e-mail or newsgroups. Click on "Tools|Message|Rules Mail" (or "News"). In Mail or News, you can set up rules by checking boxes for 1) the conditions for your rule—for example, where the From line contains people, or where the Subject line contains specific words—and 2) the actions for your rule—for example, move the message to a specified folder, or delete the message, etc. You define values as the last step; for example, if you are filtering by names in the From line, you list the names one at a time that you wish to filter.

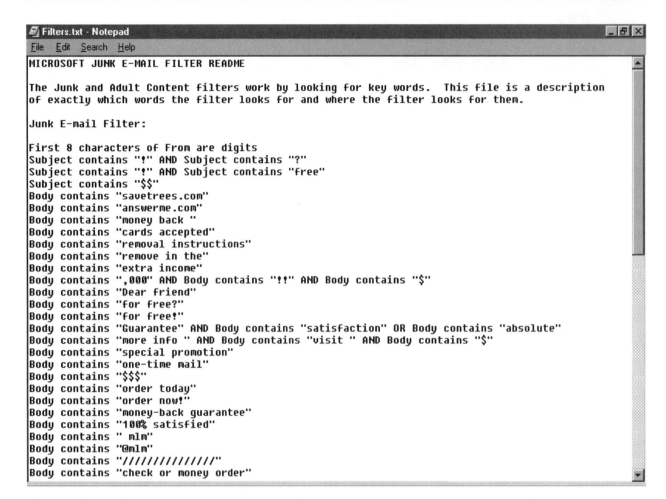

```
Filters.txt - Notepad                                                    _ 8 X
File  Edit  Search  Help
MICROSOFT JUNK E-MAIL FILTER README

The Junk and Adult Content filters work by looking for key words.  This file is a description
of exactly which words the filter looks for and where the filter looks for them.

Junk E-mail Filter:

First 8 characters of From are digits
Subject contains "!" AND Subject contains "?"
Subject contains "!" AND Subject contains "free"
Subject contains "$$"
Body contains "savetrees.com"
Body contains "answerme.com"
Body contains "money back "
Body contains "cards accepted"
Body contains "removal instructions"
Body contains "remove in the"
Body contains "extra income"
Body contains ",000" AND Body contains "!!" AND Body contains "$"
Body contains "Dear friend"
Body contains "for free?"
Body contains "for free!"
Body contains "Guarantee" AND Body contains "satisfaction" OR Body contains "absolute"
Body contains "more info " AND Body contains "visit " AND Body contains "$"
Body contains "special promotion"
Body contains "one-time mail"
Body contains "$$$"
Body contains "order today"
Body contains "order now!"
Body contains "money-back guarantee"
Body contains "100% satisfied"
Body contains " mlm"
Body contains "@mlm"
Body contains "///////////////"
Body contains "check or money order"
```

Figure 23–4: Some of the suspect words and phrases included in the *Filters.txt* used by Microsoft Outlook

STOPPING SPAM WITH HOTMAIL AND YAHOO!

Both Hotmail and Yahoo! mail systems enable you to filter messages based on name, subject, and address. Suspect e-mail can be moved to any folder you choose, including the trash folder. In addition, Yahoo! allows you to filter text contained in the body of the message.

To filter messages in Hotmail, click on the "Options" located on the toolbar and then select "Filters." You are given the option of setting 11 different filtering profiles. In each one, you can choose a mail header field (subject, name, or address) and then specify how specific words are to be handled and where the suspect e-mail should be sent. By going back to "Options" and clicking on "Inbox Protector," you can list e-mail addresses you want to block. To filter messages in Yahoo! Mail, click on "Options," and then select "Filters, Create."

E-MAIL ETIQUETTE

E-mail is a medium of communication that mixes two older forms of communication. In one sense it's like writing a letter, but in another sense it's like making a phone call—somewhat spontaneous and informal. If you apply common courtesy and the Golden Rule, which is "do unto others as you would have them do unto you," you should have no problems. Keep in mind that although it may seem like you are talking to a computer, you are indeed talking to other people when using communication services like e-mail.

SMILEY FACES

After your first few days of e-mail discussion, you'll no doubt learn something about *smileys*, expressions you can send in your e-mail messages. Those of you who were raised during the time of flowing ink and writing paper may find it a little odd at first, but over time you get used to it. :-) (Tilt your head 90 degrees to the left to see the two eyes, nose, and smile.)

There are hundreds of smileys representing different emotions and facial expressions, such as winking ;-) and surprise. :-0. If you'd like more information on smileys, run a keyword search on the words **smiley faces** or **emoticons** once you are connected to the Internet. AltaVista, a Web search engine described in Chapter 12, is sure to turn up some interesting hits. You can view dozens of emoticons at the ComputerUser High-Tech Dictionary site at *www.computeruser.com/resources/dictionary/emoticons.html*.

INAPPROPRIATE ACTIVITIES

Some activities on the Internet will bring the wrath of others upon you. *Flaming* occurs when someone sends an angry e-mail response. A flame might just be a strong statement or opinion. It might also include "!SHOUTING!," which is text typed in uppercase letters, or it may include profane language.

SPEWING AND BLATHERING

After spending some time online in the newsgroups and mailing lists, you may begin to recognize these two character types: spewers and blatherers. *Spewing* occurs when you're on a newsgroup or in a chat room and one of the participants goes on and on typing the same thing repeatedly. Spewers think that what they have to say is interesting or relevant and they say it as often as possible (to everyone else's dismay). *Blatherers* are people that have a hard time getting to the point. They may blather for pages, going on and on about a simple thought that could have been stated clearly in a single paragraph.

POPULAR UNIX E-MAIL PROGRAMS

Providing complete documentation for every available e-mail program is impractical and beyond the scope of this book. If you work on a Unix system, determine which software is running on your system and then obtain whatever support documentation is available.

To learn more about a mail program called elm, for example, you could enter the UNIX **man** (manual) command followed by the name **elm**. UNIX displays a brief description of the program and its command line options. In many cases, the online help screens in the mail program constitute your main source of documentation.

UNIX systems are the most widely used systems on the Internet and two of the more popular e-mail programs you find running on UNIX accounts are elm and Pine.

Pine is designed for inexperienced users and offers a simple and straightforward menu from which to pick commands. One of Pine's more notable features is that it has MIME capabilities (Multipurpose Internet Mail Extensions), which allows it to send and receive multimedia e-mail. Elm, like Pine, is also a full-screen, interactive mail system. Although Elm is easy to use, it offers advanced mail management features. For a detailed explanation of how to use Pine, see pp. 282–287 in *Connecting Kids and the Internet*, Second Edition, by Allen C. Benson and Linda M. Fodemski (1999. New York: Neal-Schuman Publishers, Inc.).

SETTING PREFERENCES FOR E-MAIL IN NETSCAPE COMMUNICATOR

If you have a direct connection or SLIP/PPP account and you want to use Netscape Communicator for managing your e-mail, you can use these instructions for setting the preferences in Netscape Navigator 4.0:

1. Pull down the "Edit" menu, click on "Preferences" and the Preferences window opens. Now expand the category "Mail & Groups" to see five sub-categories including Identity, Messages, Mail Server, Groups Server, and Directory. While you are in the main category you can set your preferences for quoted text and threading.

    When you reply to a message, by default the original text is included in your reply and quoted by placing a greater than (>) symbol at the beginning of each line. In the "Mail and Groups" window you can specify the font size and style of the quoted text in your message. Click on the "Messages" sub-category to specify whether you want your replies to quote original messages and whether you want copies of messages sent to yourself or others.

2. Click on the "Identity" sub-category and enter your name and e-mail address. You establish what your user ID is when you set up your account, but the domain name that follows the @ sign will be provided to you by your ISP.

    If you'd like a signature attached to all of the e-mail you send, insert the pathname where your signature file can be found in the "Signature File" field. *Signature files* are a few lines of information (generally not over four) about you that comes at the end of every e-mail message you send. They include informa-

---

Online Resource

For a list of answers to questions that have been posted in Netscape discussion groups, see The Netscape Unofficial FAQ page, *www.ufaq.org/*. FAQs are organized under these headings:

FAQs for all versions
FAQs for Navigator 3.0x and below ONLY
FAQs for Communicator 4.x and Navigator 4.0x ONLY
FAQs for Macintosh 68K and PPC
FAQs for UNIX - All Platforms
Fixes, Patches, New and Old DLL's, etc.

---

tion like name, e-mail address, and Web home page address if you have one. You can also include your postal mailing address, phone, and fax numbers.

To create a signature file, use a text editor and save the file as text only with line breaks. Whenever you send an e-mail message, Communicator looks for the signature file and automatically attaches it to the end of your message. If you don't want to create a signature file, this same window gives you the option of attaching your Address Book Card.

3. Click on the "Messages" sub-category and set your message properties.
4. Click on the "Mail Server" sub-category. This displays the "Mail Server" panel. Before you can send e-mail, Netscape Communicator has to know where to access your SMTP server, which is a program assigned to processing all of your outgoing e-mail. SMTP stands for Simple Mail Transfer Protocol and is a set of rules for distributing e-mail around the Internet. Ask your ISP (Internet service provider) for the Internet address of your SMTP server and enter it in the "Outgoing Mail (SMTP) Server" field.
5. Before you can receive e-mail, Netscape Communicator has to know where to find your POP3 server. This is a computer dedicated to storing your incoming mail. POP3 stands for Version 3 of the Post Office Protocol and is a set of rules for reading e-mail from servers. You also need to ask your ISP what the Internet address is for your POP3 server and then enter it in the "Incoming Mail Server" field.

Netscape can also work with IMAP servers. IMAP stands for Internet Message Access Protocol. When you open your Inbox using IMAP, you download only the headers of messages to your local PC. The messages remain on the server.

MAILING BINARY DATA

SMTP describes how messages that contain ASCII characters can be sent and received. Another protocol currently in development is called *Multipurpose Internet Mail Extensions (MIME)*. MIME enables the transfer of binary data through the Internet mail system. The user attaches a binary file, often referred to as *richtext*, to a message containing regular text, and then transports the entire message using SMTP. In order for this system to work, however, both the sender and the receiver must be running user mail programs that support MIME. Most current mail programs that run on PCs and Macs support MIME, including those that are incorporated in Web browsers such as Netscape Navigator and Microsoft's Internet Explorer.

ENCODING BINARY DATA AS TEXT

Another way to send binary data through the mail system is to encode the binary data as text. This encoded text is then sent as a regular message. The recipient decodes the message and converts it back into its original binary format. This is a common method of transferring binary files such as images for those who have shell account access to the Internet.

A program called UUENCODE is used to encode the binary data as text, and another program called UUDECODE is used to change it back into a binary format.

If you have software (a binary file) that you want to send to a friend on the Internet, and you have to do it via e-mail on a dial-up UNIX shell account, for example, you could UUENCODE the binary file and upload it to your local host as an ASCII text file. Because the file is an ASCII file comprised of printable characters, you can incorporate it into your e-mail file and send it to your friend. When the mail file arrives at its destination, your friend downloads it to his or her personal computer and uses UUDECODE to translate the coded version of the file back into its binary state. If the file is extremely large, the coded version is automatically sent in more than one mail message. Your friend must save the multiple messages to a single file and keep them in their correct order.

The computer output that follows was extracted from a UUENCODEd document before translation back into its binary state:

```
——the file starts directly below this line——
begin 666 WAIS.res
M*#;;*$#;;W5R8V4*R4%LRII;97$S:6]N(:#:5%I%<"UN86U%((")S;F5;V:L'O+F5N<RY
M<B(#*)#IT8W M<&]R="R R,3.*#ID871;A8F%S92UN86U%(")B:6(M9&9UI+65N
M<RUR<B(#*)#I);W-T(# N,# @"'B Z8;V]S=;"UU;;FET#)#IF<F5E( H@.FUA:6YT
M86EN97(*#@(F-(;;W5N971<VYE:VMA<BYE;:G,N9G(B"'B Z9&5SS8W))I<Ô1;I;VX@
M(@I397)V97((@8W)E871;E9"!W:71H(%==!E<F%96%)92S#@;X<F5L96%S92 X(&(U+C$@;VX@
.
end
——the UUENCODED file ended just above this line——
```

A UUENCODEd file always starts with the word "begin," followed by some numbers (the file-mode) and then the UUENCODEd file name, in this case "WAIS.res." The encoded data ends with a line containing a closing quotation mark, followed by a line containing the word "end."

If you tried to read this file in its original binary state with a text editor, you wouldn't be able to because binary data consists of nonprintable characters. This example is readable and shows what the binary data looks like after it has been translated into a file consisting of printable characters.

Online Resource

A detailed introduction to decoding files is presented by Frank Pilhofer at Website *www.uni-frankfurt.de/~fp/uudeview/Introduction.html.*

OTHER DECODING SOFTWARE

Programs for coding and decoding binary files are available via anonymous FTP. To find out where these files reside on the Internet, use the Archie service (explained in Chapter 15) to search on the character strings **uuencode** or **uudecode**; or use a Web search engine, such as directhit.com. Another decoder that is a user-friendly alternative to the standard uudecode is UUdeview. Versions of UUdeview are available for UNIX, DOS, and Windows. You can download this freeware from the UUDeview Website at *zeus.infomatik.uni-frankfurt.de/~fp/uudeview/.*

Mac users can try using uulite 2.0. This utility makes uuencoding and uudecoding files quite simple and it includes an extensive online help file and also a tutorial on how to read Usenet news.

FREE E-MAIL ACCOUNTS

When the Internet first went commercial in the early 1990s, free e-mail was unheard of. Now it seems that everyone is offering free e-mail accounts. Hotmail is one of the largest and most popular services and has been around since the previous edition of this book. Web-based e-mail accounts (as opposed to that e-mail account your system administrator gave you at work) allow you to easily access your account from any computer in the world that has access to the Web. Whether you are using your desktop at home, a friend's computer, or even a computer in the "Internet Room" at the next ALA convention, you can access your Hotmail account and check your Inbox.

You can configure Hotmail to access your POP e-mail account(s), too. To set up this feature, go to the tool bar and click on "Options" and select "POP Mail." Enter your main account's server name, userID, and password. It probably isn't necessary to change the port number or server timeout settings. If you also want to check this account with another mail client, such as Netscape Communicator, click on "Leave Messages on POP Server." When you want to see if you have mail on your POP accounts, click on "POP Mail" in your Inbox.

Hotmail, and any of the other free e-mail programs available, offer librarians a unique opportunity to present patrons with their own, personal e-mail accounts and it can be done at no extra cost to either the library or the patron. If you're looking for a good public relations idea to help promote your Internet services, this may be it.

Normally, in order to offer patrons their own personal e-mail accounts you have to do the following things: a) set up individual dial-up accounts for them; b) let them share existing accounts; or c) assign them a login name and password on your LAN and let them use the library's POP and SMTP servers. The big difference with Hotmail is this: everything—including the address book, the signature file, the "In" folder, the "Sent" folder, and any other folder the user might create—resides on the Hotmail server. This goes for any of the other free e-mail accounts, too.

Registration is simple and shouldn't take more than a minute: Connect to Hotmail's home page at *www.hotmail.com*, choose a login name and password, provide name and address, and answer some simple user-profile questions. Your e-mail address follows the format *login_name@hotmail.com.*

Other popular free e-mail accounts include Yahoo! Mail *www.yahoo.com*, RocketMail *www.rocketmail.com*, Excite Mail *www.excite.com*, and Mail.com *www.mail.com*.

SENDING HOTMAIL USING OUTLOOK EXPRESS 5.0

Hotmail is Microsoft's Web-based e-mail service and can be used with Outlook Express 5.0. If you are running Outlook Express 5.0 and have a Hotmail account, you can enjoy the benefits of Web-based e-mail along with the features of a specialized e-mail client like Outlook Express. Outlook Express is Microsoft's scaled-down version of Outlook and comes free as part of Internet Explorer.

To get started, select "Accounts" under the "Tools" menu. Create a new entry for an account by clicking on the "Add" button. Follow the instructions provided by the Connection Wizard. You need to have your POP and SMTP server addresses handy. Once you finish creating a Hotmail account in Outlook Express, you can use it like any other POP mail account. You can retrieve mail from Hotmail and store it on your local hard drive using Outlook Express's filtering options, etc.

USING ANONYMOUS REMAILERS

An *anonymous remailer* is a server on the Internet that operates as a middleman between you, the person sending the e-mail, and the receiver of the e-mail. The e-mail is sent anonymously. To maintain your anonymity, the remailer assigns you a unique ID and return address. A specialized remailer called a *cypherpunk remailer* doesn't use anonymous IDs. Instead, it strips the header information off your e-mail before it arrives at its destination. The ability to trace anonymous e-mail depends on the mail programs being used on your end and the recipient's end.

You can learn more about remailers by reading André Bacard's online FAQ at *www.andrebacard.com/remail.html*. For a comprehensive list of anonymous remailers and cypherpunk remailers, go to *anon.efga.org/*.

SECURITY AGAINST VIRUSES

E-mail viruses are serious business. They can literally render your computer useless by destroying files on your hard drive. E-mail viruses arrive as attachments in your e-mail and spread when you click on the attachment to open it. The virus can send a copy of itself to everyone in your Outlook address book. If the virus is well known by the words contained in the subject line, and you are familiar with the virus's name, you can avoid infection by deleting the file. However, more recent strains of e-mail viruses have demonstrated the ability to alter the words in the subject line each time it is sent to a new recipient.

Most antivirus applications these days offer some level of support against e-mail viruses. It's important to keep up with the latest versions of software and to continuously update your virus signature file to protect your computer against the thousands of computer viruses in circulation and against the new viruses that emerge between updates. Most antivirus software vendors update files each month. Outlook 2000 and Outlook 98 both have built-in protection against viruses that spread through mail attachments. In addition, they protect against worm viruses that replicate themselves using Outlook, such as Melissa.

When purchasing antivirus software with e-mail protection, look for programs that prevent you from accessing e-mail in your inbox that has certain file types attached to it. These file types include executables, batch files, or any other files that contain executable code. Remember, macros are programs within programs. Macros can be found in all major office applications like MS Word and Excel.

In addition, you should be prompted when an external program tries to get to your e-mail program's address book or send e-mail without your permission.

For a complete list of antivirus software vendors and their corresponding Websites, refer to the CD-ROM included with this book.

INSTRUCTIONS FOR SENDING E-MAIL ATTACHMENTS

Attachments are files that you *attach* to your e-mail message before sending it off to the recipient. Thanks to a protocol called MIME (Multipurpose Internet Mail Extension), and other types of encoding systems, such as Uuencode, you can attach various file types to your e-mail message including images, spreadsheets, documents, audio files, video clips, or any other type of file. The *encoding* process converts the file in its original form to text and the *decoding* process converts it back to its original state. The process for attaching files to e-mail varies depending on type of e-mail program you use. In general, here are the basic steps to follow for attaching files to a message:

1. Open your e-mail program and begin by composing a new e-mail message.
2. Click on the attachment icon (sometimes labeled "Attach") or click on the drop-down menu "Insert" and select "File."
3. Browse your hard disk or floppy disk (wherever the file is located) and find the file you want to attach. Usually there is a button to click on labeled "Browse." A window then opens that allows you to select the file you want to attach. When you find it, click on it and then click on the "OK" button. Most systems have a limit to how large the attachment can be.

Online Resources

Dr. Bob Rankin's "Accessing the Internet by E-mail" is a study in how to use Internet e-mail-only accounts to their fullest. To receive a free copy, send e-mail to *mail-server@rtfm.mit.edu* with the following command in the body of the message: **send usenet/news.answers/internet-services/access-via-e-mail.** In Europe, Asia, etc., send e-mail to *mailbase@mailbase.ac.uk* with the following command in the body of the message: **send lis-iss e-acess-inet.txt.**

4. After this process is complete, a message usually appears notifying you that the file has successfully been attached.
5. The last step is to send your message by clicking on the "Send" icon, or by choosing "Send" from the "File" pull-down menu.

Mailing Lists

Mailing lists provide librarians with an important tool for communicating with vendors, colleagues, and friends all around the world. A *mailing list* (also called a *discussion list*) is a group or list of people with e-mail addresses. A message from one person on the list can be sent to everyone else on the list. The person sending the message has only to send one message rather than a lot of individual messages to a whole bunch of people.

Thousands of these discussion lists are currently on the Internet sharing information on subjects as diverse as potato research, accordions, dentistry, IBM AS/400 computer systems, and fuzzy logic. A selective listing of mailing lists pertaining to libraries and librarians is presented in Appendix B of this book.

ANATOMY OF MAILING LISTS

Mailing lists are made up of three components:

1. Mailing lists have a *listowner*—the person who put the idea together and got the list up and running. When you first subscribe to a list, you'll be sent a general information sheet that includes the listowner's name and e-mail address. You can communicate with a listowner, but you'd send an e-mail message to him or her only if you were having a problem with the list.

Online Resource
To stay informed about new discussion lists, subscribe to NEW-LIST by sending the message **subscribe new-list <your name> to:** *majordomo@lists.oulu.fi.*

Online Resource

The Directory of Scholarly and Professional E-Conferences is available at *n2h2.com/KOVACS*. Diane K. Kovacs and others form the Directory Team responsible for maintaining the content of this directory. The Directory can be searched or it can be browsed alphabetically by name or by subject.

---

2. To help listowners manage their lists, they use specialized software called a *mailing-list manager*. When you subscribe to a mailing list, you don't tell the listowner you want to join; instead, you tell the mailing-list manager, which is a piece of software. When you want to drop your subscription, you notify the mailing-list manager. You communicate with the mailing-list manager when you go on vacation and have your e-mail discontinued temporarily. I introduce four common mailing-list managers in the next section.

3. The last component of a mailing list is the mailing list itself—everyone who subscribes. Depending on the list, the members may number less than a hundred or up into the thousands. The group as a whole is called a *list* and they have a name called a *listname*. For example, the folks that have joined together to discuss Total Quality Management in higher education call themselves TQM-L. Professional writers and those who aspire to write belong to a list called WRITERS.

As with all mailing lists, when you want to speak to other members of the list, you send your e-mail to an address that begins with the listname. These addresses all look basically the same. They begin with a listname, followed by the @ symbol, and then an Internet address—the same domain name address as the mailing list manager. For example, if you want to communicate an announcement to all subscribers of the WRITERS list, you address your e-mail message to *writers@vm1.nodak.edu*.

MAILING-LIST MANAGERS

Various mailing-list managers are used by listowners, but they all do basically the same thing: help manage e-mail messages and respond to commands sent in by subscribers. The commands vary slightly from one list manager to the next, so it is important to understand which type of list manager you are working with. Note that when subscribing to a list where the word "request" is included in the mailing-list manager's address, you may be dealing with a human, *not* a machine. In this section, I describe four common mailing-list managers.

LISTSERV

Because LISTSERV has been around a long time, many people use the term *LISTSERV* generically to mean any mailing-list manager. Keep in mind, however, that there are several different mailing-list managers in use and each has its own name. LISTSERV lists are electronic discussion lists that are supported by a special mailing-list manager called LISTSERV. *LISTSERV*, an abbreviation of *list server*, is an automated system that facilitates one-to-many communication and is also a general-purpose file server (an application providing users with access to files).

All LISTSERV addresses look basically the same. They begin with the word *listserv*, followed by the @ symbol, and then an Internet address. For example, *listserv@ukanvm. cc.ukans.edu* is the address for the LISTSERV that handles communications for TQM-L. WRITERS communications are handled by *listserv@vm1.nodak.edu*. If you sent a message to *listserv@vm1.nodak.edu* announcing an upcoming writers' workshop, the manager wouldn't know what you were talking about. Remember, it's just a piece of software that understands and responds to a finite set of commands.

LISTPROC

ListProc (short for *listprocessor*) is a mailing-list manager written by Anastasios Kotsikonas for UNIX systems. One unique feature offered by ListProc is its FAX command. When you use this command, ListProc sends an archived file to your fax machine. It is common, but not always the case, that ListProc mailing lists use addresses that begin with the word *listproc* as in *listproc@cern.org*.

DISTINGUISHING LISTSERV FROM LISTPROC

To make things confusing, some older versions of ListProc are called Listserv and their e-mail address starts out with the word *listserv*.

PUBLIB, a mailing list that discusses public library issues, is an example. To subscribe, you send your e-mail request to *listserv@nysernet.edu*. But actually, they're running ListProc software. If you send the wrong command to a mailing-list manager, the worst that can happen is that the mailing-list manager responds with an error message at which point you are told just who it is you are dealing with!

MAJORDOMO

Majordomo, developed by Brent Chapman, is one of the newer UNIX-based mailing-list managers. You can recognize a Majordomo mailing list by its address; each subscription address begins with the word *majordomo*.

"REQUEST" MAILING-LIST MANAGERS

Another type of mailing-list manager uses the word *request* in its address. The subscription e-mail address usually follows the format *<listname>-request@host.address*. It's safe to say that you'll be dealing with a human being when sending requests to these addresses. When writing to these addresses, just type out your request using plain English. If you end up getting a response from a machine, follow whatever instructions it

Online Resource
Lyris E-mail List Server is one of the newer programs available for managing mailing lists on the Internet. One feature that makes Lyris unique is that it allows you to subscribe and respond to messages using your Web browser window. To stay up to date on its development, check out the Lyris home page at *www.lyris.com*.

gives you and try again.

MAILING LIST COMMANDS

The commands for joining and leaving a mailing list are two of the most common commands used by list subscribers. In the section that follows, these commands and others are explained for each one of the mailing-list managers. Substitute the name of the list for "<listname>" and your first and last name for "<your_name>" below:

LISTSERV COMMANDS

     subscribe = **subscribe <listname> <your_name>**
     unsubscribe = **unsubscribe <listname> <your_name>**
     request digest format = **set <listname> digest**
     stop for vacation = **set <listname> nomail**
     resume delivery = **set <listname> mail**
     list of subscribers = **review <listname>**
     copy of your posts = **set <listname> repro**
     acknowledge posts = **set <listname> ack**

For more information on LISTSERV commands, send the command **help** in the body of an e-mail message to any LISTSERV mailing-list manager; for example, *listserv@ cunyvm.cuny.edu*.

LISTPROC COMMANDS

     subscribe = **subscribe <listname> <your_name>**
     unsubscribe = **unsubscribe <listname> <your_name>**
     stop for vacation = **set <listname> mail postpone**
     resume delivery = **set <listname> mail ack**
     request digest format = **set <listname> digest**
     cancel digest = **set <listname> mail ack**
     list of subscribers = **recipients <listname>**
     copy of your posts = **set <listname> mail ack**

For more information on ListProc commands, send the command **help** in the body of an e-mail message to any ListProc mailing list manager; for example, *listproc@ listproc.bqsu.edu*.

Online Resource

To search all of the LISTSERV mailing lists via e-mail for lists relating to a particular subject, send an e-mail message to any major LISTSERV list manager with the message **list global/<keyword>**, where "<keyword>" is the subject or topic for which you are looking.

> ### What is a Digest?
>
> Most mailing-list programs support digests. A *digest* is an archive of many e-mail messages contained in one message. The digest is sent out to anyone who is subscribed to the digest version of the list. The advantage of this is that you only receive one big e-mail message rather than a lot of individual posts. The address for subscribing to the digest version of a list can sometimes be different than the normal list address. Subscribe to whichever format is best for you.

MAJORDOMO COMMANDS

subscribe = **subscribe <listname> <your_e-mail_address>**
unsubscribe = **unsubscribe <listname> <your_e-mail_address>**
digest = **subscribe <listname>-digest**
cancel digest = **unsubscribe <listname>-digest**
list of subscribers = **who <listname>**
(There is no option for vacation mode.)

For more information on Majordomo commands, send the command **help** in the body of an e-mail message to any Majordomo mailing list manager; for example, *majordomo@forum.swarthmore.edu.*

MAILING LIST ETIQUETTE

After you join a discussion list, you should learn about any rules or customs they may have and abide by them. These rules may vary from one group to the next. You can use the following general guidelines for any discussion list you might join:

- Save the first information file or message you receive for future reference.
- If you use a signature block on the bottom of your e-mail, keep it short. Include your name, e-mail address, postal address, and phone number. Don't exceed more than six lines.
- Never send mailing-list manager commands to the discussion list. If you do, your commands are distributed to every active subscriber. Send your commands to the list manager (*listserv@domain, majordomo@domain,* etc.).
- Avoid flaming (launching personal attacks).
- Before responding to a message, think about whether it would be appropriate to respond privately to the individual who posted the message or publicly to everyone in the discussion list.
- Check your electronic mailbox daily and delete any unwanted messages immediately. Transfer to disk the messages you want to save.
- When you first subscribe to a list, it's a good practice to lurk for a while. *Lurking* is when you watch what is going on without actively participating in the discussion. This is a time to observe and understand the audience, determine whether you're interested in what subscribers are talking about, and become aware of any customs or practices that are particular to that list.

Online Resources

Vivian Neou publishes the *List of Lists* on her Website at *catalog.com/ vivian/*—a project originated by Rich Zellich back in the early days of the Internet. You can download an ASCII text version of this file called *interest-groups.txt* from *FTP://CRVAX.SRI.COM/NETINFO/INTEREST-GROUPS.TXT*. A link to this site is provided on Neou's home page. This site hasn't been updated since 1997, but it offers some interesting resources along with the historical listing of discussion lists. These include a list of Internet service providers that host mailing lists, descriptions of mailing-list software packages, and an expose written by Kat Nagel in 1994 on the natural life cycle of mailing lists.

MODERATED AND UNMODERATED LISTS

As I mentioned earlier, every mailing list has an administrator, usually one person, that performs daily maintenance by keeping the subscriber address list up-to-date. This person also deals with any network problems that may arise.

A list that is *moderated* means that all of the messages go through a *moderator* who decides which messages will be posted to the list. (One person may serve as both the administrator and moderator.) Moderators may pass messages along to the mailing-list manager software without modification, they may edit postings slightly, or they may reject an off-topic posting entirely.

Moderators also intervene when things get out of hand and *flame wars* erupt. If an individual subscriber becomes too obstinate, the moderator may ask him or her to unsubscribe or forcibly delete the subscriber from the list.

Moderators also manually bring several messages together creating one neat package called a *digest*. Some even include a table of contents along with the digest. (Digesting can also be performed as an automatic function of the software.)

Unmoderated mailing lists may distribute a lot of redundant, boring messages. You may have to spend some time looking through every message in order to find a gem.

BASIC COMMANDS FOR RETRIEVING FILES

Some discussion lists archive past messages or other files and an index of these files can be retrieved by sending an e-mail request to the mailing-list manager. This section describes how to retrieve indexes and specific files.

Send commands in the body of an e-mail message to the mailing-list manager address. Leave the subject line blank.

Your e-mail request may fail if a particular discussion list requires that you subscribe before allowing you access to their database. In those instances, you are sent a message stating something like "You are not authorized to GET file <filename> from filelist NOTEBOOK."

If you'd still like to search the database, take a moment to subscribe, conduct your search, and then unsubscribe when your work is complete.

LISTSERV COMMANDS FOR RETRIEVING FILES

index <listname>—Sends you a list of archived files for the list name you designated. Send your request to the LISTSERV site where the list originates. These files usually are monthly notebooks containing all of the correspondence that has taken place between list members. Each entry on this list includes a file name and file type.
get <file_name> <file_type>—Retrieves a specific file.

LISTPROC COMMANDS FOR RETRIEVING FILES

To retrieve a list of all files contained in the PUBLIB mailing list's archive, for example, use the index command in the format **index publib listproc/publib –all**.

To retrieve a particular file, use the get command in the format **get publib listproc/publib <file_name>**.

For example, if you were interested in retrieving a file called "Appreciation of Libraries" and it is numbered 940202, you would send this command: **get publib listproc/publib 940202**.

MAJORDOMO COMMANDS FOR RETRIEVING FILES

The command "index <listname>" retrieves a list of available files. The command "get <listname> <file_name>" retrieves a specific file.

MAILING LIST DIRECTORIES ON THE WEB

With over 50,000 mailing lists in existence, the quickest, most efficient way for you or your patrons to find a mailing list by name or by subject is to use a Web search engine. This section introduces you to several mailing list databases.

CATALIST

The CataList reference site is known as the *Catalog of Listserv Lists*. It offers access to over 30,000 public LISTSERV lists. When you arrive at their home page *www.lsoft.com/lists/listref.html*, you are presented with several options for searching their database. You can search for a list that matches a particular list name (PUBLIB), host name (*SUNSITE.BERKELEY.EDU*), or list title (Public Libraries). You can browse through listservs organized by host country. When you click on the name of a country, you are presented with a list of all the listservs hosted in that country. In addition, lists are divided into two groups: lists with 10,000 subscribers or more and lists with 1,000 subscribers or more.

LISZT

Liszt *www.liszt.com/* is one of the largest databases of mailing lists, offering a searchable index of over 90,000 discussion lists. They also offer a service called Liszt Select!

that organizes hundreds of lists under popular subject headings such as Arts, Business, Computers, Culture, Education, Health, and Humanities, etc. For those who are interested, Liszt offers a directory of over 30,000 Usenet newsgroups and 25,000 IRC chat channels.

TILE.NET

TILE.NET has expanded its service considerably since the last edition of this book. Their first service offered—access to discussion and information lists—is still available. They let you search by topic or browse through three different indexes, including:

1. Alphabetical listing by description
2. Alphabetical listing by name
3. Alphabetical listing by domain name

Newly added services include a Usenet news database that can be accessed by newsgroup hierarchy (alt, comp, soc, etc.), by description, or alphabetically by name. You can now search anonymous FTP sites at TILE.NET. Browse by site content—an alphabetical listing of directory names existing on all of the sites indexed—by country, or by site name (for example, *hamlet.caltech.edu, han.hana.nm.kr, handicap. afd.olivetti.com*, etc.). A database of computer products vendors is available. You can access it by company name, country, product (a very long list), or ZIP code. Companies located in the United States are listed by state. You can access TILE.NET at *tile.net/*.

LIBRARY-ORIENTED LISTS AND ELECTRONIC SERIALS

This resource began as a work compiled by Charles W. Bailey Jr., Assistant Dean for Systems at the University of Houston. When the last edition of this book was written, Ann Thornton and Steve Bonario had completed converting this document to HTML code. In December of 1996, work on the Library-Oriented Lists was taken over by Wei Wu of the Washington Research Library Consortium (WRLC).

Library-Oriented Lists and Electronic Serials is a compilation of names and addresses of selected mailing lists and electronic serials of interest to librarians. It includes directions for accessing these resources and, when a corresponding Website is available, that information is also provided. Both a subject index and title index are made available for browsing. The subject index uses headings that are closely aligned with departments in a library, such as Acquisitions and Cataloging/Bibliographic Services. Other headings focus on library type, such as K–12 Libraries, Medical/Health Libraries, and Public Libraries.

A special feature on this site is a list of discussion groups that can be accessed using a newsreader. If you have a newsreader on your PC and it is properly configured with the necessary NNTP address (see Chapter 25 for details), your newsreader automatically connects to the newsgroup when you click on its name. To explore this site further, connect to *www.wrlc.org/liblists/*.

To find out more about a particular mailing list without subscribing, send the command **info <mailing list name>** to the mailing-list manager address of the mailing list

---

> **Online Resource**
>
> Stephanie and Peter da Silva maintain a compilation of Publicly
> Accessible Mailing Lists at *paml.net/*. This is one of those Internet
> resources with a long history, going all the way back to Chuq von
> Rospach who started it around 1981. This list can be accessed through
> a name index and a subject index. Once in the index, you can search for
> specific character strings by using the "Edit" pull-down menu in your Web
> browser and then clicking on "Find." The site also supports keyword
> searching.

in which you're interested. For example, to learn more about ILL-L, the interlibrary
loan discussion group, send the command **info ill-l** in the body of a message to
LISTPROC@LISTSERV.ACNS.NWU.EDU.

ADVANCED LISTSERV SEARCHING TECHNIQUES

LISTSERV allows you to search its message archives using Job Control Language (JCL)
commands in the body of an e-mail message. This process is called a *batch mode query*.
Job control language is a language used for telling a computer's operating system how
to handle your job. Different JCL statements define the work you want done and the
resources you need.

PERFORMING A SEARCH

The following example illustrates just one way of setting up a LISTSERV database request. There are many other ways to use JCL for searching message archives. If you
would like to research JCL further, consult "Revised LISTSERV: Database Functions"
by Eric Thomas or run a Veronica or Web search on the character string **JCL**. The combined set of JCL statements that you input to the computer is referred to as the *JCL
Stream*. A sample JCL Stream for submitting a simple query is

```
//search job echo=no
database search dd=rules
//rules dd *
search <subject> in <listname>
index
/*
```

This is the text that you would enter in the body of your e-mail message sent to the
LISTSERV, not the list. The first line simply tells the LISTSERV not to send a job re-
ceipt message when it receives your request. The next two lines set the standard rules
for your query. The next line contains the "search" command. The fifth line uses the
"index" command, which asks LISTSERV to send you a list of messages that match
your search. The "/*" on the last line marks the end of the job.

DETAILS ON USING THE SEARCH COMMAND

The syntax of the search command includes three important elements:

1. The keyword or phrase that you want to search for in the documents
2. The name of the database or "listname" you want to search
3. The name of the database to be searched is preceded by the word "in"

The statement "search minichanger in cdromlan" would find all messages in the discussion list CDROMLAN containing the string "minichanger." Case is ignored when performing the search operation. Single-word searches usually result in a large number of hits. To narrow your search, add another search statement below the first, but this time leave out the word "in." The second search statement is applied to the hit list resulting from the previous search statement.

In most cases, you will find it more advantageous searching a key phrase rather than a single word. When you submit the search statement "search document content analysis in pacs-l," LISTSERV searches each word individually. Any message that contains these words in any order will be a match. Note also that LISTSERV doesn't require that the search term be surrounded by blank space for a match to occur. The word "document" would find a match on "documentary," "documents," and "documentation," etc.

REQUESTING SPECIFIC DOCUMENTS

After submitting your query containing the index command, LISTSERV returns an index that includes document numbers, dates, and the subject of each message. Once you decide which messages you would like to see in full text, submit another JCL Stream to the LISTSERV, this time including the print command.

The print command is used to retrieve a copy of the complete message. Insert the document numbers you are interested in retrieving after the word "print." When requesting multiple documents, separate each document number with a comma. If, for example, the index you received from the PACS-L search on "document content analysis" contained three documents of interest with corresponding document numbers of 000349, 000421, and 000423, you would send the following JCL Stream in the body of an e-mail message to PACS-L's LISTSERV address at *listserv@uhupvm1.uh.edu*:

```
//search job echo=no
database search dd=rules
//rules dd *
search document content analysis in pacs-l
print 000349, 000421, 000423
/*
```

In a few minutes, the LISTSERV would return the documents you requested in the form of an e-mail message.

ADVANCED LISTPROC SEARCHING TECHNIQUES

You can search ListProc message archives using the search command. The word or phrase you're searching for can be placed in the form of a regular expression. You also have the use of these Boolean operators.

"|" is used to represent OR
"&" is used to represent AND
"~" is used to represent NOT

A *regular expression* is a description of a text string for which you'd like to find matches. These "descriptions" are somewhat cryptic when you compare them to simple keyword or subject searching supported by CD-ROM databases such as SIRS or EBSCO's Magazine Article Index. Regular expressions are powerful, however, and perform efficient searches. To learn more about regular expressions, consult a UNIX manual or if you have access to a UNIX shell account, enter the command **man egrep** at your system prompt.

To search the PUBLIB list for any messages containing the words "exhibit" and "policy," you could send the following command to the list manager: **search listproc/ publib -all "exhibit&policy"**.

This should retrieve all files in PUBLIB's message archive where the words "exhibit" and "policy" both occur in the same sentence. The pattern is placed within quotation marks to prevent the UNIX shell from misinterpreting certain characters such as the pipe character (|) used to represent the logical OR operator.

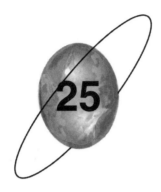

Usenet News

Usenet (User's Network) is a large collection of computers carrying something called *Usenet news*—a distributed conferencing system consisting of thousands of discussion groups. In a more abstract sense, you could think of Usenet as a huge database of conversations—on tens of thousands of diverse subjects—between millions of people worldwide. You can access and browse Usenet directly, or you can access portions of it using search engines and directories. Subjects range from geophysical fluid dynamics to baking with sourdough.

Because many Usenet participants possess a very high level of expertise in their respective fields, Usenet news can serve as a useful reference tool in answering certain queries. As a librarian, I sometimes compare this resource with the functionality of *The Encyclopedia of Associations*. When I'm presented with a highly specialized question for which there doesn't seem to be an answer in any reference source sitting on the shelf, I have often consulted a professional association. Many times the members themselves, or some other source to which they have referred me, have the answer I need. Like associations, many Usenet newsgroups bring together specialists in a particular field.

ACCESSING USENET NEWS

A connection to the Internet does not automatically give you access to newsgroups. In the case of dial-up connections, your service provider must make arrangements to re-

Online Resource
You can find the Usenet FAQ list at the Institute of Information and Computing Sciences, Utrecht University *www.cs.uu.nl/wais/html/na-dir/ usenet/.html*.

ceive Usenet files or get a "news feed" from another site that already receives them. When a server at one site provides Usenet articles to a server at another site, it is said to be providing a *news feed* or simply a *feed*.

After your local host sets up a news feed, you can access Usenet news. Many commercial providers and university systems already offer this service. You can determine whether your dial-up service, campus, or corporate computing system has a network news feed by asking the system administrator. The host organization determines the number and selection of discussion categories fed to them.

ALTERNATIVE METHODS OF CONNECTING

If your service provider doesn't receive a news feed, or you would rather subscribe through other means, there are now services on the Internet that sell access to individuals. The following two links are examples of services that offer subscription-based news feeds for individuals:

> news-service.com—*www.news-service.com/site/index.php3*
> OnlyNEWS—*www.onlynews.com/*

You can find more options listed at Premium Usenet Providers *www.exit109.com/ ~jeremy/news/providers/*.

USENET NEWSGROUPS

Internet sites can choose to subscribe or not to subscribe to a particular newsgroup. One host may carry 6,000 newsgroups, while another may carry only 2,500. Your service provider allows you to choose which newsgroups you subscribe to, but they may also subscribe you to a basic set of newsgroups. This is done automatically the first time you use their service. Typical default newsgroups include:

> news.announce.newusers
> news.newusers.questions
> news.answers

Each newsgroup specializes in a particular subject. They're organized in a tree structure, or hierarchy, with various levels of topics and subtopics. For instance, one newsgroup hierarchy called *soc* posts articles relating to social issues. The newsgroup *soc.culture.indian.telugu* is a social newsgroup concentrating on the culture of the Telugu people of India.

One collection of newsgroups, termed "World" newsgroups, is usually distributed around the entire Usenet worldwide. These newsgroups are divided into the following seven broad classifications, and each of these classifications is organized into groups and subgroups according to topic:

> *rec* (recreation)
> *sci* (science)

comp (computers)
soc (social)
news (newsgroups)
talk (debates)
misc (miscellaneous)

THE WORLD NEWSGROUPS

Under the classification of *rec* (groups oriented towards the arts, hobbies, and recreational activities), there are a number of music groups further divided into subgroups such as classical, folk, and afro-latin. Following are three examples of music newsgroups in the *rec* hierarchy:

rec.music.classical—Discussion about classical music
rec.music.folk—People discussing folk music
rec.music.afro-latin—Music with African and Latin influences

Other broad topics in the *rec* classification include arts, audio, aviation, food, games, sport, travel, etc. As with music, these groups are broken down into more specialized subgroups.

Under the classification *sci* (discussions relating to research in or applications of the established sciences) are medical groups with subgroups in AIDS and nutrition:

sci.med
sci.med.aids
sci.med.nutrition

Other groups in this classification concentrate on topics such as aeronautics, anthropology, space-related news, and virtual-worlds.

The *comp* newsgroups discuss topics of interest to both computer professionals and hobbyists, including topics in programming language, software, hardware, and operating systems, etc.

The *soc* groups address social issues; for example, religion, politics, and culture.

The *talk* classification consists of groups that are debate-oriented and contain very little useful information.

The *news* groups discuss issues relating to newsgroups (network and software).

The *misc* groups address subjects that can't easily be classified under any of the other headings.

SPECIALIZED NEWSGROUPS

You will notice several other newsgroup classifications listed on the main menu that are not part of the traditional or mainstream hierarchy of newsgroups. These are classified as "alternative" newsgroup hierarchies. Alternative newsgroups are organized into groups and subgroups similar to the traditional newsgroups. They are called alternative because they don't conform to Usenet standards. The formation of a new mainstream newsgroup is strictly controlled. An announcement must be made followed by a dis-

---

Online Resource

Before exploring the picture files residing on the various *alt.binaries. pictures* newsgroups, download a copy of the FAQ that explains all of the idiosyncrasies of posting and downloading files in this format. FTP to site *ftp.cc.utexas.edu* and get the files called *FAQ.abp.1* and *FAQ.abp.2* residing in the */gifstuff* directory. If this FTP server address changes or the files move, use Archie to search on the character string **faq.abp** to find new locations.

---

cussion and a request for people to vote. The alternative newsgroups are less strict. Anyone who knows how to start one can do so.

Examples of newsgroups in the *alt* classification include *alt.sport.bungee*, *alt.hypertext*, *alt.my.crummy.boss*, *alt.conspiracy*, and many thousands more that are bizarre and weird. *alt.bionet* is a newsgroup hierarchy for topics of interest to biologists.

The *biz* hierarchy carries information about business products, especially computer products and services. It is further subdivided into the following subgroups:

- books
- clarinet
- comp
- config
- control
- digex
- digital
- general
- jobs
- marketplace
- next
- oreilly
- pagesat
- stolen
- tadpole
- test

The *clarinet* hierarchy of newsgroups is gatewayed from Clarinet News, a commercial electronic publishing service which provides UPI, AP, and satellite news services. Groups under this classification include

- *biz.clarinet*—Announcements about ClariNet.
- *biz.clarinet.sample*—Samples of ClariNet newsgroups.
- *biz.clarinet.webnews.biz*—Business from ClariNet e.News.
- *biz.clarinet.webnews.living*—Lifestyle and entertainment from ClariNet e.News.
- *biz.clarinet.webnews.sports*—Sports from ClariNet e.News.
- *biz.clarinet.webnews.techwire*—Computers, science, and technology from ClariNet.
- *biz.clarinet.webnews.top*—Top News from ClariNet e.News.
- *biz.clarinet.webnews.usa*—News of the U.S. from ClariNet e.News.
- *biz.clarinet.webnews.world*—World news from ClariNet e.News.

Online Resource

A newsgroup called *news.announce.newusers* posts documents that are of particular interest to users that are new to Usenet. Lists of active newsgroups are posted to *news.announce.newgroups*.

- *biz.clarinet.web.sample*—Sample ClariNet news in Web (HTML) format.
- *biz.clarinet.web.xcache.large*—Large images used in *.web.sample*.
- *biz.clarinet.web.xcache.small*—Small images used in *.web.sample*.

Librarians may be interested in *K12* (Kindergarten through 12th grade), which is a collection of school-based or school-oriented newsgroups. Subgroups of *K12* include:

- chat
- ed
- lang
- library
- sys

There is presently one group within the *library* subgroup: *k12.library*, which covers discussions on implementing information technologies in school libraries.

READING THE NEWS

News articles look like e-mail messages, but they're delivered in a very different way. Usenet messages are not sent to individuals the way they are in mailing lists. Instead, a user sends, or *posts*, an article to a newsgroup on one site and the local system collects its articles and sends them as a file to adjoining Usenet sites. In a mailing list, when one subscriber mails a message to the mailing-list manager, all subscribers to that list receive the same mail message. Rather than sending many copies of one message, Usenet provides a single central copy that all subscribers can read.

Like most of the Internet services described in this book, Usenet news makes use of a client/server model. The server program manages the news feed. The client program in this arrangement is called a *newsreader* and it provides you with your interface to Usenet. There are various newsreaders available for both shell account users and those running their own Windows client software on their personal computers. Some of the more popular character-based newsreaders running on shell accounts include nn, tin, rn, and trn.

The following section provides simple reference guides for three newsreaders. For more detailed information on these or other newsreaders, consult the online help service at your site.

QUICK REFERENCE GUIDE FOR NNR

nnr is an NNTP (Network News Transfer Protocol) newsreader that I have used on IBM VM/CMS systems.

1. Enter the command **nnr** to invoke the program and display the first screen, called the PHLI/Main Screen (Primary High Level Index). This is an index of three-letter codes that fills the first screen and subsequent screens, depending on the number of newsgroups to which your host subscribes. Select a newsgroup classification by moving forward with the PF8 key.
2. When you find a newsgroup classification in the high-level index that you'd like to explore, move the cursor to its name and press **PF2** (ALL_NEWS). The next screen displayed is the SHLI/Groups (Secondary High Level Index). This index presents all of the related groups and subgroups that are available under the selected classification.
3. Move the cursor to the desired group and press **PF4** (HEADERS). This brings you to the next screen (called the Header Screen), which provides you with a list of headers or subject lines that look similar to a list of e-mail messages you may be used to seeing.
4. Move the cursor to any header that looks interesting and press **PF2** (ARTICLE) to read a specific article. This displays the Article Screen. The PFKeys you're most likely to use at this stage are these:

PF2 (Next)	Read next article in sequence
PF3 (Quit)	Exit article screen
PF4 (Previous)	Read the previous article in the sequence
PF9 (Print)	Sends the article to a printer
PF11 (Log)	Logs article in NNRLOG NOTEBOOK
PF12 (NxtGroup)	Moves to the next group in the SHLI list

Note that the documents you select for printing won't actually print until you exit nnr. If you select two or more documents during a single session, they are combined into one print job. Logging a document in a NOTEBOOK before printing it gives you the opportunity to edit it in your file list, using xedit.

QUICK REFERENCE GUIDE FOR TRN

trn is a Usenet newsreader that runs on UNIX platforms.

1. Type **trn** and press ENTER to start the newsreader.
2. The program creates a file called *.newsrc* in which all of the newsgroups you subscribe to are placed. This file also keeps track of the messages you have read.
3. The program goes through all of the newsgroups fed to your site. You have three choices for each newsgroup: view that group's articles now (press **y**), skip it for now and go to next newsgroup with unread articles (press **n**), or "unsubscribe" so you never see that newsgroup again unless you resubscribe to it at some future date (press **u**).
4. If you pressed **y**, you are presented with the first unread article. Press the spacebar to move down one page, **n** to go to the next unread article, or **q** to leave the newsgroup and go to the next newsgroup.
5. To save an article, press **s** followed by the name of the file in which you want the article saved.
6. Press **x** to unscramble a *rot13* message (see below for explanation of rot13).
7. Type the letter **h** to bring up help at any point.
8. Type **q** to quit the program.

QUICK REFERENCE GUIDE FOR ANU-NEWS

ANU-NEWS is a newsreader for VMS Systems.

1. Enter **news** at the $ prompt.
2. You are presented with one long list of newsgroups.
3. Use the down and up cursor keys to scroll through the list.
4. When you see a newsgroup you'd like to access, place the cursor on that line and press ENTER. You are presented with a list of headers for all the articles presently posted to that group. Scroll through these to choose which article you'd like to read.
5. To read an article, move the cursor to the desired line and press ENTER. To scroll through the article, press ENTER again or use the cursor keys.
6. Enter **dir/all** at the *NEWS* prompt to return to the long list of newsgroups.
7. To register (subscribe to) a particular newsgroup, move your cursor to the appropriate line and enter the word **register** at the *NEWS* prompt. The next time you enter the newsreader, the groups you registered are highlighted for easier identification.
8. Enter the command **dir/reg** at the *NEWS* prompt to view your directory of registered groups.
9. To remove a group from this list, place the cursor on the appropriate line and enter the word **deregister** at the *NEWS* prompt.
10. When you want to leave the program, type **exit** and press ENTER. The system creates a file called NEWSRC.;1, which contains information on the groups you are registered to receive.

NEWSREADERS FOR THE MASSES

The preceding section describes systems that were once the *only* newsreaders available. While some librarians still rely on these character-based newsreaders, most have switched to windows-based newsreaders running on PCs. Two of the more popular newsreaders for Windows are Free Agent and X-News. Both should be available at *www.tucows.com*. Another newsreader is called News Rover. To learn more about this newsreader, go to *www.NewsRover.com/*. In the section that follows, I explain how to install and configure Free Agent to run on your PC.

Installing and Configuring Free Agent

To access a news server (NNTP server), you need a newsreader. In this section I show you how to install a popular newsreader for Windows called *Free Agent*. It's free and you can download your copy from the Free Agent News Reader Website at *www.forteinc.com/agent/freagent.htm*. Look for the button labeled "Get Free Agent" or go straight to the Free Agent download site at *www.forteinc.com/getfa/download.htm*.

Online Resource

Denis McKeon's *Moderated Groups FAQ* discusses general and technical aspects of newsgroup moderation. You can access a copy at *www.swcp.com/~dmckeon/mod-faq.html*.

Figure 25–1: Box that shows after successfully installing Free Agent

1. After you have completed running the install program, the box shown in Figure 25–1 appears.
2. Click on "Yes." Read the software license agreement and click on "Accept" if you wish to proceed. Then the Free Agent setup window shown in Figure 25–2 pops up.
3. In the "News (NNTP) Server:" box enter the address of your NNTP server. This information is provided to you by your Internet service provider. It will be a domain name something like *news.foobar.com*.
4. Click on "OK."
5. The next window, shown in Figure 25–3, asks you if you want to go online. Click on "No." If you click on "Yes," you get the window shown in Figure 25–4. Click "OK" to remove it.

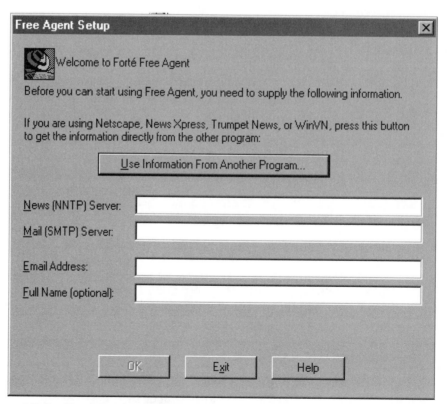

Figure 25–2: Free Agent Setup window

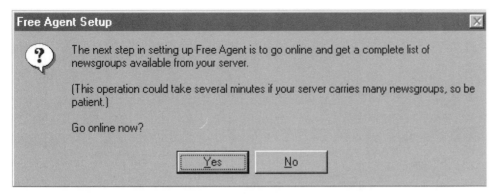

Figure 25–3: Free Agent asking if you want to go online

Figure 25–4: Free Agent 480 error message

6. If your news server is password protected, you must first tell Free Agent your username and password. You accomplish this by selecting the "Options|General Preferences" menu.
7. Enter your username and password in the "News Server Authorization" box shown in Figure 25–5. Before you can enter this information you must click on the two check boxes username and password.
8. Click "OK."
9. Next, tell Free Agent to retrieve a list of all the newsgroups that are available. Click on the "Online" pull-down menu and select "Refresh Groups List...."
10. You are asked what you want to do with extinct newsgroups. You may leave it on "Keep all extinct groups" and click "OK." Free Agent begins downloading all of the newsgroups that are available on your news server. This can take a while, depending on the speed of your connection and the number of newsgroups that have to be downloaded.

Online Resources

To help prevent newcomers from asking the same questions that newcomers before them have already asked, individual newsgroups periodically post FAQs (Frequently Asked Questions). These are text files that new users should read before attempting to post any messages.

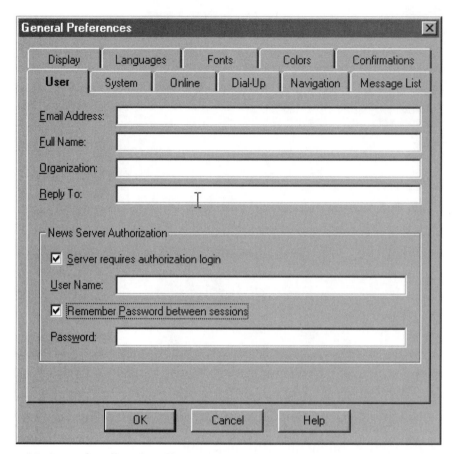

Figure 25–5:   Configuring Free Agent with your account information

11. When Free Agent has completed the download, you see the complete Usenet hierarchy of newsgroups in the upper left window on your screen.
12. Free Agent is now installed and ready to use. For additional assistance in reading news online, checkout Free Agent's Help index.

Configuring Netscape Newsreader 4.0x

Before you download and install a standalone newsreader, you might want to consider the newsreader that comes bundled with Netscape. It is not as feature rich as Free Agent, but offers all of the basic services necessary for reading and responding to news. Here are the steps necessary for setting up Netscape Newsreader.

1. Start Netscape and click on the "Edit" menu and select **"Preferences."**
2. Click on "Mail & Newsgroups."
3. In the "Mail and Newsgroups" sub-menu, click on "Newsgroup Servers."
4. The next window that opens is where you specify your news server.
5. Click on the "Add" button and enter your news server address in the server address box. This information is provided by your Internet service provider (ISP). If you do not know this information, contact your ISP. If your ISP does not offer access to a news server for Usenet news, you may subscribe to a publicly acces-

sible news server like the ones listed earlier in this chapter.

6. The default port is normally 119.

7. In the "Newsgroup Directory" box, click on "Choose." This is where you decide where all of the messages downloaded from Usenet are stored.

8. Specify the maximum number of messages that can be downloaded from one newsgroup at a time. Click on the box "Ask me before downloading more than _____ messages," and fill in the box with the maximum number of messages.

9. To read the news, click on "Communicator" and select "Newsgroups."

10. You should see the name of the news server you specified earlier located in the frame on the left side of your screen. Click on it so it's highlighted.

11. At the top of the newsreader window, click on "File" and select "Subscribe." A "Subscribe to Newsgroups" window should open.

12. Depending on how fast your connection is and how many newsgroups your service provider subscribes to, it could take a while for all of the newsgroups to load. Work your way down through the hierarchical listing of names and click on the "Subscribe" button when you find newsgroups in which you are interested.

13. When you are finished, click on "OK."

14. This brings you back to the newsreader window. The newsgroups you subscribed to should now be listed under your news server's name.

15. Click on the newsgroup whose messages you want to read.

If you have an earlier version of Netscape 3.0x, try applying the instructions outlined below.

1. Pull down the "Options" menu, click on "Mail and News Preferences," and then click on the "Servers" tab. This displays the "Servers" panel.

2. To access Usenet Newsgroups, Netscape Navigator needs to make a connection to your Internet service provider's news server. Ask your ISP if they make this service available, and if so, ask them for the Internet address of your NNTP server. *NNTP* stands for Network News Transfer Protocol and is the set of rules defining how Usenet news articles are posted and distributed around the Internet. Enter the NNTP server address in the "News (NNTP) Server" field.

3. You can specify how many news messages are transferred by entering a number in the "Get" field at the bottom of the panel. The default is 100 and the maximum that you can enter is 3,500. The larger the number, the longer it takes to transfer messages. When you click on a newsgroup name, you see a number just to the right of it that represents the total number of messages currently posted to that newsgroup. It may be anywhere from 0 to several thousand. If you enter 100 in the Get field and then click on the "*rec.gardens*" newsgroup, which may show there are 1,245 messages waiting, Netscape Navigator loads only 100 of the total available messages.

4. Click on the "Identity" tab and enter your name and e-mail address in the appropriate fields. You determine what your user ID is when you set up your account, but the domain name that follows the @ sign is provided to you by your ISP.

5. If you'd like a signature attached to all of the messages you post to newsgroups, see the section titled "Setting Preferences for E-mail in Netscape Communicator" in Chapter 23.

6. Next, click on the "Organization" tab to specify whether you want news messages threaded. By default, news messages are threaded. Threading means replies are displayed adjacent to the original message and other replies. When the messages are unthreaded, sorting is done solely by the sorting order designated in the "Sorting" panel.

7. When you reply to a news posting, by default the original text is included in your reply and quoted by placing a ">" symbol at the beginning of each line. Click on the "Appearance" tab to specify the font size and style of the quoted text in your message. Click on the "Composition" tab to specify whether you want your replies to quote original messages and whether you want copies of messages sent to yourself or others.

Online vs. Offline Readers

There is a difference between online and offline newsreaders. *Online* newsreaders require that you maintain an Internet connection during the time the program is running. When you run the newsreader, it connects to the server to see how many new messages there are in the groups to which you subscribe. You can then enter a group, and the newsreader downloads just the message headers in what looks like a mailbox. The messages themselves have not yet landed on your machine. As you scroll through the list of headers and click on a particular one, it is then that the newsreader gets it from the server. When you read a message, it is not stored on your computer unless you specifically save it to your hard drive or other storage medium.

Offline newsreaders connect to the server and then download all new messages for the newsgroups to which you currently subscribe. In addition, the newsreader uploads any posts you wrote since the last time you connected to the server. When all of this is complete, the newsreader disconnects from the server. You can then read the messages at your leisure and compose replies that will be uploaded next time you connect.

DOWNLOADING BINARY FILES

Although most newsgroups are platforms for discussion, some are distribution points for software and other binary files. Transferring binary files to or from Usenet news is trickier than transferring files from an FTP site because Usenet is a system based on ASCII text and is capable only of transmitting ASCII text files. Because images are binary files, they first must be transformed into ASCII files before they can be transferred to or from Usenet successfully. The same holds true for binary files transferred through the e-mail system.

A program called UUENCODE, explained in Chapter 23, encodes these files into ASCII format for transferring. Once UUENCODEd files arrive on your personal machine, you transform them back into binary format using a program called UUDECODE. These programs, and others like them, enable people to send files such as spreadsheets, WordPerfect documents, and executable files.

Two examples of newsgroups that distribute encoded binary files are *comp.binaries.ibm.pc* and *comp.binaries.mac*. To retrieve a binary file from one of these newsgroups, first save the file to your personal computer's hard drive. Then run it through the appropriate decoding program to transform it back into a usable state.

ROT13 CIPHER

Some files on Usenet look like gibberish and they are not encoded files. These files have likely been transformed with a program called rot13, which replaces each letter in the text of the document with the letter that is 13 places ahead of it or behind it (rotates 13 positions in the alphabet). For example, A becomes N, N becomes A, B becomes O, and so on. rot13 is not really meant to create an indecipherable code; it's more a matter of politeness. Articles that may be offensive or that might give away the ending to a book or movie are encoded in rot13. There may also be a warning given in the article's subject line such as "Offensive to Native Americans," or "Offensive to Germans," etc.

If you are using Netscape's newsreader, you can view images as they download. Microsoft's newsreader gives you the ability to open pictures once the entire file has been downloaded. Neither of these newsreaders is very good at dealing with multi-part postings, where the file spans more than one newsgroup posting. To retrieve files of this nature you may want to try using a standalone newsreader like Free Agent, discussed earlier in this chapter.

If you are using newsreaders other than Netscape, they should offer a choice that allows you to download binary files. Most Windows-based newsreaders today support downloading image files. Images are decoded automatically and the newsreader can put together the different parts of a post.

SEARCHING AND DIRECTORY SERVICES

With the advent of the Web, different services are becoming available that can help you sort through the millions of messages that are posted to Usenet newsgroups daily. One of these services is described here: Deja.com.

Deja.com, formerly Deja News, is a newsgroup service on the Web that offers several features, including these:

- The ability to post messages to Usenet newsgroups (you must first become a member and have a valid e-mail address)
- Browse Usenet news by newsgroup hierarchy
- Read and bookmark Usenet news articles
- Run keyword searches on all newsgroups or just those in which you're interested
- Access lots of online hints and useful information relating to newsgroups

---

Online Resources

If you are interested in creating your own newsgroup, check out these documents that explain the process:

Guidelines: The Big Eight Newsgroup Creation Process, by Russ Allbery—*www.eyrie.org/~eagle/faqs/big-eight.html*

How to Format and Submit a New Group Proposal, by Russ Allbery—*web.presby.edu/~jtbell/usenet/newgroup/how-submit.faq*

The User's Guide to the Changing USENET, by John Stanley—*cil-www.oce.orst.edu:8080/users.guide*

The beginners guide to creating new alt.* groups, by Imran G.—*usenet.cjb.net/*

Online Resource
Access several Usenet documents through the Usenet Info Center at the University of North Carolina's Sunsite *metalab.unc.edu/usenet-i/*.

Deja.com allows you to use these services without having a newsreader or access to your own news server. The disadvantage of accessing Usenet news in this manner is the speed at which Web pages load. When you use a newsreader to link to a news server, you are dealing primarily with text files that load quite fast. When you access newsgroups through a Web interface like Deja.com, you have to wait for the site's graphics and banner ads to load each time you move to a new page. You can speed things up a bit when you get to the messages themselves by clicking on "View original Usenet format" located at the bottom of the message window.

To explore Deja.com further, connect to their Website at *deja.com/usenet/*.

Part VI

YOUR LIBRARY AS AN ELECTRONIC PUBLISHER

Some forms of expression that can't be reproduced in paper format adapt well to electronic format. A lecture on playing the hammered dulcimer is a good example. In paper format, you could read text explaining how to play the instrument and see photographs of historic instruments and illustrations showing how to hold the sticks. In electronic format, the lecture could be transformed into a lecture and demonstration. You could still read text and view images, but you could also hear and see a musician performing on the dulcimer.

The Web adds yet another element to publishing that's unique even to online publishing called hyperlinks. *Hyperlinks* enable you to link any word, phrase, or image in one Web document to another Web document accessible anywhere on the Web. For example, say there is a sentence in the hammered dulcimer lecture/demonstration that reads, "The dulcimer is of Persian origin." If there were a Web document anywhere on the Web with additional information on Persia that you wanted to bring to the reader's attention, you could do so by linking the word *Persian* to that document. The phrase, "Sound boards are usually made of Sitka Spruce," could be linked to a site describing the Sitka Spruce tree, or a site on instrument building, etc. This presents the reader with an opportunity to make choices and interact with the document.

With the advent of the Web and Web browsers that support fully integrated video, audio, 3–D, and Internet telephone communications capabilities, scholarly electronic journals like *The World Wide Web Journal Of Biology epress.com/w3jbio/* are given the capability of transmitting information to researchers that would otherwise be unavailable in paper format. Digitizing information not only enables researchers to transmit charts, graphs, photographs, illustrations, sound files, and video clips, but they can also transmit data files, project them as 3–D images, and interact with them.

Many software applications and levels of electronic-document formatting can be used to prepare documents for distribution on the Internet. To make a document "Web ready," the main requirement is that you present the document in HyperText Markup Language, or HTML for short. Chapter 26 concentrates on explaining the basics of HTML and describes how to design and construct a simple home page for your library. Also, I introduce you to a specialized program that creates portable documents. These are documents that retain their original fonts, type size, layout, and graphics regardless of the platform on which they are viewed.

It has become essential to offer visitors to your Website the ability to not only browse for information, but also search. In Chapter 27 I introduce you to five search and indexing systems that are all free. While four are somewhat complex and require a lot of set up and configuration time on the servers themselves, there is one that can be implemented by even novice users in a matter of minutes. Chapter 27 also introduces an easy-to-use Web-based database system capable of cataloging text, images, sound clips, and video clips.

Chapter 28 is all about digital libraries. In that chapter, I provide you with a guided tour of digital libraries, electronic bookstores, newsstands, and magazine racks.

Publishing on the Web

Web browsers provide libraries with an effective and innovative platform for making resources and services known to both staff and library patrons. With an Internet audience numbering in the millions, the potential for reaching a much broader audience is also available.

In this chapter, I introduce you to the basics of Web publishing. I explain the different levels of publishing, such as posting your home page to a local PC or an Internet service provider's system. I also explain how to create a basic home page by using either an HTML editor or a home page generator for librarians. I also introduce the concept of *virtual servers*—servers that appear to be your own hardware and software, but in reality are rented hard drive space on someone else's computer. While these services may not be free, the savings are monumental when compared to owning and managing your own server-class computers. The chapter closes with an introduction to portable documents with explanations of what they are and how to create and read them.

FOUR LEVELS OF PUBLISHING

Depending on your budget, how sophisticated your system is, and the breadth of the audience you would like to reach, publishing your home page can be handled one of these four ways:

1. Create your home page and store it on your own in-house Web server. In this scenario, Web users worldwide could connect to your home page by linking to your Web server. (Explaining how to set up and configure your own Web server is beyond the scope of this book.)
2. Set up a virtual Web server. A virtual Web server is one that is run and maintained by an outside source. To those who are connecting to your home page, it

appears that you have your own Web server and your own dedicated connection to the Internet. Virtual servers are explained in more detail later in this chapter.

3. Connect with an Internet service provider (a local or national Internet service provider or community Free Net) who will "launch" your Web page for you. You could also use one of the many free Web hosting services introduced in Chapter 20. In this setting, you create your home page and then store it on your service provider's computer. When Web users want to link to your home page, they are connecting to your service provider's computer or Web hosting service.

4. Create your home page and simply load it on a local hard disk. In the first three examples, your Web page can be accessed by other computers anywhere on the Web. If your home page is merely stored on a local computer's hard disk, then only local access would be available. This access could be gained either through a local area network, or, if there is no network, only on the computers storing copies of your HTML documents.

This level of publishing still would enable users to link to other Web sites from your home page as long as you were connected to the Internet through a direct link or dial-up SLIP/PPP connection. You might resort to this level of publishing as a temporary fix if there were problems that prevented you from getting your home page mounted properly on your service provider's computer. Instructions for mounting home pages on local hard disks are given in the section that follows.

MOUNTING YOUR HOME PAGE ON YOUR PC'S HARD DISK

Web browsers running on a PC can be used as tools for accessing and viewing files stored on that PC's hard disk. To demonstrate what I mean, click on the "Open" button in Netscape and enter *file:///C* in the "Open Location:" dialog box. (Normally you'd be entering a Web page URL.) When you click on the "Open" button, your hard disk's directory tree appears in the Netscape window. Your files and directories look similar to those on a Gopher or FTP server when viewed through Netscape. Small icons identify folders and file types. In Internet Explorer, simply enter *C:* in the address box located at the top of the screen.

When you click on an HTML file, your browser displays it in the browser window. If you click on an MS Word or Excel file, Netscape launches the appropriate application to view the selected file.

In the sections that follow, I explain how to configure your Web browser and create links in your Web pages so that you can access files stored on your local hard disk. You discover that even without an Internet connection, you can use Web browsers to create customized in-house information systems.

WHAT IS A DEFAULT HOME PAGE?

When you start up your browser, it automatically links to a site on the Web. This is called the *default home page* and is usually the Website of the organization that developed your browser. For example, when you first install Netscape Navigator, it automatically links you to Netscape's home page at *home.netscape.com*. Mosaic links you to the National Center for Supercomputing Applications at the University of Illinois in Urbana-Champaign at *www.ncsa.uiuc.edu/SDG/Software/WinMosaic/HomePage.html*. NCSA Mosaic for the Macintosh links to *www.ncsa.uiuc.edu/SDG/Software/MacMosaic/*. (Neither of these sites has been updated since 1997.)

RESETTING YOUR DEFAULT HOME PAGE

You can reset your default home page in the latest versions of Netscape by clicking on the "Edit" pull-down menu and selecting "Preferences." Click on the "Navigator" category and you see a location box in the right-hand window where you can insert the home page address. In older versions of Netscape, select the "Options" pull-down menu and click on "General Preferences." You see a Preferences dialog box open. Click on the "Appearance" tab at the top of the dialog box. Reset the preferences by typing in a new path statement in the Home Page Location field.

To set your home page to a file residing on the PC's hard disk drive, the path statement should begin with the word *file* followed by three forward slashes, a *C*, the pipe (l) character, and another forward slash. For example, if you name the file *index.htm* and placed it in a subdirectory called LIBRARY, the full path statement would look like this: *file:///C\LIBRARY/index.htm*. When you finish, click on "OK" to save your changes.

Resetting the default home page in Mosaic is just as simple. Begin by selecting the "Options" pull-down menu and then click on "Preference." When the next window opens, click on the tab labeled "Document" and then replace the current NCSA Mosaic home page address with *file:///C\LIBRARY/index.htm* or with whatever pathname you choose. When finished, click on the "OK" button to save your changes.

WHY STORE YOUR HOME PAGE LOCALLY?

Creating your own home page gives you the opportunity to customize what library patrons see when they first login to a public access PC. A custom home page can provide immediate access to Websites that are in demand. These worldwide links can be listed right alongside links to local files that are pertinent to your own library such as policy statements or announcements for upcoming events. With your home page stored right at home, your browser connects to it almost immediately. Future editing is simple and can be done offline.

ACCESS RESTRICTIONS

Your custom home page and the local files it links to cannot be accessed by Web surfers just anywhere in the world. When you load your home page on your own personal computer's hard disk, only users of that specific computer will have access to it. If your PC is on a local area network, you could store the *index.htm* file in a shared directory that other computers could access locally; but still, no one from the outside world will be able to login and gain access to it.

CREATING LINKS TO OTHER HTML DOCUMENTS

Even if you aren't connected to the Internet while using this procedure, you can still link to other HTML documents stored on your hard disk from links set in your default home page. Follow this format when embedding URLs into your home page: If you would like to link from your home page to a file called *hours.htm* and you have stored this file in the *\LIBRARY\HOMEPAGE* subdirectory, type your URL as *file:///C\/LIBRARY/HOMEPAGE/hours.htm*.

VIRTUAL WEB SERVERS

A *virtual Web server* is a server that appears to be yours, but in reality is someone else's. In fact, it may not even be an individual computer, but rather a space reserved for you on a very powerful computer that maintains several virtual server accounts. Virtual servers are run and maintained by an outside source such as an Internet service provider. Virtual servers provide you with an opportunity to maintain a highly sophisticated presence on the World Wide Web without having to maintain your own server or full-time connection. Today, the term *virtual server* is used interchangeably with *Web hosting service*.

FEATURES OF A VIRTUAL SERVER

A virtual server account relieves you of the responsibility and expense of setting up your own server, yet it enables you to set up and run your own Website on the Internet. To those who are connecting to your home page, it appears that you have your own Web server and your own dedicated connection to the Internet.

Just as though you had your own server, virtual servers also let you access detailed statistics about who is visiting your Website and how often.

VIRTUAL SERVER PRICING

Virtual server accounts can cost less than $10/month or in the hundreds of dollars per month depending on the features you choose. Usually there is a one-time setup charge ranging from $20 to $150. Monthly fees vary depending upon two main factors: disk space and traffic. The amount of disk space offered on a virtual server varies from one provider to the next and you are charged accordingly. Typically, accounts are available with as little as 10MB of permanent storage to 100MB and more. In this disk space, you store your Web pages, graphics, audio and video clips, and CGI scripts.

Based on your monthly charge, some service providers limit how much data can be downloaded or "transferred" from your Website every month. The less expensive monthly packages allow for 2GB to 5GB of traffic. More expensive accounts allow up to 20GB of traffic and more. If you exceed your allotted amount, some services charge in the range of $.05 to $.15 per megabyte over your base allotment.

APPLYING FOR A DOMAIN NAME

If you don't already have a domain name, you have to apply for one. Some service providers procure a domain name for you free of charge except for the standard $70 two-year InterNIC Registration Fee ($35 each year after). Some service providers procure a domain name for you free of charge and others charge a fee. A domain name provides an Internet address for your organization and gives your organization its own identity on the Internet. For example, the Washoe County Library System has as their Web address *www.washoe.lib.nv.us/*.

When you don't have your own domain name, your address appears differently. For example, the Pocahontas Public Library in Pocahontas, Iowa, has as their Web address *www.ncn.net/~pokypl/*. The tilde sign (~) preceding "pokypl" signifies they have an account on someone else's system, in this case an ISP named Northwest Internet Services in Havelock, Iowa, and they are using that organization's domain name address, which is *www.ncs.net*.

BUSINESSES OFFERING VIRTUAL SERVER ACCOUNTS

Following is a small sampling of services on the Internet that offer virtual server accounts. With several of my projects I have used a hosting service called WestHost at *www.westhost.com*. The monthly fee is $8.95 for 25MB of disk space. Setup fee is $19 and domain name registration is the standard $70 for two years, $35 each year thereafter. Here is a small sampling of Websites that can assist you in finding other hosting services on the Net.

FINDaHOST.com *www.findahost.com/hosts/default.cfm*
HostFinders.com *www.hostfinders.com/*
Host Investigator *www.hostinvestigator.com/go.asp*
HostReview.com *hostreview.com/*

WEB AUTHORS' AND PUBLISHERS' RIGHTS

Publishers on the Internet own the copyright to any original text they create. They also own the copyright to any original images they create. If librarians want to use graphics or CGI scripts from someone else's home page, they should ask for permission. These same rights can possibly extend to the design of the home page itself. This is especially true when Web publishers combine graphics and text to form original home page designs.

One issue that is less clear concerns the rights to links. A *link* is just an address pointing to another site on the Web. Some publishers on the Web do nothing more than assemble collections of links that serve as a table of contents to other sites on the Web. If librarians do build a link to another piece of information on the Web, they should try to make it clear that the user will be linking to something created by someone else—another publisher.

A good example of this is William Cross's All-In-One home page at site *www.AllOneSearch.com/*. This page consists of nothing but links to search engines, but each link is clearly labeled and there is no doubt as to whose service it is you are using.

Online Resource

Style Guide for Online Hypertext, written by Tim Berners-Lee, discusses all aspects of Web page design. It is one of the earliest documents on the Web addressing this subject and it can be accessed at *www.w3.org/ hypertext/WWW/Provider/Style/Overview.html*.

If a publisher adds value to their collection of links by organizing and structuring the collection in a special way, adding their own information to it, and then offering it to others, they may deserve some protection against copying by other Web publishers. Librarians should consult with their lawyers for clarification on this and other issues relating to publisher's rights on the Web.

For additional information on copyright issues, librarians may refer to P.J. Benedict O. Mahoney's *The Copyright Website* at *www.benedict.com/*.

FIRST STEPS IN PUBLISHING A HOME PAGE

The first step in creating a home page is deciding what it is you want to say and what graphics you would like to include, if any. Once you have all of the raw data gathered together, then you can go about designing the page and learning the language used for creating Web pages.

I'll cover the basics here, but as your imagination grows you can begin exploring other features not covered here. Most everything you need to know in terms of "how-to" information is available online free of charge. Resources are listed at the end of this section.

INFORMATION GATHERING AND PAGE DESIGN

A home page is not just a single hypertext document, it is a hypertext environment. When you decide what information to include on your home page, you should not only consider the files you create locally, but also the files available on the millions of hosts connected to the Internet.

At the outset, understand that you will be creating a number of separate documents. These documents are linked to other documents you create and, in some cases, to external resources located on other Web servers. As you plan, decide what topics you would like to cover in your opening home page and what information you would like to link to your home page.

One of the more traditional formats includes a short welcome statement accompanied by an image. (Web pages require images in GIF or JPEG format.) Some sites also include a disclaimer notifying patrons they are responsible for the choices they make when deciding which Websites to access. The opening statement is followed by a list of broad topics that link to other documents. Following are ideas for broad topics relating to libraries that you might consider listing on your home page:

- About the Library
- Library Hours

- Library Events and Programs
- The Branch Libraries
- Online Library Catalog
- Holiday schedule
- Applying for Library Cards
- Library Policies
- Library Services
- Library Board Minutes

You can broaden your topics to include information that goes beyond the library's resources and services, such as:

- Community Information
- Online Genealogy Resources
- Internet User's Guides
- State and Federal Government Information

From this initial list of broad topics, readers make selections and connect to lists of narrower topics or to the information itself. For example, the link called "Library Policies" would connect to a document that lists the individual policies that are available. The list might look something like this:

- Borrowing privileges
- Shelving
- Smoking, food, and drink
- Use of computers
- Meeting rooms
- Gifts and donations

These links would connect readers to text files containing the individual policies. Again, because the Web is a hypertext environment, words or phrases within the text files themselves can link to resources anywhere on the Web.

It's your responsibility as a home page designer to piece all of this information together in a manner that makes sense to your library staff and patrons. You can learn more about what works and what doesn't by exploring what other libraries are doing with their home page designs. An excellent starting point is Thomas Dowling's *LibWEb* home page at *sunsite.berkeley.edu/Libweb/*. Here Dowling maintains a list of links to more than 3,700 pages from libraries in over 100 countries.

Online Resource

Bobbie Peachey is the Guide for Web clip art at About.com. She maintains her own collection of original clip art onsite at *webclipart. about.com/internet/webclipart/library/weekly/blclpmen.htm*. This clip art is free for anyone to use on personal or commercial pages. They are not free to use in any other manner, for example, stationery and greeting cards, or in any collection that is offered to others for use.

Levels of HTML

HTML Specification, version 2.0, is the minimum level of HTML supported by browsers and editors. Version 2.0 includes text, hyperlinks, fill-in forms (for collecting information from users), and linked graphics. There are earlier levels of HTML, levels 0 and 1, which offer a basic set of features.

HTML 3.2 is the standard for HTML tags when the last edition of this book was written. It was essentially HTML 2.0 plus more advanced features such as fully formatted tables and colors.

HTML 4.0 is the newest version of HTML. Version 4.0 adds several improvements to the earlier 3.2 version of HTML. Version 4.0 supports Cascading Style Sheets that enable you to create precise formatting. Web developers now move formatting information out of the HTML text and use Cascading Style Sheets when possible. *Cascading Style Sheets*, or CSS for short, allow developers and readers to attach style to HTML documents. You can control elements of style such as fonts, colors, leading, and margins.

Other improvements make it easier to control frames. The <FRAME>, <IFRAME>, and <FRAMESET> elements are now part of the official specifications. In addition, HTML 4.0 supports a different character set than earlier versions of HTML. Now there are more than 65,000 characters available, providing support for additional languages and scientific or mathematical symbols.

For more information on HTML 4.0 and CSS, visit the Web Developer's Virtual Library at *wdvl.com/*.

INTRODUCTION TO HTML

The next step is to get your message out on the Web. To do this, you have to use the language of the Web, *HyperText Markup Language*, or HTML. This is the language used by Web browsers to transfer things like text and images to the screen.

HTML documents are plain ASCII text files that consist of a set of descriptors, or "tags," that provide formatting instructions for the document. HTML tags enable you to mix graphics with text, manipulate the way text appears, and create hypertext documents that link with other documents on the Web. In the section that follows, I introduce you to the basics of HTML tagging and applications called *HTML editors* that make the whole process quite easy. You could, however, forgo using a specialized editor and create Web documents by using a simple text editor like Notepad. You might try basic coding, like that presented in this chapter, using something like SimpleText on a Mac or Notepad on a Windows PC. Then, once you know the basics, move on and try a WYSIWYG editor (a What You See Is What You Get editor). This would help you understand some of the underlying principles of HTML before using an editor.

HTML EDITORS

In order to give your text a certain look when viewed on the Web, you have to embed special descriptors in the text called *tags*. Although HTML editors make the process of writing Web pages relatively easy, it may take some time to learn a new program and understand what it is capable of doing. Three of the most popular editors are FrontPage *www.microsoft.com/*, DreamWeaver from Macromedia *www.macromedia.com/*, and HomeSite *www.allaire.com/* from Allaire.

Other good sources for HTML editors include:

- 32–Bit Basic HTML Editors from Consummate Winsock Apps *cws.internet.com/ 32html.html*—Stroud's Consummate Winsock Apps is a valuable site for locating new software. This page lists HTML editors for creating personal Web pages and entry-level Websites for small businesses. Includes reviews, downloads, and links to developer's pages.
- AOLpress *www.aolpress.com/press/index.html*—AOLpress was designed to help make Web authoring more accessible to those just starting out. AOLpress supports WYSIWYG editing capabilities and easy-to-use menu-, dialog-, and palette-based user interfaces for creating and editing Web pages. Download is free.
- BBEdit Tips and Tricks *www.anybrowser.org/bbedit/*—BBEdit is a popular editor used by Macintosh Web designers and programmers. This site offers tips and tricks for those using BBEdit to write HTML code and Perl script.
- HTML Editor Reviews *homepage.interaccess.com/~cdavis/edit_rev.html*—Carl Davis takes a detailed look at many of the HTML editors currently on the market. A comparison matrix shows each product's details side-by-side.
- ixla Web Easy *www.ixla.com/products/webeasy.htm*—Web authoring software for beginning-level authors. Includes system requirement details, add-on downloads, try-before-you-buy downloads, FAQs, and order forms. Special link takes you to sites created by individuals using ixla Web Easy software.
- Microsoft FrontPage *www.microsoft.com/frontpage/*—Microsoft's Website creation and management tool. This site includes a gallery of FrontPage-based Websites, 45–day trial download, technical information, case studies, pricing and ordering, and an e-mail newsletter.
- TableMaker *www.bagism.com/tablemaker/*—Use this handy tool to make tables for Netscape and other browsers.

Even though HTML editors shield you from writing most of the HTML code yourself, you'll need to know a few basic principles before you start. A tag looks like this: <B>. Most HTML functions use an opening tag and a closing tag. These control the text that is located between them. For example, if you want a word or phrase to appear in boldface type, you would type the start tag <B> before the word or phrase and the stop tag </B> at the end. Using an HTML editor, you would simply highlight the text you want bolded, and then click on the button labeled "B" for bold type. The HTML editor automatically inserts the <B> and </B> in the correct locations.

File Naming Conventions

The convention on UNIX systems is to name HTML documents with a four-letter *.html* extension, for example, *index.html*. Windows-based editors generally default to the three-letter extension *.htm* that is the convention for Windows NT Internet Information Server. In spite of this convention, file names with three-letter *.htm* extensions still work on UNIX systems and files named with *.html* extensions work fine when they are being edited on Windows-based computers.

Most Web servers are set to recognize either *index.htm* or *index.html* as the default file name for your home page. In rare instances either *default.htm* or *default.html* are set as the default file names for home pages. If you have control over your Web server's configuration, you can set the server to recognize *any* file name as the default home page. When you use the required default file name, then visitors to your Website can use the shortened version of your URL. For example, if your home page URL is *www.library.org/index.htm* and the default home page file name is *index.htm*, then visitors can use the shortened version of your URL *www.library.org/* to reach your site.

UNIX systems are case sensitive, so be careful how you name your files and how you reference them in your HTML documents. A file named *Policies.html* is different from a file named *policies.html*. On a Windows-based server, your browser can read either file name, but on a UNIX system these are seen as two different files. For this reason, it is a good practice to use all lower-case characters when naming files.

UNIX can support long file names, but it cannot support spaces in file names. If you name a file *circulation policy.htm*, for example, you can read it on your local PC, but the link will break when you upload it to a UNIX server. Replace with space with a dash or underscore like this: *circulation_policy.htm* or *circulation-policy.htm*.

CREATING AN HTML DOCUMENT

In this section, I present you with enough information to create a very basic HTML document using Microsoft Notepad. If you want to learn more, refer to one of the many books now available on Web publishing. You can also go online and find a lot of useful tutors that are available at no cost. Lastly, you can learn more about Web page design and HTML tags by viewing what other people are doing. When you see a page you like, you can study the HTML tags used to create that page by clicking on Netscape's "View" menu and then choosing "Source."

You can construct a basic Web page in nine easy steps. Before you start, open Notepad and save your document by choosing "Save" from the "File" menu.

Step 1: HTML documents start with the tag <HTML> and ends with the tag </HTML>. The remainder of the document consists of two main sections: The HEAD and the BODY. The *HEAD* is the text that comes at the very top of the browser window. In this sample Web page, we'll insert the phrase "Calico Rock Library" between the <TITLE> and </TITLE> tags as shown here:

```
<HTML>
<HEAD>
<TITLE>Calico Rock Library </TITLE>
</HEAD>
<BODY>
</BODY>
</HTML>
```

The title identifies the document and only appears in the browser's title bar, not in the browser's display area. The title is also displayed as the bookmark text when the document is bookmarked.

Step 2: The main text of the document is located between the <BODY> and </BODY> tags. The first text you should insert is the heading for your document. This is the text that appears at the top of the document and on our sample home page; it could say "Welcome to the Calico Rock Library."

Headings come in six different sizes: <H1>, <H2>, <H3>, <H4>, <H5>, <H6>. Web authors usually type their document heading using the largest heading size—an <H1> heading. Use the heading tags as shown here:

```
<HTML>
<HEAD>
<TITLE>Calico Rock Library </TITLE>
</HEAD>
<BODY>
<H1>Welcome to the Calico Rock Library</H1>
</BODY>
</HTML>
```

Step 3: Add body text to your document. The bulk of your hypertext documents consist of body text—text you use for paragraphs that don't require any special formatting tags.

In the body text below your <H1> heading, tell your readers something about your library or its mission. As you type text in the HTML editor, let the text wrap naturally. HTML doesn't understand hard carriage returns, so you must insert paragraph tags (<P>) to set off a paragraph.

So far, our home page looks like this when viewed in Notepad:

```
<HTML>
<HEAD>
<TITLE>Calico Rock Library </TITLE>
</HEAD>
<BODY>
<H1>Welcome to the Calico Rock Library</H1>

<P>The mission of the Calico Rock Library is to provide unrestricted access to resources
and services that meet the information needs of the citizens of Calico Rock.</P>
```

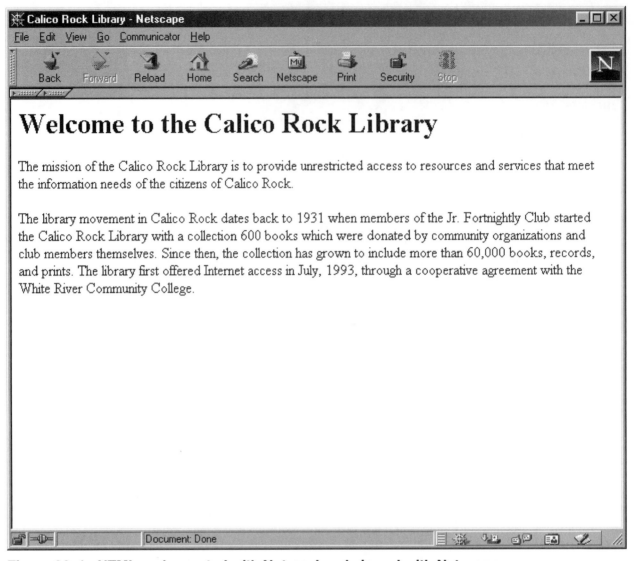

Figure 26–1: HTML code created with Notepad and viewed with Netscape

<P>The library movement in Calico Rock dates back to 1931 when members of the Jr. Fortnightly Club started the Calico Rock Library with a collection 600 books which were donated by community organizations and club members themselves. Since then, the collection has grown to include more than 60,000 books, records, and prints. The library first offered Internet access in July, 1993, through a cooperative agreement with the White River Community College.</P>

</BODY>
</HTML>

Figure 26–1 shows what the home page looks like so far when viewed in a Netscape browser

Step 4: Create a list of library resources and services. With HTML, you can create either a numbered list (ordered list) or a bulleted list (unordered list). Start with the list shown here:

> Library Hours
> Library Events and Programs
> Online Library Catalog
> Holiday Schedule
> Applying for Library Cards
> Library Policies
> Library Services
> Library Board Minutes

To create a bulleted list, highlight the list and then click on the "Bulleted List" button on the toolbar. This adds the required tags as shown below:

> <UL>
> <LH></LH>
> <LI>Library Hours
> <LI>Library Events and Programs
> <LI>Online Library Catalog
> <LI>Holiday schedule
> <LI>Applying for Library Cards
> <LI>Library Policies
> <LI>Library Services
> <LI>Library Board Minutes
> </UL>

The <LH></LH> tags can be ignored, or you can place text between them if you'd like to add a heading above your list.

Step 5: Add your address at the bottom of the page using the <ADDRESS> tag. It's customary to add the name and e-mail address of the individual responsible for creating the home page and the date the home page was last updated. Insert this information just before the </BODY> tag as follows:

<ADDRESS>This document was created by Allen C. Benson (acbenson@calico.lib.us). Last updated 01/15/00.</ADDRESS>

Step 6: Add a hyperlink to the list. This is where HTML tags become confusing, which is why someone invented HTML editors. In this sample exercise, add a hyperlink to the item Library Policies that links to a document called *policies.htm* located in the same directory as your home page. With an HTML editor, you would highlight the line "Library Policies" and then click an "External Hypertext Link" button somewhere on the button bar. Then you would fill-in a text box with the file name to which you are connecting, in this case *policies.htm*. Since we are building a Web page by hand using Notepad, you would type the following text on the Library Policies line:

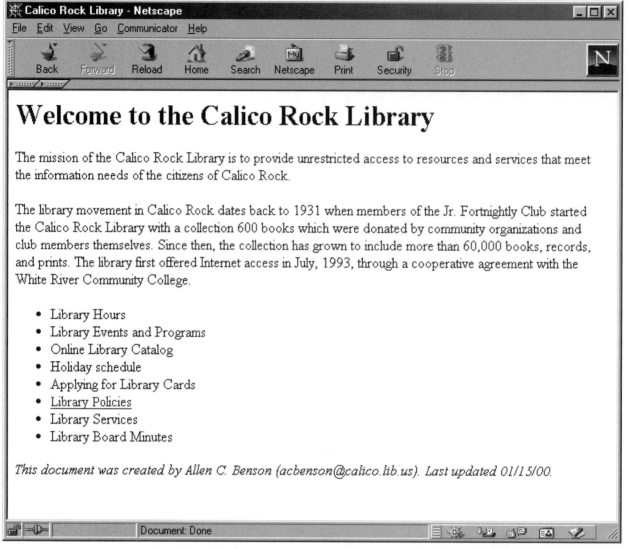

Figure 26–2: As new HTML code is added, click on the "Reload" button on your browser to view the changes

<A HREF="policies.htm">Library Policies</A>

Now when you view your Web page in a browser, it will look something like the image shown in Figure 26–2.

Step 7: Create another HTML document called *policies.htm.* This might look something like the following:

<HTML>
<HEAD>
<TITLE>Policies</TITLE>
</HEAD>
<BODY>

<H1>Policies for the Calico Rock Library</H1>

<UL>
<LI>Borrowing privileges
<LI>Shelving
<LI>Smoking, food, and drink
<LI>Use of computers
<LI>Meeting rooms
<LI>Gifts and donations
</UL>

</BODY>
</HTML>

This uses tags that were introduced earlier for creating a bulleted list.

Step 8: Create a hyperlink to the full text of one of the policies, for example, "Gifts and donations." The gifts and donations document can be named *gifts.htm*. Your final line with tags would look like this:

<A HREF="gifts.htm"> Gifts and donations</A>

Step 9: The final step is to create the text document containing the policy itself. A new tag introduced in this document is called the line break <BR>. Because browsers ignore carriage returns, the only way to get items a., b., and c. to each start on a new line is to insert a <BR> tag at the end of each of those lines. An excerpt from the Gifts and Donations Policy might look something like this:

<HTML>
<HEAD>
<TITLE>Gifts and Donations Policy</TITLE>
</HEAD>
<BODY>
<H1>Gifts and Donations Policy for the Calico Rock Library</H1>
<P>1. The Calico Rock Library is pleased to accept gifts and/or memorial gifts from patrons. Gifts are gratefully and willingly accepted as long as no restriction is placed upon their use. No commitment to accept gifts shall be made by anyone except the Librarian and Board. All such offers made indirectly shall be referred to the Librarian. In respect to gift books, this policy shall be followed: the library maintains the right to decide whether or not any gift is to be added to the collection, sold, or discarded.</P>
<P>2. It should be made clear to the donor that:
a. The Library is not obligated to retain any gifts which fail to meet its criteria for selection.
b. The Library has the right to discard any gifts in poor physical condition (e.g., brittle paper, water or mildew damage, underlining in the text, torn and/or missing pages.
c. The Library has the right to sell any gifts which duplicate materials already in the collection that are not needed for replacement or duplicate copies.
</P>
</BODY>
</HTML>

Online Resource

A Beginner's Guide to HTML, developed by NCSA (National Center for Supercomputing Applications), has become one of the standards on writing HTML documents. It is written for users who have never designed a Web page before. This guide can be accessed freely at site *www.ncsa.uiuc.edu/General/Internet/WWW/HTMLPrimer.html*.

NEW HORIZONS IN WEB PUBLISHING

Many new programs and programming languages are being developed that enhance the interactive possibilities of the Web. As a librarian, it isn't so important that you understand the code-level details of these new languages, but you should become familiar with the terms and what benefits they bring the end user. In this section, I briefly introduce four of the newer publishing tools: Java, CGI, XML, and JavaScript.

WHAT IS JAVA?

Java, developed by Sun Microsystems, is a multimedia tool that allows you to see and interact with animation built into Web pages. One of its main features is its portability—that is, its ability to run on many different systems. When you go to a site that has Java, something called an applet is temporarily transferred to your computer. *Applets* are small, downloadable applications embedded in the Web page that run inside your Web browser window. Applets perform such tasks as calculations, animation, displaying continually updated stock quotes or sports scores on a scrolling banner, and more. You can stay up-to-date with the latest developments in Java by visiting Sun Microsystems, Inc. at *java.sun.com/*. From this page you can access an online Java tutorial and several demo applets.

To learn more about which browsers are Java-enabled, check out the table compiled by Dina M. Medina at site *www.javaworld.com/jw-04_1996/jw-04_browsertable. html*.

WHAT IS CGI?

Website developers create interactive Websites using CGI scripts. *CGI* stands for Common Gateway Interface, which is a set of rules. These rules govern how a client passes data to and receives data from a Web server. *CGI scripts* are programming languages such as C++ and the language of choice—Perl. CGI scripts are used to collect and process information. For example, when you send a virtual postcard, or sign a guest book, a CGI script running on the server system receives your information and processes it. In the case of the guest book, the program simply stores your input in a database. In the case of a virtual postcard, the program generates a response showing you how the card will look before sending it. The card is sent in the form of an HTML file, which the program sends first to the Web server and then from there it goes to the recipient.

A Web page may include *Input Forms*—forms that permit you to input data into a Web page. After you enter the requested information in one of these forms, the Web page acts on the information using a CGI script. An example of a simple form is the

URL-minder, a free service made available by NetMind. To learn more about how this CGI program works, connect to *www.netmind.com/URL-minder/URL-minder.html*. Home pages that offer this service usually have a link that reads something like "Register your e-mail address to receive e-mail when this page is updated!" When the user clicks on this link, a form appears. Data entered into this form is sent to a CGI program. Once the user is registered, he or she is notified by e-mail whenever changes are made to that home page.

Another example of an Input Form is the Interlibrary Loan form at *www.asumh.edu/library/ILL/article.html* used by the Norma Wood Library at Arkansas State University Mountain Home.

CGI scripts are classified as server-side languages because they execute on the server computer, not on your personal computer. Scripting languages, such as JavaScript, run within your browser on your own computer and are considered a client-side language. Client-side languages only need your Web browser to run.

One advantage JavaScripts have over CGI scripts is that they make it possible to respond to actions more quickly. For example, when you click on a button, your action doesn't have to be communicated to a remote Web server.

WHAT IS XML?

XML, a project of the World Wide Web Consortium (W3C) *www.w3.org/*, is a language for describing other languages. XML, which stands for Extensible Markup Language, describes data, not how data is displayed. HTML, on the other hand, is a predefined language that describes how a document is displayed. Take a look at the following HTML example:

```
<B>Books About Log Cabins</B>
<P>
Walter Bernard Hunt. <BR>
<I>Building a log cabin.</I><BR>
Milwaukee, Wisconsin:<BR>
The Bruce Publishing Company, c[1947].<BR>
```

Librarians can recognize right away that this information describes a book: its author, title, place of publication, publisher, and date of publication. The tags I used to describe this book, the <B></B>, <P>, <BR>, and <I></I>, don't make this clear. These tags simply describe how the text should appear. The author is on one line, the title is in italics and comes on another line, and so on. The Web browser, and in many cases the viewer, have no idea what the meaning of this data is. Now take a look at this example in XML. There is a book that's description includes an author, title, place of publication, publisher, and date. In XML, these pieces of information each have their own element, for example, <BOOK>, <AUTHOR>, <TITLE>, etc.:

```
<BOOK>
    <AUTHOR>
        <FIRST>Walter</FIRST>
        <MIDDLE>Bernard</MIDDLE>
```

```
        <LAST>Hunt</LAST>
</AUTHOR>
<TITLE>Building a log cabin.</TITLE>
<PLACE>
        <CITY>Milwaukee</CITY>
        <STATE>Wisconsin</STATE>
<PUBLISHER> The Bruce Publishing Company</PUBLISHER>
<DATE>c[1947]</DATE>
</BOOK>
```

The XML version defines the structure of the data. It can be thought of as a hierarchical structure, or *family*. It includes a parent, or *root*, which is the "book." The book object has children, which include *author, title, place, publisher*, and *date*. Some of these first-generation children have their own children, analogous to grandchildren. For example, the *first*, *middle*, and *last* child elements are under the first generation *author* child element.

WHAT IS JAVASCRIPT?

JavaScript is a scripting language developed by Netscape Communications Corp. and Sun Microsystems. *Scripting* languages are programming languages that consist of commands written in plain text. Most scripting languages are not compiled. Instead, you use an interpreter to execute the script. Netscape 2.0 and Internet Explorer 3.0 are the earliest versions of these applications that support JavaScript. A common method of embedding JavaScript in an HTML document is to place it between a <SCRIPT></SCRIPT> tag pair. Developers use JavaScript to add interactivity to their Websites, for example, games, pop-up windows, animation, current date and time, and more.

Librarian's Homepage Creator

Please fill in all the blanks and select at least one item from each section.
You can delete these items from your homepage later, it you like.

About your organization

Note: The contact information will appear at the end of your page. Do not leave blank lines. You can change or delete this information from your homepage later.

```
        Organization: [                    ]
     Web Page Title:  [                    ]
            Address:  [                    ]
     City/State/Zip:  [                    ]
          Telephone:  [                    ]
              Email:  [                    ]
```

Describe your library or organization

Note: There's no wordwrap. Hit ENTER to start a new line. Don't get too fancy with formatting - it will not be copied to your homepage.

Figure 26–3: View of LibPage, the librarian's home page generator

LIBPAGE: THE LIBRARIAN'S HOME PAGE GENERATOR

Home page generators are Web pages that enable you to create your home page by simply filling out forms and clicking on choices. When finished, you click on a button labeled something like "Create Page." A moment later your new, custom-designed home page appears on the screen.

The advantage of using a generator is that all of the HTML tags discussed earlier in this chapter are inserted automatically for you. This is especially useful when it involves extensive use of hyperlinks to other sites on the Internet. The only drawback to using a home page generator is that your home page content is limited to the choices offered by the generator.

There is a home page generator sponsored by Metronet called LibPage that is designed just for libraries. In this section, I describe briefly how to connect to LibPage and create your own custom-designed home page.

- Start up Netscape Navigator and enter the following address in the "Location" box near the top of the screen: *www.metronet.lib.mn.us/libpage/libpage2.htm*. This will connect you to LibPage shown in Figure 26–3.
- After filling out the LibPage form, click on the "Create a Page" button.
- If you'd like to make any changes, click on the "Back" button, make your changes, and then click on the "Create a Page" button again.

Online Resource

One of the best ways to promote your Website is by registering your site with search engines. Learn how to get the best possible placement in search results lists and other Website marketing tips from an excellent article on Cnet at *www.cnet.com/Content/Features/Howto/Promote/*.

- To save your home page, pull down the "File" menu and click on "Save as." Choose the folder in which you want to save the HTML file. You can name the file *index.htm*.
- To save the graphic you chose to place at the top of your home page, place your cursor on the middle of the image, click the right mouse button, and select the option to "Save this image as." Store the image in the same directory as you store your HTML file.
- To view your home page locally, pull down the "File" menu and click on "Open File." To make your home page available on the Internet, upload the HTML file and images to your Internet service provider's computer.

DEVELOPING MULTIMEDIA FOR WEB PAGES

Librarians have the option of contracting graphics jobs out to professional art studios or doing the work in-house. One side benefit of investing in the hardware and software to do the work in-house is that the equipment can also be made available to the public for their use. The downside, of course, is that you must be able to support this new software and hardware. If everyone is already stretched to their limits with understanding and applying new technology, there may not be enough resources to formally support yet another application or hardware peripheral.

In Chapter 21 I introduce you to the tools used for creating and editing sound, images, and motion pictures. For further insight and reviews of the latest products, consult the following online resources.

- Benchin Software Review *www.benchin.com/cgi-bin/nph-$index.exe*—This site reviews 12 categories of hardware including accessories, communications hardware, computer systems, input devices, mass storage devices, memory and processors, multimedia hardware, networking connectivity hardware, power protection, printers and plotters, supplies, and video displays and adapters.
- CNET Hardware Reviews *computers.cnet.com/hardware/0–1016.html*—CNET offers a wide range of information on hardware peripherals. For example, their page containing information on scanners includes reviews of the top five scanners, a buyer's guide to scanners, links to manufacturers, and links to additional resources relating to scanners.
- ComputingReview.com *www.computingreview.com/*—This site offers product reviews for computers, digital cameras, monitors, scanners, servers, sound cards, printers, and more. Features a Hall of Fame and a Hall of Shame.
- CPUReview.com *www.cpureview.com/*—CPUReview.com covers processors, motherboards, video cards, and other PC related technology.

Online Resource

Information City provides a free metatag generator at *www.freereports.net/ metatags.html*. Using metatags helps optimize your Web pages for indexing by robots. You simply enter your information for title, author, subject, description, and keywords, and then click the "Create Metatags" button. The metatag generator automatically creates the HTML code you need to copy and paste between the head tags at the top of your page.

- HardwareCentral www.hardwarecentral.com/hardwarecentral—Go here to find reviews, previews, interviews, and how-to documents on the latest hardware products.
- ZDNet *www.zdnet.com*—Check out Ziff-Davis's home page for reviews of the latest software and hardware. Keyword search ZDNet's entire site, or browse Reviews, Tech News, Downloads, Tech Life, Shopping, Help & How-To, and Developer categories. Link to online editions of any one of their computer publications, especially *PC Magazine*.

In a small library where Web development is the responsibility of the director, or maybe an individual on the staff or a volunteer that has the reputation of being the local "computer expert," it may be best to invest in applications that are designed for the casual user. Medium- to large-size libraries that have several professional librarians working as a team on Web page development may choose to go with applications that are designed for graphics professionals.

VIEWING AND CREATING PORTABLE DOCUMENTS

Just about any information that's printed on paper can be transformed into electronic format, but there are some tradeoffs. Although digitized documents on the Internet can be easily indexed, searched, and transferred between computers, it is hard to control exactly how those documents will look. Elements such as paper size and composition are difficult, if not impossible, to translate into an electronic format. Issues like type size and style and how words and images are positioned on the page can be controlled with special software.

The sections that follow explain how this can be done using a program developed by Adobe Acrobat. The documents this program creates are referred to generically as portable documents because they can be viewed on any platform and still retain their original layout and design.

WHAT IS A PORTABLE DOCUMENT?

In the past, anyone who wanted to distribute a document had only three choices:

- They could distribute it as paper.
- They could distribute it as a digital file saved as ASCII text only.

- They could deliver it in a native-file format such as WordPerfect or Microsoft Word with all of the required fonts and graphics. In this instance, recipients could view the document only if they had the same application.

With the introduction of portable documents, you are given another option for distributing documents. *Portable documents* are platform-independent electronic file formats that preserve all of the visual aspects of a formatted document including the fonts, graphics, and colors. For example, this technology enables you to create a flyer on your Mac with text and graphics and then view it on a computer running Windows. The font display and graphics would appear the same on each computer.

One example of portable documents online can be found at a site on the Internet maintained by the IRS. The IRS makes tax forms available at Website *www.irs.ustreas.gov/ prod/forms_pubs/forms.html*. These tax form files can be viewed by both Mac and Windows users. Portable documents also utilize hypertext links and can be used for navigating the Web just as easily as Web pages.

WHAT ARE DOCUMENT VIEWERS?

Document viewers are the applications that enable you to view, navigate, and print portable document files. When you come across a portable document on the Internet, you have two options for viewing it: You can either view it seamlessly while running a Web browser, or you can download the file and then open it in a viewer application independent of your browser. In the first scenario, you would use a plug-in version of the viewer. In the second scenario, you would use an external helper application.

You can download the viewer as freeware on the Internet, or you can purchase a software package that enables you to both view and create portable documents.

DOWNLOADING AND INSTALLING VIEWERS

Most of the portable documents on the Internet are saved as PDF (Portable Document Format) files. This is the file format developed by Adobe Acrobat. There used to be another program available called Common Ground that named its portable documents DigitalPaper.

HOW TO DOWNLOAD ADOBE ACROBAT FOR WINDOWS

The Acrobat Reader 4.05 is free and available for Windows 2000, Windows 95/98, Windows 3.1, Windows NT 4.0 and 3.51, Macintosh, OS2, and different flavors of UNIX. In the Windows and Macintosh versions, Acrobat Reader is available in 12 different languages. To download, enter the following address in your browser's address window: *www.adobe.com/products/acrobat/readermain.html*. Look for Acrobat Reader in the "Downloads" area.

CREATING PDF FILES

If you're interested in publishing PDF documents, you must buy Adobe Acrobat—a suite of developmental tools. Included in the package are the tools required for searching, modifying, bookmarking, password protecting, and printing electronic documents in the Portable Document Format (PDF). Acrobat tools also let you add hyperlinks within a document, hyperlinks to other PDF documents, and hyperlinks to HTML documents on the Web.

The process of actually creating a PDF document is quite simple. Using the Acrobat PDFWriter driver (which comes with the package), you create a PDF file from within any application (Excel, WordPerfect, CorelDRAW, etc.) by using the "print" command to print the document to a PDF file. In other words, instead of choosing a printer, such as HP DeskJet, on LPT1 in "Print Setup," choose Adobe PDFWriter. (This print driver is automatically installed when you install Adobe Acrobat.)

CREATING PDF DOCUMENTS ONLINE

You can create Adobe Acrobat PDF documents by either purchasing Adobe Acrobat, or by subscribing to their new online service. Create Adobe PDF Online located at *cpdf1.adobe.com/* is a Web-hosted service that lets you convert Microsoft Office files, Web pages, graphic files, and other file types into Adobe PDF files that anyone can view using Acrobat Reader. You are limited to processing times not exceeding 15 minutes and file sizes not exceeding 50MB. It is simple to use, but if you have a slow connection to the Internet you may not want to wait for files to upload. To use the service, you upload your file or specify a URL. After the file is uploaded it is converted into a PDF document. It can then be downloaded or sent to you as an e-mail attachment.

Implementing Web-Based Search Engines and Databases

Since the last edition of this book was published, numerous opportunities have become available that make publishing on the Web exciting for even novice users. Services that were once out of reach because of their cost and complexity are now available free of charge and can be easily implemented without having any background in programming and system administration. This means that librarians, on their own, can now build Websites housing textual documents and offer search engines that are capable of searching their site's holdings. Web-based database systems are also available that make it easy to build simple, low-cost digital libraries. Because they are accessed on the Web and viewed in browsers, they can support file types browsers support. For example, multimedia documents including video and audio clips.

In Chapter 27, I introduce you to services that can help you organize and access the data you have stored on your Website. The chapter starts out with brief explanations of some of the more complex search and indexing systems designed for advanced users. These four applications all share one unique element in common. They are all free and can be downloaded from the Internet. I follow these explanations with a more detailed look at a system called whatUseek that is Web-based, free of charge, and can be set up and made operational without any experience in programming. In minutes, you can learn how to add search boxes to your Web page that are capable of searching only your site. The chapter concludes with information on how you can organize digital objects, such as images and audio clips, by using a simple, Web-based database system.

FREE SEARCH AND INDEXING SYSTEMS

Search engines are great value-added services you can add to your Website for no additional charge. They do require considerable time to install and configure properly, but the end results make the effort worthwhile. My purpose in introducing search engines is to help you gain controlled access of your own local document collections. Search engines can be made to *spider*, that is, index sites out on the Web, or they can build databases by searching only local intranets.

Search engines have one component that indexes the files you specify, and another component that searches the index and brings back the results. One approach would be to use these engines for full-text indexing and searching. Another, more controlled approach would be to use metatags in HTML documents and focus indexing on metadata. Versions of some of the engines described below run on both UNIX and Windows 95/98/NT.

ALTAVISTA SEARCH

AltaVista Search Free 3000 is a fully functional engine, but limited in terms of how many Web pages and files it can index. There is no built-in time limit with the program, but you are limited to indexing only 3,000 pieces of information at a time. For many, this ceiling presents no problems and offers a great opportunity to get started with indexing. The free version of AltaVista Search runs on various systems, including Windows NT, and is provided "as is", with no special warranties or official support. For a complete listing of system requirements, go to *doc.altavista.com/business_solutions/search_products/search_intranet/specs_requirements.shtml*.

Why might you choose one engine over another? For starters, AltaVista is easier to manage for novices. You configure the indexing parameters in a Web interface with mouse clicks. Swish-E, another search engine, is configured using a text editor. Help manuals in Swish-E don't explain things in great detail and scripts can be somewhat cryptic. Another advantage AltaVista *Search* has over Swish-E is that AltaVista indexes every word, allowing for exact phrase and keyword searching. AltaVista was designed to handle the large information sets resulting from this type of indexing. AltaVista also handles multiple languages. All of these features translate into a large file size, over 28MB to download.

To learn more about how you can build your own AltaVista search engine, visit their site at *doc.altavista.com/business_solutions/search_products/search_intranet/intranet_intro.shtml*, or look for a link pointing to AltaVista Search Products off their main page at *www.altavista.com*.

SWISH-E

Swish-E, or Simple Web Indexing System for Humans-Enhanced, is a program that indexes files and then lets you search those indexes. Kevin Hughes created the original program Swish, which was later enhanced by a development team at University of California at Berkeley resulting in Swish-Enhanced (Swish-E). This is the search engine used by the Librarians' Index to the Internet maintained by Carole Leita, *sunsite.berkeley.edu/InternetIndex/*.

Swish-E can index Web pages or other text files. It doesn't index formatted Word documents. A *user.config* file enables you to specify various levels of control on how indexing takes place and what gets indexed. When indexing Web pages, Swish-E can be told to ignore some tags while giving greater relevance to other tags.

Swish-E has been ported to various platforms including FreeBSD, IRIX, and OS/2. All can be accessed at *sunsite.berkeley.edu/SWISH-E/Ports/*. You can download source code and binary executables files for Windows NT from *www.webaugur.com/wares/files/*. The latest version at the time of this writing was *swishe-winnt-x86_132.zip*. Swish-E's main site is at *sunsite.berkeley.edu/SWISH-E/*. There you can find demonstrations of Swish-E, documentation, a Swish-E bulletin board, and CGI programs for helping you access your indexes. You can also download the source code and *user.config* file from this site.

I successfully ran Swish-E on a Windows 98 PC. I downloaded John Millard's Perl gateway interface (CGI) to Swish-E at *staff.lib.muohio.edu/~millarj/software/* and installed a version of Swish-E compiled for Windows NT. I also had good luck installing and configuring Swish-E to run on LINUX. The greatest challenges come in *tweaking* the user configuration file that determines the indexing rules and the CGI script that gets input from the user through an HTML form.

HT://DIG

Another free search and indexing system that runs on UNIX is ht://Dig. It is the system used by The WWW Virtual Library at *vlib.org/*. Complete details about ht:Dig are provided at *www.htdig.org/*. The underlying processes that enable ht://Dig to complete its work include Digging, Merging, and Searching.

Digging is the process of creating a database that contains all of the documents that are going to be searched. Other systems call this stage harvesting or spidering. The *harvester* goes to an HTML document and then proceeds to follow all hyperlinks that it comes across, or at least those in a specified domain. The result of this process creates two files: one that contains a list of all the words and another that contains the URLs and information about the URLs.

The Merging process converts these databases into a form that can be understood by the search engine. This process also creates a fuzzy word index. *Fuzzy searches* are searches that use algorithms to find matches. ht://Dig supports *exact, soundex, metaphone, common word endings,* and *synonyms.*

The last process is Searching. This is where the end user searches all of the information collected during the Digging and Merging stages. The result is a list of hits presented in HTML format.

ROADS

ROADS, common in the U.K. higher-education community, is a set of software tools that allow you to create a *subject gateway*—a catalog of searchable and browsable Internet based resources. Subjects can be anything you wish, but are usually built around academic subject headings.

You can view ROADS in action at various United Kingdom sites. ADAM *adam.ac.uk/* —the Art, Design, Architecture & Media Information Gateway—is a searchable cata-

---

Microsoft Index Server

Microsoft Windows NT Sever versions 4.0 and later support an application called Microsoft Index Server. If you are running Internet Information Services (IIS) as your Web server, and the Index Server has been installed, Microsoft FrontPage automatically utilizes the Index Server when you use a search from FrontPage.

---

logue containing 2,546 Internet resources selected and catalogued by librarians. Biz/ed *www.bized.ac.uk/* is a catalog of business and economics service for students and teachers. SOSIG *www.sosig.ac.uk/* is an Internet catalog of social science resources. ROADS is perfect for creating a robust resource discovery tool that targets specific audiences. To learn more about ROADS, visit their Website at *www.ilrt.bris.ac.uk/roads/*.

FIND WHATUSEEK

What I am about to describe would have been beyond the reach of most librarians in small libraries one year ago—the ability to set up and configure a search and indexing system for a Website. Either the expense or the learning curve would have prevented it. Now there are free search and indexing tools available that enable visitors to search only your site. I had difficulty deciding where in this book to introduce this kind of service. I was afraid it would be lost in the chapter 20 "Virtually Yours for Free," so I decided to incorporate it into this chapter on electronic publishing. If you are publishing textual documents on the Web, a search and indexing system like the one I describe here can add search functionality to your site.

This section focuses on one service in particular called whatUseek developed by What-U-Seek of Northville, Michigan. whatUseek consists of a search and indexing system called *intraSearch* that not only supports searching, but also reporting so you are given some insight into what visitors to your site are looking for and what they found. whatUseek offers other search-related services from their Website at *www.whatuseek.com/*, all part of the whatUseek Network. These include a meta search engine called Chubba.com, meta searching of online auctions through SuperAuction.com, and an e-newsletter directed towards Webmasters.

SPIDERING YOUR SITE

Setting up an account is easy. Point your browser to *www.whatuseek.com/* and click on the link labeled "intraSearch." All you have to do to register is provide your e-mail address and the URL for the site you want to index, or have spidered. You are immediately assigned a password that gives you access to your account management area. This is where you go to change your password and work on customizing how your search results page looks.

The spidering process involves *crawling* your Website and building an index. This is handled automatically by whatUseek. It may take a few hours to complete, so be patient. You know the spidering is complete when you can insert search terms in the search box on your Web page, run a search, and get results!

INSERTING A SEARCH BOX IN YOUR HOME PAGE

After you register, you are given a password to your account and instructions on how to insert a search box on your home page. These are the search box options you have:

1. JavaScript Search Box—When you use this option you can update how your search box looks from your whatUseek account management area. It requires that you copy and paste HTML code into your Web pages.
2. Hyperlink to Search Box—This is the simplest method. Visitors to your site hyperlink to a page on the whatUseek site and it is there that they have access to your search box.
3. HTML Search Box—This advanced option requires a good understanding of HTML forms and allows for lots of customization of the search box.

Going with the last option gives you the most flexibility and, if you have a basic background in working with HTML code, I recommend this option.

CONFIRMING YOUR URL

After you copy and paste the necessary code into your Web page, visit your management area and take care of some housekeeping details. You can automatically login during the second stage of your registration process. The first order of business is confirming that whatUseek has the right URL for your site. Next, decide if there is any secondary URL entry points or URLs you wish to exclude from the indexing process.

A *secondary entry point* would be another server where you store content besides the primary URL for your Website. Other examples of secondary entry points are *frames* that have their own URLs and documents that are reached via Java or JavaScript rather than the standard <A HREF> tag. In the latter case, you would enter every document URL as a secondary entry point that is reached via Java.

Exclusion URLs and *masks* are URLs that you do not want indexed. Any pages you list as exclusion URLs will not be crawled (indexed) by the whatUseek spider. A mask is just part of a URL, for example, a file name or directory path statement. When the spider comes across any URL that contains a mask, it ignores it just as it ignores exclusions.

SITE LIMITATIONS

whatUseek is free because it is advertiser supported. There is another option available, however, called the Premium Option which removes the banner ads from your search results page. This service costs anywhere from $5 to $40 per month depending on how many pages you have on your site. The free "Basic Option" package is limited to 1,000 pages and places an ad on your search results page.

As part of the registration process, after you designate secondary and exclusion/mask URLs, you choose whether you want the ad-based option or Premium Option package. Discounts are offered to government, nonprofit, and educational institutions.

Figure 27–1: The default search box created by whatUseek

SUPPORT AND FINISHING TOUCHES

The next step in the registration process gives you a chance to request assistance in the form of an e-mail message sent to your e-mail box. The only thing you may need help with is copying and pasting HTML code into your Web page. You can specify which HTML editor you use and/or which free Web service you use for specialized help in this area. If you are not interested in receiving additional help, skip this page and finish the registration process.

The last step is telling the system whether you want it to remember your e-mail address and password for the login process. If you exercise this option, your browser remembers these two items and logs you in automatically next time you visit.

From this point forward, if you want to edit your account information or change options, simply go to *www.whatuseek.com/*, login with your e-mail address and password, and make the necessary changes.

The default search box that is created on your Web page when choosing option three (see the section covered earlier called "Inserting a Search Box in Your Home Page") looks like the image shown in Figure 27–1.

The HTML code behind this image is shown in Figure 27–2.

MODIFYING YOUR SEARCH BOX

Here are some simple alterations you can apply to modify how the search box looks. In the following code, I added a number at the beginning of each line to make it easier to reference. Keep in mind, wherever you place the code in your Web page that is where the search box appears.

1) <form method="get" action="http://intra.whatUseek.com/query.go" TARGET="_self">
2) <table border="2" cellspacing="0" cellpadding="0">
3) <tr>
4) <td width="100%"><table cellspacing=0 cellpadding=2 border=0>
5) <tr>
6) <td align="center"><font><small>Search </small></font><font size="1"><input type="radio" value="02534f9a50311bb3" checked name="crid">This
7) Site <input type="radio" name="crid" value="web">
8) The Web </font><font> </font></td></tr>
9) <tr>
10) <td align="center"><input type="text" NAME="query" SIZE="15" VALUE

Figure 27–2: The HTML code created by whatUseek that forms the image of the search box shown in Figure 27–1

```
<form method="get" action="http://intra.whatUseek.com/query.go" TARGET="_self">
<table border="2" cellspacing="0" cellpadding="0">
<tr>
<td width="100%"><table cellspacing=0 cellpadding=2 border=0>
<tr>
<td align="center"><font><b><small>Search </small></b></font><font size="1"><input
type="radio" value="02534f9a50311bb3" checked name="crid">This
 Site <input type="radio" name="crid" value="web">
 The Web </font><font> </font></td></tr>
<tr>
<td align="center"><input type="text" NAME="query" SIZE="15" VALUE
MAXLENGTH="100"> <input type="submit" value="Search" name="B1"></td></tr>
<tr>
<td align="right">
 <p align="center"><a href="http://intra.whatUseek.com?synd=box&chan=1"><font
size="1">Get a Search Engine
 For Your Web Site</font></a></p>
</td></tr>
</table>
</td>
</tr>
</table>
 </form>
<img src="http://intra.whatUseek.com/htmlbox.go?crid=02534f9a50311bb3" width=1
height=1>
```

```
        MAXLENGTH="100"> <input type="submit" value="Search" name="B1"></
        td></tr>
11)     <tr>
12)     <td align="right">
13)     <p align="center"><a href="http: intra.whatUseek.com?synd=box&chan=1">
        <font size="1">Get a Search Engine
14)     For Your Web Site</font></a></p>
15)     </td></tr>
16)     </table>
17)     </td>
18)     </tr>
19)     </table>
20)     </form>
21)     <img src="http://intra.whatUseek.com/htmlbox.go?crid=02534f9a50311bb3"
        width=1 height=1>
```

Figure 27–3: Increasing the border width around the search box

Increasing the Border Size

In line 2 of the example code above, the text that reads "<table border ="2" " deter-mines the width or thickness of the border in pixels. To increase the width, increase the number. In Figure 27–3, you can see the original box with the border set at "2" com-pared to the same search box with the border set to "6".

Increasing the Size of the Cell

Cellpadding affects the distance between the cell wall and the contents. In line 4 of the sample code you see that cellpadding is set to "2". When you increase this to 10, it appears as shown in Figure 27–4.

Lengthening the Text Box

In line 10 of the sample code above, there is a "SIZE="15"." This sets the size of the text box in characters. By default it is set to 15 characters long. If you increase it to 30, you give visitors a larger viewing window and it appears like the example shown in Figure 27–5.

Editing Text

It is nice to let others know where you found this great search and indexing system, but if you want to remove the link to whatUseek, simply delete lines 13 and 14. Now the search box looks like the one shown in Figure 27–6. I have also lengthened the text box in this example.

Figure 27–4: Increasing the size of the cell

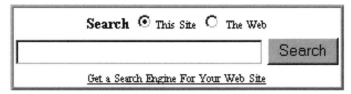

Figure 27–5: Increasing the length of the text box

Centering the Search Box on the Page

If you want to center the search box on your Web page, replace line 2 with the following code:

<table align="center" border="2" cellspacing="0" cellpadding="0">

The only change I made was I added "align="center" " to position the entire table on the center of the page.

LOGIN FOR MAINTENANCE AND CONFIGURATION

After you have your account set up and you have waited a few hours to make certain your site has been crawled by the whatUseek spider, go to your Web page and run a search. This gives you an opportunity to see what the default settings are in how the search results are displayed on the page. I installed the whatUseek intraSearch service on the files included on the CD-ROM accompanying this book. My search results on the phrase **search engine** are shown in Figure 27–7.

To change how your site is indexed and how the search results are presented on the results screen, login to your account and click on the tab labeled "spidering options." The options that are available can be viewed in Figure 27–8. As you can see from the spidering options that are available, this is where you go to re-index your site—something you should do when you change or add new information. You can use the "search box options" tab to change the way your search box looks, rather than *hacking* by hand as I described earlier in this section. In addition, this is where you go to view usage reports.

CHANGING THE RELEVANCY RANKING

whatUseek allows you to weigh four different elements:

1. data found in the description metatag
2. data found in the keywords metatag
3. data found in the title tag
4. data found in the body tag

Figure 27–6: Deleting text from the search box

search engines | This Site ▼ | seek

Documents 1 - 5 of 5 matches, best matches first.

Databases

... Alex Catalog of Electronic Texts - http://www.lib.ncsu.edu/staff/morgan/alex/alex-index.html **Search** digital documents conatined in this catalog of English literature, American literature, and Western ...

http://eagletower.artshost.com/dat.htm - 10k - 2000-08-09

Graphics

... . Images are sorted by color and motif. Alta Vista Photo Finder - http://www.altavista.com/ **Search** millions of pictures and images(Unfiltered version also available). Animation Factory - http ...

http://eagletower.artshost.com/gra.htm - 5k - 2000-08-09

Webmaster Resources

... Perl, JavaScript, XML, Design, Web Graphics, Streaming Media, Site Management, Affiliate Programs, **Search Engines**, and Intranets. Registrar Directory - http://www.internic.net/regist.html Browse ...

http://eagletower.artshost.com/web.htm - 5k - 2000-08-09

META Tags

... (RDF) integrates various metadata activities on the Web including sitemaps, collecting data for **search engine**, digital library collections, and others. This site includes links to recommended readings ...

http://eagletower.artshost.com/met.htm - 4k - 2000-08-09

Cataloging

... Journals/Newsletters/Citation Sources, Discussion List Archives, Other Sources, and Internet **Search Engines**. Created and maintained by Ann Ercelawn.   Copyright © 2000 Allen C. Benson ...

http://eagletower.artshost.com/cat.htm - 4k - 2000-08-09

Figure 27–7: Screen shot showing search results using whatUseek intraSearch

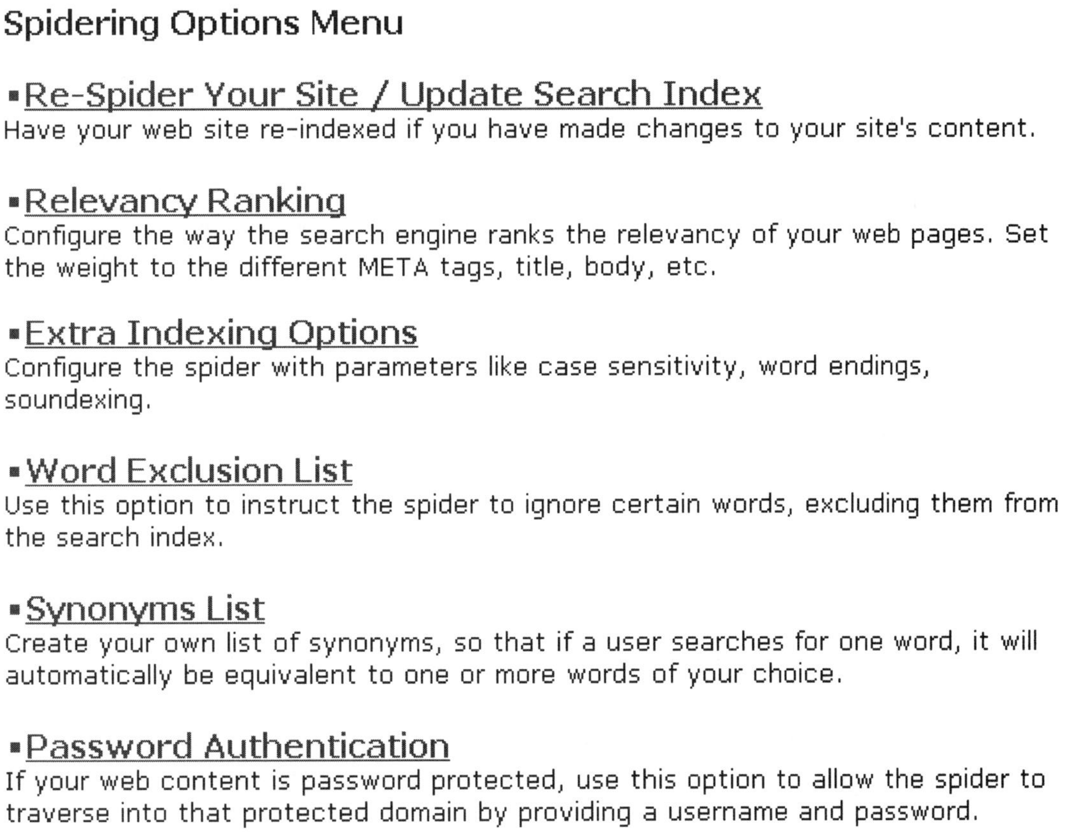

Spidering Options Menu

•Re-Spider Your Site / Update Search Index
Have your web site re-indexed if you have made changes to your site's content.

•Relevancy Ranking
Configure the way the search engine ranks the relevancy of your web pages. Set the weight to the different META tags, title, body, etc.

•Extra Indexing Options
Configure the spider with parameters like case sensitivity, word endings, soundexing.

•Word Exclusion List
Use this option to instruct the spider to ignore certain words, excluding them from the search index.

•Synonyms List
Create your own list of synonyms, so that if a user searches for one word, it will automatically be equivalent to one or more words of your choice.

•Password Authentication
If your web content is password protected, use this option to allow the spider to traverse into that protected domain by providing a username and password.

Figure 27–8: View of the "Spidering Options Menu"

To take full advantage of this feature, all of your documents should contain the keyword and description metatags along with the body and title tags. For more information on metatags, see the sidebar "Describing Networked Resources: Questions and Answers About Metadata" in Chapter 18.

Relevancy ranking is the process of ranking documents for keyword searches—telling the search engine what elements in the document are important and what their level of importance is. When you assign a lot of importance, or *weight*, to an element, you assign it a high number. You have the numbers 0 through 5 with which to work. For example, if you want the spider to consider the data in the keywords metatag to be the most relevant, you assign this element a "5". If you want the title element to be least important in ranking search results, you assign that element a "0". The default settings are good, giving the description and keyword metatags the greatest weight.

CHANGING THE SEARCH RESULTS PAGE

Click on the "search results customization" to change the way your search results page looks. You have two options: basic and advanced. In the basic options menu you are given a choice of pre-designed menus that offer different colors, logos, and backgrounds, etc. In the advanced options menu you have the ability to go in and change the HTML code, modifying the search results template however you wish.

This part of whatUseek's configuration options is unique. To change how search results are presented in locally run search and indexing systems, like those described earlier in this chapter, is fairly advanced. By using whatUseek's menu options, you can make significant changes by simply clicking on options in a drop-down menu. For example, the output shown in Figure 27–7 uses the default setting that shows the text that matches the query. In other words, it shows you where in the text the keywords "search engine" occur—taking a few words on each side of the keywords and displaying those in the results. A pull-down menu makes it easy to change this. You can change it so that either the data contained in the description metatag is displayed, the opening text in the document is displayed, or have nothing but the title displayed. You can even limit the summary's length in bytes (characters). By default it is set at 200 bytes. Other options available are showing or not showing the URL, document size, and modification date.

FUTURE CONSIDERATIONS

If you can begin building your site from scratch, I highly recommend adding keyword and description metatags to all of your documents. It is the best way to control not only how your site is indexed, but also how search results are displayed. You may decide at some future date that you want to move to a more sophisticated search and indexing system run locally. The metatags contained in your documents will remain important control elements in determining how your data is indexed and displayed in the new system.

WEB-BASED DATABASE SYSTEMS

Three or four years ago, porting a database to the Web was considered a formidable task for most librarians. Even I struggled with off-the-shelf applications like FileMaker Pro, trying to get it to support multimedia objects in container fields. The whole process of making databases accessible via the Web is becoming simpler each passing year; but for now, nothing is as simple as an online service called Bitlocker. *Bitlocker*, a private company founded in 1997 and located in Palo Alto, California, has created an easy-to-use Web-based solution. Like all Web-based applications, it doesn't run as fast as a system running on your local PC or server, especially if you have a dial-up connection. Further, it isn't as robust as a full-fledged database application, such as Microsoft Access. It has its place, however, and what it can do is pretty phenomenal when you consider it takes only minutes to set up and it's free! Login to Bitlocker's site at *www.bitlocker.com/* to begin registration.

WHAT IS A DATABASE?

A *database* is a collection of related information. It is organized in a manner that makes it easy to find what you are looking for. You can also update, sort, and print this information as needed. A database can be textual; for example, the names and addresses of all the patrons who use your library. Databases can be *image libraries*—collections of scanned photographs with keywords and descriptions. They can be audio libraries or a mix of different types of media including text, images, audio clips, and video clips.

A database may contain only one file, for example, the name, address, telephone number, and barcode number of every patron in your system. Using a *relational database*, you can join information between two or more files. For example, one file could show you that patrons are registered to use your library and a related file could show you invoices for lost items checked out by patrons.

WHY DO YOU WANT A DATABASE?

Are you sure you need a database? Especially a Web-based database? Not only should you think about your organization's needs, but the patrons you serve. If you work in a college library and the art faculty is storing lots of digital images online, maybe a Web-based database system would help organize their collection and make it more accessible to students. The library may have a small special collection of documents and/or images that could be digitized and made available via the Web. It is important to think about your needs in advance because it can help in the design of the record. A *record* is a component of a database file. Files contain one or more records. Each record contains information about one subject. For example, one record in a patron database would contain the name and address of only one patron. One record in an image database would contain the title and description of only one image.

The following basic information is needed before you start any database project:

- A name for your database
- Decide what the unit of information (record) is going to be. Can you break your information up into chunks that fit into records and fields? For example, if you have a collection of photographs, the record will be an image with a description. The fields can be title, keywords, creator, date created, etc. The record can simply describe the image, or you can have a container field in which you place the image itself.
- Determine what the fields are for each record
- Decide on a login ID and password (if needed)
- Set up quality controls, such as naming rules and formats for entering dates, etc. If you are creating digital documents to place in the database, you can set rules for file size, resolution, and file type, etc. If you are assigning keywords or subjects, use a list of standardized words, a controlled vocabulary from an existing thesaurus.
- Think about how much information you are going to enter into the database. Most systems have limitations.

WHAT ARE WEB-BASED DATABASES?

A Web-based database runs on a server that you access using the Web. The server might be located close by, or it might be thousands of miles away. No matter where the database is located, you access the system using the Internet and a Web browser. The system featured in this section also allows you to manage the information on your Website dynamically using a Web browser. A unique feature of Web-based databases is that you can view file types supported by your browser's plug-ins or helper applications. For example, if you include a movie clip in your database, depending on the format, Windows Media Player, RealPlayer, or QuickTime can view it.

WHAT DOES BITLOCKER OFFER?

Bitlocker provides two basic services. Free access to a Web-based database application called DatabasePlus and access to small business and political campaign applications. You can begin building your own custom database using a new Database Plus template or you can use one of the Business or Home templates already made up. Here is a complete listing of the current templates available:

- Advertising Schedule
- Book Library
- Bug Tracker
- Class Registration
- Customer Feedback
- Employee Evaluation
- Event Planner
- Food Diary
- Gift List
- Interview Feedback
- Journal
- Meeting Minutes
- Movie Library
- Music Collection Library
- News Clippings
- Online News Sources
- Photo Album
- Product Registration
- Recipe Catalog
- School Activities
- Wedding Planner
- Wine Cellar

Bitlocker also offers access to the following small business applications and political campaign applications:

- ApplicantPlus
- AssetPlus
- ContactPlus
- LeadPlus
- ContributorPlus
- VolunteerPlus

Bitlocker gives you 25MB of storage space for your data. You can control who accesses your database and what tasks users can perform.

CAN YOU IMPORT PRE-EXISTING DATABASES INTO DATABASEPLUS?

Bitlocker supports importing text files, HTML, and Dbase tables into your database. With database and spreadsheet applications you would begin by exporting your records into a tab-delimited text file. To import a file into DatabasePlus, you begin by clicking on an "Edit" button and then choosing the "Import" command. Before you begin, you must create a database using the same fields as in your original database.

You can also export files you create with DatabasePlus. You click on the "Edit" button and then choose "Export." You are given three text file formats from which to choose: tab delimited, comma delimited, or HTML table.

DOES DATABASEPLUS SUPPORT MULTIMEDIA?

DatabasePlus supports a field type called File, which allows you to upload pictures and any file into a database record. GIF and JPEG files automatically display as thumbnails. Sound files can be placed in this field if the file type is supported by Windows Media Player, or a browser plug-in or helper application.

The URL field type makes it possible for you to link to other sites and services. If for some reason you can't store your information in DatabasePlus, you might be able to link to it using a URL.

BUILDING A BASIC MULTIMEDIA DIGITAL LIBRARY

After you register, you can begin building your first database. In the section that follows, I briefly explain how this is done. More detail can be accessed online at Bitlocker's site.

SETTING UP YOUR DATABASE

Bitlocker presents its home page in a pretty straightforward manner. You have three tabs from which to choose: Home, My Bitlockers, and What's New. The "My Bitlockers" tab takes you to the area you begin building your own database. Under the heading "Blank Template," there is a button labeled "Create." Click on this to get started and then follow these three simple steps.

1. First you name your database, briefly describe it, and decide on security settings. The security features allow you to control who can view your database and what they can do with your data. There are three variables in the security settings.
    1. Task
    2. Access
    3. Audience
   What you choose for a task setting defines the access rights. For example, if you set the task at "Personal Organization," the access rights automatically become "Only you can view, add, modify and delete your records." The Audience options include "Private," "Public," and "Workgroup." Click the "Save" button when you are finished.

2. Create the fields you want to include in your records. You are asked to name the field, describe it, determine its type (for example, Text, Number, True/False, Date, etc.), and add a value list if you so choose. A *value list* is a menu that you define. It can be presented as a scrolling list box or set of radio-button options. Value lists are meant to speed up data entry. If, for example, you are building a database of journals holdings, you could make a value list for *frequency*. Your scrolling list box would include Daily, Weekly, Monthly, Quarterly, Irregular, etc.

   Click on the "Create" button to create a new field. When you are finished creating all the fields you want, click on the "Save" button.

   In this example of building a multimedia digital library, you might consider creating these fields:

   Item: This would be the *container* field in which you place the digital object itself. Be sure to set this field to type "File." This enables you to browse your hard drive to locate and insert the object, whether it is a sound clip, video clip, text file, or image. Remember that you are limited in how much file space you are allotted. You might include a URL field to point at other servers where you have video clips stored, for example.

   Creator: This field would be a text field listing who created the text file or who took the snapshot, etc.

   Title: This field gives the object a name. It could be the title of a paper or the name for a photograph, etc.

   Subject: If you want to add a level of vocabulary control, you could add a subject field in which you enter Library of Congress subject headings, for example.

   Description: This field describes the object in detail.

   Date: This field is for the date the object was created. If you have things for which the creation date is unknown, you may want to leave this field a text field rather than making it a date field that must follow a particular data format.

   File type: Here you can describe the file format and its size, and for images, the resolution and pixel dimensions.

3. After you click on the "Save" button in the previous step, you are presented with a blank record listing the fields you specified. You can now begin inputting data. You can click on "add another" to add another record. Click on "Save" when you are finished. You might begin by adding one record for every type of media you wish to include in your digital library to see how it works. In my experimental database I built, I included a MIDI sound recording, a JPEG image, an MPG video clip, and an HTML document. My browser supported the image and HTML document. The MPG video clip and the MIDI sound clip were supported by helper applications and plug-ins that came preloaded with my system.

Once you are this far, you can go back and begin adding new records, modifying, or deleting records. You can also change views. By default, your database records are presented in table view. This presents your data in rows and columns. You can switch to card view, which displays records one at a time.

BUILDING AN ONLINE EXHIBIT

With the information presented in this chapter and the free services described in Chapter 20, you can now experiment with building complete, full-service Websites using free resources. Find a free Webspace service you like and try building an online exhibit that includes images and HTML documents. It could be an exhibit telling visitors about historical landmarks in your town, or the special collections in your library. To add more functionality to your site, include a search and indexing system like the one described earlier in this chapter. To top it all off, add a link to a DatabasePlus database where you house several cataloged items of interest that relate to your online exhibit. You can use these free, user-friendly services to teach patrons and staff alike the basic principles of Website design, search and indexing systems, and Web-based databases.

Digital Publishers and Digital Libraries

More and more librarians are offering their patrons access to digital materials both in-house and from remote sites. In Chapter 28, I explore what is currently happening on the Internet in the realm of publishing digital information and creating repositories for storing and accessing this information. I introduce you to a digital library project called American Memory; explore various e-text repositories, including the commercial NetLibrary and the freely accessible Project Gutenberg; and offer pointers to digital library meta sources, or "lists of lists." I then go on to explore electronic journals and newspapers and tell you where some of the better-known newsstands and magazine racks are located around the Web. The chapter closes with information on where to find library-related e-journals.

THE DIFFERENCE BETWEEN DIGITAL LIBRARIES AND ONLINE LIBRARIES

When I presented online libraries in Chapter 16, I focused on libraries that made their catalogs available online. For the most part, what you are given access to in an online library are bibliographic records representing the holdings of a collection, not the bibliographic items themselves. When you search an online catalog, you retrieve records that display elements such as call number, main entry, title, place of publication, etc.

Digital libraries differ in that they are collections of digitized materials—books, newsletters, magazines, etc.—that you can view online. Where an online library only links you to a bibliographic item's cover, a digital library links you to the bibliographic item itself. When you search a digital library, you retrieve an entire book or journal article in digital format. You can view the item online, download it, and print it. For a more

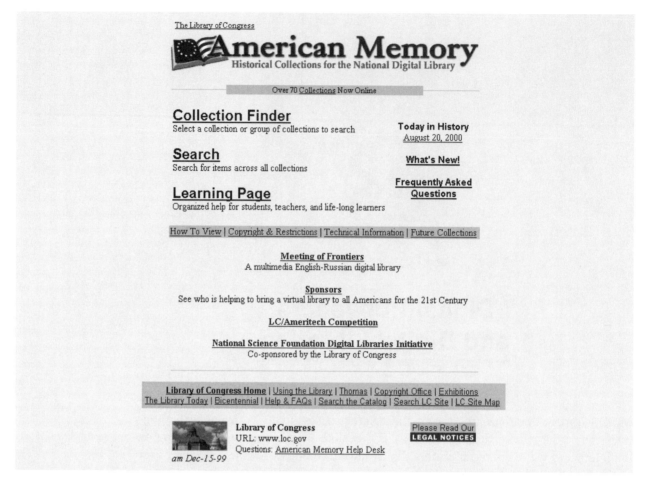

Figure 28–1: The American Memory project's home page maintained by the Library of Congress

detailed look at the meaning and purpose of digital libraries, refer to the Association of Research Libraries' *Definition and Purpose of Digital Libraries* at *sunsite.berkeley.edu/ ARL/*.

With the advent of the Web, digital libraries and Web-based library catalogs now house interactive multimedia documents. These are documents that not only present text, graphs, charts, and other images, but also sound clips, animation, 3–D imaging, and hyperlinks to related materials in the same collection or other collections distributed across many databases. One of the better-known national digital library projects is American Memory.

AMERICAN MEMORY

American Memory *memory.loc.gov/* is the Library of Congress's contribution to the historical collections of the National Digital Library Program. American Memory is a collection of materials relating to American history. When you link to the American Memory home page shown in Figure 28–1, you are given two choices for accessing the collection:

1. You can browse individual collections by topic, for example, Agriculture or Education, or you can browse by format. The format choices include written materials, maps, motion pictures, photos and prints, and sound recordings. When you click on photos and prints, you are given a variety of choices ranging from Baseball Cards to photographs of the Great Plains.
2. You can search individual collections or search all of the American Memory collections at once.

There is a feature called "What's New" on the home page that spotlights new collections. Other features on the home page include links to "Future Collections" and "Background Papers and Technical Information." Clicking on the link labeled "Learning Page" links you to the American Memory Learning Page. Here you find links to educational resources such as lesson plans plus links to tutorials, pathfinders, and related Websites.

On the Technical Information page, a document that may be of particular interest to researchers is *Privacy and Publicity Rights*. This paper discusses issues concerning privacy and publicity as they relate to researchers using letters and diaries found in library collections. If you are interested in digital imaging, this page provides an excellent training guide for reviewing images. *Quality Review of Document Images* covers image types, file formats and compression, viewing software, and more.

American Memory and the National Digital Libraries Initiative forms unique partnerships between academic and nonprofit institutions, and private organizations. The academic institutions involved with the digital library project include the following participants with their projects:

1. University of California at Berkeley *elib.cs.berkeley.edu* with their environmental planning and geographic information systems
2. University of California at Santa Barbara *alexandria.sdc.ucsb.edu/* with The Alexandria Project: Spatially-Referenced Map Information
3. Carnegie Mellon University *informedia.cs.cmu.edu/* with their Informedia Digital Video Library
4. University of Illinois at Urbana-Champaign *dli.grainger.uiuc.edu* with the Federating Repositories of Scientific Literature
5. University of Michigan *www.si.umich.edu/UMDL* with their research in using intelligent agents to locate information
6. Stanford University *www-diglib.stanford.edu* exploring resource discovery, retrieving information, interpreting information, managing information, and sharing information.

Steps in the Digitization Process is an outline published by the Library of Congress as part of the National Digital Library Program. The last time I looked, it had not been updated for four years, but still it offered relevant information on which steps are taken in preparing your collection, the conversion process, quality control, and preparing material for Web publishing. You can access this document at *lcweb2.loc.gov/ammem/ award/docs/stepsdig.html*.

THOMAS: LEGISLATIVE INFORMATION ON THE INTERNET

Thomas, named after Thomas Jefferson, is another digital library project sponsored by the Library of Congress located at *thomas.loc.gov/*. This collection offers access to current legislation, congressional record text, committee reports, directories, bills in the news, historical documents, and more.

PROJECT GUTENBERG

Project Gutenberg *www.promo.net/pg/*, directed by Michael S. Hart, is an online database containing numerous electronic texts. The purpose of Project Gutenberg is to encourage the creation and distribution of English language e-texts. The original goal set by Project Gutenberg was to release 10,000 titles and distribute them to one trillion people by the year 2001. Beginning in 1971 with the United States' Declaration of Independence as their first e-text, they are the granddaddy of e-text libraries and now make over 2,680 e-texts available on their publicly accessible Internet site. This is up from 800 when the previous edition of this book was published.

Due to copyright law, many of the works contained in this e-text collection are books written prior to 1920. Titles already released include classic literature such as *A Christmas Carol*, *Red Badge of Courage*, *Alice in Wonderland*, *The Scarlet Letter*, *The War of the Worlds*, *Tom Swift*, and *Rebecca of Sunnybrook Farm*.

Individuals that are interested in keeping informed about Project Gutenberg may view the Project Gutenberg newsletter online at *www.promo.net/pg/newsletters.html*.

To view the e-texts that are available, you can visit FTP sites all around the world listed at *www.promo.net/pg/list.html*. In the United States, the main Project Gutenberg FTP site is housed at the University of North Carolina *ftp://metalab.unc.edu/pub/docs/books/gutenberg/*. Each FTP site contains files that explain Project Gutenberg and provide access to subdirectories where the e-texts are stored. The */etext90* subdirectory is where all of the e-texts prior to 1991 are stored. Project Gutenberg e-texts are also available from other FTP sites. You can locate these by using Archie to search on the text string **gutenberg**, or use one of the many search engines available on the Internet such as ArchiePlex at *http://src.doc.ic.ac.uk/archieplexform.html*.

HIGHWIRE PRESS

Stanford University Library manages a sophisticated electronic journal publishing house called HighWire Press. It began in 1995 with the online edition of the *Journal of Biological Chemistry* and has since expanded to include over 200 titles online. The scope of their collection covers scholarly science, technology, and medicine journals. HighWire Press's electronic versions include all of the features you would expect in a hypertext document, including images, author, article, and citation links, multimedia, and interactivity.

The HighWire Press publishes their holdings online and specifies which journals offer free trial copies, free issues, or a free site. To learn more about HighWire Press, point your browser to *www-science.stanford.edu/intro.dtl*.

DIGITAL LIBRARY META SOURCES

On the Internet, you find thousands of subject indexes and directories created by individuals and organizations. Some are small with links to primary sources, while others are large lists with links to other lists. On the Internet, these "lists of lists" are referred to as *meta indexes*, *meta pages*, or *meta sources*. One of the best meta sources on digital libraries is the *Digital Library Related Information and Resources* site. This site is maintained by Ben Gross and can be found at *interspace.grainger.uiuc.edu/~bgross/digital-libraries.html*. Gross lists dozens of annotated links relating to digital library resources organized under these headings:

- The Digital Library Initiative (DLI)
- Select Digital Library Related Projects
- Upcoming Digital Library Conferences
- Previous Digital Library Conferences
- Previous Digital Library Related Conferences and Online Proceedings
- Full Text of Other Digital Library Related Publications
- Other Digital Library Related Resources
- Digital Library Funding, Coordination, and Policy Organizations
- Intellectual Property
- Human Computer Interaction (HCI)
- Computer Supported Cooperative Work (CSCW)

D-LIB FORUM

Under "Full Text of Other Digital Library Related Publications," Ben Gross links you to one of the most important full-text digital library e-journals on the Net known as *D-Lib Magazine*. You can access *D-Lib Magazine* at D-Lib Forum's home page *www.dlib.org/*. This site brings people together who are interested in the technology associated with building digital libraries and developing standards that make it possible to join together individual collections in remote locations with varying formats.

You can also link to the D-Lib Test Suite from *www.dlib.org/*. This consists of six testbeds coordinated by The Corporation for National Research Initiatives (CNRI). CNRI has had a lot of experience in managing online information and digital archives. They manage another innovative project known as Stackworks. The Stackworks project is an information service that involves itself with creating professionally managed online archival collections. There are plans to move the *D-Lib Magazine* collection to Stackworks.

D-Lib Forum is also a point of departure for accessing the D-Lib Working Group on Digital Library Metrics. This working group states as their purpose "...to develop a consensus on an appropriate set of metrics to evaluate and compare the effectiveness of digital libraries and component technologies in a distributed environment. Initial emphasis will be on (a) information discovery with a human in the loop, and (b) retrieval in a heterogeneous world." You can read their complete charter at *www.dlib.org/metrics/public/metrics-charter.html* along with other documents including *The Scope of the Digital Library,* a draft prepared by Barry M. Leiner for the D-Lib Working Group on Digital Library Metrics, January 16, 1998. Revised October 15, 1998.

D-LIB MAGAZINE

D-Lib Magazine is a monthly e-journal that focuses on research and innovation in digital libraries. It is produced by the CNRI and is sponsored by the Defense Advanced Research Projects Agency (DARPA). They make the current and back issues of *D-Lib Magazine* available free of charge at *www.dlib.org/*. Back issues can be accessed by browsing or searching. You can browse by year going back to 1995, or access articles, editorials, and briefings through author and title indexes. You can search the monthly magazine and reference pages.

BERKELEY DIGITAL LIBRARY SUNSITE

The purpose of the Digital Library SunSITE is to provide support for individuals and organizations that wish to build digital libraries, museums, and archives. Digital Library SunSITE does this through sponsorship by The Library of the University of California, Berkeley, and Sun Microsystems, Inc. They can be accessed online through their home page at *sunsite.berkeley.edu/*. Here you can find links to text and image collections in digital format, digital library catalogs and indexes, software for building electronic libraries, resources for learning, and much more.

While not directly related to digital libraries, their "Catalogs and Indexes" link connects you to several interesting resources that are under the umbrella of SunSITE. Included in this list are resources listed elsewhere in this book or on the CD-ROM accompanying this book. Some of the better known are the Alex Catalog of Electronic Texts *sunsite.berkeley.edu/alex/*, KidsClick! *sunsite.berkeley.edu/KidsClick!/*, Librarians' Index to the Internet *lii.org/*, and Libweb *sunsite.berkeley.edu/Libweb/*.

SunSITE's "Text and Image Collections" lists digital library collections hosted by the Digital Library SunSITE. These include, for example, the Emma Goldman Papers. This is a collection of documents and photographs relating to Emma Goldman's life and work. This collection also organizes thousands of other documents and photographs pertaining to Emma Goldman located all around the world. The Online Medieval and Classical Library (OMACL), headed up by Douglas B. Killings, is a collection of literary works of Classical and Medieval civilization. You can search this collection or browse it by title, author, subject, and genre.

E-JOURNALS

An *e-journal* is an electronic serial created and distributed in electronic format. E-journals cover a wide spectrum of subjects ranging from news items to scholarly refereed articles. Many e-journals are available free of charge on the Internet. Others are pro-

---

Online Resource

The Digital Library Federation is a consortium of research libraries and archives working together to bring digital materials to students, faculty, and citizens everywhere. Their Website is located at *www.clir.org/diglib/dlfhomepage.htm*.

duced privately and online users must pay a subscription fee to have them delivered to their electronic mailbox. E-journals come in various formats including journals, magazines, e-zines, and newsletters. E-zines, the most esoteric of formats, are discussed later in this chapter.

One of the advantages that e-journals offer over print journals is the speed with which they can be delivered. The results of new research and news of current events can be published within just days or hours of their occurrence rather than weeks or months. Another advantage is that e-journals can be designed as interactive multimedia documents with sound, images, and hyperlinks to other documents on the Web. The other advantages are well known in this digital, networked environment in which we now live and work.

- You can add and store e-journals to your collection without costly expansion of your physical space and storage facilities
- You can eliminate costs associated with replacing missing, stolen, and damaged issues
- You can track usage through statistical tracking programs
- You have access to your e-journals twenty-four hours a day, seven days a week
- Content can be accessed through keyword and/or subject searching

Following are examples of e-journal sites and services supported by libraries and commercial organizations on the Internet.

The University of British Columbia Library—The University of British Columbia Library offers an integrated view of their online journal holdings at *toby.library.ubc.ca/ejournals/ejournals.cfm*. They offer a solution to a problem faced by many libraries: How do you present library users with a single, integrated view of all your online holdings when in reality the journal holdings are managed by a variety of vendors. This library uses *tables* to organize information into columns. Visitors to their library can view journal titles, the service that offers access—for example, ABI/Inform Global, or EBSCO, etc.—and they provide holdings information. Titles can be browsed in a title index. The whole package is accessible via the Web.

The TriUniversities Group located in Southwestern Ontario, Canada—This collaborative group includes the University of Guelph, University of Waterloo, and Wilfrid Laurier University. Their collective journal indexes, which include more than 4,600 titles, can be accessed at *www.tug-libraries.on.ca/index.html*. Access to their collection is by alphabetical title index and four broad subject indexes. Like The University of British Columbia Library, they use the Web and HTML tables to organize their holdings. The TriUniversities Group is unique in that they use icons to distinguish between access groups and include databases freely accessible by anyone. A "globe" icon distinguishes these resources. Following are three examples of databases included in their "Science & Technology Topics" class.

- Agricola *www.nal.usda.gov/ag98/ag98.html*
- AIDSLine *igm.nlm.nih.gov/* and other National Library of Medicine Resources.
- Annual Reviews Index *www.AnnualReviews.org/* (click on the "Search" button)

TITLE: Drain e-Zine

URL:
email message to: sfarrug@caticsuf.csufresno.edu SUBSCRIBE Drain e-Zine [name and address]

✉

ABSTRACT: Information and discussion on the computing world.

PUBLISHER:

ISSN:

FREQUENCY: Irregular

START DATE:

END DATE:

COST: Free

PEER REV'D: No

CONTACT: Shaun Farrugia

E-MAIL: sfarrug@caticsuf.csufresno.edu

TELEPHONE:

ADDRESS:

SUBJECT HEADINGS: Computers

Computers -- Public Opinion

Computer Industry

Figure 28–2: Custom bibliographic records help organize information in the CIC's e-journal collection

CIC Electronic Journals Collection—The Committee on Institutional Cooperation (CIC) offers this prototype e-journal management system for anyone to use that has an Internet connection. This system incorporates freely distributed scholarly e-journals that can be accessed online. When you visit their site at *ejournals.cic.net/*, you are presented with three access methods: searching, browsing by title, and browsing by topic. Entries link to bibliographic records that provide relevant information about each resource. The record that accompanies one resource named *Drain e-Zine* is shown in Figure 28–2.

THE ELECTRONIC NEWSSTAND

The Electronic Newsstand at *www.enews.com/* is one of the largest collections of commercial magazines on the Web. It provides you with links to over 1,000 magazine titles and enables you to place online orders and free trial subscriptions for many titles. The collection can be accessed by browsing or searching.

DIRECTORY OF ELECTRONIC JOURNALS AND NEWSLETTERS

The Association of Research Libraries (ARL) makes the *Directory of Electronic Journals and Newsletters* available on their Web server at *www.arl.org/scomm/edir/index.html*.

ARL-EJOURNAL is a discussion list sponsored by ARL that focuses on all aspects

BUBL Journals

Contents, abstracts or full texts of over 200 current journals and newsletters

BUBL Journals A-Z by Journal Title

BUBL Journals arranged by subject:
Library and Information Science
Computing and Information Technology
Agriculture and Food Science
Business and Marketing
Social and Medical Services

Search BUBL journals:

| | Search |

Search Help

BUBL Journals Updates
New journals added to BUBL each week

BUBL Archive Journals
Journals no longer abstracted by BUBL

Journals Held Elsewhere
Additional journal sources including projects,
HE publications, services, publishers and magazines

BUBL's Journal Exchange Scheme
LIS staff can fill gaps in journal holdings and offer
available material via this cooperative venture

BUBL Information Service, Andersonian Library, Strathclyde University, 101 St James Road, Glasgow G4 0NS, Scotland
Tel: 0141 548 4752   *Email*: bubl@bubl.ac.uk

Figure 28–3: BUBL Journals offers free access to over 200 current journals and newsletters

of the management of electronic journals by libraries. Topics discussed include archiving, pricing, licensing, indexing, file formats, and more. You can subscribe by pointing your browser to *www.cni.org/Hforums/arl-ejournal/*.

NEWJOUR DISCUSSION LIST

A list called NEWJOUR publishes announcements of new electronic journals as they become available. To subscribe, send e-mail to *listproc@ccat.sas.upenn.edu* and in the body of the message, type **subscribe newjour <your first name and last name>**. The listowners are Ann Shumelda Okerson of Yale University and James J. O'Donnell of the University of Pennsylvania. You can subscribe online via their Website at *gort.ucsd.edu/newjour/*. You can search archived messages at this same address or browse messages by subject line organized in alphabetical order.

LINKS TO MAJOR ELECTRONIC JOURNAL SITES

BUBL, pronounced as *bubble*, no longer stands for anything. In its early days, when it began as an experimental project, the acronym meant Bulletin Board for Libraries. It was a labor of love for librarians in Glasgow and Strathclyde. In 1995 it became a funded project of the U.K. government information service. Now it is accessed by more than one million people a month.

BUBL Journals includes the contents, abstracts, or full texts of over 200 current journals and newsletters. By linking to BUBL's Web server at *bubl.ac.uk/journals/*, you are presented with the menu items shown in Figure 28–3. The information presented in

BUBL Journals is freely available to anyone without the need to register. Since their beginning in 1990, BUBL has been a continuous source of electronic newsletters and journals.

E-TEXT ARCHIVE AT THE WELL

These days, it's almost impossible to find a Gopher server that is still up and running. The WELL's Gopher is one of the few remaining Gophers still alive and kicking. The WELL has its roots in the San Francisco Bay Area and was founded by the people who created the Whole Earth Catalog. The WELL started out as a computer conferencing system, and to this day it remains a collection of electronic villages where people from all walks of life come to meet and talk. You can access their site via the Web at *www.well.com/* or through Gopher by Gophering to *gopher.well.sf.ca.us.* If you threw away that old Gopher client years ago, or never had one to begin with, you can still access the WELL's Gopher using your Web browser and this address: *gopher:// gopher.well.sf.ca.us.*

The full-text collections aren't being kept up-to-date, but you can still find some interesting artifacts at this site. At the main menu, choose *Authors, Books, Periodicals, Zines (Factsheet Five lives here!)/.* This brings you to the menu shown here:

> About the Publications area
> AIDSwire Digest
> Authors: Writings grouped by author name
> Book Sellers (from *gopher.std.com*)
> Electronic Serials archive at CICNet
> Factsheet Five, Electric
> FYIFrance, by Jack Kessler
> Gnosis Magazine—ToC, Back Issues, and Guidelines
> Natural Literacy Publishers—Environmental Publications
> Incunabula
> LOCUS Magazine—Tom Maddox reports on the Electronic
>   MicroTimes
> Miscellaneous Cyberprose
> MONDO 2000
> Online Zines
> Poetry
> Whole Earth Review, the Magazine
> Zine and Book catalogs

As you look around the site, you discover articles by Tom Maddox going back to 1992 from the science fiction newspaper *Locus.* You can read about Steve Jobs in the *MicroTimes,* or catch a glimpse of cyberprose, like the excerpt from *Virtual Romance* by Paulina Borsook that begins, "I was at a conference with the usual assortment of tech-weenies, dweebs, programmer geeks, wireheads, and brainy-type science guys."

In case you are interested, membership fees to join the WELL are between $10 and $15 per month. Membership gives you access to their online conferencing system through the Web and via telnet.

VIRTUAL NEWSPAPERS

For an extensive listing of online newspapers, go to Yahoo!'s home page at *www.yahoo.com* and follow the path "News|Newspapers." This brings you to an alphabetized listing of newspapers beginning with *Arizona Republic and Phoenix Gazette* and ending with the *Washington Times*. In addition, from this page you can link to thousands of newspapers arranged by region (countries, regions, states), alternative news weeklies, college and university newspapers, tabloids, and more.

My Virtual Newspaper at *www.refdesk.com/paper.html* covers weather conditions in every state, U.S. newspapers, national news sites, worldwide news sites, and Canadian newspapers.

THE IPL'S LINKS TO MAGAZINES AND NEWSPAPERS

The Internet Public Library (IPL) reading room offers access to online serials and newspapers. Access to magazines and serials is made easy by providing a search mode and the ability to browse by topic and subtopics. Newspapers can be found by searching or by browsing according to geographic location. You can explore IPL's collections at *www.ipl.org/*.

ZINES

Zines, micro-zines, e-zines, fanzines, and *cyberzines* are all names that describe a special underground, alternative magazine format. *Zine*, which is short for magazine, comes from the word *fanzine—fan* meaning "fanatical." Zines can be devoted to a single theme or include a mix of personal stories, poetry, reviews, unique art, and comics. *The "E" Ticket*, published by Leon and Jack Janzen, is devoted to Disneyland and other Disney company theme parks. *Aluminum Anonymous* is published by a roadside can collector, Dennis W. Brezina, who ponders the habits of drivers. More mainstream zines include *The Amateur Computerist*, a zine published by Ronda Hauben that explores the history and future of computer networking technologies, and *Sipapu*, a newsletter written for librarians by a librarian named Noel Peattie. *Sipapu* was known for its reviews of small and alternative press publications. After 28 years in print, *Sipapu* ceased publication in 1996.

Zines are small publications generally created by one person as a labor of love. Typically, publishers exchange their zines for other zines or charge $1 or $2 per issue plus stamps. Some are hand-written, copied on Xerox machines, and then stapled together. Others are printed on an offset press and perfect-bound.

THE E-ZINE LIST

Today, zines are also published in electronic format on the Internet. An electronic zine is called an *e-zine* for short. John Labovitz is the author of the definitive *E-zine List*, a document that has been published in various formats since the early 1990s. You can access it on the Web at *www.meer.net/~johnl/e-zine-list/*. The latest edition was updated

March 8, 2000, and contains 4,392 zines. The last time I checked, John Labovitz was looking for a successor to carry on his work. The site is still up and running, but no longer being kept up-to-date.

Other e-zine sites to explore on the Web include:

The Book of Zines *www.zinebook.com/*
Zine Net *www.zine.net/*
Textfiles.com *scene.textfiles.com/*
Super Magazines *www.platform.net/*
LOW bandwidth *www.disobey.com/low/archives/*
Insound *www.insound.com/*

FACTSHEET FIVE

Factsheet Five is the premier source of zine reviews. Each issue arranges reviews alphabetically by subject and includes several hundred listings. "Editor's Choice" titles receive lengthier reviews. To subscribe, write to Factsheet Five Subscription, Box 170099, San Francisco, CA 94117–0099. Subscription fee is $20 for six issues, $40 for institutions. Issues can be purchased individually for $6. An online version of this review journal called *F5 Web Edition* can be viewed on the Web at *www.factsheet5.com/*.

THE ALEX CATALOG OF ELECTRONIC TEXTS

Alex is a catalog of electronic texts covering American literature, English literature, and Western philosophy. Alex enables you to locate and retrieve the full-text electronic documents that are part of the catalog and are located on the Internet. The catalog incorporates works from the English Server at Carnegie Mellon University, the On-Line Book Initiative, portions of the Oxford Text Archive, Project Gutenberg, and other digital libraries. A complete list of hosts can be accessed in Alex's Gopher interface discussed later in this section.

The Alex cataloging project, originally started by Hunter Monroe, is currently hosted by Berkeley Digital Library SunSITE and maintained by Eric Lease Morgan. A recent service he has added to the site is Alex Bookcases. This service allows you to manage your favorite texts in the Alex catalog by annotating and organizing them on virtual bookshelves.

SEARCHING ALEX

Begin by connecting to site *www.infomotions.com/alex/*. This links you to the Alex Catalog of Electronic Texts home page.

1. Begin your search by clicking on the dialog box and typing in your search terms. When finished, click on the "Search" button. If you have any questions, click on the link labeled "Context-sensitive help" located just below the dialog box. To access a full-featured search screen, click on the link labeled "full-featured interface." In this example, I searched on the phrase **tom and sawyer**.

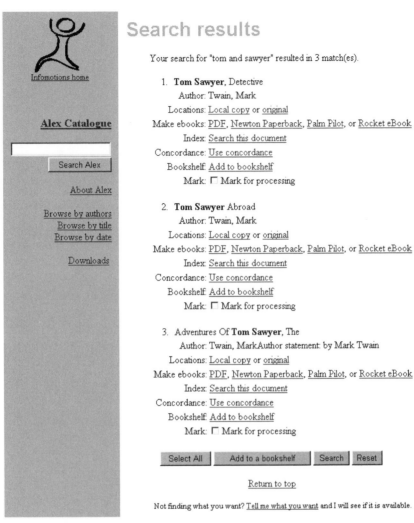

Figure 28–4: Search results from the Alex Catalog of Electronic Texts

2. Alex runs the search and displays its findings as shown in Figure 28–4. You are given various options, including viewing full text, searching the document, and using a concordance.

3. Next, click on the link labeled "Link to full record" located at the bottom of the first record for "Tom Sawyer, Detective." This brings you to a detailed record as shown in Figure 28–5. At this point, you can read the document online by clicking on "Archive," print out the document, or save it to disk. To save it to disk, click on "Make PDF." You can also save it in various e-book formats including Newton Paperback, PalmPilot, and Rocket eBook.

If you are viewing it in your browser, you can print it out by pulling down the "File" menu and clicking on "Print," which opens a Print window. Designate whether you want to print the entire document, or just portions of the document. If you're interested only in excerpts, your Web browser may allow you to cut and paste from the text. If not, then save it to disk, bring the file into a word processor, and then cut and paste.

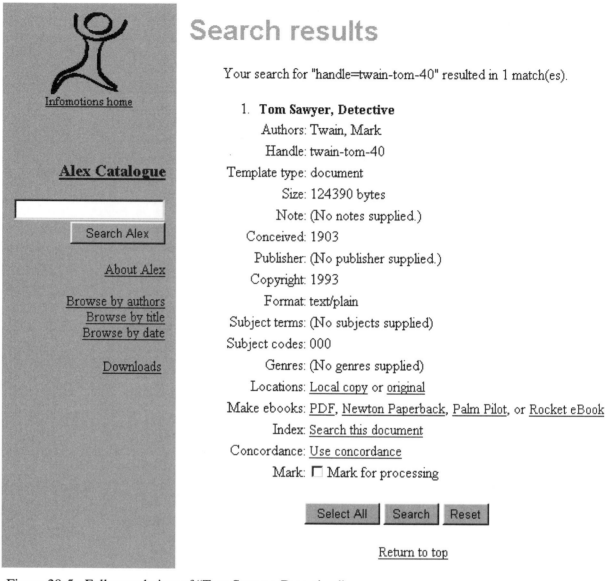

Figure 28-5: Full record view of "Tom Sawyer, Detective."

JUST HOW MANY PAGES IS THIS DOCUMENT?

If you're curious just how large any of these full-text documents are in terms of pages, pull down the "File" menu in Netscape browser and click on "Print Preview." This displays the first full page of text as it appears when printed. The total number of pages is noted in the lower left corner of the first page. In the case of "Tom Sawyer, detective," it reads 1 of 50. The print size is too small to read unless you zoom in. On the "Print Preview" screen, you see a button labeled "Zoom In." Click on this until the number in the lower left corner of the document becomes readable. As of version 5.5, Internet Explorer also supports this feature.

NETLIBRARY'S E-TEXTS

NetLibrary is a new company that buys electronic publishing rights from book publishers and creates e-texts for sale to libraries. The e-texts are available online and can be integrated with libraries' online Web-based catalogs. If your OPAC supports MARC 856 tags, search results that include netLibrary e-texts present hyperlinked URLs that link library patrons to the e-texts themselves.

Currently, the average price of a netLibrary e-text is $38. In addition to the cost of the e-text, there is an access charge. You can buy perpetual rights or annual rights to these full-text, graphics-rich e-texts. In the case of computer technology books, for example, you would probably opt for annual access. Perpetual access is prepaid at a rate of 50 percent of the book's cost.

There are a number of purchase plans for adding e-books to your collection:

- Begin with a collection of 500 titles in a selected subject area or preferred publisher
- Promotional offerings, for example, *Choice Magazine*'s outstanding academic titles with 200 books minimum
- Shared collection through a consortium. (Be sure to explore whether there are consortia licensing agreements available in your area. The savings are considerable.)

At present, the purchase options are geared for large library systems with substantial budgets. When I last spoke to a company representative, they were in the process of designing purchase options that meet the needs of smaller public libraries and two-year community colleges. By the time you read this you should have the option of building your e-text collection one book at a time, or start with a small base collection of 100 titles.

The public can go to netLibrary's Website at *www.netlibrary.com/* and freely access a collection of 4,000 public domain e-texts. If you are interested in seeing what netLibrary has available, point your browser to *www.netlibrary.com/booklist.asp*. Here you can access title lists in Excel or tab-delimited format. Currently, netLibrary has 19,000 e-texts to choose from. They offer specialized collections for academic and corporate libraries. For pricing options and title availability, contact a netLibrary representative via e-mail from their Website at *www.netlibrary.com/*.

Online Resource

The Institute on Digital Library Development was a five-day workshop sponsored by the U.S. Department of Education and The Library, University of California, Berkeley. The workshop, held in July and August of 1996, introduced librarians to the tools that are available and the skills that are required for building digital libraries. Some of the training materials used in this workshop are available online at *sunsite.berkeley.edu/IDLD/*.

LIBRARY-RELATED E-JOURNALS

An excellent source of information on dozens of library-related e-journals and newsletters is maintained by Thomas Parry Library, Llanbadarn Fawr, Aberystwyth in the U.K., on their Website at *www.aber.ac.uk/~tplwww/e/*. The service is called PICK and resources can be accessed through a contents list, subject browse, classmark browse, and keyword search.

The contents list breaks down resources into these categories:

- Libraries and Related Organizations
- Librarianship and Information Science
- LIS Documents
- Full-text Documents
- Use of Networks

Under the heading "LIS Documents," topics are further subdivided under these headings:

Major LIS Journals—
    Full details and highlights
    Brief alphabetical listing
All the Journals and Newsletters:
    General LIS journals—full text
    Focused LIS journals
    General LIS journals
    Reviewing and abstracting services
    Professional bodies newsletters
    National libraries newsletters
    Academic and public libraries newsletters
    Other newsletters
    Collections of LIS journals
    Other interesting journals
    Internet journals
Electronic Journals: The Issues
    Glossary
    Bibliography
    Finding electronic journals
    Styles of publication
PUP—Tables of Contents of Electronic Journals

Another excellent source for online e-journals relating to library and information science is BUBL Journals *bubl.ac.uk/journals/*. BUBL Journals has conveniently grouped all of the library and information science journals in one location *bubl.ac.uk/journals/ lis/*. They specify whether a journal offers abstracts, contents, or full text and the starting date for holdings. Journals can be searched or browsed by subject. Subject browsing is made easy by listing titles under the following headings:

- General librarianship and information management
- Information science and research
- Acquisitions
- Cataloging and indexing
- Document management and supply
- Electronic information and the Internet
- Library systems and technology
- Libraries in schools and colleges
- National and regional libraries
- Societies and associations
- Specialist libraries and information services
- Computing and information technology

The following list introduces you to some of the most popular online e-journals and newsletters for librarians. They are all free and can be accessed on the Web or via e-mail.

- Ariadne—Evaluates Internet resources and services *www.ariadne.ac.uk/*
- Associates—Electronic journal for library support staff *bubl.ac.uk/journals/lis/ae/associates/*
- Chinese Librarianship—International electronic journal covering topics of interest to Chinese librarians *www.whiteclouds.com/iclc/cliej/*
- Computers in Libraries—Provides a practical look at information technology in libraries *www.infotoday.com/cilmag/ciltop.htm*
- Current Cites—Annotated bibliography of selected articles, books, and digital documents on information technology *sunsite.berkeley.edu/CurrentCites/*
- DeLiberations—Platform for discussing educational development *www.lgu.ac.uk/deliberations/home.html*
- *D-Lib Magazine*—Information concerning digital libraries *www.ukoln.ac.uk/mirrored/lis-journals/dlib/dlib/*
- EDUCAUSE Online—Summary of news and information published on the EDUCAUSE Website *cause-www.niss.ac.uk/pub/educause_online.html*
- Edupage—Free e-mail newsletter sent three times a week summarizing developments in information technology *cause-www.niss.ac.uk/pub/edupage/edupage.html*
- E Journal—Journal delivered via e-mail that focuses on topics relating to electronic text *www.hanover.edu/philos/ejournal/home.html*
- Information Today—Newspaper covering news and trends in the information industry *www.infotoday.com/it/itnew.htm*
- Internet Resources Newsletter—Monthly newsletter for academics, students, engineers, scientists, and social scientists *www.hw.ac.uk/libWWW/irn/irn.html*
- Interpersonal Computing and Technology—Focuses on computer-mediated communication *jan.ucc.nau.edu/~ipct-j/*
- Issues in Science and Technology Librarianship—Forum for sci-tech librarians to publish research and bibliographies, discuss successful programs, and talk about current topics of interest *www.library.ucsb.edu/istl/about.html*
- The Journal of Academic Media Librarianship—Forum for librarians interested in academic media librarianship *www.ukoln.ac.uk/mirrored/lis-journals/mcjrnl/mcjrnl/*

Online Resources

Extensive collections of online magazines can be accessed on Yahoo!'s site. Start at their home page *www.yahoo.com*. Begin with any of the broad subject headings in the main menu—for example, News & Media or Computers & Internet—and go one level down and you see Magazines listed as a subtopic in that category. Online literary journals are located at *dir.yahoo.com/Arts/Humanities/Literature/Magazines/*.

- Journal of Digital Information—Offers papers on management, presentation, and uses of digital information *jodi.ecs.soton.ac.uk/*
- The Journal of Electronic Publishing—Written for publishers, librarians, scholars, and authors with an interest in electronic publishing *www.press.umich.edu:80/jep/*
- Journal of the American Society for Information Science—Concerned with all matters relating to generating, storing, retrieving, and disseminating information *www.asis.org/Publications/JASIS/*
- Library Journal Digital—Digital version of *Library Journal* covering news, commentary, features, and book reviews *libraryjournal.com/*
- Libres—Library and Information Science Research Electronic Journal *www.ukoln.ac.uk/mirrored/lis-journals/libres/libres/*
- Multimedia Schools—Covers multimedia technologies in K–12 schools *www.infotoday.com/MMSchools/default.htm*
- Newsletter on Serials Pricing Issues—Covers journal pricing projections, cancellation projects, price reduction efforts, electronic publishing, news, and events *www.lib.unc.edu/prices/*
- PACS—Public Access Computer Systems Review *info.lib.uh.edu/pacsrev.html*
- RIS—Review of Information Science, a peer-reviewed e-journal promoting academic research in information science *www.inf-wiss.uni-konstanz.de/RIS/*
- Searcher—Covers issues of importance to database searchers. Includes searching tips and techniques *www.infotoday.com/searcher/default.htm*

Part VII

APPENDIXES

Part VII consists of seven appendixes. Appendix A is a glossary of Internet-related terms. Appendix B contains a selective list of mailing lists of interest to librarians. Appendix C provides information on how to use the Internet to access schools of library and information science. Appendix D offers pointers on how librarians can go job hunting online. Appendix E discusses the various file types that are found on the Internet and it explains how to convert these file types into usable form. Appendix F includes descriptions of the various organizations that are concerned with issues like Internet services, standards, security, and operations. This section closes with Appendix G, which offers information on new sources of information and where to go to keep up with what's new on the Net.

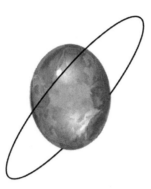

Appendix A: Glossary of Terms

Here are the most important technical terms, phrases, and acronyms originating in the world of computers, global networks, and elsewhere. Entries are arranged alphabetically with brief definitions. If you don't find the word you're looking for here, check the CD-ROM accompanying this book for online dictionaries. You can find them listed under the heading "Reference."

32–bit computing
The ability of a computer's CPU to handle 32 bits of data within one clock cycle, such as the Pentium processor.

64–bit computing
The ability of a computer's CPU to handle 64 bits of data within one clock cycle, such as IBM's PowerPC, Intel's IA-64–based Merced chip, and Compaq's Alpha processor. A 64–bit processor is billions of times more powerful than a 32–bit processor.

Acceptable Use Policy (AUP)
Rules applied to how a network may be used. Enforcement of AUPs varies from network to network. Go to site *http://gilligan.esu7.k12.ne.us/~esu7web/resources/aups.html* to view schools' AUPs and other AUP resources.

agent technology
"Intelligent" programs that are capable of finding and evaluating information on the Internet. Also referred to as *bots*. Amazon.com's service called "Shop the Web" uses agents to help consumers compare book prices. *Bot* is short for *robot*, which refers to robot-like software that methodically searches the Web.

animated GIF
Like a regular GIF image, except it contains two or more frames that are played back in sequence when viewed in a Web browser or other image viewer capable of displaying animated GIFs. *See also* GIF.

anonymous FTP
A set of rules for transferring files on the Internet that enable a user to connect to a site, and search and download files, without first setting up an account.

ANSI
ANSI (pronounced "an-see") stands for American National Standards Institute. This organization develops standards for the purpose of eliminating variations that might cause problems when programs are transported between computer systems.

anti-virus software
Programs that detect and remove computer viruses.

applet
A small program written in Java that can be distributed as an attachment in a World Wide Web document and executed by a Web browser.

application program
An application, or *app* for short, is a self-contained computer program that performs a special function. Text editors and spreadsheets are examples of common applications. Telnet, Gopher, FTP, Archie, and e-mail are common Internet applications.

Archie
Archie is a searching tool used for finding files on the Internet.

ASCII
ASCII (pronounced "ass-kee") stands for American Standard Code for Information Interchange. The ASCII character set consists of 128 seven-bit codes (the binary equivalents of the numbers 0, or "null," through 127) that represent the upper- and lowercase alphabet, numbers, standard keyboard characters such as ?, ;, !, $, etc. and certain control characters like the carriage return and line feed.

asynchronous
A method of transmitting data where each character is transmitted independently and is framed by a start bit and a stop bit.

backbone
A backbone is a central network that has the ability to transfer data at very high speeds and with great reliability.

bandwidth
The volume of information that a computer or transmission device can handle in a given period of time.

baud rate
Back when modem speeds were 300 baud, the terms *baud* and *bits per second* (bps) could be taken to mean the same thing. At today's higher modem speeds, however, the baud rate is much slower than the number of bits per second. Technically speaking, baud rate is the rate at which the state of the line changes every second. ("State" can refer to frequency, amplitude, phase, or voltage.)

BBS
Bulletin Board System, BBS, a program that runs on a personal computer and enables a user to call in through modems to download files, leave messages, or talk with other users in "real time."

binary
This is a numbering system based on "two" where only "0" (zero) and "1" are used to represent all possible mathematical values. Computers "speak" in binary. The values of "0" and "1" represent "off" and "on" switches.

bit
Computers understand only two electrical states: on and off—a pulse of electricity or no pulse. This on/off system based on 0s (zeros) and 1s (ones) is called the *binary number system*. A single 0 or 1 is called a *bit* (short for binary digit), the smallest unit of information that can be represented in binary notation.

blatherers
People communicating in newsgroups or mailing lists that have a hard time getting to the point. They may blather for pages, going on and on about a simple thought that could have been stated clearly in a single paragraph.

Boolean logic
This is a system used for searching text on computers. The terms AND, OR, and NOT are combined with keywords to sort through data. For example, searching the text string "dog and food" will return documents that include both the terms "dog" and "food," where "dog or food" would return documents with the word "dog" or with the word "food."

bots
See agent technology

bps
Bits Per Second, bps, is used to measure how fast modems transfer data.

browser
Browsers are Internet applications that enable you to search documents that are all linked together on the World Wide Web.

bulletin board
See BBS

byte
Eight bits, for example 01000010, are considered a basic unit of measurement called a *byte* (pronounced "bite"). A byte is the equivalent of one of the characters on your keyboard such as the "A" or "f" or "$."

Campus Wide Information System
Campus Wide Information System (CWIS) is an information system designed for university sites and accessible locally and on the Internet. Services typically include calendars of events, phone books, information on student services, and course descriptions, etc.

CD
Compact Disc, a medium for storing digital information.

CD-R
Compact Disc-Recordable, the term used to describe the technology associated with CD-R discs, equipment, and software.

CD-ROM
Compact Disc-Read Only Memory, format used to store sound, image, and text. (Music CD players cannot play CD-ROMs, but CD-ROM players can play music CDs.)

CD-RW
Compact Disc-Rewritable. Data stored on a CD-RW can be erased and overwritten many times.

CERN
The European Laboratory for Particle Physics. Birthplace of the World Wide Web.

CGI
Common Gateway Interface, which allows a Web server to pass data from an HTML document to a CGI script that runs various programs.

chat channels
Online services that enable many to communicate or "chat" with one another in real-time.

chatting
Chatting is real-time conversation on the Internet. Participants "talk" by typing messages at their keyboards and "listen" by reading what others type.

Class A Network
Part of the Internet Protocol addressing scheme; a network that can accommodate 16 million hosts.

Class B Network
Part of the Internet Protocol addressing scheme; a network that can accommodate 65,000 hosts.

Class C Network
Part of the Internet Protocol addressing scheme; a network that can accommodate 256 hosts.

client
The term *client* refers to a piece of hardware or software that sends a request for service to a server. For example, when you retrieve an image of the moon from an FTP site, you're making the request with a piece of software you run called a *client* and another piece of software called a *server* responds to your request.

codec
Codec is short for coder/decoder. System for coding (*co*) and decoding (*dec*) information to compress a file. Streaming audio and video products are codecs consisting of two parts: a compressor that encodes the data for transfer over the Internet and a decompressor that plays the audio stream.

command
A word or string of characters, such as *get* or *sz-b qrx.zip*, that when entered into a computer causes the computer to perform a specific function.

communication software
Also called *comm software*, this software enables one computer to communicate and share information with another computer via telephone lines.

conferencing
The communication that occurs when people meet online to discuss a topic of common interest.

cookies
Your Web browser generates a text file on your computer that allows an Internet site to exchange and record information in the background as you move around the Web. What this other Internet domain learns about you, it may use next time you visit. For example, the site may track what you do when you visit and use that data to choose banner ads that you would be interested in seeing.

cracker
A person who carries out malicious acts on another person's computer.

CSU/DSU
Customer Service Unit/Digital Service Unit. A piece of hardware that looks something like a modem and provides a digital interface between your LAN and a leased line connection. Unlike modems that modulate and demodulate analog signals (voice signals), CSU/DSUs deal with digital signals at both ends of the connection.

cyberspace
A term coined by William Gibson to describe the world created by all of the computers interconnected worldwide through telecommunications.

data warehousing
Analyzing internal corporate data to measure a company's performance and to create reports, for example, on how many units sold, the return on investment, costs and profits, etc. *See also* Web farming.

Digital Video Disc
Digital Video Disc, or DVD for short, is an optical disc technology that uses layering techniques and two-sided manufacturing to attain very large storage capacities. Digital Video Disc readers are also capable of reading CD-ROMs.

DNS
Domain Name System, which matches domain names—such as *dialog.com*—to their numeric IP addresses (*192.132.3.234*).

download
To receive, or "get," a file from one computer and bring it to another.

DSVD
Digital Simultaneous Voice and Data. Modems that support DSVD technology permit users to carry on two-way conversations on the modem while at the same time transmitting data.

dumb terminal
A monitor and keyboard with no microprocessing unit that you typically see with a personal computer system. Dumb terminals usually display only characters and numerals, no graphics.

DVD
Acronym for Digital Video Disc. *See* Digital Video Disc.

Ebone
A European backbone network.

e-mail
E-mail, short for *electronic mail*, is an Internet service that enables people to exchange electronic messages much as they would conventional mail, but with many added conveniences, such as speed.

encryption
The process of transforming information into a secret code for security reasons.

Extranet
Where intranets replace private Local Area Networks (LANs), extranets replace private Wide Area Networks (WANs). Also called a VPN (Virtual Private Network), extranets use the Internet for communications instead of private leased lines.

e-zine
An e-zine, or electronic zine (pronounced "zeen"), is a digital magazine published on the Web.

FAQ
A text file that contains answers to Frequently Asked Questions—questions that are commonly asked by Internet newbies.

file server
A computer whose primary purpose is to store files and provide network users access to these files.

finger
An Internet application that searches for information about users on your system and remote systems.

firewall
Combination of hardware and software designed to protect a local area network from security break-ins coming in through an Internet connection.

forms
Forms are a feature of Web browsers. They allow users to give information back to the server by typing in a text box and clicking on radio buttons, reset buttons, and submit buttons, etc.

FQDN
Fully Qualified Domain Name, the official domain name assigned to a computer. A public library system might register a name, such as *hennepin.lib.mn.us*. They then assign names to individual machines on their network, such as *athena.hennepin.lib.mn.us* or *tornado.hennepin.lib.mn.us*.

Free-Nets
"Free-Net" is a servicemark of NPTN (National Public Telecommunications Network). Free-Nets are computerized, civic information systems that enable members of communities to share information with each other. NPTN offers specialized network services to its members.

FTP
File Transfer Protocol, an Internet service that enables users to transfer files from one computer on the Internet to another.

gateway
A gateway is a computer that connects incompatible networks or applications so they can communicate with each other. The term is also used to describe a computer system that offers access, for example, in the form of menu choices to other remote systems on the Internet.

gbps
Gigabits Per Second. A unit for measuring the transfer rate of information. One gbps equals 1,073,741,824 bits per second.

ghost site
A site that was once available on the Web, but can no longer be reached.

GIF
Graphics Interchange Format, a file format developed by CompuServe used for compressing graphics. *See also* Animated GIFs.

gigabit
Approximately 1 billion bits (1,073,741,824 bits).

gigabyte
Abbreviated GB, equivalent to about 1,000,000,000 bytes (1,073,741,824 bytes or 1024 megabytes).

Gopher
This service enables you to organize and navigate information via the Internet by choosing items listed in menus. It is built on a client server architecture like other Internet applications. Gopher enables data to be organized hierarchically. Since the advent of the Web, use of Gopher services has almost entirely disappeared.

GUI
GUI (pronounced "gooey") stands for Graphical Users Interface. It is an interface that uses graphics and a mouse in addition to characters and keystrokes. Windows is a GUI interface and DOS is a text-based interface.

hacker
A person who is a very knowledgeable and technically sophisticated computer user.

hierarchical menu
Menu system that starts with broad subject headings, then moves down through submenus and narrower terms. Sometimes called *tree-structured menus*.

home page
Home page is the hypermedia document that loads when you first open your Web browser.

host
A computer system that provides services to outside users. If you have a dial-up account, the computer you dial into is your host.

HotJava browser
A World Wide Web browser written entirely in Java.

HTML
HyperText Markup Language, a text-based markup language used for creating files that can be displayed on the World Wide Web.

HTTP
HyperText Transport Protocol, a set of rules designed to distribute information quickly to many users.

hyperlink
A "connector" that quickly links you to another item on the Web when you click on highlighted words and special graphics.

hypermedia
The joining together of text, graphics, sound, animation, photos, and video, forming a unique association of topics that are independent yet related. Users jump between formats and topics in search of information.

hypertext
A form of document on the Internet with built-in links to other documents. Hypertext documents can link to documents located on the same computer or to documents located on computers thousands of miles away.

information architecture
How information is designed, organized, and labeled so it can be more successfully navigated, searched, and managed by people.

interface
A computer program screen. For example, Netscape Navigator provides an interface to the World Wide Web.

Internet
A self-governing global network that joins together millions of individuals, commercial, and nonprofit organizations.

Internet telephony
Transmitting voice communications between telephones connected to computers. The computers convert the voice signal to a digital signal and the transmission takes place over the Internet or private network. *See also* PC-to-PC Telephony.

Internet 2
A next generation, world-class network that will support the national research community.

Intranet
Network that uses Internet standards and Web server software for managing an organization's internal information and communications. Intranets are cordoned off from the rest of the Internet through software applications called *firewalls*.

IP Address
Internet Protocol address, a unique address for each computer connected to the Internet made up of four numbers separated by dots; for example, *190.167.12.2.*

IRC
Internet Relay Chat, an Internet service that makes it possible for users to communicate in "real time" over the Internet. Conversations take place on hundreds of different topics. Each topic has its own "channel," or room in which two or more people communicate using their keyboards.

ISDN
Integrated Services Digital Network, technology used for transmitting digital information. It is replacing the less-efficient analog phone lines and modems.

Java
A programming language developed by Sun Microsystems that is well suited for the World Wide Web. Java programs are written in the form of small, platform-independent programs called Java *applets*.

JPEG
Joint Photographic Experts Group, the name of a format for compressing full-color or gray-scale digital images.

kbps
Kilobits Per Second. One kilobit represents 1,024 bits of information. In some applications, such as ISDN, 1 kbps represents 1,000 bits per second.

kBps
Kilobytes Per Second. One kilobyte represents 1,024 bytes and one byte is eight bits.

keyword
Words used when searching online for documents.

kilobyte
A kilobyte is another basic unit of measurement that equals roughly 1,000 bytes (1,024 bytes). The abbreviation 16KB is read as 16 kilobytes, which is roughly equivalent to about 16,000 bytes.

line noise
Line noise is interference on the communications lines. It usually shows itself as garbage characters on your screen when you're working in terminal mode (when dialed-up to a shell account). Sometimes it can be so bad your connection is broken.

login
Once connected to a computer, this process identifies you to the computer or online service. The login process usually consists of entering a user ID and password.

lossless compression
Compression reduces a file's storage size. Lossless compression does it without losing any data. GIF and the newer PNG formats both use lossless compression algorithms. This means the image you start with is the same after compression; nothing is lost.

lossy compression
When you reduce the size of an image using lossy compression, some data is lost. JPEG, which is well suited for photographs, uses a lossy compression scheme.

lurkers
People who only read messages in mailing lists, newsgroups, and forums, and never participate in any discussions.

mailing list
People with e-mail addresses linked together forming an electronic discussion group sharing common interests.

mbps
Mega Bits Per Second. One mega bit represents 1,024 kilobits per second or 1,048,576 bits per second.

megabyte
Abbreviated as MB, equivalent to about 1,000,000 bytes (1,048,576 bytes or 1,024 kilobytes). This is the common unit of measurement for personal computer memory.

metadata
Data about data, sometimes machine-readable. For example, keyword and description metatags in HTML documents that help robots index Web pages.

MIME
Multiple Internet Mail Extensions, a process that enables a server to tell a client what type of file it is sending; for example, RealAudio, Shockwave, Adobe Acrobat PDF, etc.

mirror site
Some of the more popular FTP sites are difficult to access because there are so many people trying to "connect" to them at the same time. To help alleviate the traffic jams result, the FTP site copies their holdings to other sites around the Internet, called "mirror" sites.

modem
Acronym for MOdulator/DEModulator. A device that connects computers together via telephone lines. Modems translate the digital signals a computer generates into analog signals a telephone line can transfer, and vice versa.

Mosaic
A hypermedia Web browser enabling users to point-and-click their way around the Web. Developed by the National Center for Supercomputing Applications (NCSA) *www.ncsa.org/*.

MPEG
Moving Pictures Experts Group, the organization that manages the MPEG format for digital videos that allows movies to be played on a computer.

NCSA

The National Center for Supercomputing Applications located at the University of Illinois in Urbana-Champaign.

Netscape Navigator

Deemed the "killer application," Netscape is a hypermedia Web browser enabling users to run FTP, Archie, telnet, WAIS, view Usenet newsgroups, Gopher, Veronica, and e-mail—all through one interface.

newsgroups

A distributed conferencing system consisting of thousands of discussion groups organized hierarchically by topic.

node

A node is a computer connected to the Internet and it has its own Internet address.

NSFnet

An acronym for National Science Foundation Network. NSFnet provides backbone service on the Internet.

PC-to-PC telephony

Like Internet telephony, but instead of using telephones, this system uses microphones and speakers connected to PCs. *See also* Internet telephony.

ping

An Internet application that tells you whether another entity on the Net is connected.

plug-in

Plug-ins are software applications that merge seamlessly into their host. They provide additional features that go beyond what the host can do on its own. An example would be RealAudio, an audio player plug-in that enables Netscape Navigator to play audio files in real-time.

PNG

PNG (pronounced "ping") is the Portable Network Graphics format. PNG images are typically smaller in size than GIF images, but can offer the same bit depth (number of bits defining each pixel) as JPEG. PNG's official Website is at *www.libpng.org/pub/png/*.

POP

Point of Presence. In the world of Internet service providers, a POP is the geographic location where you connect to their service.

POP3

Post Office Protocol, a mail protocol on the Internet whereby your mail is held until you connect to the POP3 server and request to see it.

PPP

Point-to-Point Protocol, a protocol that enables computers to use TCP/IP over a serial connection such as a telephone line that is directly attached to the Internet. It functions somewhat like SLIP, but is more advanced.

protocol
A set of formal rules describing how something should be done. On the Internet, there are protocols that describe how to transmit data across a network.

push delivery
A technique used by PointCast, Inc., and other Webcasting services, direct e-mailers, and corporate intranets where a computer "pushes" information files out to you. A "push technology" is any technology that delivers personalized information from the Internet or corporate intranets.

RFC
Request for Comments. Provides background information on various technical details relating to the Internet.

robots
See spiders

router
A hardware device that connects two or more networks—for example, your main library's LAN to a branch library's LAN, or your library's LAN to the Internet.

server
The unit in a client/server model that stores data and responds to requests from clients. Server also refers to a class of computer hardware and software found on networks. *See also* file server.

SGML
Standard Generalized Markup Language, an international standard and encoding scheme for creating textual information. HTML is a subset of SGML.

shareware
Software that you can copy and distribute to others for evaluation purposes during a specified period of time. If after trying it you like it, you then pay the author for the software in order to continue using it.

shell account
A shell is a utility program that expects you to type commands at a prompt in order to interact with the computer's operating system. A shell "account" refers to a shell on another machine that you connect to that is in turn connected to the Internet.

signature file
A text file that contains a few lines of text for your signature. A "signature" consists of your name, e-mail address, and maybe a short quote and is automatically attached to the end of your e-mail messages being sent out.

SLIP
Serial Line Internet Protocol, a protocol that enables computers to use TCP/IP over a telephone line.

SMTP
Simple Mail Transfer Protocol, a set of rules that enables you to transfer e-mail over the Internet.

spamming
To mass distribute unwanted e-mail messages to many different mailing lists or newsgroups.

spewing
When you're on a newsgroup or in a chat room and one of the participants goes on and on typing the same thing repeatedly.

spiders
Also known as *robots* (*bots* for short) and *knowbots*, Spiders are programs that travel around the Web searching for something. Some create indexes; others collect statistics.

stack
A collection of network programs that work together to support one or more network protocols.

T1
An Internet line that transfers data at speeds up to 1.536 million bits per second (1.536Mbps).

T3
An Internet line that transfers data at speeds up to 45 million bits per second (45Mbps).

TA
Terminal Adapter, the interface used to connect your computer to an ISDN connection.

TCP/IP
Transmission Control Protocol/Internet Protocol, the software that implements the rules that enable computers to communicate on the Internet.

telnet
Telnet is an Internet tool that enables you to connect to a remote computer. The most common uses of telnet are connecting to library card catalogs and other large databases and participating in real-time games on the Internet called MUDs, MUSHes, and MOOs.

terabyte
A terabyte is roughly equal to about 1 trillion bytes.

TIFF
This acronym stands for Tag Image File Format. TIFF is a format used for storing image files.

UART
Universal Asynchronous Receiver-Transmitter, chips that handle communications between your modem and your PC.

upload
To transmit, or "send," a file from one computer to another.

URL
Uniform Resource Locator, an addressing format used on the World Wide Web.

Usenet newsgroups
Usenet is the Internet's news/discussion service. Information is sorted by topics into entities called *newsgroups* of which there are over 9,000. Conversations usually focus on a particular topic or "thread." Anyone who joins in can read responses from others and jump in with their own comments.

Veronica
The name of a program that searches for information on Gopher servers.

WAIS
Wide Area Information Server. This Internet service allows you to run searches on full-text databases using keywords and phrases.

Webcasting
Internet-style broadcasting that uses "push delivery" for delivering near-continuous updates of information over the Internet.

Web farming
An emerging field that combines *data warehousing*—internal data analysis—with external data available on the Web. For example, combining stock market information, monetary exchange rates, political events, legislation, emerging competitors and old competitors going out of business, etc., with an organization's business data. *See also* data warehousing.

Webspace
All of the documents on all of the Web servers worldwide. A broader definition of Webspace would include everything accessible with a Web browser including files on FTP and Gopher servers.

white papers
A technical paper describing a product. The paper is usually less than 20 pages in length, and is often presented in PDF format on the Web. White papers usually go into more detail about a product's features than does a brochure. Sometimes multiple white papers are created for a single product, each one presenting a different point of view.

World Wide Web
Also called the *Web*, *WWW*, and *W3*, the World Wide Web is a collection of cross-linked documents, or "pages," stored on computers all around the world.

WRN
World Radio Network, a 24–hour news and information network which broadcasts segments of programming from 25 of the world's leading public and international broadcasters.

Xanadu
Ted Nelson, who originally invented the word "hypertext," has had a long-standing dream that all the world literature would be accessible in one global online system. Nelson's work relating to hypertext became known as the Xanadu project.

Z39.50
Networking standard used in libraries and for searching databases. Allows an application on one computer to query a database on another computer.

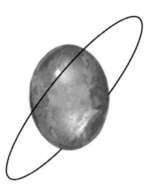

Appendix B: Library Discussion Lists

This appendix contains a selective list of mailing lists relating to libraries. These lists are managed by a variety of mailing list managers including LISTSERV, ListProc, and Majordomo. Commands for these mailing-list managers are explained in Chapter 24 of this book. Sometimes you won't see the words Majordomo or LISTSERV in the e-mail address. For example, the address for Conservation DistList is *consdist-request@lindy.stanford.edu*; a forum for Texas librarians has the address *loanstar-request@twu.edu*; and a law librarian discussion list has the address *law-req@ucdavis.edu*. When you sign-on to these lists, you are communicating with a person, not a piece of software. Still, send the basic information: your name and the name of the list to which you'd like to subscribe. For more complete listings of library-related lists online, see Library-Oriented Lists and Electronic Serials at *www.wrlc.org/liblists/* or search on the keyword **library** using the mailing list director Liszt at *www.liszt.com/*. Search CataList for *listserv* mailing lists. Connect to their site at *www.lsoft.com/lists/list_q.html* and search on the keyword **library**.

LIBRARY RELATED DISCUSSION LISTS

ACQNET-L	Acquisitions Librarian's Electronic Network
	listserv@appstate.edu
	www.library.vanderbilt.edu/law/acqs/acqnet.html
ADVANC-L	The Geac Advance Library System for online services
	listserv@listserv.boisestate.edu
AFAS-L	African American Studies & Librarianship
	listserv@listserv.kent.edu

AJCUIL-L	Law Librarians/Interlibrary Loan
	listserv@listserv.georgetown.edu
ALA	For a complete list of ALA's discussion groups (currently 117),
	visit their Website at *www.ala.org/membership/lists.html.*
ALA-WO	ALA Washington Office Newsline
	listproc@ala.org
ALANEWS	ALA News Releases
	listproc@ala.org
ALAOIF	ALA Intellectual Freedom Discussion List
	listproc@ala.org
ALF-L	Canadian Academic Librarians Forum
	listserv@yorku.ca
ANSS-L	Library issues among specialists in anthropology, sociology, and
	related fields.
	listserv@uci.edu
ARCHIVES	Archives & Archivists List
	listserv@miamiu.muohio.edu
ARIE-L	Users of RLG Ariel Document Transmission System
	listserv@listserv.boisestate.edu
ARLIS-L	Art Libraries Discussion List
	listserv@luky.edu
ASIS-L	American Society of Information Science
	listserv@asis.org
ATLAS-L	Data Research ATLAS Users
	listserv@tcubvm.is.tcu.edu
AUTOCAT	Library Cataloging & Authorities Discussion
	listserv@listserv.acsu.buffalo.edu
BI-L	Bibliographic Instruction
	listserv@listserv.byu.edu
BIBSOFT	Bibliographic Databases & Formatting Software
	listserv@listserv.iupui.edu
BUSLIB-L	Business Library Issues
	listserv@listserv.boisestate.edu
	www.willamette.edu/~gklein/buslib.htm
CARL-L	Carl Users Forum
	listserv@uhccvmits.hawaii.edu
CDROM-L	CD-ROM User List
	listserv@uccvma.ucop.edu
CDROMLAN	CD-ROM Use on a Network
	listserv@listserv.boisestate.edu
CIRCPLUS	Circulation Department Issues
	listserv@listserv.boisestate.edu
COLLDV-L	Collection development list
	listserv@usc.edu
CONSALD	Committee on South Asian Libraries & Documentation
	listserv@mcfeeley.cc.utexas.edu
CONSDIST	Conservation preservation
	e-mail to: *consdist-request@lindy.stanford.edu*

DIGLIB	Digital Libraries Research
	listserv@infoserv.nlc-bnc.ca
DLDG-L	Dance Librarians Discussion List
	listserv@iubvm.ucs.indiana.edu
DOC-L	OCLC Documentation
	lsitserv@oclc.org
DYNIX-L	Dynix Users List
	majordomo@sbu.edu
ELDNET-L	Engineering Libraries
	listserv@ukanvm.cc.ukans.edu
ELEASAI	Open Library/Information Science Research forum
	listserv@utkux.utk.edu
EXLIBRIS	Rare Book & Special Collections Forum
	listserv@library.berkeley.edu
FIRSTSEARCH-L	FirstSearch and Other OCLC Offerings
	listserv@oclc.org
FISC-L	Fee-based Information Services in Academia
	listserv@listserv.nodak.edu
GAY-LIBN	Gay/Lesbian/Bisexual Librarians Network
	listserv@.usc.edu
GEONET-L	Geoscience Librarians & Information Specialists
	listserv@iubvm.ucs.indiana.edu
GOVDOC-L	Federal Deposit Libraries
	listserv@psuvm.psu.edu
GSLISTEC	Library Technology Issues, University of Washington
	listproc@u.washington.edu
GUTNBERG	Project Gutenberg E-mail List
	listserv@postoffice.cso.uiuc.edu
ILL-L	Interlibrary Loan Discussion Group
	listserv@listserv.acns.nwu.edu
INDEX-L	Indexer's Discussion Group
	listserv@bingvmb.cc.binghamton.edu
INNOPAC	Innovative Interfaces OPAC & Related
	listserv@innopacusers.org
	cooley.colgate.edu/InnovativeUsersGroup
INTLAW-L	Foreign and International Law Librarians
	listserv@tc.umn.edu
KIDLIT-L	Children and Youth Literature
	listserv@bingvmb.cc.binghamton.edu
KUTUP-L	Discussion among Turkish Libraries
	listerv@vm.cc.metu.edu.tr
LAW-LIB	Law Librarians List
	listserv@ucdavis.edu
LIBADMIN	Issues of Library Administration and Management
	listserv@umab.umd.edu
LIBEVENT	Library Information Services List
	listserv@usc.edu

LIBJOB-L   Job Announcements for Librarians
                    listserv@infoserv.nlc-bnc.ca
                    www.nlc-bnc.ca/ifla/II/lists/libjobs.htm

LIBMASTR   Library Master Bibliographic Database Program List
                    listserv@listserv.appstate.edu

LIBNT-L   Implementation and Administration of Windows NT in Libraries
                    listserv@utkvm1.utk.edu

LIBPER-L   Library Personnel Issues
                    listproc@gsaix2.cc.gasou.edu

LIBRARY   Libraries and Librarians
                    listproc@listproc.bgsu.edu

LIBREF-L   Changing Environment of Reference Services
                    listserv@listserv.kent.edu

LIBRES   Library and Information Science Research Electronic Journal
                    listserv@listserv.kent.edu

LIBSOFT   Software of Interest to Librarians
                    listserv@mail.orst.edu
                    www.orst.edu/groups/libsoft/

LISA-L   Forum for Library and Information Science Students
                    listserv@ulkyvm.louisville.edu

LIS-L   Library and Information Science Student Discussion Group
                    Listserv@postoffice.cso.uiuc.edu

LITA-L   The Library and Information Technology Association
                    listproc@ala.org

LM_NET   School Library/Media Services
                    listserv@listserv.syr.edu

MAPS-L   Maps and Air Photo Systems
                    listserv@uga.cc.uga.edu

MEDLIB-L   Medical & Health Science Libraries
                    listserv@ubvm.cc.buffalo.edu

MLA-L   MusicLibrary Association
                    listserv@iubvm.ucs.indiana.edu

NETADMIN   Library Network Administration List
                    listserver@leo.vsla.edu

NOTIS-L   NOTIS Users List
                    listserv@uicvm.uic.edu

NOTISACQ   NOTIS Acquisition List
                    listserv@cuvmb.columbia.edu

NOTISSER   NOTIS Serials Discussion List
                    listserv@ukcc.uky.edu

NOTMUS-L   NOTIS Music Library List
                    listserv@ubvm.cc.buffalo.edu

OCLC-JOURNALS Information about OCLC Electronic Journal Publishing
                    listserv@oclc.org

OCLC-NEWS   OCLC Press Releases
                    listserv@oclc.org

OFFCAMP   Off-campus Library Services
                    listserv@lists.wayne.edu

PACS-L   Public Access Computer Systems forum
                  listserv@listserv.uh.edu
PACS-P   PACS-L Publications Only
                  listserv@listserv.uh.edu
PROCITE   ProCite Bibliographic Software Users List
                  listserv@iubvm.ucs.indiana.edu
PUBLIB   Public Library Discussion Group
                  listserv@sunsite.berkeley.edu
                  sunsite.berkeley.edu/PubLib/
PUBLIB-NET   Use of Internet in Public Libraries
                  listserv@sunsite.berkeley.edu
PUBYAC   Youth Services in Public Libraries
                  listserv@nysernet.org
SERCITES   Citations for serial literature
                  listserv@sun.readmore.com
SERIALST   Serials in Libraries–user discussion
                  listserv@list.uvm.edu
SHARP-L   History of the Printed Word
                  listserv@listserv.ucs.indiana.edu
SLAEDD-L   SLA Education Division
                  listserv@nervm.nerdc.ufl.edu
SLAJOB   Special Librarians Association Job Listings
                  listserv@iubvm.ucs.indiana.edu
SLAPA-L   Special Libraries Association
                  lists.psu.edu
TECHBUL-L   OCLC Technical Bulletins
                  listserv@oclc.org
UNCOVER   UNCOVER Discussion List
                  listserv@uhccvm.uhcc.hawaii.edu
UNICRN-L   SIRSI/UNICORN Automated Library Systems
                  listserv@psuorvm.cc.pdx.edu
WEB4LIB   Creation and Management of Library-Based Web Servers and Clients
                  listserv@sunsite.berkeley.edu

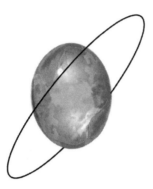

Appendix C: Online Access to Schools of Library and Information Science

Appendix C provides a list of library schools around the world and their corresponding Web addresses. These Websites offer more than faculty profiles and course information; many provide details about ongoing research projects, calendars of events, information about student organizations, student and alumni directories, employment resources, and student-created Web projects.

School	Web Address
Archivschule Marburg (Germany)	*www.uni-marburg.de/archivschule/*
The Catholic University of America, School of Library and Information Science (Washington, D.C.)	*http://slis.cua.edu/*
Charles Sturt University, School of Information Studies (Australia)	*www.csu.edu.au/faculty/sci agr/sis/admin/sishome.htm*
Charles University–Prague Institute of Information Studies and Librarianship (Czech Republic)	*http://dec59.ruk.cuni.cz/%7Eskenders/uisk/*
City University, Department of Information Science (U.K.)	*http://web.is.city.ac.uk/*

School	Web Address
Curtin University of Technology Technology Department of Information Studies (Western Australia)	*http://smi.curtin.edu.au/*
Drexel University College of Information Science and Technology	*www.cis.drexel.edu/*
Emporia State University, Kansas, School of Library and Information Management	*http://slim.emporia.edu/*
Florida State University School of Library and Information Studies	*www.fsu.edu/~lis/*
The Hebrew University of Jerusalem, School of Library, Archive and Information Studies	*http://sites.huji.ac.il/slais/*
Indiana University at Bloomington, School of Library and Information Science	*www-slis.lib.indiana.edu/*
Kent State University, School of Library and Information Science	*http://ariadne.slis.kent.edu/*
LIBLABWeb, Library and Information Science Laboratory, Link_ping University (Sweden)	*www.ida.liu.se/labs/liblab/*
Loughborough University, Department of Information and Library Studies (U.K.)	*http://info.lut.ac.uk/departments/dils/*
Louisiana State University, School of Library and Information Science	*http://adam.slis.lsu.edu/*
McGill University, Graduate School of Library and Information Studies (Canada)	*http://132.206.199.40/*

School	Web Address
North Carolina Central University, School of Library and Information Sciences	*www.slis.nccu.edu/*
Pratt Institute, New York, School of Information and Library Sciences	*www.pratt.edu/index.html*
Queensland University of Technology, School of Information Systems (Australia)	*www.fit.qut.edu.au/InfoSys/*
Robert Gordon University–Aberdeen, School of Information and Media (U.K.)	*www.rgu.ac.uk/~sim/sim.htm*
Royal Melbourne Institute of Technology, Department of Information Management (Australia)	*www.bf.rmit.edu.au/Dimals/*
Royal School of Librarianship (Copenhagen, Denmark)	*www.db.dk/*
Rutgers, The State University of New Jersey, School of Communication, Information and Library Studies	*www.scils.rutgers.edu/*
San Jose State University, School of Library and Information Science	*http://witloof.sjsu.edu/*
Simmons College, Graduate School of Library and Information Science (Boston)	*www.simmons.edu/programs/gslis/*
Syracuse University, School of Information Studies	*http://istweb.syr.edu/*
Texas Women's University, School of Library and Information Studies	*www.twu.edu/slis/*

School	Web Address
Universite de Montreal Ecole de Bibliotheconomie et des sciences de l'information	*www.fas.umontreal.ca/EBSI/*
University at Albany (SUNY), School of Information Science and Policy	*www.albany.edu/sisp/*
University College London, School of Library, Archive and Information Studies (U.K.)	*www.ucl.ac.uk/~uczcw11/slais/slais.htm*
University of Alabama, School of Library and Information Studies	*www.slis.ua.edu/*
University of Alberta, School of Library and Information Studies (Canada)	*www.ualberta.ca/dept/slis/homepage/slis.htm*
University of Arizona, School of Library Science	*http://timon.sir.arizona.edu/*
University of British Columbia, School of Library, Archival and Information Studies	*www.slais.ubc.ca/*
University of California at Berkeley, School of Information Management & Systems	*http://info.sims.berkeley.edu/*
The University of Hawaii –Manoa, School of Library and Information Studies	*www2.hawaii.edu/slis/*
University of Illinois at Urbana-Champaign, Graduate School of Library and Information Science	*http://alexia.lis.uiuc.edu/*
University of Iowa, School of Library and Information Science	*www.uiowa.edu/~libsci/*

School	Web Address
University of Kentucky, School of Library and Information Science	*www.uky.edu/CommInfoStudies/SLIS/*
University of Michigan, School of Information	*www.sils.umich.edu/*
University of North Carolina–Chapel Hill, School of Information and Library Science	*http://ils.unc.edu/ilshome.html*
University of North Carolina–Greensboro, Department of Library and Information Studies	*www.uncg.edu/lis/*
University of Oklahoma, School of Library and Information Studies	*www.ou.edu/cas/slis/*
University of Oulu, Department of Information Studies and Sociology (Finland)	*http://syy.oulu.fi/*
University of Parma, Institute of Library Science and Paleography (Italy)	*www.aldus.unipr.it/*
University of Pittsburgh, School of Information Sciences	*www.lis.pitt.edu/*
University of St.Gallen, Institute for Information Management (Switzerland)	*www-iwi.unisg.ch/*
University of Sheffield, Department of Information Studies (U.K.)	*www.shef.ac.uk/uni/academic/I-M/is/home.html*
University of South Florida, School of Library and Information Science	*http://nosferatu.cas.usf.edu/lis/index.html*
University of Strathclyde, Glasgow, Department of Information Science (Scotland)	*www.dis.strath.ac.uk/*

School	Web Address
University of Tampere, Department of Information Studies (Finland)	*www.info.uta.fi/home.html*
University of Tennessee School of Information Sciences	*http://pepper.lis.utk.edu/*
University of Texas at Austin, Graduate School of Library Information Science	*http://fiat.gslis.utexas.edu/*
University of Toronto, Faculty of Information Studies	*www.fis.utoronto.ca/*
University of Washington, Graduate School of Library and Information Science	*www.ischool.washington.edu/slis/*
University of Western Ontario, Graduate School of Library and Information Science	*www.fims.uwo.ca/lis/*
University of Wisconsin at Madison, School of Library and Information Studies	*http://polyglot.lss.wisc.edu/slis/*
University of Wisconsin–Milwaukee School of Library and Information Science	*www.uwm.edu/Dept/SLIS/*
Victoria University of Wellington, Department of Library and Information Studies (New Zealand)	*www.vuw.ac.nz/dlis/*
Wayne State University, Library and Information Science Program	*www.libraries.wayne.edu/*

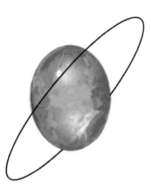

Appendix D: Job Hunting Online for Librarians

The Internet now provides a cost-effective, efficient way to go job hunting online all over the world. Libraries with Internet connections are still placing their recruitment ads in print sources, but many are also uploading job announcements to the Net. Although the print versions of display and classified ads can be expensive, in most cases the only cost associated with Internet announcements is the cost of your connection and the time it takes to upload the ad.

POSTING JOBS ON MAILING LISTS

Some mailing lists, such as LIBJOBS and SLAJOB, are set up for the sole purpose of distributing job announcements. Many times recruiters post announcements to other library-related mailing lists that discuss issues relating to a particular job description. For example, job announcements for reference librarians are often posted on LIBREF-L, a mailing list read by reference librarians; and job announcements for a children's librarian are posted on PUBYAC, a mailing list that discusses youth services in public libraries.

An excellent online resource for determining which mailing lists might match a particular department in your library is the "Library-Oriented Lists and Electronic" Serials Web page.

This resource began as a work compiled by Charles W. Bailey Jr., Assistant Dean for Systems at the University of Houston. When the last edition of this book was written, Ann Thornton and Steve Bonario had completed converting this document to HTML code. In December of 1996, work on the "Library-Oriented Lists" was taken over by Wei Wu of the Washington Research Library Consortium (WRLC). You can access the site at *www.wrlc.org/liblists/*.

Look for the link labeled "subject index." This takes you to a directory of mailing lists organized under headings such as Acquisitions, Cataloging/Bibliographic Services, Children's Librarianship, Interlibrary Loan, K–12 Libraries, Law Libraries, and many others.

HOW APPENDIX D IS ORGANIZED

The job services described in this appendix are organized under these headings:

- Academic Libraries
- General (Includes public, academic, and school libraries, etc.)
- Government Libraries
- Special Libraries

All of the information presented here is summarized in Tables D-1 through D-4, placed at the end of this appendix. For information relating to online job hunting in general, check out Monster.com *monster.com/*. Monster.com is a comprehensive source for job listings and career resources. *Flip.Dog.com* and *HotJobs.com* are two other big job sites that can help you and your patrons sort through thousands of job listings. About.com is a good place to start for general job searching in all areas of librarianship. You can find their job links listed at *librarians.about.com/careers/librarians/blwherejobs.htm*.

ACADEMIC LIBRARIES

In this section, I present ACADEME THIS WEEK, College & Research Libraries News-Net, LITA/LAMA National Conference Placement Center Job Listings, the Academic Position Network, EDUCAUSE Job Posting Service, university library job postings, and ARL Career Resources.

ACADEME THIS WEEK

ACADEME THIS WEEK is a complimentary online service of *The Chronicle of Higher Education*. ACADEME THIS WEEK carries all of the job listings found in *The Chronicle*. A new edition of ACADEME THIS WEEK comes out every Tuesday at precisely 12 noon (U.S. Eastern Time). You don't have to be a subscriber to *The Chronicle* to read the job ads posted in ACADEME THIS WEEK.

Finding ACADEME THIS WEEK

ACADEME THIS WEEK can be accessed on the Web at *chronicle.merit.edu*. Look for the link "Jobs" located on *The Chronicle of Higher Education's* home page. The most recent issue of *The Chronicle* can be accessed by *Chronicle* subscribers. There is online help that explains how to get a password. Job announcements from previous issues can be accessed free of charge.

You can browse through job listings using *The Chronicles'* list of job titles. Follow the path "Professional Fields I Library science." On the day I checked for job openings for librarians, there were a variety of positions posted including Director of Public Services, The University of Oklahoma; Instructor/Reference Librarian, Shepherd College; Assistant Librarian, University of Maryland Eastern Shore; Assistant Director, Public Services, University of Missouri; Collection Management Services, Marywood College; Director of Libraries, Bryn Mawr College; Reference, Xavier University of Louisiana; and dozens more.

Searching ACADEME THIS WEEK

The Chronicle also offers you the opportunity to search their entire database of job listings by keyword or phrase, or you can limit your search to a certain section of the country. To launch a search from their Web server, click on the link labeled "Jobs" and then look for your search options and the box for entering your search term(s).

COLLEGE & RESEARCH LIBRARIES NEWSNET

By going through the ALA's Web address *www.ala.org*, you can access the electronic component of *College & Research Libraries News* called College & Research Libraries NewsNet. Beginning at the main page, click on the link called "Employment." On the next page you should find a link under Employment called "Academic Librarian Positions from *College & Research Libraries NewsNet.*"

Jobs are grouped by month. In the most recent listings I viewed, C&RL NewsNet listed openings for Information and Technology Coordinator, Claremont Colleges (California); Reference/Instructional Librarian, North Harris College Library (Texas); Head, Systems Department, The University of Memphis (Tennessee); Dean of Libraries, Baylor University (Texas); Director, Library Information Systems, California State University; and many others.

While you are at the ALA Website, you may also be interested in exploring their other Job Line services including:

- Link to LITA, which lists jobs in library and information technology. This site lists people looking for jobs and people posting jobs.
- Conference job listings
- Guide to library placement sources
- Library Job Postings on the Internet, compiled by Sarah L. Nesbeitt
- Job openings at the American Library Association

THE ACADEMIC POSITION NETWORK

The Academic Position Network (APN) posts job notices for academic positions including faculty, staff, and administrative positions. APN also announces openings for post-doctoral positions and graduate fellowships and assistantships.

You can access APN via the Web at *www.apnjobs.com*. Job announcements are organized under state headings for browsing or you can run keyword searches on the entire database.

EDUCAUSE JOB POSTING SERVICE

The EDUCAUSE Job Posting Service posts job openings for teaching and other academic positions, including librarians. This database isn't particularly large, but it does cover all levels of management positions, technical and customer service positions, and faculty/instruction positions. To focus-in on library-related jobs, use their search engine and search on the keyword **library.** On the day I explored EDUCAUSE, I found 35 library-related job openings. A wide variety of interests were covered including university management positions and technology positions.

To learn more about EDUCAUSE Job Posting Service, point your Web browser at *www.educause.edu/* and click on the link labeled "Job Postings." This brings you to a page where you can either run a keyword search or browse listings by job type or geographic location.

UNIVERSITY LIBRARY JOB POSTINGS

Many of the larger university library systems have their own Web pages announcing job openings. A good example is The University of California, San Diego, Library Human Resources at *orpheus-1.ucsd.edu/fac/postions.htm*. You can find several job listings at any given time under the following headings:

- Executive and Management Positions
- Administrative Professional
- Academic Librarian Positions
- Staff Positions
- Positions Elsewhere

In addition, checkout the job postings at Columbia University Library Jobs *www.Columbia.edu/cu/libraries/inside/hr/libjob.html*, Duke University Library Job Vacancies *www.lib.duke.edu/jobs/index.htm*, University of Michigan Library Student Jobs *www.lib.umich.edu/libhome/newnow/stujob.html*, University of Pennsylvania Library Employment *www.library.upenn.edu/services/employment/employment.html*, and Yale University Human Resources Department *www.library.yale.edu/htmldocs/emp_idx.htm*.

ARL CAREER RESOURCES

The Association of Research Libraries offers information about job opportunities to members and non-members alike. Job announcements are grouped by geographical region and by area of specialization. Announcements can be written online by filling out a form located on their Web page at *db.arl.org/careers/index.html*. This service is free to members of ARL. The fee for non-members to post a vacancy announcement for 45 days is $250.

GENERAL LIBRARIES

In this section, I describe job services that cater to all types of libraries, including ALA Jobline, LIBEX, LIBJOBS, The Colorado State Library Jobline, and examples of graduate school job lines.

ALA JOBLINE

ALA Jobline offers online access to current job listings from *American Libraries* magazine at site *www.ala.org/education/*. Jobs are listed under broad subject headings including Academic Library, Federal Agency, Internet Reference, Library Network, Library System, Medical Library, Music Library, Public Library, Publishing, Research Library, School Library, State Agency, and Vendor/Utility.

LIBEX

LIBEX posts job openings for library and information professionals interested in working in other countries. LIBEX is run by the Thomas Parry Library, University of Wales, Aberystwyth, and can be accessed on the Web at *www.inf.aber.ac.uk/tpl/Libex/intro.asp*.

LIBJOBS

LIBJOBS is the Library and Information Science jobs mailing list. You can subscribe to the list by sending the command **subscribe libjobs <your_name>** to *listserv@ infoserv.nlc-bnc.ca*.

LIBJOBS on the Web

The friendliest interface for accessing LIBJOBS is the Web. LIBJOBS is part of the IFLANET LWGate, a mailing list WWW gateway that makes joining lists and viewing archives quite easy. By linking to LIBJOBS' Web page *www.ifla.org/II/lists/libjobs.htm*, you can subscribe to the list using forms and you can view the LIBJOBS archives in hypertext format.

The LIBJOBS Archive

The LIBJOBS archive stores job announcements going back to August 1995. Because it is updated daily, you may want to forgo joining the mailing list and instead check in with this site whenever it is convenient for you. You can access the archive from the LIBJOBS home page by either browsing or searching the hypertext index. Job announcements are for a wide variety of positions and locations.

Posting Recruitment Ads

If you want to post a position opening in your organization, join the LIBJOBS mailing list and send your announcement to *libjobs@infoserv.nlc-bnc.ca*.

THE COLORADO STATE LIBRARY JOBLINE

The Colorado State Library Jobline is a service that lists library positions available in Colorado and out-of-state. The list is updated daily and maintained by the Colorado

State Library. You can access this jobline at *jobline.aclin.org*. This site offers links to other job sources including other library jobs Websites in Colorado and general job resources. When I last looked at this site, there were job openings posted for a wide variety of positions in locations ranging from Alaska to New York.

GRADUATE SCHOOL JOB LINES

Some library schools offer online placement services. An example is the University of Illinois at Urbana-Champaign, Graduate School of Library and Information Science. The GSLIS Placement Office receives as many as 180 new job announcements each month and posts them bi-weekly in their Online Placement Bulletin.

To access the GSLIS Placement Office via the Web, go to site *http://carousel.lis.uiuc.edu/~jobs/*. The Web interface enables you to view notices under the following headings:

- Experience Level
- Employer
- Job Title Keywords
- Job Type
- Library Type
- Location or Region

The School of Information Management Systems at the University of California at Berkeley supports a Web-based mailing list where messages are posted for all to read. You can access this service at *www.sims.berkeley.edu/resources/mailing-lists/jobs/*. When I last checked, job postings were listed covering the period April 1997 through the present date. A wide variety of openings were available, including part-time librarian positions, information architect positions, digital resources librarians, and more.

The Library Job Resources site maintained by the School of Information Studies at the University at Buffalo, The State University of New York, is quite extensive. You can access it at *wings.buffalo.edu/sils/alas/usamap/index.html*. Here you can explore job listings organized by state and specialty, as well as other job resources.

GOVERNMENT LIBRARIES

In this section I describe three resources: Jobs in Government, the Defense Technical Information Center, and job opportunities at the U.S. Office of Personnel Management. You can also find references to library jobs in Federal Agencies at ALA's Website *www.ala.org/education/*.

JOBS IN GOVERNMENT

This site provides a comprehensive listing of public sector jobs. The main purpose of this site is to help the 80,000 public sector agencies fill jobs. This could amount to quite a few openings considering there are millions working in the public sector. When you visit their site at *www.JobsInGovernment.com/*, you are given the option of searching, posting or editing resumes, or viewing an employer list.

You search this site by filling out a form that includes the job category "Library."

They also ask you to specify a state or province, salary range, job term (part time, full time, etc.), and any keywords you care to enter.

DEFENSE TECHNICAL INFORMATION CENTER

The Defense Technical Information Center *www.dtic.mil/dtic/joas/* lists job opportunities at any of the DTIC offices. The last time I checked, there were only four openings posted and three of these were for Technical Information Specialist.

U.S. Office of Personnel Management

The official site for jobs with the U.S. government can be located at *www.usajobs.opm.gov/ index.htm*. Look for the link labeled "CURRENT JOB OPENINGS" and then jump to "Alphabetical Job Search." Clicking on "L" takes you to library openings all around the United States.

SPECIAL LIBRARIES

In this section, I describe the Special Libraries Association's SLA Job Search-ONLINE, SLA's News Division Job Announcements on the Web, job opportunities at OCLC, the American Association of Law Libraries Placement Services, and the Medical Library Association job site MLANET.

SLA JOB SEARCH-ONLINE

SLA Career Services Online is a service available to Special Libraries Association members and non-members alike. To access the SLA job listings, go to SLA's Website at *www.sla.org/* and click on the link labeled "Strategic Learning/Careers." On the next page look for the link called "SLA Career Services Online." To see what job listings are available, you can browse by viewing all jobs, or you can conduct a search.

SLA'S NEWS DIVISION JOB ANNOUNCEMENTS

Webmaster Chandra Pierce, along with many other contributors, maintains the News Division home page of SLA at *sunsite.unc.edu/slanews,* where job hunters can access job and internship notices.

   Their clearinghouse is a service for anyone interested in posting or searching for librarian positions in the news business. You can post positions on the NewsLib mailing list at *listproc@listserv.oit.unc*. Questions about NewsLib and how to join are answered by clicking on the link labeled "NewsLib mailing list" or by going directly to *metalab.unc.edu/journalism/newslib.html*. Additional questions may be directed to the list owner, Barbara P. Semonche, at *semonch@metalab.unc.edu*. All of the services associated with NewsLib are free.

Table D-1: Online job resources for librarians: academic libraries	
Service	**Address**
Academe This Week	http://chronicle.merit.edu/
Academic Position Network	www.apnjobs.com
ARL Career	http://db.arl.org/careers/index.html
C & RL NewsNet	www.ala.org/
EDUCAUSE	www.educause.edu/
LITA	www.lita.org/jobs/
Columbia University	www.Columbia.edu/cu/libraries/inside/hr/libjob.html
Duke University	www.lib.duke.edu/jobs/index.htm
University of California	http://oorpheus-1.ucsd.edu/fac/postions.htm
University of Michigan	www.lib.umich.edu/libhome/newnow/stujob.html
University of Pennsylvania	www.library.upenn.edu/services/employment/employment.html
Yale University	www.library.yale.edu/htmldocs/emp_idx.htm

EMPLOYMENT OPPORTUNITIES AT OCLC

OCLC maintains a Web page at *www.oclc.org/oclc/jobs/jobtoc.htm* where they maintain a list of current job openings with their firm. This list includes jobs both related and unrelated to library and information science.

AMERICAN ASSOCIATION OF LAW LIBRARIES PLACEMENT SERVICES

The American Association of Law Libraries maintains a Career Hotline Listing on the home page at *www.aallnet.org/index.asp*. By clicking on the link labeled "Career Op-

Table D-2: Online job resources for librarians: general libraries	
Service	**Address**
About.com	http://librarians.about.com/careers/librarians/blwherejobs.htm
American Libraries	www.ala.org/education/
GSLIS, University of Illinois at Urbana-Champaign	http://carousel.lis.uiuc.edu/~jobs/
LIBEX	www.aber.ac.uk/~tpl www/libex.html
LIBJOBS	listserv@infoserv.nlc-bnc.ca
LIBJOBS	www.ifla.org/II/lists/libjobs.htm
The New England Library Jobline	telnetvmsvax.simmons.edu
Colorado State Library Jobline	http://jobline.aclin.org
Graduate School Jobline	http://carousel.lis.uiuc.edu/~jobs/
Graduate School Jobline	www.slims.berkeley.edu/resources/mailing-lists/jobs/
University at Buffalo	http://wings.buffalo.edu/sils/alas/usamap/index.html

Table D-3: Online job resources for librarians: government libraries	
Service	**Address**
ALA	*www.ala.org/education/*
Defense Technical Information Center	*www.dtic.mil/dtic/joas/*
Jobs in Government	*www.JobsInGovernment.com/*
United States Office of Personnel Management	*www.usajobs.opm.gov/index.htm*

portunities," you can then access a page that links to AALL's Career Hotline Listing. Job openings for information professionals are updated every Friday.

On the day I read AALL's Job Hotline, I found descriptions for positions that included Collection Development/Copyright Librarian, Law Library Directors, Catalog Librarian, and Research Librarian. Any employer can post job openings with AALL, even if they are not members of AALL.

MEDICAL LIBRARY ASSOCIATION MLANET

The Medical Library Association takes jobs posted in *MLA News* and publishes them on their Website MLANET at *www.mlanet.org/jobs/*. Soon this service will be available only to members. You can find out how to join MLA at this same Website address.

Table D-4: Online job resources for librarians: special libraries	
Service	**Address**
American Association of Law Libraries	*www.aallnet.org/index.asp*
Medical Library Association	*www.mlanet.org/jobs/*
OCLC	*www.oclc.org/oclc/jobs/jobtoc.htm*
SLA Career Services Online	*www.sla.org/*
SLA's News Division	*http://sunsite.unc.edu/slanews/*

Appendix E: File Types and the Software That Creates Them

When downloading files on the Internet, you'll see several different file name extensions—the part of the file name coming after the dot. Each extension provides a clue as to the type of format in which a particular file has been saved. These extensions also tell you what processes, if any, must be performed before a file can be made usable.

In Appendix E, I describe what the various file formats are and explain how to deal with them. In order to view a text or image file or listen to a sound file on the Internet, you need a certain program designed just for that purpose. Rather than list specific places to go for these special-purpose programs—information that will change over time—I present only the file name and the actual name of the program. You can locate a download site by searching on these text strings using Archie or one of the search engines introduced in Chapter 12. You can also try one of these software super-sites on the Web:

Stroud's CWSApps List   *cws.internet.com/*
TUCOWS *www.tucows.com/*
Jumbo!   *www.jumbo.com/*

If you search on a specific file name, for example "pk361.exe," and you get zero hits, it could be because that specific version of the software is no longer available. If this is the case, broaden your search by using the application name. In the above example, "pk361.exe" would be replaced with "pkunpak."

WHAT ARE COMPRESSED FILES?

Compressed files are files that have been compressed and reduced in size. For practical exercises in working with compressed files and a program called PKUNZIP, see the section "File Compression" in Chapter 13. In this section, I introduce other programs for decompressing files.

COMPRESSED FILES (.Z AND .GZ)

One compression program found on UNIX systems is called *compress*. When compress is used to make a file smaller, it also creates a new file name by adding the extension .Z to the end of the original file name (note this is an uppercase Z). If you retrieve a file whose name ends with a .Z extension, you will have to uncompress it before you can use it. To uncompress it, you use a program called *uncompress*. Thus, if you have retrieved a file called *<filename>.Z* and you are working on a machine running the UNIX operating system, the following UNIX command will uncompress the file: **uncompress <filename>** where "<filename>" is the name of the file you want to uncompress. The .Z extension may be left on or off.

If you are on a UNIX machine, it is likely that compress for UNIX is already running on it. If you intend to download a .Z file to your PC or Mac and then uncompress it, you need one of the following programs:

- MS-DOS users should use *comp430s.zip*. The syntax for uncompressing a file with this program is A:\> **comp430d -d <filename>.Z**, where "<filename>.Z" is the name of the file you want to uncompress. The .Z extension must be included with the file name.
- Mac users should use *maccompress-32.hqx*. Files with a *.gz* extension are files created with another UNIX system compression program called *gzip* (GNU zip). Its counterpart, *gunzip*, uncompresses files. The gunzip program can also uncompress .Z files and *.zip* files. MS-DOS users need the file called *gzip124.zip* and Mac users need the file called *gzip.hqx*.
- Windows users can use WinZip, which is excellent at handling many different archiving and compression formats.

ARCHIVE FILES (.ARC)

To "archive" a group of files is to compress and combine several related files into a single, easy-to-manage file and to do it in such a way that the individual files may later be recovered intact. *PKPAK* is a program that is used to compress files when adding them to an archive. *PKUNPAK* will expand them upon extraction. When downloading files with the *.arc* extension, you will need a copy of *pk361.exe*. This is a *self-extracting* archive; this means that when you run the program, it will unpack itself. There isn't any need for any additional programs to make this program useful.

pk361.exe unpacks itself to become nine distinct files. The main extraction program is called *PKUNPAK.EXE*. To unpack an archived file called *callback.arc*, you would enter the following command: a:\> **pkunpak callback**

Mac users can use a program called *arcmac*. Look at FTP sites for a file called *arcmac.hqx*.

ARJ FILES (.*ARJ*)

ARJ is a program that creates archive files and automatically compresses the files when adding them to an archive. For files with an *.arj* extension, you need a copy of *ARJ241.EXE* to extract the files. *ARJ241.EXE* is a self-extracting archive. When you run the program, it will create *ARJ.EXE* and other related documentation. To unpack an ARJ archive called *foo.arj*, you would type the command a:\> **unarj e foo**

It isn't necessary to supply the *.arj* extension when typing the file name. If you're an MS-DOS user, look for a file called *arj241a.exe*. If you're a Mac user, look for a file called *unarjmac.cpt.hqx*.

LHA FILES (.*LZH*)

LHA is another program used to create and maintain file archives. To extract files that have the *.lzh* extension, you need a copy of *LHA213.EXE*. This is a self-extracting file, so when you run the program it will produce *LHA.EXE* and other related documentation. To unpack a file with the *.lzh* extension, type: a:\> **lharc e <filename>**

You don't have to specify the *.lzh* extension on the file name. For MS-DOS, get the file called *lha213.exe*. For a Macintosh, get a copy of *maclha2.0.cpt.hqx*.

ZOOFILES (.*ZOO*)

ZOO is an archiving program similar in function to PKPAK and ZIP; however, it cannot be used to unpack files created with PKPAK and ZIP. A unique feature of ZOO is that it can produce archives with long pathnames in them and it can store comments about each file. If you want to unarchive a ZOO file, you will need a copy of *ZOO.EXE*. Following is an example of the ZOO syntax for extracting a file: a:\>**zoo e <filename>**

The *.ZOO* extension does not have to be specified. To find a copy of ZOO for Macintosh, look for the file called *maczoo.sit.hqx*. MS-DOS users should look for the file called *zoo210.exe*.

SQUEEZED FILES (_*Q*_)

Nusq110.com is a program used to squeeze and unsqueeze files that have a "Q" as the middle letter of the file extension. Files with this letter in the extension were squeezed with *sqpc12a.com*, or something similar. If you download a file that has been squeezed you will need a copy of *NUSQ110.COM* to unsqueeze it before it can be used. The syntax to unsqueeze a file would be a:\>**nusq110 <filename>.tqt**, where "<filename>.tqt" is the name of the file you want to unsqueeze. Here it is important to supply the full file name and the type of file (the extension).

To obtain a copy of this program for MS-DOS, look for a file called *sqpc12a.com* (squeeze) and *nussq110.com* (unsqueeze).

Files with the extension *.sqz* are also "squeezed" files, but they are different from the above file types. For a version of this squeeze program for MS-DOS, locate a copy of *sqz1083e.exe*.

TARFILES (*.TAR*)

Tarfiles are archived files that must be unpacked by using the *tar* program. Tarfiles usually consist of multiple files and sometimes directories. To obtain a copy of tar for MS-DOS, look for a file called *tar4dos.zip*. For a Macintosh version, download the file called *tar-30.hqx*.

COMPRESSED TARFILES (*.TAR.Z*)

Sometimes compression programs are combined with tar to create compressed archives. Files that are packed into an archive and then compressed will have two file extensions. On UNIX systems, files with the format *filename.tar.Z* have been archived by tar and then compressed. Tar is not a compression program. It just combines several files, creating one. The tarfile is then compressed with another program, like *compress*, which creates a *tar.Z* file. When you retrieve files like this, you must first uncompress them and then untar them.

Let's say, for example, that you have downloaded the UNIX version of HYTELNET from the archive site at the University of North Texas (*ftp.unt.edu* in directory */pub/library/hytelnet* filename *unix*). This file consists of multiple files that have been packed together into one file called *hytelnet.tar.Z*. First you create a directory and move the compressed tarfile into that directory. Once the file is there, you uncompress the file and then you unpack it. If, after viewing the directory, you see that the process worked and all of the files were converted properly, you can delete the original tarfile.

If you transfer a file *ka9qbin.8.tar.Z* from a site and it arrives at your computer as *ka9qbin.8*, it is still a compressed and tarred binary file. The file name has just been truncated to meet DOS file name standards. You must still uncompress the file first, and then untar it. The name change does not change the file type.

If you try to uncompress the file and it doesn't work, try renaming the file by adding the *.Z* extension again.

WHAT IS MACBINARY? (*.BIN*)

Macintosh files consist of two parts: a data fork and a resource fork. In some instances, the data fork contains the main part of the file—text if it is a document, or the actual image if it is a GIF file—and the resource fork contains the icon and other data relating to the main file. In other instances, such as applications, the main part of the file is stored in the resource fork and the data fork is usually empty. Individuals who want to store Macintosh files on non-Macintosh computers have to convert them to a MacBinary format before transferring them.

MacBinary is the name of a program used for converting files to and from MacBinary format. The newer Macintosh telecommunications programs have a built-in feature capable of converting and unconverting these files. Files with the extension *.bin* are binary images of Macintosh files in MacBinary format. These files will only be useful to you if you are using a Macintosh computer. It isn't necessary to use MacBinary to transfer GIF images because GIF files don't contain any information that's specific to Macintosh computers. Encoding them in MacBinary format would just make it impossible for non-Macintosh users to use them.

BINHEX FILES (.HQX)

Most of the Macintosh files you'll find on the Internet are stored in BinHex (Binary/ Hexadecimal) format. These are ASCII text files containing an image of a Macintosh file. There is a common practice of labeling such files with *.hqx* extensions. The BinHex process does what MacBinary does, plus it converts binary files into ASCII text. This enables you to transfer the file via the Internet mail system or as Usenet news.

To download *.hqx* files and use them on a Macintosh computer, you must first run them through a program that converts them from *.hqx* format into a regular Macintosh file. If you do this conversion process on a Unix system before transferring the program to your Macintosh, you can use the MCVERT program. The file name for this program is *mcvert.shar*.

If you've transferred the BinHex files to your Macintosh, you'd run a de-binhexing utility to convert the *.hqx* files into either real Macintosh files or compressed files. If they are compressed, use one of the decompression programs to decompress it.

Some of the popular programs that allow you to convert BinHex files into applications and documents right on your Macintosh are StuffIt, BinHex 4.0, and Compact Pro. To download a copy of BinHex 4.0, look for a file named *binhex4.bin*. This file is a MacBinary version of BinHex 4.0. Make sure you issue a "binary" command on the FTP server before downloading or you'll get a corrupted file.

MAC TOOLS FOR COMPRESSING FILES

The most common Macintosh compression tools include StuffIt, StuffIt Lite, and StuffIt Deluxe—all of which create files with *.sit* extensions—and Compact Pro, which creates files with *.cpt* extensions. The above utilities also create self-extracting archived files with *.sea* extensions. Another Macintosh compression program, called PackIt, creates files with *.pit* extensions.

As a Mac user, if you would like to compress files for uploading or decompress files created by DOS or UNIX computers, StuffIt Deluxe is a commercial program with very versatile file-handling capabilities. The program also will convert files from BinHex format. It is produced by Aladdin Systems, Inc., e-mail *cust.service@aladdinsys.com*; the Web *www.aladdinsys.com/*.

StuffIt Files (.sit)

StuffIt files usually appear with the *.sit* extension. Stuffit is a Macintosh program that performs an operation similar to a PC archiver; it compresses and collects several files together into a single file. Files with *.sit* extensions may also be created with compression programs called StuffIt Lite and StuffIt Deluxe.

To download a copy of StuffIt for Macintosh, search FTP sites for the file name *stuffit-lite-30.hqx* or go to Aladdin Systems' home page listed earlier. If you need to unstuff a file using an MS-DOS utility, use *unsit30.zip*.

PackIt Files (.pit)

Files with a *.pit* extension can be made usable with PackIt for Macintosh. Depending on the latest version, the file name will look something like *stuffit-151.hqx*.

Compact Pro Files (.cpt)

Files with a *.cpt* extension were made with Compact Pro for Macintosh. You can find this program in a file named *compact-pro-133.hqx*.

Self-Extracting Files (.sea)

To extract a file with the *.sea* extension, you simply run the file. To practice this procedure, use Archie (on the Web try Nexor's Archie services at *http://pubweb.nexor.co.uk/public/archie/servers.html*) and run a search on the text string **sea.hqx**. This will retrieve a list of files that consists of multiple files that have been packed into a self-extracting archive (*.sea*) and then converted into BinHex format (*.hqx*).

The *.hqx* at the far right tells you the first thing you must do before you can use this file is convert it from BinHex format. (Run it through one of the BinHex programs mentioned earlier.) The second thing you must do is unpack the resulting *<filename>.sea* file. The *.sea* extension indicates that the file is of the self-extracting variety, so you can unpack the file by simply running the program.

AUDIO FILE FORMATS

The most popular audio file formats include AIFF, AU, MOD, MPEG Audio, and WAV. These formats were originally designed to play on a specific platform, but now there are hundreds of sound tools available that make it possible to listen to these formats on any system.

AUDIO SOFTWARE

There are different classes of programs associated with sound files. *Players* are sound tools that allow you to play sound files. *Editors* are programs that help you edit prerecorded sound. *Converters* enable you to change an audio file recorded in one format to a different format. *Authoring* programs are designed to help you create sound files.

In Table E-1, I describe the most popular audio file formats and tell you their file name extensions and what they mean. Three of the more popular programs for Mac users that support these formats are SoundApp, Sound Tracker, and PlayerPro. Two of the better sound players available for Windows include WHAM (Waveform Hold and Modify) and MIDAS. Shareware versions of most of these programs are available for under $50.

When searching for sound players on the Internet, either search on the player's name or search on the word **player**. Searching on the word "player" will help you zero-in on FTP sites that maintain directories containing sound players.

Table E-1: Audio file formats and their meanings		
Sound Format	**File Extension**	**Description**
u-Law	*.au*	Developed by Sun Microsystems, u-Law files are fairly popular on the Web because of their size. While the sound quality is not that good, these compressed files are quick to download.
AIFF	*.aiff*	AIFF is an acronym for Audio Interchange File Format. AIFF sound files are Mac-based sounds.
MPEG Audio	*.mp2, .mp3*	MPEG represents both the name of an organization—the Moving Pictures Expert Group—and a file format. The organization's purpose is to develop standards for digital video and audio compression.
MIDI Files	*.mid or .midi*	MIDI is an acronym for Musical Instrument Digital Interface. CompuPic by Photodex is a Windows program that lets you listen to music stored as MIDI files. Mac users can use a converter program called All Midi to convert *.mid* files into Mac QuickTime movies ((*.mov*), which are playable on any QuickTime movie player.
MOD	*.mod, .s3m,* and *.mtm*	The term MOD (short for module) refers to a group of sound formats. Some of the more popular MOD formats are MOD, S3M, and MTM.
RealAudio	*.ra* and *.ram*	To listen to RealAudio sound files you need a RealAudio Player. RealAudio Players can be downloaded free of charge from *www.realaudio.com.*
System 7	*.snd*	System 7 sound files are as common to Mac Sound users as WAV files are to Windows users. System 7 sounds, when uploaded to the Internet, are usually done so in a compressed format (*.sea, .sit*, etc.)
VOC File	*.voc*	Sound Blaster soundboards have their own audio file format called VOC. Because Creative Lab's Sound Blaster is so popular, VOC files are supported by most sound players.
Wave Format	*.wav*	The WAV sound format was created by Microsoft.

OTHER FILE FORMATS

In this section, I cover miscellaneous other file formats including portable documents, graphics, and video.

BITMAP (*.BMP*)

You can view BMP files with Microsoft Paint. LViewPro also views BMP files, along with most other graphic files. Although Web browsers are already equipped to view GIF and JPEG graphics, they cannot handle BMP graphics. If you install a program called FIGleaf Inline by Carberry Technology, Netscape Navigator will then be capable of supporting BMP files.

DIGITALPAPER (*.DP*)

DigitalPaper is a file format created with Common Ground. DigitalPaper files have a *.dp* file extension. You can view them with a Common Ground MiniViewer, which is available free of charge from Common Ground at *www.commonground.com*.

GIF (*.GIF*)

GIF is an acronym for Graphics Interchange Format. GIF is a file format used for compressing graphics. You can view GIF files with a freeware program called JPEGView. LViewPro also views GIF files along with most other graphic files.

HTML (*.HTML* OR *.HTM*)

HTML (HyperText Markup Language) is the file type commonly found on the Web. Web browsers can interpret the code in HTML files. You could view an HTML file in any text editor, but the HTML code would also appear mixed in with the text.

JPEG (*.JPG* OR *.JPEG*)

JPEG is an acronym for Joint Photographic Experts Group. It is a format for compressing full-color or gray-scale digital images. JPEGView is a freeware graphic viewer that reads GIF, TIFF, JPEG, and PICT files. LViewPro also views JPEG files along with most other graphic files.

MPEG (*.MPEG* OR *.MPG*)

MPEG (Moving Pictures Expert Group) is a subcommittee of the ISO (International Standards Committee) and their purpose is to develop standards for digital video and audio compression.

Online Resource
Tom Lane maintains a JPEG image compression FAQ in two parts at *www.faqs.org/faqs/jpeg-faq/*. Some of the basic questions addressed include: • What is JPEG? • Why use JPEG? • When should I use JPEG, and when should I stick with GIF? • How well does JPEG compress images? • What are good "quality" settings for JPEG? • Where can I get JPEG software? • How do I view JPEG images posted on Usenet?

PORTABLE DOCUMENT FORMAT (.*PDF*)

Portable Document Format files are created with Adobe Acrobat and have a *.pdf* extension on their file names. You can view a PDF file with an Acrobat Reader. Acrobat Reader is free and can be downloaded from *www.adobe.com*.

PORTABLE NETWORK GRAPHICS (PNG)

PNG (pronounced "ping") is a format for storing images in computers. PNG has its own Website at *www.libpng.org/pub/png/*. The site is divided into four areas: General Information, Applications that Support PNG, Programming Resources, and PNG Images.

POSTSCRIPT FILES (.*PS*)

The file extension *.ps* stands for PostScript. *PostScript* is a programming language that is used to generate images on a printer. To view these text files they must be printed on a PostScript printer. You may want to explore a program called GhostScript that claims to print PostScript documents on non-PostScript printers.

QUICKTIME MOVIE (.*MOV* OR .*QT*)

QuickTime is a multimedia format developed by Apple Computer that supports audio and video over the Net. You can download QuickTime players from Apple's home page at *quicktime.apple.com/*.

SELF-EXTRACTING FILES (.*EXE*)

Although this looks like a normal executable program, it sometimes represents a self-extracting file. Simply run these files to unpack the archive.

Online Resource
A comprehensive listing of file types and file name extensions can be found in the CCI Dictionary at *www.currents.net/resources/dictionary/ filetypes.html.*

TEXT FILE (*.TXT*)

Files with a *.txt* extension are plain ASCII text files. They can be viewed with any text editor.

TIFF (*.TIFF* OR *.TIF*)

TIFF stands for Tag Image File Format. TIFF is a format used for storing image files. You can view TIFF files with a freeware program called JPEGView. LViewPro also views TIFF files along with most other graphic files. To enable Netscape Navigator to view TIFF files, install a program called FIGleaf Inline from Carberry Technology.

WORLD FILES (*.WRL*)

World files are virtual reality files created with Virtual Reality Modeling Language, or VRML. Netscape comes with a VR viewer already installed called Live3D. Live3D also supports files with a *.wrl.gz* extension. These are world files that have been compressed. Other VR viewers that support WRL files include WebSpace by Template Graphics Software, VR Scout by Chaco, Vrealm by Integrated Data Systems, and WorldView by Intervista.

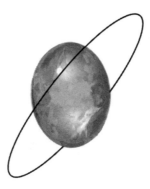

Appendix F: Organizations Involved in Network Activity

Although the Internet is not a centralized establishment and on the whole is self-governing, there are certain organizations that do exert influence over the Internet and coordinate many of the Internet's activities. The following list introduces organizations and explains their basic functions.

CLEARINGHOUSE FOR NETWORKED INFORMATION DISCOVERY AND RETRIEVAL (CNIDR)

CNIDR was established in 1992 as a support center for the development of wide-area information retrieval tools such as World Wide Web, Wide Area Information Servers, and Gopher. With so many information resources available on the Internet, resource discovery or information discovery has become a critical issue. CNIDR provides a repository for such systems. It is also active in the development of standards and provides continuing education for Internet users. For further information, contact their Website at *cnidr.org/*.

DOMAIN NAME SUPPORTING ORGANIZATION (DNSO)

DNSO is responsible for making recommendations on new generic top-level domains (gTLDs) to the Internet Corporation for Assigned Names and Numbers board. DNSO maintains a Website at *www.dnso.org/*.

THE ELECTRONIC FRONTIER FOUNDATION, INC. (EFF)

The Electronic Frontier Foundation was established to make the new telecommunications technology useful and available not just to the technically elite, but to everyone. In keeping with the belief that the individual's constitutional rights should be preserved, the society places a high priority on maintaining the free and open flow of information and communications. EFF publishes an electronic bulletin called *EFFector Online* along with a hardcopy version called *EFFector*. The online version can be viewed at Website *www.eff.org/pub/EFF/Newsletters/EFFector/*. For further information, contact their home page at *www.eff.org*

THE FEDERATION OF AMERICAN RESEARCH NETWORKS (FARNET)

Established in 1987 as a nonprofit corporation, FARNET's mission is to promote research and education in a computer network environment. Among other things, they offer members educational programs and assistance in improving information services. FARNET publishes a monthly online newsletter for its members called *FARNET's Washington Update*. For further information, contact their Website at *farnet.org*.

THE GLOBAL INFORMATION INFRASTRUCTURE COMMISSION (GIIC)

The GIIC is a worldwide network of more than 50 CEOs, policymakers, and academics representing telecommunications, computers, cable, software, broadcasting, satellite, media, policy, and education. According to the GIIC FAQ, which you can access at *www.giic.org/faq5.html*, the GIIC officially began in July 1995, with their main goal being to, "Reinforce the role of the private sector as critical to the development of the global information infrastructure." A listing of GIIC books and reports are listed on the GIIC Website. Topics include the global information economy, Asian social and economic development, data privacy, electronic commerce, and the information infrastructure in India and Africa.

IEEE

IEEE (read "I Triple E) is a not-for-profit association with more than 330,000 members in 150 countries. Its main activities are developing standards and publishing literature in electrical engineering, computers, and control technology. Their Website at *www.ieee.org/* offers access to periodicals, books, conference proceedings, electronic products, videos, self-study courses, and the most up-to-date topical listing of IEEE standards.

INFORMATION TECHNOLOGY ASSOCIATION OF AMERICA (ITAA)

ITAA is a trade association of over 11,000 direct and affiliate members representing leaders in the IT (information technology) industry. The ITAA Website at *www.itaa.org/* offers information about the IT industry, publications, and announcements about meetings and seminars.

THE INTERNET ARCHITECTURE BOARD (IAB)

Back in the early 1980s when this organization was first formed, it was known as the Internet Activities Board. Its goals were to "coordinate research and development of the TCP/IP protocols and to give other research advice to the Internet community." Today, the IAB is responsible for the "oversight of the architecture of the worldwide multiprotocol Internet." IAB receives reports from the Internet Engineering Task force and the Internet Research Task Force. IAB meeting minutes are published on their Website at *www.iab.org/*.

INTERNET ASSIGNED NUMBERS AUTHORITY (IANA)

Every computer on the Internet has a unique IP number. Operated by the University of Southern California Information Sciences Institute, IANA coordinates this system by allocating blocks of IP addresses to regional registries. These include ARIN in North America, RIPE in Europe, and APNIC in the Asia/Pacific region. You can learn more about the generic top-level domains and the country code top-level domains on their Website at *www.iana.org/*.

THE INTERNET CORPORATION FOR ASSIGNED NAMES AND NUMBERS (ICANN)

The new nonprofit corporation that is responsible for IP address space allocation, protocol parameter assignment, domain name system management, and root server system management. ICANN's Domain Name Supporting Organization is responsible for making recommendations on new generic top-level domains (gTLDs). To learn more, visit their Website at *www.icann.org/*.

INTERNET ENGINEERING TASK FORCE (IETF)

This group specializes in the development and approval of specifications that become Internet standards. Ideas begin as working documents called *Internet Drafts*. Many Internet Drafts are technical in nature, but some are more practical and along the lines of how-to texts. For more information, visit their Website at *www.ietf.org/rfc.html*. From this site you can link to a directory list of RFCs. RFC 1718 explains how the IETF works.

THE INTERNET RESEARCH TASK FORCE (IRTF)

This is a research wing of the Internet Architecture Board. The IRTF is made up of research groups that work on topics relating to developing technologies that may be needed in the future. Topics currently under consideration include resource discovery, network management, routing, and secure multicast. One research group that would be of particular interest to librarians is the Internet Resource Discover research group. This group is chartered to develop a model for describing resources on the Internet. To learn more about this research group and others, visit the IRTF Website at *www.irtf.org/.*

THE INTERNET SOCIETY (ISOC)

The Internet Society is a nonprofit organization whose purpose is to facilitate and support the technical evolution of the Internet as a research and education tool. The Internet Society publishes a bimonthly publication for its members called *OnTheInternet*. A selection of articles from this magazine can be accessed at their Website *www.isoc.org/.* Also of interest on their Website is a link to Babel, the ISOC's Website dedicated to the Internationalization of the Internet.

THE WORLD WIDE WEB CONSORTIUM (W3C)

The W3C is a joint initiative of the Laboratory of Computer Science at MIT, the French National Institute for Research in Computer Science and Control (INRIA), and the European Laboratory for Particle Physics (CERN). The W3C focuses on Web technology and the development of protocols, standards, and prototypes. You can access their home page at *www.w3.org/.*

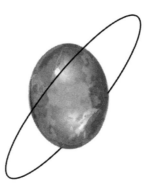

Appendix G: Keeping Up With What's New

This section describes Internet services that help keep you abreast of the latest changes in Internet-networking technology and all of the new Internet resources and services that are coming online daily.

NEW SITES ON THE WORLD WIDE WEB

One way librarians can keep up with what's new on the Web is by checking out the "What's New?" or "New" departments on major directory sites like Yahoo! at *www.yahoo.com/new/* and its sister site for kids, Yahooligans! at *www.yahooligans.com/new/*. Netscape also offers updates on what's new on their Web page *www.netscape.com/home/whats-new.html*.

NET-HAPPENINGS

One of the best sources for keeping up-to-date with new sites on the Net is a mailing list called Net-Happenings. Gleason Sackman maintains this list, which points to dozens of new Internet resources every day, including Websites, corporate information, new Internet books and software, mailing lists, and more.

To subscribe, go to the Classroom Connect Website at *listserv.classroom.com/archives/net-happenings.html*, choose which mailing lists you want to subscribe to, and then enter your name and e-mail address.

To avoid the onslaught of mail you receive from mailing lists, why not access this same information through the Web? Point your Web browser to *listserv.classroom.com/*

archives/net-happenings.html where you can browse or keyword search the Net-Happenings archives.

WHAT'S NEW TOO!

The What's New Too! service is maintained by Manifest Information Services at site *newtoo.manifest.com/*. What's New Too! claims to post an average of over 500 announcements per day within 36 hours of submission. They offer a dialog box for entering keyword searches on all of their current listings. Each entry includes the name of the site, a subject heading, the developer's name and address, and a short description of the site.

NEWS AND INFORMATION SERVICES FOR LIBRARIANS

The following news and information services keep readers up-to-date on the latest happenings in the library profession.

LIBRARY NEWSFLASHES/WILSON NEWS

Library NewsFlashes, H.W. Wilson's news service for librarians, lists library-related announcements such as library openings, closings, exhibits, awards, retirements, appointments, who's reading what, a sig file quote of the day, pertinent political issues, and ALA-related news. This site is updated once weekly. The NewsFlashes page can be found at *www.hwwilson.com/libnews/libnews.htm*. To submit your news to NewsFlashes, send e-mail to Roseward Sky, Editor, at *rsky@hwwilson.com*. Fax: 718–588–1230. Voicemail (24 hours): 800–367–6770 x2272. Snailmail: Roseward Sky, NewsFlashes, H.W. Wilson, 950 University Avenue, Bronx, NY 10452–4224.

METRONET

Metronet, centered in Minneapolis/St. Paul, Minnesota, offers a wide variety of news and information services for librarians and other information specialists on their home page at *www.metronet.lib.mn.us/*. Services include such things as:

- The Metronet Calendar, a list of events of interest to librarians
- Kids Connect @ the Library, a site just for kids interested in authors, writing, and Websites.
- Kids Logon @ the Library, a selective listing of fun and educational sites for kids.
- Web Design Tools, including a link to the Librarian's Homepage Creator.
- Archives of METRONET@LISTSERV.NODAK.EDU, which includes discussions about library-related Internet resources and services and notifications to subscribers about Metronet. You can subscribe to the list on their Website at *listserv.nodak.edu/archives/metronet.html*.
- *LIBCAT: A Guide to Library Resources on the Internet*, a resource guide that provides hyperlinks to thousands of library catalogs, electronic newsletters and journals, listservs, and library-related Websites. You can access LIBCAT directly by pointing your browser to *www.metronet.lib.mn.us/lc/lc1.cfm*.

CURRENT CITES

The Berkeley Digital Library SunSITE, sponsored by the Library of the University of California at Berkeley, offers *Current Cites*, an annotated monthly bibliography of selected articles, books, and electronic documents on information technology edited by Teri Andrews Rinne. *Current Cites* can be accessed two ways:

1. To view on the Web, point your browser to site *sunsite.Berkeley.EDU/ CurrentCites/*.
2. When new issues are released they are distributed to both the PACS-L and PACS-P mailing lists. You can subscribe to PACS-L at *info.lib.uh.edu/pacsl.html* and PACS-P at *info.lib.uh.edu/pacsp.html*.

Use the Bibliography on Demand service to build your own bibliographies from information contained in the *Current Cites* database. You can access this service directly at *sunsite.berkeley.edu/CurrentCites/bibondemand.cgi*.

HERIOT-WATT'S *INTERNET RESOURCES*

Internet Resources is a monthly newsletter edited by the Heriot-Watt University Library staff and published by Heriot-Watt University Internet Resource Centre. The purpose of the newsletter is to keep readers informed about new Internet resources, especially those that are relevant to the research interests at Heriot-Watt University. This newsletter can be read at Website *www.hw.ac.uk/libWWW/irn/*.

TECHNOLOGY ISSUES

Edupage, the Center for Democracy and Technology, FindLaw, and New York Times: Technology help keep you up-to-date on news and Web links relating to information technology and related legislation.

EDUPAGE

Edupage offers a collection of article summaries on issues relating to information technology, telecommunications, and higher education. To read *Edupage* online, connect to their site at *www.educause.edu/pub/edupage/edupage.html*. You can subscribe to the Edupage mailing list through a link included on the home page listed above. Edupage is a service of Educause *www.educause.edu/*—an organization that focuses on information technology in higher education.

CENTER FOR DEMOCRACY AND TECHNOLOGY

The Center for Democracy and Technology is concerned with a variety of Internet issues and legislation. Go to their site at *www.cdt.org/* to stay up-to-date on issues relating to free speech, data privacy, writetapping, and cryptography.

FINDLAW

FindLaw *cyber.findlaw.com/* is an online law center offering information relating to cyberspace law, intellectual property, and telecommunications. Their site features top headlines and news archives. Look for a link called "Legal News" to access the latest headlines.

THE NEW YORK TIMES: TECHNOLOGY

The New York Times: Technology *www.nytimes.com/yr/mo/day/tech/* publishes stories taken from the print's daily and weekly edition "Circuits," which focuses on different aspects of digital technology. In addition, it includes *CyberTimes* which is only published on the Web. CyberTimes covers e-commerce, cyber law and legislative developments.

MAGAZINES COVERING THE INTERNET

The publications listed in this section can help keep you up-to-date on the latest Internet developments. If you had to choose one print edition and your budget was limited, *PC Magazine* offers good, overall coverage of the latest developments in hardware, software, and telecommunications.

Some of the magazines listed here are sold on newsstands or through subscriptions, but others, such as *c\net online* and *HotWired*, are only available in electronic format.

> *BETA Magazine www.betamag.com/*
> *Boardwatch Magazine www.boardwatch.com*
> *c\net online www.cnet.com*
> *The Cook Report on the Internet cookreport.com/*
> *HotWired hotwired.lycos.com/*
> *Internet Shopper www.internet-shopper.com/*
> *ISP Business News www.ispbusinessnews.com/*
> *Internet Magazine www.internet-magazine.com/home/index.html*
> *Internet World www.internetworld.com/*
> *.net magazine www.netmag.co.uk/*
> *Netguide Magazine www.netguide.com/*
> *Netsurfer Digest www.netsurf.com/nsd/*
> *Online Magazine www.online-magazine.com/index.htm*
> *WEBsmith www.ssc.com/websmith/*
> *Wired www.hotwired.com/wired/*

LIBRARY JUICE

Library Juice *www.libr.org/Juice/* is a news digest for library and information science students edited by Rory B. Litwin. Go here for news, announcements, book reviews, calls for papers, and pointers to Web resources. You can subscribe to Library Juice and have issues sent to you via e-mail. Either sign-up on their Website at *www.libr.org/Juice/ subscribe.html*, or send e-mail to *Juice-request@libr.org*, with "subscribe" in the subject line of the message.

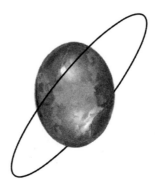

Index

The *Neal-Schuman Complete Internet Companion for Librarians* CD-ROM

To access the more than 500 specially selected sites arranged on the CD-ROM, follow these steps.

WHAT'S ON THE CD?

A completely portable, indispensable subject directory created for librarians and other information specialists. The following figure illustrates the *index.htm* file as it will appear in your browser.

Neal-Schuman
Complete Internet Companion For
Librarians
Second Edition
by Allen C. Benson

Online Resources for Librarians

Acquisitions
Publishers, Services & Supplies,
Powell's Books, Rocket eBooks,
Book Sale Finder...

Associations & Consortiums
ALA, ACRL, LITA, PLA, SLA,
American Society of Indexers...

Business
Data warehousing, Information
architecture, Information brokerage,
Knowledge management...

Cataloging
MARC, Serials, CORC, Library
of Congress, AUTOCAT,
Technical Services Unlimited...

Circulation
Electronic Course Reserves,
Barcode technology, 3M Library
Systems...

Collection Development
NetLibrary, Statistics and policies,
Licensing digital information,

Copyright
Resources, U.S. Copyright Office,
The Coalition for Networked
Information (CNI)...

Databases
AskERIC, CARL UnCover, Invisible
Web, Medscape...

Document Delivery
Ariel, Suppliers...

Education
Bibliographic Instruction,
Library Schools...

Employment
Academe This Week, EDUCAUSE,
LIBJOBS, SLA Job Search...

Government Documents
Citing Documents, GODART,
Government information on
the Internet, Thomas...

Internet
Filtering, News, Technology,
History, World Wide Web...

Libraries
Digital, Online Catalogs, Cool
Library of the Week, Public
Library Locator...

Mailing Lists
Library Lists, Mailing list software,
Finding mailing lists...

Policies
ALA Documents, Information
Policies, Electronic resources
policies...

Reference
Citation Guides, Dictionaries,
Encyclopedias, Experts,
Internet Resources...

Serials
BUBL, EBSCO, ISSN, E-Journals,
Serials in Cyberspace, HighWire
Press, Newspapers...

Special Collections
Society of American Archivists,
Rare Books & Manuscripts
Book Arts, CoOL...

Supplies & Services
Archival, Online Warehouse...

Website Development
· Authoring Software
· Free Services
· Graphics
· Metatags
· Programming
· Special Characters
· Webmaster Resources
· Website Hosting

Hardware
· Device Drivers
· Learning
· Buying Computers &
Peripherals
· Product Reviews
· Upgrading

Software
· AntiVirus
· Finding Software
· Freeware &
Shareware
· Library-Related
· Multimedia
· Reviews
· Security

Copyright © 2001 Allen C. Benson.

To view this page and its resources, you will need a version 4 or higher browser.
Microsoft Internet Explorer or Netscape Navigator.

To view the information stored on the CD-ROM, PC users should follow these steps:

1. Establish your Internet connection.
2. Insert the CD-ROM into your computer's CD-ROM drive.
3. Start your Web browser.
4. After your browser opens, click on the "File" pull-down menu and select the "Open" or "Open Page" command.
5. An "Open" dialog window appears in which you can enter the path to the *index.htm* file located on the CD-ROM. For example, if your CD-ROM drive is mapped to "D", enter **D:\index.htm**. If your CD-ROM drive is mapped to "E", enter **E:\index.htm**.
6. After you enter the path statement, click on the "Open" or "OK" button. The *Online Resources for Librarians* page should appear in your browser window.
7. As an alternative, you can browse to find the CD-ROM drive by clicking on the "Browse" button. The "Browse" button is located in the "Open" dialog window that appears in step 5 above. After clicking on "Browse", find the small CD-ROM icon and double-click on it. Now scroll down through the file names until you find the *index.htm* file. Double-click on the file name and then click "OK". The *Online Resources for Librarians* page should appear in your browser window.

If you are operating a Mac, follow these instructions:

1. Establish your Internet connection.
2. Insert the CD-ROM into your computer's CD-ROM drive.
3. Start your Web browser.
4. After your browser opens, click on the "File" pull-down menu and select the "Open" or "Open Page" command.
5. An "Open" dialog window appears. Locate the CD-ROM icon and double-click on it. You can now view the contents of the CD-ROM.
6. Scroll down through the file names until you come to the *index.htm* file. Double-click on the file name.
7. The *Online Resources for Librarians* page should now appear in your browser window.
8. As an alternative, when you insert the CD-ROM into your CD-ROM drive, a CD-ROM icon appears on the Mac desktop. You can double-click on this icon to view the contents of the CD-ROM. Scroll down until you find the file *index.htm*. Double-click on the file name. If your Mac understands that Web browsers read files with *.htm* extensions, your browser automatically opens and displays the *index.htm* file. If this association has not been established, you are presented with a window that lists all of the programs you have at your disposal to "play" an *.htm* file. Scroll through the list until you find your browser's name, for example, Internet Explorer or Netscape. Double-click on the application's name and your browser should open displaying the contents of the *index.htm* file.

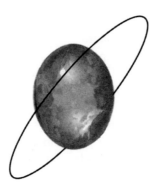

About the Author

Allen C. Benson is the Director of Library Services at Arkansas State University Mountain Home. He earned his Master of Library Science degree from the University of Alabama, where he was also awarded the Faculty Scholar Award in 1993. Benson is known throughout the U.S. for his pioneering work in integrating Internet services into traditional library practices. He is the author of the national bestseller *The Complete Internet Companion for Librarians* (Neal-Schuman Publishers, Inc., 1995), *Securing PCs and Data in Libraries and Schools* (Neal-Schuman Publishers, Inc., 1997) and co-author of *Connecting Kids and the Internet* (Neal-Schuman Publishers, Inc., *Second Edition,* 1999).